NEW AGE RELIGION
AND WESTERN CULTURE

SUNY Series, Western Esoteric Traditions
David Appelbaum, editor

NEW AGE RELIGION
AND WESTERN CULTURE

ESOTERICISM IN THE MIRROR
OF SECULAR THOUGHT

BY

WOUTER J. HANEGRAAFF

STATE UNIVERSITY OF NEW YORK PRESS

This research was supported by the Foundation for Research in the Field of Philosophy and Theology in the Netherlands, which is subsidized by the Netherlands Organization for the Advancement of Research.

Published by
State University of New York Press

© 1998 State University of New York

For information, address the State University of New York Press, State University Plaza, Albany, NY 12246

Marketing by Nancy Farrell
Production by Bernadine Dawes

Library of Congress Cataloging-in-Publication Data

Hanegraaff, Wouter J.
    New Age religion and Western culture: esotericism in the mirror of secular thought / Wouter J. Hanegraaff.
        p.   cm. — (SUNY series, western esoteric traditions)
    Originally published: Leiden ; New York : E. J. Brill, 1996, in series: Studies in the history of religions.
    Includes bibliographical references and index.
    ISBN 0-7914-3854-6 (pbk. : alk. paper)
    1. New Age movement. 2. Occultism. I. Title. II. Series: SUNY series in Western esoteric traditions.
BP605.N48H36   1998
299'.93—dc21   97-37707
                                                                         CIP

1   2   3   4   5   6   7   8   9   10

Denn die einen sind im Dunkel
Und die andern sind im Licht
Und man siehet die im Lichte
Die im Dunkeln sieht man nicht

Bertold Brecht, *Dreigroschenoper*

PREFACE

The experience of having finished a large project produces strange effects in the psyche of the author. During the boring process of making an index, I found myself musing over the past and wondering what made me decide, years ago, to make a study of the New Age movement.

One memory fragment tells me that, as a boy, I stood with my father before the shop-window of a second-hand bookseller in Amsterdam. For some reason my attention was drawn by a book on "gnosticism", written by Hans Jonas, and I asked my father (a theologian) what this word meant. I do not remember his explanation, but I do recall a vague feeling of fascination.

Years later I lived in the small Dutch town of Zwolle. I remember strolling into a newly-opened shop one afternoon, curious about the combination of pastel tints, tensionless music, and a smell of incense coming out of the open door. Later I would learn to identify the phenomenon as a "New Age bookshop", but at the time I was merely puzzled to find books of Bhagwan and Meister Eckhart, quantum physics and witchcraft, psychology and astrology, standing brotherly side by side in a manner which seemed to suggest that they had something in common.

Years later again, I stumbled across a book, the title of which claimed that "the third component" (besides "faith" and "reason") of the European cultural tradition consisted in something which the editor referred to as "gnosis". This claim fascinated me, but this time no longer vaguely and in passing. I had been frustrated for some years by the fact that the Christian faith of my upbringing and the rationalism dominant in western culture and society were unable to account for my conviction that music, art, and literature—my principal interests at the time—dealt in some sort of "truth" rather than merely in "beauty". Could this thing called "gnosis" perhaps provide a clue?

This question provided the impetus for an intellectual quest of which, I hope, this book is merely a first result. I have found that the question just formulated brings a whole range of other questions in its wake. Essentially, my investigation of the New Age movement has done no more than provide answers to some of these subsidiary questions. Without wishing to denigrate the value which New Age spirituality may have for its adherents, I privately had to draw the conclusion that (with a few nonrepresentative exceptions) this particular manifestation of the "third component" is conspicuously lacking in artistic sensitivity. This conclusion is irrelevant to the argument of my book, which restricts itself to empirical and historical questions; and I realize that it will probably be of little interest to most of my readers. It is highly relevant, however, in terms of the underlying motivations which originally impelled me to take up the subject; and those who read this book out of a primary interest in the dynamics of western culture might keep it in the back of their minds particularly while reading the Third Part.

Many people have helped me during the years in which this book was written, and their support has taken various forms. Since I have already thanked most of them at greater length elsewhere, I will here express my gratitude merely by mentioning their names in alphabetical order: Prof.Dr. Herman Beck (Tilburg), Drs. Hans van den Berg (Utrecht), Prof.Dr. Bert Blans (Utrecht), Dr. Christoph Bochinger (München), Prof.Dr. Roelof van den Broek (Utrecht), Prof. Antoine Faivre (Paris), Anneke Huyser (Utrecht), Drs. Peter Jans (Utrecht), Drs. Joop van Klink (Alphen a/d Rijn), Prof.Dr. Ria Kloppenborg (Utrecht), Dr. Reender Kranenborg (Amsterdam), Prof.Dr. L. Leertouwer (Leiden), Dr. Robert A. Segal (Lancaster), Prof.Dr. Jan Snoek (Leiden), Leo Spee (Utrecht), the Rev.Dr. Peter Staples (Utrecht), Prof. Garry W. Trompf (Sydney), Dr. Lieteke van Vucht Tijssen (Utrecht), and Drs. Auke Wouda (Arnhem). In addition, I want to mention all my colleagues at the Faculty of Theology, Utrecht University, and especially those with whom I had the pleasure to share room 1014b while working on this book. And finally I want to mention three more people: my parents, and Hester Munniksma, for reasons best known to them. Cliché or not, the truth is that without them this book could not have been written.

Wouter Hanegraaff
Utrecht, May 1996

TABLE OF CONTENTS

Part One

ORIENTATION: MAJOR TRENDS IN NEW AGE RELIGION

Part Two

EXPOSITION: THE VARIETIES OF NEW AGE EXPERIENCE

Part Three

INTERPRETATION: NEW AGE RELIGION AND TRADITIONAL ESOTERICISM

INTRODUCTION

During the 1980s, and continuing into the 1990s, there has been much talk in western society about the New Age movement. The term "New Age" has entered the standard vocabulary in discussions about ideas and practices regarded as alternative *vis à vis* dominant cultural trends, especially if these ideas and practices seem to be concerned with "spirituality". In spite of the popularity of the term, its actual content remains extremely vague. This is largely due to the fact that the New Age is not an organization, which could be unambiguously identified or defined on the basis of self-proclaimed leaders, official doctrines, standard religious practices, and the like. The initial fact about the "New Age" is that it concerns a *label* attached indiscriminately to whatever seems to fit it, on the basis of what are essentially pre-reflective intuitions. As a result, the New Age means very different things to different people. This observation provides the proper—if sobering—starting point of the present study. My purpose will be to characterize and delineate the New Age movement on the basis of an analysis and interpretation of its implicit structure of beliefs. This seems to presuppose, however, that we already know in advance what it is and, even more important, what it is not. In other words, defining the term "New Age" is a necessary condition for finding out how it may be understood. That this apparent paradox is not insurmountable will be discussed below.

Whatever the precise nature of "New Age", its cultural and religious significance—in terms of the popularity of ideas and practices associated with the label—can not be doubted[1]. An awareness that the New Age movement constitutes a major phenomenon in popular religion is reflected by the sheer number of books and articles which have been written about the movement in recent years. These publications fall into several categories.

---

[1] Due partly to confusion about definitions, precise statistics are notoriously difficult to come by. For an overview and discussion, see Heelas, *New Age Movement*, ch. 4. James R. Lewis has rightly mentioned the scarcity of quantitative data ('Approaches', 11). Polls about religious beliefs can give an indication (see for instance the U.S.A. figures given by Lattin, '"New Age" Mysticism strong in Bay Area'). Another important indication is the sale of books. In Germany, books classed as (!) New Age/esotericism comprised 10% of the total sale in 1988 (Stenger, 'Der "okkulte" Alltag, 119; but cf. Bochinger, *"New Age"*, 126-127 nt 112). Yet another indication is the number and distribution of New Age centers (see for the Dutch situation Strijards & Schreuder, 'Nieuwe Spiritualiteit', 119). Eileen Barker ('The New Age in Britain', 332) estimates that 'a million Britons (2% of the population) would themselves admit to some kind of commitment to New Age ideas and practices, but many more will have been subjected to New Age influences and still more will claim to be sympathetic to many of the concerns'.

First, there are the products of journalistic activity. New Age frequently attracts the attention of the media, and this has given rise to a proliferation of information. The popular image of the New Age among outsiders is largely based on these sources, which have an inherent proclivity to the sensational and the controversial and seldom attempt to go beyond the surface aspects of the movement. Although media sources can teach us much about how the New Age movement is perceived in the wider society, they cannot be said to have contributed to a deeper understanding of its nature and essence[2].

Second, there are many publications written from the perspective of religiously committed outsiders, almost always of a Christian persuasion[3]. This body of texts is extremely diversified both in general approach and in quality. We find here the whole gamut between attempts at a serious theological dialogue between the churches and the New Age on the one hand, and extremely hostile attempts to unmask the movement as satanic on the other. Although typical products of the "demonizing" approach may occasionally contain some useful insights, the information they provide is often unreliable from a scholarly point of view, while their interpretations tend to tell us more about the religious views of their authors than about those of the New Age movement[4]. Moving towards the other extreme, we find much superficial and insufficiently-researched literature, but also some well-documented analyses and interpretations which significantly contribute to clarifying important aspects of the New Age[5].

A third category of literature is written from the "skeptical" point of view. In the U.S.A., this perspective has been represented since 1976 by the *Committee for the Scientific Investigation of Claims of the Paranormal* (CSICOP) which has its own publishing firm and runs a popular magazine[6]. In many other countries, organizations modeled on CSICOP have emerged. Only nominally committed to scientific research, skeptics have in fact concentrated on influencing the popular media[7]. They have extended their attention from claims of the paranormal to alternative religious views and tend to criticize religion in general on the basis of a secular-humanistic ideology. The New Age movement has been a major target since the second half of the 1980s. At one extreme of the skeptical literature about the New Age we find publications with no apparent goal other than to ridicule and make fun of the movement[8]. At the

---

[2] Cf. Lewis, 'Approaches', 10-11 and his note 23. Books written by journalists usually suffer from the same defect, although there are exceptions such as D'Antonio, *Heaven on Earth*.

[3] One example from a different religious perspective is Neve, *"New Age" als Ablenkung?*.

[4] For instance, Marrs, *Dark Secrets*; id., *Mystery Mark*. Cf. Hexham, 'Evangelical Response'.

[5] For instance, Sudbrack, *Neue Religiosität*.

[6] Cf. Clark, 'Skeptics and the New Age', 417-427; Hansen, 'CSICOP and the Skeptics', 19-63.

[7] Clark, 'Skeptics and the New Age', 418-419; Hansen, 'CSICOP and the Skeptics', 19, 40-41, 43-45.

[8] For instance Gordon, *Channeling into the New Age*.

other end of the spectrum, we find some useful studies in which an effort is made at serious research[9].

To the three categories summarized above, we could add a fourth one consisting of studies in which New Age is studied less in itself than as an illustration of sociological theories; and a fifth consisting of literature written from New Age perspectives. Generally speaking, we can conclude that in the overwhelming majority of writings the subject has been approached from strongly committed religious or ideological positions, and that scholarly standards of research have seldom been observed. If we look for serious scholarly studies written from a detached point of view, we find comparatively few[10]. It is this unsatisfactory situation which has provided the motivation for the present study.

METHODOLOGY

The methodology followed can for the most part be inferred from the considerations outlined above.

– *Historical/contextual*. New Age research has usually been conducted in the context of the study of New Religious Movements (NRM's) in general. One less fortunate result is that certain lacunae resulting from the latter's strong sociological emphasis can also be observed in most of the literature about the New Age movement. There exists a marked lack of (1) in-depth analyses of the worldviews and theologies of alternative movements[11] and (2) a historical perspective on their origins and cultural background[12]. For the New Age movement specifically, there does not yet exist a study in which these dimensions are treated in sufficient detail. Therefore they will be at the center of attention in the present study. I will look at the New Age movement from the perspective of the history of (religious) ideas. An effort will be made to put the movement into its proper historical context, as a necessary presupposition for adequately interpreting its worldview and theology. To this end, considerable attention will be given to certain religious traditions in western culture which have largely been neglected by historians of ideas and of religion.

---

[9] Cf. the anthology edited by Basil, *Not Necessarily the New Age*.

[10] Notably: Schorsch, *New Age Bewegung*; York, *Emerging Network*; Melton, Clark & Kelly, *New Age Encyclopedia*; Lewis & Melton, *Perspectives*; Bochinger, *"New Age"*; Heelas, *New Age Movement*; Steyn, *Worldviews in Transition*.

[11] A pioneering exception is Bednarowski, *New Religions*. In the foreword to this study, Catherine L. Albanese emphasizes that Bednarowski is 'among the first to offer a sustained description and analysis of the religious thought of these communities without reflecting the normative bias of an apologist, an opponent, or an apostate', adding some pertinent remarks on the disdain with which the theologies of these movements tend to be regarded by members of the academic community (Albanese in Bednarowski, *New Religions*, vii).

[12] Cf. the sharp remark by Zwi Werblowsky: 'The trouble with most writings on the new ... religious groups is that their authors seem to have forgotten, or never learned, history' ('Religions New and not so New', 33). The most notable exception is Ellwood & Partin, *Religious and Spiritual Groups*.

– *Restriction to written sources*. I will focus on the religious ideas of the New
Age movement such as can be found in a representative sample of written
sources. As a matter of principle, sociological and anthropological research
methods, like interview or participation techniques, have not been used. This
is not because these methods are regarded as less important. Quite the reverse:
they are essential for a complete view of the New Age movement in which all
its different aspects and dimensions are taken into account. The aims of the
present study, however, are more modest. We will concentrate on religious
ideas, knowing full well that a definitive and complete view of the New Age
movement would require the combination of several methodologies, focusing
on different dimensions of the New Age[13]. An attempt to take account of all
these dimensions in one single study would surely be over-ambitious and likely to result in a confounding of methods hardly conducive to clarity.
It may be necessary to point out explicitly that the choice to work from an
analysis of written sources was in no way inspired by a conviction that
researchers should remain clinically detached from their subjects. No chance
has been left unused to get to know the New Age as well as possible, including frequent contacts and discussions with adherents and sympathizers as well
as occasional participation in New Age activities. These contacts have often
proved very useful in providing a "living" background to my research. Nevertheless, my arguments and discussions will refer to the written sources alone,
and will have to justify themselves without recourse to other kinds of information.
– *Empirical*[14]. The empirical study of religions can be distinguished from theological, positivist-reductionist or religionist approaches by its practice of permanent *epochè* (suspension of normative judgment), also known as methodological agnosticism[15]. According to the positivist-reductionist approach, the
religious views under study are delusions. This view (represented in the case
of New Age research by the skeptical literature) rests on an ideological foun-

---

[13] For instance, the ideas of many New Age adherents may be far more vague than those of
New Age authors. The results of the present study will therefore have to be critically compared
with the results of studies based on interviews with representatives of the general New Age public. Strijards & Schreuder, who have done this kind of research in the Netherlands, observe: 'As
regards the ideology of the adherents of the New Age religion, we had to conclude first of all
that among our respondents we have not been able to find systematically ordered, nuanced and
rounded theories. What is more, their thoughts are vaguer than the concepts of the New Age-
authors whom they read.' ('Nieuwe Spiritualiteit', 121). Referring to recent research results about
Dutch religious beliefs in general, Strijards & Schreuder note that in this respect the general New
Age believer is not different from the general member of a christian church.
[14] For an extensive discussion of empirical method as understood in this study, see Hanegraaff, 'Empirical Method'.
[15] For a clear and succinct overview of the empirical, religionist and positivist-reductionist
modes of the study of religions, see the first chapter of Platvoet, *Comparing Religions*, esp. par.
1.6. See also id., 'Definers Defined'; and Hanegraaff, 'Empirical Method'.

dation, the truth of which can be neither verified nor falsified by inductive methods[16]. The same holds true for the religionist perspective, which is based on *a priori* assumptions about the truth and validity of religion (cf. the "perennialist" school in Religious Studies[17]); and for the approach of Christian theology which is based on the truth of the Christian faith as perceived by the theologian in question. In contrast to all these approaches, the empirical approach to the study of religions holds that it is impossible to answer the question of ultimate religious or metaphysical truth on scientific grounds, and that it cannot therefore be the business of the researcher to adjudicate on the validity of the believer's truth. In Platvoet's words:

> This does not imply that a religion can only be studied in its externals, and not 'in itself' ... But it does imply that a religion 'in itself' can be studied only indirectly: i.e., on the basis of statements of belief, ritual actions and other religiously inspired behaviour of the believers. The meta-empirical part of a religion is as such completely outside the grasp and scope of an empirical scientist of religions. He can make no statement, affirmative or negative, about its ontological qualities: whether or not it is real and active. Nor can he pronounce on the truth-claims of a religion. He must not, therefore, introduce any prejudiced argument, or personal belief, or probability reasoning that 'proves', or tends to 'prove', any opinion which he may hold privately about religion or about a particular religion. But he must also show that the meta-empirical beings of a religion are very real to its adherents[18].

This last point requires emphasis. Unfortunately, it is sometimes suggested by adherents of the "religionistic" approach that the empirical mode of research is itself reductionist or positivist, because it adopts an agnostic position with regard to ultimate questions and restricts itself to what can be objectively asserted by scientific and scholarly means. This is a misunderstanding of both the underlying motivation of empirical research and its methodology[19].
As regards the first point: this criticism fails to recognize that the empirical approach is inspired by the wish to do full justice to the integrity of the believer's worldview, to an extent which is not possible for positivist-reductionists. The empirical mode aspires to objective[20] knowledge which should be equal-

---

[16] Platvoet, *Comparing Religions*, 15-16.
[17] This school subscribes to what it perceives as the "transcendent unity of religions", or to a universal core of truth to be found in all religions, and uses this as the basis for research. One example relevant to the New Age movement is the typology of New Religious Movements developed by Dick Anthony. See Anthony & Ecker, 'Anthony Typology'. Cf. also Hanegraaff, 'Empirical Method', 110.
[18] Platvoet, *Comparing Religions*, 16-17.
[19] Reversely, reductionists often accuse empiricists of religionism. My 'Empirical Method' begins with a refutation of this argument as formulated by Segal, 'In Defense of Reductionism'. About the misunderstandings among religionists and reductionists about the nature of empirical research, see especially pp. 105-107.
[20] See Platvoet, *Comparing Religions*, 4-6 about the meaning and the limits of objectivity in the empirical study of religions. Notice that empirical research *aspires to* objective knowledge,

ly acceptable to believers, critics and declared foes, and may thus be of service in improving the quality of the discussions between them. The information offered by empirical research can assist in discarding incorrect perceptions among outsiders (resulting from lack of familiarity with the religion in
question), but it may also unveil aspects of that religion which are unknown
and surprising (and not necessarily welcome) to the believers themselves. In
view of the heated but often poorly informed controversies surrounding the
New Age movement and its religious views, empirical research certainly has
an important mission to fulfill.

Secondly, the empirical mode of research, if correctly understood, presupposes an acute awareness of the special requirements of research in the humanities, as opposed to the natural sciences. In Platvoet's words, 'Its methods of
collecting data and interpreting them have a hermeneutical setting: they are
operated in a two-way framework of interpretation intimately linked to the person of the investigator and necessarily involving his or her subjectivities in
their operation.'[21] A certain tension between the aim of objective knowledge
on the one hand and the awareness of the necessary role of hermeneutics on
the other is characteristic of research of this kind. The principal theoretical tool
to safeguard scientific legitimacy in this situation is the distinction between
emic and *etic*[22]. Emic denotes the 'intersubjective patterns of thought and symbolic associations of the believers[23]' or, expressed more simply, the "believer's
point of view". An accurate presentation of the religion under study as
expressed by the believers themselves must be the basis of research. On the
part of the researcher, the reconstruction of this emic perspective requires an
attitude of empathy which excludes personal biases as far as possible. Scholarly discourse about religion, on the other hand, is not emic but etic. This means
that it may involve types of language, distinctions, theories, and interpretive
models which are considered appropriate by scholars on their own terms. Scholars may introduce their own terminology and make theoretical distinctions
which are different from those of the believers themselves. The final results
of scholarly research should be expressed in etic language, and formulated in

---

without necessarily claiming to *furnish* such knowledge. Cf. Hanegraaff, 'Empirical Method',
108. Some of the same methodological points are made, with special reference to the sociological study of New Religious Movements, by Eileen Barker, 'The Scientific Study of Religion?
You Must Be Joking!', *Journal for the Scientific Study of Religion* 34:3 (1995), esp. 294-296.

[21] Platvoet, *Comparing Religions*, 6.

[22] For discussions of this distinction as understood here, see Platvoet, *Comparing Religions*,
4-5, 21, 29, and *passim*; Snoek, *Initiations*, 4-8, and *passim*. Notice that the relation between the
distinction as understood here and as originally presented by Kenneth Pike and Marvin Harris is
in need of further clarification (see Pike, *Language in Relation to a Unified Theory*, 38-39, and
passim; Harris, *Cultural Materialism*, ch. 2; for discussion, see Richters, *De medisch antropoloog*,
234-240; Faivre & Voss, 'Western Esotericism and the Science of Religions', 66-67.)

[23] Platvoet, *Comparing Religions*, 4-5.

such a way as to permit criticism and falsification both by reference to the emic material and as regards their coherence and consistency in the context of the general etic discourse[24].

The structure of this study reflects the order in which the actual research was done. First, a representative sample of New Age literature was analyzed in detail; the results of this descriptive analysis make up Parts One and Two of the book. Second, an attempt was made to interpret the material of Parts One and Two from a historical perspective, in order to reach a comprehensive view of the nature of New Age religion[25]. This concluding synthesis is presented in Part Three. Although it would be pointless to deny that certain ideas and expectations about possible directions for interpretation were already present during the first phase (Parts One and Two) of the research, the systematic (re)construction of a historical context for interpretation was deliberately undertaken *after* the analytic part had been concluded, in order to minimize the risk of the interpretative context influencing the analysis—or even the choice of sources—beforehand.

A PRELIMINARY DEMARCATION OF THE FIELD

Because my complete argument will rest on the representative value of the written sources selected for analysis, the criteria used for selection are crucial to the whole endeavour. As noted in the Introduction, we are not dealing with the relatively comfortable situation of a religious movement the boundaries of which can be defined beforehand on the basis of normative doctrines, generally recognized leaders, and organizational structures or common practices. Before we can study the beliefs of "the movement" it will therefore be neces-

---

[24] A clear distinction between the two levels is essential to empirical research, but it should be added that this does not imply that they necessarily have to be presented separately in the publication of such research. In this study, I will take care to present my research in such a way as to make it evident to the reader at each point whether it is the New Age movement or the present author whose opinions are being expressed.

[25] The use of the term "New Age Religion" is not meant in any way as a premature statement about the measure of internal coherence of the New Age movement (such as would be implied by speaking about "*The* New Age religion", which is not done here). Terms such as "New Age Religion" will be used quite loosely and pragmatically (along with such terms as "New Age movement" or simply "New Age") as a recognition of the fact that New Age concerns obviously belong to a sphere widely regarded as "religious" according to common parlance (even though many New Agers would prefer the term "spirituality" over "religion"). Such an approach does not necessarily presuppose an answer to the tricky theoretical question of the definition of religion. Similarly, people involved in the New Age will be variously referred to by such designations as "New Age believers", "New Age adherents" or "New Agers". None of these terms is intended to carry any content more specific than "people involved, in some way or another, in the New Age movement".

sary to make choices about what to include and what to exclude. At first sight, this may seem to invite arbitrariness and circular arguments. In fact, however, the task—although admittedly delicate—is less impossible than it may seem. What is required is a dialectical approach which starts with a well-founded but sufficiently inclusive preliminary demarcation while allowing for adjustments in the course of the research process.

J.A.M. Snoek, in an important study of classification and definition theory in the study of religions, notes that in situations such as the present one, three attitudes can be regularly observed[26]. The "essential-intuitional" method does not recognize the need to begin with a preliminary demarcation at all, because it assumes that we already know what we are talking about. According to the "inductive" method we should start with specific examples, and build up general definitions by generalizing conclusions about these examples. According to a third approach, we should start with a definition, because 'in the absence of definitions there can be no inquiry—for it is the definition ... which designates the phenomenon to be investigated'[27]. The first approach would imply that we start discussing the New Age movement as if no problem of definition exists. The second approach would entail the paradox of studying "specific examples" of a movement yet to be defined. Starting with a definition, finally, would mean defining the New Age before investigating it.

Snoek disagrees with these three standard approaches:

> The methodological error in all three approaches is that they see definition as an analytical process, whereas in fact it is usually a dialectical one. In most cases we deal with terms that already exist in our language, and have some meaning there, though this may be vague and ambiguous. When we start investigating a subject, we cannot but approach it with this vague "essential-intuitional" concept in mind. Such a preliminary study enables us to better formulate our impression of what we are dealing with. In later work, we state this as a definition at the beginning, showing clearly what it is that we intend to investigate further. This subsequent research may lead to a still more refined definition, and so forth. However, such an approach would be sterile if we regard the definitions from which we start as uncrossable barriers. Most progress in insight is often reached precisely by studying border-line cases, explicitly allowing for adjustment of the originally assumed border.[28]

Recognizing the dialectical nature of our endeavour, we may therefore start with a preliminary demarcation of the New Age movement provided it is sufficiently inclusive[29]. The material falling within these boundaries may then be

---

[26] Snoek, *Initiations*, 8-9. It should be noted that Snoek investigates *etic* terms, while I investigate *emic* beliefs in order to reach results which can be formulated in *etic* terms. Snoek's discussion of the dialectical process is however perfectly applicable to both situations.

[27] Spiro, 'Religion', 90.

[28] Snoek, *Initiations*, 9.

[29] Cf. Snoek's quotation of Van Baaren, about the preferability of wide rather than restricted

analyzed. It is not impossible that the results of this analysis will lead to the conclusion that some materials which were included first will have to be excluded from the field of "New Age" later. Reversely, the possibility cannot be excluded beforehand that the view of the New Age movement which emerges from the analysis may afterwards (although probably not in the present study) be compared with certain groups excluded at the outset, and that this comparison will lead to the conclusion that these groups resemble the New Age sufficiently to include them after all.

We now return to the empirical situation which provided the starting point of our study. It is true that "New Age" is primarily a poorly defined label which has different meanings and connotations for different people. However, there is a substantial number of authors who would be regarded as belonging to the New Age movement by any external[30] standard. It is in defining the boundaries of the New Age, then, rather than its core, that we encounter difficulties. Nor do we need to draw the radical conclusion that "anything goes" in the sense that any use of the term is equally valid. Some random examples may be helpful to illustrate this last point.
– If M. Gorbachev's political reforms in the former Sovjet Union are hailed by some New Age-believers as a sign of the coming of the New Age, and Gorbachev himself as the chosen instrument of higher powers, this must be noted as part of New Age beliefs[31]. It would obviously be an error, however, to infer from this that we need to study Gorbachev's bestselling book *Perestrojka* as a statement of New Age doctrine.
– Both outsiders and insiders sometimes associate certain older movements in the occultistic tradition, for instance Anthroposophy, with the New Age. Such

---

preliminary demarcations: 'I would rather take the risk of bringing something into the discussion that afterwards turns out to have to be excluded, than that I run the risk of missing an aspect or element. I would rather be a little too liberal, than that I am opinionated and want to know from the start what I can only take in in its full breadth and depth in the end.' (Van Baaren, *Uit de Wereld der Religie*. Translation in Snoek, *Initiations*, 184).

[30] On the basis of internal, emic opinions of New Agers about the "true" nature of the New Age (rather than an external observation of its empirical phenomena) this is different. Both David Spangler and Shirley MacLaine must be considered important as declared spokes(wo)men for the New Age who cannot be omitted in any neutral account, but their views of the movement are very different. In fact, Spangler claims that the New Age as represented by MacLaine and others is a degeneration of the original movement (Spangler, *The New Age*). Some researchers have adopted such emic views in defining what they consider to be New Age (for instance, Mary Farrell Bednarowski accepts Spangler's definition in her *New Religions*, 15-16). However, if we followed such a procedure, we would have to exclude many people who are generally regarded as central to the New Age, simply because they have come to dislike the label. This is increasingly the case as a result of negative media coverage during the 1980s (Cf. Lewis, 'Approaches', 1-2; Bochinger, *"New Age"*, 103, 115, 128, 517; Heelas, *New Age Movement*, ch. 1, 'The term "new age"').

[31] Cf. Anon., 'Capra und Gorbatschow', 152-154; Riordan, 'Channeling', 107.

an application of the term is unwarranted for several reasons. Anthroposophy is a clearly demarcated organisation which emerged and developed into its current shape far earlier than the period in which the term New Age began to be used as a general label. Furthermore, Anthroposophists will usually reject the label "New Age" as unrelated to the specific teachings of their founder Rudolf Steiner. Nevertheless, the fact that outsiders or New Age believers associate these movements with each other (which is reflected by the presence of anthroposophical literature in most New Age bookshops) is in itself highly significant. It may alert us to the possibility of affinities between the religious views of Anthroposophy and New Age, or of a historical connection between the two. – If New Age believers suggest that the essence of Buddhism is synonymous with the essence of the New Age, this fact can teach us much about New Age belief, but it does not imply that we need to study, say, the Pali canon in order to find the meaning of the New Age there. Rather, a study of sources in which modern New Age believers establish the connection is required.

In cases like these, the decision to exclude certain phenomena is based essentially on common sense. By analyzing the criteria implicit in such decisions, we can formulate two initial guidelines for deciding which sources to include and exclude beforehand. These guidelines provide the minimum restriction required in order to reduce the wealth of existing material to manageable proportions without leaving out essential texts. Basically they involve a restriction of the *time period* to which the sources should belong, and of their *cultural/geographical context*. They determine, in other words, where the New Age movement will be considered to be situated in time and space.
Added below are two other guidelines which further restrict the field. The first of these is necessary in order to clarify the relation between New Religious Movements in general and the New Age movement. A final guideline concerns the usefulness of specific texts in terms of the aims of the present study. I will discuss these guidelines in some detail.

A. Restrictions according to Time Period

The New Age movement is commonly, and rightly, regarded as rooted in the so-called counterculture of the 1960s. Indeed, many of the concerns which can still be found in the movement of the 1980s and the early 1990s were present already in the 1960s, including the expectation of a New Age—the "Age of Aquarius" as celebrated in the musical *Hair*—which would replace the culture of the status quo. For this reason, some commentators employ the term "New Age" to cover the complete alternative movement from the 1960s to the present day. By the same token, some studies of the early alternative movement (1960s and early 1970s) are still quoted as authoritative in relation to the New

Age movement as a whole[32]. Although this broad definition is not unnatural in view of the many uncontested similarities and continuities between the early and the later period, it tends to obscure some crucial changes which took place during the 1970s. As a result of these changes, the New Age movement of the 1980s looks very different from the earlier movement in important respects.

The early alternative movement was dominated by adolescents rebelling against the values of the older generation. Bob Dylan's well-known saying that "you can't trust anyone over thirty years old" neatly describes the sentiments which prevailed in the counterculture. The New Age movement of the 1980s, on the other hand, no longer represents a specific generation but attracts people of all ages. While many people who were young in the 1960s have over the years developed into adherents of the New Age movement, others no longer wish to be identified with it because they feel it has betrayed the ideals of the counterculture.

Some of these ideals were of a political nature. The left-wing political beliefs of the counterculture and its commitment to radical action are no longer characteristic of the New Age movement of the 1980s. The writings of Marx, Che Guevara or Mao Tse-tung are completely absent in the modern New Age bookshop, and New Age spokesmen do not usually call on their audiences to take political action in the streets (they may, however, organize group meditations for world healing).

One of the most characteristic elements of the counterculture was the widespread use of psychedelic drugs. It has often been noted that most of the New Religious Movements which enjoyed their heyday in the wake of the counterculture (late 1960s and early 1970s) strongly discouraged or flatly forbade the use of drugs. Instead, they emphasized meditation and other spiritual techniques as alternative means of expanding consciousness. This same approach has become typical for the New Age movement of the 1980s, which no longer encourages the use of psychedelic drugs as part of its religious practices[33].

This combination of predominantly young members, left-wing political engagement and the use of psychedelics resulted in a characteristic, easily recognizable social movement which is now generally associated with the period of "the sixties". Although the terms "New Age" or "Aquarian Age" did belong to its vocabulary, the movement was not generally known under the name "New Age movement". This last indication came into use only in the latter part of

---

[32] For instance Roszak, *Unfinished Animal*; Rossman, *New Age Blues*.

[33] However, recent developments in the direction of a "high-tech" New Age (sometimes labeled "New Edge") involve the use of so-called "smart drugs", as well as "brain machines" for the artificial production of psychedelic experiences. This trend, which is still too recent to put into clear perspective, falls outside the scope of our study. Elsewhere, we will discuss the transpersonal psychologist Stanislav Grof's experiments with LSD.

the 1970s and developed into the dominant and generally used label during the
1980s[34]. For the reasons discussed above, I will therefore restrict the enquiry
to written sources that were either published, or enjoyed popularity, *after* the
first half of the 1970s. Sources that were popular in both the period before ánd
after (roughly) 1975 qualify for inclusion in the analysis, but sources which
are characteristic of the earlier period and declined in popularity during the
1970s will be excluded. In the rest of this study, the term "New Age movement" will therefore be taken to refer to *a movement which emerged in the second half of the 1970s, came to full development in the 1980s and is still with
us at the time of writing.*
It is important to note that in this distinction between the movements (roughly) before and after 1975 the emphasis lies on their character as *social entities*
rather than as groups of people sharing certain beliefs. There are, no doubt,
very strong continuities between both periods in terms of beliefs and ideas. At
this point, however, we are concerned with demarcating the "New Age" on the
basis of some general considerations, rather than with answering the question
of the ultimate originality of its ideas and beliefs. Whether or not the different social entities of counterculture and New Age will ultimately have to be
considered one single movement in terms of their ideas is a question which
can only be answered *after* these ideas have first been analyzed.

B. Restrictions according to Cultural/Geographical Context

The New Age is originally a movement of modern western, industrialized society. Although there are some signs that New Age ideas have begun to spread
beyond this domain[35], the movement's foundations lie in the United States and
Western Europe[36]. Within this field, I have restricted the analysis to American
and English sources for the following reasons. Most of these sources are also
accessible (either in the original language or in translation) in the other countries mentioned, while Dutch and German sources in particular are seldom
translated and therefore remain unknown abroad. It is the English and American literature which has clearly set the trends for other countries. Because this
study aims at an interpretation of New Age religion as such, rather than of possible regional variants, there would be no point in partly basing it on sources
which are relevant to only one particular country. Judging from the Dutch sit-

---

[34] Cf. Bochinger, *"New Age"*, 126: in Germany the label did not come to be generally known
until 1984.
[35] Cf. Hackett, 'New Age Trends in Nigeria'; Mullins, 'Japan's New Age'; Oosthuizen, '"Newness" of the New Age in South Africa'; Steyn, *Worldviews in Transition*.
[36] Michael York speaks of an 'especially an American-Canadian-British-Dutch-West German-
Australian-New Zealand phenomenon' ('New Age Movement in Great Britain', 150). This list
can be further expanded with areas such as France, Italy and the Scandinavian countries. Cf. Heelas, *New Age Movement*, ch. 4.

uation, and to some extent from the German one, there seems to be no reason to assume that such regional variants would lead to significant new insights. Nor is there any indication that specific Dutch or German authors have made contributions to New Age thought crucial enough to necessitate the inclusion of their work. The body of New Age ideas seems to be an English-American affair by any standards, and this will be reflected in the study.

On the other hand, the fact that the research was conducted in the Netherlands has exercised some limited influence on the choice of texts, especially in relation to the American situation. The supply in Dutch New Age bookshops is not a literal copy of the American supply plus Dutch additions. Rather, the different cultural climate tends to filter out some American sources which booksellers apparently do not expect will "catch on" among Europeans. The present survey includes such American sources as are indispensable for a balanced view of the American New Age but are largely or completely unknown in the Netherlands (the books based on messages from Ramtha channeled by J Z Knight are a case in point). Nevertheless, American readers may find that the final choice of sources represents a compromise between the American and the European—in particular the Dutch—cultural climate. This, however, has been considered an advantage rather than a disadvantage in the study of a movement which derives its importance partly from its apparent ability to transcend narrow cultural boundaries and adapt to different societies.

Cultural differences are important in a different sense as well. In New Age bookshops we find a considerable amount of literature with a cultural background different from either of the countries listed above. Primarily these are books about the great religious—especially mystically-oriented—traditions, and translations of original texts from these traditions. In the New Age subculture there appears to be a substantial market for books dealing with various aspects of Buddhism, Hinduism, Sufism, Jewish mysticism, gnosticism, native American religions, as well as comparative mythology and traditional folklore. To the extent that books in these categories are not explicitly written to promote a New Age perspective, these sources will be excluded from our analysis as a matter of principle. The reason is simply that, although they happen to be on sale in New Age bookshops, their contents have nothing to do with the New Age movement specifically. Nevertheless, as noted above, the high level of interest for such subjects among a New Age readership is highly significant in itself; the reasons for this interest can, however, be inferred easily from more specific New Age sources which refer to these traditions within their own context.

C. Restrictions vis à vis New Religious Movements

It is of crucial importance to have criteria for distinguishing the field to be regarded as representative of the New Age movement from the wider field of

New Religious Movements (NRM's), including the alternative movements dating from the nineteenth or the first half of the twentieth century which are sometimes referred to as the "old new religions"[37].

It is typical of the confusion surrounding the label "New Age" that two conflicting approaches to the relation between New Age and NRM's exist side by side. On the one hand, there is a tendency to regard all NRM's, at least if they are not explicitly Christian, as New Age. The unfortunate result is that New Age becomes a synonym for culturally deviant NRM's in general, including those which do not accept the label or are indifferent to it. On the other hand, there is an equally strong tendency to present the New Age movement as one NRM among others. However, the discussion in such cases usually makes it abundantly clear how badly the New Age in fact fits this mold[38]. Whatever the nature of the New Age movement will turn out to be, the absence of generally recognized leaders and organizations, normative doctrines and common practices effectively distinguishes it *as a whole* from the many movements which do have these characteristics. However, it cannot be doubted that there exist many clearly organized movements with leaders, specific doctrines and practices which do describe themselves explicitly as "New Age", side by side with movements which are often associated with New Age by others although they refer to themselves by more specific designations (for instance Transcendental Meditation, Hare Krishna, Rajneeshism).

This confusing situation is well accounted for by the concept of the "cultic milieu" as developed in a seminal article by Colin Campbell[39]. Campbell discusses the way in which Ernst Troeltsch's tripartite division of religious phenomena (church religion, sect religion and mysticism) was developed by later theoreticians into a model which allows for a sharp distinction between *sect* and *cult*. On the basis of Campbell's discussion[40], we could represent this distinction as follows:

---

[37] Wilson, 'New Religions'.

[38] As also noted by Heelas, *New Age Movement*, Introduction. One example is Barker, *Practical Introduction*, 188-192. Although Barker lists the New Age movement along with other NRM's, she explicitly says that it is not in fact a "movement" at all but a collection of phenomena grouped together on the basis of Wittgenstein's celebrated concept of "family resemblance" (Barker, *Practical Introduction*, 189). Snoek (*Initiations*, 29-31) has called attention to the fact that Wittgenstein's concept lays at the basis of the distinction between polythetic classes (i.e., classes based on family resemblance) and monothetic classes (i.e., classes based on a minimal number of required characteristics) in general classification theory. Applying this to our subject, most NRM's would constitute monothetic classes while the special character of the New Age movement lies in the fact that it is a polythetic class.

[39] Campbell, 'Cultic Milieu', 119-136.

[40] Campbell, 'Cultic Milieu', 121.

Cult	*Sect*
Individualistic	Collectivist
Loosely structured	Tightly structured
Few demands on members	Many demands on members
Tolerant	Intolerant
Inclusivist	Exclusivist
Transient	Stable
Undefined boundaries	Clearly circumscribed
Fluctuating belief systems	Stable belief systems
Rudimentary organisation	Stable organization
Highly ephemeral	Persisting over time

Campbell has made a seminal contribution to the sect-cult discussion by introducing the concept of the "cultic milieu". In view of the crucial importance of this concept for our concerns, I will quote Campbell's own description in full.

> Given that cultic groups have a tendency to be ephemeral and highly unstable, it is a fact that new ones are being born just as fast as the old ones die. There is a continual process of cult formation and collapse which parallels the high turnover of membership at the individual level. Clearly, therefore, cults must exist within a milieu which, if not conducive to the maintainance of individual cults, is clearly highly conducive to the spawning of cults in general. Such a generally supportive cultic milieu is continually giving birth to new cults, absorbing the debris of the dead ones and creating new generations of cult-prone individuals to maintain the high levels of membership turnover. Thus, whereas cults are by definition a largely transitory phenomenon, the cultic milieu is, by contrast, a constant feature of society. It could therefore prove more viable and illuminating to take the cultic milieu and not the individual cult as the focus of sociological concern[41].

According to Campbell, the cultic milieu, despite its diversity, can be regarded as constituting a single entity[42].

> At the basis of the unifying tendencies is the fact that all these worlds share a common position as heterodox or deviant items in relation to the dominant cultural orthodoxies. This fact gives rise to a common consciousness of deviance and the need to justify their own views in the light of the expressed ridicule or hostility of the larger society. The spokesmen for the various cultic movements thus have a common cause in attacking orthodoxy and in defending individual liberty of belief and practice. Arising from this there is a prevailing orientation of mutual sympathy and support, such that the various cultic movements rarely engage in criticism of each other. On the contrary they display a marked tolerance and receptivity towards each others' beliefs which, although partly stemming from this common concern with liberty of belief and resistance to any suggestion of dogmatism, also receives a great stimulus from the presence of the mystical tradition. Since this tradition emphasizes that the single ideal of unity with the divine can be attained by a diversity of paths it tends to be ecumenical, super-ecclesiastic, syncretistic and tolerant in outlook. These tend, in fact, to be characteristics of

---

[41] Campbell, 'Cultic Milieu', 121-122.
[42] Campbell, 'Cultic Milieu', 122.

the the cultic milieu in general whether or not the belief content is mystical in the sense of pursuing the goal of ecstatic experience. As a result, the fragmentary tendencies present in the milieu because of the enormous diversity of cultural items are more than counteracted by the continuing pressure to syncretization.[43]

This tendency towards syncretization is further reinforced by the overlapping communication structures of the milieu. 'More than anything else, the cultic world is kept alive by the magazines, periodicals, books, pamphlets, lectures, demonstrations and informal meetings through which its beliefs and practices are discussed and disseminated.'[44] These media are generally open, rather than restricted to the beliefs of a particular collectivity. Finally, the cultic milieu is united by the shared ideology of "seekership", a concept applied to 'persons who have adopted a problem-solving perspective while defining conventional religious institutions and beliefs as inadequate'[45].

The (religious) culture of the cultic milieu, according to Campbell, is most prominently characterized by mysticism in the Troeltschean sense, but also includes pre-Christian pagan traditions and deviant science and technology[46]. Campbell's identification of the "cultic milieu" provides us with a solid foundation for determining what should and what should not be regarded as New Age within the wider field of NRM's. Reading his article during the early 1990s, it is almost impossible to miss its relevance to the New Age movement as it initially presents itself to the outside observer. The very difficulty of "catching" and defining the New Age—its vagueness and fluency which provided the starting point of our study—strongly suggests cultic rather than sectarian characteristics. The fact that New Age clearly transcends the boundaries of a specific religious organization, while leaving room within its own domain for such organizations to develop and disappear, further indicates how perfectly it fits Campbell's description.

Finally, a survey of the secondary literature about the New Age movement tends to confirm the profile of the cultic milieu on every page. With all the available evidence pointing in the same direction, it is natural to conclude that the New Age is *either* synonymous with the cultic milieu *or* that it represents a specific historical stage in the development of it. In view of the time restrictions discussed above, the latter alternative would seem to be preferable. Michael York, one of the first specialists to have drawn attention to the connection between the New Age movement and the cultic milieu, suggests something like this in characterizing the former as 'possibly an attempt to unify to some extent the great diversity and amorphousness which is that milieu and

---

[43] Campbell, 'Cultic Milieu', 122-123.
[44] Campbell, 'Cultic Milieu', 123.
[45] Campbell, 'Cultic Milieu', 123. Campbell uses the concept of seekership as developed especially by Lofland & Stark, 'Becoming a World-saver, 862-875.
[46] Campbell, 'Cultic Milieu', 124-126.

bring its related tenets and activities together under a single label and organization; in a word, to bring the cultic milieu together as a new religious movement'[47]. The use of the words "organization" and "new religious movement" seems somewhat unfortunate in this context as it tends to obscure the very character of the cultic milieu which, by definition, is not organized and transcends specific NRM's. It would therefore be more correct to say that the *New Age is synonymous with the cultic milieu* **having become conscious of itself** *as constituting a more or less unified "movement"* (although not a "New Religious Movement" in the normal sense of the word). This addition ties in perfectly with the restrictions of time period given above. Campbell's analysis of the cultic milieu was published in 1972; that is, before the emergence of the New Age movement as understood in this study. That the characteristics of the cultic milieu which would later be called "New Age movement" were apparently already present at this time confirms the connection of the New Age with the counterculture of the 1960s, which attracted its adherents from the same milieu. The birth of the New Age movement in the sense we will use in this study is marked by the phenomenon that people on a wide scale began to recognize the existence of what Campbell calls the cultic milieu. As a result, they began to refer to this milieu as a "movement", and began to perceive themselves and others as participating in this movement. This development took place in the period after 1975[48], and stimulated attempts from within the movement itself to reflect on and define the central concerns of the New Age movement considered as a whole[49].

On this basis, we are justified from the outset to exclude from our study all movements displaying the sect characteristics listed above, while including in principle all movements of the cult variety. It should be noted, however, that these two polar opposites are in fact ideal types, between which there is room for many varieties. In his argument for the cultic milieu rather than the cult as the central phenomenon of the "cultic" variety, Campbell even goes so far as to suggest an inherent tension between cult characteristics and the cults themselves. The latter necessarily display certain "sectarian" characteristics which

---

[47] York, 'New Age Movement', 147.

[48] Marilyn Ferguson's *Aquarian Conspiracy* can be considered the most typical expression of this development.

[49] The increasing commercialization of the New Age movement in the 1980s has by the beginning of the 1990s led to a reverse development among many erstwhile New Agers. The label "New Age" has acquired negative connotations, and many people no longer want to be associated with it. As noted by Lewis ('Approaches', 2), '...one can no longer simply ask respondents in a straightforward manner whether they consider themselves part of the New Age'. This development does not necessarily imply that these people no longer see themselves as part of a "movement", but it does mean that the term "New Age" will probably not survive the twentieth century as a generally-used label for that movement. The present study is basically concerned with the period from the later 1970s until the early 1990s, and therefore retains the term New Age.

make them less than fully representative of the cultic milieu: '...it would appear as if the organizational form most typical of the cultic milieu is not the cult but the 'society of seekers'. Indeed the cult, in the form of a group offering a particularized and detailed revealed truth, represents something of an aberration from the basic principle of tolerance and eclecticism which is prevalent in the milieu in general...'[50] This is particularly the case with the so-called revelatory cults, 'which have adherents rather than seekers and promulgate *the* truth as it has already been revealed'[51]. With these nuances in mind, I will follow the general rule that sources qualify as New Age *the more* they diverge from sect characteristics and approach the cultic profile. Furthermore, sources representative of "transorganizational" New Age currents will be considered preferable to sources representative of specific organizations (i.e., cults). This last criterion, however, will not be applied as a matter of strict principle but rather as a general guideline from which it is possible to deviate in specific cases.

D. Restrictions according to the Research Aims of this Study

Our focus is on the religious ideas of the New Age movement as they can be found—either explicitly or implicitly—in New Age sources. This means that a great deal of literature with purely practical purposes can be excluded from the analysis. For instance, astrological handbooks intended for the calculation of birth charts and the like will be excluded, while more reflective literature about the religious or psychological value of astrology may be included. By the same token, medical or psychological handbooks concentrating on methods of treatment will be excluded, while more general reflections on health and healing, in which the ideas behind the procedures are explained will definitely be included. Also, while the New Age belief in crystals as transformers of cosmic energy is very relevant to our inquiry, it would be useless for our concerns to study picturebooks in which the different kinds of crystal are listed together with descriptions of their accompanying virtues.

A considerable part of the literature offered for sale in New Age bookshops is in fact little more than the written reflection of New Age practices. This purely practical dimension of New Age religion is of great importance for a complete view of the movement. As noted in the introduction, however, its study would require the use of methods and research strategies which differ from those of textual analysis and historical interpretation concentrated on in the present study. While fully aware that a combination of different approaches will be needed in order to produce a reasonably complete description, I will

---

[50] Campbell, 'Cultic Milieu', 127.
[51] Campbell, 'Cultic Milieu', 127. Cf. the discussion as continued on Cambell's page 128.

concentrate on the ideas and leave the systematic study of practices to other researchers.

It is important to give explicit attention to the nature of the preliminary demarcation arrived at in this way. Snoek[52] has called attention to the important distinction between what he calls association by contiguity and association by similarity. A cluster of phenomena which are associated by contiguity do not need to be similar at all. They are associated not on the basis of shared characteristics, but on the basis of the structural or functional relationships between them, which bring them together in a single *Gestalt* (a general example would be "all organisms living on a certain plot of land"[53]). The empirical situation of the New Age movement displays the characteristics of a cluster of phenomena associated by contiguity. They are classified together on the basis of various structural or functional relationships (either or not of a social nature), but there is no logical implication or guarantee that the various beliefs referred to as "New Age" will display any intrinsic similarities. The same also applies to the restricted field resulting from our preliminary demarcations. All the arguments used (age, commitment to political action, use of drugs, time period, geographical situation, cultural provenance, and sect/cult characteristics) are extrinsic to the *beliefs* of participants. It remains to be seen whether it will be possible to speak of *one* New Age movement on the basis of association by similarity (of beliefs). This question, which is the one we seek to answer in the present study, therefore remains untouched by the preliminary demarcations.

The criteria discussed above proved sufficient to reduce the overwhelming—and continually expanding—supply of material to manageable proportions and to select circa one hundred representative books which together cover the complete field. During approximately two years (summer 1990-autumn 1992) a number of leading New Age bookshops in the Netherlands were visited on a regular basis (this included the large New Age section of an American bookshop in the Netherlands, which allowed for an adequate impression of the American supply). During travels over a period of several years I further had occasion to visit bookshops in Germany, France, and England. During these visits, the supply of books was systematically surveyed. The proprietors were consulted for advice about which books were especially popular among their clients. This procedure resulted in the textual corpus which forms the foundation of the present study.
The materials fall into five categories, corresponding to the major trends which I found can be discerned in the New Age movement. These are: 1. Channel-

[52] Snoek, *Initiations*, 33-34.
[53] Snoek, *Initiations*, 33.

ing; 2. Healing & Growth; 3. New Age Science; 4. Neopaganism; 5. New Age in a restricted and in a general sense. It must be emphasized that these different trends, although clearly identifiable, are far from being rigidly separated and therefore display a considerable overlap. For instance, part of the material based on channeling (cat. 1) is concerned with information about healing (cat. 2). As a result, certain books can turn up in more than one category. The five categories will be introduced in Part One. This way of subdividing the New Age material emerged naturally in the course of this research. It must derive its justification from its practical heuristic value and its ability to chart the field in an elegant and comprehensive way.

In spite of all criteria, the choices which had to be made from the wealth of material will inevitably remain vulnerable to criticism. It can be predicted that some readers will regret the absence of this or that book which they feel is absolutely essential, and that others will find that I included some books which they consider less important. This would no doubt happen in any case, regardless of the choices made. I am fairly confident, however, that all the essential authors are represented and that the choice among the lesser ones has resulted in a balanced and adequate spectrum. At a certain point in the research I found the number of new and unexpected ideas starting to diminish, until finally the reading became increasingly repetitive, with books presenting already familiar notions in different wordings. This has been taken as an indication that a sufficiently complete overview had been obtained.

The aim of the next five chapters (Part One) is to provide the reader with a general orientation to the field. The five major trends discerned in New Age religion will be introduced one by one, with reference to the available secondary literature. An effort will be made to put each of these trends into perspective from the point of view of the systematic study of religions. Finally, the authors and sources selected as representative for each category will be briefly introduced. The corpus as a whole will then be analyzed in Part Two.

PART ONE

ORIENTATION:
MAJOR TRENDS IN NEW AGE RELIGION

CHAPTER ONE

CHANNELING[1]

Joan: I hear voices telling me what to do. They come from God.
Robert: They come from your imagination.
Joan: Of course. That is how the messages of God come to us.

G.B. Shaw, *Saint Joan*

CHANNELING: A BRIEF CHARACTERISTIC

The term channeling refers to the conviction of psychic mediums that they are able, under certain circumstances, to act as a channel for information from sources other than their normal selves. Most typically, these sources are identified as discarnate "entities" living on higher levels of being, but the complete range of channeled sources mentioned in the literature contains almost everything to which some kind of intelligence might be attributed[2]. In many cases, a state of trance appears to be required, during which the entity takes possession of the medium's body to communicate either by the speech organs or (less usual in the New Age context) by automatic writing. The trance in such cases may vary from a state of complete or almost complete dissociation, during which the medium has no conscious knowledge of what happens, to a very light trance in which part of the medium's consciousness remains able to witness the channeling process as an outside observer. If all channeling phenomena could be associated with trance, we would be permitted to regard channeling as a special case of the well-known—if still insufficiently understood—phenomenon of religious dissociation, which under different and not always compatible labels (such as "ecstasy", "trance", "spirit possession", "mediumship") has been the object of much research[3]. However, some of the phe-

---

[1] Relevant general sources: Klimo, *Channeling*; id., 'Channeling Research'; Anderson, 'Channeling'; Babbie, 'Channels to Elsewhere'; Hughes, 'Blending'; Riordan, 'Channeling'; id., 'Channeling: A New Revelation?'; Hanegraaff, 'Channeling-literatuur'; Hastings, *Tongues*.

[2] Not only such entities as ascended masters, spirit guides, angels, extraterrestrials, various historical personalities (Jesus, Paul, etc.), God/the "Ultimate Source", gods and goddesses of antiquity, and the collective unconscious or Universal Mind, but also "group entities", incarnate or discarnate animals (dolphins, whales), nature spirits or "devas", gnomes, fairies, plants, and finally the "higher self" of the channel. One particular channel even claimed to be in contact with "The Committee": a geometrical consciousness comprised of a line, a spiral and a multidimensional triangle (Ridall, *Channeling*, 9).

[3] The terminology is far from fixed. See for different approaches and theories, as well as case studies, Lewis, *Ecstatic Religion*; Tart, *Altered States of Consciousness*; Bourguignon, *Religion, Altered States of Consciousness and Social Change*; id., *Possession*; Crapanzano & Garrison, *Case Studies in Spirit Possession*; Sharma, 'Ecstasy'; Crapanzano, 'Spirit Possession'; Goodman, *Ecstasy, Ritual, and Alternate Reality*.

nomena classed as channeling do not seem to involve trance at all, notably the cases of inner dictation in which the medium hears a voice dictating messages which (s)he writes down in a fully conscious state. If, following the emic view of New Age believers, we accept both these phenomena and trance communications as different aspects of channeling, the only common denominator appears to be the fact that people receive information—messages—which they interpret as coming from a source other than their own normal consciousness. We may slightly specify this by adding that this source is believed to represent a level of wisdom or insight superior to that of most humans (although it is not necessarily or even usually regarded as all-knowing and infallible). Communication with such sources is sought for the purpose of learning and guidance. In contrast, communication with spirits of the recently departed—as in classical spiritualism—is not characteristic of New Age channeling.

CHANNELING AS ARTICULATED REVELATIONS

In the literature about the phenomenon, an effort is usually made to define channeling in abstract terms. According to Jon Klimo,

> Channeling is the communication of information to or through a physically embodied human being from a source that is said to exist on some other level or dimension of reality than the physical as we know it, and that is not from the normal mind (or self) of the channel[4].

Arthur Hastings refers to channeling as

> ...a process in which a person transmits information or artistic expression that he or she receives mentally or physically and which appears to come from a personality source outside the conscious mind. The message is directed toward an audience and is purposeful[5].

The differences between these two definitions are not without significance, but the implications do not need to concern us here. Of more immediate interest is the fact that historians of religions, if presented with these definitions, would probably recognize both as attempts to demarcate the general class of "religious revelations" rather than "channeling" specifically. This somewhat sobering realization provides us with a good starting point for evaluating the nature of channeling from the perspective of the study of religions.

Unfortunately, although one might expect the comparative study of religious revelations to be of obvious importance in the systematic study of religions, remarkably little research has in fact been done in this area. We do not yet possess a usable cross-cultural theory or typology of revelations, and this makes

---

[4] Klimo, *Channeling*, 2.
[5] Hastings, *Tongues*, 4.

it difficult to reach an adequate evaluation of channeling. Th.P.van Baaren's 1951 dissertation about *Conceptions of Revelation*, one of the very few studies of the subject, suffers from an excessively inclusive definition of revelation, and from a methodical concentration on the source (or "author") of revelation which betrays a theological background[6]. Given the fact that only the form and content of revelations, as mediated by human beings, is accessible to others (whether believers or researchers), a modern comparative study of revelations might more fruitfully focus on this form and content than on the supposed author. Nothing essential would be lost in such an approach, because all relevant information about the author is necessarily contained in the form and content itself. However, I know of no major attempts in this direction.

Still, one particular terminological distinction can be made which is implicit in the work of Van Baaren. This is the identification of "inspiration" as a special, and prominent, mode of revelation. Van Baaren defines inspiration as '...oral or written communications from a deity to the world, in which the former uses a human being as medium.'[7] This definition is confirmed by G.Lanczkowski: 'The concept of inspiration ... indicates a form of revelation, which is ultimately based on the conception of a substantial conveyance of the divine spirit .... As immediate divine action, inspiration results in knowledge and communication of supernatural insights.'[8] On the basis of such definitions, it is clear that channeling must be regarded as belonging to the general class of religious inspiration[9]. Regarding channeling as "inspiration" has only one disadvantage. The secularization of its original meaning has resulted in a close association of "inspiration" with the realm of artistic and literary creation. The underlying belief that artistic creation is, indeed, the result of divine revelation is no longer dominant today. Consequently, "inspiration" has become a rather weak term to use for the phenomena under discussion. For this reason, I prefer to speak of "articulated revelations", which has the added advantage of making its status as a subgroup of religious revelations explicit.

Articulated revelations may come to human beings in different forms. Although it would be tempting to compare the different channeling modes with the modes

---

[6] Van Baaren, *Voorstellingen van openbaring*. See definition on p. 12.

[7] Van Baaren, *Voorstellingen van openbaring*, 97.

[8] Lanczkowski, 'Inspiration: Religionsgeschichtlich', 773-775 (my transl.). Cf. also Carpenter, 'Inspiration', 256-259.

[9] This requires that we understand terms like "deity" or "divine", as used by Van Baaren and Lanczkowski, in a wide sense. Since angels, for instance, apparently qualify as dispensers of divine revelation although they are not "deities" or "divine" themselves, the "higher entities" contacted in channeling must also qualify because they represent the "higher world". Strictly spoken, the terms used by both Van Baaren and Lanczkowski are problematic because they display hidden theological presuppositions. A metaphysically neutral alternative would be "meta-empirical beings", as proposed by Platvoet, *Comparing Religions*, 30.

of receiving articulated revelations found in other religions, the absence of a
general comparative study and typology of revelations puts such an endeavour
beyond the scope of this study. However, there is one particular way of putting
channeling "into context" historically which we do need to discuss. This is
because the approach is both widely accepted and manifestly wrong.

Instead of regarding New Age channeling as an example of the general category of (articulated) revelations, there is a strong tendency to turn the argument around and claim that all revelations of the past are to be regarded as
channeling. This view was introduced by Klimo in his pioneering study of
1987, and has been rather uncritically adopted by almost all commentators
since[10]. It asserts that "channeling" is a universal phenomenon which can be
found in most or all religions throughout history. This claim has considerable
popular appeal, because it strongly suggests that the New Age phenomena give
us a new and exciting perspective on the real nature of old stories about revelations. By studying the process of channeling in its modern manifestation,
or so it is suggested, we will be able to find out what really happened to the
Old Testaments prophets, to Muhammed, and many others. Channeling, in
effect, is perceived as the master key to understanding religion.

Now, as a *hypothesis* the idea that channeling and other revelations share the
same etiology is completely valid and indeed very interesting. It certainly
deserves serious and unbiased study. However, our present state of knowledge
does not permit us to regard it as more than an hypothesis. First, the scarcity
and inherent limitations of sources about ancient religious revelations make
their identification as "channeling" highly speculative: we do not know for
sure what happened, and we should not pretend that we do. Second, and more
important, neither do we know to what extent the different channeling phenomena, and *a forteriori*, religious (articulated) revelations in general have to
be attributed to, and can be explained in term of, one single process. At the
moment, both channeling and "articulated revelations" are mere container concepts which do not necessarily imply a deeper similarity between the phenomena falling under them. "Association by similarity" in this case would
require that we understood, beyond reasonable doubt, the processes involved
in the production of revelatory phenomena, and were able to explain them in
a unified way. The fact that we do not possess such an explanation is obscured
in most studies of channeling by a characteristic argumentative strategy. Typically, authors do not start with empirical descriptions but with abstract definitions of "channeling". These definitions—two of which were quoted above—
use the production of information apparently coming from other sources as a
sole criterion, while ignoring differences in the way this information is ob-

---

[10] Anderson, 'Channeling', 6; Babbie, 'Channels to Elsewhere'; Riordan, 'Channeling', 97;
id., 'Channeling: A New Revelation?', 105-106; Hastings, *Tongues*, 6.

tained. Such a procedure is quite legitimate for delimiting the otherwise pluriformous category of "articulated revelations", but it does not imply any deeper connection between the phenomena belonging to this category. Nevertheless, these definitions are then used to jump to the arbitrary conclusion that the phenomena belonging to the category thus defined are essentially *one*, in other words, that there is one basic *process* responsible for the appearance of revelatory information. A provisory association on the basis of abstract criteria is thus wrongly presented as proof that the phenomena in question are similar in essence. When this has been succesfully accomplished, it is easy to point out that revelations outside the New Age context also fall under the definition, that they are therefore also examples of "channeling", and that a study of contemporary New Age channeling can lead to the identification of the process behind revelations in general.

When the arbitrariness of this procedure is recognized, the glamorous implications of "channeling throughout the centuries" are perceived to be premature at the very least. Our conclusion about the status of channeling in the context of the study of religions is less exciting: *"channeling" is an emic term used in the New Age context to refer to the general etic category of "articulated revelations"*. It is no more and no less than that. The attempt to present channeling as an etic term must be dismissed as an apologetic strategy for convincing the public of the validity of New Age channeling.

This conclusion has, of course, no bearing on the validity of New Age channeling as such. It may or may not be a valid source of revelation regardless of its similarity or dissimilarity to other reported revelations. Whatever the final verdict on channeling will be, at least there can be no doubt about its central importance in the genesis of New Age religion. Many of the fundamental New Age beliefs, as we will see in Part Two of this study, have first been formulated in channeled messages. It is therefore fair to say that, in spite of the tendency among New Age believers to emphasize personal experience as the exclusive basis of religious truth, New Age religion must to a large extent be considered a religion of revelation (*Offenbarungsreligion*).

CHANNELING MODES AND DEVELOPMENTAL PROCESSES

The phenomena classed as channeling fall into several groups. First, we have cases of trance channeling, in which the depth of the trance may vary from very light to complete or almost complete dissociation. Second, we have various kinds of automatisms, like the ouija board and automatic writing[11]. Third,

---

[11] Anderson ('Channeling', 6) uses "automatism" as a general term for both groups, defining it as 'behavior, usually speaking or writing, for which the subject denies voluntary control'.

there are cases of clairaudient channeling, either or not combined with clairvoyant vision of the communicating entity. As a fourth group, we may decide to include what Jon Klimo refers to as "open channeling". This concept will be explained and discussed below[12].

As noted above, the ultimate nature of these different modes—let alone how they are related—is far from clear at the moment. Although they are obviously different, they are probably not distinct in an absolute sense. There are many examples of mediums starting in one mode and switching to another in the course of a gradual process of development. Usually, they end up specializing in one particular mode. I will discuss some examples of such developments found in the literature. The comparison of these cases appears to suggest a certain correlation between the different channeling modes on the one hand, and the extent to which the medium is able to control the channeling process on the other. Although this correlation may not be strict and absolute, it provides a preliminary outline for a phenomenology of channeling.

Channeling may be either *intentional* or *spontaneous*[13]. In cases of spontaneous channeling, the channel is more or less at the mercy of the comings and goings of the revelations. Intentional channels have control over the phenomenon and can usually produce it at will, either or not using specific techniques. Because it is widely believed in New Age circles that channeling is a natural ability which is latent in everybody, the phenomenon of intentional channeling has resulted in the publication of do-it-yourself books with instructions for getting in touch with one's personal guide[14]. However, it is not denied that some people are more gifted than others. Most of the revelations central to New Age religion have been produced by "natural channels". In most of these cases the channeling process started spontaneously, taking the medium by surprise. Jane Roberts, one of the undisputed "classics" of channeling, describes how she received her first revelation on september 9, 1963, while quietly sitting at the table:

---

[12] Klimo (*Channeling*, 185-201) describes some more channeling modes. His category of "physical channeling", in which the medium or entity affects the physical environment (healing of illnesses, materializations, moving or bending of objects), does not involve the 'communication of information' and is therefore not covered by Klimo's own definition. Moreover, this group is very characteristic for classical spiritualism, but not for New Age channeling. I also exclude dream channeling. It is true that people may interpret dreams as revelations, and that New Age believers often attach great importance to dreams as carriers of intuitive insights. There is therefore some justification in Klimo's opinion that dreams qualify as channeling, but this is not what is commonly understood by the term even in the New Age subculture itself. Klimo's category of "sleep channeling", finally, involves higher knowledge believed to be "implanted" in the brain during sleep and remembered later. This, also, qualifies as channeling according to Klimo's definition only in a technical sense. It appears to refer to a belief rather than to a phenomenon or experience.

[13] Klimo, *Channeling*, 185-186.

[14] For instance Ridall, *Channeling*, and OtC (abbreviations like this one refer to the New Age sources analyzed in Part Two. Cf. the list in the appendix).

Between one normal minute and the next, a fantastic avalanche of radical, new ideas burst into my head with tremendous force, as if my skull were some sort of receiving station, turned up to unbearable volume. Not only ideas came through this channel, but sensations, intensified and pulsating ... It was as if the physical world were really tissue-paper thin, hiding infinite dimensions of reality, and I was suddenly flung through the tissue paper with a huge ripping sound. My body sat at the table, my hands furiously scribbling down the words and ideas that flashed through my head. Yet I seemed to be somewhere else, at the same time, traveling through things. I went plummeting through a leaf, to find a whole universe open up; and then out again, drawn into new perspectives.

I felt as if knowledge was being implanted in the very cells of my body so that I couldn't forget it—a gut knowing, a biological spirituality. It was feeling and knowing, rather than intellectual knowledge ... When I came to, I found myself scrawling what was obviously meant as the title of that odd batch of notes: The Physical Universe as Idea Construction. Later the Seth Material would develop those ideas, but I didn't know that at the time.[15]

Seth was the name of the entity who would later introduce himself as responsible for this revelation. The first message was apparently received by automatic writing, but Roberts describes how she gradually developed via some intermediate stages into a full-trance intentional channel displaying the typical characteristics of "spirit possession". After Roberts had entered a deep trance, Seth would use her body for the purpose of verbal communication. During a channeling session Roberts's general behaviour and facial expression would become distinctly male, and her voice would drop dramatically.

While Roberts claimed to have been completely unprepared for the revelation of September 1963, other channels suggest that the revelation had been announcing itself for a long time. One of the most famous New Age channels, J Z Knight, describes her whole early life as a preparation for the meeting with her entity "Ramtha". At a certain moment, a clairvoyant predicted that she would meet "the One" in the near future, and another saw "an awesome power walking with her", whom she described as "on the same scale" as Jesus Christ[16]. Nevertheless, the decisive revelation came as a complete surprise: one evening while she and her husband were in an extremely silly mood playing with paper pyramids.

In jest, I grabbed one of the rejects off the floor, held it over my head, and proclaimed, "Attention, attention please, you are now about to witness a miracle. We are about to place our new brain machine upon the willing victim, upon whom nature did not smile with great intelligence. Carefully we place the pyramid in the aligned position, encompassing the entire head and face. In moments, gentlemen, you will witness a truly magnificent transformation."

I placed it on my head, and through peals of laughter from myself and [my husband], I mumbled, "I sure hope it works". After a few moments, I lifted the end of the pyramid just to eye level and, laughing so hard that tears were streaming

[15] SM 11-12.
[16] SoM 244-245.

from my eyes, I caught the glimmer of a bright light at the other end of my kitchen. The light was blurred by the tears, so I reached for a tissue and wiped the tears away. I blinked, and to my utter shock and amazement, there stood a giant man at the other end of my kitchen... just standing there, aglow.
This...thing...was made all of light, like golden glitter dropped through a ray of sunlight. His shoulders came to the top of the door, and it was as if the ceiling had disappeared to make room for his head. It was beautiful. ...
A smile so divine parted his lips to reveal glistening, immaculate teeth. "I am Ramtha, the Enlightened One. I have come to help you over the ditch". The words were delivered in a most melodious manner.[17]

Here we have an example of a channel who claims to be able to actually see "her" entity. However, like Jane Roberts, Knight would later develop into a full-trance channel with Ramtha using her speech organs to communicate with the audience. In both cases what started as spontaneous channeling later developed into intentional channeling. Sometimes, however, the channel never gets used to the process and keeps resisting it, although without succes. During the early 1960s, psychologist Helen Schucman began to experience visions and to hear an distinct "inner voice", both in her dreams and while awake. In October 1965 it started to tell her 'This is a course in miracles. Please take notes'[18]. When she finally and reluctantly obeyed, the voice proceeded to dictate the opening paragraph of what was to become, over a period of eight years, the 1188 pages of *A Course in Miracles*. Over the years the voice proved to be remarkably consistent, stopping the dictation when interrupted (by telephone calls etc.) and continuing at the next opportunity, if necessary in the middle of a sentence. Although Schucman finally resigned herself to the daily routine of taking dictation, she never really accepted the role which was forced upon her against her choice, and which conflicted with her atheistic persuasion. Her attitude is reflected in a remark she once made to a friend: "'I know the Course is true, Bill", she said—and then after a pause, "but I don't believe it"'[19]. In Schucman's case, the channeling process remained essentially spontaneous and never developed into trance channeling.

I discussed examples of spontaneous channeling which do or do not develop into intentional channeling. However, according to do-it-yourself books, intentional channeling can also be learned "from scratch", i.e., without any previous experiences of spontaneous channeling. It must be noted, however, that not one of the channels whom I studied (including those who authored do-it-yourself books) appears to have actually learned to channel in a purely intentional way, simply by applying techniques. They invariably report having had spontaneous psychic and/or channeling experiences beforehand. Edgar Cayce saw

---

[17] SoM 10-12.
[18] Skutch, *Journey*, 54.
[19] Skutch, *Journey*, iv.

angels, invisible playmates and other "little folk" when he was a child[20]. The voice of an angel helped him discover his psychic abilities[21]. Eva Pierrakos's abilities appear to have appeared spontaneously in the form of automatic writing[22]. David Spangler had a powerful experience—similar to the one described by Roberts—at the age of seven. After he had tried to develop his abilities by practicing meditation, channeling experiences continued to appear spontaneously from time to time[23]. Sanaya Roman had psychic experiences since her teens and spontaneously started to hear a voice when she was seventeen[24].

Of course, no definite conclusions can be drawn on such an impressionistic basis, but the above seems to suggest that channeling indeed requires a natural aptitude, more or less comparable to musical talent. Although everybody can learn to make music, it requires talent to reach an adequate level of performance. Similarly, it may require a certain natural sensitivity to perform adequately as a channel[25]. Furthermore, the evidence seems to suggest that while the trance and automatism varieties of channeling require some training on the part of the channel, who must learn to use and control his/her talents to achieve maximum effectivity, the hearing of inner voices does not require such training.

So what about completely intentional channeling on the basis of do-it-yourself techniques? Many New Agers claim to have learned channeling in this way; but, although they certainly do produce messages, few if any of these seem to have commanded wide popularity. While the most influential channeled texts appear to have been produced by "natural" channels, the messages of purely intentional channels seem on the whole to be rather unremarkable. If correct, this impression confirms the comparison with musical talent. Untalented players can certainly learn to make music in a technical sense, but only the ones with talent deserve to be called musicians. Comparably, it requires talent to become a real channel, but even the untalented may be able to learn channeling at least in a technical sense. If this comparison is valid, then what is it that purely intentional channels are really doing?

This is where Klimo's concept of "open channeling" may come in useful. While channeling as normally understood concerns communications from 'anomalous but identifiable sources'[26], open channeling in Klimo's terms refers to 'tapping information from other than individual identifiable sources.'[27]. In this

---

[20] TiR 27, 37-39, 45.
[21] TiR 47.
[22] PST 240.
[23] RS 61-63 and 65-66.
[24] LJ 2.
[25] For channeling as "performance", cf. Spangler, *Channeling*, 14-15.
[26] Klimo, *Channeling*, 186.
[27] Klimo, *Channeling*, 186.

way, Klimo wishes to accomodate into channeling 'traditional concepts of intuition, insight, inspiration, and imagination'[28]. His motivation to do this is revealing: 'The importance of open channeling is that, by definition, it allows anyone to participate in the experience of channeling'[29]. At first sight, this seems a particularly doubtful way of "proving" the universal significance of channeling, and it is not surprising that most later authors have dismissed Klimo's concept of open channeling as over-inclusive[30].

However, it seems to me that the concept of "open channeling" can indeed be very well defended as relevant for New Age phenomena. Klimo does not say that anyone who feels inspired is in fact channeling; he says that the concept of open channeling *allows* everybody to channel. What is more, by including the crucial words 'is said to' in his definition of channeling, Klimo has made it quite clear that the decision whether a given phenomenon is to be regarded as channeling ultimately depends on the personal belief of the channel (or his/her clientele)[31]. In referring to religious revelations, which are emically mediated in principle, this is indeed the only correct procedure[32]. It follows that, in terms of Klimo's own definition, the answer to the question whether "intuition, insight, inspiration and imagination" qualify as channeling must depend upon how these phenomena are experienced and interpreted by the person in question. If someone emically explains his inspirations as coming from a source existing 'on some other level or dimension of reality than the physical as we know it, and ... not from the normal mind (or self) of the channel' (= Klimo's definition) then for him these inspirations will be channeled revelations; but if he prefers to attribute them simply to the abilities of his own normal mind, then they will not. In principle, this argument applies to other forms of channeling as well, and to "articulated revelations" generally.

"Intuition, insight, inspiration and imagination" may therefore be emically regarded as channeling, and they qualify as examples of "articulated revelations" to the extent that they result in messages. Now, if we analyze the techniques offered for developing channeling abilities, we find that they consist largely of techniques for awakening and using natural intuitive abilities[33]. They

---

[28] Klimo, *Channeling*, 199.

[29] Klimo, *Channeling*, 199.

[30] Notably Hastings, *Tongues*, 5-6, who remarks that 'it is not clear that the process of spontaneous creativity or intuitive thinking is the same process as one in which there appears to be an outside personality or entity'. This is correct but, as noted above, neither is that the case for the different channeling modes which are included by Hastings.

[31] Klimo calls attention to this himself: 'Jeffrey Mishlove ... points out that a great deal rests on the phrase "is said to" in this definition. Clearly, it is the channels, their alleged sources, and the various followers of the phenomenon who comprise the rapidly growing worldwide channeling subculture, who say that the sources being channeled come from another level of reality.' (Klimo, *Channeling*, 2).

[32] Cf. Van Baaren, *Voorstellingen van Openbaring*, 12.

[33] Cf. for instance Kautz & Branon, Channeling; Ridall, Channeling; Klimo, *Channel-*

appear to concentrate on setting aside or circumventing rational "ego" control
by various means, allowing imagination and the "stream of consciousness" to
express itself freely in speech. In principle, this does not require special talents but only the ability to trust oneself and "let go". For instance, it is sometimes asserted that talking aloud *as if* one were channeling, without judging
the contents, will help to trigger real channeling[34]. Such procedures may easily result in messages, either or not attributed to specific other beings, but it
is only to be expected that their content will often be rather close to the medium's own beliefs. However, if we conclude from this that the source of these
messages is "just the imagination" of the channel, we are making an emic statement, reflecting certain presuppositions about the nature of the mind which
the medium is under no obligation to share. Indeed, many intentional New Age
channels will emically assert—like Shaw's Joan of Arc—that the faculty of the
imagination is the medium for "divine" revelations. This presupposes a different set of presuppositions about the nature of the mind, which will be discussed in more detail in chapter eight. In the meantime, we may conclude that
the concept of "open channeling"—understood as techniques for accessing normal intuitive abilities—is useful to account for purely intentional channeling.

This leads us to some general and preliminary conclusions and suggestions.
Trance channeling and automatisms seem to belong together to a considerable
extent. These phenomena display an obvious similarity with "spirit possession"
as known from shamanic contexts[35]. In both cases, the shaman/medium typically starts his career with spontaneous experiences and/or possession symptoms. The person in question is thereby started on a development which results,
in the succesful cases, in the ability to control the phenomena and turn them
into socially useful directions[36]. This similarity provides a promising starting
point for further comparative research.
The hearing of inner voices and the occasional seeing of visions, without trance
and without the symptoms of spirit possession, seems to be a different phenomenon. It is not clear from the evidence that this subgroup of "channeling"
involves a development resulting in increasing control over the experiences;
they seem to retain an essentially spontaneous character. Rather than with
shamanism and spirit possession, these channeling modes seem to be associ-

---

ing, part 4, which significantly discusses open channeling and channeling techniques in close
connection.

[34] Ridall, *Channeling*, 109. Cf. Hastings, *Tongues*, 159, about 'channels who speak impromptu or intuitively and consider this channeling'.

[35] In spite of the imagery evoked by the term "channeling", however, New Age mediums may
experience it not as "possession" by an alien entity, but rather as "blending" with another consciousness. This is argued by Dureen Hughes, 'Blending'.

[36] Eliade, *Shamanism*; Lewis, *Ecstatic Religion*.

ated with mysticism[37]. Again, further comparative study of this connection would be welcome.

Finally, there are cases of channeling in which the medium is simply sitting quietly and relaxedly, usually with eyes closed, and talks to the audience in a normal voice. There are no obvious symptoms of spirit possession (seizures, voice alterations, etc.). Some degree of dissociation may be involved, resulting from deep meditative relaxation, but the extent to which such a state may be described as "trance" is probably a matter of definition. These kinds of channeling do not necessarily start with spontaneous phenomena and experiences: they usually result from practicing techniques for developing intuition and minimizing rational control, with or without the explicit aim of developing channeling.

Obviously, these distinctions are of a preliminary character. While I am reasonably convinced that the second type is different from the others, the relation between the first and the third is less clear. They may turn out to be different in essence, but it is also possible that they in fact represent two opposite poles of a continuum. Scholarship is probably not yet in a position to decide which is the case. Also, it must be noted that some cases of channeling do not seem to fit so well, notably Edgar Cayce's practice of providing information while apparently asleep. So, many puzzles remain, which will not be solved here. More definitive answers will require a polymethodological approach combining the perspectives of (para)psychology and consciousness research, neurology, anthropology and religious history. In the meantime, the above distinctions must suffice for providing some orientation.

THE SOURCES

I will now briefly introduce the channeling sources selected for analysis in the present study. The abbreviations are used for reference in the rest of this study, especially in Part Two[38].

EDGAR CAYCE[39]

TiR   Thomas Sugrue, *There is a River: The Story of Edgar Cayce*
SP   Jess Stearn, *Edgar Cayce: The Sleeping Prophet*
SOS   Harmon Hartzell Bro, *Edgar Cayce: A Seer out of Season*
ECR   Hugh Lynn Cayce, *The Edgar Cayce Reader*

---

[37] See for instance the discussion of "voices and visions" in Underhill, *Mysticism*, 266-297.

[38] For a complete alphabetical list of all abbreviations, see the appendix.

[39] For general information about Cayce, see TiR, SP and SOS. TiR is the most complete biography and SOS adds information about Cayce's last years. SP largely concentrates on Cayce's prophecies. For more objective information about Cayce, his son and grandson and the A.R.E. (see text), see Melton, Clark & Kelly, *New Age Encyclopedia*, 88-93. Cf. also Klimo, *Channeling*, 113-116. For a favourable theological analysis, cf. Drummond, *Unto the Churches*.

ECRe   Noel Langley, *Edgar Cayce on Reincarnation*
ECMM   Henry Reed, *Edgar Cayce on Mysteries of the Mind*
ECSU   Lin Cochran, *Edgar Cayce on Secrets of the Universe*
ECA   Edgar Evans Cayce, *Edgar Cayce on Atlantis*
ECDS   Glenn D. Kittler, *Edgar Cayce on the Dead Sea Scrolls*
ECSJ   Jeffrey Furst, *Edgar Cayce's Story of Jesus*
ECJC   Anne Read, *Edgar Cayce on Jesus and his Church*

Edgar Cayce (1877-1945) is one of the most famous psychics of this century. In 1900 he developed laryngitis and lost his voice. When an amateur hypnotist put him into a trance, Cayce appeared to be able to correctly diagnose his own illness and prescribe a cure. News of the phenomenon spread, and people began to ask him for help with their illnesses. Cayce turned out to be able to give correct diagnoses even over great distances, and the accuracy of his "readings" (as the session transcripts were called) eventually made him famous. In 1923 Cayce met Arthur Lammers, an enthusiast of theosophy and the occult who introduced him to the idea of reincarnation. Subsequently, Cayce began to describe past lives while in trance, often explaining illnesses with reference to them. These past life readings eventually resulted in detailed information about historical and biblical events, forgotten cultures, and the like. Cayce would also give predictions of future events. All the readings were systematically taken down in shorthand by a secretary, which has resulted in a mass of written material. The publication in 1942 of the biographical novel TiR led to an unprecedented flood of requests for health readings; the resulting overwork probably hastened Cayce's death in 1945.

Cayce's son Hugh Lynn Cayce took charge of his father's heritage, reorganizing the *Association for Research and Enlightenment* (A.R.E.) which had been founded in 1931 for the purpose of studying and disseminating the readings. His agressive publishing policy resulted in a wide popularity of books based on Cayce's readings. The A.R.E. has published verbatim transcripts of the readings in the "Edgar Cayce Library Series"[40], but better known are the many books in which key themes in the readings are compiled, commented upon and interpreted by others. Some of these sources seem to emphasize Cayce's own personal perspective, others stick closely to the actual text of the readings, and many others bear a heavy personal stamp of the author or compiler. ECR, for instance, strongly emphasizes Cayce's own conservative Christian beliefs. ECSJ largely lets the readings speak for themselves. In many of the most popular Cayce books, however, it is often difficult to distinguish between Cayce's ideas and those of his interpreters. ECMM, in particular, is basically a book by Henry Reed, who only seems to use the Cayce material as a pretext for presenting his own views. Over the years, Cayce's conservative Christian beliefs seem to have been increasingly ignored while the esoteric aspects of the mate-

[40] See SOS 403.

rial have been emphasized. For our purpose, this onesided reinterpretation by later commentators is important to note, but not crucial. We will be concerned with the *Wirkungsgeschichte* of the Cayce books in the New Age context, rather than with an attempt to recover the original meaning.

Although Cayce lived long before the emergence of the New Age movement, the books based on his readings have crucially influenced the development of the latter. They have been popular at least since the 1960s and have remained so up to this day. Many of the more recent books based on his readings are fully representative of modern New Age thought. The question remains to what extent his manner of conveying information can be called channeling[41]. Cayce only occasionally channeled personified sources (notably the archangel Michael[42]). Normally no individual source was identified, but it is widely believed by Cayce's supporters that he in fact tapped into the collective unconscious of mankind. The Cayce phenomenon remains a borderline case both with regard to the source of the information and, as noted above, with regard to the process involved in the communication. Cayce is normally regarded as a channel in the New Age context, however, and we will follow this opinion here.

EVA PIERRAKOS[43]

PST   Eva Pierrakos, *The Pathwork of Self-Transformation*

Eva Pierrakos (1915-1979), daughter of the Jewish writer Jakob Wassermann, emigrated from Austria to the U.S.A. after the Nazi takeover. She married John Pierrakos, a co-founder of bio-energetics. Her mediumistic abilities first manifested themselves as automatic writing, but 'by meditating for long hours, changing her diet, and making the commitment to use her gift only for helping people ... she eventually succeeded in becoming a pure channel so that a spirit entity of high wisdom like the Guide was able to manifest through her and offer us the gift of his teachings'[44]. This Guide never gave his name. Judging from the Pathwork material he seems to have answered questions, which suggests that the process was a form of trance channeling. No information is given about the time period during which the messages were received. An organisation seems to have emerged around Pierrakos, concentrating on public channeling sessions and workshop-like applications of the material, which is basically about healing and personal growth. Pathwork was incorporated as a non-profit educational foundation in 1972. At her death, Pierrakos left hundreds of channeled lectures, which were disseminated separately at first and seem to have influenced many people in this way. The compilation PST

---

[41] Cf. SOS 107-108; ECSU 147ff.
[42] ECSJ 342, 345.
[43] A very brief biographical sketch is included in PST 240-241.
[44] PST 240-241.

appeared in 1990. There are two Pathwork centers (New York and Virginia), and several study- and working groups in the U.S.A. and abroad.

JANE ROBERTS/SETH[45]

SM   Jane Roberts, *The Seth Material*
SS   Jane Roberts, *Seth Speaks: The Eternal Validity of the Soul*
NPR   Jane Roberts, *The Nature of Personal Reality: A Seth Book*

We have seen how poet and science-fiction writer Jane Roberts (1929-1984) came to be a channel for the "energy essence personality" Seth. The Seth books, based on the material as written down in shorthand by Roberts's husband Robert Butts, are undisputed "classics" of modern channeling. Almost all of the later New Age channels mention Seth, together with Cayce, among their chief sources of inspiration. During the 1970s, when such literature was still relatively scarce, Roberts's example encouraged many to take their own experiences with channeling seriously. The influence of the Seth books was no doubt enhanced by Roberts's considerable literary talents. Hastings rightly remarks that 'her writing is excellent and more poetic and imagistic than Seth's. If he drew on her skills, he fared well'[46]. Indeed, both Roberts's own books[47] and those based on Seth's words make fascinating reading. Both "authors" come across as highly intelligent, and this is reflected in the considerable complexity of the material. In Part Two of this study we will see that several of the basic metaphysical concepts which were to become normative in the New Age Movement were probably first introduced by Roberts/Seth. It remains an unresolved but highly relevant question to what extent these concepts reflect Roberts's own earlier science fiction work.

A COURSE IN MIRACLES[48]

CiM   *A Course in Miracles: The Text, Workbook for Students and Manual for Teachers*
        T   Text
        WfS   Workbook for Students
        MfT   Manuel for Teachers

If we were to select one single text as "sacred scripture" in the New Age movement, the sheer awe and reverence with which *The Course*—as it is fondly

---

[45] For general overviews, see Melton, Clark & Kelly, *New Age Encyclopedia*, 274-275; Klimo, *Channeling*, 28-34; Hastings, *Tongues*, 72-78. An analysis of Seth's teachings is given in Hanegraaff, 'Channeling-literatuur', 12-20.

[46] Hastings, *Tongues*, 72-73.

[47] See, for instance, *God of Jane*.

[48] General information: Melton, Clark & Kelly, *New Age Encyclopedia*, 129-132; Klimo, *Channeling*, 37-42; Hastings, *Tongues*, 98-113 and Skutch, *Journey*. For analyses of the teaching: Hanegraaff, 'Channeling-literatuur', 28-33; Koffend, 'Gospel according to Helen', 74-90. A good commentary is Wapnick, *Meaning of Forgiveness*. Other books based on the "Course" have been written by Wapnick, F. Vaughan & R. Walsh, G. Jampolsky and Tara Singh.

called—is discussed by its devotees would make this huge volume the most obvious choice. Indeed, it is among those channeled texts which refute the often-heard opinion that channeling only results in trivialities. Although less original in content than the Seth messages, the *Course* impresses by its flawless consistency over a length of more than 1100 pages, and by the poetic quality of its language. Amazingly, several long parts of the text were later discovered to be written in Shakespearean blank verse (Iambic pentameters).

The text implies that its author is Jesus Christ. The intention of the material is 'removing the blocks to the awareness of love's presence, which is your natural inheritance'[49]. To this end, the main text (622 pp.) is supplemented by a workbook consisting of 365 exercises, one for each day of the year, and a brief manual for teachers. The "career" of the *Course* has been extraordinary. At first it was only disseminated by photocopies to some friends of Helen Schucman and her companion Bill Thetford, but as the fame of the *Course* was spread by word of mouth, the number of copies in circulation grew explosively. A nonprofit *Foundation for Inner Peace* was founded, which in 1975 published the *Course*. The original three volumes were later followed by a paperback, which has been a publishing success ever since. Large numbers of people profess to have been deeply influenced by the teachings[50]. Many small groups have emerged in which the *Course* is respectfully studied, and an extraordinarily large number of commentaries have been published.

DAVID SPANGLER[51]

RBNA   David Spangler, *Revelation: The Birth of a New Age*
CNA   David Spangler, *Channeling in the New Age*

The American David Spangler may be regarded as the "theologian in residence" of the influential New Age community Findhorn in Scotland. Spangler, who reports having had psychic experiences since childhood, came to Europe in 1970 after his "inner guidance" had told him that he would find the keys for a next cycle of work there. Findhorn proved to be his destination. On July 31, 1970, Spangler began channeling an entity calling itself "Limitless Love and Truth"[52]. This resulted in seven so-called "transmissions" about the coming of the New Age, which form the core of RBNA. Under the inspiration of his guide, Spangler added a commentary which shows a profound influence of Theosophy in the tradition of Alice Bailey. RBNA was published by Findhorn.

---

[49] CiM Introduction.
[50] Cf. the video *The Story of A Course in Miracles. Part 1: 'The Forgotten Song', Part 2: 'The Song Remembered'*. The second part contains a great number of personal testimonies.
[51] General information: Melton, Clark & Kelly, *New Age Encyclopedia*, 428-429; cf. Bednarowski, *New Religions and the Theological Imagination in America*, Bloomington/Indianapolis 1989; an interesting analysis is Rhodes, 'New Age Christology of David Spangler', 402-418.
[52] RBNA 39-43; cf. Hughes, 'Blending': Spangler's description of his channeling experiences seems to confirm Hughes's preference of the term "blending" over "channeling".

When Spangler returned to the U.S.A. in 1973, he discovered that the book had become a basic text in the emerging New Age subculture. This was somewhat embarrassing to him, because he disliked being looked at as a "psychic medium". He decided to publish a second version of RBNA, with a new introductory part and some added transmissions received in 1975 from an entity called "John". I have used this second version. Spangler's reservations were to grow stronger over the years, as his New Age philosophy gradually outgrew its original theosophical framework, but he has never renounced his early work[53]. In CNA, published in 1988, Spangler does show himself very critical of the popular channeling craze of the 1980s. Evidently worried about being lumped together with "talkshow-channels" like J Z Knight and others, he attempts to distinguish valid forms of channeling from phenomena merely representative of "New Age glamour".

Spangler's later work, which is very different from RBNA and not explicitly based on channeling, will be discussed in chapter five. RBNA, regardless of its status in the context of Spangler's personal development, must be regarded as one of the foundational texts of the New Age Movement.

RAMALA[54]

RR	*The Revelation of Ramala*
WR	*The Wisdom of Ramala*
VR	*The Vision of Ramala*

The so-called Ramala messages were channeled by an anonymous English couple ("David and Ann"). The revelations started somewhere during the sixties and were made public in pamphlet-form. The compilation RR was published in 1978 in response to growing public demand. In the meantime the channels, led by their "inner guidance", had moved to Chalice Hill House in Glastonbury, one of the focal points of New Age activity in England[55]. This house was subsequently transformed into a succesful New Age center.

"Ramala" is the "soul name" of the channeling couple, who appear to have developed a form of light trance channeling[56]. The teachings are believed to come from about ten different anonymous "Masters"—as the entities are called —, but the majority of them has been given by a core group of three. It is believed that these Masters do not restrict their attention only to Ramala, but are also speaking through other channels all over the world. To Ramala, they give brief lectures (20-30 minutes) on a wide variety of topics, often in reac-

---

[53] Cf. Spangler's chapter 'Formative forces and the higher dimensions of spirit' in RW (cf. chapter five).

[54] For an analysis of the teaching, see Hanegraaff, 'Channeling-literatuur', 23-28.

[55] For background see Hexham, '"Freaks" of Glastonbury', and Bowman, 'Drawn to Glastonbury'.

[56] RR xiv; WR Introduction.

tion to prior requests. Afterwards, David's personal guide, who calls himself Zen Tao, takes over to answer questions and engage in discussions with the audience. In RR these questions and answers are omitted; in WR and VR a selection of them is included after each lecture. The messages were selected 'on a purely subjective basis[57]', and the originals have been rather heavily edited and condensed; but, we are told, 'always with strict regard to the original meaning'[58]. The teachings ended abruptly on June 11, 1989, when the "last channeling" was received. After this, the Masters have withdrawn, claiming that now is the time to live the message rather than just talk about it.

J Z KNIGHT/RAMTHA[59]

R   *Ramtha*
RI   *Ramtha: An Introduction*
RIC   *Ramtha Intensive: Change, the Days to Come*
SoM   J Z Knight, *A State of Mind: My story—Ramtha: The Adventure Begins*

J Z Knight (1946) tells the story of her life in SoM. We saw how she first met Ramtha, an ancient warrior from Atlantis who attained enlightenment during his only life on earth. Knight later developed into a full trance channel, who is completely unaware of what happens while Ramtha uses her body (she claims not to be aware of any time interval between the beginning and the end of a session). Her appearances on television talkshows and in Shirley MacLaine's books have made her one of the best-known channels in the U.S.A. As one of the most publicly visible mediums, Knight has strongly contributed to the popular image of channeling criticized by Spangler as "New Age glamour". Channeling has made her a star and brought in millions of dollars. Ramtha himself encouraged Knight to accept money in order to stem the flood of requests for help and guidance, also pointing out that it would be reasonable to expect some compensation for the large parts of her life irretrievably "lost" while channeling. Critics have, of course, found in these material rewards of the spiritual an occasion for cynical commentary. But Ramtha has become controversial within the New Age community as well. The increasingly dark and frightening, rather than positive and uplifting content of his messages has given rise to the speculation that, whoever the original Ramtha may have been, his place has now been taken by a less benign entity[60].

---

[57] WR Introduction.
[58] RR xiv.
[59] General information: Melton, Clark & Kelly, *New Age Encyclopedia*, 376; Klimo, *Channeling*, 42-45; and SoM.
[60] Klimo, *Channeling*, 44.

SANAYA ROMAN[61]

OtC   Sanaya Roman & Duane Packer, *Opening to Channel: How to Connect with your Guide*
LJ   Sanaya Roman, *Living with Joy: Keys to Personal Power and Spiritual Transformation*
PPA   Sanaya Roman, *Personal Power through Awareness: A Guidebook for Sensitive People*
SG   Sanaya Roman, *Spiritual Growth: Being your Higher Self*

Sanaya Roman is a well-known trance channel for the entity Orin, whose messages are basically about healing, personal transformation and inner growth. OtC, published together with Duane Packer, who channels DaBen, is one of the better known do-it-yourself channeling guides. The other three books, classed together as "The Earth Life Series", contain channeled material including practical exercises.

SHIRLEY MACLAINE (KEVIN RYERSON, J Z KNIGHT, e.o.)[62]

OL   Shirley MacLaine, *Out on a Limb*
DL   Shirley MacLaine, *Dancing in the Light*
IAP   Shirley MacLaine, *It's All in the Playing*
GW   Shirley MacLaine, *Going Within: A Guide for Inner Transformation*

Shirley MacLaine is not known as a channel herself, but some of the best known New Age channels have become famous by figuring in her books. The Swedish medium Sturé Johanssen ("Ambres") figures only in OL, and Jach Pursel ("Lazaris") plays some part in IAP but remains in the background. J Z Knight and Ramtha are introduced in DL; MacLaine's reaction to Ramtha was extremely emotional, and her spontaneous feeling that she had been his sister during his Atlantean life was confirmed by Ramtha[63]. But MacLaine's favourite was the full-trance channel Kevin Ryerson with his entities "Tom McPherson" and "John". Ryerson plays a crucial part in OL, and returns in DL and IAP. All these books contain extended descriptions of the channeling sessions which provided MacLaine with the basic elements of her New Age convictions. Ryerson is also important because MacLaine's TV-miniseries *Out on a Limb* (1987) featured him going into a trance and channeling McPherson and John *live* before the camera. Millions of people in the U.S.A. and abroad were thus first introduced to the channeling phenomenon by Ryerson's example.

---

[61] For some biographical information, see LJ and Klimo, *Channeling*, 141-144.

[62] General information: Melton, Clark & Kelly, *New Age Encyclopedia*, 270-272. Most material about MacLaine is written from the skeptical perspective. See Gardner, 'Issness is her Business'. Gordon, *Channeling into the New Age* should be mentioned for the sake of completeness, but can hardly be taken seriously as scholarship.

[63] DL 119.

CHAPTER TWO

HEALING AND PERSONAL GROWTH[1]

> Si c'est à l'illusion que je dois la santé dont je crois jouir,
> je supplie humblement les savants, qui voyent si clair, de ne
> le pas détruire; qu'ils illuminent l'univers, qu'ils me lais-
> sent mon erreur, et qu'ils permettent à ma simplicité, à ma
> faiblesse et à mon ignorance de faire usage d'un *agent invis-*
> *ible et qui n'existe pas, mais qui me guérit*[2].

THE ALTERNATIVE THERAPIES

The proliferation of what may loosely be called "alternative therapies"
undoubtedly represents one of the most visible aspects of the New Age Movement. The confusing variety of practices and perspectives, however, makes this
field particularly difficult to categorize. One of the very few generalizations
that can be made with some certainty is that all the ideas and activities belonging to this category share a concern with *healing*. This, at least, is the term
most practitioners will emically use, or agree to, for describing their practices.
The same term "healing", however, can also be understood in a more precise
etic sense, and this is the meaning I will adopt in this chapter. In using "healing" as an umbrella term (the addition "personal growth" will be discussed
below), I will adopt the terminology introduced by Arthur Kleinman, which is
widely used in the field of medical anthropology[3]. Kleinman makes a theoretical distinction between disease and illness, which has been summarized as
follows:

> DISEASE refers to abnormalities in the structure and/or function of organs and
> organ systems; pathological states whether or not they are culturally recognized;
> the arena of the biomedical model.
> ILLNESS refers to a person's perceptions and experiences of certain socially dis-
> valued states including, but not limited to, disease.[4]

Diseases are biophysical conditions, and medical practitioners are concerned
with *curing* these conditions. Illness, in contrast, has to do with 'the complex

---

[1] A good introduction of the general field is given by Beckford, 'Holistic Imagery and Ethics';
id., 'World Images'. A popular but informative introduction is Drury, *Elements of Human Potential*. See also the long discussion of healing in Heelas, *New Age Movement*, ch. 3.
[2] Response to the Report (1784) of the French Commission entrusted with investigating Mesmerism; quoted in Podmore, *Mesmerism and Christian Science*, 65.
[3] A useful overview and criticism is given by Young, 'Anthropologies of Illness and Sickness', 257-285.
[4] Young, 'Anthropologies', 264-265.

social, psychological, and spiritual condition of the sick person'[5], and constitutes the proper domain of *healing*. This distinction between disease/curing and illness/healing is particularly relevant for understanding the relation between modern western medicine on the one hand and traditional medical systems on the other. While the healing of illness is central to the medical practice of traditional cultures, modern western medicine is characterized by its increasing concentration on curing relatively isolated diseases. Critics of the latter maintain that the progress of scientific medicine has exacted a heavy price: 'It has been said that contemporary medicine has made great progress in the science of curing but, in so doing, it has lost the art of healing'[6].

Widespread dissatisfaction with this situation is certainly one of the main reasons for the growth of alternative healing approaches. These therapies typically aim at healing the whole person, rather than just curing the disease. For this reason they seek to give attention to the interaction between physical, emotional, mental and spiritual aspects of the patient's experience, as well as to social factors and the influence of the wider environment. The scope of factors relevant to healing, illness and health is therefore extended far beyond the horizon of official western medicine.

In their implicit criticism of official western medicine, New Age healing practices not surprisingly evince a rather close affinity to those of traditional cultures which western medicine has sought to replace. Because of their emphasis on the overall situation of the sick person rather than on a narrowly defined disease, neither traditional healers nor their New Age counterparts accept a rigid dichotomy between physical and mental illness[7]. Equally important is the fact that both traditional and New Age approaches to healing share a concern with *meaning*. In traditional healing systems, the illness is typically given symbolic form by being interpreted in the context of general cultural beliefs. Therefore, as one scholar puts it, 'illness is not a simple biophysical fact but— through symbolic interpretation—is shaped into a human experience.'[8] As we will see, the same applies to New Age healing. Again, it is important to emphasize the contrast with modern western medicine. The secularization of health and healing in modern society has resulted in

> the notion that health, illness, and dying have no real meaning beyond their biophysical reality determinable by empirical, rational means. Institutions of the private sphere are allowed to provide meaning, as voluntary and purely subjective interpretations, only so long as that interpretive scheme does not interfere with the medical dominance and its biophysical treatment of the disease[9].

---

[5] McGuire, 'Religion and Healing', 270.
[6] Foster & Anderson, *Medical Anthropology*, 137.
[7] Foster & Anderson, *Medical Anthropology*, 81.
[8] McGuire, 'Religion and Healing', 272.
[9] McGuire, 'Religion and Healing', 272-273.

Alternative approaches to healing, in contrast, offer general interpretive contexts for giving meaning to illness. These contexts are generally of a religious
(or "spiritual") nature. In this way the new therapies attempt to reinstate the
close connection between religion and healing abandoned and rejected by
scientific western medicine.

HEALING AS A RELIGIOUS PHENOMENON

The link between religion and healing is undoubtedly a natural one. Both
domains, after all, share a concern with providing alternatives to human weakness and suffering. As observed by the Dutch scholar of religion C.J. Bleeker,
'Man feels weak, often powerless, mortal, foolish, sinful, guilty. He longs to
be whole, happy, spiritually strong and pure. Religion meets this desire. Every
religion is a religion of salvation.'[10] This notion of religion as responding to
the experience of human weakness and suffering by promising "salvation" can
easily lead to reductionistic conclusions[11], but that implication is not necessary. Regardless of how one thinks about the ultimate nature and explanation
of religion, or of particular religions, empirical evidence does confirm Bleeker's statement that religions generally give answers and prescriptions for dealing—either practically or conceptually—with human weakness and suffering[12].
If we add to this the observation that religious salvation is typically conceptualized as a condition in which all suffering and "lack" has been left behind,
it is only natural to conclude that religious salvation in fact amounts to a radical form of "healing". The natural affinity between the domains of religion
and healing based on this constellation is further confirmed by the fact that
central figures or symbols in religious traditions are very often also the source
of healing[13]. The very fact of healing, at least if practiced by persons endowed
with religious charisma, carries salvational overtones.

Apart from religious salvation considered *as* healing, religion is also often
a crucial element *in* healing. This is most evident in the case of so-called personalistic healing systems. In these systems, 'illness is believed to be caused
by the active, purposeful intervention of a sensate agent who may be a super-

---

[10] Bleeker, *Godsdienst voorheen en thans*, 127-128. My translation.
[11] The most famous example is, of course, Marx's statement: 'Religious distress is at the same
time the expression of real distress and a protest against real distress. Religion is the sigh of the
oppressed creature, the heart of a heartless world, just as it is the spirit of a spiritless situation.
It is the opium of the people.' (Marx & Engels, as quoted in Morris, *Anthropological Studies of
Religion*, 34.
[12] The teachings of the Buddha, which take the fact of suffering as their point of departure,
are of course a case in point. For the Western context, see for instance Keith Thomas's acclaimed
study Religion and the Decline of Magic.
[13] Sullivan, 'Healing', 226.

natural being (a deity or a god), a nonhuman being (such as a ghost, ancestor, or evil spirit) or a human being (a witch or sorcerer)'[14]. If illness is caused by supernatural agents, then naturally the healer must be accorded a corresponding religious status. The most typical example is the shaman, who acts as a mediator between the world of the spirits and the human community[15]. The religious background is less obvious in the alternative category of naturalistic systems, where

> illness is explained in impersonal, systemic terms. Naturalistic systems conform above all to an equilibrium model; health prevails when the insensate elements in the body, the heat, the cold, the humors or *dosha*, the yin and yang, are in balance appropriate to the age and condition of the individual in his natural and social environment. When this equilibrium is disturbed, illness results[16].

Still, even in these systems, the philosophy of nature presupposed in healing is traditionally closely interwoven with the general religious worldview of the society in question. The meaning of illness in such cases lies in a disturbance of the natural balance between the elements of the human organism[17]. Because the human body is usually regarded as modeled on the wider universe, medicine has its natural place in a general cosmological or metaphysical context. For this reason, it is common for the domain of healing to shade into the sphere of the religious *per se*.

I will not make an attempt to categorize the different types of healing that can be found in religions generally. As in the case of "revelations" discussed in the previous chapter, there does not yet seem to exist a cross-cultural study and typology of healing in religions, although the field of medical anthropology has laid important foundations on which the study of religions could build. In the absence of such a typology, it suffices to summarize what is basic to healing in traditional religious contexts. The central feature, from which the rest follows, is the relevance accorded to the whole context (physical, psychological, spiritual, social, religious) of illness rather than only to the disease. Religion is often included in this context as relevant to both curing and healing. This inclusive approach to illness, furthermore, encourages the fusion rather than the separation of the domains of physical and mental illness. Concerned with more than just "fixing" isolated problems, healing is regarded as promoting harmony in the world and therefore carries at least implicit salvational overtones[18].

It is advisable to look at New Age healing from a historical and cross-cultural perspective along the lines given above, rather than considering it as a

---

[14] Foster & Anderson, *Medical Anthropology*, 53.
[15] Foster & Anderson, *Medical Anthropology*, 67.
[16] Foster & Anderson, *Medical Anthropology*, 53.
[17] Foster & Anderson, *Medical Anthropology*, 126.
[18] Cf. Fuller, *Alternative Medicine*, ch. 6.

historically isolated and more or less anomalous phenomenon within modern society. Certainly, modern New Age healing approaches may look "alternative" and strange from the perspective of modern secular health care, and their spiritual overtones may seem superfluous for the hard business of curing disease. From the perspective of religious history, however, the development of modern scientific medicine appears as "alternative" and anomalous. Although strongly influenced by certain modern developments in medicine and especially in psychology, which have led to the introduction of novel techniques, the basic approach of New Age healing is definitely traditional.

Concern with healing is the first general characteristic of our field. It can be further defined on the basis of a second characteristic, which reflects a more specific religious worldview. This is the element of "personal growth"[19], the precise nature of which will be analyzed in detail in Part Two of this study. In a general sense, "personal growth" can be understood as the shape "religious salvation" takes in the New Age movement: it is affirmed that deliverance from human suffering and weakness will be reached by developing our human potential, which results in our increasingly getting in touch with our inner divinity. Considering the general affinity between salvation and healing, the close connection between personal growth and healing in the New Age Movement is hardly surprising in itself. It is important to note, however, that therapy and religious "salvation" tend to merge to an extent perhaps unprecedented in other traditions. In many cases it is all but impossible to draw the line and decide whether a given practice or technique is religious or therapeutic in nature[20]. Later in this study, we will return to this point.

While the field as such is sufficiently circumscribed and characterized by the terms "healing and personal growth", one additional observation must nevertheless be made. Many New Age-believers would emphasize that their aim is not the elimination of suffering, but the promotion of *health*. This subtle shift of perspective is important to note. It contains a polemical thrust aimed at official health care, which is criticized for focusing on "fixing" diseases while promoting an unhealthy lifestyle at the same time. The official approach, according to a New Age perspective, betrays the hidden conviction that disease is a natural phenomenon. Perfect health is therefore an essentially unnatural condition which must be wrested from nature, so to speak. This turns the medical enterprise into a continuous fight of man against nature[21]. The New Age movement, in contrast, strongly tends towards the view that illness is a

---

[19] Cf. Ruitenbeek, *New Group Therapies*, 182; Beckford, 'Holistic Imagery', 263.
[20] Cf. Nüchtern, *Sehnsucht nach Heilung*, 15.
[21] Cf. the historical precedents discussed in Fuller, *Alternative Medicine*, esp. 14.

disruption of the balance of nature. Not disease, but health is the natural state of the world and of living beings. Illness results precisely when (as in official health care, according to the New Age perspective) we work against, instead of with nature. In this respect also, the New Age healing movements echo the worldview of naturalistic healing systems in traditional societies. According to both, the meaning of illness can be found in a disruption of a natural state of balance.

If "illness" is a condition which, ultimately, includes all domains of living, then it is clear that "health" must also be more than just the absence of problems. Rather, it must refer to a general, and natural, condition of blessing and abundance. The implications of this view, although logical as such, are nevertheless surprising. Not uncommonly,

> Good health is classed with any kind of good luck: success, money, a good job, a peaceful home. Illness, on the other hand, may be looked upon as just another undesirable event, along with bad luck, poverty, unemployment, domestic turmoil and so on. The attempted manipulation of events [by individuals] therefore covers a broad range of practices that are carried out to attract good, including good health, and to repel bad, including bad health.[22]

This quotation is based upon a study of American folk medicine, but precisely the same phenomenon can be found in a particular development of the "healing and growth" movement, often referred to as "prosperity consciousness". In certain American healing systems it is assumed that the attainment of the natural, even divine, state of "perfect health" will also include worldly success in the widest sense of the word, including material prosperity. Although this phenomenon of an apparent "spiritual materialism" is frequently used by critics to highlight the absurdity of the New Age Movement, it must be admitted that it can be seen as a natural—if indeed rather extreme—implication of the basic premises of "healing". To a more limited extent, the same applies to one further extension of the "healing and growth" movement, known as the quest for "physical immortality". If death is the ultimate illness, then perfect health should imply the abolition of death. This line of reasoning has brought certain New Age adherents to the conviction that it is not necessary to die[23]. Even with such admittedly extreme cases we are still in the sphere of ideas and practices concerned with health in the sense of radical "well-being", which is the proper aim of healing as well as of personal growth.

---

[22] Loudell F. Snow, quoted in Foster & Anderson, *Medical Anthropology*, 77.

[23] A good source for both prosperity consciousness and the belief in physical immortality is RNA (below) 150-170 & 196-216. Prosperity consciousness is a major focus of attention in Heelas, *New Age Movement*.

MAIN CURRENTS

As observed above, the healing and personal growth movement is extremely difficult to categorize. The terminology is not fixed: different authors use different terms for the same trends, or use the same terms in different ways. In what follows, I will make a rough distinction between the *Human Potential Movement*, on the one hand, and the *Holistic Health* movement, on the other. This distinction rests on the relative emphasis on psychological healing in the former and on physical healing in the latter. However, considering the substantial overlap between the movements, which both aspire to heal "body and soul" as a whole, this distinction must be understood largely as an idealtypical and heuristic device. Within the field of the Human Potential Movement, special attention will be given to its theoretical wing known as *Transpersonal Psychology*. Again, the distinction is not clearcut; nor is it implied that the transpersonal perspective is absent in the Holistic Health sector. Finally, some attention is given to the *Shamanic consciousness* movement, which can be considered as an offshoot from the transpersonal field but also overlaps with neo-paganism (chapter four).

At the core of the *Human Potential Movement*[24] lies a widespread dissatisfaction with the way most of us live our lives in modern society. Very early in life we learn to adjust to the demands of our social environment and, in the process, to suppress much of our natural human potential. Spontaneity gives way to an increasing conformity to the demands and expectations of society. The price we pay for social acceptance is the impoverishment of our inner life and the repression of abilities which are our natural birthright. Modern society, in particular, produces lonely and alienated individuals who have lost touch with their inner selves and are at a loss to find deeper meaning in their lives. Hendrik Ruitenbeek, in a useful study of the early group therapies, notes that 'the great problem ... is the absence of feelings among many, either young or old. The detachment, the coldness, the absence of human feelings are, to our distress, very relevant to many people in our society today'[25]. This situation produces all kinds of complaints. The basic goal of the Human Potential movement is to help people get in touch with themselves, i.e., with those parts which have been alienated and suppressed[26]. The ideal is to restore the human being

---

[24] Ruitenbeek, *New Group Therapies*; Rosen, *Psychobabble*; Stone, 'Human Potential Movement'; Raschke, 'Human Potential Movement'; Wallis, 'Betwixt Therapy and Salvation'; Küenzlen, 'Psychoboom und Weltanschaaung'; Drury, *Elements of Human Potential*. I have not listed the many case-studies that have been published about specific Human Potential movements, particularly about *est*.

[25] Ruitenbeek, *New Group Therapies*, 144.

[26] This focus on the "self" has given rise to a Freudian interpretation of the Human

to his/her original wholeness and integration, and thus to enable him/her to live a full and meaningful life. In accordance with our discussion of healing (above), the Human Potential Movement sees health and wholeness as the natural condition of life: not nature but society (to the extent that it restricts the unfolding of human potential) produces illness. The link with the countercultural values of the 1960s is therefore not surprising. A defender of the pioneering Human Potential center Esalen points out the implications for therapy: 'It is the concern of psychiatry to adjust people to the social environment. Esalen, rather, is concerned with those who are too well-adjusted, too tight and controlled. It attempts to release them for growth and greater integration'[27]. Evidently, the Human Potential Movement radically re-defines the nature of health and illness. Health is far more than the absence of disease, and this has consequences for the type of patient attracted to alternative therapies. Although the movement does include therapeutic methods for treating psychiatric disorders, most people who attend Human Potential groups do not suffer from mental illness. Many suffer from a lack of meaning and fulfillment in their lives. They long to be whole. And even those who are reasonably happy may nevertheless choose to "work on themselves" because they believe that inner growth and development is of the essence of human life. For such individuals—often the ones most consciously committed to New Age beliefs—, nothing short of complete enlightenment and God-consciousness fully deserves to be called "health".

This last observation already indicates the elasticity of the term "Human Potential", which has taken on an increasingly spiritual connotation over the years[28]. This is parallelled by the development of the Human Potential Movement from a basically therapeutic movement to an increasingly religious one. In the first phases of its development, spiritual aspects were largely implicit. From its origins in the Sensitivity Training of the later 1940s, the movement developed into the group therapies of the 1960s[29]. Under the impact of Bioenergetics and Gestalt (as practiced by Esalen) there emerged an increasing focus on a wide variety of neo-Reichian "Bodywork" methods. By the 1970s, the term "Human Potential Movement" had come into use as an umbrella term to cover the pletho-

---

Potential movement as "narcissism", and the rise of the movement has been described as symptomatic of cultural degeneration (Marin, 'New Narcissism'; Lasch, *Culture of Narcissism*). This interpretation has met with criticism from specialists on the movement. According to Beckford ('Holistic Imagery', 263), the narcissistic interpretation is 'a misunderstanding based on the separation of ideas about the self from other aspects of the holistic outlook.' Lewis ('Approaches', 11) speaks of a '*simplistic generalization*'.

[27] Ruitenbeek, *New Group Therapies*, 122.

[28] Donald Stone speaks of 'a change in emphasis from the self-transcendence of going beyond the routines of everyday life to the self-transcendence of merging with infinite cosmic energy or ground of all being' ('Human Potential Movement', 96).

[29] Stone, 'Human Potential Movement', 95.

ra of practices that had developed. In spite of the spiritual elements already present at this time, the general approach and terminology was nevertheless still predominantly psychotherapeutic. This was changed decisively during the 1970s by the increasing assimilation of Oriental religious ideas and the development of the transpersonal perspective (see below). As a result, the Human Potential movement developed a strong focus on spirituality and religious imagery, and a correspondingly expanded vision of "Human Potential". In the early period, the term chiefly referred to such faculties as 'awareness, creativity, insight, empathy, emotional expressivity, capacity for experience and exploration, and the like'[30]. In the later period, the same term—while also retaining the earlier meaning—became associated with such states as "cosmic awareness" and transcendental insight. The full development of a person's Human Potential is now understood to include conscious awareness of the transcendental ("transpersonal") realms experienced in altered states of consciousness. These experiences are sought not merely for themselves, but are also believed to possess strong therapeutic value.

Transpersonal Psychology[31] can be regarded as the theoretical wing of the Human Potential Movement. Abraham Maslow—who also coined the term "Human Potential"—is generally credited with having given the impetus to the development of the transpersonal perspective within the field of humanistic psychology, in a 1967 lecture entitled "The Farther Reaches of Human Potential"[32]. Two years later, Anthony Sutich defined the new perspective as follows:

> Transpersonal (or "fourth force") psychology is the title of an emerging force in the psychology field by a group of psychologists and professional men and women from other fields who are interested in those ultimate human capacities and potentialities that have no systematic place in positivistic or behaviorist theory ("first force"), classical psychoanalytic theory ("second force"), or humanistic psychology ("third force"). The emerging transpersonal psychology ("fourth force") is concerned specifically with the empirical, scientific study of, and responsible implementation of, the findings relevant to becoming, individual and species-wide meta-needs, ultimate values, unitive consciousness, peak experiences, B-values, ecstasy, mystical experiences, awe, being, self-actualization, essence, bliss, wonder, ultimate meaning, transcendence of the self, spirit, oneness, cosmic awareness, individual and species-wide synergy, maximal sensory awareness, responsiveness and expression, maximum interpersonal encounter, sacralization of everyday life, transcendental phenomena, cosmic self-humor and playfulness, and related concepts, experiences, and activities. As a definition, this formulation is to be understood as subject to optimal individual or group interpretations, either wholly or in part with regard to the acceptance of its content as essentially naturalistic, theistic, supernaturalistic, or any other designated classification.[33]

---

[30] Wallis, 'Betwixt Therapy and Salvation', 24.
[31] Walsh & Vaughan, *Beyond Ego*; Valle, 'Emergence of Transpersonal Psychology'.
[32] Valle, 'Emergence of Transpersonal Psychology', 260.
[33] Quoted in Valle, 'Emergence of Transpersonal Psychology', 261.

Certainly, this "definition"—which has been called 'one of the earliest descriptions of what would later become the New Age'[34]—was delivered in the playful spirit of the late 1960s (Sutich himself relativized his impressive list by adding 'How's that for a nice ride on "Astro-Bike" or perhaps better still, "Inner Space Bike"'[35]). The intent, however, was quite serious. Transpersonal psychology has developed since this period as that branch of psychological theory which takes religious and mystical experiences seriously as constituting a domain *sui generis*, refusing to follow the reductionistic interpretations widely accepted in other psychological schools. In doing so, it claims well-known authorities like William James and Carl Gustav Jung as predecessors. Transpersonal psychologists have devoted themselves to both empirical and theoretical research. The empirical branch has largely concentrated on the field of so-called Altered States of Consciousness (ASC's) induced either by drugs or by various mind-expanding techniques. Theoretical work has concentrated on devising all-embracing "cartographies of consciousness" which distinguish a hierarchy of levels in the psyche. The premise is that the traditional psychological schools adress the lower levels of the psyche, but are largely inadequate for dealing with the higher or transpersonal levels. The latter are seen as the proper domain of spiritual traditions, especially those of Oriental origin. Transpersonal psychology thus aims at a theoretical synthesis of western psychology and Oriental spiritual systems and technologies.

This attempt to integrate religiously-based theories into secular psychology has brought transpersonal psychologists into conflict with dominant views of science. Referring to Thomas Kuhn's famous *Structure of Scientific Revolutions*, they have therefore called for a new scientific paradigm to replace the outdated "Cartesian-Newtonian" framework. Very significantly, most transpersonalists go beyond the basically empirical approach to "transpersonal experiences" as exemplified by William James and others, in affirming that the new paradigm should accept the essential *truth* of the so-called perennial philosophy as axiomatic for research[36]. Both the new paradigm and the perennial philosophy will be discussed in more detail in Part Two of this study. At this point, it suffices to conclude that the transpersonal school, positing the perennial philosophy as the proper foundation of scientific research, has resulted in an openly religionist psychology[37]. As such, its influence has spread

---

[34] Drury, *Human Potential*, 38-39.

[35] Drury, *Human Potential*, 39.

[36] Cf. Valle, 'Emergence of Transpersonal Psychology', 260: 'This new approach not only embraced the values of humanistic psychology, but went beyond our ordinary boundaries to transcend the limits of the ego-self. This position reemphasizes the need to live by and for "intrinsic values" and to reject the view that true science needs to be value-free or neutral.'

[37] There are also scholars of religion who affirm the relevance of transpersonal research

beyond the strictly psychological domain to the field of religious studies and beyond[38].

Shamanic Consciousness[39] is closely connected to the transpersonal movement. It is based on the view of the shaman as a specialist of altered states of consciousness who is able to mediate between the transpersonal realms of spirits and gods and the world of humans. Nevill Drury, in an overview of Shamanism from the New Age perspective, defines the shaman as 'a person who is able to perceive [the] world of souls, spirits and gods, and who, in a state of ecstatic trance, is able to travel among them, gaining special knowledge of that supernatural realm'[40]. However, in the democratic New Age-context shamanic consciousness is supposed to be accessible to anyone, not just the traditional specialist. Under the influence especially of Michael Harner, an anthropologist-turned-shaman, shamanic techniques for inducing ASC's have become popular in New Age healing & growth groups. Drury testifies to their efficacy: '...one thing never ceases to amaze me—that within an hour or so of drumming, ordinary city folk are able to tap extraordinary mythic realities that they have never dreamed of'[41].

According to the German historian of religions Hartmut Zinser, New Age shamanism actually has little in common with "real" shamanism as found in traditional cultures[42]. Some of his arguments (notably his criticism of Eliade's universalistic interpretation of Shamanism[43], which is widely accepted in New Age circles) merit serious consideration. Others reflect aprioristic and reductionistic models of interpretation, which ignore the emic religious context of the New Age movement as not worthy of being taken seriously[44]. Somewhat

---

for the study of religions while rejecting the religionistic framework. See Crownfield,'Toward a Science of Religion'. Cf. also Alexander, 'William James'.

[38] The perennialist perspective in religious studies goes back to the work of the perennialist "triumvirate" of Ananda Coomaraswamy, Frithjof Schuon and René Guénon (Sharpe, *Comparative Religion*, 262-266). It took on new impetus under the impact of transpersonalism and has been adopted by well-known scholars like Huston Smith and the sociologist of New Religious Movements Dick Anthony (Anthony & Ecker, 'Anthony Typology').

[39] Drury, *Elements of Shamanism*; Zinser, 'Schamanismus'; cf. Zinser's 'Zur Faszination des Schamanismus'.

[40] Drury, *Elements of Shamanism*, 6.

[41] Drury, *Elements of Shamanism*, x.

[42] Zinser, 'Schamanismus', 319.

[43] Zinser, 'Zur Faszination des Schamanismus', 49-50.

[44] Zinser's interpretation of New Age shamanism as escapist ('Schamanismus', 320) mirrors the popular interpretation of the Human Potential movement as "narcissist". James R. Lewis's comments to the effect that the latter interpretation reflects the focus of the researcher rather than the expressed aims of the movement ('Approaches', 11) is equally applicable to Zinser's interpretation. If the complete context of the New Age worldview is taken into serious account (cf. Beckford, 'Holistic Imagery', 263)—rather than a context believed in by the researcher but alien to the believers under study—then what first looks like escapism may as plausibly be viewed as a legitimate (although not necessarily successful) attempt to use transpersonal insights in order

surprisingly, one prominent difference between New Age shamanism and its traditional models is not mentioned by Zinser. This is the strong tendency in New Age shamanism to emphasize visits of the Shaman to the other world, while downplaying the complementary element of the spirits visiting the human world by possessing the body of the shaman[45]. Most specialists emphasize that *both* directions are typical for traditional shamanism[46], and in the previous chapter we saw that defenders of New Age channeling tend to mention the shaman as a typical example of a "channel". Nevertheless, enthusiasts of New Age shamanism generally stress what they see as the "active" dimension of shamanism, while playing down the more "passive" practice of trance possession, which they assign to the separate field of mediumship or channeling[47]. So there appears to be a certain tension within the New Age movement between the channeling subculture, on the one hand, and the shamanic consciousness movement, on the other, which leads—among other things—to a different evaluation of channeling phenomena.

As a healing approach, New Age Shamanism differs from most other Human Potential practices by its personalistic rather than naturalistic framework. Illness is conceptualized as the result of "harmful intrusions" invading the body of a person. These "hostile energies" are extracted by the Shaman by various techniques, often involving the use of "spirit helpers".

Holistic Health[48] is the most common name for the alternative approaches to health care that gained momentum in the 1970s. Detailed histories are not yet available, but it is clear that Holistic Health, which arose out of the free clinic movement of the 1960s, developed in close connection with the Human

---

to bring healing to the everyday world. Unfortunately, however, Zinser seems not prepared to take his subjects seriously at all, which occasionally leads to statements that are unnecessarily arrogant and factually misleading: 'It is true that in these tracts there is much talk about healing, but what healing is can usually no longer be said. As content and goal of healing, of enlightenment or however this condition is called, appears then the void or the nothing. And because the authors themselves cannot imagine anything by it, we promptly find references to Buddhist conceptions as evocation of a hardly doubtable authority'. ('Schamanismus', 323). I do not see how Zinser can be so sure about the (in)validity of the inner experiences of New Age believers, nor how he can escape the implication that the Buddha also—and Buddhist practitioners generally—did and do not know what they are talking about. The statement that New Age believers "cannot imagine anything" by their own experiences is mainly suggestive, but remains unsupported by any sort of proof (undoubtedly because such proof is impossible in principle). The statement that New Age believers cannot explain what "healing" means to them is simply not true, as anyone can verify by studying the sources.

[45] Drury, *Elements of Shamanism*, 11, 30-31.

[46] For instance Lewis, *Ecstatic Religion*, 43-44.

[47] Drury, *Elements of Shamanism*, 11, cf. also 30-31.

[48] Kunz, *Spiritual Aspects*; Reisser, Reisser & Weldon, *New Age Medicine*; Fuller, *Alternative Medicine*; Kelly, 'Holistic Health'; Eibach, *Heilung*; Ernst, 'New Age'; Nüchtern, *Sehnsucht nach Heilung*.

Potential movement and shares most of the latter's concerns[49]. At the core of the movement is the conviction that 'every human being is a unique, wholistic interdependent relationship of body, mind, emotions and spirit'[50]. In this context, healing is 'a process in which a person becomes whole physically, emotionally, mentally and at deeper levels, resulting ideally in an integration with the underlying inward power of the universe'[51]. As we saw, this fits in very well with the definition of healing as used by medical anthropologists, while being very different from the notion of curing as prevalent in official health care. Rising criticism of the latter therefore played an essential part in the development of the Holistic Health movement too[52].

A central characteristic of Holistic health is the important role that the mind plays in physical healing. The immunity system or, alternatively, the Indian chakra system, is seen as the connection between the spiritual, mental and emotional faculties, on the one hand, and the physical body, on the other. By way of this connection, stress and other psychological factors can disturb the physical organism and cause illness. Reversely, physical diseases can be cured by changing the psychological conditions that caused them. In this way, everyone is personally responsible for "creating" his/her illness or, alternatively, for creating health. The individual is challenged to find the deeper *meaning* of his/her illness and thus to use it as an instrument for learning and inner growth instead of taking the passive role of the victim. The concept of "taking responsibility" for one's illness is central to the Holistic Health movement, and accordingly there is a heavy emphasis on the individual character of therapy. This individualization of health care, in which not an abstract "disease" but the unique individual in his/her undivided wholeness is at the center of attention, is arguably the most central characteristic of the movement[53]. The fact that the full weight of the responsibility for illness is also thrown on this same individual has given rise to vehement attacks by critics[54]. These will be discussed in Part Two.

The variety of approaches for promoting Holistic Health is enormous. Among the more important ones are acupuncture, biofeedback, chiropractic, kinesiology, homeopathy, iridology, massage and various kind of bodywork (such as orgonomy, Feldenkrais, reflexology, Rolfing, polarity massage, therapeutic touch etc.), meditation and visualization, nutritional therapies, psychic heal-

---

[49] See Kelly, 'Holistic Health', 216-217.

[50] Quoted in Fuller, *Alternative Medicine*, 92.

[51] Weber, 'Philosophical Foundations and Frameworks for Healing', 21.

[52] Especially Dubos, *Man, Medicine, and Environment*, and Illich, *Medical Nemesis*.

[53] Cf. Reisser, Reisser & Weldon, *New Age Medicine*, 17ff (precept 3); Kelly, 'Holistic Health', 217 (nrs. 2-4); Ernst, 'New Age', 17 (nrs. 2-4).

[54] In the Netherlands, for instance, a lively public debate was incited by Spaink, *Het strafbare lichaam*.

ing, various kinds of herbal medicine, healing by crystals, metals, music or colours, reincarnation therapies and, finally, twelve-step programs modelled on Alcoholics Anonymous. For detailed descriptions I must refer to the literature[55].

THE SOURCES

EVA PIERRAKOS

PST   Eva Pierrakos, *The Pathwork of Self-Transformation*

Pierrakos was introduced in the previous chapter. The information she received from "the Guide" concerned a method of self-transformation referred to as "Pathwork", which is now being practiced in special therapeutic centers. Pathwork teaches that unitive consciousness, or awareness of our divine being, can be accomplished by honestly confronting our own negativity. PST presents the method for the general public.

KEN KEYES[56]

HHC   Ken Keyes, *Handbook to Higher Consciousness*

Ken Keyes has developed a method for achieving happiness and personal fulfillment called the "Living Love Way". It is based on the idea of "deprogramming" the human mind. Most of us suffer from "negative programming", usually dating back to early childhood. This programming consists of "emotion-backed desires" referred to as "addictions". We suffer because we are addicted to certain things happening or not happening in our lives. By changing our addictions into "preferences" we reprogram the mind into an attitude of total acceptance of "the here and now". In this way we achieve higher consciousness and total fulfillment. The Living Love Way is taught in Ken Keyes college in Oregon, and has influenced Shakti Gawain and other well-known New Age thinkers.

LEONARD ORR & SONDRA RAY[57]

RNA   Leonard Orr & Sondra Ray, *Rebirthing in the New Age*

Rebirthing, originally invented by Leonard Orr, is one of the better-known Human Potential therapies. Its basic premise is that we all suffer from the

---

[55] For instance Reisser, Reisser & Weldon, *New Age Medicine*; Fuller, *Alternative Medicine*; Ernst, 'New Age'; several contributions in Kunz, *Spiritual Aspects*. For more detailed descriptions of the last mentioned approach, see Kurtz, 'Alcoholics Anonymous'; Kelly, 'Twelve-step Programs'; and Fuller, *Alternative Medicine*, 99-103.

[56] Cf. Melton, Clark & Kelly, *New Age Encyclopedia*, 249-251.

[57] Cf. Rosen, *Psychobabble*, 118-135; Melton, Clark & Kelly, *New Age Encyclopedia*, 377-378. Rebirthing has been criticized by other representatives of the Human Potential Movement (Schmidt, 'Rebirthing').

effects of the birth trauma. By consciously re-experiencing this trauma we can release it and become free. Other factors play an additional part in producing suffering: the parental disapproval syndrome, certain "specific negativities", the unconscious death urge and influences from former lives. The method consists of special rhythmical breathing procedures—practiced either "wet" (while lying in a tub) or "dry"—accompanied by so-called affirmations (positive sentences which are believed to have a strong influence on the subconscious). RNA is an updated edition of Orr & Ray's original book, and still reflects much of the atmosphere of the 1960s. Rebirthing is widely practiced in many New Age centers.

SHAKTI GAWAIN

CV	Shakti Gawain, *Creative Visualization*
LL	Shakti Gawain, *Living in the Light: A Guide to Personal and Planetary Transformation*
RG	Shakti Gawain, *Return to the Garden: A Journey of Discovery*

Shakti Gawain's books are very typical examples of popular New Age approaches to healing and growth. CV focuses on the use of visualization techniques for personal fulfillment, happiness and healing. LL shows a stronger emphasis on spirituality. A general New Age worldview is outlined in the first part; the second part contains practical advice about subjects such as intuition, feelings, various psychological mechanisms, relationships, sexuality, money, health and a perfect body, and life and death. Like CV, LL contains many practical exercises, with a central role for affirmations. RG is a sort of autobiography which presents Gawain's views in a more narrative context. Gawain has applied her ideas in many popular workshops about personal development and healing.

SANAYA ROMAN

OtC	Sanaya Roman & Duane Packer, *Opening to Channel: How to Connect with Your Guide*
LJ	Sanaya Roman, *Living with Joy: Keys to Personal Power and Spiritual Transformation*
PPA	Sanaya Roman, *Personal Power through Awareness: A Guidebook for Sensitive People*
SG	Sanaya Roman, *Spiritual Growth: Being your Higher Self*

In the previous chapter we saw that Roman's books are based on channeled communications. These messages are generally about personal development and spiritual growth. The central theme is that we create our own reality and that we should therefore learn to "take responsibility" for our development. The books (which stress that "growing is fun") include "playsheets" with exercises at the end of each chapter. Roman's activities do not seem to include workshops or seminars, but the end of each book does include extensive advertisements for audio cassette tapes with messages and guided meditations by Orin, crystals said to be charged by Orin with spiritual energy, and further books. Roman's overtly commercial attitude is officially sanctioned by another book containing Orin's advice about *Creating Money: Keys to Abundance*. This is a strong example of the "prosperity consciousness" mentioned above.

HENRY REED/EDGAR CAYCE

ECMM   Henry Reed, *Edgar Cayce on Mysteries of the Mind*

As noted under the discussion of Cayce's work in chapter one, ECMM is very much the personal product of Reed, although inspired by Cayce. The basic theme is the power of the mind to change, and even create, its own reality. Reed outlines a complete transpersonal model of the mind and discusses its various implications for healing and growth.

JEAN HOUSTON[58]

PH   Jean Houston, *The Possible Human: A Course in Extending your Physical, Mental, and Creative Abilities*

Jean Houston is director of the Foundation for Mind Research in New York. PH is probably the most representative example of her intelligent blend of empirical research and practical application, in which much attention is given to mythology and the powers of the creative imagination. The book is structured as a course in Human Potential development in the fullest sense, with theoretical chapters and practical exercises for "awakening" the latent faculties of the body, the senses, the brain and the memory, as well as integrating the traces of evolutionary history still present in the brain, and developing creativity and transpersonal awareness. In this way, Houston covers the complete "spectrum of consciousness", from the physical body up to unitive consciousness.

STANISLAV GROF[59]

BB   Stanislav Grof, *Beyond the Brain: Birth, Death and Transcendence in Psychotherapy*
AS   Stanislav Grof, *The Adventure of Self-Discovery: Dimensions of Consciousness and New Perspectives in Psychotherapy and Inner Exploration*

Grof is the leading empirical researcher in transpersonal psychology. During his early career in Prague he conducted several thousands LSD sessions in a clinical psychiatric setting. He concluded that LSD, far from producing drug-specific hallucinations, in fact greatly facilitated access to the subconscious.

---

[58] Cf. Melton, Clark & Kelly, *New Age Encyclopedia*, 220-222.
[59] Crownfield, 'Religion in the Cartography of the Unconscious'; Bonin, 'Reinkarnationserfahrung'; Kampschuur, 'Zelfhelende proces'.

His research convinced him of the strong therapeutic value of LSD. After emigrating to the U.S.A. he continued his research, but eventually had to discard the use of LSD due to changes in the legal system. He then developed a new technique called "holotrophic therapy" to replace LSD. This approach—which combines breathing techniques with music—is said to be somewhat less efficient, but to result in basically the same experiences as those induced by LSD. Grof came to distinguish four distinct levels in the experiences reported by his subject. The first level, called the *sensory barrier*, has little or no therapeutic significance, as it consists simply of a heightened but random activation of the sensory organs. The second, or *recollective-biographical* (*psychodynamic*) level contains biographical material displaying well-known Freudian characteristics. The third, or *perinatal* level contains experiences related to the birth trauma. The therapeutic significance of this level confirms Otto Rank's thesis about the centrality of the birth trauma, and of course it also fits well with Rebirthing[60]. The perinatal level can be further subdivided into four therapeutically significant "perinatal matrices". The fourth, or *transpersonal* level contains an extremely wide variety of experiences which share as a common characteristic the fact that they transcend the personal ego of the experiencing subject. They include such experiences as apparent memories of former lives, personal identification with other individuals, with groups or even with mankind or with other biological species, encounters with various Jungian archetypes and experiences of cosmic unity and bliss. Both the perinatal and the transpersonal levels are replete with religious imagery[61]. Grof's cartography of the unconscious, with its non-reductionistic approach to the "higher" levels of experience, has become one of the pillars of transpersonal psychology in general.

KEN WILBER[62]

SoC   Ken Wilber, *The Spectrum of Consciousness*
NB   Ken Wilber, *No Boundary*
AP   Ken Wilber, *The Atman Project: A Transpersonal View of Human Development*
UfE   Ken Wilber, *Up from Eden: A Transpersonal View of Human Evolution*

Ken Wilber is regarded as the foremost theoretician in the transpersonal movement. All his publications are characterized by a brilliant ability to combine information from a wide variety of sources into an at times stunningly elegant synthesis. In SoC, he introduced his basic idea of the "Spectrum of con-

---

[60] Rebirthing and Holotrophic therapy seem to be rather similar. Although Grof admits the similarities in the practice, he rejects Orr's theories and terminology (Kampschuur, 'Zelfhelende Proces', 17).

[61] Cf. Crownfield, 'Religion in the Cartography of the Unconscious'.

[62] Amrito, *Struikelen over waarheid*; Schmidt, 'An Ontological Model of Development'; Schneider, 'Deified Self'; Melton, Clark & Kelly, *New Age Encyclopedia*, 495-496.

sciousness". The different Western psychological schools are not mutually exclusive but complementary. They adress different levels of consciousness, and each approach is valid as long as it remains within its proper domain and does not claim to be able to explain other, particularly higher, levels. The different levels of consciousness and their attendant psychologies can be arranged in a hierarchy, and the psychological dynamics which govern their relationship can be logically explained. The higher levels have been largely ignored by western psychology. Here, we have to resort to Oriental spiritual schools, which are in fact psychological systems adressing the higher levels of consciousness. In this way, a hierarchical spectrum of consciousness emerges which combines eastern and western approaches under the umbrella of the perennial philosophy. NB is a popular version of SoC, and probably Wilber's best-known book among the wider New Age public. In AP, Wilber applies the spectrum-approach to the cycle of human development from the womb to "total realization". This is Wilber's most strictly psychological book. It contains some essential new elements, notably an added emphasis on dynamic processes of development (in contrast to the somewhat static scheme of SoC) and the crucial distinction between *pre*personal and *trans*personal states. Psychologically regressive states are sometimes wrongly interpreted as mystical consciousness, and genuine mysticism is regularly confused with infantile regression. However, while prepersonal states are "not yet" personal, transpersonal states have transcended the personal. The failure to recognize this difference results in the "pre/trans-fallacy" which haunts both psychology and popular religion (including the New Age movement). UfE applies the scheme of development outlined in AP to the evolution of consciousness as reflected in cultural history. Humanity has progressed from the prepersonal to the personal, and is now in the process of entering the transpersonal stage.

MICHAEL HARNER[63]

WS   Michael Harner, *The Way of the Shaman*

Michael Harner is a professor of anthropology who, during a trip to the Amazon, was initiated into shamanic consciousness by drinking *Ayahuasca*, the sacred potion of the Conibo Indians. Since then, Harner has been active promoting shamanism as a method of healing and personal growth by organizing workshops in the context of the Human Potential movement. WS gives an overview of his approach.

---

[63] Cf. several parts in Drury, *Elements of Shamanism*.

ROGER WALSH

SSh   Roger N.Walsh, *The Spirit of Shamanism*

Walsh has published widely on a range of subjects in the transpersonal field. SSh, written in a popular scholarly style, is representative of the connection between the transpersonal perspective and New Age shamanism.

LOUISE L. HAY[64]

YHL   Louise L. Hay, *You can Heal your Life*

YHL is one of the most popular New Age healing guides. It teaches that all diseases can ultimately be reduced to negative attitudes about ourselves. By changing the negative thoughts that underly those attitudes we can attain health, happiness, personal success and fulfillment on all levels. Louise Hay has attracted much media attention by organizing the so-called "Hayrides", workshops for AIDS-patients.

CHRIS GRISCOM

TI   Chris Griscom, *Time is an Illusion*
ENF   Chris Griscom, *Ecstasy is a New Frequency*

Chris Griscom is a healer from New Mexico who became famous as a result of Shirley MacLaine's *Dancing in the Light*, in which MacLaine describes her past-life regression sessions with Griscom. Griscom founded the "Light Institute" in Galisteo as a center for healing and growth. Originally, she and her co-workers used an unconventional technique of acupuncture resulting in visions of past lives and communication with the "Higher Self". Later they dispensed with the needles and now use only their hands to obtain similar effects. Griscom's popular books, which have been appearing since 1986, are based on seminar notes and informal talks given during workshops.

SHIRLEY MACLAINE

GW   Shirley MacLaine, *Going Within: a guide for inner transformation*

Shirley MacLaine's sixth book is presented as a guide for healing and inner transformation. It is based on a series of New Age seminars which were organized and led by her throughout the U.S.A. MacLaine discusses such subjects as stress, meditation, getting in touch with the superconscious and the Higher Self, the chakra system and its corresponding colours and sounds, the use of crystals, sexuality etc. She also describes her contacts with the painting medium Luis Gasparetto, the healing medium Mauricio Panisset, the Phillipine psychic surgeon Alex Orbito and the physicist Stephen Hawking.

---

[64] Cf. D'Antonio, *Heaven on Earth*, ch. 2.

FRITJOF CAPRA

TP   Fritjof Capra, *The Turning Point*

The long chapters about healing and psychology in this book, which will be further introduced in chapter five, justify its inclusion in this chapter. The contrast between traditional health care and the new holistic health movement is described in detail. These chapters in TP may be regarded as among the most clear and well-known theoretical expositions of the case for holistic health.

CHAPTER THREE

NEW AGE SCIENCE[1]

Daß ich erkenne, was die Welt
im Innersten zusammenhält,
Schau alle Wirkenskraft und Samen
und tu nicht mehr in Worten kramen

J.W. von Goethe, *Faust I*

THE QUEST FOR A UNIFIED WORLDVIEW

One of the notable characteristics of New Age thinking is its high regard for modern science. This may seem surprising at first sight because New Agers also tend to distrust and reject academic rationalism; but, in fact, the contradiction is only apparent. Modern scientific developments—especially in theoretical physics—appeal to New Age concerns for two reasons. On the one hand, they are interpreted in such a way as to legitimate a spiritual worldview; but, at the same time (and for the very same reasons) they also serve as weapons to attack the existing scientific consensus. This is possible because the "old" and the "new" science are perceived as radical opposites, if not in practice then at least in principle. Traditional science—associated with the academic establishment—is thoroughly condemned as materialistic and conducive to human alienation, but the New Age has discovered the new science as a potential ally against it. Following Thomas Kuhn's *Structure of Scientific Revolutions*[2], New Age believers claim that established science reflects an outdated reductionistic paradigm bound to be replaced by a new paradigm based on a holistic perspective. The suggestion that the evolutionary thrust of science now leads it to reject the very materialism it once helped to create is as inspiring to some people as it is outrageous to others. That New Age Science diverges from mainstream science is recognized by critics and sympathizers alike, but both interpret this fact differently. Critical outsiders prefer to speak of "fringe science", an appellation which reflects their conviction that these approaches are borderline cases of genuine scientific research, if not nonsensical pseudo-science pure and simple. Defenders, on the other hand, turn the fact of their marginal

---

[1] Briggs & Peat, *Looking Glass Universe*; Chowdhury, Wiskerke, van Zoest & van der Zwan, *Holisme en New Age-bewustzijn*; Hemmering, 'Über Glaube und Zweifel; Griffin, *Reenchantment of Science*; Gladigow, 'Pantheismus'; Templeton & Herrmann, *God Who would be known*; Mutschler, *Physik—Religion—New Age*; Grim, *Philosophy of Science and the Occult*, Sect. IV: Quantum mysticism; Sperry, 'Search for Beliefs'.
[2] Kuhn, *Structure of Scientific Revolutions*.

position into an advantage by re-labeling their perspective as "leading edge science". They see themselves as the avant-garde of scientific progress: pioneers of a radical new worldview.

In order to put "New Age science" into context we must, first of all, evaluate its status as *science*. Surely most of its central proponents are, or have been, practicing scientists. Some of them (David Bohm, Ilya Prigogine) enjoy general recognition for their contributions to fundamental research, while others (Peat, Jantsch) hold or held university posts while also writing books for a general public. A few authors (Capra, Sheldrake) started their career as scientists but, as a result of the popular success of their books, largely or completely abandoned fundamental research for a career in the lecture circuit. It is undoubtedly the case that the authors' scientific credentials have served, in the eyes of the general public, to lend authority to the views expressed in their books[3]. Nevertheless, there can be no doubt that the literature of New Age science does not primarily aim at keeping the public informed about the current situation of scientific research, or at disseminating knowledge about new scientific discoveries. Rather, New Age science is typically concerned with developing *unified worldviews*. It shares this ambition with many popular expositions of modern science. Stephen Hawking's *A Brief History of Time*[4], to give one well-known example, culminates in the perspective on a Grand Unified Theory (GUT) which, if and when it will be discovered, is expected to deal the final death blow to theism and to metaphysics generally[5]. In fact, the appeal of popular science books *in general* seems to be based largely on the exciting suggestion that science is on its way to know the "Mind of God"[6]. In its secular variety, such as represented by Hawking, the premise is that such knowledge would prove the superfluity of traditional theologies and the vacuity of religion; the New Age variety, in contrast, suggests that science can shed light on, even explain, the workings of the divine in the cosmos and thus secure a scientific basis for religion. It is hardly surprising that both alternatives presuppose different conceptions of God. The appeal of the secular variety rests on its (quasi-)polemical relation to a christian theism characterized by the traditional attributes of omniscience and omnipotence. The New Age counterpart is not concerned with christian theological conceptions but emphasizes, instead, the ubiquity or immanence of the divine in the cosmos.

New Age science is, therefore, characterized by the search for a unified worldview which includes a religious dimension. This religious dimension— the specifics of which will be discussed in Part Two of this study—may be

---

[3] Cf. Mutschler, *Physik—Religion—New Age*, 16; O'Hara, 'Of Myths and Monkeys', 70-71.
[4] Hawking, *Brief History of Time*.
[5] Hawking, *Brief History of Time*, 166-169.
[6] Cf. Davies, *Mind of God*.

quite explicit or only implicit, but it is invariably present in some form. The point to be emphasized here is that such religiously inspired worldviews necessarily represent an *interpretation* of research data, rather than a direct and obvious implication of those data. One of the most frequent criticisms of New Age science is that its authors tend to blur this distinction between science, on the one hand, and philosophical or religious interpretations of scienctific findings, on the other, by suggesting that modern science *proves* mysticism or a particular holistic worldview[7]. It is certainly the case that many readers of New Age science ultimately come to believe that this is what it all comes down to, and that fact is crucial for understanding the popularity of modern science in the wider New Age movement. However, the authors of the books themselves are often more cautious. On close reading, many of them appear to be concerned with demonstrating a mutual harmony or parallellism, rather than a one-to-one connection, between a particular unified holistic worldview and the results of modern scientific research. The incontestably correct core of their argument is that, even if it is granted that we can never *infer* a comprehensive worldview from science, it is still the case that we cannot help but *interpret* research findings. The way most traditional scientists view the world, it is argued, is as much the result of secondary interpretation as the alternatives proposed by New Age science. The question then is which interpretation is the more appropriate, both theoretically and in terms of its implications for human life in the world. Certainly, it is normal and legitimate for people to try and "make sense" of scientific results; nor can it be disputed that our view of the world should preferably be consistent with what science has to tell us about that world. But precisely this, according to the New Age view, is no longer the case today. Modern scientific research, particularly in physics, yields results which are radically at odds with common sense assumptions or, alternatively, it fails to produce results in certain areas because accepted assumptions prevent scientists from investigating some theoretical options. We need, then, a new worldview: both in order to accomodate and "make sense" of modern science and in order to open up new directions for research.

New Age Science as *Naturphilosophie*

So it is evident that, although New Age scientists are strongly interested in disseminating new scientific facts, they consider these not as goals in themselves. Their guiding motivation is the search for a new worldview. For this reason the term "New Age science" is actually a misnomer: its real domain is not natural science, but *philosophy of nature*. The essence and specificity of this

---

[7] For an example of this criticism, see Vanheste, 'Berichten'.

endeavour has been succinctly characterized by Antoine Faivre:

> In the West, "natural philosophy" and "philosophy of nature" have developed side
> by side and at times have been confused because of an ever-present ambiguity.
> They differ in principle, however: the first has been defined by Galileo, Comte,
> and Darwin as the pursuit of a total but essentially objective knowledge of phe-
> nomena, whereas the second has oriented such thinkers as Leibniz, Hegel, and
> Bergson toward an intuitive approach that nevertheless strives to be rigorous
> regarding the reality that underlies data derived from observation.[8]

In order to prevent confusion with other approaches this "philosophy of nature"
is often referred to by the german word *Naturphilosophie*, and I will follow
this convention here. Faivre's definition of *Naturphilosophie* as "a both intuitive and rigorous approach focusing on the reality underlying phenomenal
reality" precisely characterizes the central concern of New Age science. This
has not escaped historians of traditional *Naturphilosophie*[9], but somewhat surprisingly it has remained largely unnoticed by both critics and defenders of the
new paradigm[10]. The likely reason, as Faivre wrily observes, is that 'our own
traditions, even in these areas, are generally unknown'[11]. Here, Faivre refers
not only to the tradition of *Naturphilosophie* which is the subject of his article, but more generally to the field of "western esotericism" of which he is the
leading authority. Indeed, of the three main periods which may be distinguished
in the western history of *Naturphilosophie*—the Pre-Socratics, the Renaissance
and German Idealism[12]—the second and the third are closely interwoven with
precisely this tradition, which remains one of the most neglected areas in the
history of religions. We will return to this "western esotericism" in Part Three
of this study. At this point it suffices to point out that *Naturphilosophie* has
always been closely associated with a religious or mystical mode of thinking[13].
The attempt to separate its specific philosophical speculations from their religious context in order to relegate both to different academic spheres is therefore articifial and misleading. *Naturphilosophie* is not a secular but a religious
philosophy, whether or not its defenders try to present it as such[14].

---

[8] Faivre, 'Nature', 328. Reprinted as 'Speculations about Nature'.

[9] Faivre, 'Nature', 336; Yates, 'Hermetic Tradition', 273-274; Böhme, 'Einleitung', 10;
Gladigow, 'Pantheismus', 233.

[10] With an occasional exception. David Bohm's remarks that '... in earlier times, science was
called natural philosophy and this corresponded perfectly with the way I saw the whole field'
(SOC 3).

[11] Faivre, 'Nature', 336.

[12] Joël, *Ursprung der Naturphilosophie*. Cf. Böhme, 'Einleitung', 7.

[13] For splendid illustrations, see Faivre & Zimmermann, *Epochen der Naturmystik*.

[14] Mutschler, in his otherwise very informative study, fails to make due allowance for this
historical fact. This makes his fundamental distinction between science (the level of natural laws),
philosophical interpretation or metaphysics of nature (the level of meaning-disclosure) and religion or nature-mysticism (level of meaning-fulfillment) less than convincing (*Physik—Religion—
New Age*, 41).

If this is understood, and if the interpretation of New Age science as a species of *Naturphilosophie* is correct, then the discussion about its validity must take a different turn. The ability to generate new knowledge is essential for strictly scientific theories, but for *Naturphilosophie* it is not a central concern. Therefore if New Age science fails to produce practical results this is not a sufficient reason to reject it as irrelevant, although if it occasionally does lead to testable hypotheses (as in Sheldrake's theory) that may be considered a welcome bonus. The real criteria for judging *Naturphilosophie* lie in such arguments as internal consistency, philosophical elegance and religious profundity. Ultimately, such philosophies are convincing to the extent that they are perceived to "make sense" of the world of experience. By the same token, the validity of *Naturphilosophie* does not crucially depend upon scientific proof, although specific theories may be vulnerable to empirical falsification. In order to be convincing, a theory must merely be able to demonstrate its *consistency* with accepted scientific knowledge and it must interpret this knowledge in such a way as to show its relevance for human concerns. If a particular *Naturphilosophie* has heavily invested in certain scientific theories, however, subsequent falsification of these theories will seriously impair its ability to convince (although the "true believer" will probably be able to counter cognitive dissonance by the expectation that future discoveries will put thing right).

The fundamental problem in debates about New Age science is that defenders *and* critics alike tend to invoke "science" as the ultimate authority, while all of them, including the few authors who approach the subject from a philosophical perspective, tend to ignore the specific character of *Naturphilosophie*. The confusion on both sides leads to a strange situation. Critics usually attack New Age science *as science*. Because this is the wrong target, or at most half of the target, their arguments are predictably unsuccesful in convincing, or rather, converting, their New Age opponents. However, because both critics *and* defenders share a strong belief in "science" as an arbiter of truth, New Age scientists coin their replies in scientific terms which, in turn, of course do not convince or convert the critics. Simply asserting an *a priori* belief that certain speculative principles are necessary as the foundation for an adequate interpretation of scientific results is apparently felt to be equal to admitting defeat[15]. Thus, an ideological battle between opposing worldviews is fought out in the arena of *science*, which is simply the wrong place. And when the fight occasionally takes place in the arena of philosophy, this is usually a philosophy which insists on reason as the exclusive arbiter of truth: a rationalist epistemology which *Naturphilosophie* does not accept. The result is a discus-

---

[15] An important exception, as we will see, is David Bohm (WIO, first part of chapter 1).

sion *about* rather than *with* the accused party who, of course, is under no obligation to accept the results.

The implication of the above discussion is clear. So-called "New Age science" is to be placed within the field of irreducible *belief systems*[16], which is
the proper domain of the study of religions. For this reason I will not attempt
to enter the usual discussions about scientific and rational validity or sufficient proof, except for purely descriptive purposes. New Age science will be
approached as a system of *emic* beliefs. The scientific arguments of its
authors—even if they seem entirely convincing—will be approached as integral parts of the belief system. This means that they will be taken at face value, as ways of reasoning which carry conviction for New Age believers but the
legitimacy of which it is not our business to judge[17].

MAIN ORIENTATIONS

The varieties of New Age science can be reduced largely to two strongly different schools of *Naturphilosophie*; two scientific theories with philosophical
and metaphysical implications; and one popular literary genre. The two systems are the "holographic paradigm" associated with David Bohm and Karl
Pribram, and the "paradigm of self-organization" associated with the school
of Prigogine. The theories are Sheldrake's hypothesis of "formative causation"
and Lovelock's Gaia-hypothesis. The literary genre is known as "parallellism",
and is primarily associated with Fritjof Capra. I will briefly characterize these
different currents.

The so-called "holographic paradigm" is based upon controversial theories
independently developed by physicist David Bohm and neurologist Karl Pribram, both generally recognized authorities in their respective fields. Bohm
has, over several decades, developed his theory of the "implicate order". One
of several metaphors he uses to explain this theory is that of the hologram.
This is a device for making three-dimensional images of objects, by converting these into a frequency pattern and then "reading out" the original object
from that pattern. Holography has the peculiar characteristic that each fragment of intermediate frequency pattern contains the information of the whole
object. Bohm's theory suggests that, in a similar way, the whole of the universe is implicit in each of its parts. Pribram, for his part, has proposed a theory according to which memory fragments are not locally stored in the brain.

---

[16] In order to prevent confusion: I do not wish to defend a religionistic doctrine of "irreducible
religion", but simply to remind the reader that it is not possible for empirical research to adjudicate upon the truth or appropriateness of religious beliefs.

[17] Cf. the second criterion of empirical research discussed in Hanegraaff, 'Empirical Method',
102-104.

Instead, each memory fragment is distributed over the whole of the brain so that each fragment of the brain, reversely, contains the information of the whole. Bohm and Pribram acknowledge the similarity between their theories, but they seem not to have further collaborated, and neither do they normally refer to their theories as the "holographic paradigm". This has been done by popular New Age authors since Marilyn Ferguson (cf. chapter five). Pribram's theory is known among the New Age audience primarily in second-hand accounts by Ferguson and others; he has not himself published popular books. Bohm, on the other hand, has written a number of books which, in spite of their difficulty, enjoy considerable popularity. Other than Pribram, he has developed a fully-fledged and carefully argued holistic worldview which has a far-reaching influence within the New Age movement. Several influential New Age authors, such as Michael Talbot and F. David Peat, have based their own work on Bohm. Peat has also co-authored a work with Bohm.

The second "big theory" in New Age science is based on the work of Ilya Prigogine, and has been promoted especially by Erich Jantsch. More recent celebrities of New Age science, like Francisco Varela, stand in the same tradition. While the holographic cosmology has a certain timeless quality about it, the theory of the "self-organizing universe" is basically a theory of evolution. Prigogine's central pre-occupation is the irreversibility of time. While time in classical physics is a reversible parameter, Prigogine emphasizes the ubiquity of the "arrow of time" in nature. By re-introducing historical time into physics he hopes that the alienation between the "two cultures" of the natural sciences and the humanities may be overcome. His theory of "dissipative structures" explains how random fluctuations can result in the emergence of qualitatively new orders of increased complexity in the universe. In this way, the universe may be seen as evolving by way of an essentially open-ended process of creative self-organization. Both Prigogine and Jantsch are difficult authors to read, and the influence of their theories is due largely to popularization by others. The main reason for their influence is undoubtedly the fact that they give scientific legitimacy to the optimistic idea of a process of creative evolution of the cosmos, in which man can be seen to play an essential part. It is far from clear to what extent the basically non-temporal holographic paradigm and the time-oriented theory of the self-organizing universe contradict each other. This question is seldom explicitly adressed by New Age authors; usually a possible convergence of the two schools in a future synthesis is hinted at, but the obvious problems which should be adressed to achieve this are not identified, let alone discussed.

An encompassing *Naturphilosophie* is suggested, but not fully developed, in the books of the biologist Rupert Sheldrake. The basis of his work is a neovitalist hypothesis, developed to account for certain unsolved problems in biology and for anomalies to which orthodox science has not been able to find an explanation. This "hypothesis of formative causation" postulates the existence of invisible organizing fields which operate by "morphic resonance". The controversial nature of the theory, and its fascination for New Age believers, lies in the fact that if the hypothesis were proved, this would have far-reaching consequences for our view of the world. Certain basic postulates of established science would have to be abandoned, and replaced by radical holistic alternatives. There can be no doubt that this, rather than its possible contribution to science (i.e., to the problems of biological morphogenesis, crystallization, learning processes etc.), is what motivates Sheldrake to explain his theory book after book and in lectures all over the world. The hope is that his theory—not unlike Darwin's theory one century ago—will cause a revolution in our view of the world and of ourselves which will open the doors for developing a completely new outlook[18].

The second influential scientific theory, Lovelock's Gaia-hypothesis, states that the earth functions like a living organism, to the extent that both are self-regulating systems. The influence of the hypothesis in the New Age movement rests largely on the popular inference that the earth *is* therefore a living organism. We will encounter this adaptation in the work of several authors discussed below.

Finally, there is the popular literary genre of "parallellism", which claims that there are significant parallels between modern physics, on the one hand, and oriental mysticism, on the other. The best-known example is Fritjof Capra's *Tao of Physics*. The parallellist approach to the interpretation of modern physics is both bolder and more modest than the currents discussed above. It is bolder because it is quite explicit about its aims: nothing less than the reconciliation, within one unified whole, of what have traditionally been regarded as extreme opposites. In contrast, all the theories discussed above are presented primarily as scientific or philosophical proposals, the possible mystical implications of which are left for the reader to work out. They are not explicitly presented as "master keys" for healing the cleft between science and religion, although ambitions in this direction are certainly not alien to their inventors. On the other hand, parallellism is more modest, because it does not develop a complete all-encompassing *Naturphilosophie*, and does not even pretend to make a contribution to scientific progress. Capra himself would be the first to admit that he is not an original, innovative thinker like David Bohm or like his own mentor Geoffrey Chew. He merely points out parallels which he believes suggest the need for a new worldview. He leaves it to others to work out such a theory.

While the above currents cover the main categories of New Age science,

---

[18] Not surprisingly, one of Sheldrake's most recent books is called *Seven Experiments That Could Change the World*.

there are some authors who do not quite fit into them. Ken Wilber (cf. chapter two) is important because he defends a transpersonal worldview which
qualifies as "New Age", while at the same time sharply *rejecting* both parallellism and the holographic paradigm. As a dissenter from within the New Age
movement itself, his position is rather unique. The intellectual quality of his
criticism has induced several leading authors to think again about some of their
basic assumptions, and the discussion would be incomplete without his contribution.
I have also included, with some hesitation, the work of Arthur M. Young. Young
seems a rather isolated figure, and his *Naturphilosophie* rests on foundations
entirely different from those of other authors of New Age science. It does not
belong to the "big theories" in terms of influence within the New Age movement or within New Age science, but his approach is sufficiently interesting
to be included here as a borderline case.

THE SOURCES

DAVID BOHM[19]

WIO   David Bohm, *Wholeness and the Implicate Order*
UM   David Bohm, *Unfolding Meaning*
SOC   David Bohm & F. David Peat, *Science, Order, and Creativity*
euu   David Bohm & Renée Weber, 'The enfolding-Unfolding Universe' (In: HP)
pm   David Bohm & Renée Weber, 'The Physicist and the Mystic' (In: HP)
isio   David Bohm & Renée Weber, 'The Implicate and the Super-Implicate Order'
        (In: Renée Weber (ed.), *Dialogues with Scientists and Sages: The Search for
        Unity*)
mmc   David Bohm & Renée Weber, 'Mathematics: The Scientist's Mystic Crys-
        tal' (In: Weber, o.c.)
smdm   David Bohm & the Dalai Lama, 'Subtle Matter, Dense Matter' (In: Weber,
        o.c.)

David Bohm's theory of the implicate order is the outcome of a development
which started in 1951. In this year he published what would become a classic
textbook on quantum mechanics (*Quantum Theory*, 1951). A discussion with
Einstein about this book set Bohm on a trail of thought which led him to develop his "causal interpretation of quantum theory". This theory was presented
in *Causality and Change in Modern Physics* (1957), which already contains
many of the elements of his later thought. Between the publication of this book

---

[19] Feyerabend, 'Professor Bohm's Philosophy of Nature'; Temple, 'David Bohm'; Bohm,
'Hidden Variables'; Russell, 'Physics of David Bohm'; Griffin, 'Bohm and Whitehead'; Peters,
'David Bohm'; Bohm, 'Response'; Restivo, *Social Relations*, esp. 121-125; Van der Zwan, 'New
Age, holisme en theologie'; Hiley & Peat, 'General Introduction'; Goodwin, 'Science of Quali-
ties'; Pylkkänen, *Search for Meaning*; Sharpe, 'Relating the Physics'; Mutschler, *Physik—Reli-
gion—New Age*, 140ff.

and his third one (*The Special Theory of Relativity*, 1965), and while continuing to refine his theories, Bohm came into contact with the work of the Indian thinker Jiddu Krishnamurti. He met Krishnamurti in 1961, and they eventually got to know each other well. The relationship with Krishnamurti has led to the publication of several books containing transcripts of their discussions[20], and there can be no doubt about the importance of Krishnamurti's influence on Bohm's subsequent development. Bohm first started to go beyond the domain of strict science to discuss larger questions of human nature and culture in 1968[21]. In 1980, he published WIO, which can be regarded as the ripe synthesis between his scientific theories and his concern with larger questions stimulated by Krishnamurti. While *Causality and Change in Modern Physics* had already earned him a following of enthusiastic admirers, it is WIO on which Bohm's popularity in the New Age movement is based. It presents the outlines of a worldview according to which the phenomenal world is perceived to "unfold" from a more fundamental "implicate" order characterized by unbroken dynamic wholeness (the holomovement). The theory will be discussed in more detail in Part Two of this study. WIO is presented as the interim result of a work in progress, and in his later publications Bohm has expanded the theories of WIO, describing a hierarchy of orders beyond the implicate (the super-implicate order, the generative order, etc.), and developing a theory devised to reconcile the domains of matter and meaning (referred to as the theory of "soma-significance").

Although the quality of Bohm's earlier work is generally recognized by his colleagues in physics, his later development has resulted in an increasing alienation from mainstream physics. The reasons for this rejection of his mature work are complex. They seem to involve a combination of purely theoretical objections, certain widespread misunderstandings about his theory[22], and of course the deep mistrust among many scientists of the "mysticism" of persons and movements (Krishnamurti, New Age science) with which Bohm has allowed himself to become associated.

F. DAVID PEAT

S   F. David Peat, *Synchronicity*

F. David Peat is a prolific author of popular science books. Together with John P. Briggs he wrote the best existing popular introduction to New Age science

---

[20] Krishnamurti & Bohm, *Ending of Time*; id., *Future of Humanity*. Cf. Hanegraaff, 'Krishnamurti'.

[21] Temple, 'David Bohm', 364.

[22] According to Temple ('David Bohm', 364), most physicists use a standard work by Jammer, *Philosophy of Quantum Mechanics* as their main source of information about Bohm. Jammer, however, allegedly failed to understand Bohm in some crucial ways, and presented him as a determinist.

(see note 1); he co-authored *Science, Order, and Creativity* with David Bohm; and he has been deeply influenced by the latter. Peat's worldview is similar to Bohm's, but also incorporates influences from Prigogine, Sheldrake and others[23]. In so doing, it makes use of the theory of "Synchronicity" which was developed by C.G. Jung in collaboration with the theoretical physicist Wolfgang Pauli. The fact that this theory resulted from the combined efforts of a psychologist and a physicist, and gives a strongly holistic account of the interdepence of mind and matter, makes it extremely fascinating for New Age scientists. Peat's book is highly imaginative and speculative, culminating in the perspective on a coming transformation of man and society.

MICHAEL TALBOT

MNP   Michael Talbot, *Mysticism and the New Physics*
BQ   Michael Talbot, *Beyond the Quantum*
HU   Michael Talbot, *The Holographic Universe*

Talbot's work is representative of a trend in popular New Age science to convince the reader by simply overwhelming him with a mass of accumulated facts, theories, conjectures and speculations. The net effect is the impression that mainstream science is hopelessly inadequate in accounting for what is actually going on in the world. Talbot is especially interested in the interface between physics and parapsychology. In MNP his favoured scientific framework is the so-called "Many worlds-hypothesis", an interpretation of quantum mechanics developed by H. Everett and J. Wheeler. In his later books the holographic paradigm moves increasingly into the center of attention, but Talbot also draws on a wide range of other theories which are presented as somehow pointing in the same direction. BQ is the most systematic exposition of his views. In general Talbot's books promote a worldview similar to the one presented by Peat.

ILYA PRIGOGINE[24]

OC   Ilya Prigogine & Isabelle Stengers, *Order out of Chaos*
rn   Ilya Prigogine, 'The Reenchantment of Nature' (In: Weber, o.c.)

Ilya Prigogine, a Belgian scientist of Russian descent, won the Nobel Prize in 1977 for his work on the thermodynamics of nonequilibrium systems. His fame in the New Age movement is slightly puzzling, considering that OC is actually a very difficult book, large parts of which are inaccessible to readers without a scientific training. The same can be said, to a slightly lesser extent, of the works by his follower Erich Jantsch (next section). It seems that Prigogine's

---

[23] Cf. Briggs & Peat, *Looking-glass Universe*, which attempts to demonstrate the possibility of a synthesis between these different thinkers and their paradigms.
[24] Mutschler, *Physik—Religion—New Age*, 106-119 and *passim*; Van Kampen, 'Determinism and Predictability', 273-281.

ideas have been disseminated among the wider New Age audience primarily by popular authors like Marilyn Ferguson (see chapter five) and by New Age scientists like Peat. Another probable factor is Prigogine's frequent appearances as a speaker for New Science audiences. However, in contrast to his most prestigious counterpart David Bohm, Prigogine refuses to speculate about mysticism or about most other subjects with which his New Age admirers are concerned. His chief non-scientific interest, as noted above, is the reconciliation between the natural sciences and the humanities by re-introducing historical time into the former.

ERICH JANTSCH[25]

SOU   Erich Jantsch, *The Self-Organizing Universe*

If Prigogine is the architect of the paradigm of self-organization, it is Erich Jantsch (1929-1980) who has developed it into an encompassing theory of evolution[26]. Although more accessible than Prigogine's *Order out of Chaos*, SOU is still an academic rather than a popular science book. Its perspective can be characterized as a process-oriented general systems theory. With a naturalness that is typical for such approaches, physical, biological, and socio-cultural "systems" are presented on a continuum and are assumed to answer to the same laws. Thus, Jantsch's story of evolution starts with the big bang and ends with a mystical epilogue ("Meaning") about God.

RUPERT SHELDRAKE[27]

NSL   Rupert Sheldrake, *A New Science of Life*
PP   Rupert Sheldrake, *The Presence of the Past*
RN   Rupert Sheldrake, *The Rebirth of Nature*
mf   Rupert Sheldrake, 'Morphogenetic Fields: Nature's Habits' (In: Weber, o.c.)
mmf   Rupert Sheldrake & David Bohm, 'Matter as a Meaning Field' (In: Weber, o.c.)

Rupert Sheldrake first presented his controversial theory in NSL. The book, although presented so as to make it interesting and accessible to a general public, is almost completely scientific in content. Only in the final chapter does Sheldrake discuss some possible metaphysical frameworks which might account for his theory. The new edition of 1985 includes a long appendix documenting the controversies which followed the original publication in 1981, including *Nature*'s editorial calling NSL "a book for burning", and the *New Scientist*'s inquiry whether this meant that *Nature* had abandoned the scien-

---

[25] Fabel, 'Dynamic of the Self-organizing Universe'.
[26] Cf. also Jantsch & Waddington, *Evolution and Consciousness*; Jantsch, *Evolutionary Vision*.
[27] Wilber, 'Sheldrake's Theory'; O'Hara, 'Reflections'; Sanders, '"Morphische Felder"'; Ertel, 'Sheldrake's morfogenetische velden getest'.

tific method for "trial by editorial". It also includes information about experiments to test the hypothesis. In general, the results of the latter seem to have
been encouraging but not yet fully conclusive, and this has been confirmed by
independent research[28]. It seems that Sheldrake's basic hypothesis has not been
significantly changed or expanded since NSL. PP presents much of the material from NSL in a different form, and Sheldrake also looks at the theory from
a wider philosophical and historical perspective. This trend of going beyond
the strictly scientific domain is continued in RN. This is Sheldrake's most typical "New Age" book, with long sections about ecological concerns, the quest
for a new worldview, and reflections about religious implications. Here, Sheldrake comes closest to developing his initial hypothesis into an encompassing
Naturphilosophie.

FRITJOF CAPRA[29]

ToP   Fritjof Capra, *The Tao of Physics*
topr   Fritjof Capra & Renée Weber, 'The Tao of Physics revisited' (In: HP)

ToP is no doubt the epitome of New Age science in the eyes of the general
public. The basic idea of a parallellism between modern physics (quantum
mechanics) and various traditions of Oriental mysticism is well known and has
been hotly debated. Somewhat surprisingly, however, there has been comparatively little attention to the fact that Capra actually ends up defending a consistent philosophical worldview which would merit attention in its own right,
i.e., regardless of the credibility of the parallellism-thesis. This is the so-called
"bootstrap philosophy" of the physicist Geoffrey Chew, which has been found
to be strikingly similar to Leibniz's Monadology[30]. The "early Capra" is a boot-
strap-philosopher. It is significant that Capra's later development, represented
by *The Turning Point* (see ch. five), has led him to reject certain premises of
ToP. Capra has never rejected the bootstrap philosophy, but in *The Turning
Point* it is no longer the foundation of his *Naturphilosophie*. That place has
been taken over by Gregory Bateson's systems theory. Therefore, in terms of
Capra's own development, ToP represents an early phase of development, some
weaknesses of which have been corrected in his later work. This should be kept
in mind while evaluating the position of ToP within New Age science, and
within the New Age movement generally.

---

[28] An overview of the research is given by Ertel. He concludes that morphic resonance has
not been proven beyond doubt, but that the results suggest that it must be considered eligible as
a very serious explanation ('Sheldrake's morfogenetische velden getest', 42).
    [29] Restivo, *Social Relations*; Van Zoest, 'New Age-beweging'; Chowdhury, 'Holisme en par-
allellisme'; Wiskerke, 'New Age-holisme'; Clifton & Regehr, 'Toward a Sound Perspective';
Mutchler, *Physik—Religion—New Age*; Bochinger, *"New Age"*, 421-511.
    [30] Gale, 'Chew's Monadology', 339-348.

KEN WILBER

HP	Ken Wilber (ed.), *The Holographic Paradigm and other Paradoxes*
npr	Anonymus, 'A new perspective on reality'
cr	Marilyn Ferguson, 'Karl Pribram's changing reality'
f	Karl Pribram, 'What the fuss is all about'
cht	Div., 'Commentaries on the holographic paradigm'
EtE	Ken Wilber, *Eye to Eye*
QQ	Ken Wilber, *Quantum Questions*

Ken Wilber, who studied biochemistry before turning to transpersonal psychology, has evinced a strong interest in New Age science. Contrary to almost all other New Age authors, however, he has expressed strong reservations. His criticism is based on the incompatibility he perceives between the holographic paradigm and his own belief in (a modern version of) the *perennial philosophy*, which describes reality as a hierarchy of different levels. The holographic paradigm, according to Wilber, commits hierarchy collapse and is ultimately an example of semi-pantheistic reductionism. Wilber's criticism has contributed to an increased awareness among New Age scientists of the dangers of reductionism. Wilber's own alternatives, while very important within the transpersonal movement, definitely remain a minority view within New Age science. Wilber's importance for the latter lies in the fact that his criticism has presents one of the very few real theoretical polemics (although a onesided one) within the New Age movement. The holistic and syncretistic orientation of the New Age subculture is not congenial to conflicts. It tends to minimize differences in the name of a deeper all-encompassing truth, and discussions among New Age scientists often become occasions for the "sharing" of viewpoints rather than for rigid intellectual debate. Wilber's attacks on this holistic consensus have forced New Age scientists to think again about some fundamental premises of their theories. This makes his voice an important one.

ARTHUR M. YOUNG[31]

RU   Arthur M.Young, *The Reflexive Universe*

As noted above, Young is a borderline case of New Age science. He has become known outside the alternative community as the inventor of the first helicopter to be awarded a commercial license (Bell Model 47). His real ambition, however, was to construct a theory of the universe, and he saw his helicopter as a mere metaphor for the "psycopter": the evolving spirit or "winged self"[32]. RU is the final result of his efforts. In contrast to most New Age scientists, Young is quite uninhibited about admitting the non-scientific foundations of his theory (modern theosophy in particular). Science is used whenever Young needs

---

[31] For autobiographical backgrounds: Young, *Bell Notes*.
[32] Young, *Bell Notes*, 3.

it, but it is as easily dismissed wherever it is deemed inadequate in comparison with "higher insights" of an esoteric nature. The ultimate authority is evidently not science but esotericism. This results in a broadly theosophical, speculative *Naturphilosophie* which incorporates modern science within a wider framework. The theory has impressed leading New Age spokesmen, notably Stanislav Grof, who has called it 'a serious candidate for a scientific meta-paradigm of the future'[33].

---

[33] BB 63.

CHAPTER FOUR

NEOPAGANISM[1]

THE PHENOMENON OF NEOPAGANISM

As a general term, "neopaganism" covers all those modern movements which are, firstly, based on the conviction that what Christianity has traditionally denounced as idolatry and superstition actually represents/ represented a profound and meaningful religious worldview and, secondly, that a religious practice based on this worldview can and should be revitalized in our modern world. The very use of the term "neopaganism" as a self-designation clearly contains a polemical thrust towards institutionalized Christianity[2], which is held responsible for the decline of western paganism and the subsequent blackening of its image. The problems of the modern world, particularly the ecological crisis, are regarded as a direct result of the loss of pagan wisdom about man's relationship to the natural world, and a recovery of this wisdom is regarded not only as desirable but as urgently needed. The focus on ecological problems is particularly prominent in contemporary neopaganism, but it should be noted that—given the above definition—the phenomenon of neopaganism as such is not in fact synonymous with its postwar "New Age" manifestation. Commentators of the contemporary neopagan movement(s) usually seem unaware of the fact that the term neopaganism is also used in quite different contexts, particularly in connection with certain religious and philosophical developments in prewar Germany[3]. The general definition of neopaganism given above encompasses both these often politically suspect movements and tendencies, and the contemporary "New Age" phenomenon. Of course it does not follow that the latter is therefore fascistic, although that opinion has sometimes been

---

[1] General sources and special studies relating to neopaganism in general: Adler, *Drawing down the Moon*; Anon., 'Witchcraft (Wicca), Neopaganism and Magick'; Ruppert, *Die Hexen kommen* (also printed as 'Magie und Hexenglaube heute'); Luhrmann, *Persuasions*; id., 'Persuasive Ritual'; id., 'Witchcraft, Morality and Magic'; Eilberg-Schwartz, 'Witches of the West'; Kelly, 'Neopagans and the New Age'; Burnett, *Dawning of the Pagan Moon*; Hough, *Witchcraft*; York, *Emerging Network*, spec. 99-144; Weissmann, 'Erwachen'; Kelly, 'Update'.

[2] Christianity as such is not necessarily rejected. Surprisingly many neopagans, including well-known figures as Caithlín Matthews or Maxine Sanders, consider themselves both pagan and christian. They believe that the true esoteric core of Christianity is perfectly compatible with the pagan worldview and that it is therefore not Christianity as such which is to be rejected, but only a particular interpretation which happens to have become dominant in church institutions. These christian pagans find inspiration in Catholic ritual or in the remnants of Celtic Christianity, and generally regard christian gnosticism in a positive light.

[3] Cancik, 'Neuheiden und totaler Staat'; Faber, 'Einleitung'; Spindler, 'Europe's Neo-paganism'. Cf. especially Von Schnurbein, *Religion als Kulturkritik*.

voiced[4]. It does imply that, in a strict sense, the term "neopaganism" is not sufficient in itself as a designation for the movements studied here. "New Age" neopaganism should be distinguished from other (earlier or contemporary) attempts to revitalize the worldview of pre-christian European cultures. When in the rest of the discussion I refer to "neopaganism", I will be referring to the New Age variety only.

However, speaking of a "New Age variety" of neopaganism—and indeed, discussing neopaganism as part of the New Age movement—is to invite criticism. Aidan A. Kelly, for instance, states that 'The Neopagan movement ... parallels the New Age movement in some ways, differs sharply from it in others, and overlaps it in some minor ways'[5]. Obviously, such a categorical statement is possible only if both movements are already clearly defined and demarcated. It is a basic assumption of the present study, however, that at least the New Age movement is not. Kelly's comparison between the "New Age" and the "neopagan" perspective indeed turns out to be based on a rather selective view of the former, which occasionally exerts gentle pressure on the evidence[6]. It is difficult to escape the impression that his attempt to separate neopaganism from the New Age as much as possible is inspired by apologetic considerations—Kelly is not only a well-known researcher, but also a neopagan—rather than by empirical ones. Tanya Luhrmann, in her ground-breaking study of magical groups in London, appears not to have encountered anything like Kelly's distinction: 'In whatever form magicians practice magic, they situate it within what is proclaimed the "New Age"'[7]. Luhrmann's characterization of

---

[4] There is some justification for associating contemporary neopaganism with fascism in the case of so-called "Norse paganism", which uses Norse/Germanic mythology as a source of inspiration. Predictably—considering that neopagans are naturally interested in the mythological heritage of their own country—this variety is especially prominent in Germany, but it also exists elsewhere. Adler notes (*Drawing Down the Moon*, 273) that some groups use Norse paganism as a front for right-wing or outright Nazi activities, but blanket generalizations on the basis of such cases should be warned against. Each specific group should be judged on its own merits (or the lack thereof). Cf. Adler, *Drawing Down the Moon*, 273-282, and Weissmann, 'Erwachen'. In any case, Norse paganism is of only marginal significance for the present study.

[5] Identical quotation in Kelly, 'Neopagans and the New Age', 311, and 'Update', 136.

[6] For instance, it is true that neopagans 'reject the dualism of Eastern traditions' ('Neopagans and the New Age', 314), but so do many New Age believers. In general, Kelly ascribes a far stronger respect for traditional Eastern notions (such as the role of the guru) to the New Age than the evidence permits. Furthermore, when he says that '*Many* New Agers assume ... that...' ('Neopagans and the New Age', 314. My emphasis) he implicitly admits that not all of them do, but he nevertheless contrasts these assumptions to neopaganism, suggesting a far greater consensus among New Agers than in fact exists. A comparably artificial consensus is suggested by the statement that neopagans are 'not particularly interested in a New Age in the future' ('Neopagans and the New Age', 314). As Part Two of this study will show, directly disconfirming evidence can easily be found in most of the standard neopagan literature. Finally, Kelly's statement that 'New Age bookstores rarely have sections labeled magic or witchcraft' ('Neopagans and the New Age', 313) is disconfirmed by my own observations in the Netherlands, Germany and England.

[7] Luhrmann, *Persuasions*, 30.

the New Age, it should be added, is basically the same one as I have outlined in my Introduction.[8] My own research confirms Luhrmann's conclusion that neopaganism is part of the New Age in this general sense at least. Having stated this, however, it must also be said that neopaganism definitely has its own distinctive flavour which sets it apart from other New Age trends. Kelly's position is therefore not totally unfounded, but is best regarded as an overstatement resulting from the exaggeration of real differences at the expense of similarities. The complicated relationship between New Age in general and neopaganism has been adequately summarized by Michael York.[9] York expresses no final opinion for or against the inclusion of neopaganism in the New Age, but his discussion illustrates the importance of both the similarities and the differences. The picture presented by York is confirmed by my own research. Considering the demarcations proposed in my Introduction, the neopagan movement should be treated as part of the New Age movement, but it should nonetheless be seen as a special, relatively clearly circumscribed subculture within that movement.

If our subject is a special case of both neopaganism in general and of the New Age movement, then it may be asked what exactly constitutes its uniqueness. This question can only be conclusively answered on the basis of a detailed analysis of the sources, and therefore has to be postponed to Part Two of this study. Very briefly (and predictably) it can be said that the special character of contemporary neopaganism in relation to neopaganism in general is precisely its use of New Age concepts, while its special position within the New Age movement derives from the fact that the specifically neopagan perspective—as defined in the first section of this chapter—is not particularly prominent in the rest of the New Age. In other words, it is precisely the overlap between the two movements/perspectives which constitutes the uniqueness of "New Age" neopaganism.

NEOPAGANISM AS MAGIC

Looking at neopaganism from the perspective of the study of religions, we are confronted with the notorious problem of the conceptual status of *magic*[10]. Rit-

---

[8] Luhrmann describes New Age as 'a broad cultural ideology, a development of the countercultural sixties, which privileges holistic medicine, 'intuitive sciences' like astrology and tarot, ecological and anti-nuclear political issues, and alternative therapies, medicines and philosophers. The 'New Age' has become a widely accepted catch-phrase for this matrix of concerns ...' (*Persuasions*, 30).

[9] York, *Emerging Network*, chapter 4 'New Age and Neo-paganism: Similarities, Contrasts and Relationships'.

[10] For overviews of the magic-science-religion debate, cf. Wax & Wax, 'Notion of Magic'; Middleton, 'Theories of Magic'; Versnel, 'Some Reflections'; Tambiah, *Magic, Science, Religion*.

ual magic is the central neopagan practice and, according to neopagan self-understanding, it is the key to the pagan worldview. However, to what extent is it legitimate for us to adopt this emic view and describe the essence of neo-paganism as "magic" in an etic sense?

The classical distinctions between magic, religion and science as essentially different pursuits (Tylor, Frazer, Malinowski etc.) have long been discredited as projections of western ethnocentrism[11]. But if these distinctions are no more than the product of intellectual imperialism, it becomes extremely doubtful whether the term "magic" can be retained at all. Because all traditional definitions have depended on an implicit or explicit contrast with either religion or science, the very concept of "magic" appears to collapse together with these distinctions; any further use of it seems to imply support for scientifically untenable theories. Nevertheless, the concept has proven to be remarkably resistant. H.S. Versnel, in a highly perceptive analysis, remarks that contemporary theoreticians find it extremely hard to do without the term "magic" even if they are convinced of the need to do so: 'Practically no one escapes moments of reduced concentration when they suddenly fall into using unsophisticated common sense concepts, though they sometimes betray their awareness of the lapse by putting the term magic between inverted commas or adding "so-called".'[12] Because of the impracticality of avoiding the term "magic" in an etic sense when discussing phenomena emically known under that name[13] (after all, the word did not originate in scholarly discourse), some authors have proposed to retain it on a pragmatic common-sense level. Cl. Kluckhohn has drawn a comparison with such terms like 'boy, youth, man, old man, which neither physiologists nor psychologists will wholly discard but which they will also not attempt to include among the elementary units and basic concepts upon which they rear their sciences'[14]. Not dissimilarly, Versnel proposes to use "magic" as an etic term referring to a polythetic class of religious phenomena[15].

> Just like religions, 'magical' practices or expressions may share some though not all family resemblances. This means that we may accept a 'broad, polythetic or

---

[11] See for instance Wax & Wax ('Notion of Magic', 500): 'these conceptualizations have been subjected to severe criticism: the critics have been eminent; their data have been excellent; and their critique has never been refuted. ... [it has become] clear that the basis of the distinctions between magic and religion (or magic and science) is not the attitudes and conduct of the primitive peoples in whose lives magic plays such a major role. Rather, these distinctions stem from the rationalistic orientation of Western civilization (and its highly rational scholars).'

[12] Versnel, 'Some Reflections', 181.

[13] Cf. Versnel: '...you cannot talk about magic without using the term magic' ('Some Reflections', 181).

[14] Cl. Kluckhohn, 'Universal Categories of Culture'. Quotation according to Wax & Wax, 'Notion of Magic', 499.

[15] The concept of polythetic classes was discussed in the Introduction.

prototypical' definition of magic, based on a "common sense" collection of features, which may or may not, according to convention and experience, largely correspond to the items listed in the first part of this introduction: instrumental, manipulative, mechanical, non-personal, coercive, with short-term, concrete and often individual goals etc., and employ this as a provisional ideal-typical standard, coined by *our* cultural universe, and just see what happens.[16]

According to such an essentially pragmatic approach, magic can be seen either as different from religion or as a special phenomenon *within* religion. The important point, in Versnel's view, is not to make a distinction between magic and religion, but between magic and non-magic[17]. In principle, this makes his proposal compatible with a quite different approach, which sees magic as a form of religion and contrasts both to "science". A strong tradition has emerged which posits a broad, universal dichotomy between two contrasting mentalities or worldviews, suggesting that it is a certain worldview—rather than certain practices regarded in isolation—which holds the key to understanding magic. Lévy-Bruhl distinguished the "prelogical" or "mystical" mentality from the "logical" mentality of modern man[18]. S.J. Tambiah has more recently developed a similar, but no longer ethnocentric, duality between worldviews based on "participation" or on "causality"[19]. Wax & Wax, following Sigmund Mowinckel, contrast the "magical world view" with the worldview of Western man[20]. Several other typological dichotomies have been developed, which all share a basic similarity. They see non-western humanity as living in an "enchanted" world of "participation", without sharp divisions between persons and things, in which actions can have immediate effects not mediated by instrumental causality. Western society, in separating man and world, replaces this intimate participation and mutuality by an "impersonal" relationship based on instrumental causality. The first type of worldview is favourable to the development of magical practice, while the second is not. The implication of this approach is that magic can no longer be seen as competing with "science",

---

[16] Versnel, 'Some Reflections', 186. Versnel himself applies his common-sense distinction to the interpretation of the so-called *defixiones* (short curse-texts, usually inscribed in lead tablets) from Graeco-Roman antiquity, and concludes that it makes good sense to describe these as examples of "magic".

[17] Versnel, 'Some Reflections', 187.

[18] Cf. Tambiah, *Magic, Science, Religion*, 84-90. Lévy-Bruhl still displays the traditional ethnocentric bias in seeing the logical mentality as superior. For a recent defense of his basic framework, cf. Wiebe, *Irony of Theology*.

[19] Tambiah, *Magic, Science, Religion*, 105-110.

[20] Wax & Wax, 'Notion of Magic', 501-503, and their 'The Magical World View'. While studying Max Weber's descriptions of the Hebrew prophets attacking the so-called "primitive worldview", the Waxes 'realized that *magic*—in the most significant sense of the term—was but this world view presented with the emphasis upon rite. The previous scholarly attempts to interpret magic had failed because in their concentration upon ritual, incantation, or wish-fulfillment, they had not truly understood how the persons in question conceived the world and the place within it of wish, spell, emotion, or ritual' ('Notion of Magic', 501).

because the two do not share a common "world" in which a comparison could be made on the basis of mutually acceptable premises.

Although this approach is attractive, it must be admitted that it leaves the relation magic—religion (or magic—non-magic within the "first world") somewhat vague. One almost gets the impression that religion has now become a special case of the magical worldview rather than the reverse. As before, the danger exists that religion is opposed to magic according to a definition which is as culture-specific as any of the traditional definitions[21]. To round off this brief discussion of the debate about magic, I would like to highlight the contribution made in 1963 by the Dutch scholar of religion Jan van Baal. This is because it seems to me that Van Baal's article contains, *in nuce* at least, the seeds of an elegant approach which manages to avoid most of the traditional dilemmas[22].

Van Baal defines religion as including 'all those ideas relating to a reality which cannot be determined empirically and all those acts which imply the presence of such ideas'[23], and magic as 'all those acts and spells directed towards furthering a certain aim by employing another reality than the empirically determinable one, in which process this other reality is not independently active but is an instrument manipulated by the active person'[24]. It is clear that this makes magic a special case of religion while retaining a manageable distinction. From Van Baal's further discussion one can infer that he does not conceive of the distinction as absolute and rigid, but as idealtypical and pragmatic. He claims that the supposed belief in the effectiveness of magic (magic as coercion) has been far too heavily emphasized in existing theories, at the expense of the far more frequent 'ordinary magic' of everyday life. This ordinary magic is quite similar, for instance, to prayers for a good harvest. Although such prayers are taken quite seriously by the persons involved, belief in their effect is highly conditional. If the harvest fails this is not regarded as disconfirmation of the existence of God or of his ability to act. Now, in interpreting prayer we are usually inclined to concentrate not on what is expected of it (as if prayer were an alternative to practical manipulation), but on what it *express-*

---

[21] Cf. Tambiah, *Magic, Science, Religion*, 18-24. Discussing the central thesis of Keith Thomas's celebrated *Religion and the Decline of Magic*, Tambiah wonders about the implications: 'If the distinctions between religion and sacramental magic, between prayer and spell, between sovereign deity and manipulable divine being, were the product of a specific historical epoch in European history and its particular preoccupations stemming from Judaeo-Christian concepts and concerns, can these same categories (embedded in and stemming from an historical context) fruitfully serve as universal, analytical categories and illuminate the texture of other cultures and societies?'.

[22] Van Baal, 'Magic'.

[23] Van Baal, 'Magic', 11. In his later work, van Baal has changed the formulation: 'All explicit and implicit notions and ideas, accepted as true, which relate to a reality which cannot be verified empirically' (Van Baal & van Beek, *Symbols for Communication*, 3).

[24] Van Baal, 'Magic', 10.

es. Van Baal proposes that we should do the same with regard to magic. His position appears to be that magic, exemplified in particular by the spell, both expresses and reconfirms a distinct view of—or way of experiencing—the world. The effect of the magical spell is 'that it evokes the weird atmosphere of mystery, in which things have power, in which things are more than they are and hold out to man danger and promise at the same time.'[25]. Symbols are of crucial importance for magical man, as 'a means of expressing his experience of and against an uncertain, power-charged world, which makes its mystery felt in that uncertainty'[26]. Like the authors mentioned above, Van Baal regards a "participatory" worldview—which does not rigidly separate persons and things—as crucial for magic. The subjective persuasiveness of this worldview is not too surprising, according to Van Baal, if seen in the light of Bergson's observation that 'all resistance we meet with in life tends to be experienced as intentional by nature each time the event acquires significance in relation to our own ego'[27]. Traces of this "magical" intentionality in everyday life are still present when we say, for instance, that our engine "refuses" to start or the tram "will not come"[28]. Finally, Van Baal claims that magic is expected to produce results not primarily in the pragmatic sphere but 'in the atmosphere of mystery and intentionality surrounding the object'[29].

It is the atmosphere of mystery which distinguishes the magical worldview from our modern Western one: 'In our own culture the atmosphere of mystery has become a rarity ... the mysterious is a category too tenuous for systematic research and scientific knowledge. It flourishes only where systematic analysis is absent[30]'. The persistence of magic in our world—difficult to explain if magic is regarded only as a means to reach pragmatic results, which in that case has to compete with science—is understandable precisely because of this contrast:

> It permits people to live not in a cold world of cause and effect but in a world which, for all its faults, is one of which one may expect anything. ... It is a world full of intimacy and, for all its terrors, it is nevertheless familiar and dependable too. The mystery of such a world is not only threatening, but also full of promise. Anyone who knows that mystery and is a party to the weird words that express and influence it holds the key to all kinds of possibilities.[31]

Van Baal's perspective deserves more attention than it has received. On the

---

[25] Van Baal, 'Magic', 16.
[26] Van Baal, 'Magic', 18.
[27] Van Baal, 'Magic', 17.
[28] Van Baal, 'Magic', 17-18.
[29] Van Baal, 'Magic', 19. Against Malinowski, Van Baal holds that a magical result is not a substitute for a technical one.
[30] Van Baal, 'Magic', 16-17.
[31] Van Baal, 'Magic', 19-20.

basis of exceptionally lucid definitions of religion and magic, he manages to give the basic outlines of a synthesis which makes sense of the evidence while avoiding most of the traditional theoretical deadlocks. For us, it is significant that his theory, although based on fieldwork in non-western traditional societies, is very illuminating for understanding neopaganism. The defense of "magic" by neopagans is very clearly based on a rejection of the 'cold world of cause and effect' in favour of an "enchanted" world of the kind described by Lévy-Bruhl, Wax & Wax, Tambiah and Van Baal. Van Baal's emphasis on the atmosphere of mystery as crucial to magic is strongly confirmed by the neopagan evidence. Neopagan magic indeed functions as a means of invoking and reaffirming mystery in a world which seems to have lost it; the subjective attraction and persuasiveness of this practice is convincingly explained by Van Baal. Finally, Van Baal's downplaying of the importance to be attached to magical efficacy, and his observations on "ordinary magic", accord perfectly with the anthropological analysis of contemporary magic offered by its most knowledgeable and sophisticated analyst, Tanya Luhrmann.

We can conclude that neopaganism may legitimately be regarded as a religious movement based on magic in the sense of a certain ritual practice (i.e., as defined by Van Baal) which expresses a comprehensive worldview (or, conversily, a 'worldview presented with the emphasis upon rite'[32]). However, it should be added immediately that neopaganism is a special case of magic in at least one crucial respect. Neopagan magic is different from traditional magic in that the magical worldview is *purposely adopted* as a reaction to the "disenchanted" world of modern western society. It is not just the case that the characteristics which enable neopaganism to be identified as "magic" can be discerned analytically from a comparison with the "scientific" worldview; rather, neopaganism is based on a conscious rejection of that worldview. There is a certain irony in the fact that the scientific study of religion—with its frequent descriptions of magic as opposed to science—has itself significantly contributed to this phenomenon. By confirming the popular view that magic is the natural alternative for the modern western worldview, scholarship has made itself into a powerful factor in the very emergence and persistence of neopaganism as a new religious movement[33]. Neopagans are avid readers[34] and it is in the scholarly literature, and its semi-scholarly spin-off, that they have found and continue to find much of the information enabling them to revive or reinvent the world of magic.

The other major source of inspiration has not been touched upon yet, although

---

[32] As elegantly formulated by Wax & Wax, 'Notion of Magic', 501 (cf. note 20).

[33] Jencson, 'Neopaganism and the Great Mother Goddess'; Hanegraaff, 'From the Devil's Gateway'.

[34] Luhrmann, *Persuasions*, 86; Jencson, 'Neopaganism', 4.

it is highly relevant to the discussion. Neopaganism is a continuation of nine-teenth-century occultist ritual magic, which in turn has its historical roots in the hermetic revival of the sixteenth century. In Part Three of this study I will make reference to the centrality of popular and intellectual magic to this tradition[35]. If the above discussion has yielded an affirmative answer to the question whether neopaganism can be described as "magic" in a theoretical sense, these roots of neopaganism are reason for characterizing it as magic in a historical sense as well (i.e, as a continuation of what was traditionally—emically—known as "magic" in the west). The theoretical relevance of an historical perspective on western magical traditions has been recognized only recently. The meaning of "magic" in the context of the Renaissance, in particular, has been largely neglected in anthropological theories of magic, and the recovery of this chapter of western history might have significant implications for the theoretical debate[36]. Investigation of the meaning of *magia* in the Renaissance period, in particular, will probably strengthen the notion of magic as a worldview, while further weakening the traditional emphasis on practice regarded out of context.

MAIN ORIENTATIONS

The most convenient way to bring some order into the variety of New Age neopagan perspectives is to start with the original founding movement of modern witchcraft known as *Wicca*[37], and to picture neopaganism in general as "fanning out" from this relatively clearly circumscribed center into increasingly syncretistic and nondogmatic directions. It could be argued that Wicca as such is somewhat closer to the "sect" profile outlined in the Introduction than most other New Age groups (although it is definitely non-sectarian as regards intolerancy and exclusivism, at the very least), and in that respect the movement would have to be regarded as a borderline case within the present study. Indeed, if Wicca had remained the relatively self-contained, England-based occultist religion which it originally was, I might have decided not to include it in the present study. As it is, however, the Craft—as it is also called—was exported to the U.S.A. by Raymond Buckland during the 1960s[38]. In its new environment, it was interpreted and developed in increasingly unorthodox and syncretistic directions. The most important influence on the development of the movement beyond its original boundaries has been a section of the feminist

---

[35] For a brief impression, cf. Culianu, 'Magic'.

[36] A first step in this direction is made by Tambiah, *Magic, Science, Religion*, 24-31.

[37] Apart from relevant parts of sources mentioned in note 1, cf. Russell, *History of Witchcraft*, ch. 9; Kelly, *Crafting*.

[38] Adler, *Drawing Down the Moon*, 92-93; Kelly, 'Update', 137.

movement known as *women's spirituality*[39]. The cross-fertilization between Craft traditions and spiritually-oriented feminism resulted in a type of neopaganism which is often referred to as the *Goddess movement*[40]. This development, finally, has not remained without influence on the women's spirituality movement as such, which has to some extent adopted neopagan and general New Age elements. However, women's spirituality is in itself just a loose and unspecific term[41], and it is here in particular that the boundaries become most seriously blurred. If Wicca is at the center of neopaganism, and the Goddess movement represents a heterodox divergence from that center, then women's spirituality can be located partly at its circumference and partly (perhaps mainly) beyond the neopagan and New Age domain altogether.

It is probably superfluous to emphasize that this picture is no more than a crude idealtypical approximation, justified only by its heuristic usefulness. The three domains of *Wicca*, Goddess movement and women's spirituality very much blend into each other, and the boundaries between the second and the third are particularly fuzzy. A further complication results from the fact that traditional Wicca, in particular, is rooted in traditional occultist ritual magic, and still retains much of that legacy[42]. Again, the boundaries are fuzzy. Luhrmann, in her study of magic in contemporary London, makes a rough distinction between four domains, of which "witchcraft" (mainly Wicca) and "western mysteries" (occultistic ritual magic) seem to be the most clearly circumscribed alternatives. The other two groups (*ad hoc* ritual magic and non-initiated paganism) can be regarded as less tightly organized variations of these two basic types[43]. In practice, these different orientations are part of one and the same subculture, and while different in theory they are often difficult to separate in fact. The complicating factor with regard to our concerns is that Wicca is a neopagan development of traditional occultistic ritual magic, but that the latter movement is not itself pagan. In other words, within the context of "magical groups" as described by Luhrmann, neopaganism (Wicca) gradually and almost imperceptibly shades into a non-pagan domain. This "western mysteries" movement as such, however, falls outside the scope of the present study[44].

---

[39] Cf. Spretnak, *Politics*; Borsje, 'Vrouwenspiritualiteit'; King, 'Voices of a New Spirituality', in: *Women and Spirituality*; Lanwerd, 'Zur Bedeutung'; Bednarowski, 'New Age Movement and Feminist Spirituality.

[40] Cf. Dijk, 'Goddess Movement'; Weaver, 'Who is the Goddess'; Adler, 'Response'; Mollenkott, 'Evangelical Feminist'; Roberts, 'Is there a Future for the Goddess?'; Harvey, 'Avalon from the Mists'.

[41] Bednarowski, 'New Age Movement', 168.

[42] For an overview of this tradition, see King, *Ritual Magic in England*.

[43] Luhrmann, *Persuasions*, 32ff. Women's spirituality and Goddess religion are predominantly American phenomena, and for that reason do not figure in Luhrmann's London-based research.

[44] Except for WW2 (see below), which is part of a two-volume publication illustrative of the

We can conclude that there are two ways in which neopaganism overlaps with something else. The overlap with occultistic ritual magic is a legacy of the historical roots of Wicca in English occultism. The overlap with women's spirituality is a later, essentially American development.

Wicca is a new religious movement founded in september 1939 by a retired British civil servant named Gerald Gardner. It was essentially an attempt to revive the medieval Witchcraft religion as described in Margaret Murray's *The Witch-cult in western Europe*[45]. Gardner claimed to have been initiated into Wicca by a member of a secret coven[46] tracing its lineage back to the period of the witchcraft persecutions. In fact, as Aidan Kelly has conclusively demonstrated[47], Gardner did not revive an old religion but created a new one. His main sources of inspiration were occultist ritual magic in the tradition of Aleister Crowley and the *Hermetic Order of the Golden Dawn*[48], and popular works about folklore and mythology such as Frazer's *Golden Bough*, Charles Leland's *Aradia* and, of course, Margaret Murray's works. Gardner published several books about witchcraft and initiated new members, who would eventually "hive off" to start their own covens when the original one became too large. This continuing process resulted in a mushrooming of "Gardnerian" covens. Gardnerians trace their lineage back to Gardner's own original coven, using the rituals and "Craft laws" as laid down by Gardner in the so-called *Book of Shadows*. An alternative Wiccan tradition, known as "Alexandrian", resulted from

---

close links between neopaganism and "western mysteries". It would have been artificial to include the first volume and exclude the second. PR, it could be argued, hovers somewhere on the border between both domains. In spite of existing connections and affinities, the "western mysteries" should not be regarded as part of the New Age movement. Firstly, most of these groups are direct continuations of much older and quite separate traditions, and secondly, these relatively secretive and self-contained groups approach the "sect" profile even closer than Wicca does. Luhrmann's statement, quoted above, that all magicians situate magic within the "New Age" might be considered a counter-argument. I used her words as a disconfirmation of Kelly's thesis, but this does not oblige me to follow her in all other respects. The demarcations outlined in my Introduction are necessary precisely with respect to these admittedly ambiguous cases.

[45] Murray, *Witch-cult in Western Europe*. Murray's central thesis that the witches persecuted by the inquisition were members of a secret pagan fertility religion is now generally discredited by scholars. This has led to the so-called "Murrayite controversy" among neopagans. Some continue to believe that Murray was right after all and that Wicca is the continuation of an ancient pagan tradition, but many neopagans are quite comfortable seeing themselves as members of a newly founded religion which is connected with ancient paganism only "in spirit". The "Murrayite controversy" is summarized by Adler, *Drawing Down the Moon*, 47ff.

[46] "Coven" is the usual neopagan name for a circle of witches, ideally 13 in number.

[47] Kelly, *Crafting*.

[48] The "Hermetic Order of the Golden Dawn" is an occultist magical order of the turn of the century. All twentieth-century groups practicing ritual magic are dependent on the impressive system of rituals which was developed by its most creative member, Samuel Liddell McGregor Mathers (cf. Howe, *Magicians of the Golden Dawn*. Aleister Crowley, the most (in)famous magician of this century, was briefly a member of the order. His influence on twentieth-century occultist groups of all kinds is equally large.

the innovations of Alex Sanders. Sanders, the self-proclaimed "King of the Witches", was to attract considerable media attention since the 1960s. His personal brand of Wicca shows a stronger influence of Crowley and the Golden Dawn than the Gardnerian original, but the differences are relatively minor and have grown less over the years.

Wiccan rituals and mythology are centered around the Goddess and her male partner, the Horned God. The polarity of male and female expressed by these divinities (or, as many neopagans will say, archetypes) is basic to the Wiccan worldview. The primary characteristic of the American *Goddess movement*, as it developed in America, is the feminist perspective which often brings with it a relatively strong, sometimes exclusive, emphasis on the Goddess. This has consequences, of course, for the role accorded to polarity in human beings, nature and the universe as a whole. Goddess-worshippers tend to emphasize the immanence of the Goddess as the one fundamental principle permeating all reality. If the Wiccan emphasis on polarity encourages men to discover their female side and women their male side, the emphasis on immanence of the Goddess movement encourages both to discover the world and the body (rather than the heavens and the spirit) as embodiments of the divine. These are differences in emphasis rather than clear-cut distinctions, but they result in relatively different symbolic expressions and ritual forms. Another distinction exists between the "myths of origin" of both movements. While Wicca tends to look especially to the putative European witchcult (along the lines of Margaret Murray) for their mytho-historical roots, the Goddess-worshippers are more interested in historical and archeological evidence for a prehistoric matriarchy centered on worship of the Goddess[49]. Again, the differences are not clearcut. Both accounts can easily be combined by seeing the witchcult as a survival of matriarchal religion. In both orientations, also, "patriarchy"—exemplified especially by institutionalized Christianity—is clearly the enemy. However, the emphasis on polarity determines whether the reign of patriarchal values is perceived as the result of a lack of balance between the male and the female element (the first eclipsing the second), or of the overthrow of matriarchy as the principle of balance and harmony by the pattern of oppression and violence inherently characteristic of patriarchy.

---

[49] I deliberately speak of "mytho-historical" roots. There is a tendency in neopaganism to blur the distinctions between mythical narrative and historical fact (Bowman, 'Reinventing the Celts'). Although neopagans would undoubtedly prefer the idea of matriarchy and of a witchcult to be historically validated, many feel that historical truth is less important than mythical truth. Cf. King's comment ('Voices', 142), which is somewhat puzzling because she is not herself a neopagan: 'For the purpose of feminism the historical debate as such is perhaps less important than the need to construct a theory of matriarchy for contemporary women whose aim it is to create a new social order'. On the other hand, many pagans *do* feel that genuine historical roots are important. For the debate on matriarchy, see Spretnak, *Politics*, 541-561 ('Are Goddesses and Matriarchies merely Figments of Feminist Imagination?').

The *women's spirituality movement* as such is only partly pagan-oriented. Women trying to develop a spirituality that is true to female experience may find inspiration in neglected aspects of Judaeo-Christian traditions as well as in other religions. They may emphasize the divine as female without necessarily worshipping a pagan Goddess. These forms of Judaeo-Christian women's spirituality, and the closely linked movement of christian feminist theology, are basically internal developments within Judaism and Christianity and fall outside the scope of the present study in principle. Again, the boundaries are not sharp. Nothing prevents Judaeo-Christian women's spirituality from feeling inspired by the neopagan tendencies in the wider women's spirituality movement, and such cross-fertilization does indeed occur frequently.

THE SOURCES

JANET & STEWART FARRAR[50]

WWD   Stewart Farrar, *What Witches Do: A Modern Coven Revealed*
WW   Janet & Stewart Farrar, *The Witches' Way: Principles, Rituals and Beliefs of Modern Witchcraft*
LTMW   Janet & Stewart Farrar, *The Life and Times of a Modern Witch*

The Farrars are among the best-known contemporary representatives of British Wicca. They have put much energy in attempting to improve the popular image of witchcraft by writing introductory books for a general audience combined with frequent appearances in the media. WW is undoubtedly the most complete general introduction to Wicca currently available. Together with the companion volume *Eight Sabbats for Witches* (devoted mainly to descriptions of rituals, and not included here), it forms a complete compendium of the movement and its ideas and practices. The earlier volume WWD was written by Stewart Farrar during the period in which he himself first became involved in the Craft. It illustrates his development from an interested outsider/observer to a fully committed initiate. It is interesting to compare WWD with WW, because the former volume represents the Alexandrian branch while WW is more universal. LTMW, a more recent introductory volume, contains many overlaps with the earlier books. It is interesting because it contains the results of a questionnaire sent by the Farrars to witches all over the world, in order to learn their ideas about the essence of modern witchcraft. The answers give a good impression both of the common core of the movement and of the wide variety of attitudes and orientations found in the Craft as a whole.

---

[50] Some information is given in Drury, *Occult Experience*.

VIVIANNE CROWLEY[51]

W   Vivianne Crowley, *Wicca: The Old Religion in the New Age*

This book has strongly contributed to stimulating interest in Wicca among a
wider New Age audience. Crowley (no relation of Aleister Crowley) introduces
the reader to how Wicca is practiced in her own coven, which is a mixture of
Gardnerian and Alexandrian traditions. Crowley is a Jungian psychologist, and
part of the attraction of W lies in the way she interprets Wiccan teachings and
rituals from a Jungian perspective. Actually, this perspective is so strong that
readers might be forgiven for concluding that Wicca is little more than a religious and ritual translation of Jungian psychology. W is therefore a particularly good example of the pervasive influence of Jung in the New Age movement.

STARHAWK[52]

SD   Starhawk, *The Spiral Dance: A Rebirth of the Ancient Religion of the Great
         Goddess*
DD   Starhawk, *Dreaming the Dark: Magic, Sex and Politics*
TD   Starhawk, *Truth or Dare: Encounters with Power, Authority, and Mystery*

Starhawk (ps. of Miriam Simos) is probably the best-known, and certainly the
most influential American witch. Her work, which represents a blend of traditional Wicca and Goddess spirituality, has exerted an enormous influence on
the development of feminist Witchcraft in the U.S.A. According to Margot
Adler, SD and DD 'have perhaps reached more women and men than any other books written by a Pagan'[53]. Starhawk writes powerful books, which combine profound conviction with a passionate sense of social and ecological justice. SD, her first publication, is the one most specifically focused on witchcraft. It is a comprehensive discussion of the different aspects of the Craft, outlining its basic worldview and containing all the information necessary for
founding one's own coven. As such, SD has been highly successful. According to Adler, it has been estimated that SD 'has *alone* created a thousand
women's covens and spiritual groups'[54]. Although DD does not add much news
about witchcraft specifically, it is important for emphasizing the connections
Starhawk perceives between Goddess spirituality, on the one hand, and social
and political action, on the other. Feminist and ecological concerns are presented as closely connected within the general framework of neopaganism. TD
is basically similar to DD but longer, more varied (containing stories, poems,
rituals etc.), and even more politically-oriented than its predecessor.

---

[51] York, *Emerging Network*, 117-122.
[52] Albanese, *Nature Religion*, 180-185; York, *Emerging Network*, 106-113.
[53] Adler, *Drawing Down the Moon*, 413.
[54] Adler, *Drawing Down the Moon*, 227-228.

ZSUZSANNA BUDAPEST[55]

HBWM   Zsuzsanna Budapest, *The Holy Book of Women's Mysteries: Feminist Witch-craft, Goddess Rituals, Spellcasting, and Other Womanly Arts*

Z Budapest (as she is usually called) is the strongest exponent of radical feminist separatism within the Goddess movement. Where Starhawk and others accept both women and men within the coven, Budapest sees witchcraft basically as "wimmin's religion"[56]. Men are generally regarded with suspicion, at the very least, and are not permitted to take part in rituals. Budapest is equally uncompromising with regard to Christianity. Most neopagans, in the tolerant spirit characteristic for the movement, tend to see Christianity as containing at least a core of truth which is compatible with paganism, and they generally regard Jesus in a positive light as an inspired teacher whose spiritual teachings were perverted by the church. For Budapest, however, Christianity is the sworn enemy of wimmin's religion, and Jesus is a welcome target for sarcastic remarks. This militant hostility to everything regarded as patriarchal makes Budapest less than fully representative of the New Age movement and neopaganism, but as an extreme example of the latter she cannot be ignored.

MARIAN GREEN[57]

MAA   Marian Green, *Magic for the Aquarian Age: A Contemporary Textbook of Practical Magical Techniques*
EAM   Marian Green, *Experiments in Aquarian Magic: A Guide to the Magical Arts and Skills that will Unlock the Secrets of the 'Gods for the Future'*
GAAM   Marian Green, *The Gentle Arts of Aquarian Magic: Magical Techniques to Help you Master the Crafts of the Wise*
WA   Marian Green, *A Witch Alone: Thirteen Moons to Master Natural Magic*

Marian Green is an important figure in the English neopagan scene, and a very clear example of the way in which the neopagan perspective can be assimilated within the New Age movement. Her approach is different from many other forms of neopaganism in that she primarily adresses people who want to practice magic *alone*, rather than in a coven. This individualistic emphasis, and the concomitant reliance on books rather than direct personal instruction for "learning magic", is in itself rather characteristic of the New Age subculture. Indeed, Green explicitly states that "Aquarian magic"—the magic appropriate for the New Age—is individualistic rather than collectivist. The expectation of a New Age to come figures prominently in her work[58].
There have been subtle but significant changes in Green's perspective over the years. One gets the impression that she originally came to magic via the 1960's

---

[55] Drury, *Occult Experience*, 67-72; Christel Manning, 'Restoring the Goddess', 183-200.
[56] By writing "woman" as "womon" and "women" as "wimmin" in earlier editions, Budapest wants to avoid the word "man" (men) as much as possible.
[57] York, *Emerging Network*, 151-154.
[58] Cf. York, *Emerging Network*, 151-154, for examples from Green's periodical *The Quest*.

counterculture. MAA as a whole, and especially the first parts, looks far more
like a standard Human Potential guide than a specifically neopagan book. The
"magic" is presented within the general context of meditation and visualization exercises of a very general kind. The difference in atmosphere with books
of Starhawk, Budapest or the Farrars is rather striking. In both MAA and EAM,
the main influence seems to be western occultism in a general sense, rather
than Wicca or neopaganism specifically. In GAAM, however, there is a new
emphasis on "natural magic" which becomes even stronger in WA. In these
books, Green appears to be primarily interested in the simple, common traditional wisdom of the countryside. She is rather averse from the pretentious-
ness of many "high magicians" in the western mysteries tradition, and stresses that natural magic is essentially simple and common-sense. Real natural
magic cannot be written down: it consists of highly practical arts wich people
in traditional societies acquire quite naturally while growing up. We moderns,
having lost touch with natural wisdom, have to rediscover these arts via the
artificial medium of writing.

CAITLÍN & JOHN MATTHEWS[59]

WW1   Caitlín & John Matthews, *The Western Way: A Practical Guide to the West-
       ern Mystery Tradition. Vol. 1: The Native Tradition*
WW2   Caitlín & John Matthews, *The Western Way: A Practical Guide to the West-
       ern Mystery Tradition. Vol. 2: The Hermetic Tradition*

The Matthews are prolific authors in the English magical subculture. Their
perspective comprises both the "western mysteries" and specifically neopagan
ideas. The two volumes of *The Western Way* serve as a semi-scholarly introduction, written from a committed point of view, into the traditions of modern occultism. The Matthews are well-read, and their understanding of the historical backgrounds of modern occultism compares favourably with most similar books. WW1 presents the neopagan strand of occultism, and WW2 discusses the hermetic tradition and its connection with modern magical movements. Both volumes strive to combine theory and historical exposition with
practical application in the contemporary context, by showing the continuing
relevance of old traditions for the modern world. To this end, the books contain a number of exercises enabling the reader to train his/her imaginative faculties by making use of traditional symbols and stories.

MURRY HOPE

PR   Murry Hope, *The Psychology of Ritual*

The title of this book is rather misleading. In fact, in spite of the author's
attempts to sound "professional" and even scholarly, it is a loose collection of

[59] Cf. Joscelyn Godwin's discussion of the Matthews's in 'New Series from Britain', 74-80.

scarcely related items of information and reflections about rituals, occultism, religion, psychology etc. Hope finds it difficult to resist the temptation to drift away from any subject she is supposed to be discussing at any moment. The result of her extremely associative way of thinking is that we find her chatting happily about anything which happens to catch her attention while writing. At the same time, she constantly attempts, as one neopagan reviewer puts it, 'to convince the reader that her tentacles extend beyond the milky way and before Atlantis'[60]. Nevertheless, Hope is a popular author, not least thanks to her books about different magical systems (Celtic, Egyptian, Greek). PR was chosen because it is less specific than these, and thus gives a general impression of Hope's views.

---

[60] Lankester, Review, 18-19.

CHAPTER FIVE

NEW AGE IN A RESTRICTED AND IN A GENERAL SENSE

> It is necessary to throw all political, moral and economic
> theories into the fire and to prepare for the most astonish-
> ing event ... FOR THE SUDDEN TRANSITION FROM
> SOCIAL CHAOS TO UNIVERSAL HARMONY.
>
> Charles Fourier[1]

INTRODUCTION

In the previous chapters I discussed the first four main categories which can be discerned in the New Age movement. They have in common the fact that, although they belong to the New Age as demarcated in the Introduction, they can also be defined in a more specific sense. Thus, chapter one discusses a phenomenon which is "New Age" in a general sense but has to be referred to as "channeling" in a specific sense. Likewise, the other chapters discuss specific, rather clearly definable movements which also happen to be part of the wider "cultic milieu" referred to as New Age. The final category discussed in this chapter is slightly different. It comprises those books which not only belong to the New Age movement in a general sense, but in which "New Age" *as such* is the specific concern. This category falls into two parts, corresponding to two possible meanings of "New Age". First, there are those books which concentrate on the expectation of an imminent "Age of Aquarius", and in which everything centers around the vision of a transformed, or at least significantly improved world. Second, there are those books which are about the New Age as an innovative *movement* in a general sense. Briefly: the first group is about the "New Age" as a future era; the second about "New Age" as a contemporary movement (the very movement which is the subject of this study). The movement concentrating on a "New Paradigm" can be regarded as a special development within the second group.

AN HISTORICAL SKETCH

Although an historical perspective on the New Age movement and its implications for the interpretation of the latter is the subject of Part Three of this

---

[1] Quoted in Darnton, *Mesmerism*, 143.

study, it is necessary at this point to give at least some rough outlines, which will be amplified later[2].

J. Gordon Melton has repeatedly emphasized that the New Age movement is rooted in what he calls the metaphysical-occult community, a religious tradition going back at least to the eighteenth century[3]. In order to find the historical roots of the New Age movement I suggest we should look, more specifically, at the so-called UFO-cults which flourished in the 1950s and have continued to exist since[4]. The UFO groups of the 1950s generally held strongly apocalyptic beliefs. David Spangler, one of the "fathers of the New Age", became involved in them in the late 1950s and has given an eloquent description of their belief system:

> The earth was entering a new cycle of evolution, which would be marked by the appearance of a new consciousness within humanity that would give birth to a new civilization. Unfortunately, the present cultures of the world were so corrupt and locked into materialism that they would resist this change. Consequently, the transition from one age to another would be accomplished by the destruction of the old civilization, either by natural causes such as earthquakes and floods, or by a great world war, or by social collapse of an economic and political nature, or by combinations of these. However, those individuals whose consciousness could become attuned to and one with the qualities of the new culture would be protected in various ways and would survive the time of cataclysms and disasters. They would then enter a new age of abundance and spiritual enlightenment— the Age of Aquarius, as astrologers call it—in which, guided by advanced beings, perhaps angels or spiritual masters or perhaps emissaries from an extraterrestrial civilization whose spacecraft were the UFO's, they would help to create a new civilization.[5]

The metaphysical-occult worldview of these UFO-cults drew on many sources of inspiration, but special mention must be made of the Theosophical system of Alice A. Bailey. Bailey's influence on the New Age movement, especially in its early phase, is pervasive; it is she who is also generally credited with having introduced the term "New Age"[6]. Considering the belief system as sum-

---

[2] Cf. Hanegraaff, 'New Age en cultuurkritiek', 3-5; id., 'Verschijnsel New Age'; id., 'Nieuwe Religieuze Bewegingen'. My emphasis on England rather than America, as the historical basis of the New Age movement is also found in Lewis & Melton, 'New Age', 248.

[3] Melton, 'New Age Movement'; id., 'History of the New Age Movement'; Lewis & Melton, 'New Age'.

[4] There does not exist a comprehensive history of UFO-groups as a religious tradition. For brief overviews I refer to Jacobs, 'UFOs and the Search', and McIver, Ufology. A good collection of essays on the religious dimensions of the subject is Lewis, The Gods have Landed. It should be noted that, as both Jacobs and McIver emphasize, occultist UFO-cults should not be confused with UFO-research groups of the same period.

[5] RS 17-18 (see end of this chapter). For a complete description of the belief system of an UFO-cult of the 1950s, see Festinger, Riecken & Schachter, When Prophecy Fails. Cf. the analysis of their "Ifo-Sananda" religion in Platvoet, Comparing Religions.

[6] Bochinger ("New Age", 30 nt 12, 76 nt 172, 109; and compare his valuable overview, 119-123) attaches great importance to denying this claim, pointing instead to William Blake's

marized above, I propose to regard the UFO-cult movement of the 1950s as a
kind of *proto-New Age movement*.

The 1960s saw the emergence of alternative, countercultural communities
of various kinds, with Findhorn in Scotland as probably the most famous[7].
David Spangler, who became a central figure in Findhorn and has been involved
in many comparable communities, has emphasized their initial similarity with
the UFO-cults. Both were part of the same cultic milieu, and they shared a
similar apocalyptic view of the future. However, it was precisely this apocalyptic element which was to be largely discarded, or at least nuanced, in the
later development of the alternative communities. As the predicted apocalypse
failed to arrive, there developed an increasing resistance to the passive attitude
of "waiting for the big event". The development of Findhorn in this regard has
been paradigmatic for a similar change of direction in many comparable groups.
Spangler and his associate Myrtle Glines

> ...suggested that Findhorn not become aligned with an apocalyptic perspective.
> This was echoed by others in the group. ... The real questions were not when and
> how the new age would come but what kind of people we would be when it came
> and what kind of a world we would wish to build and live in. If we had that vision,
> then what was stopping us from being that kind of person and working to create
> that kind of world right now? Instead of spreading warnings of apocalypse, let
> Findhorn proclaim that the new age is already here, in spirit if not in form, and
> that anyone can now cocreate with that spirit so that the form will become man-
> ifest.
> Because all at that meeting felt the same way about this issue, this philosophy of
> "we are creating the new age now" became Findhorn's policy ... As a model of
> the new age, it was qualitatively different from the image that I had first encoun-
> tered in Arizona some fourteen years earlier.[8]

Although (as we will see in Part Two of this study) apocalypticism has certainly not died out in the New Age movement, its seems that this change of
direction has occurred in the majority of New Age communities. Apocalypti-

---

use of the term in the preface to *Milton* (1804) (o.c., ch. 6.3.1). It is true that Blake used the
words (only *once* in his whole oeuvre, however, as noted by Bochinger himself: o.c., 282), and
that Theodor Roszak repeatedly quotes Blake in his books about the counterculture and the
"Aquarian Frontier" (the lines on the New Age appear as the motto to *Making of a Counter Culture*; cf. the repeated allusions to Blake in Roszak, *Unfinished Animal*) and may have been instrumental in introducing him into the alternative subculture (cf. o.c., 306 nt 106). However, the mere
fact that he seems to have been the first one to speak of a "New Age"—in itself a quite unspecific millenarian term—is hardly sufficient to assign to Blake a major key function (second only
to Swedenborg) as historical precursor of the New Age Movement, as is done by Bochinger. A
similar argument is in order with respect to Bochinger's extended discussions of A.R. Orage and
the journal "The New Age" (o.c., 293-299). About the history of the term "New Age", cf. also
chapter 1 of Heelas, *New Age Movement*.
   [7] Cf. Hawken, *Magic of Findhorn*; Rigby & Turner, 'Findhorn Community'; Clark, 'Myth,
Metaphor, and Manifestation'; Riddell, *Findhorn Community*. A comparable center is Glastonbury in Somerset. Cf. Hexham, '"Freaks" of Glastonbury'; Bowman, 'Drawn to Glastonbury';
an analysis of an American commune is given by Trompf, 'Cargo and the Millennium'.
   [8] RS 34-35.

cism was gradually replaced by a kind of pioneer attitude: people in alternative communities tried to live "as if the New Age had already come" in an effort to be the vanguard of the radically new. I propose to refer to this early, idealistic movement as *New Age sensu stricto* (i.e., New Age in a restricted sense). This movement had its roots primarily in England, a country where Theosophy and Anthroposophy have traditionally been strongly represented. Accordingly, the New Age *sensu stricto* showed a strong Theosophical and Anthroposophical flavour. Typical for this New Age *sensu stricto* is the absolute centrality of the expectation of a New Age of Aquarius. All activities and speculation circle around the central vision of a new and transformed world.

The New Age *sensu stricto* has survived as a rather clearly recognizable part of the *New Age sensu lato* (i.e., in a wide sense), which is the subject of the present study[9]. As defined in my Introduction, this wider New Age movement emerged when increasing numbers of people, by the later 1970s, began to perceive a broad similarity between a wide variety of "alternative" ideas and pursuits, and started to think of these as parts of one "movement". This movement, as argued before, can be regarded—referring to Colin Campbell's terminology—as *the cultic milieu having become conscious of itself as constituting a more or less unified "movement"*. The New Age *sensu stricto*, as it survived into the late 1970s and the 1980s, can be regarded as one of its components. In spite of the name, and in contrast to the New Age *sensu stricto*, the expectation of an Aquarian Age is not necessary in order for a movement or trend to be part of the New Age *sensu lato*. Furthermore, the New Age *sensu lato* has a comparatively strong American flavour and has been profoundly influenced by the Californian counterculture. Theosophical and anthroposophical influences are not particularly prominent. Instead, the influence of typically American movements in the "metaphysical" and "New Thought" tradition is strong[10]. All these historical connections will be dealt with more extensively in Part Three of this study.

---

[9] It should be noted that some researchers, notably Mary Farrell Bednarowski, obscure this fact by presenting the movement which I refer to as New Age *sensu stricto* as representative for the New Age *sensu lato* (*New Religions*, 15). In the Introduction I already noted that in doing so she somewhat uncritically adopts the emic conviction of Spangler as a basis for delimiting the New Age. In the context of Bednarowski's otherwise important study, this confusion has rather important implications because she makes a systematic comparison between Theosophy and the New Age movement. Considering the profound influence of Theosophy on the historical emergence of the New Age *sensu stricto*, the similarities between both movements are hardly surprising, but a comparison between Theosophy and the New Age *sensu lato* would undoubtedly lead to completely different results.

[10] Cf. the distinction arrived at by Bochinger, independently from my own research, in the conclusions of his *"New Age"*, 515 (and cf. 517): 'In the 1970s the expression ["New Age"] appeared firstly in translations of English books which derived from various subcultural (religious or social) movements, in particular the scottish Findhorn movement and the American centres connected with it, as well as from the American "counterculture" of the later 1960s, the

At first sight, it might seem that the quest for a *New Paradigm* which should replace the old one is a variation on the quest for a New Age of Light which should follow the present age of darkness. However, the major architects of the New Paradigm derive their inspiration from other sources than the English-based, Theo-/Anthroposophically oriented New Age *sensu stricto* and, unlike the latter, their perspective cannot properly be called millenarian. The quest for a New Paradigm is essentially an American phenomenon concerned with defining, in theoretical terms, the essentials of the new worldview which is believed to be taking shape in our midst. To this end, the different dimensions of the new paradigm are discussed in detail, which leads to a picture essentially similar to the one furnished in the early "manifesto" of the New Age *sensu lato*, Marilyn Ferguson's *Aquarian Conspiracy*.

NEW AGE *SENSU STRICTO*: THE MILLENARIAN VISION

While the New Age movement *sensu lato* is at least nominally concerned with the "pursuit of the millennium", it is only in the New Age *sensu stricto* that the expectation of an imminent new era is the focus of attention[11]. For this reason it is natural to look at this particular movement from the perspective of millenarian scholarship[12].

The terminology in this field is far from fixed. Hans Kippenberg discusses *apocalypticism*, *messianism* and *chiliasm* (as a near synonym for millenarianism[13]) as analytically distinct concepts, but emphasizes their limitations: 'often the facts simply do not fit into the prepared compartments[14]'. It is important, nevertheless, to emphasize the relative difference between apocalypticism and millenarianism. In the typical apocalyptic vision, the new world comes as 'a catastrophe over what exists'[15] and replaces the worldly order by a radical-

---

reception of which in the German context took place with a delay of ca. 10 years. Between 1978 and 1984 the term—together with its synonym "Aquarian Age"—became the covering concept of a new religious thematic field ...'. Bochinger, too, associates this second phase primarily with Ferguson's *Aquarian Conspiracy* and Capra's *Turning Point*, and in addition with the German magazine *Esotera*.

[11] This fact is somewhat obscured in Lemesurier, *This New Age Business*, an attempt to put the New Age movement in the broad context of the history of millenarian movements.

[12] Cohn, *Pursuit of the Millennium*; Mühlmann, *Chiliasmus und Nativismus*; Sierksma, *Nieuwe hemel*; Thrupp, 'Millennial Dreams'; Shepperson, 'Comparative Study of Millenarian Movements'; Lanternari, *Religions of the Oppressed*; Desroche, *Sociology of Hope*; Jansma & Schulten, 'Inleiding'; Talmon, 'Pursuit of the Millennium'; Schwartz, 'Millenarianism'; Trompf, 'Introduction'; Hoynacki, 'Messianic Expectations'; Kippenberg, 'Apokalyptik...'. Cf. the extensive discussions in Bochinger, *"New Age"*, 6.1.

[13] Other synonyms are millennialism and millenarism (Schwartz, 'Millenarianism', 521; Hoynacki, 'Messianic Expectations').

[14] Kippenberg, 'Apokalyptik...', 9.

[15] Kippenberg, 'Apokalyptik...', 10, with reference to Gershom Scholem.

ly different, *transcendent* order. According to Kippenberg, 'the more this transcendent character of the new world decreases, the more we move into the
direction of Millenarianism'[16]. The typical millenarian dream is one of a perfect, *earthly* realm of peace and plenty, without injustice and suffering. While
apocalypticism implies that this world "passes away" in order to be replaced
by a qualitatively different one, the millennium, in contrast, is logically possible only if there is a world left in which to realize it. Defined in this way, the
alternatives seem straightforward enough; but, as Kippenberg's last-quoted sentence indicates, the distinction is in fact relative rather than absolute. The more
an earthly realm of "love and light" differs from the world we are used to—in
fact: the more perfect it is—the more it will be perceived as "transcending"
that world. It is difficult, probably impossible, to draw the line exactly: how
strongly may an earthly "new age" differ from the old order without losing its
this-worldly character?[17] A world of peace and plenty, in which spiritually
evolved human beings walk hand in hand with the angels certainly looks more
like heaven than earth. We will encounter this ambivalence in the discussion
of New Age-conceptualizations in Part Two of this study. Furthermore, a slightly moderated apocalypticism is possible, which envisions widespread cataclysms but not the complete destruction of the world. According to this scenario, the apocalypse may be seen as the period of "cleansing"—to use a popular New Age expression—which prepares the way for the millennium. It is in
this sense, rather than the radical one, that I referred to the UFO-cults as "apocalyptic".

Closely connected to the above is the oft-quoted, but somewhat unclear distinction between *pre- and post-millenarianism*[18]. Desroche's distinction is relatively sharp. According to the pre-millenarian scenario, the coming of the
Kingdom of God is abrupt and violent, as a result of one-sided otherworldly
intervention. Human beings can only react to this event when it happens, but
of themselves they can do nothing to bring the kingdom closer. Humanity is
dependent on the initiative from the other world. In post-millenarianism, on
the other hand,

> ...the kingdom of God is progressively installed by an *evolutive* process, inte-

---

[16] Kippenberg, 'Apokalyptik...', 10. I have taken the liberty to translate the German "Chiliasmus" as "millenarianism".

[17] Talmon ('Pursuit', 41-42) implicitly rejects the transcendence-immanence distinction, when
she states that millenarian movements view salvation as 'a merger of the spiritual with the terrestrial. The millenarian view of salvation is transcendent and immanent at the same time'.

[18] Thrupp, 'Millennial Dreams', 44; Desroche, *Sociology of Hope*, 93-94; Hoynacki, 'Messianic Expectations'. This last author adds a third possibility: *amillennialism*, which 'simply
advances a figurative representation of the heavenly reign of God's blessed with Christ', but does
not envision an earthly millennium. It therefore seems somewhat out of place in this context, and
other authors indeed seldom mention it. Note also that according to Hoynacki, *chiliasm* should
be used as a synonym for premillenialism, as distinguished from postmillenialism.

grating itself in the succession of historical facts ..., and directing the world, by
the internal logic of its social and religious evolution, towards the point of maturity where it will bear the millennial or messianic kingdom as a tree bears fruit.
... The religiously motivated and controlled action of man is not only not opposed
to this final advent, it is such that it speeds up its rhythm: in any case the millennium comes after (*post-*) this collective human effort, and this is one of its pre-
requisite conditions.[19]

Following Desroche's exposition, we can conclude that the *proto-New Age*
movement of the UFO-cults—which waited passively for the Kingdom to come
in the form of an apocalyptic cataclysm—was of a premillenarian character.
The *New Age sensu stricto* which emerged from this milieu changed its focus
to a post-millenarian perspective. The view that the New Age will emerge, carried by human commitment, as the result of a (super)natural evolutionary
process—although probably steered during the critical transition by superhuman assistance—has remained the dominant one in the *New Age sensu lato*.

Up to this point, I have ignored the third component of the millenarian complex, i.e. messianism. Although one could theoretically conceive of a millennium without a savior figure, ever since the New Testament Book of Revelation the two have been closely connected in practice. The New Age movement,
as we will see, is no exception. It is significant that the ambivalent relation
(see above) between a transcendent Kingdom of God and an immanent millennium is also mirrored in the phenomenon of messianism. Thus, Hoynacki
distinguishes two types of messianic figures:

> One represents a social phenomenon in that human charismatic visionaries rise
> up from among the people and achieve some dimension of "divinity" either by
> self proclamation or devotee acclamation. They usually emerge as symbols of
> leadership and hope during periods of intense oppression and misrule. The other
> represents a spiritual phenomenon in that divine saviors will appear out of the
> transcendent world of deities. Their expected appearance among men will signal
> the imminent end of time and the emergence of a new utopian era of joy, peace,
> and prosperity.[20]

A valuable addition to this distinction is Shepperson's concept of the "messiah mechanism". Shepperson uses this mechanical analogy in order to accomodate cases of impersonal messianic agencies. Interestingly, he mentions flying saucers as an example: '...if there is no individual, personal messiah, an
invariable part of all millennial-style movements seems to be some "trigger-
ing-off" agency, apparently from outside the society or group concerned, in
forms as various as invading American soldiers and flying saucers.'[21]

---

[19] Desroche, *Sociology of Hope*, 93-94.
[20] Hoynacki, 'Messianic Expectations'. As examples of the first type, Hoynacki discusses cargo cults, various Islamic messianic movements, and the mid-nineteenth century Chinese T'ai-
p'ing movement. As examples of the second type, he discusses examples in Zoroastrianism, Hinduism and Buddhism.
[21] Shepperson, 'Comparative Study', 47.

To regard invading soldiers as a messianic agency might well be regarded as rather far-fetched. However that may be, Shepperson's proposal is interesting because of its remarkable relevance to the case of New Age messianism. Our first observation about the latter must be that New Age messianism clearly belongs to the second variety of messianism distinguished by Hoynacki. When messianism occurs in the New Age context, it always concerns a superhuman, spiritual agency, not a charismatic personality invested with divine qualities by devotees[22]. In the context of the New Age *sensu stricto*, which is the primary *locus* of New Age messianism, this agency is almost invariably referred to as "the Christ". The interesting point in relation to Shepperson's "messiah mechanism" is the fact that the Christ is quite often described as a "principle" or "energy" rather than as a person in the traditional sense. In Part Two of this study I will analyze the idea of "the Christ" on the basis of the sources. Here, I must restrict myself to the observation that this particular New Age conception of the Christ is, on the whole[23], very strongly dependent upon Theosophical and especially Anthroposophical speculation, but with an additional tendency—particularly in the later period—towards impersonal conceptualizations influenced by New Paradigm science. The conclusion at this point is that, although New Age believers may talk about the "second coming of the Christ", they do not necessarily believe that this event will involve the appearance of a visible person. Some of them do (for instance the Scottish New Age theosophist Benjamin Creme, who has been announcing "Maitreya the Christ" for two decades now) but others expect the second coming to be a purely spiritual event which will be felt and experienced within, rather than seen with physical eyes.

A further comment to make about the New Age *sensu stricto* as a millenarian movement is the fact that millenarianisms are always embedded in general, largely implicit "macrohistorical" views[24]. Although some authors have stated that millenarianism as such presupposes a linear view of history[25], it is not obvious that this link is necessary outside of the Judaeo-Christian context. The

---

[22] Messiahs of the first type do appear in some sectors of the alternative subculture which fall outside the New Age as demarcated in this study. One obvious example is the Indian guru Sathya Sai Baba. A figure like Bhagwan Shree Rajneesh—a borderline case with regard to the New Age movement—could also be mentioned. However, in both cases the connection between the messiah figure and the New Age millennium is insignificant. These gurus are not heralded as the savior of the world who will lead humanity into the New Age, or who will rule the world in the future.

[23] Matthew Fox's concept of the "Cosmic Christ" is a case apart.

[24] The concept of macro-historical ideas has been central to many publications by G.W. Trompf. See for instance his 'Future of Macro-Historical Ideas' and 'Macrohistory and Acculturation'.

[25] For instance Talmon ('Pursuit of the Millennium', 40): 'Perhaps the most important thing about millenarism is its attitude towards time. It views time as a linear process which leads to a final future'.

New Age movement, at any rate, does not regard the Aquarian Age as a final and definite conclusion of history. As is well known, New Age believers generally see the coming of the New Age as closely connected to large astronomical cycles, which are interpreted astrologically[26]. Thus, the last ca. 2000 years, dominated by Christianity, are referred to as the Age of Pisces (and the fact that the early church used the fish as a symbol for Christ is, of course, seen as highly significant[27]). The Age of Aquarius which will follow the Age of Pisces will also last approximately 2000 year, presumably to be followed by yet another and quite different Age. There is a certain discrepancy between the general, implicit acceptance of this macrohistorical view of recurring cycles, on the one hand, and the remarkable lack of interest in developing this macrohistory in a systematic way, on the other[28]. All attention goes to the coming New Age and its contrast to the preceding one. Ideas about preceding cycles are extremely vague and sketchy at best, and the question what kind of period will follow the Age of Aquarius is apparently considered irrelevant. As we will see, overall theories about the meaning and end of history do exist, but their relation—if any—to the theory of astrological cycles is far from clear. From a theoretical perspective, this situation creates interesting problems which might well turn the millenarianism debate into new directions. This is obviously not the place for such a discussion. We must restrict ourselves to pointing out the importance of asking ourselves what kinds of relation—if any—exists between practical millenarian expectations, their implicit macrohistorical suppositions, and the theoretical implications of these assumptions. As for the subject of this section, it suffices to emphasize the special character of New Age millenarianism from the perspective of macrohistorical presuppositions[29].

Finally, in evaluating New Age expectations it is relevant to call attention to a remark made by Sylvia Thrupp in 1962:

> ...the most serious single deficiency in our knowledge of millennial movements relates to those types that have not produced very clear-cut doctrines nor extremist leaders, that is, the movements whose members are content to await the consummation of their hopes quietly. This gap is not due to lack of evidence but rather to a failure to exploit it. The literature is heavily biased towards the more dramatic types of movement, those that alarm civil and religious authorities or openly clash with them[30].

---

[26] David Spangler states the theory in RBNA 92-94. A critical discussion from a skeptical point of view is given by Culver & Ianna, *Astrology*, ch. 6 'The Age of Aquarius'. For an extensive historical discussion, see Bochinger, "*New Age*", 308-370.

[27] This connection was already proposed by Jung, *Aion*, 72-94 (Chapter "The Sign of the Fishes"), which also speaks of the coming Age of Aquarius.

[28] This interest was not lacking, however, in the Theosophical sources from which the idea of the New Age has emerged.

[29] An extensive discussion of these problems is included in chapter 7 of Christoph Bochinger, "*New Age*".

[30] Thrupp, *Millennial Dreams*, 14.

On the whole, New Age millenarianism seems to belong to this quiet type. This is another reason why it is an interesting subject to explore with a view to expanding the framework of existing theories.

NEW AGE *SENSU LATO*

The other major group in this chapter is mentioned here only for the sake of completeness. The New Age *sensu lato* is the subject of this study, and an interpretation from the perspective of the study of religions will be the subject of the third and final part of this book. Therefore such an interpretation cannot be given here, but must be based on *all* the sources introduced in the five chapters of Part One. The books selected as examples of New Age *sensu lato* in the present chapter will take their place among these other sources in the systematic analysis which follows in Part Two, and on which the interpretation will be based.

We may summarize the argument thus far by concluding that the New Age *sensu lato* is a complex movement, the various components of which can be regarded as particular manifestations of cross-cultural phenomena well-known in the study of religions. Channeling is a popular medium for "revelations", which concentrates on the transmission of articulated messages from invisible beings to humanity. New Age healing & growth movements are structurally similar to healing practices known in traditional societies. New Age science is a contemporary form of *Naturphilosophie*. New Age Neopaganism is rooted in a worldview which may be described as "magical". And the New Age *sensu stricto* is an example of millenarianism. In none of the cases, however, is the New Age manifestation just a repetition of traditional phenomena. They were all developed in characteristic, often historically unique directions under the impact of an overarching New Age worldview. The nature and structure of that worldview is our central concern. The question whether and, if so, how the different elements of the New Age compound relate to one another in a structural way, as well as the question whether the inherent logic of such a structure might explain the absence of other theoretically possible phenomena, will have to wait until Part Three. At this point, we have attempted no more than to bring some *order* into the confusing variety of New Age concerns. Whether or not there is also a *structure* in the New Age movement remains to be seen.

THE SOURCES

DAVID SPANGLER[31]

RBNA   David Spangler, *Revelation: The Birth of a New Age*
RS   David Spangler, *The Rebirth of the Sacred*
NA   David Spangler, *The New Age*
CNA   David Spangler, *Channeling in the New Age*
RW   David Spangler & William Irwin Thompson, *Reimagination of the World: A Critique of the New Age, Science, and Popular Culture*

David Spangler is sometimes referred to as the Father of the New Age, primarily because of RBNA, which is one of the foundational texts of the early New Age movement (*sensu stricto*). This text, which is based on channeled information, has already been introduced in chapter one. It is interesting to observe that the strongly Theo-/Anthroposophical contents of RBNA are replaced by a far more "down to earth" perspective in RS. In fact, both books are so different in content and atmosphere that they almost seem to be written by different authors. It seems that Spangler has made a deliberate effort to dissociate himself from the "cultic" atmosphere of RBNA in order to become acceptable to a wider public. Thus, in RS we encounter a quite "reasonable", commonsense Spangler, who speaks in tones of quiet authority about the need to create a better world. This change of direction does not mean, however, that the mature Spangler has renounced his youthful work. In RW, when pressed by his audience about the apparent discrepancy between the "esoteric" and the "exoteric" Spangler, he admits that he has moved beyond the traditional theosophical cosmology[32]. Hierarchical concepts betraying a limited nineteenth-century perspective should be replaced by more up-to-date holistic and holographic alternatives. However, although the conceptualization and the terminology has changed, Spangler claims that the basic ideas remain the same. The "moderate" vision of RS must therefore be seen as just one side of the coin: even in the early 1990s the traditional occultist picture remains very much alive in Spangler's mind[33]. Nevertheless, it remains the case that RS is a book which might well be quite acceptable even to people who would reject all occultist metaphysics. To that extent it might even be considered mildly misleading with regard to Spangler's actual intentions.

If RS is an example of Spangler's efforts to steer a diplomatic middle course between occultism and commonsense rationality, in the small booklets NA and CNA he similarly tries to find the golden mean between the latter and the popular New Age movement (*sensu lato*) of the 1980s. Spangler is appalled by what he calls the "New Age glamour" of talkshow channelers, healing crys-

---

[31] Cf. Rhodes, 'The New Age Christology'; Bednarowski, *New Religions*.
[32] RW 118.
[33] See RW 125-126.

tals, and the like. The superficial, commercialized pursuits which have come to characterize New Age in the eyes of the public are presented as having little if anything to do with the serious vision of a transformed world which inspires Spangler's work. Popular "New Age glamour" should be sharply distinguished from the genuinely transformative vision at the heart of the New Age movement; likewise, popular New Age channeling should not be confused with genuine spiritual communications such as received by Spangler himself. NA and CNA are obviously inspired by Spangler's worries about being lumped together with a New Age of the Shirley MacLaine-variety, and with channels like J Z Knight. However, his argumentation fails to be fully convincing to the outsider, particularly with regard to channeling.

RW contains lectures given by Spangler and the American New Age author William Irwin Thompson, and discussions with the audience. The text gives abundant additional information about various points of Spangler's (and Thompson's) views, including a somewhat surprising enthusiasm on Spangler's part for the recent "high-tech" developments sometimes referred to as "New Edge".

GEORGE TREVELYAN

VAA   George Trevelyan, *A Vision of the Aquarian Age*
OR   George Trevelyan, *Operation Redemption: A Vision of Hope in an Age of Turmoil*
EiG   George Trevelyan, *Exploration into God*

It might be argued with some justification that Sir George Trevelyan is the most typical "New Age" author discussed in this study. The subject of his books is the 'immensely broad movement of spiritual awakening that characterizes our age'[34], and which will usher in a new civilization of peace, love and light. In contrast with Spangler, Trevelyan makes no effort to present his message in a way which will make it sound more acceptable to a wider audience. His highly idealistic spiritual worldview is unfolded without reservations, and the reader has no other choice than to "take it or leave it". Trevelyan's work, which retains much of the hippie-flavour of the 1960s and early 1970s, is fully characteristic of the New Age *sensu stricto*. First of all, the millenarian vision of the coming Aquarian Age is quite central to his thought. Secondly, Theosophical and particularly Anthroposophical influences permeate his books. Several chapters are completely Anthroposophical. Thirdly, Trevelyan's work is unmistakably English. English Romantic idealism is the backbone of his vision, and all his books are sprinkled with quotations from mostly English Romantic poetry. VAA, OR and EiG, which span the period between 1977 and 1991 are basically very similar, even interchangeable books: Trevelyan's ideas seem

---

[34] VAA 2.

to have remained very much the same throughout the 1970s and 1980s.

GARY ZUKAV

SoS   Gary Zukav, *The Seat of the Soul*

Gary Zukav became well-known for his best-selling *The Dancing Wu-Li Masters*[35], which is usually regarded as the best popular introduction to modern physics. SoS is completely different. It contains the outlines of a general New Age worldview, presented in a rather extreme *ex cathedra* mode: there are no notes, no arguments, just statement after statement. The whole book makes the impression of a channeled text, especially because of the typical style of assumed authority: Zukav does not talk with the reader, but only lectures *to* him. The general picture is clearly Theosophical in nature, with additional influences from such New Age classics as the Seth books and *A Course in Miracles*. The basic message is that, right now, humanity is in the process of evolving from "five-sensory consciousness" to "multi-sensory consciousness". Zukav describes what is involved in the new, multi-sensory reality.

MARILYN FERGUSON[36]

AC   Marilyn Ferguson, *The Aquarian Conspiracy: Personal and Social Trans-
        formation in the 1980s*

This is one of the most frequently quoted books about the New Age movement. In our context, it can still be regarded as the most characteristic manifesto of the New Age *sensu lato*. However, some reservations must be made about the tendency among commentators and critics of the New Age movement to take AC as their main or even their only point of reference. AC appeared as early as 1980, and is representative of the intermediate period between the countercultural engagement of the 1960s/early 1970s and the New Age movement as it took shape in the 1980s. It represents the phenomenon of the earlier cultic milieu "becoming conscious of itself as a movement" in the later 1970s, but this does not necessarily make it authoritative about developments which took place after its publication. This is frequently forgotten by authors who write about New Age. Substantial parts of AC are indeed no longer very relevant for the New Age movement as a historical current, because they represent characteristic attitudes of the 1960s and 1970s which have not survived into the 1980s. Many typical elements of the New Age movement of the 1980s,

---

[35] Gary Zukav, *Dancing Wu-Li Masters*. This book is often mentioned together with Fritjof Capra's ToP as an example of physics-mysticism parallellism. However, although Zukav is no doubt in sympathy with Capra's approach, *Dancing Wu-Li Masters* refers to mysticism only briefly and in passing. It is only because of the title and these occasional remarks that the book could be mistaken for a parallellist book.

[36] See also the discussions in York, *Emerging Network*, 48-53.

futhermore, are not represented. In sum, AC must be regarded as an important statement about a particular historical phase of the New Age movement, not as a comprehensive guide to understanding the complete movement.

The central thesis of AC is that a powerful transformation of society is now occurring, which starts with the individual but will lead to radical social change. Ferguson believes that the "Aquarian conspiracy", consisting of non-hierarchical networks of likeminded people, will ultimately change the foundations of modern industrialized society. Of course, her expectation that this change would take place in the 1980s has not been confirmed by events, and in a reprint of the early 1990s the subtitle has significantly been changed to 'personal and social transformation in our time'. AC can be seen as a specimen of the literary genre of popularized cultural analysis for a wide public. It represents the optimistic counterpart to such more recent examples of cultural pessimism as Bloom's *The Closing of the American Mind* or Lasch's *The Culture of Narcissism*. Only afterwards, and in contrast to these, AC acquired the status of the "manifesto" of a self-proclaimed "movement".

FRITJOF CAPRA[37]

TP   Fritjof Capra, *The Turning Point: Science, Society, and the Rising Culture*
UW   Fritjof Capra, *Uncommon Wisdom: Conversations with Remarkable People*

TP, which appeared in 1982, is often mentioned in one breath with AC as a basic source of information for evaluating the New Age movement. In that respect, similar reservations must be made as in the case of AC. Capra adopts the concept of the New Paradigm, which was already introduced by Ferguson, as a basic framework. According to Capra, western society is in a state of crisis due to its basis in an outdated mechanistic Newtonian/Cartesian paradigm. Newtonian/Cartesian presuppositions permeate our way of thinking and looking at the world, deeply influencing everything we do, including our ways of trying to deal with global problems. Because our present problems are a direct result of this outdated Newtonian/Cartesian paradigm, we need a radical new perspective in order to be effective in changing the course of events. This new perspective is the holistic and ecological "systems view" of reality, which is presented as in essential agreement with both modern scientific developments and ancient mystical traditions. The old paradigm is now in an irreversible process of decline, while the new, holistic culture (which started as a counterculture) is on the rise. We are approaching the "turning point" at which the rising culture will become dominant and a new society will accordingly take shape. This new society will be holistic, open to the spiritual dimension of reality, and "healthy" in all its dimensions. The structure of TP is built upon a systematic opposition of the old and the new paradigm. In particular, Capra

---

[37] Cf. Wiskerke, 'New Age-holisme'; Bochinger, *"New Age"*, 521-511.

discusses in detail the implications of the paradigm change in the fields of biology, medicine/healing, psychology and economics.

UW is an autobiographical companion volume to TP. Capra describes his personal intellectual development as exemplified by ToP and TP, and describes his meetings with the people who influenced his thinking. Of particular importance is the role of Gregory Bateson and his systems view of reality. In ToP, Capra saw the new physics as an ideal model for new concepts and approaches in other disciplines. Eventually, however, he came to realize that by presenting physics as a model for other, quite different disciplines he had 'fallen into the very Cartesian trap that I wanted scientists to avoid'[38]. Capra discovered in Bateson's systems view of reality a more appropriate theoretical framework which enabled him to avoid the reductionism implicit in his earlier approach. Accordingly, in TP the new physics is no longer presented as a model for other sciences but 'as an important special case of a much more general framework, the framework of systems theory'[39]. This development of Capra's thinking from the new physics to Batesonian systems theory makes for a major difference between ToP and TP. Whether Capra (or, for that matter, Bateson) has really succeeded in avoiding reductionism will be discussed in Part Two of this study.

PETER RUSSELL

AE   Peter Russell, *The Awakening Earth: The Global Brain*

Peter Russell's book is roughly comparable to Capra's *Turning Point*. It is about the possibility for a great 'evolutionary leap' to occur in the very near future, which will totally transform our world. It is one of the clearest examples of how recent scientific theories (in particular the Prigoginian theory as presented by Erich Jantsch in *The Self-Organizing Universe*) may be combined with a concern for meditation (Transcendental Meditation in this particular case) and other popular New Age practices, within one sweepingly optimistic vision of the coming transformation of mankind. AE is also a particularly good example of the often-mentioned influence of Teilhard de Chardin's thought on the New Age movement.

WILLIS HARMAN

GMC   Willis Harman, *Global Mind Change: The Promise of the Last Years of the Twentieth Century*

This is one more example of "new paradigm" books along the lines of Ferguson, Capra and Russell. Willis Harman heads the influential Institute for Noetic Sciences, concerned with the need for a change in basic underlying assump-

---

[38] UW 74.
[39] TP 74.

tions about reality in order to deal with the world crisis we are witnessing now. Harman's basic thesis is that in the last third of the twentieth century we are going through a "global mind change" comparable to the Copernican revolution of the seventeenth century.

SHIRLEY MACLAINE[40]

OL   Shirley MacLaine, *Out on a Limb*
DL   Shirley MacLaine, *Dancing in the Light*
IAP   Shirley MacLaine, *It's All in the Playing*
GW   Shirley MacLaine, *Going within: A Guide for Inner Transformation*
DWYC   Shirley MacLaine, *Dance While You Can*

If Ferguson's *Aquarian Conspiracy* is the manifesto of a hoped-for new culture, MacLaine's bestselling autobiographies represent the subculture which actually emerged. From one perspective, they are probably the best examples of the "New Age glamour" rejected by David Spangler. From a different angle, MacLaine's story of how she learned to "get in touch with herself"[41] will be understandable and sympathetic to many who experienced a similar development during the 1980s. OL contains the story of MacLaine's gradual and reluctant "conversion" to a New Age perspective, as it occurred in her early forties. It is no doubt superior to her later books in terms of dramatic structure: skilfully building up tension towards the final chapters, and ending with a "back to earth" epilogue according to the best movie traditions. DL is a follow-up to OL in which MacLaine now speaks from a firmly committed New Age point of view. Probably the most important part of the book is her description of past-life regression sessions with Chris Griscom, culminating in MacLaine's succesful attempt to contact her own "Higher Self", which appears to her in the form of an androgynous being. IAP is about the process of making a TV miniseries of OL. This miniseries itself has done even more than MacLaine's books to bring the New Age perspective to the attention of a mass audience, and the airing of *Out on a Limb* in January 1987 has often been referred to as a crucial moment in the history of the New Age movement. The peculiarity of "recreating her own reality" on screen provides MacLaine with the opportunity of speculating about the ambivalent relation between fact and fiction, dream and reality. GW, based on a series of New Age seminars organized and led by MacLaine, is conceived as a kind of practical Human Potential guide. It also contains autobiographical material about meetings with the painting medium Luis Gasparetto; the healing medium Mauricio Panisset; the psychic surgeon Alex Orbito; and (oddly out of place in this context) the physicist Stephen Hawking. DWYC, finally, is a rather boring follow-up of the earlier

---

[40] York, *Emerging Network*, 74-81; Gardner, 'Isness is her Business'; and for the sake of completeness, Gordon, *Channeling into the New Age*.
[41] OL 5.

books, with the experience of getting older as the central theme. If the signs
do not deceive, MacLaine's enthusiasm about the New Age has become more
moderate and she is moving away from a spiritual into a more strictly psychological direction.

MATTHEW FOX[42]

OB   Matthew Fox, *Original Blessing: A Primer in Creation Spirituality Present-
        ed in Four Paths, Twenty-six Themes, and Two Questions*
CCC   Matthew Fox, *The Coming of the Cosmic Christ: The Healing of Mother
        Earth and the Birth of a Global Renaissance*
CS   Matthew Fox, *Creation Spirituality: Liberating Gifts for the Peoples of the
        Earth*

The so-called "creation spirituality" of the controversial dominican priest
Matthew Fox (turned Presbyterian in 1994) is to some extent a special case in
the present chapter. Fox's work is concerned with the need for a *religious* paradigm shift. It is different from the one proposed by Capra and others in being
explicitly based on an appeal to western traditions of mystical Christianity.
Fox's basic framework is the opposition between the "fall/redemption theology" which became dominant in western religion especially under the influence
of Augustine, and the "creation spirituality" which Fox believes is far older,
and solidly rooted in the oldest Jewish roots of Christianity. Fox is very concerned about the current world crisis, especially the destruction of the environment. He believes that the crisis is ultimately the result of fall/redemption
thinking, and that a revival of creation spirituality is the only solution. A charismatic personality, Fox has become a major voice in the American New Age
movement in recent years.
OB, the very title of which is a polemic against the doctrine of original sin,
can be regarded as the basic program of creation spirituality. It contains meditations on twenty-six themes grouped in four "paths": the via positiva, via
negativa, via creativa and via transformativa. CCC is Fox's most elaborate theological statement. Its basic theme is the archetype of the Cosmic Christ and
the need for recovering a 'living cosmology' in our time. CS is a comparatively brief overview of the basics of creation spirituality, with an additional
emphasis on connections with liberation theology. Actually, creation spirituality is presented as a "liberation theology for first world peoples".

---

[42] Peters, 'Matthew Fox'; id., *Cosmic Self*, 119-131; Brearley, 'Matthew Fox'.

PART TWO

EXPOSITION:
THE VARIETIES OF NEW AGE EXPERIENCE

CHAPTER SIX

THE NATURE OF REALITY

1. Introduction: Attitudes to Experiential Reality

In this chapter we will look at general New Age theories and speculations about the nature of reality. This is a convenient starting point, because most of the beliefs discussed in later chapters presuppose certain ideas about what kind of universe we are living in. Arguably, such ideas will only carry conviction for specific individuals to the extent that they resonate with how they feel about living in the world of daily experience. Therefore I will begin this chapter with some remarks about the attitudes New Age adherents take to experiential reality.

These attitudes vary along a scale from *this-worldliness,* on the one hand, to *otherworldliness,* on the other. I use the distinction between these two poles in the sense of A.O. Lovejoy's classic study *The Great Chain of Being*[1]. Lovejoy explains that otherworldliness does not refer to 'a belief in and a preoccupation of the mind with a future life'. On the contrary, such a preoccupation betrays a strong this-worldly focus, hoping for 'a prolongation of the mode of being which we know in the world of change and sense and plurality and social fellowship, with merely the omission of the trivial or painful features of terrestrial existence, the heightening of its finer pleasures, the compensation of some of earth's frustrations'[2]. Otherworldliness, rather, refers to

> the belief that both the genuinely 'real' and the truly good are radically antithetic in their essential characteristics to anything to be found in man's natural life, in the ordinary course of human experience, however normal, however intelligent, however fortunate. ... the human will, as conceived by the otherworldly philosophers, not only seeks but is capable of finding some final, fixed, immutable, intrinsic, perfectly satisfying good .... Not, however, in this world is either to be found, but only in a 'higher' realm of being differing in its essential nature, and not merely in degree and detail, from the lower[3].

Of the temporal, sensible, essentially divided world, an otherworldly view of reality may give any one of three accounts. This world may be regarded as no

---

[1] Lovejoy, *Great Chain*. I will repeatedly refer to Lovejoy's work, because his discussions prove surprisingly relevant to New Age thought. Lovejoy provides us with a number of systematic tools for analyzing the essential structure of New Age views of reality. The backgrounds to this phenomenon will become clear from Part Three of this study.
[2] Lovejoy, *Great Chain*, 24.
[3] Lovejoy, *Great Chain*, 25-26.

more than an illusion, as is the case in monistic Vedânta philosophy[4]. Or it may be stated that, although this world is real, it *ought* never to have come into existence. This is the position of the dualistic gnosticism of late antiquity, which sees the creation of the world as a disaster.[5] Finally, the otherworldly-minded may simply refuse to discuss the nature of the world because this is deemed irrelevant to the sole aim of salvation from that world. Such is the case in early Buddhism[6].

The alternative, this-worldly attitude can be found even in societies which officially espouse otherworldliness. According to Lovejoy, this is simply because people living in such societies

> have never quite believed it, since they have never been able to deny to the things disclosed by the senses a genuine and imposing and highly important kind of realness, and have never truly desired for themselves the end which otherworldliness held out to them. The great metaphysicians might seek to demonstrate its truth, the saints might in some measure fashion their lives in accordance with it, the mystics might return from their ecstasies and stammeringly report a direct experience of that contact with the absolute reality and the sole satisfying good which it proclaimed; but Nature in the main has been too potent for it. ... the plain man ... has manifestly continued to find something very solid and engrossing in the world in which his own constitution was so deeply rooted and with which it was so intimately interwoven; and even if experience defeated his hopes and in age the savor of life grew somewhat flat and insipid, he has sought comfort in some vision of a better 'this-world' to come, in which no desire should lack fulfilment and his own zest for things should be permanently revitalized.[7]

I have quoted Lovejoy's ornate descriptions at some length, because we will find again and again that a correct view of this distinction is crucial for understanding the nature of New Age religion.

Implicit in Lovejoy's description of this-worldliness is a distinction between a focus on our world of experience *as such*, or on a better "this-world" to come which is modeled on the present world, but better. I propose to refer to the first variety as "strong this-worldliness" and to the other as "weak this-worldliness". Within this weak variety, again, the better "this-world" may be envisaged either as located on this earth (which amounts to some form of millenarianism) or in another reality beyond death.

On the strong this-worldly pole we find, first of all, many neopagans, particularly those of a strongly Goddess-centered perspective. Neopagans generally emphasize the beauty and splendour of the natural world, and show relatively little interest in non-empirical realities other than the "inner worlds" of the

---

[4] Lovejoy, *Great Chain*, 96-97; cf. 30-31, 92.
[5] Lovejoy, *Great Chain*, 97.
[6] Lovejoy, *Great Chain*, 97.
[7] Lovejoy, *Great Chain*, 26-27.

mind. They often explicitly attack New Age tendencies to escape from this world either spatially (into "higher spiritual spheres") or temporally (into past-life experiences or expectations of future bliss), emphasizing that our business is the here and now. The primary neopagan symbol of this-worldly spirituality is the *Goddess*, the essence of which is poetically evoked by Z Budapest:

> This is God, children, listen up well. The beautiful blue planet, our mother, our sister. She moves with 200 miles per second, yet imperceptible; she offers the quiet of the lakes and the rushing of her rivers, the vast expanse of her oceans, the echoes of her mountains. This is God, children... listen up well. Lift your eyes to the heavens, and you behold her sisters the stars, and her cousins the suns and nebulas, and fill your senses with her infinite beauty. This is God, children... and she has made no other heaven but the heavens where you already reside, and she has made no hell except the one you insist to create for yourself. Here is paradise. Here is destiny. Here is infinite grace. This is God. When you seek her she is beneath your feet. When you seek her she is food in your mouth. When you seek her she is love in your heart, pleasure in your body. You share her heartbeat.[8]

Essentially similar sentiments can be found outside the neopagan community, very prominently in Matthew Fox's Creation Spirituality[9] but also, less expectedly, in the teachings of the channeled entity Ramtha[10].

Before discussing the varieties of "weak this-worldliness", I first focus on the radical opposite to strong this-worldliness. Although repeated allusions in New Age sources to the importance of the unitive experience of ultimate reality might make one expect otherwise, true other-worldliness is very rare in the New Age movement. The only unambiguous example in our corpus is *A Course in Miracles*. According to this text—which has correctly been characterized as a Christianized version of non-dualistic Vedânta[11]—our world is just an illusory chimaera, which has nothing to offer but violence, sorrow and pain[12]. We must awaken from the bad dream of separation, and reunite with God. Then the world will cease to exist[13]. Although many other New Age sources routinely use the Oriental concept of "maya" and refer to the world of space-time as ultimately illusory, they seldom come close to the uncompromising world-rejection found in the *Course*. The more usual view is that, in the final analysis, the world may well be an illusion, but that it is a *meaningful* illusion: one which should be used and worked with constructively rather than simply escaped from or dispelled. Thus, the "illusionism"-view is accomodated to an

---

[8] HBWM 298. It is no doubt for poetic reasons that the Goddess, who is obviously female, is here referred to as "God".
[9] For instance OB 59-61
[10] RI ch. 9 'If this isn't Heaven'.
[11] Skutch, *Journey*, 72.
[12] Cf. Wapnick, *Meaning of Forgiveness*, 20-24.
[13] CiM:MfT 35-36.

attitude of weak this-worldliness (to be discussed below). The second other-worldly position distinguished by Lovejoy, i.e., "gnostic" world-rejection, is remarkably absent from New Age thought. Although many New Age sources regard ancient gnosticism in a favourable light, this never includes its world-rejecting dualism, which is sometimes explicitly refuted[14]. Finally, Lovejoy's "Buddhist" variety is of marginal importance in New Age sources, although traces of it can be found, again, in *A Course in Miracles*[15].

Although New Age thinking is on the whole more congenial to strong this-worldliness than to otherworldliness, most typical of the movement is a weak this-worldliness. Both varieties distinguished above may be found: either a bet-ter "this-world" located on our earth, or such an existence located in "higher" realms. Most typical for the last variety is the view that, although this world is not perfect, it is to be valued positively as a *means* for reaching the higher realities beyond. Although in New Age sources we find various degrees of "earth plane" devaluation, these are seldom of a radical kind. According to the most common view, physical reality is characterized by a *relatively* "dense" and limited level of consciousness. This implies a hierarchical universe con-sisting of levels of spirituality, in which pure spirit on the one hand and dense matter on the other are two poles of a continuum rather than radically sepa-rate and opposed principles. Our own level of existence is generally regarded as among the lowest and most material. Incarnation on earth, then, is not exact-ly a pleasant experience: 'Imagine that one day you put on many layers of shirts, trousers, and socks, then added to those several heavy sweaters and over-coats. How would you feel? This is what it feels like for your Higher Self to come into a physical body. You wonder why you feel so heavy at times!'[16].
In spite of such unpleasantness, life on earth is not on that account seen as negative. The world is essentially regarded as *a domain for learning and growth* (often referred to quite literally as a "school"[17]), and the troubles associated with it must be approached as *tasks*. The school-analogy is actually very close

[14] OB 76-77, 112, 307; SS 479-480. Seth, among others, is very concerned with refuting world-rejecting attitudes, emphasizing repeatedly that 'spirituality is a thing of joy and of the earth'. This does not prevent him from developing a theory of multidimensional reality which is this-worldly only in a weak sense.
    [15] See for instance its refusal to discuss subjects like reincarnation, because 'theoretical issues but waste time' (CiM:Mft 57-58).
    [16] SG 149. Cf. Shakti Gawain: 'Being a very evolved spirit in a relatively unevolved form is quite uncomfortable. It accounts for most of the problems we are having. It's as if we are gods and goddesses living in little mud hovels and driving around in clunky, funky, old jalopies. It can be frustrating and demeaning—especially when nobody even realizes who we are!' (LL 39)
    [17] For instance IAP 337; RBNA 102; RU 180. Cf. related formulations like "learning envi-ronment" (SoS 28), "learning lessons" (RR 15-21), doing a "course" or "curriculum" (CiM Intro-duction).

and illuminating. As indicated by the quotation above, entering the school of earth does mean that limits are imposed on an individual's freedom of movement and expression. But these are *meaningful* restrictions which serve a purpose, as indeed they do in any other school. New Age authors tell us that we are here to learn lessons which cannot be learned otherwise, and once we have learned them we will be free to leave the school and pass on to a higher level of development. As long as we have not absorbed the lessons, we are stuck with earth existence and have to make the best of it. Accordingly, the attitude of many New Age sources to life on earth is characterized by a certain ambiguity, not dissimilar to common feelings about attending school. Some love it because there is so much to learn. Some hate it, because they feel constricted by it. Mostly, however, one finds a mixture of both emotions. The essential point is that New Age authors—whether they hate it or love it or just take it as it comes—see it within a larger perspective. Just as school is only a preparation—but a necessary one—for "real life", life on earth is also just one stage in a much larger evolutionary process. Earth life must be seen as a stepping stone to larger realities, which is why we will not be able to leave it before having experienced it to the fullest. Strong world-affirming or world-denying elements may occasionally be accomodated within this "school"-view, with varying degrees of success[18]. Mostly, however, one finds an attitude in which everyday reality is simply accepted as something to be dealt with in a positive spirit, against the background of a larger, cosmic life which gives meaning to the relatively limited existence on earth.

Both the representatives of the New Paradigm, on the one hand, and those authors who focus on the coming of the Age of Aquarius, on the other, look for a better "this-world" on our earth. Nevertheless, from our present perspective these two groups must be rather sharply distinguished. The believers in an Age of Aquarius tend to combine their expectation of an imminent earthly millennium of Love and Light with an equally strong belief in higher realities and intelligences beyond this world. There is an element of contradiction is this: if heaven were to descend on earth then presumably humans would no longer need to ascend to heaven, and the reverse. It also is difficult to see how a world of pure bliss and harmony could continue to be effective as a "learning environment". We will return to these problems in due course. At this point I just call attention to the characteristics of this form of weak this-worldliness. The essential point is the expectation of an imminent transformation of both humanity *and* the world. Both will be transferred to a new, higher state of being and a "higher level of vibration". It is not just that humanity will change its

---

[18] For instance Ramtha, who exalts the beauties of nature but whose spiritual authority derives from his attainment of enlightenment during his only life on earth, after which he no longer needed to be incarnated in that world he praises in such glowing terms.

ways and restore the world to its former state of harmony and beauty, although this is also involved. The transformation will be more radical and unprecedented, even involving changes in the atomic structure of the world which result in a spiritualization of matter as such. The whole world, together with humanity, will be transported "into a higher octave".[19] In these expectations we recognize a form of this-worldliness which may be called even "weaker" than the preceding view of the world as a "learning environment". Although prophets of the Age of Aquarius may exalt the beauties of nature unspoilt by man[20], in the final analysis even this natural world appears to be in need of redemption[21].

Such is not the case with the typical "New Paradigm" literature. Although representatives of this category seldom celebrate the beauties of the natural world as poetically as Z Budapest, they are equally concerned with its preservation; they tend to talk of "spirituality" in terms of living in harmony with nature and its laws rather than in terms of other spiritual realities beyond this world. Defenders of the New Paradigm share with those who expect the Age of Aquarius a strong dissatisfaction with the present state of the world. This dissatisfaction, however, is not with the world as such, but only with our present culture. The ecological crisis has been created by a society based on fundamentally flawed presuppositions. Humanity has to change its way of thinking, perceiving and acting, and then it will hopefully still be possible to heal the world. It is on such a positive transformation of *humanity* that representatives of this category focus their attention. A transformation of the *world*, however, is not necessary: the earth must just be restored to its former natural beauty and balance. We have to conclude that in this New Paradigm variety the boundary between strong and weak this-worldliness is blurred. New Paradigm and Neopagan views about nature, although expressed in different literary styles and terminologies, are fundamentally compatible. The question whether the balance tilts slightly in favour of either strong or weak this-worldliness in specific cases is of minor importance here.

It can be concluded that otherworldly thinking and world-rejection, at least in its stronger forms, is not typical of New Age thinking. On the whole, New Age-adherents are this-worldly oriented, either completely or somewhat ambivalently. Weak forms of this-worldliness dominate, but strong forms can count on widespread approval even by weak this-worldy New Agers. It will be seen

---

[19] For instance RBNA 99-109; VAA 111, 114-116, 118.

[20] See Trevelyan's frequent quotations of Romantic nature poetry, in particular his favourite poem 'God's Grandeur' by Gerald Manley Hopkins (EiG 191).

[21] Cf. George Trevelyan, *Operation Redemption* (OR). See for instance OR 181-182, which illustrates that, in spite of his exaltation of natural beauty, he is almost exclusively concerned with the destiny of *humanity*. Sorrow and indignation about the destruction of nature, so prominent in Matthew Fox's Creation Spirituality, is strikingly absent in Trevelyan's work.

later that these conclusions have important consequences for various aspects of New Age religion, such as the view of reincarnation. First, however, we will look at general New Age ideas about the nature of reality and its relation to the world of experience.

2. THE MEANINGS OF HOLISM

There is no doubt that the quest for "wholeness" at all levels of existence is among the most central concerns of the New Age movement. "Holism", a term originally invented by the South-African statesman J.C. Smuts[22], has been adopted as a universal catchword for this orientation. However, it is important to emphasize from the outset that the term "holism", in a New Age context, does *not* refer to any particular, clearly circumscribed theory or worldview. The only thing which demonstrably unites the many expressions of "holism" is their common opposition to what are perceived as *non*-holistic views, associated with the old culture which the New Age movement seeks to replace or transform. Such non-holistic orientations boil down to two categories which can be referred to as *dualism* and *reductionism*[23]. The main forms of dualism for which the New Age movement tries to develop holistic alternatives are: 1. The fundamental distinction between Creator and creation, i.e. between God and nature and between God and man; 2. The distinction between man and nature, which has traditionally been conceived as a relation based on domination of the latter by the former; 3. The dualism between spirit and matter in its various derivations, from Christian asceticism to Cartesian dualism. It is generally assumed in the New Age movement that such dualistic tendencies are ultimately based on the Judaeo-Christian roots of western civilization. Reductionism is a more recent development, associated with the scientific revolution and the spirit of modern rationalism. Its main forms are: 1. The tendency to fragmentation, which treats organic wholes as mechanisms that can be reduced to their smallest components and then explained in terms of the latter; 2. The tendency to reduce spirit to matter, so that spirit becomes merely a contingent "epiphenomenon" of essentially material processes. In all these five domains, the New Age alternatives are called "holistic". The only common characteristic of these alternatives is that they systematically attempt—with varying degrees of success—to avoid and replace dualism and reductionism.

Holism, in this sense, pervades the New Age movement: from its concern with Holistic Health to its quest for unitive consciousness, and from ecological awareness to the idea of global "networking". In this chapter, we are con-

---

[22] Smuts, *Holism and Evolution* (cf. Steyn, *Worldviews in Transition*, 123-124) Contrary to what one might expect, Smuts's book has been almost completely ignored by New Age authors.
[23] Cf. Hanegraaff, 'New Age en cultuurkritiek'; id., 'Verschijnsel New Age'.

cerned with holistic views of reality as such. While discussing the most important theories and speculations which have been developed, I will attempt to
make a rough distinction between the main structural types of holism which
underlie these theories. I will argue that holism can be conceived in abstract
terms as: 1. based on the possibility of reducing all manifestations to one "*ultimate source*"; 2. based on the *universal interrelatedness* of everything in the
universe; 3. based on a universal dialectic between complementary *polarities*;
4. based on the analogy of the whole of reality, or of significant subsystems,
with *organisms*. I will not address the philosophical question to what extent
these types can be combined with each other in principle; it suffices that, in
the work of specific New Age thinkers, they *are* sometimes combined, although
one type usually dominates quite strongly. The first two types, finally, are
undoubtedly the most important in a New Age context. They will be treated in
separate sections, while the others will be discussed more briefly.

A. The Ultimate Source of Manifestation

One of the most pervasive assumptions to be found in the New Age movement
is that all reality is ultimately derived from one Ultimate Source. The great
diversity of phenomena found in the world of manifestation must, at some deep
level, be linked together by virtue of a common Origin. This One Source of
all being thus guarantees the ultimate wholeness of reality. The capitals are
appropriate, because the Source is inevitably regarded as, or immediately associated with, God. A typical New Age statement of "Ultimate Source Holism"
is the following passage from George Trevelyan:

> Behind all outwardly manifested form is a timeless realm of absolute conscious-
> ness. It is the great Oneness underlying all the diversity, all the myriad forms of
> nature. It may be called God, or may be deemed beyond all naming—and there-
> fore, as in the East, be called THAT. If one is of agnostic turn of mind, one can
> refer to it as 'creative intelligence'. But from it derive all archetypal ideas which
> manifest in the phenomenal world. For that world issues ultimately from spirit,
> and its forms might be conceived as frozen spirit. The quality of Being perme-
> ates everything, suffuses everything. Divinity is therefore inherent everywhere.[24]

Rupert Sheldrake, in his first book, cautiously presents the idea of an ultimate
source as an hypothesis:

> If this transcendent conscious being were the source of the universe and of every-
> thing within it, all created things would in some sense participate in its nature.
> The more or less limited 'wholeness' of organisms at all levels of complexity
> could then be seen as a reflection of the transcendent unity on which they depend-
> ed, and from which they were ultimately derived.[25]

---

[24] VAA 5.
[25] NSL 210. Some other examples of the same idea: ToP 233; CV 39; S 188-189; RBNA 29-
30.

Although it may not be immediately apparent, such statements contain an inner ambivalence which considerably complicates the character of "Ultimate Source Holism". We note that Trevelyan's quotation, with its clear pantheistic tendencies, also states that the Source resides in a "timeless" sphere. Sheldrake speaks of creation "participating in" and "reflecting" a source which is, nevertheless, transcendent. In other words, both transcendence and immanence are affirmed to varying degrees. As a guideline for analyzing their relation in New Age holism of the present type, I again refer to Lovejoy. The central argument of his *Great Chain of Being* is summed up as follows:

> The most noteworthy consequence of the persistent influence of Platonism was ... that throughout the greater part of its history Western religion, in its more philosophic forms, has had two Gods ... The two were, indeed, identified as one being with two aspects. But the ideas corresponding to the 'aspects' were ideas of two antithetic kinds of being. The one was the Absolute of otherworldliness—self-sufficient, out of time, alien to the categories of ordinary human thought and experience, needing no world of lesser beings to supplement or enhance his own eternal self-contained perfection. The other was a God who emphatically was not self-sufficient nor, in any philosophical sense, 'absolute': one whose essential nature required the existence of other beings, and not of one kind of these only, but of all kinds which could find a place in the descending scale of the possibilities of reality—a God whose prime attribute was generativeness, whose manifestation was to be found in the diversity of creatures and therefore in the temporal order and the manifold spectacle of nature's processes.[26]

This paradox of God as the self-sufficient Absolute *and* as the generative source of Being, combined in one and the same tradition, led to a pervasive ambiguity about ultimate values.

> If the good for man was the contemplation or the imitation of God, this required, on the one hand, a transcendence and suppression of the merely 'natural' interests and desires, a withdrawal of the soul from 'the world' the better to prepare it for the beatific vision of the divine perfection; and it required, on the other hand, a piety towards the God of things as they are, an adoring delight in the sensible universe in all its variety, an endeavor on man's part to know and understand it ever more fully, and a conscious participation in the divine activity of creation.[27]

In other words, the pervasive duality between otherworldliness and this-worldliness is parallelled by a duality between two conceptions of Ultimate Reality/God as either radically transcendent or immanent in creation. Lovejoy's study documents the uneasy marriage of these two contradictory strains in Western intellectual and religious history. From our perspective, it is extremely interesting to note that substantial and essential parts of Lovejoy's book (first published in 1936) read as if he had the New Age movement specifically in mind.

---

[26] Lovejoy, *Great Chain*, 315.
[27] Lovejoy, *Great Chain*, 316.

The similarities are so close and numerous that we can only conclude that Platonism, with its attendant problems, apparently extends its influence into the heart of the New Age movement. In Part Three of this study we will explore the historical background of this phenomenon. At this point we are interested in the ambivalent coexistence of otherworldly and this-worldly elements, epitomized by the concentration on a Transcendent Absolute or a Generative Source.

Given the this-worldly rather than otherworldy orientation of New Age thinking, it is to be expected that the conception of God as a "generative source" will be more common than its self-contained alternative. And this expectation is indeed confirmed by the sources. Particularly clear examples are the "creation myths" found in various New Age sources, all of which are actually myths of emanation from one Original Source[28]. They describe how an original absolute Oneness gave birth to the richness and diversity of creation. This process is generally presented as a *positive* event, not as a fall from perfection. Although these mythical stories differ in detail, they usually follow a similar basic pattern[29]. A comparatively sophisticated, but representative and extremely influential version, is given by the channeled entity Seth, who refers to God as "All That Is" and explains his purpose in creating the world:

> The purpose is, quite simply, *being* as opposed to nonbeing. I am telling you what I know, and there is much I do not know. ... Now—and this will seem like a contradiction in terms—*there is nonbeing*. It is a state, not of nothingness, but a state in which probabilities and possibilities are known and anticipated but blocked from expression. Dimly, through what you would call history, hardly remembered, there was such a state. It was a state of agony in which the powers of creativity and existence were known, but the ways to produce them were not known. This is the lesson All That Is had to learn, and that could not be taught. This is the agony from which creativity originally was drawn, and its reflection is still seen. ... All That Is retains memory of that state, and it serves as a constant impetus— in your terms—toward renewed creativity. ... the agony itself served as an impetus, strong enough so that All That Is initiated within Itself the means *to be*. ... The first state of agonized search for expression may have represented the birth throes of All That Is as we know It. ... Desire, wish, and expectation rule all actions and are the basis for all realities. Within All That Is, therefore, the wish, desire, and expectation of creativity existed before all other actuality. The strength and vitality of these desires and expectations then became in your terms so insup-

---

[28] TiR 306-308; RG 3ff; OL 145; S 206-209; R 79; SD 31-32. See also chapter eleven, section 2, under "Cosmogonic Myths".

[29] Usually, God is posited as the primary unitive reality, and manifestation starts with the emergence of a duality in the original oneness (RG 3; S 190-191: cf. R 79; SD 31-32); sometimes, alternatively, God himself must first be "born" out of a primary Ground (TiR 306-307; SM 266: 'birth throes of All That Is as we know It'). In all cases, once the original unity has become a duality, the basis for further pluralization is given and creation unfolds in a kind of self-generating process.

portable that All That Is was driven to find the means to produce them. ... At first, in your terms, all of probable reality existed as nebulous dreams within the consciousness of All That Is. Later, the unspecific nature of these 'dreams' grew more particular and vivid. The dreams became recognizable one from the other until they drew the conscious notice of All That Is. And with curiosity and yearning, All That Is paid more attention to Its own dreams. It then purposely gave them more and more detail, and yearned toward this diversity and grew to love that which was not yet separate from itself. It gave consciousness and imagination to personalities while they still were but within Its dreams. They also yearned to be actual. ... All That Is saw, then, an infinity of probable, conscious individuals, and foresaw all possible developments, but they were locked within It until It found the means. This was in your terms a primary cosmic dilemma ...

The means, then, came to It. It must release the creatures and probabilities from Its dream. To do so would give them actuality. However, it also meant 'losing' a portion of Its own consciousness, for it was in that portion that they were held in bondage. All That Is had to let go. ... With love and longing It let go that portion of Itself, and they were free. The psychic energy exploded in a flash of creation. ... It, of Itself and from that state, has given life to infinities of possibilities. From its agony, It found the way to burst forth in freedom, through expression, and in so doing gave existence to individualized consciousness. Therefore is It rightfully jubilant. Yet all individuals remember their source, and now dream of All That Is as All That Is once dreamed of them. And they yearn toward that immense source ... and yearn to set It free and give It actuality through their own creations.[30]

The extremely ambivalent character of this last sentence once more reflects the inner paradoxality of Lovejoy's "two Gods". It is difficult to imagine a more explicit example of God as the "generative source" of reality than the theology/cosmology of *The Seth Material*. Still, the intuitive longing to "return to the source" is also given its due, even though such a return would obviously mean the reversal and frustration of the creative process, in the name of an otherworldly rejection of the world of manifestation. This illustrates how difficult it is to dispel otherworldly sentiments even from a strongly and consistently this-worldly doctrine like Seth's, which celebrates reality as an ongoing feast of cosmic creativity.

The principle of a Generative Source generally leads to the conception of a hierarchical cosmos constituted by levels of spirituality, inhabited by intelligent beings on corresponding levels of spiritual development. Such a view of the cosmos is indeed extremely common in New Age thought[31]. All intelligent entities—discussed in detail in the next chapter—are engaged in a process of spiritual evolution which will, presumably, ultimately lead them back to the Ultimate Source. Again we encounter the ambivalence analyzed by Lovejoy: individual intelligences emanate from the Ultimate Source in a "downward" (or "outward") process of creative generation, so that these intelligences can

---

[30] SM 264-268.
[31] ECSU 60; WW 216-217; WWD 124; ENF 82; PR 73; RR 201-208; R 54-67; OtC 35ff; RBNA 29-30; VAA 6-7; SoS 97.

start on the "upward" (or "inward") journey back to the source which transcends creation. Many New Age authors, especially the representatives of this-
worldliness in its weakest—and therefore most ambivalent—varieties, such as
George Trevelyan, do not appear to perceive any problem, and are able to affirm
the splendour of creation *and* the need to transcend it in the same breath. Others, especially those of a stronger this-worldly orientation, appear to have
noticed the ambiguity. Their favoured solution is to affirm that the possibilities for future evolution are *infinite*. Seth, again, is a clear example of such a
consistently this-worldly view. If the purpose is "being as opposed to nonbe-
ing", then there can be no question of an ultimate re-absorption of individuality into the One Source: 'There is nothing more deadly than nirvana. ... it
offers you the annihilation of your personality, in a bliss that destroys the
integrity of your being. Run from such bliss!'[32] and 'You are not fated to dis-
solve into All That Is. ... All That Is is the creator of individuality, not the
means of its destruction'[33]. Instead, Seth offers the prospect of an infinite
process of creative expansion: 'I offer no hope for the lazy, for they will not
find eternal rest ... You will discover the multidimensional love and energy that
gives consciousness to all things. This will not lead you to want to rest upon
the proverbial blessed bosom. It will instead inspire you to take a better hand
in the job of creation'[34]. The great goal of existence is for human beings to
become fully conscious "co-creators with God". This is a theme found throughout our New Age corpus, and it is linked immediately to what may well be
regarded as the second pervasive theme of New Age thinking in addition to
the theme of holism, i.e. the idea of *"creating our own reality"* (see chapter
eight, section 3B).

   As we will see, the conviction that we are, somehow, the creators of our
own reality is no less pervasive in the New Age literature than the theme of
holism. Like the latter, it takes different forms in different contexts and cannot be considered as denoting any single, clearly circumscribed theory. Both
"holism" and "creating our own reality" are catchwords or -sentences referring to very deep convictions or longings which are far more basic than any
explicit formulation. Below (chapter seven), much more will be said about this
second great New Age theme. At this point, however, we are more interested
in its relevance to "Ultimate Source Holism". It is clear that Seth sees human
beings as active participants in the creative energy which gave birth to the universe, and this same conviction is reflected throughout the New Age literature[35]. While *All That Is* is also referred to as "Primary Energy Gestalt", indi-

---

[32] NPR 163 (footnote).
[33] SS 412. This view is rather commonly shared in the New Age corpus (see for instance TiR
308-309; EiG 12), although the tendency rejected by Seth is not completely absent.
[34] SS 460.
[35] For instance ENF 168; GW 100.

vidual beings are referred to as "Energy Essence Personalities". Our very being therefore consists of creative energy. It is, in effect, only *through us* that *All That Is* is able to create manifested realities. Seth tells us that although we may be unaware of it, we are constantly creating our reality as naturally as we breath. The nature of our reality is a direct reflection of our conscious and unconscious *beliefs*. Because most of us hold limiting and restricting beliefs about the world, the universe confirms these convictions. If we nevertheless change our beliefs, we will find that reality changes with it. Actually, there are no limits to the realities we can imagine and "make real" if only we believe they are possible. Thus the many-leveled cosmos emanating from the generative source of *All That Is* is actually constituted of realities created by individual "entities" participating in the universal creative energy. The levels of reality reflect the extent to which they have become aware of their own creative potential. Human beings live in their own self-created dreams, and the apparent stability of "physical reality" is conditioned only by the intersubjective consensus of many individuals believing in a similar reality[36]. Seth's worldview is thus a perfect example of the way in which, as noted above, ideas about the ultimately illusionary character of reality are accomodated to a basically this-worldly perspective. The traditional Oriental view of "maya" implies that the illusion of this world must be dispelled in order to reach the ultimate "Real" beyond. In Seth's strongly contrasting views, the recognition that reality is a self-created illusion serves as an impetus to create ever better realities: *not* to flee from illusion altogether. God's creation exists as an incredibly rich and dazzling kaleidoscope of "imaginary worlds". These worlds are there to be enjoyed to the fullest, and to be made ever more beautiful and diverse; they are not to be dispelled in the name of some bleak otherworldly Absolute. This central message of the Seth material has been of enormous influence in the New Age movement. We find his worldview mirrored in many later authors[37], although seldom developed with the intellectual rigor which characterizes Seth's formulations. Evidence of Seth's consistency is his insistence on the *infinity* of God's creative expansion. Not only is such infiniteness necessary, as we saw, in order to avoid the image of God as an other-worldly final term of individual evolution; it is also a necessary implication of the very nature of creativity: 'Ultimately a completed or finished God, or All That Is, would end up smothering His creation. For perfection presupposes that point beyond which development is impossi-

---

[36] On a higher level not accessible to normal consciousness, individuals participating in the "same" reality are believed to be in permanent telepathic contact. They reach a consensus about their shared reality by emphasizing all the similarities between their respective realities while ignoring the differences. Intersubjective reality is thus to be seen as a telepathically mediated compromise (SM 202; SS 457-459).

[37] His influence is particularly strong in the work of Shakti Gawain, Chris Griscom, Louise L. Hay, Shirley MacLaine, Sanaya Roman and probably Michael Talbot.

ble, and creativity at an end.'[38] In Seth's Romantic cosmology, which is based
on the supremacy of the Creative Imagination, there is no room for a perfect,
self-sufficient, and therefore otherworldly Absolute.

Special attention has been given to Seth's view of reality because it is paradigmatic of Generative Source-holism in its most highly-developed New Age
form. We find here the essential picture of a hierarchical cosmos emanating
from a generative source (a traditional Platonic concept) combined with a quite
modern emphasis (reminiscent of Science Fiction) on the infinity of multidimensional, creatively expanding worlds which are, furthermore, created by the
imagination of their inhabitants (participating in the divine creativity) on the
basis of their conscious and unconscious beliefs. These are absolutely basic
tenets for large and fundamental sectors of the New Age movement. Seth's pivotal role in the development of New Age thinking has not yet been sufficiently recognized by scholarship. However, in the context of "revelations" as discussed in chapter one, the Seth messages must be regarded as a fundamental
revelatory source for the New Age movement. It is hardly an exaggeration to
regard Jane Roberts as the Muhammad of New Age religion, and Seth as its
angel Gabriel. Without their metaphysical teamwork, the face of the New Age
movement of the 1980s would not have developed as it did.

While the "Generative Source" variety of "Ultimate Source Holism" is far more
typical of New Age thinking than the "Self-sufficient Absolute" variety, the
role of the latter should not be underestimated. However, it is seldom presented
explicitly in the sources. The most important exception is, again, *A Course in
Miracles*, which was singled out above as the only example of strong otherworldliness in our New Age corpus. The importance of the idea of a "self-sufficient Absolute" in a New Age context lies primarily in the way it tends to
recur as loose references in very different, sometimes surprising and even logically incompatible contexts. In order to better understand this phenomenon, I
refer again to A.O. Lovejoy's work. Lovejoy introduces the concept of "metaphysical pathos", prominent examples of which are the "eternalistic" and
"monistic or pantheistic" pathos. Both are exemplified in Shelley's lines quoted by Lovejoy:

> *The One remains, the many change and pass,*
> *Heaven's light forever shines, earth's shadows fly ....*

Commenting on the peculiar 'aesthetic pleasure which the bare abstract idea
of immutability gives us', Lovejoy comments dryly:

> It is not self-evident that remaining forever unchanged should be regarded as an

---

[38] SS 340.

excellence; yet through the associations and the half-formed images which the mere conception of changelessness arouses ... a philosophy which tells us that at the heart of things there is a reality wherein is no variableness nor shadow that is cast by turning, is sure to find its response in our emotional natures, at all events in certain phases of individual or group experience.[39]

The same is true of the varieties of monistic or pantheistic pathos, with an obvious relevance for New Age holism:

That it should afford so many people a peculiar satisfaction to say that All is One is, as William James once remarked, a rather puzzling thing. What is there more beautiful or more venerable about the numeral *one* than about any other number? But psychologically the force of the monistic pathos is in some degree intelligible when one considers the nature of the implicit responses which talk about oneness produces. ... again, when a monistic philosophy declares, or suggests, that one is oneself a part of the universal Oneness, a whole complex of obscure emotional responses is released.[40]

If we accept the frequent allusions to "self-sufficient Absolutes" in New Age sources as examples of the instinctive emotional appeal of metaphysical pathos, this has important implications for our analysis. The point is that there is a difference in conceptual status between an explicitly formulated worldview on the one hand, and expressions of metaphysical pathos on the other[41]. The former generates more or less consciously-held convictions about the nature of reality, expressed as propositions; the latter signals the existence of deep-seated and essentially pre-reflective wishes and longings. Although holistic worldviews in general are usually defended by people susceptible to a corresponding kind of metaphysical pathos, the two categories should not be confused. If, in many New Age sources, we find examples of eternalistic or monistic pathos expressed in the terminology of self-sufficient Absolutes, then the pre-reflective and emotional character of these utterances precludes the automatic inference that the authors therefore *believe* in a worldview based on such an Absolute. On the contrary, the susceptibility of authors to eternalistic or monistic pathos may equally well lead them, in the process of reflection, to develop a "generative", or indeed any other kind of holistic worldview. And this, as we have seen, is precisely what we find in the great majority of New Age sources. Eternalistic and monistic pathos is prominently present; but it surprisingly seldom gives rise to otherworldly-oriented worldviews according to which peace will be found only in the pure One. Real otherworldliness remains very much restricted to the emotional sphere, and almost never survives the transition to theoretical speculation.

---

[39] Lovejoy, *Great Chain*, 12.
[40] Lovejoy, *Great Chain*, 13.
[41] I have elsewhere defined this same distinction in terms of "latent mental dispositions" versus "explicit views of life", in a study of the nature of gnostic views of life (Hanegraaff, 'Dynamic Typological Approach').

B. Universal Interrelatedness

First of all, the difference between this second category of holism and the former must be precisely defined. It is not the case, of course, that universal interrelatedness is absent from "Ultimate Source Holism". On the contrary: everything in the universe is related to everything else by virtue of the fact that everything participates in, or emerges from, the same Source. This situation can be envisaged as a pyramid hierarchy with the Source at the top and the increasing diversity of manifestation "fanning out" from that One Center or, alternatively, with the Source at the center and manifestation radiating to all sides like the rays of the sun. Universal Interrelatedness as understood in this chapter is characterized, however, by *the absence of a Source or other ontologically privileged Center*. The appropriate picture is one of a network in which every point is connected to every other point but in which no point has a privileged status. A traditional parallel, which brings out the religious appeal of Universal Interrelatedness, is the image of God conceived as a sphere whose center is everywhere and circumference nowhere[42]. An important result of the absence of a Source with privileged ontological status is that Universal Interrelatedness tends to be of an unambiguously monistic character[43]. In this kind of holism, questions about the ultimate *origin* of the universe usually receive less attention than questions focused on its *present nature and constitution*. It is perhaps not surprising, given this more practical interest, that the foundations of holism in the sense of "universal interrelatedness" are almost exclusively found in the domain of New Age Science. However, it must be emphasized that the ideas developed in this domain, in various degrees of popularization or simplification, are widely influential throughout the New Age movement as a whole. Furthermore, the idea of holism in the sense of "universal interrelatedness" also recurs in contexts other than the "nature of reality", for instance in ecological or social theories of a New Age orientation.

Parallellism and Bootstrap Philosophy

In the first of his two influential books, *The Tao of Physics*, Fritjof Capra argues that there are significant parallels between modern physics—especially quantum mechanics—and Oriental mysticism. Capra's central thesis is that 'a consistent view of the world is beginning to emerge from modern physics which

---

[42] This formulation, associated with thinkers like N. Cusanus, among others, originated in a Hermeticist tract of the late 12th century called the *Liber viginti quatuor philosophorum* (Faivre, 'Ancient and Medieval Sources', 31).

[43] This kind of monism is, of course, different from the otherworldly monism encountered in the previous chapter, according to which only the transcendent Source is real and the rest is illusion. In the case of Universal Interrelatedness, which is generally this-worldly, the monistic character derives from the tendency to accept only one ontological substance in the universe.

is harmonious with ancient Eastern wisdom'[44]. A similar concern underlies several other books which enjoy some popularity in the New Age[45], but there is no doubt that Capra is the recognized champion of popular New Age "parallelism"[46]. It is not my intention to enter into the debate about the validity of this genre as such, or the merits (or lack of them) of Capra's particular contribution[47]. The important point for us is that Capra's type of physics-mysticism parallellism, whether valid or not, has unquestionably become one of the cherished beliefs of the New Age movement.[48] This adaptation of parallellism tends to produce "pop" versions of what is in itself already an example of "popular science", exemplified most typically by assertions to the effect that "modern science proves mysticism". It can be demonstrated that Capra himself, at least in the *Tao of Physics*, is more cautious. His claim is that Oriental mysticism provides a consistent and relevant *philosophical background* to the theories of contemporary science[49]; and he emphasizes that the parallels strictly apply only to the level of *verbal formulations*[50]. Therefore the ultimate reality experienced by mystics cannot simply be identified with the quantum field of modern physics[51]; although, of course, the similarity is quite suggestive. Rather than in adducing "proof" for mysticism, the importance of the parallels lies in their implicit criticism of current non-holistic (dualistic and reductionistic) assumptions about the nature of reality. The suggestion of the *Tao of Physics* is that Oriental philosophical worldviews are able to *make sense* of the data of quantum physics, by assimilating them within a consistently holistic framework. The reigning western scientific paradigm is not able to do so, because its very presuppositions are directly refuted by the evidence of advanced physics.

Here, we are less interested in the credentials of parallellism than in the intrinsic nature of the worldview defended by Capra. His version of holism has

---

[44] ToP 12.

[45] For instance MNP which, other than Capra's book, favours the so-called "many-worlds hypothesis" in quantum mechanics. Zukav's *Dancing Wu-Li Masters*, as I argued, is not really a parallellist book at all. LeShan's *Medium, the Mystic, and the Physicist* is concerned with the paranormal rather than with mysticism.

[46] As pointed out by Sal Restivo in his important study of the subject, parallelism as such is by no means restricted to the New Age context. Rather, it is 'a recurring strategy in intellectual conflict' to be found already in the Renaissance and in Weimar Germany (Restivo, *Social Relations*, 91ff).

[47] See Restivo, *Social Relations*; Chowdhury, 'Holisme en Parallellisme'; Clifton & Regehr, 'Toward a Sound Perspective'; Wilber, 'Introduction: Of Shadows and Symbols', in: QQ; and Capra's response to his critics in 'Tao of Physics Revisited: A Conversation with Renée Weber' (in: HP).

[48] See for instance DL 323-329; AE 128.

[49] ToP 30, 54.

[50] ToP 52.

[51] ToP 233. It seems that Capra later changed his mind and came to believe in the actual identity of the realities disclosed by mystical experience and by physical research (ToPR 218-220).

two significant features. The first of these is the unity and universal interrelation of all phenomena, which leads to the view of the universe as an *interconnected web of relations*. The second is the *intrinsically dynamic* nature of this universe[52]. The argumentation of the *Tao of Physics* culminates in a defense of the so-called *Bootstrap theory* in physics, which is presented as a perfect exemplification of this kind of holism. Bootstrap theory was created by the physicist Geoffrey Chew as a philosophical framework to account for the research results of quantum mechanics. Interestingly, a close similarity has been demonstrated to Leibniz' Monadology; Chew's quarrel with the corpuscularian metaphysics of classical physics may well be regarded as a re-enactment of the historical dispute between Leibniz and Newton[53]. Capra describes the essence of the bootstrap philosophy as follows:

> According to this bootstrap philosophy, nature cannot be reduced to fundamental entities, like fundamental building blocks of matter, but has to be understood entirely through self-consistency. All of physics has to follow uniquely from the requirement that its components be consistent with one another and with themselves. This idea constitutes a radical departure from the traditional spirit of basic research in physics which had always been bent on finding the fundamental constituents of matter. At the same time it is the culmination of the conception of the material world as an interconnected web of relations that emerged from quantum theory. The bootstrap philosophy not only abandons the idea of fundamental building blocks of matter, but accepts no fundamental entities whatsoever—no fundamental constants, laws, or equations. The universe is seen as a dynamic web of interrelated events. None of the properties of any part of this web is fundamental; they all follow from the properties of the other parts, and the overall consistency of their interrelations determines the structure of the entire web.[54]

There should be no mistake about the radical implications of this view. Even more clearly than in Capra's description, the full meaning of "overall consistency" is brought out in the following observations, from an academic study of Chew's philosophy, about the nature of hadrons (i.e., strongly interacting particles constituting the atomic nucleus):

> ...the model of the hadrons is very peculiar. Hadron x is composite. Its constituents are y and z. But both y and z are also composite. Among their constituents is x. Thus each hadron is constituted by other hadrons, which it in turn constitutes. This network is possibly infinite in extent. Moreover, on this view, each single hadron can be, and probably is, individual, with its individuation being given by its precise mirroring of the total situation of all other hadrons, particularly those which immediately determine it. ... In other words, each particle helps to generate other particles, which in turn generate it. In this circular and violently nonlinear situation, it is possible to imagine that no free, or arbitrary, variables appear and that the only self-consistent set of particles is the one found in nature.[55]

---

[52] ToP 30; cf. TP 87.
[53] Cf. Gale, 'Chew's Monadology', 339-348.
[54] TP 92-93. Cf. ToP 316-317.
[55] Gale, 'Chew's Monadology', 345-346.

This is exactly the conclusion drawn by Capra:

> the whole set of hadrons generates itself in this way or pulls itself up, so to say, by its 'bootstraps'. The idea, then, is that this extremely complex bootstrap mechanism is self-determining, that is, that there is only one way in which it can be achieved. In other words, there is only one possible self-consistent set of hadrons—the one found in nature.[56]

What we have, then, is a view of physical reality based on universal interrelatedness in its most radical sense. At the subatomic level, everything in the universe quite literally participates in everything else. Of course, such a view raises many questions. A problem not adressed by Capra is how one should deal with the seemingly unavoidable conclusion of an absolute determinism. Another problem is the fact that bootstrap holism deals exclusively with physical realities, and would appear to leave no room for the spiritual. It is not clear, moreover, how interrelatedness at the ultimate subatomic level—however total—could be relevant to the macroscopic level of human life in the phenomenal world. These problems did occur to Capra, and have resulted in an interesting change of direction between the *Tao of Physics* and his second fundamental contribution to New Age literature, *The Turning Point*.

Capra has described this change in his autobiographical volume *Uncommon Wisdom*. In *The Tao of Physics* he saw the new physics as 'the ideal model for new concepts and approaches in other disciplines'[57]. A casual remark from the systems theorist Gregory Bateson, communicated to Capra by a common friend, made him realize that this thinking contained a 'major flaw'. Bateson had said jokingly: 'Capra? The man is crazy! He thinks we are all electrons'. Reflecting on this remark, Capra came to realize that 'by presenting the new physics as a model for a new medicine, new psychology, or new social science, I had fallen into the very Cartesian trap that I wanted scientists to avoid'[58]. Presenting physics as a model for other domains implied that physical phenomena were the primary reality and the basis of everything else. In other words: the bootstrap holism of the *Tao of Physics*, taken by itself, amounted to a species of materialist reductionism. This shocking realization led Capra to develop, over the course of several years, a new approach which 'no longer presented the new physics as a model for other sciences but rather as an important special case of a much more general framework, the framework of systems theory'[59].

Capra appears to be confident about the success of this reorientation, the final result of which is *The Turning Point*. Before discussing the systems view devel-

[56] ToP 327-328.
[57] UW 73.
[58] UW 74.
[59] UW 74.

oped in that book, however, it seems relevant to call attention to another chapter of *Uncommon Wisdom*, which sheds additional light on the problem of reductionism. In the context of his research for the chapter about economics in *The Turning Point*, Capra visited the economist E.F. Schumacher, well-known for his book *Small is Beautiful*. After explaining his new systems approach, which he believed to be in fundamental accord with Schumacher's views, Capra expected a positive response. However, Schumacher strongly disagreed. The core of his argument was that science cannot solve the problems of our time because it cannot entertain the qualitative notion of higher and lower levels of being. Both bootstrap physics and the systems view accept only one fundamental level of reality and are therefore ultimately reductionist.

> In the long discussion that followed Schumacher expressed his belief in a fundamental hierarchical order consisting of four characteristic elements—mineral, plant, animal, and human—with four characteristic elements—matter, life, consciousness, and self-awareness—which are manifest in such a way that each level possesses not only its own characteristic element but also those of all lower levels. This, of course, was the ancient idea of the Great Chain of Being, which Schumacher presented in modern language and with considerable subtlety. However, he maintained that the four elements are irreducible mysteries that cannot be explained, and that the differences between them represent fundamental jumps in the vertical dimension, 'ontological discontinuities', as he put it. 'This is why physics cannot have any philosophical impact', he repeated. 'It cannot deal with the whole; it deals only with the lowest level'.
> This was indeed a fundamental difference in our views of reality. Although I agreed that physics was limited to a particular level of phenomena, I did not see the differences between various levels as absolute. I argued that these levels are essentially levels of complexity which are not separate but are all interconnected and interdependent.[60]

The Capra-Schumacher discussion exemplifies a fundamental rift in New Age thinking between two contradictory views of reality: a monistic and a hierarchical one. The dividing issue is whether the former can manage to avoid reductionism. It is significant, in this context, that Capra explicitly rejects Schumacher's view of the different levels as "irreducible" mysteries, apparently not realizing that this literally implies a belief in reductionism. It will be useful to keep this problematic in mind in the following discussions of systems thinking and the holographic paradigm. We will return to this issue at the end of this chapter, in discussing the debate initiated by Ken Wilber.

Systems Thinking
General Systems Theory emerged from Cybernetics as an attempt to correct the failings of positivism. Making no fundamental distinction between such apparently different domains as nature, social reality or the products of engi-

---

[60] UW 228-229.

neering, its basic analytical concept in all these areas is the "system", defined as a whole that is more than the sum of its constituent parts. Instead of explaining systems in terms of mechanical interactions between discrete units it emphasizes overall patterns of relationship. Of particular importance is the fact that "mechanical" descriptions of systems in terms of matter and energy exchange are replaced by descriptions based on the fundamental concept of *information*. Leading proponents of systems theory[61] have claimed that the shift to a system-oriented society constitutes a revolution which actually brings in a "New Age": the "postindustrial" System Age which is based on the interlocking global networks of information technology[62]. Nevertheless, our first observation must be that what might technically be called the "holism" of General Systems Theory has no specific relation to the New Age movement. As a result of the information revolution of the 1980s, the holistic idea of a global information network has actually become a reality. Some New Age proponents, notably Marilyn Ferguson, have interpreted this as a sign of the emergence of a planetary New Age. Those more specific systems approaches which have achieved popularity in the New Age movement are, however, by no means fully representative of the phenomenon of systems thinking as such. It is significant in this respect that Capra, in the crucial chapter of the *Turning Point* about "The Systems View of Life", mentions the founding fathers of General Systems Theory only casually. Although he sometimes refers to Laszlo in a footnote, none of the founders is even mentioned in the text. Capra's Systems theory turns out to be a personal blend of the ideas of only two thinkers: Gregory Bateson and Ilya Prigogine[63].

Bateson (1904-1980), sometime husband of Margaret Mead, is an extremely original but enigmatic thinker. During the last years of his life, which he spent at the Human Potential center Esalen, he seems to have become a sort of cult guru of the alternative movement[64]. It is perhaps regrettable that he allowed this to happen. Bateson has been labeled a New Age thinker because of his association with Esalen, but there is little doubt that few of his admirers understood his ideas[65]. Bateson's daughter recalls her father's irritation:

A great many people, recognizing that Gregory was critical of certain kinds of

---

[61] See in particular Von Bertalanffy, *General Systems Theory*; Laszlo, *Introduction to Systems Philosophy*; id., *Systems View of the World*; Ackoff, *Redesigning the Future*.

[62] Schuurman, *Technische overmacht*, 24.

[63] UW 215.

[64] UW 75.

[65] Cf. UW 79: 'Even the few people who *thought* they understood him, *he* did not think understood him. Very, very few people, he thought, understood him' (quotation of R.D. Laing). Bochinger (*"New Age"*, 417-418) provides an incorrect presentation of Bateson's position vis à vis New Age on the basis of superficial analogies between Bateson's interdisciplinary interests and the various domains of New Age speculation.

materialism, wished him to be a spokesman for an opposite faction, a faction advocating the kind of attention they found comfortable to things excluded by atomistic materialism: God, spirits, ESP, "the ghosts of old forgotten creeds". Gregory was always in the difficult position of saying to his scientific colleagues that they were failing to attend to critically important matters, because of methodological and epistemological premises central to Western science for centuries, and then turning around and saying to his most devoted followers, when they believed they were speaking about these same critically important matters, that the way they were talking was nonsense[66].

Whether Capra belonged to this last group is difficult to decide with certainty. Capra's own memories of his encounters with Bateson, in spite of his own assertions to the contrary, hardly convey the impression of substantial intellectual discussions in which Bateson accepted Capra as a serious partner[67]. To ascertain whether Capra fully and correctly understood Bateson's thinking would require a detailed comparative analysis beyond the scope of this study. My impression is that the differences between the two outweigh their points of agreement. Capra remains very much the physicist who tries to overcome the Cartesian split by finding a way to include the dimension of consciousness in an essentially material universe. Bateson, as an anthropologist and biologist, was primarily interested, as he put it, in "living things". He actually mistrusted physicists[68]. Capra seems to have been fascinated by Bateson primarily for two reasons. First, the overall monistic and holistic quality of Bateson's systems thinking seemed congenial to his own bootstrap philosophy. Second, and more importantly, Bateson appeared to have found a way out of the Cartesian dilemma. His definition of *Mind* permitted a completely new perspective on the problem of "Mind and Nature", demonstrating that they formed "a necessary unity"[69]. However, it seems that Capra disregarded at least two other important aspects of Bateson's thinking. First, while the concept of *Mind* is central to his work, Bateson consistently refused to discuss *consciousness*. This, he said, was 'the great untouched question, the next big challenge'[70]. Compared to Bateson himself, who shrank from "rushing in"[71] to this domain, Capra often appears over-confident in proposing solutions on the basis of Bateson's own premises. Secondly, Capra all but ignores Bateson's fundamental distinc-

---

[66] Bateson & Bateson, *Angels Fear*, 6. Compare the attack on a whole range of New Age concerns in *Angels Fear*, chapter 5. Nevertheless, both Bateson himself and his daughter appear to have permitted the publication of their work in the series "Bantam New Age Books".

[67] See UW 75ff.

[68] UW 76.

[69] See subtitle of Bateson, *Mind and Nature*.

[70] UW 88. Cf. Bateson, *Mind and Nature*, 137. Bateson would finally adress the problem of consciousness in *Angels Fear* which, however, appeared posthumously in 1987, i.e., five years after the publication of *The Turning Point*.

[71] Cf. Bateson & Bateson, *Angels Fear*, 1.

tion between the two "worlds" of *creatura* and *pleroma* (terms Bateson borrowed from C.G. Jung) which may be described as corresponding roughly to "mind" and "substance"[72]. Capra himself quotes a passage from *Mind and Nature* in which Bateson, in his characteristic style, emphasizes that his work is restricted to the former realm: 'In my life I have put the descriptions of sticks and stones and billiard balls and galaxies in one box ... and have left them alone. In the other box, I put living things: crabs, people, problems of beauty...'[73]. Bateson's theories applied to the *creatura*: the realm of "living things" which is the realm of mind. This would suggest that Bateson's systems view of Mind does not adress the realm of physics *qua* physics. Capra, however, does not seem to have accepted that message.

This much about Bateson's contribution. Biochemist Ilya Prigogine (the winner of a 1977 Nobel prize for his work on the thermodynamics of nonequilibrium systems) will be discussed in section three of this chapter, on evolutionary perspectives. In making use of Prigogine's ideas (mediated to him through Erich Jantsch) Capra found himself on far more familiar ground, and there is no reason to doubt that his presentation is basically correct.

In the *Turning Point*, Capra points out that the new systems view covers all domains of reality (not just physics and mysticism) and that its implementation will therefore lead to a new kind of society.

> The new vision of reality ... is based on awareness of the essential interrelatedness and interdependence of all phenomena—physical, biological, psychological, social, and cultural. It transcends current disciplinary and conceptual boundaries and will be pursued in new institutions. At present there is no well-established framework, either conceptual or institutional, that would accomodate the formulation of the new paradigm, but the outlines of such a framework are already being shaped by many individuals, communities, and networks that are developing new ways of thinking and organizing themselves according to new principles.
> In this situation it would seem that a bootstrap approach, similar to the one that contemporary physics has developed, may be most fruitful. This will mean gradually formulating a network of interlocking concepts and models and, at the same time, developing the corresponding social organizations. None of the theories and models will be any more fundamental than the others, and all of them will have to be mutually consistent. They will go beyond the conventional disciplinary distinctions, using whatever language becomes appropriate to describe different aspects of the multileveled, interrelated fabric of reality. Similarly, none of the new social institutions will be superior to or more important than any of the others, and all of them will have to be aware of one another and communicate and cooperate with one another.[74]

---

[72] See Bateson's fundamental article 'Form, Substance, and Difference', in: *Steps*, 456. Note that it is a simplification to conclude that the "hard sciences" deal with the pleroma and the "sciences of the mind" with the creatura.
[73] UW 76.
[74] TP 265.

Although this account is obviously closely modeled on Chew's bootstrap physics, the latter is now seen as just a special case of the general systems view of life, which is described by Capra as follows:

> The systems view looks at the world in terms of relationships and integration. Systems are integrated wholes whose properties cannot be reduced to those of smaller units. Instead of concentrating on basic building blocks or basic substances, the systems approach emphasizes basic principles of organization.[75]

Although natural systems are the most obvious examples (Capra mentions organisms in general, cells, and the human brain), the same aspects of wholeness are exhibited by social systems (such as anthills, beehives or human families) and by ecosystems. The two basic characteristics of wholeness which were already emphasized in the *Tao of Physics*—interrelatedness and dynamic quality—are equally fundamental to the systems approach:

> All these natural systems are wholes whose specific structures arise from the interactions and interdependence of their parts. ... Systemic properties are destroyed when a system is dissected, either physically or theoretically, into isolated elements. Although we can discern individual parts in any system, the nature of the whole is always different from the mere sum of its parts.
> Another important aspect of systems is their intrinsically dynamic nature. Their forms are not rigid structures but are flexible yet stable manifestations of underlying processes. ... Systems thinking is process thinking; form becomes associated with process, interrelation with interaction, and opposites are unified through oscillation.[76]

Capra relies heavily on the concept of "self-organization" as used by the school of Prigogine and advocated by Erich Jantsch. Although living systems are most clearly exemplified by organisms, some modern cybernetic machines also display organismic properties so that the distinction between machine and organism becomes 'quite subtle'[77]. The real distinction is not between natural organisms and human constructions, but between those systems that display the characteristics of "self-organization" and those that do not. The former, whether organic or not, can be regarded as "living systems"[78]. This is a crucial move which has wide-ranging implications, as we will see. Whether something is *living* or not now depends on whether it satisfies a set of formal criteria for self-organization. The most important of these are the following. 1. While a machine (for instance a clockwork) is an essentially closed system which does not need to interact with the environment in order to function, living systems

---

[75] TP 266.

[76] TP 266-267.

[77] TP 268.

[78] See for instance TP 271 about Prigogine's favorite experiment with certain chemical systems displaying the characteristics of self-organization (the so-called "chemical clocks"). Capra notes that whether or not one regards these chemical reactions as living organisms is 'ultimately, a matter of convention'.

are *open* systems. In order to stay alive they need to maintain a continuous exchange of matter and energy with the environment. 2. This exchange process (metabolism) keeps the system in a permanent state of *nonequilibrium*. Systems in equilibrium, in contrast, are dead systems. 3. Nevertheless, living systems display a high degree of stability. This is not the static kind of stability displayed by systems in equilibrium but, rather, a *dynamic stability*. 4. Living systems are capable of *self-renewal*: they can repair damage, adapt to changing circumstances, and many have even developed a method of "super-repair" in order to deal with death. This, of course, is what we refer to as sexual reproduction in the organic world.

The radical implications of these criteria for the definition of "living systems" become apparent as soon as we realize that, for instance, social organizations such as cities, or abstract systems such as "the economy"[79], must now be regarded as "living". This appears to be quite acceptable to Prigogine, Jantsch, Capra and others thinking along similar lines[80]. Following Capra's association of Prigogine with Bateson, we have to draw an even more radical conclusion: cities, economies etc. are not only living, they also possess "mind".

The crucial step in Capra's development of a systems view of life came when he realized that the Prigoginian criteria for self-organization (life) were extremely similar to Bateson's criteria for Mind, as described in the latter's book *Mind and Nature*[81]. Bateson himself confirmed to Capra that 'Mind is the essence of being alive'[82]. By combining the systems approaches of Prigogine and Bateson, Capra tells us, 'everything fell into place'[83]. Whether or not Capra is right in his conclusion that these two sets of criteria are structurally similar need not concern us here: we are interested in Capra's interpretation of Bateson rather than in Bateson's philosophy as such. Bateson's criteria are extremely formal and abstract and cannot be understood without a comprehensive discussion of his complete philosophy. Significantly, Capra himself makes no attempt to compare both sets of criteria, or to furnish proof for his statement that they are similar or identical[84]. He does not even reproduce or summarize Bateson's criteria, but jumps directly to his conclusion:

Gregory Bateson proposed to define mind as a systems phenomenon characteris-

---

[79] TP 392: 'According to the systems view, an economy, like any living system, will be healthy if it is in a state of dynamic balance ...'.

[80] Cf. OC 196-203; SOU 71-72; BQ 112-115.

[81] Bateson, *Mind and Nature*, ch. 4 'Criteria of Mental Process'. For Capra's description of his discovery, see UW 87-89, 215.

[82] UW 88.

[83] UW 216. Erich Jantsch, who is mentioned by Capra in this connection, is most probably the one who originally proposed this connection. In *The Self-Organizing Universe* he explicitly connects the Prigoginian principle of self-organization with Bateson's concept of Mind (SOU 162-165).

[84] Neither does Jantsch (SOU 162).

tic of living organisms, societies, and ecosystems, and he listed a set of criteria which systems have to satisfy for mind to occur. Any system that satisfies those criteria will be able to process information and develop the phenomena we associate with mind—thinking, learning, memory, for example. In Bateson's view, mind is a necessary and inevitable consequence of a certain complexity which begins long before organisms develop a brain and a higher nervous system.

Bateson's criteria for mind turn out to be closely related to those characteristics of self-organizing systems which I have listed above as the critical differences between machines and living organisms. Indeed, mind is an essential property of living systems[85]. As Bateson said, "Mind is the essence of being alive". From the systems point of view, life is not a substance or a force, and mind is not an entity interacting with matter. Both life and mind are manifestations of the same set of systemic properties, a set of processes that represent the dynamics of self-organization. This new concept will be of tremendous value in our attempts to overcome the Cartesian division. The description of mind as a pattern of organization, or a set of dynamic relationships, is related to the description of matter in modern physics. Mind and matter no longer appear to belong to two fundamentally separate categories, as Descartes believed, but can be seen to represent merely different aspects of the same universal process.[86]

Having included the dimension of Mind in a general systems view of life, Capra has now laid the foundation for a holistic worldview based on "universal interrelatedness", which covers a much wider spectrum of phenomena than the earlier model based on the bootstrap philosophy in physics[87]. The connection between "living" systems, on the one hand, and the whole of reality, on the other, is made with reference to the concept of "stratified order":

> The tendency of living systems to form multileveled structures whose levels differ in their complexity is all-pervasive throughout nature and has to be seen as a basic principle of self-organization. At each level of complexity we encounter systems that are integrated, self-organizing wholes consisting of smaller parts and, at the same time, acting as parts of larger wholes[88].

This notion of "systems within systems" can be extended *at libitum* in the direction of the infinitely small and the infinitely large[89]. Capra emphasizes

---

[85] Note that Capra covers up the essential move from organisms in the normal sense of the word to "living systems" in the Prigoginian sense. In fact, he has discussed the difference between organisms and "classical" (i.e., non-cybernetic) machines on TP 268-269, after which he moves on to a separate discussion of the differences between self-organizing and other systems.

[86] TP 290. Compare these last sentences with my observations about Bateson's distinction between *pleroma* and *creatura*. Capra appears to use Bateson's systems view as a means to unite both domains, which had been kept carefully separated by Bateson himself. Accordingly, Bateson talked about the unification of Mind and Nature, which *both* belong to the order of "living things". Capra, in contrast, speaks of a unification of Mind and *Matter*, which is something completely different.

[87] One is left with the question of whether Capra believes it covers *all* phenomena. Where do non-living systems (for instance, clocks) fit in?

[88] TP 280.

[89] It is interesting to compare this with very similar ideas found in the Ramala messages (RR 28-29, 147-148).

especially Lovelock's "Gaia-hypothesis" according to which the earth itself is to be seen as a living organism, i.e. as a living system containing smaller living systems. But, of course, there is no reason to stop at that level, and Capra indeed takes the systems holism of universal interrelatedness to its logical conclusion:

> In the stratified order of nature, individual human minds are embedded in the larger minds of social and ecological systems, and these are integrated into the planetary mental system—the mind of Gaia— which in turn must participate in some kind of universal or cosmic mind. The conceptual framework of the new systems approach is in no way restricted by associating this cosmic mind with the traditional idea of God. In the words of Jantsch, "God is not the creator, but the mind of the universe". In this view the deity is, of course, neither male nor female, nor manifest in any personal form, but represents nothing less than the self-organizing dynamics of the entire cosmos[90].

There is no compelling reason to object to the labeling of this theology as "pantheistic" in the full monistic sense of the word, as long as it is fully realized that Mind (God) is *not* seen as a "substance" but as an abstract pattern of relationship. This, at least, was Bateson's view[91]. Whether Capra does full justice to the latter remains doubtful. Notice that, in any case, there is no suggestion that God is conceived as an "ultimate source" of reality. God is completely immanent in the universe: he is its very dynamics of self-organization or, in Bateson's terms, "the pattern that connects".

The Holographic Paradigm
Perhaps the most widespread New Age vision of the nature of reality is inspired by a technique called holography. The hologram is regarded as a perfect model for understanding the nature of reality and the role of consciousness in perceiving that reality. Holography is originally a technique for making three-dimensional representations of objects. Laserlight is reflected onto a photographic plate from two sources: one source consists of light reflected directly by the object itself, the other consists of light reflected from the object to the plate by way of a mirror. The interference of these two beams on the photographic plate produces a pattern of apparently meaningless swirls, the so-called "holographic blur". This blur has no similarity whatsoever to the object. However, when a laser beam is shined through this photographic film, a three-

---

[90] TP 292. Bateson himself similarly associates the universal Mind with "God" ('Form, Substance, and Difference', 461).

[91] There is reason to suspect that Capra blurs the distinction between traditional panpsychism and Bateson's system view. At the end of the chapter, Teilhard de Chardin is presented as in essential accord with Capra's systems view (TP 304). Bateson, however, expressly objected to an interpretation of his philosophy as a Teilhardian panpsychism which even ascribes a mental character or potentiality to atoms. Bateson, in contrast, saw the mental as 'a function only of complex *relationship*' ('Comment on part V', 465 footnote).

dimensional image of the original object appears behind it. This technique has two characteristics which have fired the imagination of New Age scientists and New Age believers generally. Firstly, holography suggests that it is possible to convert objects into frequency patterns, and frequency patterns back into objects[92]. The object is implicitly present in the seemingly chaotic frequency pattern. The latter apparently possesses a hidden order which can be regarded as the "deep structure" underlying the object in its manifested form. Secondly, there is not a simple one-to-one relationship between the object and the blur, so that each part of the blur would contain the information needed to reconstitute the corresponding part of the object. Instead, if the film is cut into pieces *each* fragment appears to contain all the information needed to reconstitute the *complete* object (although the smaller the fragment, the vaguer the image). In other words: the whole is present in each of the parts. This property of the hologram is difficult to reconcile with commonsense assumptions about the continuum of absolute space associated with the Cartesian/Newtonian worldview. It does, however, evoke associations with ancient prescientific and/or mystical worldviews[93]. The most famous example in New Age circles, which is quoted or referred to throughout its literature, is the Buddhist *Avatamsaka Sutra*:

> In the heaven of Indra, there is said to be a network of pearls, so arranged that if you look at one you see all the others reflected in it. In the same way each object in the world is not merely itself but involves every other object and in fact *is* everything else. 'In every particle of dust, there are present Buddhas without number'[94].

The parallellist implication is clear: modern science has apparently rediscovered a truth which was already known to the ancient mystics[95].
According to defenders of the so-called holographic paradigm, reality is structured on holographic principles (or at least according to principles for which

---

[92] Of course, it is only an illusionary *image* of a real object that is reconstituted. This aspect, as we will see, tends to be ignored by adherents of the holographic paradigm.

[93] The traditional view of the macrocosmos reflected in the microcosmos is mentioned remarkably seldom in connection with the holographic paradigm. Leibniz's monadology, in contrast, is mentioned several times (WIO 207; HP:euu 91; HP:npr 13; PH 188; ToP 329-330). The last passage recalls a suggestion by Joseph Needham that Leibniz may actually have been influenced by the *Avatamsaka Sutra* (see text).

[94] This is the fragment as rendered by Capra in ToP 328, from C. Eliot, *Japanese Buddhism*, 109-110. Ferguson (AC 202) leaves out the last sentence and misquotes the end of the preceding one ('everything else') as 'in every other object'. Jean Houston (PH 188) gives a wildly imaginative version which she presents as her own translation. Other sources in which the same fragment is referred to or quoted include HU 290-291, RW 137, HP:cr 25.

[95] Reading the fascinating introductory essays to the German translation of the Avatamsaka Sutra, Doi, *Kegon Sutra*, which emphasize the "philosophy of interpenetration" as the central theme of the Sutra, it is almost impossible not to be impressed by the force of the similarities. The quotation about Indra's heaven is certainly representative of its context.

the hologram furnishes a striking model). The paradigm is formulated with reference to the theories developed in their respective fields by the neuroscientist Karl Pribram and the theoretical physicist David Bohm.

Karl Pribram is regarded as one of the leading authorities in his field. Although most of his work is highly technical and deals with localized brain functions, his popularity in New Age circles rests on his theory that the brain stores memory according to holographic principles. This means that each memory fragment is distributed over the whole of the brain so that each part of the brain, reversely, contains the information of the whole. Moreover, a similar principle is said to be at work in the way the visual centers process information. Pribram's conviction that the brain works by holographic principles is not just based upon superficial analogies. The inventor of holography, Dennis Gabor, used a type of mathematical calculus known as Fourier transforms, and the brain seems to be using these same Fourier transforms to analyze frequencies and convert them into visual images[96]. To Pribram, this similarity suggested that perceived reality might be of an order similar to the holographic image: an ultimately illusionary spectre created by the brain out of a domain of pure frequency. This is how Marilyn Ferguson presents Pribram's "holographic supertheory" in her influential *Aquarian Conspiracy*: '...our brains mathematically construct 'hard' reality by interpreting frequencies from a dimension transcending time and space. The brain is a hologram, interpreting a holographic universe'[97]. Michael Talbot formulates the same idea even more provocatively:

> The question that began to bother [Pribram] was, if the picture of reality in our brains is not a picture at all but a hologram, what is it a hologram of? ... Which is the true reality, the seemingly objective world experienced by the observer/photographer or the blur of interference patterns recorded by the camera/brain? Pribram realized that if the holographic brain model was taken to its logical conclusions, it opened the door on the possibility that objective reality—the world of coffee cups, mountain vistas, elm trees, and table lamps—might not even exist, or at least not exist in the way we believe it exists. Was it possible, he wondered, that what the mystics had been saying for centuries was true, reality was *maya*, an illusion, and what was out there was really a vast, resonating symphony of wave forms, a "frequency domain" that was transformed into the world as we know it only *after* it entered our senses?[98]

---

[96] HU 27-28.

[97] AC 198.

[98] HU 31. Nobody seems to notice, rather surprisingly, that the holographic model "if taken to its logical conclusions" does *not* imply that the holographic blur is the "true" reality. The true reality in actual holography is the original object. This object is transformed into frequencies, and these frequencies are then re-converted into an illusionary image. Surely the model taken to its logical conclusion would imply that our reality is an image of another, essentially similar although more "true" reality. The frequency domain would then function only as a medium of

For the New Age audience, to pose the question is to answer it. Again we
encounter the picture of the world as an illusion, but again without the traditional corollary of ascetic otherworldliness. The frequency domain is often
associated directly with unitive reality as experienced in mystical states (an
association which again evokes the suspicion of reductionism[99]). However, the
typical conclusion drawn by New Age thinkers is that as human beings our
goal is not to take permanent residence in that amorphous realm, but that the
"wholeness" of that realm should be the guiding model and inspiration for living our lives in everyday reality. Our world is described as fragmented and
broken, and therefore "out of phase" with the wholeness in which it is ultimately grounded. Our goal must be to restore the world to wholeness. This
recurring theme evokes the obvious question how one is to picture a world that
exhibits the complete "wholeness" reigning in the frequency domain, and yet
can be distinguished from the latter. One person fully convinced of the possibility of such a world is the other major thinker associated with the holographic
paradigm, David Bohm.

Bohm has been elaborating his theory of the implicate order for several
decades[100], and at his death in 1993 his philosophy of nature still remained
very much a "work in progress". It must be said from the outset that, in the
present context, it will be impossible to do justice to the subtleties of Bohm's
work and the development of his views over the years. While his colleagues
in physics have largely reacted to his philosophical and spiritual excursions
with suspicion and ridicule, Bohm has been recognized as an important and
original thinker by philosophers and theologians interested in science and society. This has provoked a flood of commentaries and discussions, only a part
of which can be associated with the New Age movement[101]. In this study, I
have to restrict myself to a quite general characterization of Bohm's main ideas.
   Bohm's philosophical work can be characterized as a result of the convergence of two very different systems of thought. Firstly, there is Bohm's work
in theoretical physics which, from the very beginning, appears to have been
inspired by an underlying intuition of the wholeness of the universe[102]. Since
his youth, Bohm never accepted the distinction between natural science and

---

translation between both realities. If the New Age interpretation were correct we would be forced,
in the case of actual holograms, to regard both the image *and* its original as equally illusionary.
This demonstrates that the holographic worldview is not actually derived from holography; rather,
the latter is used as a convenient argument to defend an already existing intuition.
   [99] Pribram himself, making no distinction between the paranormal and mysticism, seems to
endorse the view that the implicate order (see below) 'has ... apparently been explored experientially by mystics, psychics and others delving into paranormal phenomena' (HP:f 34).
   [100] For Bohm's development, see Temple, 'David Bohm'; Bohm, 'Hidden Variables'.
   [101] See the literature quoted in chapter three, under Bohm.
   [102] SOC 3.

philosophy of nature, and it seems that his early physical theories already anticipated what was later to become the philosophy of the implicate order[103]. Secondly, there is his fascination with the Indian thinker Jiddu Krishnamurti. Bohm discovered Krishnamurti's work in 1959, and met him in person in 1961[104]. Their discussions, which have been recorded on videotape and published in book-form, give important sidelights on Bohm's philosophical work[105]. The acquaintance with Krishnamurti seems to have stimulated Bohm to explore connections between his physical theories and larger question of human nature and culture[106]. Ever since, his governing theme has been the problem of "Fragmentation and wholeness", as formulated in his most important book:

> The title of this chapter is 'Fragmentation and wholeness'. It is especially important to consider this question today, for fragmentation is now very widespread, not only throughout society, but also in each individual; and this is leading to a kind of general confusion of the mind, which creates an endless series of problems and interferes with our clarity of perception so seriously as to prevent us from being able to solve most of them[107].

> What I am proposing here is that man's general way of thinking of the totality, i.e. his general world view, is crucial for overall order of the human mind itself. If he thinks of the totality as constituted of independent fragments, then that is how his mind will tend to operate, but if he can include everything coherently and harmoniously in an overall whole that is undivided, unbroken, and without a border (for every border is a division or break) then his mind will tend to move in a similar way, and from this will flow an orderly action within the whole.[108]

Bohm believes that fragmentation in society results from an incorrect way of thinking, which is out of touch with the wholeness of existence. In order to restore wholeness to the world, humanity must learn to think in a completely new way. This need for a radical restructuring of the mind is the central theme of Krishnamurti. As a physicist, Bohm's special interest is in developing a philosophical view of reality—a *Naturphilosophie*—which both legitimates *and* reflects radical holistic thinking. A comprehensive worldview which legitimates holistic thinking by providing it with a solid conceptual framework is necessary as an alternative to the mechanistic worldview based on classical physics. Bohm repeatedly expresses his amazement at the fact that his colleagues are able to continue thinking in terms of a mechanistic and reduc-

---

[103] Bohm, 'Hidden Variables', 113; SOC 3: 'I was never able to see any inherent separation between science and philosophy. Indeed, in earlier times, science was called *natural philosophy* and this corresponded perfectly with the way I saw the whole field'.

[104] Temple, 'David Bohm', 363.

[105] Krishnamurti & Bohm, *Ending of Time*; id., *Future of Humanity*.

[106] Bohm's ventures beyond physics started with two essays written in 1968 (Temple, 'David Bohm', 363-364) which deal, interestingly, with creativity and art.

[107] WIO 1. Readers familiar with Krishnamurti's work will immediately recognize the influence of the latter's characteristic style.

[108] WIO xi.

tionistic worldview, even though this worldview is explicitly falsified by the very theories they professionally know to be correct[109]. A new holistic "paradigm" or worldview is needed to replace the outdated fragmentary one. In contrast to some other holistic thinkers, however, Bohm is acutely aware that the world will not be restored to wholeness if we simply replace one theory for another. A theory can only succesfully legitimate holistic thinking, and promote wholeness in society, if its very nature reflects a consistently holistic outlook and if that nature is correctly understood by those who use it. Now, even the most holistic theory necessarily introduces distinctions (conceptual, terminological, etc.). If we see these as reflecting reality as it "really" is, then we are in fact affirming that fragmentation is real. Therefore, the only consistently holistic way of looking at theories is to consider them not as descriptions of reality but as transitory "forms of insight" into a reality which transcends any explicit theory.

> ... a theory is primarily a form of *insight*, i.e. a way of looking at the world, and not a form of *knowledge* of how the world is. ... all theories are insights, which are neither true nor false but, rather, clear in certain domains, and unclear when extended beyond those domains. ... So, instead of supposing that older theories are falsified at a certain point in time, we merely say that man is continually developing new forms of insight, which are clear up to a point and then tend to become unclear. In this activity, there is evidently no reason to suppose that there is or will be a final form of insight (corresponding to absolute truth) or even a steady series of approximations to this. Rather, in the nature of the case, one may expect the unending development of new forms of insight (which will, however, assimilate certain key features of the older forms as simplifications, in the way that relativity theory does with Newtonian theory).[110]

If theories are merely forms of insight, the validity of which rests on the extent to which they "clarify" reality, then we cannot simply point to the "facts" for confirmation of how reality is. Rather, 'the factual knowledge that we obtain will evidently be shaped and formed by our theories'[111]. Bohm regards it as a crucial mistake to 'confuse the forms and shapes induced in our perceptions by theoretical insight with a reality independent of our thought and our way of looking'[112]. Pointing to the "fact" of fragmentation in the world, therefore, does not disprove the axiom of the wholeness of reality:

> ...some might say: 'Fragmentation of cities, religions, political systems, conflict in the form of wars, general violence, fratricide, etc., are the reality. Wholeness is an ideal, toward which we should perhaps strive.' But this is not what is being said here. Rather, what should be said is that wholeness is what is real, and that fragmentation is the response of this whole to man's action, guided by illusory

---

[109] For instance HP:euu 53-54.
[110] WIO 4-5.
[111] WIO 5.
[112] WIO 6.

perception, which is shaped by fragmentary thought. In other words, it is just because reality is whole that man, with his fragmentary approach, will inevitably be answered with a corresponding fragmentary response. So what is needed is for man to give attention to his habit of fragmentary thought, to be aware of it, and thus bring it to an end. Man's approach to reality may then be whole, and so the response will be whole. For this to happen, however, it is crucial that man be aware of the activity of his thought *as such*; i.e. as a form of insight, a way of looking, rather than as a 'true copy of reality as it is'.[113]

This is important for a correct understanding of Bohm's theory of the implicate order. The theory is based on the *a priori* assumption of the wholeness of reality. This assumption is regarded as justified for at least two reasons. Firstly, the two competing "big theories" in modern physics (relativity and quantum mechanics), are said to share, each in their own manner, a rejection of the "fragmenting" tendencies implicit in Newtonian physics and a corresponding tendency toward wholeness[114]. Secondly, the assumption that reality is fragmented and that therefore fragmentation is "natural" is perceived as having negative consequences in society, while the assumption that reality is whole is expected to have a healthy influence. Bohm's theory is, moreover, to be understood not as a fixed doctrine but as a form of "insight" that tries to attain a clearer perspective on the relation between the "nonmanifest" realm of subatomic reality, on the one hand, and the "manifest" realm of our macroscopic world, on the other. Bohm's constant revisions and refinements of the theory should therefore be seen as attempts to attain progressively clearer levels of "insight". Bohm evidently did not foresee an end to this process. He did claim, however, that his theories were at least a great deal more adequate than those still based on Newtonian presuppositions, and that their general acceptance would stimulate a movement towards wholeness in society. Finally, it may be added that Bohm's philosophy of nature has its direct counterpart in his strictly physical theory known as the "causal interpretation of quantum theory" which includes a theory of so-called "hidden variables"[115].

According to Bohm, the key feature of holography, which makes it a useful analogy to his theory of the implicate order, is the remarkable fact that the form and structure of the orginal object are *enfolded* within each region of the photographic record, and can in turn be *unfolded* from each region. Bohm's proposal is that a new kind of order is involved here: one which is strongly different from the mechanical order. This is the implicate order:

---

[113] WIO 7. The statement that man can be "aware" of the fragmentary nature of his thought and thus "bring it to an end" is again typical Krishnamurtian jargon.

[114] WIO 172-176.

[115] See WIO chapter 4, which is technical and, because of the frequent use of formulae, inaccessible to the lay reader. Cf mmc 140-141 about the different reactions of scientists to the philosophical exposition of the implicate order theory, on the one hand, and the scientific one, on the other.

In terms of the implicate order one may say that everything is enfolded into every-thing. This contrasts with the explicate order now dominant in physics in which things are *unfolded* in the sense that each thing lies only in its own particular region of space (and time) and outside the regions belonging to other things.[116]

The limitation of the holographic analogy lies in the fact that a hologram is static. Reality is dynamic, and Bohm therefore refers to his concept of "ulti-mate reality" as the *holomovement* (or, sometimes, as the "flux"):

> Our basic proposal [is] that *what is* is the holomovement, and that everything is to be explained in terms of forms derived from this holomovement. Though the full set of laws governing its totality is unknown (and, indeed, probably unknow-able) nevertheless these laws are assumed to be such that from them may be abstracted relatively autonomous or independent sub-totalities of movement (e.g., fields, particles, etc.) having a certain recurrence and stability of their basic pat-terns of order and measure. Such sub-totalities may then be investigated, each in its own right, without our having first to know the full laws of the holomovement. This implies, of course, that we are not to regard what we find in such investi-gations as having an absolute and final validity, but rather we have always to be ready to discover the limits of independence of any relatively autonomous struc-ture of law, and from this to go on to look for new laws that may refer to yet larg-er relatively autonomous domains of this kind.[117]

It appears contradictory to speak of the holomovement as containing "parts". If each part contains the whole, a distinction between parts and whole becomes logically impossible. This holomovement, which is obviously of a dimension-ality inconceivable to us (at least at present, and probably in principle[118]), con-tains the whole of our reality in "enfolded" (implicit) form. The domain of experience investigated by classical (mechanistic) physics is a particular sub-totality "unfolded" (explicated) from this whole. Thus, we get the fundamen-tal picture of an *implicate order* (a frequency domain in the holomovement) from which is unfolded an *explicate order* (our world[119]). The mechanistic fal-lacy consists in the assumption that this explicate order, which consists of sep-arate and independently existing interacting entities, is the basic reality. Mech-anistic science starts with the parts and tries to explain wholes in terms of these parts and their interactions. Scientific research in terms of the implicate order, in contrast, begins with the undivided wholeness of the universe and defines its task as deriving parts through abstraction from the whole[120]. Newtonian

---

[116] WIO 177.

[117] WIO 178.

[118] Cf. WIO 189: the dimensionality of the holomovement is 'effectively infinite'.

[119] Our world may be no more than a comparatively insignificant pattern of excitation with-in an immense sea of energy. Bohm repeatedly refers to the Big Bang as no more than a 'little ripple' (cf. WIO 192).

[120] WIO 179. An electron, for instance, must be understood through 'a total set of enfolded ensembles, which are generally not localized in space. At any given moment one of these may be unfolded and therefore localized, but in the next moment, this one enfolds to be replaced by

physics remains roughly appropriate for dealing with the explicate order, but its limitations are now clearly defined. The laws of the holomovement (referred to as *holonomy*) which, among other things, provide for the relative stability of the explicate order, are not mechanical. Rather, they 'will be in a first approximation those of the quantum theory, while more accurately they will go beyond even these, in ways that are at present only vaguely discernible'[121]. The process of unfoldment of our world from the implicate order apparently takes place not in a random or chaotic but in an orderly fashion, resulting as it does in the relative stability and permanence of explicate reality. There must be a force of necessity behind this process, but the laws defining this necessity are unknown to us.

> An understanding of its origin would take us to a deeper, more comprehensive and more inward level of relative autonomy which, however, would also have its implicate and explicate orders and a correspondingly deeper and more inward force of necessity that would bring about their transformation into each other[122].

However, following the publication of *Wholeness and the Implicate Order,* Bohm has not been able to resist the temptation to explore the logical possibility that the implicate order is itself organized by a deeper order which, in turn, is organized by an even deeper one, and so on *ad infinitum*. In Bohm's later work, the comparative simplicity and elegance of the original implicate/explicate scheme is progressively obscured by a proliferation of additional orders: the super-implicate, super super-implicate and so on[123]. The situation becomes even more complicated by the introduction, in *Science, Order, and Creativity*, of the not very clear concept of a "generative order", which appears to have resulted from the attempt to account for the domains of art and creativity[124]. The details of these later developments are of minor concern here. The New Age audience has retained not much more from it than the general picture of "infinite dimensions".

More important are Bohm's views about the possibility of an ultimate order or ground of being which might be associated with "God". Bohm repeatedly alludes to an ultimate "ground" beyond the holomovement, from which spring both matter and mind, and which he associates with absolute "intelligence". This notion of intelligence is derived from Krishnamurti and, like the latter, Bohm is extremely cautious about associating it with God. An example of this is the following fragment from an interview with Renée Weber:

---

the one that follows. The notion of continuity of existence is approximated by that of very rapid recurrence of similar forms, changing in a simple and regular way ... Of course, more fundamentally, the particle is only an abstraction that is manifest to our senses' (WIO 183).

[121] WIO 181.
[122] WIO 195-196.
[123] Cf. isio 33; SOC 182-184.
[124] SOC 151ff.

We're not saying that any of this is another word for God. I would put it another way: people had insight in the past about a form of intelligence that had organized the universe and they personalized it and called it God. A similar insight can prevail today without personalizing it and without calling it a personal God.
WEBER: Still, it's a kind of super-intelligence and you've said elsewhere that that is benevolent and compassionate, not neutral.
BOHM: Well, we can propose that.[125]

Although Bohm seems a bit embarrassed about Weber's reminder, it is true that the description of the ultimate Ground as a compassionate intelligence appears repeatedly in his later work, as for instance in this passage: 'When I see the immense order of the universe (and especially the brain of man), I cannot escape feeling that this ground enfolds a supreme intelligence. Although it is not quite so evident, I would say also that this intelligence is permeated with compassion and love'[126]. Bohm is aware that this belief (which emerged from his discussions with Krishnamurti) cannot be justified on physical or even philosophical grounds. However, as it became increasingly clear during the 1980s that the scientific community was not prepared to take his philosophy of nature seriously anyway, one gets the impression that Bohm has come to care less about justifying to the skeptics.

The combination of Pribram's and Bohm's holographic theories leads to the picture of a universe in which the whole is "implicated" in each part, and which is interpreted by a brain functionally modeled on that same universe. The basic reality is pictured as a non-localized "frequency domain" characterized by unbroken, dynamic wholeness. Reality as we perceive it is "read out" of this domain by our brains (Pribram) or "unfolds" from it on the basis of unknown holonomic laws. Beyond even the holomovement may be an ultimate "ground" characterized by intelligence, compassion and love. It might be argued that the picture of many "orders" unfolding from an ultimate "Ground" is closer to "Ultimate Source Holism" than to "Universal Interrelatedness". However, Bohm claims that his series of "orders" represents levels of abstractions instead of a hierarchy with levels of graded ontological status[127]. Bohm's orders are not higher or lower, but merely different. The quality of the "Ground" permeates all being, although most people are unaware of it. It is not an Ultimate Reality beyond our world, but should rather be seen as a "state of mind" accessible in *this* world. Bohm claims that such an awareness of the Ground is not a privileged kind of "mystical" experience, but rather a state of being "open"

---

[125] isio 39-40.

[126] Bohm, 'Hidden Variables', 124. Cf. UM 148-149.

[127] HP:pm 191-194. In spite of Bohm's rejection of hierarchical schemes, his introduction of an ultimate Ground produces a sufficient amount of ambivalence to permit his follower F. David Peat to describe Bohm's Ground entirely as a "generative source" (see S 185-213: ch. 'The Creative Source'). Peat speaks of a 'limitless series of levels' (S 187), but also accepts the idea of an "order of orders", beyond which is the Ground (S 188).

to the real depth of *ordinary* reality[128]. In the context of Bohm's (and Krishnamurti's) philosophy, such a state of "awareness" is not a merely subjective experience, but a state in which one is receptive to the objective reality of the Ground. A further problem is the relation between the brain's process of "constructing reality" out of the frequency domain (Pribram) and the physical process of "unfoldment" out of the holomovement (Bohm). Are these two ultimately one? Pribram's view, as we saw, clearly implies that the world is "maya"; reading Bohm's work, however, one is not quite sure.

As is usual with the popular reception of philosophical worldviews, the conceptual complications of the holographic paradigm hardly bother the larger New Age audience. While intellectuals like Pribram, Bohm and others were still grappling with the logical implications of their ideas, the New Age population had already taken possession of them. To Marilyn Ferguson, the holographic paradigm heralds the end of the alienation occasioned by the Cartesian split: 'we are indeed participants in reality, observers who affect what we observe'[129]. Like Michael Talbot, she is particularly interested in the holographic paradigm as legitimating the paranormal. Matthew Fox incorporates the holographic theory into an enthusiastic vision of cosmic spirituality culminating in the assertion that 'to explore the cosmos is to explore God'[130]. Jean Houston asserts that 'If the hologrammatic-Buddhist-monadic-Cabalistic theory[131] is true, then you are literally ubiquitous throughout the universe and are being sent out as an interference pattern through the flow emulsion of the ether ... to all possible places in the matrix of space-time'[132]. To Chris Griscom, the holographic paradigm means the collapse of the three-dimensional spacetime continuum, and of all the conventional distinctions associated with it (such as subjective-objective, mind-matter, inner-outer, man-God, past-future). Griscom's enthusiastic combination of the holographic perspective with Seth's teachings about a multidimensional reality is typical for New Age perspectives[133]:

> The major transformation of reality comes from the realization of our intrinsic participation in all that is. When we experience the power of synergistic relationships in which energy (thoughts, emotions, patterned pulsations) translates

[128] HP:pm 196, 198. It is interesting to compare this with Capra's discussions with R.D. Laing. Capra tends to put mystical experience in a class apart, while Laing defends a view more like Krishnamurti (UW 142-143).
[129] AC 198.
[130] OB 69-70.
[131] Note that the worldviews of the holographic paradigm, the Avatamsaka Sutra, Leibniz's monadology, and also Jorge Luis Borges's story about the Cabalistic symbol of the "Aleph", are all regarded as synonymous.
[132] PH 190.
[133] Some other examples: PR 193-194; DL 310; GW 311; ECMM 270-273; RW 118-119.

into matter—crystallizations that create the actual experience of form (health, disease, catastrophe, ecstasy)—the true hologram begins to emerge.[134]

The reality of the multidimensional self is manifested through the hologram. We do not "reach" the hologram; we *are* the hologram. What happens is that we become fixated at different spots on the hologram, and we lose our understanding that there's something across the circle. We have no idea that we're connected to something across the circle, just as we have no idea that we can pull a string and tap the unconscious. We don't realize that we are in a fluid medium. We might call that the body, the universe; let us learn to call that the hologram. In the hologram, we can recognize that we are here right now, and yet we have also lived many lives. We can experience and access the energy of those lifetimes, and that's the experiential aspect of the hologram. It is what the hologram really represents to us. It is not something out there to be tamed; it is simply that the more we become conscious of the hologram, the more we become God. ... We can understand the connection to the God force, rather than having that perception, that concept that God is separate out there, or that anything else out there is separate. At the Institute [the Light Institute in Galisteo], we create a threshold for people to begin accessing the hologram, to recognize that anything they see or experience is part of themselves.[135]

Finally, it must be noted that the holographic model clearly has its own "metaphysical pathos". This particular kind seems extremely similar to the metaphysical pathos responsible for the appeal of science fiction literature, as may be illustrated by the following burst of enthusiasm:

The self is a meeting place of eternity and time, the holographic mind in the evolutionary body. Each nervous system tells the story of Bethlehem. The encoded information of the cosmos is incarnate in every historical body. A human being is a gateway to the beyond. When the question of self is placed in the context of the mystical-scientific view of the cosmic-evolutionary self the vistas and possible adventures of self-love are staggering. How much can we learn from ourselves? How much of the encoded information that resides in our bodies and minds can be recovered and brought into awareness? What can we know of happenings in distant galaxies and of animal wisdom by tuning into our own nervous systems? Can we slip out of the prison of time and space and travel into the beyond which is the source from which all things flow? Can we travel backwards and forwards in time? Once we see that the self is not merely a captive to the phenomenal world, not a mere prisoner of this time and space, of this body, the possibilities become endless. The adventure of self-knowledge takes us to the edges of every unknown.
How far can we travel? Who knows. We are at the beginning of a new age of discovery. The marriage of science and mysticism will open new possibilities and release potentialities we can scarcely imagine.[136]

Having discussed the holographic paradigm, I briefly call attention to the ambivalent position of Seth's worldview. Chris Griscom, as we saw, appears to

---

[134] TI 211.
[135] ENF 148-149.
[136] HP:cht 117-118 (Sam Keen, 'Self-Love and the Cosmic Connection').

have no difficulty combining Seth's metaphysics, discussed in the context of "Ultimate Source Holism", with the holographic paradigm which is an example of "Universal Interconnectedness". Indeed, it may be argued that Seth has managed to accomplish a convergence of both types: although everything springs from an ultimate creative Source, it is equally true that *every* single consciousness is actually the creative source responsible for its own realities. This view will be discussed in more detail below. At this point I only call attention to the similarities between Seth's multidimensional holism and the holographic paradigm. Reality "as it really is" exists, according to Seth, outside time and space. It must therefore be pictured as a radical singularity containing the potential for all creation. All realities in all dimensions are relatively illusionary creations "read out" of this singularity, which seems similar to the holographic frequency domain. Each single human mind is the central *locus* or center of this process of reality-creation, and therefore its very own center of the universe, so to speak. This image evokes the familiar catchphrase that the human brain is "a hologram interpreting a holographic universe", and indeed each mind must on these premises be pictured as containing all the information of the whole. Taking Seth's vision to its logical conclusion, Chris Griscom and many other "holographic" New Age thinkers ultimately go beyond Seth in discarding the concept of an ultimate, creative "God" source altogether and making each individual mind the center of the universe:

> There is, within all that movement of the eternal pulsation with all the ever-changing, ever-creating patterns that are going on, a center. Our multidimensional soul has that center; it is enlightenment. What we mean by enlightenment is our capacity to receive, to see the latticework. Just as everything about us is interwoven in all of these interdimensional realities, the center of the latticework is multidimensional and it's integral[137].

This center or source is often called "God" in Griscom's books; but, rather than meaning that we all participate in or spring from one ultimate divine force, she seems to mean that we *are* that source in a far more literal way. *We* create the universe. It is true that, if we fully realize that, we also see that "we" are all one; but this "one source" (of divine energy, etc.) seems to have no independent ontological reality, let alone authority. Although Griscom often uses words like "God" or "divine", God in any traditional sense (as a reality which is somehow greater than man, and transcends or precedes man) is strangely absent in her writings. It is only man himself (and the world) that is greater than he himself normally realizes. Seth's metaphysics was an example of a multidimensional universe governed by "universal interconnectedness", but which still sprang from an ultimate creative source. When that Source is discarded by later writers, only radical holographic interconnectedness remains.

---

[137] ENF 74.

C. Other Meanings of Holism

As noted earlier, "Ultimate Source Holism" and "Universal Interrelatedness" are by far the most important types of New Age holism. Two other varieties may be discussed more briefly.

There exists a rather pronounced tendency in New Age thinking to describe the holistic nature of reality in terms of a dynamic harmony of opposites. Dualistic conceptions based upon the opposition of separate, mutually exclusive opposites are replaced by the concept of a creative tension between complementary poles which together constitute a dynamic whole. The principle of complementarity is asserted to be at work on all levels of reality. It provides the foundation for both explaining the workings of nature and a nondualistic ethics (to which more attention will be given in chapter ten). Janet and Stewart Farrar express the idea very clearly:

> The Theory of Polarity maintains that all activity, all manifestation, arises from (and is inconceivable without) the interaction of pairs and complementary opposites—positive and negative, light and dark, content and form, male and female, and so on; and that this polarity is not a conflict between 'good' and 'evil', but a creative tension like that between the positive and negative terminals of an electric battery. Good and evil only arise with the constructive or destructive *application* of that polarity's output (again, as with the uses to which a battery may be put).[138]

Fritjof Capra maintains that his systems view of reality is in fundamental accord with the yin-yang polarity expounded by the *I Ching*. Capra, like the Farrars, sees the male-female distinction as a prominent example[139]. However, he warns against a "patriarchal" interpretation according to which yang/masculine is pictured as active and yin/feminine as passive. According to Capra, ancient Chinese thought did not entertain the idea of passivity as understood by us. Both the masculine and the feminine pole are active, but yin corresponds to 'responsive, consolidating, cooperative activity', and yang to 'aggressive, expanding, competitive activity. Yin action is conscious of the environment, yang action is conscious of the self.'[140] Capra further associates these with two 'kinds of knowledge, or two modes of consciousness'[141]: the intuitive and the rational. In all cases, the point is that a destructive imbalance occurs when we choose

---

[138] WW 107. Cf. DL 246-247.

[139] Cf. also Shakti Gawain: RG 3ff.

[140] TP 38.

[141] TP 38. Cf. the table of opposites on this page: Yin: feminine, contractive, conservative, responsive, cooperative, intuitive, synthesizing; Yang: masculine, expansive, demanding, aggressive, competitive, rational, analytic. Later in his book (TP 293) Capra mentions the well-known theory of the two brain hemispheres, which is extremely popular in the New Age movement and will be discussed in chapter eight, section 2B.

to concentrate on only one pole to the exclusion of the other. Healthy, natural states of being are the result of a creative tension between both poles, which hold each other in balance. Domination by only one pole produces static and rigid results, while the interaction between both poles leads to systems characterized by dynamic flexibility. The former constellation ultimately means death, the latter life. It is held that this principle applies to all aspects of reality: to the cosmos as a whole, as well as to ecology or individual health.

Like all other kinds of holism, this theory of polarity or complementarity is proposed as an alternative to dualism. Although "polarity-holism" has many dimensions, the association of the two poles with masculine and feminine appears to be particularly strong in the minds of New Age adherents. In terms of Jungian psychology (*animus* and *anima*), men are encouraged to discover their feminine, and women their masculine side; the goal is to achieve a healthy balance. It is a common New Age assumption that the dominant culture leads both men and women to repress and alienate their nondominant sexual pole, in order to conform to the sexual stereotypes of a dualistic society. The ideal of the "whole" person, on this premise, implies the harmonious integration of both poles. On the other hand, there also exists a rather different New Age tendency of emphasizing the need for women to rediscover their authentic femininity, and this has been followed somewhat later by a corresponding search among men[142]. Here, the premise is that the one-sided patriarchal orientation of western society (which is built on dualistic assumptions itself) has had negative effects on popular ideas of what is a "real" woman or a "real" man. Women are expected to be either submissive and supportive of male expectations or, more recently, to cultivate an attitude of aggressive assertiveness and independence which is itself modeled on masculine models. They are not encouraged to discover their authentically feminine "power" in their own terms. Men, in turn, are expected to conform to onesided "macho" stereotypes of masculinity, which are equally constricting. If the problem of dualism and patriarchy is approached from this angle, men and women, rather than cultivating their latent sexual polarity and striving for harmonious integration, should discover the real meaning of their dominant sex. While the former perspective logically tends towards the androgyne, the latter would produce "strong" women who experience their femininity as power instead of weakness, and men who do not need macho behavior to feel secure in their masculinity. We may summarize the distinction by saying that the first type asserts that holistic complementarity must be realized "within" each human being, while the second tries to realize it in society. The first view is most characteristic for what might be called "mainstream" New Age (i.e., the kind of approach exemplified most

---

[142] Kelley, 'An Update', 149.

typically by Shirley MacLaine[143]); the second is mainly found in the domain of women's spirituality (and its complementary offspring, men's spirituality) and neopaganism.

In the latter case, there is a direct connection with wider neopagan views of reality. *Wicca* is basically a fertility religion based upon a worldview constituted by sexual polarities. They are exemplified in particular by the female Goddess and her male partner, the Horned God. Neopagans in general tend to think of the universe as polarized between masculine and feminine energies, as exemplified by the above quotation from Janet and Stewart Farrar or the following from Starhawk:

> The view of the All as an energy field polarized by two great forces, Female and Male, Goddess and God, which in their ultimate being are aspects of each other, is common to almost all traditions of the Craft. ... The Male and Female forces represent difference, yet they are not different, in essence: They are the same force flowing in opposite, but not opposed, directions. ... Each principle contains the other: Life breeds on death, feeds on death; death sustains life, makes possible evolution and new creation. They are part of a cycle, each dependent on the other.
> Existence is sustained by the on-off pulse, the alternating current of the two forces in perfect balance. Unchecked, the life force is cancer; unbridled, the death force is war and genocide. Together, they hold each other in the harmony that sustains life, in the perfect orbit that can be seen in the changing cycle of the seasons, in the ecological balance of the natural world, and in the progression of human life from birth through fulfillment to decline and death—and then to rebirth.[144]

This passage also exemplifies the neopagan emphasis on natural cycles of birth, death and rebirth. Women are naturally linked to the Goddess and share in her natural rhythms. The moon, with its three stages of waxing, fullness and waning is a prominent symbol of the "triple Goddess" who grows from young to mature to old, and then dies and is reborn again. Individual women may exemplify these three phases of the Goddess as Maiden, Mother and Crone. The same cyclical pattern can be seen in all of nature and is a reflection of the rhythms of the cosmos. Symbolic associations of this kind are responsible for the fact that neopaganism, in spite of all efforts towards inclusiveness, is and remains oriented primarily towards the feminine polarity. Witches like Z Budapest take this tendency towards its logical conclusion by claiming that witchcraft is synonymous with "women's mysteries", and therefore not the business of men. But, even in less extremist groups, the symbolism of the Horned God is inevitably somewhat less developed and his role in the neopagan worldview is less immediately obvious than that of the Goddess. The relation between

---

[143] Very characteristically, when Chris Griscom brings MacLaine into conscious contact with her "Higher Self", MacLaine perceives it as an 'almost androgynous' human being (DL 334-335). Another clear example is Shakti Gawain, for instance RG 24.

[144] SD 41. Starhawk later came to change her mind about polarity. See SD 8, 216-217.

the masculine and feminine pole in modern witchcraft recalls the image of the small sperm in relation to the large egg-cell: the masculine element is necessary for creation, but its role is very much limited to the single task of fertilization. Once it has fulfilled its role, the egg-cell can go on autonomously without further masculine assistance. Similarly, in Wicca, the masculine element represented by the God is necessary because of the polarized nature of reality; for the rest, it is the feminine element which dominates that reality[145].

Another variety of holism takes its inspiration from organic models. In itself, this connection is hardly surprising. We have seen that the New Age rejects mechanistic models and sees organicistic models as the natural alternative. We also saw that, in systems approaches, the notion of "organism" is subtly extended: the distinction between organisms and machines is replaced by a distinction between systems that do and systems that do not display the characteristics of self-organization. This criterion of self-organization is also central to the most prominent example of "organicistic holism" in the New Age movement, i.e., the so-called "Gaia-hypothesis".
The Gaia-hypothesis is tied to the name of the biochemist James Lovelock[146]. It claims that 'Life defines the material conditions needed for its survival and makes sure that they stay there'[147]. The earth, taken as a whole, is a complex system which functions according to the principles of self-organization. In that sense, it is not essentially different from an organism. Like an organism, the earth persists in a remarkably stable state of chemical and thermodynamic non-equilibrium, and is able to regulate the planetary environment in such a way that optimum conditions for life are maintained. The dynamic stability exhibited by the earth over long periods of time is impossible to explain on the usual premises of linear, mechanical causality. Lovelock et al. point out that 'If the temperature or humidity or salinity or acidity or any one of a number of other variables had strayed outside a narrow range of values for any length of

---

[145] Cf. Janet & Stewart Farrar: 'Every woman, if she can free herself from the conditioning imposed by the patriarchal stereotype, is a natural witch. Most men, unless they have a well-integrated and fully functioning Anima, have to work harder at it. Witches work primarily with the 'gifts of the Goddess'—the intuitive, psychic functions, the direct awareness, by sensitivity at all levels from bodily to spiritual, of the natural order of things. All this is a woman's immediate inheritance; on the whole, a man approaches it best *via* the woman (...). ... That is why Wicca is matriarchal, and the High Priestess is the leader of the coven—with the High Priest as her partner. They are essential to each other, and ultimately equal (...), but in the context of Wiccan workings and of their present incarnation, he is rather like the Prince Consort of a reigning Queen.' (WW 169)
[146] Lovelock first proposed the hypothesis together with Sidney Epton ('Quest for Gaia'). Later, he has collaborated with the microbiologist Lynn Margulis. The best-known exposition of the theory was, however, published under his name only (Lovelock, *Gaia*).
[147] Lovelock & Epton, 'Quest for Gaia', 304.

time, life would have been annihilated'[148]. The hypothesis that the earth functions as a living organism (with obvious implications for a holistic ecology)
was named after the ancient Greek Goddess of the earth, Gaia.

In our New Age corpus, several interpretations of the Gaia hypothesis can be
found. At a very moderate level, which is probably closest to Lovelock's intention, it is merely asserted that the functioning of the earth can be understood
along the analogy with an organism, because both meet the criteria for self-
organization. New Age sources almost never stay at this level, however; at the
very least they use the Jantsch/Capra strategy of equating self-organization
with Bateson's concept of mind to assert that earth therefore has "mind"[149].
More usual for New Age thinking is a silent acceptation of the premise that
each self-organizing system is an organism (which, as we saw, is misleading)
and to conclude that earth therefore not only functions as a living organism,
but actually *is* a living organism[150]. Usually, an immediate further step is made,
i.e., that this living organism possesses not just "mind" but consciousness, and
even that it is intelligent. Connections are often made (most explicitly by Peter
Russell) with Teilhard de Chardin's concept of the *noosphere*: the "thinking
layer" of the earth comprised by the unified consciousness of humanity[151]. As
a result of the global networks of information technology, a "planetary consciousness" is emerging: this signals a momentous evolutionary process in
which Gaia becomes conscious of herself. Global society unified by information technology is described as a planetary nervous system, and the emerging
unified consciousness of humanity as a "Global Brain"[152]. However, in view
of the ecological crisis, Peter Russell wonders whether humanity might now
be in the process of actually frustrating these goals of evolution, exhibiting the
characteristics of a "planetary cancer" rather than a global brain[153]. It may well
be that we have become parasites on the body of Gaia, and we should not be
surprised if she finally takes steps to exterminate us. The present situation of
the earth constitutes a test for humanity: 'If we do pass, we may move into our
next evolutionary phase—our integration into a single being. If we fail, we will
probably be discarded as an evolutionary blind alley, an experiment which for
one reason or another did not quite work out. Humanity will be spontaneously aborted ...'[154] Towards the end of his book, however, Russell shows himself
optimistic about a good ending.

---

[148] Lovelock & Epton, 'Quest for Gaia', 304.
[149] SOU 164.
[150] TP 285; WW 128.
[151] AE 83-84. Although Marilyn Ferguson's *The Aquarian Conspiracy* does not yet mention
the Gaia hypothesis, she uses Teilhard de Chardin's work to convey essentially the same idea.
[152] AE 77-79.
[153] AE 18-19, and *passim*.
[154] AE 207.

The idea that the earth is a conscious, living organism naturally evokes the question of whether the same applies to the other planets and heavenly bodies. When this happens, Gaia-speculation moves close to certain theosophical ideas which have profoundly influenced the New Age *sensu stricto*. David Spangler, George Trevelyan, and the Ramala books all closely follow the theosophist Alice Bailey in describing the sun and the planets as conscious, divine or semi-divine beings[155]. Our solar system is an actual Body governed by the "Solar Logos", who lives in the sun and who is the entity we refer to when we talk of "God". However, the Solar Logos and his body—the Solar System—is in turn just a part of a larger galactic body which possesses a greater and more encompassing consciousness. This body is, again, part of yet another body and so on: apparently *ad infinitum*. This "chinese boxes" scheme appears to be open-ended in both directions. The earth, while being a part of the Solar Body, is itself the body of the "Earth Logos". Our own bodies, while being parts of the Earth body, in turn contain even smaller beings who experience our body as their "Solar Body". The very atoms of our body are quite literally minute Solar Systems inhabited by conscious beings, and so on *ad infinitum* again[156]. As might be expected, the New Age *sensu stricto* has gratefully adopted Lovelock's Gaia hypothesis as scientific corroboration of its theosophical metaphysics[157]. The theosophical Earth Logos is usually reinterpreted as female and identified with "the Goddess", and "Gaia" is used as an appropriate name to address her[158]. Peter Russell, although apparently not directly influenced by theosophy or by the New Age *sensu stricto*, develops his Gaia-speculation into a strikingly similar direction. Throughout his book the idea is developed that in order for a new level of evolution to emerge in any system, that system must have reached the threshold number of 10^{10} (ten billion) constituting units. Russell calculates that our galaxy, which contains some 10^{11} stars, must therefore contain a sufficient number of 'potential Gaias' in order to make possible the eventual 'emergence of some galactic super-organism whose cells are awakened Gaias'[159] and which would possess an appropriate kind of super-consciousness[160]. And, of course, having come that far, Russell does not stop here. Ultimately, the emergence of more than 10^{10} such super-conscious Galactic Beings might result in the universe as a whole becoming a single Universal Super-Organism[161], which Russell identifies with *Brahman*.

In sum, "Organicistic holism" of the above kind is based on either one of two

---

[155] RBNA 94-97; RR 28-33. Cf. Hanegraaff, 'Channeling-literatuur', 24-25; OR 33-34.
[156] RR 147-148.
[157] RS ch. 5.; OR 178-179; EiG 94-95, 187.
[158] We already noted the corresponding tendency towards divinization of the earth, and to some extent of the planets, in neopaganism. Cf. for instance HBWM 298; W 155.
[159] AE 214.
[160] AE 215: 'The Galaxy would become her equivalent of conscious'.
[161] AE 218.

different systems of thought or their combination. One kind of argument is based on the crucial move, discussed above, of describing organisms as self-organizing systems. This is the basis of Lovelock's Gaia hypothesis, which can then be extended to larger and larger, and also to smaller and smaller systems. The other argument derives its justification from the subjective persuasiveness, to certain people, of theosophical speculation. Both systems of thought may be combined in worldviews which attempt yet another marriage between metaphysics and science and which result, not surprisingly perhaps, in cosmic visions strongly reminiscent of Science Fiction[162].

3. THE EVOLUTIONARY PERSPECTIVE

All forms of New Age thinking share at least two general assumptions about the nature of reality. The first of these, discussed in section 2 of this chapter, is that reality is an unbroken, unified whole. On the basis of this Holistic Assumption, as we saw, several types of worldviews can be developed. In the context of these worldviews, the apparent evidence for fragmentation and dualism of various kinds is explained as resulting essentially from the erroneous assumption that the necessarily limited perceptions accessible to *normal* consciousness and experience provide us with sufficient evidence to draw conclusions about the whole. The whole as such, it is implied, must necessarily be inaccessible to finite perceptions (although it can perhaps be experienced in *supra-normal* kinds of consciousness and experience). From an encompassing perspective which starts from the whole, apparent cases of fragmentation and dualism lose their absolute character and can be seen as only partial manifestations of an underlying wholeness. Although reality may appear as broken and fragmented from a limited perspective, a deeper harmony is revealed from a holistic point of view.

The second general New Age assumption is that reality is engaged in a process of evolution. While the Holistic Assumption tends to emphasize the unity of space, this Evolutionistic Assumption emphasizes processes in time. Below, we will discuss the paradox that the almost universal New Age belief in evolution goes hand in hand with an equally strong tendency to regard time as an illusion, and belief in its reality as a major source of fragmentation. In this section, I will concentrate on the various types of evolutionism present in New Age literature, in sofar as they apply to the "nature of reality".

Like holism, New Age evolutionism must not be seen primarily as a theory about reality. Just as specific holistic theories are developed in order to provide the prior vision of wholeness with a theoretical underpinning, theories of

---

[162] Significantly, Peter Russell ends his book with a quotation from Olaf Stapledon's novel *Starmaker*.

evolution are formulated to account for the prior feeling that present reality cannot be finished, complete or perfect and that the future must hold the promise of successive improvements (particularly in the sense of a progressive movement towards greater and greater wholeness). Both holism and evolutionism begin as visions which, eventually, give rise to a multitude of theories. Several of them are formulated with specific reference to "the nature of reality", but evolutionism as such pervades the New Age movement as a whole and will therefore be encountered again and again in different parts of this study.

Before discussing examples of evolutionism found in the New Age corpus, I propose a general analytic framework. Notice that this is not a summary of New Age forms of evolutionism, but an etic construct proposed as an ordering principle with respect to the latter. Evolution may be pictured as taking place either in a closed or in an open system. Possible examples of *closed* systems are the earthly biosphere, the solar system or even our universe as a whole: all can be pictured as self-sufficient units constituted in such a way as to permit evolutionary processes to occur within their boundaries. A distinction can be made between different levels of such processes: natural evolution, or evolution from life to consciousness, or evolution of consciousness itself. In all cases, the possible scope of evolution within a closed system is limited by the intrinsic boundaries of the system concerned. As an alternative, it can be assumed that systems—including the earth or the universe as a whole—are *open* systems which are themselves evolving. In this case there is no prescribed boundary and consequently no necessary limit or predestined outcome of their evolution. In this case, it is almost impossible to avoid speculating about where the evolutionary dynamics themselves come from. Postulating that the universe itself is part of a more encompassing system provides no solution, because any such super-system necessarily reintroduces the idea of an ultimate limit, and so on *ad infinitum*. Paradoxes of space-time infinity seem to be unavoidable once evolution is pictured as open.

While the distinction between closed and open systems concerns the possible *scope* of evolution (either finite or infinite), we must also distinguish different *types* of evolution. First, we may think of evolution as being part of a *cyclical* process. The beginning of such a cycle is classically pictured as the appearance of some kind of duality in a primeval singularity. The result is a "downward" process of emanation (or "involution"). When emanation and manifestation reaches a natural limit, the direction is reversed and a process of "evolution" back to unity begins. If such a cycle would simply mean a regression back to exactly the same state from which all has sprung, the process would be devoid of meaning and the term "evolution" would seem to be inappropriate. In spite of occasional references to the cosmic cycles of Hinduism as an ultimately meaningless "divine play", the Nietzschean vision of an '*ewige Wiederkehr des Gleichen*' is atypical of New Age literature. In the context of both closed and open systems, however, the cyclical process as a whole may also be described in more genuinely evolutionary terms. In this case, the whole achieves a "higher" level of integration at the completion of the cycle. This higher level may be the end of the process or it may be the beginning of a new cycle. The result can be pictured as an evolutionary *spiral*, the number of cycles of which may be anything between one and infinite (in open systems).

Other types of evolution are *linear*. The theoretical option of "blind" linear evolution resulting from random causal processes (the Darwinian theory) is generally rejected in the New Age movement. This is done not only because random evolution forecloses ultimate meaning; radical contingency is also considered as scientifically falsified on the basis of evidence such as provided by Lovelock. Because of its wholesale rejection by New Age believers, it is superfluous to discuss here the forms which blind linear evolution would assume either in closed or in open systems. *Teleological* evolution, in contrast, assumes that the linear process moves towards some goal which is implicitly present from the beginning. The dynamics of evolution is based on the natural, built-in tendency of systems or parts of systems to realize or attain their *telos*. Because the *telos* defines the possible limit of evolution, the teleological option presupposes a closed system. A third type of linear evolution, which may be labeled *open-ended or creative*, differs from both former types. There is no final *telos*, but neither is evolution random and blind. Evolution is governed by a built-in tendency of *self-organization*. As a result of the dynamics of self-organization, each system strives towards ever-increasing complexity and expansion. This "purposiveness" of self-organization ensures that evolution is not random: it naturally moves from chaos to ever-increasing order. This order, however, may reach infinite levels of complexity and the precise results to which evolution will lead are unpredictable. The goal is not some final, complete state; rather, the meaning and end of evolution lies in the very creativity of evolution itself. The essence of this type is caught in Seth's words: 'Ultimately a completed or finished God, or All That Is, would end up smothering His creation. For perfection presupposes that point beyond which development is impossible, and creativity at an end.'[163].
This neat framework becomes slightly more complicated once we recognize the additional possibility of a *teleological spiral*. A spiral is, after all, a line which describes circles, and any line may be imagined to be either infinite or finite. If the line has any end at all, and if it is not based on random processes, then, after a finite number of "cycles", there must be some *telos*164. Allow-

---

[163] SS 340.

ing for this addition, and leaving out the possibilities which do not appear in New Age sources, we get the following diagram:

	Closed System	Open System
Cyclical	Teleological spiral	Open-ended Spiral
Linear	Teleological linearity	Open-ended/Creative linearity

Having distinguished these categories of evolutionism, it is hard to miss their significance in relation to the categories of holism discussed in section 2 of this chapter. Evolutionism of the "teleological spiral" type is naturally linked to "ultimate source holism": the source of all manifestation is also the *telos* of evolution within the system generated by the source. We will see that the same context is still presupposed (not entirely consistently) in the open-ended variety. Evolutionism of the "open-ended/creative linearity" type, in contrast, has found a very characteristic expression in the philosophy of self-organization developed in the context of systems theory (i.e., a prominent kind of "universal interrelatedness") which, however, also appears to have room for teleologic varieties. But these general affinities lead us only to a certain point. The holographic paradigm of Pribram/Bohm, influential though it may be, has remarkably little to say about evolution[165]. Seth, on the other hand, not only manages—as we have seen—to combine elements of "ultimate source holism" with its logical alternative "universal interrelatedness", he even succeeds in giving an evolutionary turn to the otherwise static holographic paradigm. In Seth's case, we again have to do with a variation of "open-ended/creative linearity", but now combined with the belief in an Ultimate Source. So, a strict analogy between types of holism, on the one hand, and types of evolutionism, on the other, cannot be demonstrated; but general affinities certainly exist.

Examples of the teleological spiral—naturally bound up with the hierarchical universe of "Ultimate Source Holism"—are easy to find in New Age literature. In the discussion of the latter, notice was taken of the tendency to describe the universe as a learning environment, in which separate units of consciousness have emerged from the divine source and are now on their way to becoming conscious co-creators with God (the option of re-absorption into God being rather seldom). A characteristic statement comes from George Trevelyan:

> ...man has been called 'the experiment of God'. The world of matter, ruled by gravity, is the setting necessary for this experience of separation and exercise of

---

[164] The presence of a *telos* in evolution does not automatically imply that it will ever be realized. The process may be frustrated and cut off for some reason. As we saw above, Peter Russell for instance believes that such a thing might happen in the case of the evolution of Gaia.

[165] Robert John Russell has criticized Bohm for neglecting time and evolution in 'Physics of David Bohm', 147-148. In a response, Bohm accepts this criticism as valid, adding that he is exploring a possible combination of his theory with Prigogine's work on irreversibility (Bohm, 'Response', 219). I would consider the possibility of such a combination highly implausible.

free will. Only by separation from the divine and from the realms of light can man discover his freedom. And his spiritual guides must undoubtedly watch with some anxiety what man does with his self-consciousness and the freedom that attends it. He must prove himself worthy of the gift conferred upon him. The divine purpose seems to be that man should have the opportunity of growing into a companion and co-creator with God. To date, however, he has tragically abused the trust reposed in him[166].

The universe itself—the learning environment—is mostly assumed to have emerged in an analogous way. Edgar Cayce, for example, describes the emanation of both the material universe and conscious souls; as soon as he has sufficiently accounted for the former, however, he concentrates on the latter in the rest of his discussion[167]. This is rather characteristic of "Ultimate Source Holism" in general, which is primarily interested in the spiritual dimension. Extended discussions of *natural* evolution are mostly restricted to the domains of New Age Science and the New Paradigm, where not the teleological spiral but the paradigm of self-organization dominates. If authors representative of "Ultimate Source Holism" do not simply take the material universe for granted, they mostly describe it as the creation of its own inhabitants: individual souls, as sparks of the great Creative Source, create realities as a mirror for their own development. This view, largely derived from Seth, has been discussed above and will be returned to again.

The status of the open-ended spiral variety is more difficult to assess. The idea as such fits easily within the perimeters of New Age evolutionism, for the simple reason that it combines two convictions that are popular in themselves: the idea of "cycles of learning" and the idea of infinite possibilities for development. It must also be noted that the very notion, encountered in the Trevelyan passage quoted above, that completion of the evolutionary spiral makes us into "co-creators" with God, implies that the creative process does not stop at reunion with the Source. Typically, no final end is mentioned at all. An open-ended spiral of evolution seems to be implied by theosophically-oriented holism of the New Age *sensu stricto* variety, such as the Ramala doctrine of infinite universes within universes. David Spangler, representing the same tradition, puts it like this:

> The whole solar system, from the physical level on up to the cosmically oriented levels of awareness of the Solar Logos, is like a womb in which seeds of consciousness develop and unfold into a full flowering of that unobstructed awareness and creativity that is the God-life and cosmic consciousness inherent within all creation. At that point, these consciousnesses, full-fledged beings of radiant creative Divinity, go forth as graduates of this solar system into the infinite universe beyond to become, in turn, educators for the life-streams following after

166 VAA 34-35.
167 TiR 306-308.

them and seeds for still greater manifestations of God-life yet to unfold from the potentials within Divine Mind[168].

Anticipating the discussion in Part Three of this study, we can already conclude that a large part of the New Age movement seeks to combine the "closed world" of traditional cosmologies with the "infinite universe" revealed by the Copernican revolution[169]. Basic models of evolution are derived from the former, but their scope is widened to the magnitude of the latter.

The linear types of evolutionism popular in the New Age corpus are more resolutely modern, and tend to place the evolution of consciousness within the wider context of natural evolution. Roughly speaking, the cyclical types discussed above start with a spiritual worldview and give only a limited amount of attention to the natural world within that context. The linear types, in contrast, start from nature and describe consciousness as an "emergent property" of nature. The main source of these views is the complex theory of self-organization developed by Ilya Prigogine and popularized in particular by Erich Jantsch and Marilyn Ferguson.

Ilya Prigogine is far more difficult to fit into a holistic framework than might be expected. At the core of his scientific oeuvre is the conviction that classical science, which emphasized "being", is now superseded by a new paradigm which emphasizes "becoming"[170]. Accordingly, he is extremely critical of the belief in eternal laws and cosmic harmony. Instead, he emphasizes the primacy of time, change, contingency, and the unpredictability of the future[171]:

> [The] feeling of confidence in the "reason" of nature has been shattered .... our vision of nature is undergoing a radical change towards the multiple, the temporal, and the complex. ... We were seeking general, all-embracing schemes that could be expressed in terms of eternal laws, but we have found time, events, evolving particles. We were also searching for symmetry, and here also we were surprised, since we discovered symmetry-breaking processes on all levels, from elementary particles up to biology and ecology[172].

The closing sentences of *Order out of Chaos* leave no doubt about the basic orientation of his worldview:

> The ideas to which we have devoted much space in this book—the ideas of instability, of fluctuation—diffuse into the social sciences. We know now that societies are immensely complex systems involving a potentially enormous number of bifurcations exemplified by the variety of cultures that have evolved in the relatively short span of human history. We know that such systems are highly sen-

---

[168] RBNA 95-96.
[169] Cf. Koyré, *From the Closed World*.
[170] Prigogine, *From Being to Becoming*.
[171] Cf. also his rejection of "Grand Unified Theories" (rn 192; OC 21, 47).
[172] OC 292.

sitive to fluctuations. This leads both to hope and a threat: hope, since even small
fluctuations may grow and change the overall structure. As a result, individual
activity is not doomed to insignificance. On the other hand, this is also a threat,
since in our universe the security of stable, permanent rules seems gone forever.
We are living in a dangerous and uncertain world that inspires no blind confidence, but perhaps only the same feeling of qualified hope that some Talmudic
texts appear to have attributed to the God of Genesis: "Twenty-six attempts preceded the present genesis, all of which were destined to fail. The world of man
has arisen out of the chaotic heart of the preceding debris; he too is exposed to
the risk of failure, and the return to nothing. "Let's hope it works" [*Halway
Sheyaamod*] exclaimed God as he created the World, and this hope, which has
accompanied all the subsequent history of the world and mankind, has emphasized right from the outset that this history is branded with the mark of radical
uncertainty"[173].

This quotation illustrates not only why New Age thinkers are fascinated with
Prigogine, but also why they usually follow him only up to a certain point. The
fascination derives from the excitement that comes with the vision of an infinite and open evolutionary future in which man may once more play a meaningful role. The idea that small fluctuations, including those resulting from
human activity, may drive evolution as a whole over critical thresholds into
unforeseeable new evolutionary directions, appeals to deep-seated New Age
concerns. One of these is the hope for an Age of Aquarius. It will be seen later that Prigogine's theories can be used to defend the possibility of a sudden
evolutionary transformation of society. In general, the theory is attractive
because it promotes man from the role of a passive object to that of an active
agent in the processes of nature, and suggests that even the smallest part—the
individual—can influence the whole. The disconcerting aspect of his thinking
is that the process of self-organization is neither causal nor teleological. It
therefore includes the possibility of failure at any moment. The reaction of
Renée Weber, in an interview with Prigogine, is characteristic of New Age
thinking:

> If the universe is something that is creating itself as it goes along, it is as if you
> are pulling the rug out from under us. The picture generates a sense of inse-
> curity as well as excitement. We don't know what the universe is going to do until
> it does it. There are no archetypes, no gods, no platonic ideas, no eternal laws,
> no immanence in anything, no implicate order. That seems bleak and austere[174].

While the popularity of Prigogine in the New Age movement rests on the
"excitement" generated by his evolutionary vision, the "insecurity" that comes
with it has been played down and obscured by the interpretations of his fol-

[173] OC 313. The quotation is from Neher, 'Vision du temps', 179.
[174] rn 195. Prigogine gives a double answer. Firstly, it is not his business to describe the universe as he would *like* it to be, but as it is. Secondly, the alternative of a closed and deterministic world may be even more unattractive, because it leaves no room for human freedom.

lowers. This is illustrated very clearly by the work of Erich Jantsch.

Jantsch explains how the Prigoginian paradigm differs both from Newtonian dynamics and from thermodynamics[175]. Newtonian dynamics is mechanical and treats time as reversible (for example, in mathematical descriptions of the movement of planets around the sun it makes no difference if the direction of time is reversed). The second law of thermodynamics[176] undermined Newtonian reversibility by demonstrating the existence of an "arrow of time": the universe moves towards increasing entropy (dissipation of usable energy) in a process that is basically irreversible. Classical thermodynamics thus demonstrated that historical (i.e., irreversible) time is a necessary part of physics, but it also led to the pessimistic conclusion that the universe was inevitably "running down". The progressive loss of available energy would ultimately result in universal "heat death". Prigogine's theory of dissipative structures, while based on thermodynamics, demonstrates an alternative possibility. In open systems that are far from equilibrium—for instance, organic systems—new and higher levels of increased complexity may arise suddenly and spontaneously. While classical thermodynamics implied that time inevitably moves in the direction of increasing chaos, Prigogine's theory maintains that it is precisely from chaos that new orders of higher complexity may emerge. It therefore opens the possibility for an optimistic reformulation of thermodynamics, which ascribes to the universe the ability to develop ever higher and more complex orders. Prigogine calls such orders dissipative structures, i.e., dynamic (=far from equilibrium) systems, which are not closed but open and therefore maintain constant energy exchange with the environment (=dissipation). The logical contrast to a dissipative structure is a machine, for instance a clockwork machine, which is closed and static. Such structures are subject to the Second Law of Thermodynamics: they run down over time and cannot repair themselves, let alone evolve to new levels of complexity. Dissipative structures can do all these things. Living organisms are obvious examples; but dissipative structures do not need to be organisms in the traditional sense. As noted in section 2B of this chapter, the essential distinction in systems thinking of this type is not between organisms and anorganic material structures, but between systems that display the characteristics of self-organization and systems that do not. Whether or not the former (including human artefacts) can be called "living" is regarded as no more than a matter of convention. In this way, Prigogine, Jantsch and others attempt to explain the evolution of both living organ-

---

[175] SOU ch. 1.

[176] The first law of thermodynamics states that the total energy in an isolated system is conserved. The second law states that the amount of *available* energy decreases over time. This implies, among other things, the impossibility of perpetual motion machines, and can be relabeled as the "law of increasing disorder" (Murphy, 'Time, Thermodynamics, and Theology', 360, 363-364).

isms and, for example, social systems in terms of the same basic mechanisms.

Erich Jantsch, in the bewildering mixture of scientific theory and visionary enthusiasm that is *The Self-Organizing Universe*, goes far beyond Prigogine by covertly reintroducing a range of teleological elements. An explicit defense of teleological evolution would bring Jantsch into headlong collision with the very core of Prigoginian theory. So it is not surprising that his apparent belief in a higher evolutionary purpose is expressed by means of frequent suggestive remarks rather than by explicit argument. Some examples of covert teleology are his description of the evolution of the universe as a process of "unfoldment"[177]; his mention of a "directedness" of evolution which might be recognized *post hoc*[178]; or, especially, his speculations about the "meaning" of evolution. At one level, evolution and "metaevolution" (i.e., the evolution of the evolutionary mechanisms and principles themselves[179]) generates its own meaning, in the sense that the meaning of evolution lies in the intrinsic value of creative expansion. On another level, meaning has to do with evolutionary "self-transcendence" culminating in the development of "Mind". Jantsch comes very close to an explicit teleological statement towards the end of the book: 'In self-transcendence ... the chord of consciousness becomes richer. In the infinite, it falls together with the divine. The divine, however, becomes manifest neither in personal nor any other form, but in the total evolutionary dynamics of a multilevel reality'[180]. An explicit teleological statement (reminiscent of Teilhard de Chardin's Omega Point) is avoided only by the words "in the infinite" (which however have the effect of obscuring completely what may be meant by the divine "becoming manifest"). The latent affinity with a linear teleological evolutionism, like that of Teilhard[181], is further confirmed by Jantsch' statement that primitive forms of "consciousness" must be attributed even to simple chemical structures and single cells[182]. This is another way of saying that the tendency towards mind/consciousness is built into evolution from the very beginning. It then becomes almost impossible to distinguish Jantsch' views from an explicit linear-teleological evolutionism as expressed, for example, by Willis Harman:

> Consider [the] kind of explanation which speaks of some sort of teleological "pull" in the evolutionary process, of evolution toward increased awareness, complexi-

---

[177] SOU 75.

[178] SOU 8.

[179] SOU 8.

[180] SOU 308.

[181] Note that neither Prigogine nor Jantsch refer to Teilhard at all.

[182] SOU 40: 'If consciousness is defined as the degree of autonomy a system gains in the dynamic relations with its environment, even the simplest autopoietic systems such as chemical dissipative structures have a primitive form of consciousness'. *If* that is done, Jantsch's conclusion may well be correct. However, he does not explain why we should define consciousness in that way to begin with.

ty, freedom—in short, of evolution *going somewhere* (not in a predetermined sense, but in the sense of preferred direction). In that kind of evolutionary explanation the organism developed two eyes because at some deep level of inner understanding it wanted to see better![183]

In spite of the logical open-endedness of Prigoginian evolutionism, the attraction of teleological models has, on the whole, been too strong for his New Age followers. Prigogine's 'dangerous and uncertain world' has been transformed, with reference to his own theories, into a world of inevitable progress towards a superconsciousness of cosmic dimensions. In this connection, we may also think of Marilyn Ferguson's *Aquarian Conspiracy*, which not only freely combines such radically different theories as those of Prigogine and Bohm[184], but also very frequently quotes Teilhard de Chardin. Although Teilhard is not discussed in detail, a strong presumption is created that it is his evolutionary vision which inspires more recent theories. Something similar is suggested also by Fritjof Capra[185] and Peter Russell[186]. Teilhard's role in the New Age movement is, however, ambivalent. His direct influence, in terms of specific theories, is much less than has sometimes been suggested[187]. Compared with thinkers such as Bohm and Prigogine he must definitely be considered a minor source. However, several central aspects of his thought (e.g., evolution towards Omega Point; the idea of the noosphere; the "inwardness" of matter) have their direct counterparts in New Age speculation. As a result, his name is often evoked to lend added support to ideas to which he is linked only by analogy. The peculiar combination of logical open-endedness and a suggestion of teleological directedness is often found in New Age sources. Seth has already been mentioned as an obvious example. Although there are no reasons to suppose any direct connections, Seth's and Jantsch's views of evolution are surprisingly similar. Central to both is the conviction that the meaning of evolution lies in the inherent value of creativity. The universe exists in order to unfold into ever more magnificent creations. Unlimited creativity is the beginning, the means, and the "end" of evolution; human consciousness is destined to play a crucial role in that process. It appears to be irresistible, even for a professional scientist such as Jantsch, to associate the very dynamics of creativity with

---

[183] GMC 55.

[184] It is interesting to compare the attitude of both scientists to each other's work. Bohm is interested in Prigogine and tries to incorporate his theory in his own work (SOC 137-141; David Bohm, 'Response', 219). Prigogine, from his side, shows less interest: '...I have not understood him exactly. My feeling when I hear or read him is that his is a rather conservative view, in the sense that he very much emphasizes enfolding and unfolding. To my mind enfolding and unfolding is exactly as conservative as his point of view on hidden variables. ... In spite of his great originality, and of many things which I admire in Bohm's views, I still feel he is trying to come back to a classical transparancy of nature'.

[185] TP 304.

[186] Esp. AE 83-84.

[187] For example by Sudbrack, *Neue Religiosität*.

"God". God (or *All-That-Is*) is pure creative energy; and human beings, as co-creators with God, partake in that divinity. Evolution is the process of God's infinite expansion.

4. SOME ADDITIONAL ISSUES

In this chapter, I have discussed the views about reality explicitly described or implicitly presupposed in our New Age corpus. The chapter's comparative lengthiness was predictable given the fact that it not only had to provide a sufficiently comprehensive context for the next chapters to draw on, but also because reflection on the "nature of reality" is a comparatively sophisticated intellectual enterprise. Even so, the scope and purpose of this study does not permit a really exhaustive treatment of the philosophical worldviews involved. It was necessary to pass over many interesting aspects and details. Some of these will be "filled in" in the course of the next chapters; others are marginal to the understanding of New Age religion and will be ignored, although they would be important for an in-depth interpretation of specific thinkers and their work. An obvious example is David Bohm's philosophy of nature, which would require a book-length critical monograph combining expertise in both philosophy and physics. Of more immediate importance are a number of general philosophical issues related to, or implicit in, the theories discussed above. This chapter will be rounded off with a brief survey of the most important ones.

The Transcendence of Space-Time
The "Quest for Eternity" has sometimes been highlighted as the central pre-occupation underlying a wide variety of modern "irrational" movements, from Romanticism to the New Religions[188]. The analysis of our corpus strongly confirms that in the New Age movement "time"—or, more specifically, the *belief* in time—is generally regarded as an unfortunate, limiting condition. Our textual corpus is full of suggestions that time is something to be transcended[189]. Less prominently, but still with remarkable frequency, we find the belief that

---

[188] Raschke, *Interruption of Eternity*. This study has many interesting insights to offer. The guiding definition of "gnosticism" is, however, extremely problematic: 'Over against the historicist mentality ... can be posed the theme of revolt against history, a quest for metahistorical meaning which can be classified generally as "Gnosticism" (24). This definition of "gnosticism" remains unsupported by any arguments and must be regarded as yet another source of confusion about this already seriously devaluated term'.

[189] CiM:T 5, *passim*; WIO 210-212; SOC 108-109, 197-199; ToP 197; AS 38; PR 193-194; PH 82-83; GW 199-220; S 227-237; RR 38; WR 13, 37, 226-227; ECMM 63; SM 163; SS 339-340; OtC 115, 218; RBNA 99-100; MNP 97; BQ 172; HU 197-228; SoC 98, 123; UfE 60-62; HP:cht 112; SoS 35.

the transcendence of time is to be complemented by a transcendence of space[190]. In the context of "Ultimate Source Holism", the wish to transcend the space-time continuum is directly connected to the longing for a "self-suf-ficient Absolute", and many references to time/space-transcendence can be attributed to the attendant "eternalistic pathos". In holographic theories, the wish to transcend time and space is given a theoretical underpinning by pre-senting the whole space-time continuum as "unfolding" from an implicate order beyond time and space. In the context of Seth's holographic worldview, this radical non-dimensionality is referred to as 'the spacious present'. It is impor-tant to realize that the meaning of space-time transcendence is different in both contexts just mentioned. In the first, otherworldly-oriented context, the wish to leave space-time behind seems to reflect quite simply the wish to find eter-nal peace and rest. In the holographic context, however, it is not eternal rest but eternal *creativity* that is sought. The "spacious present" functions not as a resting place, but as an archimedean point from which multidimensional real-ities can be created: 'In one respect, the body and physical objects go flying out in all directions from the inner core of the whole self'[191]. Starting from the premise that all multidimensional realities are created by conscious souls, it is indeed only logical to infer that those souls themselves must transcend the dimensions of space and time (time being the fourth dimension, as the post-Einstein generation has duly learned, if not from popular science books then from science fiction). Furthermore, if realities are created on the basis of our *beliefs*, then we are not actually constricted by the limitations of space and time, but only by the limitations of our beliefs. Expansion of consciousness means transcending those limitations and envisioning the possibility of other worlds, including higher worlds of more than four dimensions. The human mind is pictured as having the ability, at least in principle, of travelling between dimensions and realities at will, from the archimedean point of the "spacious present" beyond all creation. For illustration, I refer once more to the quota-tions about the popular reception of the holographic idea, at the end of chap-ter six section 2B. Shirley MacLaine, a strong representative of these views, emphasizes Seth's "spacious present" in her own words: 'I was learning to rec-ognize the invisible dimension where there are no measurements possible. In fact, it is the dimension of no-height, no-width, no-breadth, and no-mass, and as a matter of further fact, no-time. It is the dimension of the spirit'[192].

From this perspective of the spirit, time and space are regarded as *meaning-ful illusions*. The soul makes use of these categories to demarcate the play-

---

[190] CiM:T 361, *passim*; euu 49; ToP 197; TI 136; AS 38; OL 213; ECMM 63; SM 127, 136-137; OtC 115; RBNA 99-100; MNP 80-82; HU 229ff; SoC ch. 4. In most cases, space is just mentioned routinely in connection with time.

[191] SM 136.

[192] DL 309.

grounds it creates for furthering its own growth and expansion: 'The whole construction is like an educational play in which you are the producers as well as the actors. There is a play within a play within a play. There is no end to the 'within' of things. The dreamer dreams, and the dreamer within the dream dreams. But the dreams are not meaningless, and the actions within them are significant'[193]. We will return to this in the discussion of reincarnation. It seems clear that, on these premises, "evolution", as a process in time, can only have a limited significance: it exists to the extent that it is believed in. But, of course, this raises the question of what is the point of this whole dazzling play with illusions. If the soul is beyond time, then it seems contradictory to say that it can "evolve" by playing out its dreams. Nevertheless, this seems to be implied. Although the soul has literally "nowhere to go", it is still pictured as in a dynamic process of becoming a conscious co-creator with All That Is. Seth is very aware of this paradox, but attributes our failure to grasp it to our limited understanding: 'Everything happens at once, and yet there is no beginning and end to it in your terms, so it is not completed in your terms at any given point. Your idea of development and growth ... implies a one-line march toward perfection, so it would be difficult for you to imagine the kind of order that pervades'[194]. The paradox, in other words, is a result of category confusion: the order of multidimensional reality just cannot be grasped by a merely fourdimensional logic. All attempts to solve the contradiction are therefore futile and bound to fail. This seems to be a perfectly satisfying answer to New Age authors and their readership, and we should therefore accept it on the level of *emic* belief.

But, even if representatives of the holographic paradigm are able to give an emically convincing account of evolution "out of time", we are still left with the incompatibility of the holographic paradigm as such and the competing paradigm of self-organization. For Prigogine historical time is primary, and any sort of "illusionism" is alien to his thinking. In the process of adaptation of Prigogine's views to general New Age concerns, however, what happens is that the exciting vision of infinite evolutionary possibilities is emphasized at the expense of Prigogine's historism. To the extent that the latter is played down or ignored, the artificial impression can be created that Prigoginian self-organization, on the one hand, and holographic evolutionism of a Sethian kind (both of them being of the open-ended/creative variety), on the other, are in basic agreement. This is a very significant fact. If historical realism cannot survive even in theories of evolution, then we must conclude that the New Age aversion to historical time is deep-seated indeed.

---

[193] SM 302-303.
[194] SS 339-340.

Mind and Matter

The only thing, as was noted above (beginning of chapter six, section 2), which unites the different expressions of New Age holism is a common opposition to non-holistic views associated with the "old culture". This is particularly clear in the case of views about the relation between mind and matter. All New Age authors unanimously reject Cartesian dualism, but beyond that agreement confusion reigns. Although the harmonizing and syncretistic, rather than polemic, spirit of most New Age literature tends not to emphasize differences of opinion, on the understanding that "basically we are all talking about the same thing", in fact the alternatives to Cartesian dualism cover the whole gamut of theoretical options. I will briefly characterize the main positions found in our New Age corpus and comment on some problems related to them.

David Bohm attempts to transcend dualism by describing mind and matter as explicate orders which seem separate from the perspective of manifest reality, but are one at a deeper implicate level. The basic unification of matter and mind takes place, therefore, at a level which cannot be reduced to either of them. An "ultimate reality" which is neither matter nor mind but encompasses both as enfolded potential is, of course, not easy to assimilate within a philosophy based on the evidence of physics. However, in the course of his intellectual development, Bohm has been increasingly concerned with securing a place for "meaning" within the seemingly impersonal framework of his philosophy. To describe meaning simply as something which is attributed by human beings to (aspects of) reality seems to have been unacceptable to him from the outset. Meaning, rather, must be inherent in the very structure of reality. This realist rather than nominalist perspective has led him to extended speculations on "matter as a meaning field" and the concept of "soma-significance"[195]: 'The notion of soma-significance implies that soma (or the physical) and its significance (which is mental) are not in any sense separately existent, but rather that they are two aspects of one over-all reality. By an aspect we mean a view or a way of looking. ...there is only one flow, and a change of meaning is a change in that flow. Therefore any change of meaning is a change of soma, and any change of soma is a change of meaning'[196]. Bohm's speculations in this domain are a relatively obscure part of his philosophy. They take him further beyond physics than ever, and many of his discussions are characterized by a lack of specificity which relies heavily on "intuitive" understanding on the part of his audience. Unlike his theory of the implicate order, Bohm's ideas about meaning and soma-significance seem to have been adopt-

---

[195] Cf. the double interview with Bohm and Sheldrake, mmf; the notion of "soma-significance" dominates UM, and is discussed in a number of contributions in Pylkkänen, *Search for Meaning*. The theme of "meaning" is also a central concern for Bohm's epigone Peat, in S. Cf. further Jantsch' final chapter with the title "Meaning".

[196] UM 73 & 76.

ed only by his immediate followers (such as Peat and Talbot) without significantly influencing New Age thinking generally. They tend to be mentioned
from time to time, however, quite generally, as yet another confirmation from
a famous physicist that Cartesian dualism is bancrupt.

Only a thorough philosophical analysis of Bohm's complete oeuvre could determine the question of whether his approach to the mind-matter problem succesfully avoids materialist reductionism. Suspicions to the contrary have been
voiced even from within the New Age movement, and these will be examined
below. Here, it must be noted that materialist reductionism is indeed a strong
temptation for New Age holism. Any movement which combines the search
for a monistic alternative to mind-matter dualism with a high regard for modern science will easily develop a form of materialistic monism. However, if
such a movement also explicitly rejects reductionistic materialism and exalts
spirit, then it obviously has a problem. To escape from the dilemma, it must
claim either that science as such must be transformed so as to encompass
aspects of reality normally associated with the spiritual, or it must demonstrate
that the existence of a spiritual dimension is confirmed by advanced science[197].
Critics will object that the former option leads to bad science, and the latter
to bad spirituality. Defenders will reply that traditional notions of both science
and spirituality have been too limited all along and that the convergence of
both domains will lift both to an entirely new level. From such a perspective,
mind and matter would turn out to be superseded and ultimately meaningless
notions. This suggestion is what we actually find, not only in the work of David
Bohm, but in many other representatives of New Age science as well[198]. For
our purposes, the main thing to note is their pervasive *belief* that the mind-
matter problem can be solved in this way. If we look at the specific theoretical defenses of the belief, however, it is quite possible to argue that, in several central cases, what is presented as a solution to Cartesian dualism in fact
amounts to either materialist or spiritual reductionism[199]. A definitive judg-

---

[197] Cf. Shirley MacLaine: 'If and when science does get to establishing the Source, it will be
acknowledging spirituality as a physical reality' (OL 325).

[198] An often-quoted example is the essential role of the observer in quantum physics, which
seems to imply that mental and physical processes are aspects of one process. Frequently, however, this is—consciously or not—given an idealistic turn. This happens rather subtly in the case
of Fritjof Capra (TP 93: 'The fact that all the properties of particles are determined by principles closely related to the methods of observation would mean that the basic structures of the
material world are determined, ultimately, by the way we look at this world; that the observed
patterns of matter are reflections of patterns of mind'), and quite unsubtly in the case of Henry
Reed (ECMM 114: 'Atomic physics discovered that it is just not possible to look at an atom
without the atom's feeling an impact of the scientist's observation'). Both authors have in common that they describe a one-way movement from a mental agent to a material object and not
the reverse, which suggests that the mental aspect is primary. This seems difficult to reconcile
with the logic of Capra's theories.

[199] I have already mentioned several examples, such as Capra's early bootstrap holism (crit-

ment would require a detailed philosophical criticism, which is beyond the scope and competence of this study. Given that, we are left with the problem that it is extremely difficult to decide how to characterize the authors in question. Should we characterize them according to their beliefs or according to their actual philosophical and scientific achievements? Suppose that the suspicion of materialist reductionism turns out to be justified: would it then be right to say that such authors *believe* in a materialistic universe (but without realizing that they do) or, rather, that they only describe such a universe (but without realizing its implications)? Both could be plausibly defended. I do not intend to take a final stand on this issue, but it is an important one to mention.

A closely related position sees mind as an "emergent property" of material processes. This view is connected to evolutionary perspectives of the self-organization variety, either combined with (krypto)teleological elements or not[200]. Again, there is good reason to suspect covert or less covert reductionism; and the above comments apply equally to this category. In this connection, it is not superfluous to mention the popularity, in some quarters, of the "anthropic cosmological principle"[201]. This theory argues that there is a parallelism between the form of the human psyche and the form of the cosmos, such that 'neither could be supposed to be significantly different without supposing the other to be significantly different as well'[202]. On these premises, the answer to the question "why does the universe exhibit the features it does exhibit?" would be: "because we are here"[203]. In other words, human consciousness is regarded not as the *explanandum* but as the *explanans* of cosmic evolution. The so-called "final version" of this anthropic principle, a science fiction-like argument developed by John D. Barrow and Frank J. Tipler[204] under the inspiration of Teilhard de Chardin, is fully congruent with the more extremist kinds of New Age science[205].

If the mind-matter problem is approached from a primary interest not in matter (as is the case in the former categories, which are generally the products

---

icized by E.F. Schumacher); his interpretation of Gregory Bateson; and the Prigoginian description of "living systems". Below, the case of the holographic paradigm will be discussed in connection with Ken Wilber's criticism.

[200] Strictly speaking, the notion of "emergent property" belongs only to the theory of self-organization. Elsewhere, "unfolding property" might be more appropriate. However, the actual assimilation of teleological elements in Prigoginian self-organization renders such fine distinctions rather pointless.

[201] For an excellent discussion see Hallberg, 'Anthropic Cosmological Principle'.

[202] Hallberg, 'Anthropic Cosmological Principle', 139.

[203] Hallberg, 'Anthropic Cosmological Principle', 141.

[204] Barrow & Tipler, *Anthropic Cosmological Principle*.

[205] Cf. BQ 184-187.

of scientists or scientifically trained thinkers) but in mind, the result is usually a version of "illusionism"[206]. Only mind is real, and whatever seems essentially different from mind is "maya". A perfect example is the following statement by Stanislav Grof, related by Fritjof Capra:

> [My metaphysical system] is based on the concept of a Universal Mind, or Cosmic Consciousness, which is the creative force behind the cosmic design. All the phenomena we experience are understood as experiments in consciousness performed by the Universal Mind in an infinitely ingenious creative play. The problems and baffling paradoxes associated with human existence are seen as intricately contrived deceptions invented by the Universal Mind and built into the cosmic game; and the ultimate meaning of human existence is to experience fully all the states of mind associated with this fascinating adventure in consciousness; to be an intelligent actor and playmate in the cosmic game. In this framework, consciousness is not something that can be derived from or explained in terms of something else. It is a primal fact of existence out of which everything else arises. This, very briefly, would be my credo[207].

We note in passing that the physicist Capra quotes this statement approvingly, and apparently regards Grof's worldview as compatible with his own. In general, this idealist solution to the mind-matter problem is less problematical than the preceding one, for at least two reasons. First, it does not have to justify itself to scientific research, because whatever science may find, still belongs to the sphere of maya. And *if* science were to provide a physical description of Universal Mind that would be inconsequential: the point is that the believer simply does not need such support in order to believe in it. Secondly, while the overt explanation of mind in material terms is rejected as reductionism, the reverse explanation of matter in spiritual terms is not usually perceived as reductionistic. While scientifically-based monism, in the New Age context, is always in the difficult (if not impossible) position of having to avoid the scylla and charybdis of dualism *and* reductionism, spiritual monism can be just itself.

Finally, we must note the prominence in New Age literature of certain ambivalent terms which are used to good effect in order to suggest the unity of mind and matter. One example is Pribram/Bohm's "frequency domain": a domain of universal "unbroken wholeness" or dynamic flux from which all reality unfolds, but which is also described as the domain of the spirit. Mystical experience, on this premise, results from "tuning in" to this frequency domain[208]. While

---

[206] Gregory Bateson's theory is an exception; but he defines "mind" completely differently. Bateson (who was trained as a biologist and anthropologist) has proposed an extremely original solution to the mind-matter problem which would merit extended discussion here if it could be regarded as belonging to the New Age movement. However, as we saw, Bateson's influence in the New Age is limited to secondary interpretations of his work à la Capra.

[207] UW 150.

[208] Pribram himself confirms this (HP:f 34).

this might quite conceivably lead to a sceptical argument (the mystic thinks
(s)he experiences God, but in fact experiences only physical frequencies), New
Age authors characteristically see it as proof that mystical experience is not
illusory but "real".

The most widespread example of such ambivalent terminology, however, is
"energy". For examples of the way energy is described as both physical and
spiritual there is no better source than Shirley MacLaine. See for instance the
following conversation with her spiritual mentor David:

> "But do you really believe the soul is a *physical* force?" "Yes, exactly. But it is
> a significantly different *kind* of force from the physical atomic and molecular
> forces that comprise the body. It is a subatomic force, the intelligent energy that
> organizes life. It is part of every cell, it is part of DNA, it is in us, and of us, and
> the whole of it—everywhere—is what we call 'God'"[209].

The implications for human "co-creatorship" are obvious:

> We are literally made up of God energy, therefore we can create whatever we
> want in life because we are each co-creating with the energy of God—the ener-
> gy that makes the universe itself. ... If the pattern of that energy has order, and
> balance, and grace (which science claims it does), if it has meaning in terms of
> all life, what is to distinguish it from what the New Age calls God?[210]

Nothing, finally, summarizes the basic idea better than David's remark: 'Maybe
the God-force is really scientific'[211]. It would be superficial, in a New Age
context, to attempt to make a strict separation between the mind-matter problem and the problem of religion vs. science. If the essence of mind or spirit
(terms which are used interchangeably) is divine energy, as is commonly asserted, then naturally scientific or philosophical "proof" for the reality of mind/
spirit amounts to a legitimation of religion. Therefore it is commonly asserted in New Age sources that between science and religion there need be no conflict, and that a healing of the split between both is urgently needed. The argument usually reflects some variety of parallelism[212]. The hidden premise is, of
course, that the religion in question must be of the "right" kind, just as the science in question must be of the "right" kind. Sometimes this is made explicit: 'There appears ... to be no conflict between a mature science and a mature
religion'[213] and 'the only *real* battle is between genuine science and bogus science, and between genuine religion and bogus religion ... and the only worth-

---

[209] OL 326.
[210] GW 100-101.
[211] OL 240. Cf. OL 325: 'If and when science does get to establishing the Source, it will be
acknowledging spirituality as a physical reality'.
[212] For instance OB 10, EW *passim*; DL 323-329; GW 95-108; S 1-2, *passim*; SD 202-203;
MNP 161.
[213] GMC 102.

while battle is between genuine and bogus, not between science and religion'[214]. The problem is, of course, who decides what is "mature or immature", "genuine or bogus".

The Wilber Controversy

Sometimes the wished-for convergence of science and religion is put in the more general context of the conflict between the natural sciences and the humanities. In Prigogine & Stengers' *Order out of Chaos* this is even the central theme; the original French title *La Nouvelle Alliance* reflects the ambition of the authors to reunite the "two cultures" on the basis of a common recognition of historical time. However, we saw that it is exactly Prigogine's focus on history which has *not* been followed by his New Age admirers, so this part of his efforts must remain marginal to our present concerns. A far more crucial concern with the demarcation between different kinds of "science" is reflected in the vehement criticism of the holographic paradigm and of science-mysticism parallelism which has been voiced by Ken Wilber in several publications. Wilber's criticism is important because it is almost the only example of an intellectual controversy *within* the New Age movement, and because it illustrates a central problem area which has repeatedly been referred to above. Very briefly, Wilber argues that natural science has *no* competence to speak about spirituality. As an alternative to the monism of New Age science, which he claims cannot but result in reductionism, he proposes a hierarchical vision in which the higher levels encompass the lower but the lower cannot understand the higher. Wilber's sophisticated criticism, only the barest outlines of which can be presented here, seems to be similar to what E.F. Schumacher had in mind in his rejection of Capra's views (see above).

Wilber argues that the holographic paradigm is 'shot through with profound category errors'[215]. It fails to distinguish between fundamental levels in reality, the most important of which are the material, the mental and the transcendent realms[216]. Each of these corresponds to a specific mode of attaining knowledge, the terminology for which Wilber borrows from Bonaventura: the eye of flesh, the eye of reason and the eye of contemplation. Each level, furthermore, refers to a specific object domain, which he refers to as *sensibilia*, *intelligibilia* and *transcendelia*. The possible epistemological relationships resulting from this are presented in the following diagram:

---

[214] QQ:ss 21.
[215] EtE:pmhp 126.
[216] In other publications, Wilber has made finer distinctions within each level.

[Reprinted by arrangement with Shambhala Publications, Inc., Boston, MA]

Mode #5 represents 'simple sensorimotor cognition ... the presymbolic grasp of the presymbolic world'[217], and mode #1 represents what Wilber calls "gnosis": 'the transsymbolic grasp of the transsymbolic world, spirit's direct knowledge of spirit, the immediate intuition of transcendelia'[218]. The experience in these two modes is completely valid as knowledge, but it does not produce *theoretical* knowledge. This is done only in mode 2, 3 and 4:

> Whereas the *data* in *any* realm is itself immediate and direct (by definition), the *pointing* by *mental* data to *other* data (sensory, mental, or transcendental) is a mediate or intermediate process—it is a *mapping, modeling,* or *matching* procedure. And this mapping procedure—the use of mental data (symbols and concepts) to explain or map *other* data (sensory, mental, or transcendental)—simply results in what is known as theoretical knowledge[219].

Most sciences proceed by producing theoretical knowledge, but in principle a science based on *direct* (unmediated) knowledge is possible. Logically, this can only be the knowledge of mode #1. The word "science" is appropriate in this mode as in modes 2-4, to the extent that all are based not on dogmatic formulation but on valid procedures of data accumulation and verification. Such a procedure, as explained by Wilber, must consist of the three steps of "injunction, apprehension and confirmation"[220]. Wilber's complete argument thus results in a distinction between the following categories:

Mode #4 results in "empirical-analytic or monological (monologue) sciences". As examples, Wilber mentions physics, chemistry, biology, astronomy and geology.

Mode #3 results in "mental-phenomenological, rational, hermeneutical, semiotic, or dialogical (dialogue) sciences". Examples: 'linguistics, mathematics, experimental phenomenology, introspective and interpersonal psychology, historic-hermeneutics, logic, interpretive sociology, communicative philosophy'[221].

Mode #2 results in "mandalic sciences": 'the attempt by the mind to arrange or categorize, however inadequately, the data of transcendelia ... this would include mental cartographies of the transmental realms, rational "plausibility arguments" for spirit; verbal discussions of Godhead; and so on'[222].

---

[217] EtE:pp 67.
[218] EtE:pp 67.
[219] EtE:pp 67.
[220] See EtE:ete.
[221] EtE:pp 72.
[222] EtE:pp 72.

Mode #1 results in "noumenological or gnostic sciences": 'the methodologies and injunctions for the *direct* apprehension of transcendelia as transcendelia; direct and intuitive apprehension of spirit, noumenon, *dharmakaya*'[223].

Duly taking notice of the complicating factor of mathematics and logic in mode #3, we may conclude that the distinction between mode #4 and #3 largely corresponds to the traditional distinction between the Natural Sciences and the Humanities. Wilber's criticism of the holographic paradigm reflects an acute awareness of this distinction. Mode #2 largely corresponds to the transpersonal perspective which emerged in psychology, as was seen in chapter two, from the desire for a non-reductionistic account of mystical and related kinds of experience. Mode #1 is simply mystical *practice*, as distinguished from theory. According to Wilber, mysticism, as traditionally taught, is subject to the same epistemological structure as all valid science (i.e. "injunction, illumination, and confirmation").

It will be clear that, from a perspective that distinguishes between fundamental ontological and epistemological levels, the attempt to describe all reality in terms of one fundamental reality modeled on physics must be hopelessly reductionistic. Physicalist reductionism is therefore Wilber's basic objection to the holographic paradigm and to the parallellist enterprise:

> ...the new physics has simply discovered the one-dimensional interpenetration of its own level (nonsentient mass/energy). While this is an important discovery, it cannot be equated with the extraordinary phenomenon of multidimensional interpenetration described by the mystics. ... To put it crudely, the study of physics is on the first floor, describing the interactions of its elements; the mystics are on the sixth floor describing the interactions of all six floors. ... Further, physics and mysticism are not two different approaches to the same reality. They are different approaches to two quite different levels of reality, the latter of which transcends but includes the former. ... In the rush to marry physics and mysticism, using the shotgun of generalization, we tend to forget that quantum reality has almost no bearing whatsoever in the actual world of macroscopic processes. ... But it is precisely in the *ordinary* realm of rocks and trees that the mystic *sees* his mutual interpenetration of all matter. His basic oneness of the universe does not "start at the atomic level". When the mystic looks at a bird on wing over a cascading stream and says, "They are perfectly one", he does not mean that if we got a super microscope out and examined the situation we would see bird and stream exchanging mesons in a unitary fashion. ... Ask almost any physicist if the connections between, say, a macroscopic tree and river are as intense and unitary as those between subatomic particles, and he will say no. The mystic will say yes. That is a fundamental issue and shows, in fact, that the physicist and the mystic aren't even talking about the same world[224].

David Bohm's implicate order, according to Wilber, is very interesting but should not be seen as a transcendent reality. Rather, it "subscends" matter, and

---

[223] EtE:pp 72-73.
[224] EtE:pmhp 135-137.

is simply 'the unitary deep structure (holoarchy) or level-1'[225]. As for Pribram's holographic brain: Wilber has no doubt that memory is holographically stored, but denies that this has any spiritual implications:

> ...it is said that a shift to a "perception of the holographic blur" would produce transcendent states. ... By the account of the theory itself, I do not see that it would or could result in anything but an experience of one's own memory storage bin, properly blurred and without benefit of linear read-out. How one could jump from a blur of one's own memory to a crystal clear consciousness that transcends mind, body, self, and world is not made clear at all[226].

Popular ideas about the holographic "frequency domain" are similarly criticized:

> The transform of "things" into "frequencies" is not a transform of space/time into "no space, no time", but a transform of space/time objects into space/time frequencies. Frequency does not mean "no space, no time"; it means cycles/second or space per time. To read the mathematics otherwise is more than a quantum leap; it is a leap of faith[227].

The common belief that the new holistic theories reintroduce notions of freedom and creativity, and refute the determinism of earlier classical science, is equally groundless:

> ...even with its little bit of Heisenberg indeterminacy, the physical universe is much more deterministic than even level-2, biological beings. Any good physicist can tell you where Jupiter will be located a decade from now, barring disaster, but no biologist can tell you where a dog will move two minutes from now.
> ...
> It's a reflex thing to do—finally, after decades of saying the physical universe is deterministic and therefore human choice is an illusion, you find a little indeterminacy in the physical realm and you go nuts. ... You get so excited you forget you have just pulled the reductionist feat of the century: God is that big electron in the sky. The intentions are good, but the philosophy is so detrimental[228].

Wilber acknowledges that some of the founders of New Age holism have subsequently moved to a more sophisticated view, but is afraid that these necessarily more complicated views will never succeed in reversing the tide of 'pop mysticism and the new physics or holographic craze'[229]. Wilber's own alternative for a new paradigm would not only have to include all levels, modes of knowing and correlative methodologies, but also a 'social evolutionary stance, a social policy geared to help human beings evolve through the stage-levels of existence'[230]. It should be noted that, in Wilber's view, the only ultimate real-

---

[225] EtE:pmhp 139.
[226] EtE:pmhp 148.
[227] EtE: pmph 149.
[228] EtE:nap 169-170.
[229] EtE:nap 163.
[230] EtE:nap 196.

ity is universal spirit, and all lower levels are ultimately illusionary in relation to this final mystery[231]. Therefore his opposition to popular New Age holism can still be fitted into the general duality between science-based monism on the one hand, and idealistic "illusionism" on the other. What distinguishes Wilber is his carefully argued and psychologically sophisticated account of how the different levels of "illusion" emerge from the ultimate reality of "Mind-only", and what dynamics govern their relations to each other.

Quantum Questions (ed. Ken Wilber) is a compilation of "mystical" writings from a number of famous physicists (Heisenberg, Schroedinger, Einstein, De Broglie, Jeans, Planck, Pauli and Eddington). Wilber's aim in making this compilation is to demonstrate that these physicists all came to embrace mysticism while nevertheless *rejecting* physics-mysticism parallelism. According to Wilber, they almost unanimously declared that modern physics offers *no* positive support for mysticism or any sort of transcendentalism. They did this, moreover, not out of ignorance about mysticism; quite the contrary, their writings are 'positively loaded with references'[232] to mystics and idealistic philosophers. Their rejection of parallelism derives from an acute awareness that in their research they were looking 'at nothing but a set of highly abstract differential equations—not at "reality" itself, but at mathematical symbols of reality'[233]. Why, then, did they become mystics? The answer is that the new discoveries forced physicists to be aware of the *limitations* of physics. In Wilber's words:

> ...both the old and the new physics were dealing with shadow-symbols, *but the new physics was forced to be aware of that fact*—forced to be aware that it was dealing with shadows and illusions, not reality. ... Schroedinger drives the point home: "Please note that the very recent advance [of quantum and relativistic physics] does not lie in the world of physics itself having acquired this shadowy character; it had ever since Democritus of Abdera and even before, *but we were not aware of it; we thought we were dealing with the world itself*". And Sir James Jeans summarizes it perfectly ...: "... from the broad philosophical standpoint, the outstanding achievement of twentieth-century physics is ... the general recognition that we are not yet in contact with ultimate reality. We are still imprisoned in our cave, with our backs to the light, and can only watch the shadows on the wall". ... To put it in a nutshell: according to this view, physics deals with shadows; to go beyond shadows is to go beyond physics; to go beyond physics is to

---

[231] This position is developed theoretically in all Wilber's books, and sometimes expressed aphoristically in statements like EtE:nap 167: 'All things are not ultimately made of subatomic particles; all things, including subatomic particles, are ultimately made of God'. Cf. the preface to AP (xi): 'There follows, then, the story of the Atman-project. It is a sharing of what I have seen; it is a small offering of what I have remembered; it is also the zen dust which you should shake from your sandals; and it is finally a lie in the face of that Mystery which only alone is'.

[232] QQ:ss 6.

[233] QQ:ss 8.

head toward the meta-physical or mystical—and *that* is why so many of our pioneering physicists were mystics[234].

Wilber's rejection of popular holism seems complete, and is unusually well-
argued. It is all the more significant because it comes not from an "outsider"
but from within the broad sphere of New Age thinking, and because it clearly formulates the fundamental differences between the two main types of speculation about "the nature of reality" which we have encountered again and
again: a monistic type inspired by modern natural science and a hierarchical
and idealistic type (the first starting from a primary interest in "matter" but
concerned with saving the spiritual dimension; the second starting from "spirit" and forced to explain the apparent existence of "matter").

If we screen our New Age corpus, finally, for argued responses to Wilber's
criticism by defenders of the holographic paradigm and parallelism, the result
is rather disappointing. Only Capra and Bohm have taken the trouble to give
some kind of response, but both restrict themselves to rather impromptu observations which fail to address the fundamental philosophical problems raised
by Wilber. Bohm feels that Wilber incorrectly emphasizes transcendence at the
expense of immanence, but does not appear to have read Wilber himself, or to
be particularly interested[235]. Capra treats the matter more seriously and argues
that, contrary to what Wilber believes, mystics do not perceive interconnectedness and interpenetration in the ordinary realm: their mode of perception is
non-ordinary and because the perceived can no longer be regarded as separate
from the perceiver, it follows that the reality perceived by mystics is also non-
ordinary. Physicists, by employing sophisticated instruments, also perceive a
"non-ordinary" reality. The mystic and the physicist do not perceive the same
elements, however, but their perceptions do mirror each other because both are
based on interrelatedness. Capra then evades the real debate by saying that he
is simply studying the overlap between physics and mysticism, but that there
is much more to both sides[236]. In his observations about hierarchical models,
later on in the interview, he suggests that Wilber treats the concept of levels
somewhat too seriously. For the rest, he disposes of Wilber by simply agree-
ing with almost everything he says while refusing to draw his conclusions[237].
We can only conclude that neither Bohm nor Capra is interested in polemics,
the former probably because he is too engrossed in his own theory, the latter
because of an apparently deep-seated inclination towards harmony.

---

[234] QQ:ss 9-10.
[235] HP:pm 188
[236] HP:ToPR 233.
[237] See esp. HP:ToPR 237-238.

CHAPTER SEVEN

META-EMPIRICAL AND HUMAN BEINGS

1. INTRODUCTION

One conclusion which can be drawn from the previous chapter is that "God", particularly as the ultimate "source" or as the "mind" of the universe, is mostly an integral and necessary part of New Age ideas about the nature of reality. Part of the material strictly belonging to the present chapter has therefore already been covered, or at least referred to. I will now proceed with a more systematic exposition, covering the spectrum of beings from "God" (however defined), via semi-divine beings to channeled entities. As a comprehensive *etic* category for embracing the full range of possibilities, I have given preference to the technical term "meta-empirical" over such concepts as "divine", "spiritual" or "supernatural". Intermediate beings, such as channeled entities or angels, are not generally considered as "divinities", but in the believers' daily practice they may often function as such. It would be artificial and misleading to treat them as a category completely separate from "divine" beings in a strict sense. The term "spiritual" is more comprehensive, but seems to suggest an opposition to "material" which is particularly problematic when used in monistic contexts. The same applies to "supernatural", which presupposes an ontological division expressly denied by many of our sources. The term "meta-empirical", in contrast, simply indicates any reality beyond the empirical world accessible to common, intersubjective sense experience (or the extension of sense experience by scientific technology). The "meta-empirical" covers God, gods, angels, invisible entities, and subjectively experienced presences or non-ordinary realities.

Although the term "meta-empirical" is useful as a neutral term covering the object domain of religious belief in general[1], it should be noted that there is one particular area where it loses analytic clarity. This is the domain of subjective *psychological* experiences, which could quite plausibly be regarded as "meta-empirical" in a strict sense. The fuzzy boundary between religion and psychology logically following from this terminology has suggestive implications for theoretical reflection on the nature and definition of religion, but we will not pursue that line of research here. However, it is interesting to note that, whatever the implications in relation to other religious traditions, precisely in

---

[1] Cf. Platvoet, *Comparing Religions*, 25ff, esp. Platvoet's definition of religion on page 30; id., 'Definers Defined'.

the case of New Age religion this fuzziness is an advantage rather than a disadvantage. The reason is, quite simply, that New Age religion itself tends to blur the distinction between religion and psychology to an extent hardly found in other traditions. Several elements in this chapter therefore touch on the domain of New Age psychology, which will be analyzed in chapter eight.

2. DIVINE BEINGS

A. God

New Age ideas about God reflect a marked aversion to rigid, doctrinal definitions. The latter are associated with a narrow-minded dogmatism which lacks affinity or has lost touch with the experiential dimension. God is experienced rather than believed in, and on that basis his existence is usually regarded as fairly self-evident and non-problematic. As far as most New Agers are concerned, the burden of proof lies not with the believer but with the sceptic: it is the latter who should explain how he thinks that this incredibly rich and abundant universe could have come into existence and could have continued to exist by mere accident. To the New Ager it is obvious that there is a deeper spiritual dimension which gives meaning and coherence to the contingencies of earthly existence. This dimension, which is the guarantee for *meaning*, is unproblematically treated as synonymous with God. As a point of departure, it is useful to give attention to what is strikingly *absent*, or marginal, to New Age ideas about God.

Most importantly, God is very seldom conceived as *personal*[2]. However, we should not jump too hastily to the conclusion that New Agers *therefore* believe in an impersonal God. Many of them apparently do, but in many other cases the issue of personality is markedly ambiguous. Certainly, a personal God generally tends to be associated with anthropomorphism, and consequently rejected as much too limited and narrow. He also tends to be associated with a God who judges and metes out punishment for sins, which is incompatible with fundamental New Age beliefs about ethics and healthy psychology (see next chapter). But, in spite of all this, New Age views about God frequently contain distinctly personal elements. While it is certainly true that even the most personalized New Age divinity is not of a nature such as to engage in an I-

---

[2] The only possible exceptions are some authors with very strong personal ties to traditional Christianity. Edgar Cayce believed in a personal God (cf. for instance SOS 112-113) but, as noted in chapter one, this aspect of his work is de-emphasized by his New Age followers. Matthew Fox says that Jesus's 'panentheistic Father/Mother God is forever a personal God' (OB 124), but whether his own creation spirituality leaves room for a personal God in any traditional sense must be considered doubtful to say the very least.

Thou relationship with human individuals, to describe the New Age God as a
mere "impersonal force" is to overshoot the mark. Far more representative is
the conviction that the very distinction personal-impersonal is based on an artificial dualism. God can be experienced as either personal or impersonal, but
in reality his being transcends such limited distinctions. Eva Pierrakos's reflections on this point are quite representative:

> God is. ... Think of God as being, among so many other things, *life* and *life force*.
> Think of God as of an *electric current, endowed with supreme intelligence*. This
> "electric current" is there, in you, around you, outside of yourself. It is up to you
> how you use it. ... This concept may raise the question whether God is personal
> or impersonal, directing intelligence or law and principle. Human beings, since
> they experience life with a dualistic consciousness, tend to believe that either the
> one or the other is true. Yet God is both. But God's personal aspect does not mean
> personality. God is not a person residing in a certain place, though it is possible
> to have a personal God-experience within the self. For the only place God can be
> looked for and found is within, not in any other place. God's existence can be
> deduced outside of the self from the beauty of Creation, from the manifestations
> of nature, from the wisdom collected by philosophers and scientists. But such
> observations become an experience of God only when God's presence is felt first
> within. The inner experience of God is the greatest of all experiences because it
> contains all desirable experiences.
> This particular feeling experience might be called the *cosmic feeling*. ... I cannot
> describe this experience adequately within the limitations of human language. ...
> The oneness is total. It is an experience of bliss; the comprehension of life and
> its mysteries; all-encompassing love; a knowledge that all is well and there is
> nothing to fear.
> In the state of cosmic feeling you experience the immediacy of the *presence of
> God within*[3].

Significantly, what begins as a discussion of God's nature ends in a description of religious experience. The primacy of experience over all other considerations implies, among other things, that the question whether or not God *is*
personal is regarded as unimportant as long as he can be *experienced* as personal. Particularly clear examples can be found in the work of Shakti Gawain,
who sometimes prefers to speak of "source": 'Source means the supply of infinite love, wisdom, and energy in the universe. For you, source may mean God,
or the universal mind, or the oneness of all, or your true essence. However we
conceptualize it, it can be found here and now within each of us, in our inner
being'[4]. So, God may mean many things to many people, but these represent
only different personal perspectives on one and the same universal reality. From
certain perspectives God, or "the universe", may appear in personal form:

---

[3] PST 51.
[4] CV 39. A perspective such as Gawain's sometimes leads to the use of "the Universe" as a
synonym for God. See for instance YHL 8, *passim*, or WW2 33: 'The universe (or God)...'.

The universe has both personal and impersonal aspects: as I surrender and trust more, I find my relationship with this higher power becoming more personal. I can literally feel a presence within me, guiding me, loving me, teaching me, encouraging me. In this personal aspect the universe can be teacher, guide, friend, mother, father, lover, creative genius, fairy godmother, even Santa Claus. In other words, whatever I feel I need or want can be fulfilled through this inner connection. I seldom feel truly alone anymore. In fact, it is in physical aloneness that I often find the most powerful communion with the universe. At such times, the previously empty places inside of me are filled with the light. Here I find a constant guiding presence that tells me which move to make next and helps me to learn the lesson that lies in taking each step along my path[5].

The singular lack of interest in precise formulations, based on the absolute primacy accorded to personal experience, can be considered the central aspect of New Age beliefs about God. This tendency can take rather extreme forms, such as the assertion of Sanaya Roman's guide Orin that spiritual growth leads to connection with 'a Higher Power—the God/Goddess within and without, Christ, Allah, Buddha, the All-That-Is'[6]. This theology easily assimilates all personal perspectives on God as equally valid, on the tacit but crucial understanding that none of them has prominence over the other. Any attempt to give one particular view of God prominence over others is rejected as reflecting a restricted, limited consciousness which absolutizes its own perspectives over all others and is lacking in authentic religious experience. In other words: the criterion deciding whether one fits into the New Age religious framework lies *not* in what one believes about God, but in one's measure of tolerance towards other beliefs about God as complementary to one's own vision within the larger whole. This theology both follows from and reinforces an inclusivist and universalistic perspective on religious diversity. Particularly in neopagan contexts, the result is often a kind of "qualified polytheism":

> Wicca does not believe, as do the patriarchal monotheisms, that there is only one correct version of God and that all other God forms are false: the Gods of Wicca are not jealous Gods. We therefore worship the personification of the male and female principle, the God and the Goddess, recognizing that all Gods are different aspects of the one God and all Goddesses are different aspects of the one Goddess, and that ultimately these two are reconciled in the one divine essence. There are many flowers in the garden of the divine and therein lies its beauty[7].

The general New Age vision of God easily assimilates the perspectives of New Age science, as can be inferred from Marilyn Ferguson's summary of how her "Aquarian" informants view God:

> God is experienced as flow, wholeness, the infinite kaleidoscope of life and death. Ultimate Cause, the ground of being, what Alan Watts called 'the silence out of

---

[5] LL 8.
[6] SG 9.
[7] W 11-12. Cf. WWD 31.

which all sound comes'. God is the consciousness that manifests as *lila*, the play of the universe. God is the organizing matrix we can experience but not tell, that which enlivens matter. ... We need not postulate a purpose for this Ultimate Cause nor wonder who or what caused whatever Big Bang lauched the visible universe. There is only the experience. To Kazantzakis, God was the sum total of consciousness in the universe, expanding through human evolution. In the mystical experience there is the felt presence of an all-encompassing love, compassion, power. Individuals revived after clinical death sometimes describe a passage down a dark tunnel to an unearthly light that seems to emit love and understanding. It is as if the light itself is a manifestation of universal mind[8].

It would not be correct—at least it would be very one-sided—to say that the vagueness of New Age talk about God means merely that New Agers are not clear in their own minds about who or what God is. Rather, this vagueness is largely intentional, and results naturally from the belief that God's essence transcends the inherent limitations of human language and conceptual frameworks. Furthermore, however non-committal they may seem at first, New Age statements about God do not permit the conclusion that "anything goes". They turn out to be structured according to a limited number of rather closely connected elements. The New Age view of God is [1] strongly *holistic*, in the sense that it is God's oneness which ensures the enduring integrity of the universe. As the "Ultimate Source" of reality, God is the wholeness and oneness from which the world of apparent fragmentation and diversity springs. I refer again to the characteristic passage of George Trevelyan quoted at the beginning of chapter six, section 2A[9]. Frequently-used terms like "Ocean of Oneness", "Infinite Spirit", "Primal Stream", "One Essence", "Universal Principle" and the like are mutually interchangeable ways to assert that on the deepest level reality is whole. This universal integrating essence is [2] often described as *Mind*. God is seen as the *superconscious* Mind of the universe: '...the mind is the active force behind what we see around us. The mind is a primary reality of its own. It is a universal reality'[10]. This Idealistic view is in a matter-of-fact way associated with God as the *selforganizing* Mind of the universe. On the basis of such associations, Michael Talbot can speak of an 'overall gestalt of consciousness, a supermind', and quote the physicist Paul Davies for support: '...the universe *is* a mind: a self-observing as well as self-organizing system. Our own minds could then be viewed as localized 'islands' of consciousness in a sea of mind, an idea reminiscent of Oriental conceptions of mysticism'[11].

---

[8] AC 420-421. Cf. EAM 135-136

[9] I.e., VAA 5. Cf. also EiG 40-41, 183. Trevelyan is an example of a New Age thinker who freely mixes non-personal and personal elements. God is Life, Light, Love, the Mind of the Universe, Universal Energy etc., but also the divine I AM, the "Great Cosmic Being", the "Beloved", the "Almighty", or 'a vast Intelligence which knows what It is doing and ultimately is Love' (EiG 40).

[10] ECMM 66, cf. 53-54. Cf. TiR 307; CV 39; RR 202, 238; R 31.

[11] BQ 193-194. Cf. Erich Jantsch (SOU 308): 'God is not the creator, but the mind of

Terms like "Consciousness" or "Intelligence" are mostly used interchangeably with "Mind"[12]. God is [3] the *energy* (cf. the last part of the paragraph on "Mind and Matter", in chapter six, section 4) which keeps the universe alive and whole: 'We each form part of a universe of living energy, an immense, unified field of living, pulsating energy. If we are to speak of God, then God must comprise the totality of this universal life energy...'[13]. Because he is the energy which sustains life, God is also referred to as [4] the *Life Force*. Sometimes this connection is explicitly described in the terms of physics, as for instance in Eva Pierrakos's comparison of God as the life force with an electric current. In other instances, it is the simple experience of life itself which leads to the connection, for instance when Ramtha finds the "unknown God" in the ongoingness of nature, which never judges man's deeds but simply allows him to play out his illusions however he chooses[14]. Very importantly, the essence of the life force is [5] *creativity*, as described in orgasmic terms by Chris Griscom:

> Ecstasy soars upward, fueled by its own momentum, by its very being, transcending until it becomes an energy without a source. It becomes the source itself. This is the source which creates the worlds, creates the coalescence into thought, light, and form. This is the source which creates supernovas. Then it extinguishes itself to begin again after another cessation. It is the swelling moment of rapture, rewarded with bliss, exploded into ecstasy over and over again. It is the sourcing creative force across the entire universe. We use the nuances of these words in relationship to each other to explore the ecstatic frequency, which is itself a force field of divine energy in which we can learn to bathe our consciousness, to anchor our reality, to choose our path. The source ripples out in all directions on the current of ecstasy which knows no limitations or separations[15].

The striking emphasis of many authors on God as creative energy[16] is complemented by the complete absence of any traditional view of God as the *Creator* of the world. Creativity is a *force* (often frankly described as a physical force) which creates from *within*; the monistic framework leaves no room for a creator "outside" of creation[17]. Finally [6], the creative, intelligent life energy is often associated with *Love*. The concept of Love, in this context, is not based on relationship and can hardly be called personal. Rather than an action or an attitude it is, again, a force or energy: the 'cosmic glue' that holds the

---

the universe'. This passage is quoted approvingly by the Catholic Matthew Fox (CS 63).

[12] YHL 70; RNA 186; PST 51; VAA 62; EiG 41. Note also David Bohm's ideas about "intelligence", undoubtedly derived from Krishnamurti: UM 148; euu 70.

[13] VAA 62. Cf. also Capra's mystical experience described at the beginning of *The Tao of Physics*, when he "saw" the cosmic dance of energy and realized that this was the dance of Shiva (ToP 11).

[14] R 14-15. Other examples of God as Life force: RBNA 129; W 16; PST 50; VAA 62.

[15] ENF 168.

[16] Cf. SOC ch. 6; CV 120; WA 36; ECMM 267-268; GW 100; S 188-189; SS 339-340.

[17] LTMW 38.

universe together[18]. The entity "John", in conversation with Shirley MacLaine, can therefore say that 'God is love—which is the highest vibrational frequency of all'[19], proceeding next to deny any discontinuity between the frequencies of material energy, light, thought, and Love.

George Trevelyan, finally, sums up all the elements mentioned above in a few sentences which amount to a succinct formulation most New Agers will subscribe to:

> Now into human thinking re-emerges the vision of the sacred, the deep certainty that the Universe is mind and that behind the wisdom poured into all the diverse forms of nature is a great oneness of intelligence. And transfusing this intelligence is an endless ocean working for the harmonizing of all life in a creative on-going flow of true evolution. This is Love and it is alive, permeating everything. Each one of us is a point of consciousness in a sea of greater consciousness[20].

Finally, something must be said about the neopagan concept of the Goddess. Like the New Age God, the Goddess is not a personal being, although she may be adressed in a personal way. What is striking about neopagan statements about the Goddess is the extent to which they emically acknowledge her metaphorical nature. To an even greater extent than in other sectors of New Age religion, divinity in neopaganism is radically immanent, and the Goddess is a metaphor for that immanence. Starhawk's term "power-from-within" perfectly catches the essence of why neopagans come to speak of the Goddess.

> This book is about the calling forth of power, a power based on a principle very different from power-over, from domination. For power-over is, ultimately, the power of the gun and the bomb, the power of annihilation that backs up all the institutions of domination.
> Yet the power we sense in the seed, in the growth of a child, the power we feel writing, weaving, working, creating, making choices, has nothing to do with threats of annihilation. ... It is the power that comes from within.
> There are many names for power-from-within, none of them entirely satisfying. It can be called *spirit*—but that name implies that it is separate from matter, and that false split, as we shall see, is the foundation of institutions of domination. It could be called *God*—but the God of patriarchal religions has been the ultimate source and repository of power-over. I have called it *immanence*, a term that is truthful but somewhat cold and intellectual. And I have called it *Goddess*, because the ancient images, symbols, and myths of the Goddess as birth-giver, weaver, earth and growing plant, wind and ocean, flame, web, moon and milk, all speak to me of the powers of connectedness, sustenance, healing, creating[21].

Starhawk observes that, although they speak of her and adress her, neopagans do not "believe" in the Goddess any more than they have to believe, for instance,

---

[18] R 31. Some other examples: RBNA 129; CiM 'Introduction'; CV 39; DL 247; UM 148.
[19] OL 202-203.
[20] EiG 40-41.
[21] DD 3-4.

in rocks. Rocks are simply there and do not have to be believed in[22]. Rather, neopagans feel *connected to* the "Goddess", as the power immanent in all that is[23]. We should not conclude too hastily, however, that the Goddess must therefore be synonymous with the "Life Force" mentioned elsewhere in New Age thinking. Although both concepts can obviously be put in connection, the Goddess is far more radically immanent than the New Age Life Force: while the latter is the basic energy *sustaining* life, the Goddess is simply *life itself*. In contrast to the Life Force, the Goddess has no idealistic overtones at all and cannot be regarded as a "higher" or "more fundamental" reality beyond the world of sense experience. On the contrary, it is precisely in the world of the senses that the Goddess is experienced. Consequently, neopagans fully accept all those aspects of life which spiritual idealism attempts to "overcome". The Goddess encompasses the dark and tragic side of life, and her power is celebrated in sexuality and bodily pleasure: 'all acts of love and pleasure are my rituals'[24]. As we saw already in the quotation from Z Budapest at the beginning of chapter six, section 1, the Goddess stands for radical this-worldliness. She is therefore qualitatively different from the God found elsewhere in the New Age movement, who is clearly representative of the "weak this-worldly" perspective.

B. Christ

It is remarkable how often New Age authors talk about Christ, or *the* Christ, as a divine reality, power or person. In spite of the religious inclusivity of New Age thinking, in spite of its interest in Oriental religions, and in spite of its criticism of mainstream Christianity, it is still Christ who dominates New Age speculation wherever the need is felt to explain the relation between God and humanity by some mediating principle. Not even the Buddha, generally regarded by New Agers as a model of spiritual enlightenment, comes even close to the unique metaphysical status enjoyed by Christ[25]. Before discussing this New

---

[22] SD 91.

[23] See SD 91-92.

[24] This is an often-quoted sentence from the so-called "Charge of the Goddess". The text is derived from Gerald Gardner's *Book of Shadows* and witches have long believed it to be of ancient origin. Recently, convincing proof has been given that the Charge was invented by Gardner himself, who incorporated fragments from Charles Leland and Aleister Crowley (Kelly, *Crafting*, 54).

[25] If the Buddha is mentioned, it is either as an example of a "fully realized being", or as only one in a long line of "great souls", "enlightened Masters", "great initiates" etc. Typical for this approach is Shirley MacLaine: 'The great spiritual masters such as Christ and Buddha were totally in touch with their higher unlimited selves ... They were fully realized human beings who understood all of their incarnational experiences...' (DL 104). Cf. also R 67, RBNA 103, EfE 241, RU 203, SoS 69.

Age christology, we must distinguish it from another view which properly belongs to a later section. This is the tendency to say that Jesus Christ exemplifies what each human being will one day become. Christ is then put forward as a model of spirituality to which we should all aspire. He exemplifies the human potential for attaining, after a long process of spiritual evolution, a state of perfect spiritual enlightenment. As such, Christ is often presented as a highly evolved spiritual "master" who has progressed to a high status in the spiritual hierarchy. The distinction between human beings and Christ is thus merely a matter of degree; Christ actually becomes a spiritual "entity" of the kind discussed in chapter seven, section 3B. In this section we are interested in approaches that accord to Christ a *unique* divine status. We may interpret this viewpoint as a New Age variation on traditional views of Christ as mediator between God and humanity. These two approaches are not necessarily contradictory, and are certainly not regarded as such by New Age believers. They must be distinguished, however, for reasons of analysis.

"The Christ" in New Age parlance may mean any one of three closely connected things: (1) a supreme state of mind called *Christ Consciousness*, (2) a spiritual reality mostly referred to as the *Christ principle*, and (3) the *Incarnation* of this principle in a human form. Christ Consciousness (1) is a state of total enlightenment, love and compassion to which all human beings must aspire. Jesus developed this consciousness in himself, encouraging us to do the same. Christ Consciousness means being directly aware of one's oneness with God while living in the world of manifestation[26]. This awareness implies total unselfish love and compassion for all beings. Sources representative of the New Age *sensu stricto*, strongly influenced by Alice Bailey's modern Christian Theosophy and Rudolf Steiner's Anthroposophy, usually go one step further[27]. They claim that, by developing this supreme consciousness, we are actually aligning ourselves with an objectively existing, universal "pattern", energy or principle: the Christ Principle or Cosmic Christ (2). In the Ramala books we find descriptions such as the following:

> The basic principle of the Christ, the principle which illuminates onto this Earth, the principle which is to redeem both Humanity and this Earth, is that of sacrificial service in love. The Christ, therefore, is the spirit of service, of the sacrificing of the self, so that through the control of the lower elements of its being Humanity can rise to be an instrument of service ... The Nazarene's life was intended to show what Humanity can achieve and what Humanity may do when it, too, is Christed. Do not think, however, that the Christ dwells only in a few beings of great evolution. The Christ expression exists in all of you, and the light which

---

[26] Cf. ECMM 274-275.
[27] See also, in particular, OR 36-44, 77-78.

you shine, the Christ light, will vary according to your point of consciousness, your soul knowingness ... You are all Christs in the making[28].

That this Christ Principle must be conceived not only as an inherent human potentiality, but as an objective spiritual reality, becomes particularly clear in the early work of David Spangler. He describes the Christ Principle as an evolutionary, "educational" force or energy[29] present in all evolving life. We might regard this simply as an aspect of what is elsewhere described as the divine "life force" or "energy"; but Spangler and other representatives of the "New Age *sensu stricto*" insist that the Christ principle is something more specific. Spangler describes how the Christ Principle acts as the principal spiritual counterforce to the downward pull of merely materialistic consciousness and how, throughout history, many "great beings" have been incarnated on earth in order to assist in this great cause. Their possibilities were limited, however, because 'they were not part of the evolutionary stream of Earth. It was necessary for an agent of Earth to reach a point where he could link with the Cosmic Christ and radiate his energies'[30]. Buddha was the first to succeed: he actually contacted the Christ Energy and thus became one with the Cosmic Christ, which resulted in the release of positive energies on earth. Over the "bridge" thus built by the Buddha, the Christ could now "cross over" to humanity. At the beginning of the Age of Pisces, he finally succeeded in reaching the earth and began to blend with the evolutionary energies of the earth. At this point, the man Jesus awoke to the Christ consciousness and, going one step further than Buddha, became fully one with the Christ Principle. Thus he became the focal point for the progressive descent and anchoring of the Christ energy on earth: 'Thus began one of the greatest dramas of this planet's history, the impregnation of an aspect of the Cosmic Christ, through the consciousness of Jesus, into the physical, etheric and spiritual life of Earth'[31]. The "incarnation" of the Christ Principle (3) therefore includes Jesus's unification with the Christ, but refers far more crucially to the earth becoming impregnated with Christ energy. This impregnation signalled a turning point in history. Over the last two thousand years, the Christ energy has gradually proceeded to permeate the whole earth, finally resulting in a total transformation of the earth on the (invisible) etheric level. We may now expect a second coming of the Christ (although not necessarily in a human form) which will complete the process and bring in the New Age. In this New Age, the transformation that has *already* occurred on the etheric level will become manifest on the outer level.

We will return to the theme of the coming New Age and the return of the Christ

---

[28] RR 275-276.
[29] RBNA 101.
[30] RBNA 103.
[31] RBNA 104.

in chapter twelve. In the meantime it should be noted that the rest of this particular theory, which is found almost exclusively in sources belonging to the
New Age *sensu stricto*, is directly derived from Anthroposophy[32]. Some other
sources in the same tradition combine the Anthroposophical Christology with
more general theosophical ideas. In particular, we find the view that the
"grounding" of the Christ principle is not a unique turning point in history (as
believed by Anthroposophists) but a regular event repeated at the beginning of
every new Age of the world[33]. Throughout history, great "masters" (Moses,
Buddha, Pythagoras, Zoroaster etc.) have come to earth for this purpose, and
each of them has given a new impulse to the spiritual evolution of humanity.
Jesus, in this view, was just one "master" among many, but *all* of them shared
the "Christ" energy.

Such differences notwithstanding, all New Age authors who speak about
"the Christ" at all, tend to describe it as the energy of unselfish love and compassion rather than a divine "person" in the traditional sense. Nevertheless,
statements about the Christ are characterized by the same ambiguity over the
issue of personality which we already found in our discussion about "God".
He is neither personal nor impersonal but both at the same time. However,
while in the case of God the "impersonal" pole tends to dominate, in the case
of the Christ it is the personal element which is inevitably emphasized. The
very name of "Christ", by virtue of its traditional connotations, already has
this effect: it seems plausible that, under any other name, New Age speculations about this "Principle" would hardly have made much impact. The difference between the "energies" of God and Christ is, after all, quite subtle from
a purely theoretical point of view. It is the suggestion of personal love and
compassion, of an intimacy and warmth that cannot be so obviously expected
from "the source that creates supernovas" (Griscom), which really puts the
Christ into a separate category. As such he seems to function, quite traditionally in a sense, as a mediating reality between the Universal Source and human
beings. While God is the ultimate power and energy animating and sustaining
the universe, the Christ is that aspect of God which is "personally" involved
with the fate of humanity.

It is interesting to see how David Spangler, whose book *Revelation* is a
foundational text of the New Age movement, later came to revise and redefine
his Theosophical and Anthroposophical ideas about the Christ in order to assimilate them to his new holographically-inspired worldview. In *Reimagination of
the World*, he acknowledges that he finally found the topology of Theosophy
too limiting[34]. His attempts to redefine "the Christ" in holographic terms are

---

[32] See Olson, 'Rudolf Steiner'.
[33] RR 53.
[34] RW 118.

a particular good illustration of the ongoing New Age dilemma between the personal and the non-personal. Spangler makes clear that whatever he says about God, the Buddha or the Christ is based on direct personal experience of "presences":

> One is a presence that pervades everything else. It is beyond description, but I think of it as the absolute foundation for everything that exists. Sometimes I call this God. ... This presence is universal, transcendent, and beyond human imagining, and at the same time it is profoundly personal, immediate, and accessible.
> There is an extension or aspect of this Godhead that reaches deep into the incarnational patterns of creation and links the immanent with the transcendent, the particular with the universal. One might call it active or dynamic sacredness. I think of it generically as the avatar function. Sometimes I experience it as two separate presences. The first is a presence that, when I encounter it, is like entering a deep, deep well of peace, compassion, and serenity. It has a quality of depth to it that beggars description. This presence I have always identified as the Buddha ... The second is a presence of love and compassion as well and a presence of peace, but it possesses a powerfully stimulating energy. ... When I first encountered it, it simply said, "I am that which you have named the Christ"[35].

Elsewhere, Spangler describes the Christ as a "participative dimension":

> I experience this dimension in various ways. At times it seems like an event horizon: on the one side of it lies singularity and the merging into oneness of all the geometries and dimensions that we know of, while on the other side of it lies the multiverse in all its diversity and unfolding splendor. Yet at the same time that it is a boundary, it is also a path winding through the whole multiverse, connecting each part to the singularity—to the ultimate Source. ...
> Because this dimension is available to us, human beings have always been able to experience it. Throughout history, it has been called different things, but the name most familiar to us in our culture is the Christ. We think of the Christ as a person, and often as an energy or a state of consciousness. Moving into the inner realms, though, it can be experienced as a dimension that runs through all the enfolded and unfolded universes and dimensions, right back to the Source. ... The Christ is a way of extending ourselves and manifesting ourselves in the universe in a manner that generates qualities of empowerment, participation, communion, co-creativity, compassion, and love, to name a few. However, it may be helpful as well to see the Christ as a kind of meta-geometry or meta-topology that is accessible to every point of incarnation within creation[36].

This is certainly a far cry from any traditional notion of Christ, whether of orthodox christian or theosophical provenance. It should be noted that certainly not all believers in the Cosmic Christ have followed Spangler's evolution from theosophy/anthroposophy to holography. The Ramala books, for example, or George Trevelyan, apparently feel no need for an updated reformulation of

---

[35] RW 138. Spangler goes on to say that the preference for the name "Christ" may reflect no more than cultural conditioning, but that the presence behind it is universal.
[36] RW 123.

theosophical concepts. Another example of New Age christology, finally, attempts to reinterpret traditional Christian mysticism in holistic terms. The Roman Catholic Matthew Fox borrows a term from Gregory Bateson (who would undoubtedly be horrified by this use) in order to describe the Cosmic Christ as

> "the pattern that connects" all the atoms and galaxies of the universe, a pattern of divine love and justice that all creatures and humans bear within them. ... The Cosmic Christ will make things happen, will effect a change of heart, a change of culture, a change of ways. ... This book is about the sacred and our response to it: reverence. The sacred what? The sacred everything. The sacred creation: stars, galaxies, whales, soil, water, trees, humans, thoughts, bodies, images. The holy omnipresence of the Divine One in all things. The Western term for this image of God present in all things is "the Cosmic Christ"[37].

In the relatively recent holistic formulations of the later Spangler and of Matthew Fox it seems that, in the end, the non-personal pole once more takes the upper hand. New Age believers do feel a need for a personal relation to the divine but, very frequently, their respect for scientific monism proves stronger. It will be seen that, in the absence of a fully personal God, lesser spiritual entities may take up his function.

3. INTERMEDIATE BEINGS

A. Beings of Ambiguous Status

In a New Age context, it is not always possible to make clearcut demarcations between "Divine" beings and beings who are neither divine nor human but somehow in between. The reason is simply that New Agers tend to use terms such as "divine" or "god" quite casually. Two categories of ambiguous beings must be mentioned briefly, and a third category must be commented upon in somewhat more detail.

Some New Age sources reinterpret the Christian trinity in New Age terms. Thus, they may mention the *Holy Spirit* side by side with the Christ. These cases, however, are few and far between, and of marginal interest for understanding New Age religion[38]. Somewhat more important is the concept of

---

[37] CCC 7-8.

[38] See ECJC 108-109 (Christ = the Christ Spirit; the Holy Spirit is a synonym for Christ *Consciousness*); RNA 55 gives an idiosyncratic view of the Trinity which has not been followed by others; only *A Course in Miracles* offers a developed view on the Holy Spirit. He is *created* by God as the mediating link between God and his separated sons who makes "atonement" possible: 'He knows because He is part of God; He perceives because He was sent to save humanity [an allusion to the distinction between perfect and imperfect knowledge—divine gnosis and illusionary "perception"—developed in CiM:T 35-37]. 'He is the great correction principle; the bringer of true perception, the inherent power of the vision of Christ. He is the light in which

"planetary deities" such as found in the theosophically-inspired New Age *sensu stricto*. This kind of speculation was described in chapter six, section 2C. "God" here becomes a relative concept, within the all-encompassing divine whole called "Infinite Spirit" or "Infinite Mind". While the "Solar Logos" is explicitly described as that being we refer to when we normally speak of "God", we must conclude that he is really only one among many gods. This God is special to us simply because he happens to govern our particular solar system. Comparably, the Goddess of Earth is seen—in distinction from the usual neo-pagan view—as an intelligent being inhabiting, or embodying, the earth. The precise status of these "gods" is ambivalent: whether they are really gods or angels or just "great beings" is not something which greatly worries those who believe in them.

We saw that neopaganism knows a multiplicity of gods. All traditional pantheons of the world, but "western" ones in particular, are used as a repository of gods and goddesses eligible for being evoked in rituals. Individual neopagans may develop a special preference for a certain God(dess), but this never involves rejection of other people's preferences. On the contrary, there are, as we saw, 'many flowers in the garden of the divine and therein lies its beauty'[39]. This polytheism-cum-henotheism[40] is qualified only by the common agreement that all gods and goddesses are ultimately just particular manifestations of universal principles or energies. Ultimately, there is only one divine essence, manifesting itself under many forms. It is natural, then, to ask in what sense the individual gods/goddesses who are evoked and adressed in rituals can be considered "real" at all. The usual neopagan view about their ultimate nature is represented very clearly by the Farrars:

> To the age-old question 'Are the Gods real' ..., the witch answers confidently 'Yes'. To the witch, the Divine Principle of the Cosmos is real, conscious and eternally creative, manifesting through Its creations, including ourselves. This belief is of course shared by the followers of all religions, which differ only in the God-forms (or single God-form) which they build up as a channel of communication with Its aspects. And even these various God-forms differ less than would appear at first sight. For example, the ancient Egyptian's Isis, the witch's Aradia and the Catholic's Virgin Mary are all essentially man-conceived Goddess-forms relating to, and drawing their power from, the same Archetype. We say 'man-conceived', but the building up of a God-form or Goddess-form is of course a two-way process; even a partially adequate man-conceived symbol improves communication with the unknowable Archetype, which in turn feeds

---

the forgiven world is perceived; in which the face of Christ alone is seen. He never forgets the Creator or his Creation. He never forgets the Son of God. He never forgets you'. (CiM:Mft 85)

[39] W 11-12. Cf. WWD 31. From time to time a connection with ecology is drawn. A healthy ecology consists of many different organisms in natural balance; monoculture, in contrast, is unnatural. A healthy "religious ecology" would, accordingly, encourage religious diversity.

[40] Cf. part 2 of the 'Introduction' to Versnel, *Ter Unus*, 35: henotheism denotes 'a personal devotion to one god ... without involving rejection or neglect of other gods'.

back a better understanding of its nature and thus improves the adequacy of the God-form.

A non-religious psychologist would probably answer 'No' to the same question. He would maintain that the Archetypes, though vital to man's psychic health, are merely elements in the human Collective Unconscious and not (in the religious sense) cosmic in nature.

We stick to our own, namely the religious view of the Cosmos, which is to us the only one which makes ultimate sense. But from the point of view of the psychic value of myth, ritual and symbolism, the somewhat surprising answer to the question is, 'It doesn't matter'. Each man and woman can worry out for himself or herself whether archetypal God-forms were born in the human Collective Unconscious or took up residence there (and elsewhere) as pieds-à-terre from their cosmic home—their importance to the human psyche is beyond doubt in either case, and the techniques for coming to healthy and fruitful terms with them can be used by believers and non-believers alike.

Voltaire said: 'If God did not exist, it would be necessary to invent him'. That remark can be taken as cynical; but it can also be rephrased: 'Whether the archetypal God-forms are cosmically divine, or merely the living foundation-stones of the human psyche, we would be wise to seek intercourse with them *as though* they were divine'. Myth and ritual bring about nourishing communication with the Archetypes, and because of the nature and evolution of the human psyche, the symbolism or myth and ritual—their only effective vocabulary—is basically religious[41].

The emphasis on symbols and myths as imaginative "masks of God"[42] is most characteristic of neopaganism specifically. Of more general importance for us is the Farrars's view on the relation between religion and psychology, because it shows a structural similarity with other New Age ideas about the meta-empirical. It is here that we encounter yet another crucial aspect of New Age religion, which has been hinted at above and will be encountered again in different contexts. To a certain extent, it mediates between two other fundamental characteristics of New Age thinking, i.e., holism and the idea that we "create our own reality". In the most general terms, we can describe it as *the conviction that certain fundamental distinctions which are usually taken for granted in our culture lose all significance when applied to the divine*. Such distinctions are regarded as limiting, artificial dualisms which effectively hide reality from our view instead of clarifying it. This conviction is significant because outside the New Age sphere they are commonly regarded as doing exactly the opposite: i.e. formulating crucial distinctions that prevent confusion between basic categories of reality. One such distinction was encountered above: personal vs. impersonal. According to the New Age, this distinction breaks down if applied to God, because he is neither and both. A second, and this time absolutely crucial, distinction is that between religion and psychology. New

---

[41] WW 154-155. Cf. W 154.

[42] Cf. Joseph Campbell's four-volume anthology of mythology of that title, which enjoys great popularity in New Age circles.

Age shows a strong tendency towards a *psychologizing of religion combined with a sacralization of psychology*. This aspect will be discussed further in the next chapter. At this point I just recall the Farrars' opinion that the ultimate reality of the gods does not really matter as long as they can be addressed and their presence experienced. This is an extremely important statement, with wide implications not only for neopaganism but for New Age thinking generally. Once again we encounter the primacy of practical, phenomenal experience over theoretical considerations. Neopagans address the gods *because it works*. Whether the reality they contact is metaphysical or intrapsychic is felt to be of secondary importance. Underlying that opinion is the common New Age feeling that the alternatives themselves are false, and that the question is therefore meaningless. The relation between religion and psychology, in terms of New Age thinking, is not correctly described in terms of objective realities versus subjective experiences. The subject is conceived as an objective reality and any object as a subjective experience; what results is a psychological idealism or idealistic psychology. We will return to this "subject matter" (sic) in the next chapter.

B. Entities, Angels, and other Intermediate Beings

In this section we focus on meta-empirical beings who are not considered as divine, but as somehow mediating between the God source itself and human beings. Of course, traditional religions acknowledge a variety of such intermediaries, such as demons or angels. In the New Age context, we hear little or nothing about demons[43], but far more about angelic beings. Explicit belief in angels is, again, largely restricted to the New Age *sensu stricto*. George Trevelyan adopts a traditional angelic hierarchy, which he describes as consisting of nine levels:

> All these planes or realms interpenetrate, since each operates on a different frequency and so is invisible to those below it. The subtler planes traverse and interpenetrate the denser. So we may recover the concept of the angelic hierarchies as referring to a phenomenon of reality and important in our lives.
> The angels, the lowest of the nine heavenly hierarchies, are nearest to man. It appears that their task is to help and guide the human being while sojourning on the earth plane. Now, the angelic worlds are all part of the Thought of God. They cannot be separated from it. Their delight is to serve the Will of God as it operates harmoniously through the Divine Law. The angels are not, therefore, concerned with free will as such. That is the peculiar gift to mankind. ... Humanity has been called the Tenth Hierarchy, a great continuum of souls in evolution towards moral freedom and creativity[44].

---

[43] A relative exception is George Trevelyan, who sometimes speaks about the "dark forces", and adopts the anthroposophical theory of the demonic entities Lucifer and Ahriman.

[44] OR 61.

Note that the eight highest hierarchies are apparently represented by beings higher than angels. We hear little about them except in scattered references to the archangels such as Michael. Apart from angels, this theosophically-inspired literature is full of references to related beings with names such as Guardian Angels, Personal Guides (also called Doorkeepers), Masters, Teachers (or Controls), Contacts etc. It is pointless to discuss the differences between such beings in detail. New Age angelology is quite unsystematic and each particular description reflects the personal ideosyncrasies of the author in question. No systematic distinction can be made, furthermore, between genuinely angelic beings on the one hand, and highly-evolved human beings, on the other. Human beings, as we will see, climb up through the hierarchy in the course of spiritual evolution, and in this process they acquire progressively "angelic" characteristics. While an author like Trevelyan sees angels as a category apart because they lack free will, and Ramtha goes even so far as describing them as less evolved than human beings[45], such distinctions are as frequently blurred by other authors or even by the same author in another passage[46]. What matters about New Age angelology is simply the belief that there are "higher beings" who are aware of what is happening on earth and who are benevolently interested in the spiritual progress of humanity. Often, these beings (or certain categories of them) are seen as directly assisting earth development, particularly during the present world crisis preceding the New Age. An example is the work of Chris Griscom, whose way of describing the hierarchy underscores once more the unimportance, in the eyes of New Agers, of too precise distinctions:

> There are many levels of guides, entities, energies, and beings in every octave of the universe. There are those who are lords, just like there were Crecian lords on one octave of reality, and ascended masters on another octave of reality. There are lords of the universe, the galactic frequencies. They are all there to pick and choose from in relation to your own attraction/repulsion mechanisms. They are all orchestrating to bring this planet, which is so desperately out of balance, into balance[47].

The sentence about the higher beings being available to "pick and choose" according to one's personal "attraction/repulsion mechanisms" is significant. The underlying idea is quite similar to the neopagan view of the "gods/goddesses": one draws towards oneself those "energies" which accord with one's own current personality. These energies appear as personal beings, although their ultimate nature may be different from their phenomenal appearance.

---

[45] R 93-94.
[46] For instance the Ramala books. RR 202 describes angels as beings without free will, who automatically perform the will of the creator; RR 52, however, describes how they sinned by cohabiting with human beings, against the will of the creator.
[47] ENF 82.

The same applies also to a separate category of "intermediate beings" which is encountered almost exclusively in English sources, belonging either to neo-paganism or to the New Age *sensu stricto* (which often assimilates "pagan" elements). In these sources[48], we find mention of beings that are closely related to the natural world. The most usual names are "devas" (related to the "plant kingdom") or "elementals" (related to the four elements). Again, we encounter the by now familiar argument that the "real nature" of these beings differs from the phenomenal forms they take when they appear to human beings.

> Elementals are natural energies associated with the elements of Earth, Water, Fire and Air. We can't really be sure what they are like in their own realms, for like all beings that appear to our clouded vision, they tend to be shaped by our own imagination. ... They look like their element, flowing, streaming, illuminating, almost invisible giant vortices of power, but because they are willing to limit themselves to the stereotyped image constructed by humans, they may be perceived as nymphs or dryads or sylphs or gnomes. Once you learn to catch them unaware, by entering their worlds gently and without making cross-dimensional ripples, you may see them as they are. Do realise, though, that all these beings are huge, vast, lofty and expansive. Imagining them as little animal-like spirits diminishes them and demeans their might. They are eternal, awesome, potent and far wiser than we children of Earth[49].

It is significant that these nature spirits are described not only as powerful energies existing in the natural world but also as accessible on the "inner planes": i.e. by the use of techniques for reaching altered states of consciousness. The deeper, invisible side of nature and the inner realms of the mind appear to be one and the same. These inner realms possess an objective reality or, reversely, other domains of reality can be entered by way of the subjective psyche. Again we encounter the phenomenon of a conflation of psychology and metaphysics.

It was already suggested that, in the absence of a fully personal God, the need for personal contact with the "divine" is frequently catered for by lesser spiritual entities. Rather than praying to God, New Age believers tend to meditate in order to attain a state of trans-personal oneness with the Source. Parallel to that, a quite personal relationship can be maintained with a personal guide or guardian spirit, with "spiritual entities", and even with one's own "Higher Self". Many New Age believers feel that they receive personal guidance from a higher being, referred to as their guardian spirit, guardian angel, guide or teacher[50]: '...the invisible guide ... can speak in your thinking with the still

---

[48] RBNA 95; W 84-87; RR 156, 166, 170; WA 83-84; WWD 138-145; EiG 93-94, SoS 185.
[49] WA 83-84.
[50] RR 204-205; EiG 81, 118; SoS 99.

small voice. He can use your faculty of intuition to suggest to you a course of action into your Higher Self'[51]. The sense of guidance can also be ascribed to one's own Higher Self. This important New Age concept will be discussed in the next chapter (section 2B), but it may already be noted at this point that the Higher Self may appear to people as a separate, personal being. No one has described this more clearly than Shirley MacLaine, who encountered her own Higher Self in the shape of a quasi-androgynous being which she was able to describe in detail and which engaged in extended conversations[52]. We will return to her story below.

Apart from such personal guides, the most prominent intermediate beings in the New Age context are, of course, the "spiritual entities" known from channeling. These are often regarded as human beings who only differ from us in having progressed beyond the earthly plane[53]. They have completed the cycle of incarnations on earth and are now further developing in higher realities. From their comparatively exalted perspective they can help and advise their brothers and sisters who are still struggling for spiritual understanding within the perimeters of matter. But it is equally possible that they have another background; for example, they may have come from other planets or from other dimensions. In all cases, they are essentially like us: evolving spiritual beings who are engaged in a cosmic process of learning by experience. The general context for this conception has already been described (chapter 6, section 2A), and need not be repeated. It must be stressed once more that, although analytical distinctions between "spiritual entities" and other categories such as angels are made in a number of relevant sources, other sources quite as frequently blur all such distinctions. A good example, which also illustrates the variety of entities in terms of their provenance and in terms of their activities (giving guidance to human beings, or doing other things), is the channeled entity Orin:

> There are so many places that guides come from that they appear to be infinite. You might find it useful to classify guides into those who have been incarnated on the earth and lived at least one earth life; those who have not lived an earth life and are from dimensions outside the galaxy and stars, such as the fourth dimension; the Masters, such as St. Germain; Angels, such as Michael and Raphael, including guardian angels; and extraterrestrial entities from other galaxies and planets. There are other guides that do not fit into these categories. I, Orin, have lived one earth life very long ago in your years, so that I could better understand physical existence. I have long since evolved into pure light and spirit, having no physical body. DaBen is also a being of light and has not lived an earth life ...

---

[51] EiG 118.

[52] DL 334ff.

[53] Cf. WW2 151: the "masters" are 'Human beings like yourselves, but older. They are not Gods, nor Angels, nor Elementals, but are those individuals who have achieved and completed the same task as you have set yourselves' (quoted from the influential occultist Dion Fortune).

Not all entities from the higher realms choose to be guides, just as not all of you choose to be channels. Work on the other planes of reality is as varied as your work can be on earth. Guides are certain beings who are highly skilled at transmitting energy from their dimension into yours. ... Guides can appear to your inner eye as particular nationalities with clothing that is appropriate. I, Orin, appear to Sanaya as a radiant shimmer of light that sits around her body when she channels. She is aware that I am about eight or nine feet tall. All that she can see when she tries to see my face is brilliant white light. I often appear in robes such as your ancient monks wore.

Some report seeing their guides as color. Some perceive their guides as sounds, others feel their guides as openings into their hearts. ... Some people picture their guides as familiar figures they have known, such as Christ, Buddha, or angels, who represent great love and wisdom to them. Guides can appear as American Indians, Chinese sages, East Indian masters, or as one of the Great Masters, such as St. Germain. Guides may appear as either male or female, although in the realms of pure energy there is no polarity, so guides are not truly male or female. Guides will choose an identity that will best accomplish what they are here to do, or one that you can most relate to[54].

The last part of this quotation is very revealing. We encounter once again the distinction between "real" and "phenomenal", but there is also more than a hint that entities may engage in benevolent forms of deception. What appears as Christ may actually be an entity masquerading as Christ for paedagogical reasons. Again the underlying premise is geared to practical considerations: it does not really matter who the entity "really" is, as long as (s)he is loving and wise and gives guidance informed by spiritual insight. It should be noted that such insight, although obviously carrying authority for New Age believers, is not necessarily taken as absolute and final truth. New Age sources regularly warn against the danger of forgetting that the entities are not all-knowing. One of the Ramala masters admits that 'As I speak to you now, I can understand life only as it exists within this Solar Body. That is the limitation of my consciousness, for I cannot understand the planes of consciousness beyond that of our Creator'[55]. The final responsibility, therefore, remains with the hearer: 'At all times of communication it should be remembered, because we are not the Source, that everything that we say must be carefully considered before being acted upon. You must always use your God-given powers of discrimination. We would insist that nothing that we say is ever taken as the truth, just because it comes from our side of life'[56].

This regularly-repeated reminder fits in well with the individualism of New Age thinking, and with its sensitivity to religious authoritarianism. In theory at least, the New Age recognizes no spiritual authority higher than personal

---

[54] OtC 35-37.
[55] RR 218.
[56] VR 19.

inner experience. Genuine spiritual guides may give help and advice, but will never attempt to impose their views in an authoritarian manner. If one of them does, he should not be trusted: he may turn out to be comparatively unevolved and ignorant himself, or even to be a negative entity masquarading as a Master. Most do-it-yourself channeling books include guidelines for distinguishing highly evolved from less evolved or negative entities. Significantly, these guidelines unvaryingly describe the latter as authoritarian, given to religious exclusivism, and spiritually arrogant[57]. Roman & Packer's entities emphasize that genuine guides '...encourage you to use your own wisdom and discernment rather than blindly follow anything you are told. They never tell you that you "have to" do something or attempt to determine a direct outcome in you personal life. ... They will encourage you not to give your power to them'[58]. In a later chapter, these views will turn out to be part of a distinct ethical framework. In the meantime, we may note that nowhere in this whole hierarchy of meta-empirical beings or realities have we encountered anything or anyone with sufficient authority to overrule the free choice of human beings, to demand their unconditional allegiance, or to punish transgression of its (or his) wishes. We will see, however, that there are nevertheless believed to be laws which humans cannot break without having to suffer the consequences.

Spiritual entities, especially those referred to in theosophical parlance as "Masters", are not only accessible by channeling. They may also "incarnate" (the term is not always taken in a literal sense) on earth. In those cases they usually become part of religious history, and I will therefore discuss such incarnations in chapter eleven. Jesus is, of course, a prominent example. I referred above to the view of Christ as a highly evolved entity rather than a semi-divine "principle". Both views can be used to support the belief that the "Master Jesus" embodied the Christ. According to the first perspective, the Christ was not the divine principle of absolute love and wisdom as such, but a particular intelligent being who had attained a high level of love and wisdom. Although the sources themselves often blur such fine distinctions, they nevertheless imply them.
Spiritual incarnations apart, there is yet another category which could be discussed here but is more properly relegated to the next chapter. This is the widespread tendency to say that "man is God". This statement may be explained in several ways, as will be seen. Similarly, there is a New Age tradition which says that human beings are none other than "the gods" who originally created the universe, but in the process came to be trapped in their own creations. For completeness' sake, these different strands should at least be mentioned here, but they will be discussed more fully in chapter eleven, section 2.

[57] Cf. for instance Ridall, *Channeling*, 73.
[58] OtC 39.

CHAPTER EIGHT

MATTERS OF THE MIND

1. Introduction

It seems natural to subdivide religious worldviews into three large domains, pertaining to God, the world, and humanity respectively. More precisely, one may distinguish between the physical universe; the metaphysical reality (God, or gods) behind or beyond this physical universe; and humanity as a factor that somehow differs from both. This commonsense triad is philosophically problematical because it is loaded with implicit metaphysical presuppositions, most of which are based on some basic form of dualism[1]. On a more commonsense level, however, there is a naturalness about it that most people find hard to resist. Something in human nature rebels against the idea that humans are not, somehow, qualitatively different from the rest of nature; and although those who believe in God may think of him in different ways, at least they do not regard him as synonymous with humanity or with the world outside. Although New Age believers are certainly not different from most other people in this regard, it is remarkable to what extent they blur the distinctions between the three domains. It is often difficult, if not impossible, to make a distinction between God and the universe (not uncommonly, as we saw, the two terms are used as synonyms), and in this chapter we will encounter a similar tendency to conflate man with God and/or the universe. This tendency is found, furthermore, not only in the more intellectual and philosophical sources, but throughout our corpus. This is, in fact, remarkable. In traditional religious contexts, the philosophical critique of commonsense distinctions has usually been limited to intellectual or mystical elites, while the masses largely held far more concrete beliefs[2]. In the New Age, however, the rejection of these conventional distinctions is commonplace. In this respect, New Age intellectuals differ

---

[1] The distinction between human beings and their natural environment may be described as based on the dualism of subject versus object; but God as Creator does not quite fit in, to the extent that he is seen as the ultimate Subject in relation to his creations. Or God may be characterized as spirit and nature as matter; but human beings do not quite fit in because they take part in both. Similar arguments pertain to other dualities, such as freedom vs. determinism or personal vs. impersonal. In each case it is difficult to combine a fundamentally dualistic scheme with the triad of World-God-Man. Since it is always possible to question the dualism, the validity of the triad is open to criticism on a philosophical level.

[2] One might think, for instance, of the philosophy of the *Upanishads* or of the *Vedanta*, on the one hand, and popular Hinduism exemplified by devotional practice (*bhakti*).

from popular authors only because they express themselves in a more systematic and sophisticated way.

In spite of the above, this and the two preceding chapters are roughly based on the traditional triad. After "the nature of reality" (the universe) and "meta-empirical beings" (God, gods), the present chapter deals with the human element. We will see that, very significantly, a discussion of New Age views of human beings largely boils down to a discussion of the human *mind*, and of matters related to the mind. That an overview of religious anthropology should thus be largely dominated by religious *psychology* would not be obvious in other contexts; in the case of New Age religion, however, it is unavoidable. Given this focus on the mind, we may already point to the significance of the fact that chapter six together with the present chapter will turn out to be the two central and indispensable pillars for understanding New Age religion (which is why they are the most lengthy). In the holistic context outlined above, these two chapters must be seen as presenting complementary perspectives on what is emically perceived as *one* interrelated whole. Officially, chapter six dealt with "outer" reality and the present one deals with "inner" reality; actually, however, New Age holism implies that the two are ultimately one. God (chapter seven, section 2A) is perhaps best seen as the connecting link between the universe without and the universe within, or as the wholeness in which this seeming duality reposes.

2. Human Beings

A. The "I am God" Motif

The idea of God as universal energy, permeating the universe, naturally implies that everything participates in God's being. The more specific assertion that human beings, in particular, are divine in essence belongs to the most common beliefs of the New Age movement. Typically, formulations of this belief show the same lack of precision which we already found in general ideas about God. The intimate connection between the God Source and human beings is mostly regarded as quite natural and self-evident, and explicit arguments or explanations are therefore rather rare. Instead, we find a collection of suggestive formulas which merely convey the general idea without bothering about specifics. Most of these suggest that divinity can be found "within": human beings contain a "divine essence", "inner Godhead", "divine Self", "inner divinity", "divine spark" or "droplet of divinity"[3]. Others place less emphasis on interiority, and prefer to speak in terms of a "cosmic connection" which

---

[3] TiR 308-309; ECR 13-14; W 105; AC 420-423; CV 39; EAM 136; GMC 129; WW2 25; PST 63; RR 11-12; SG 10-11; RBNA 195; VAA 6; EiG 6; SoS 185-186.

makes human beings into potentially "perfect expressions of God", or "channels for the universe"[4]. Very often, creativity is seen as of the essence of the divine[5]. By developing our potential for "co-creating with God" we align ourselves with the dynamics of the divine: 'That is, we come back into an experience of our true selves, the God-like nature or the universal mind that is within us all. Through this experience we are eventually restored to our full spiritual power, the emptiness inside us is filled up *from within*, and we become radiant beings, sharing the light and love that comes from within us with everyone around us'[6].

Henry Reed, in his personal exegesis of the Edgar Cayce material, has given a very useful pictorial representation of the relation between the "Universal Mind" (God) and the individual mind of a human being [fig. A]. The *One Mind* is depicted in the form of a star. Each point of the star represents the *mind of an individual* (Reed gives a picture with a limited number of points, but adds that we would actually need a star with billions of points). Although these points fan out from the center, and are therefore relatively far away from that center, they remain connected to it. Each arm of the star ends in a very sharp point, which represents the *conscious* mind of an individual. 'A conscious mind is capable of very exact, penetrating focus. Yet it also becomes

Figure A. The Relation between Individual Conscious Minds and the One Mind.

---

[4] CV 39-40; OR 99; EiG 27.
[5] See for example OB 183.
[6] CV 28.

isolated from the rest of the mind by this very narrow focus'[7]. The development of individual consciousness is, in other words, bought at the price of a relative alienation from the universal source. This alienation remains only relative; ultimately, it is illusionary, because the continuity between the point of the star and its center remains unbroken.

Reed's star diagram also allows for a perspective on the role of the human unconscious. If one magnifies one tiny part of the star, one finds that two neighboring points of consciousness are connected [fig. B].

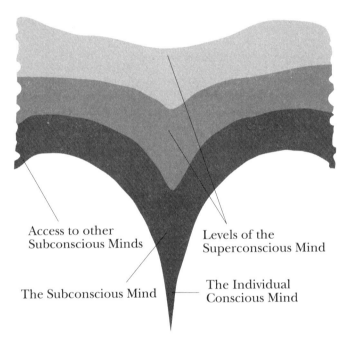

Figure B. Regions of the Mind.

They can be pictured as two mountains, connected by a valley. All these valleys together represent the *collective unconscious*[8]. Now, if one moves from the top of the "mountain" (individual consciousness) downwards, one moves from individual consciousness toward the *individual unconscious*. The further one moves from the top down, the less individuality remains. By the time one

---

[7] ECMM 54.

[8] If one were to picture the star as three-dimensional, looking down on the surface of the star one would see a grid consisting of the collective unconscious, and small ponts consisting of individual consciousnesses.

has reached the valley, one has moved into the domain of the collective unconscious. Moving upwards again on the slope of a second mountain means moving towards increased individuality again, culminating in another conscious mind represented by the top of that particular mountain. In this way, the collective unconscious is pictured as the "surface tissue" of the star. This allows for an unbroken connection between all individual consciousnesses. If one moves from that surface toward the center of the star, one reaches ever deeper levels of the *superconscious* mind.

Reed's diagram fits most easily in the framework of "Ultimate Source Holism", but defenders of "Universal Interconnectedness" do not find it difficult to describe the same constellation in the scientific terminology of self-organization:

> In a universe in which mind is software, it is possible to imagine an overall gestalt of consciousness, a supermind, existing since creation, encompassing all the fundamental fields of nature, and taking upon itself the task of ordering the laws of physics.
> Davies states, "This would not be a God who created everything by supernatural means, but a directing, controlling, universal mind pervading the cosmos and operating the laws of nature to achieve some specific purpose. We could describe this state of affairs by saying that nature is a product of its own technology, and that the universe *is* mind: a self-observing as well as selforganizing system. Our own minds could then be viewed as localized 'islands' of consciousness in a sea of mind, an idea reminiscent of the Oriental conception of mysticism..."[9].

Popular New Age beliefs, according to which every human being participates in the mind of God, mostly presuppose something essentially similar to Reed's star diagram or Talbot's "islands of consciousness"[10]. The same conceptualization can even support the statement that "everybody is God". On the basis of the star diagram, however, it is clear that this should not be understood in the most radical sense: human beings are not "fully" or exclusively God, because the very development of individual focus implies a corresponding lack of awareness of the underlying wholeness. In this connection, J Z Knight characterizes man as 'the altered state of God'[11]: a lucky formulation which catches the essence of New Age anthropology and psychology.

Few aspects of the New Age have shocked traditional religious sensitivities more (and have invited more ridicule, even from non-religious quarters) than Shirley MacLaine's notorious "I am God" exclamations[12]. MacLaine's often-

---

[9] BQ 193-194. The quotation is from Davies, *God and the New Physics*, 189.

[10] Cf. Tanya Luhrmann's highly relevant observations about occultist adaptations of Jungian psychology (*Persuasions*, 280-282).

[11] SoM 373.

[12] The statement "I am God" appears regularly in MacLaine's books, but achieved notoriety on the basis of the TV-miniseries *Out on a Limb*. In DL 111-112, MacLaine describes how she

repeated conviction that not only she herself, but everybody else as well is God, might be interpreted as just one more example of the perspective just discussed. Partly, this is indeed how she herself sees it, as shown for example in these reflections on

> the most controversial concept of the New Age philosophy: the belief that God lies within, and therefore we are each part of God. Since there is no separateness, we are each Godlike, and God is in each of us. We experience God and God experiences through us. We are literally made up of God energy, therefore we can create whatever we want in life because we are each co-creating with the energy of God—the energy that makes the universe itself[13].

However, MacLaine's "I am God" belief, based on the holistic premise that there is "no separation", is potentially more radical. Clearly intended to be provocative, it contains a polemical edge which is absent in most other authors. More importantly, within the wider context of MacLaine's beliefs, the phrase "I am God" can be seen as containing (holographically, as it were) a whole metaphysics in a nutshell. This worldview, based on the idea that "we create our own reality", will be discussed in section 3B of the present chapter. Briefly, we are dealing here with the more radical implications of the holographic paradigm. If the whole is contained in each of its parts, then each part *is* the whole. Consequently, while the "spiritual father" of New Age holography—Seth—still made a distinction between *All That Is* as the "primary energy gestalt" and smaller "energy essence personalities", the logic of holography ultimately demands that all distinctions between "part" and "whole" break down completely. If the whole is God and God is Mind, then each human mind *is* God. At one point in her development, MacLaine herself apparently realized this logic. In another notorious passage, she manages to shock even a convinced New Age audience by proclaiming radical solipsism: 'I was the only person alive in my universe'[14]. We will return to that in section 3B of the present chapter.

MacLaine's radical "I am God" belief is directly derived from two of her main influences, Chris Griscom and J Z Knight/Ramtha. At the end of chapter six, section 2B, it was already noted that Griscom, following holographic logic, goes beyond Seth in asserting that each individual mind is the center of the universe. Ramtha is less concerned with holography, but he does see it as his most important task to convince the members of his audience that each of them

---

uses "affirmations" (brief sentences meant to influence the subconscious mind; see below) such as 'I am God in action', 'I am God in health', 'I am God in fun', 'I am God in stamina', 'I am God in light'.

[13] GW 100. Cf. DL 396, where the channeled entity Tom McPherson describes the basic spiritual law of the universe as 'Everyone is God. Everyone'. MacLaine's own Higher Self has the same message (DL 343): '...you see, each soul is its own God. You must never worship anyone or anything other than self. For *you* are God. To love self is to love God'.

[14] IAP 171.

is God. On the back cover of *Ramtha: An Introduction* is a photograph of J Z Knight staring the reader straight in the face, accompanied by this text: 'You never knew how beautiful you were, for you never really looked at who and what you are. You want to see what God looks like? Go look in a reflector—you are looking God straight in the face'. What exactly is meant by this? The volume *Ramtha* begins with the story of how Ramtha, an Atlantian warrior of "Lemurian" birth, known also as "the Ram", came to discover "the Unknown God" in the ongoingness of life itself:

> It was not until I observed and pondered life and its ongoingness that I discovered who the Unknown God truly was. I reasoned that the Unknown God was not the gods created through the altered thinking of man. I realized that the gods in men's minds are only the personalities of the things they fear and respect the most; that the true God is the ongoing essence that permits man to create and play out his illusions however he chooses, and that will still be there when man returns yet again, another spring, another life. I realized that it is in the power and the ongoingness of the life-force where the Unknown God truly lies.
> Who was the unknown God? It was me... and the birds in their night nest, the frost on the reeds, the morning dawn and evening sky. It was the sun and the moon, children and their laughter, alabaster knees and running water, and the smell of garlic and leather and brass. This understanding took a long time for me to grasp, though it had been right in front of me all the time. The Unknown God wasn't beyond the moon or the sun—it was all around me! It was with this new birth of reasoning that I began to embrace life, to hold that dear to me, and to find a reason to live. I realized that there was more than blood and death and the stench of war; there was *Life*—far greater than we had ever perceived it to be.
> It was through this realization that I would understand, in the years to come, that man *is* the greatest of all things; and that the only reason the sun is ongoing while man dies, is the sun never even contemplates death. All it knows ... is to be.[15]

Ramtha began to wonder how he himself could become as ongoing as life. He wanted to *be* the Unknown God. He concluded that the wind most closely resembled the life force: 'it is ongoing, free-moving, all-consuming; it has no boundaries and no form; it is magical, exploratory and adventurous. ... and the wind never judges man. The wind never forsakes man. The wind, if you call it, will come to you... through love. Ideals should be like that'[16]. By ceaselessly contemplating the wind, Ramtha finally "became the wind". One day he discovered that he was able to leave his body and travel like the wind. Ultimately, he succeeded in entirely "reprogramming" the very cellular structure of his body, transposing it from the vibration rate of matter to the vibration rate of pure light: 'I became an unseen power that has no form, that is pulsating light, indivisible'[17]. One day he ascended before his people, and was gone.

---

[15] R 14-15. We may note, incidentally, that Ramtha's view of God comes extremely close to the neopagan view of divine "immanence".

[16] R 16.

[17] R 18.

> After I ascended is when I knew everything I wanted to know, because I went out of the density of flesh and into the fluidness of thought; and in so doing, I was not inhibited by anything. Then I knew that man truly was, in his essence, God. ... That is when peace came. That is when I began to know more. That is when I became one with the Unknown God. ... I was Ram the Conqueror. I am now Ram the God. I was a barbarian who became God through the simplest and yet the most profound of things. What I teach you is what I learned[18].

Ramtha's message that we are all God contains several elements. Firstly, it means to him that we are not sinful, guilty, flawed or wretched creatures, but that we are inherently good, beautiful and perfect. In this context, saying "I am God" is not a propositional but a performative statement[19]: it is a means of rejecting and neutralizing depreciatory self-images ingrained in our society together with the idea of a judging and punishing God. Secondly, it means that we are one with the flow of life and the essence of reality (which, according to Ramtha, is "Thought"). Third, it means that we are, literally, *gods*. We were originally perfect, divine beings. It was we who created the cosmos, in a very literal sense, only to get lost in our own creations afterwards (see chapter eleven, section 2).

Ramtha's views imply that man is intimately one with God, but he still does not completely conflate both categories. Saying "I am God" means rejecting dualism in favour of a holistic oneness of human beings and God and, maybe even more importantly, rejecting the idea that human beings are guilty or sinful and in need of salvation. This central New Age theme will be discussed in chapter ten, about ethics. It must be concluded, therefore, that Ramtha's slogan "You are God" is slightly overstated: at most, Ramtha claims that "You are *a* God" (among many others) or "You are one with God in essence" or, simply, "You are perfect and sinless". The radical "You are God" ideology, as pronounced by Shirley MacLaine, is the result of the assimilation of Ramtha's message and his "I am God" slogan within the holographic worldview of Chris Griscom. Only on that basis could "You are God" take on the meaning of "You are the source and center of the (or: your) universe".

B. The Constitution of Human Beings

In the discussion of Henry Reed's star diagram we noted how metaphysical and psychological concepts may be combined within one "transpersonal" vision of reality. The most important concepts, in such views, are the Universal Mind (also referred to as God, Mind, Superconsciousness), the Higher Self (also referred to as transpersonal Self or the soul), the collective and personal uncon-

---

[18] R 20-21.
[19] The distinction is derived from Jürgen Habermas. For a brief discussion and application to the study of religions, see Kippenberg, *Vorderasiatischen Erlösungsreligionen*, 47-54.

scious, and the individual ego. The connection between mind and matter is provided for by the concept of subtle bodies on the one hand, and by theories about the brain on the other.

The (Higher) Self

Not all New Age ideas about the Higher Self are fully consistent with each other, but the general idea is quite clear. David Spangler speaks of 'another part of myself, one that is vastly more expansive than my personality; it is a deeper self, one that participates in eternity even as my daily self participates in time'[20]. This catches the essence of the concept. The normal, daily personality we usually call "me" is not the real Self at all. The real Self possesses a vast consciousness not bounded by space and time. This Higher Self participates in the divine Mind in a way our "skin-encapsulated ego" (to use Alan Watts's famous term) does not, but at the same time it is personal in a way the universal Life Force is not. In other words, the Higher Self functions as the personal mediating link or bridge between man and God: it is more personal than God yet more universal than man[21]. This Higher Self is what really matters about human beings: it is our real identity[22]. Spiritual development means getting in touch with, and aligning oneself with one's Higher Self rather than with one's limited personality. The channeled entity Orin explains what this means: 'As you open to the higher dimensions of yourself, you will be able to lift the veils of illusion and see the world through the eyes of your Higher Self. You will link your throat[23] with your Higher Self and express truth and love in all you say. Your mind will be illumined and your emotions will be harmonious as they are blended with the light of your Higher Self'[24]. Not all New Age sources promise that much, but it is generally agreed that conscious connection with one's Higher Self leads to increased insight, spirituality, love, balance and health. One prominent way in which the Higher Self connects with the limited personality is through the intuition[25]. In chapter one we found that

---

[20] RS 64. Spangler became aware of this higher self during an impressive mystical experience at age seven. See his description in RS 61-64.

[21] George Trevelyan describes the Higher Self as our individual channel to the divine realm (OR 92). '...the I AM, the great Cosmic Being, the Beloved, is personalized for us through our Higher Self' (OR 94). Shirley MacLaine speaks of the 'personalized interface with [the] God source within' (GW 84).

[22] This, at least, is the general trend. Some authors prefer a more complicated conception. Gary Zukav presents a not uncommon variation by describing the Higher Self as the connecting link, not between the Universal Mind and the personality, but between the Soul and the personality. The soul is more than the Higher Self, but less than the Universal Mind. The personality cannot communicate with the fullness of its own soul, and needs the Higher Self as an intermediate. Similarly, Chris Griscom describes the Higher Self as the 'megaphone of the soul' (ENF 10). The soul itself, in her view, remains 'unknown and foreign' (ENF 11).

[23] Presumably a reference to the throat chakra.

[24] SG 10.

[25] Cf. SoS 86-88.

the training of intuition may gradually lead to channeling experiences. In fact, the relation between the personality and its Higher Self is, according to New Age thinking, quite similar to that between a human person and a spiritual entity. In learning to trust one's intuition and act on it, what one actually does is to open oneself to the inner guidance of one's Higher Self. Shakti Gawain, for instance, relates how she 'began to realize that "it" (my higher self) seemed to know more than "I" (my personality self) did about a lot of things. I saw that it would probably be smart to try and find out what that inner guidance was telling me and follow it. Every time I did that it seemed to work'[26]. The systematic and purposive development of intuitive capabilities may result in increasingly intimate and concrete experiences of the Higher Self. At a certain point, the Higher Self may even appear to the personality in the form of a separate being, in a manner hardly distinguishable from channeling. In the next chapter we will discuss the crucial role of the Higher Self, with its superior "transpersonal" perspective, in the process of personal reincarnation. At this point, the most important thing is to recognize the implications for religious anthropology. To believe in the Higher Self implies that we are not who we think we are. Our everyday personality is a transient shadow, and may well be described as a dream or illusion created by the real Self[27]. Our real essence is a spiritual reality about which most of us know nothing at all: we are living in a state of alienation from our real being. We are accustomed to regard ourselves as free, active agents in the world; but actually, the only real agent is the Higher Self expressing itself through our limited minds: 'The High Self stages trials and situations, allowing us free rein to hurt ourselves and to follow our whims and desires, our ambitions and self-aggrandizement, until ultimately, disillusioned, we turn and come back to Him as He waits within'[28].

The inevitable conclusion is that human beings are not as autonomous as they are normally supposed to be. They are "actors on a stage", unconsciously trying (with more or less success) to follow a script written by their own Higher Self. Nobody has brought this out more clearly than Shirley MacLaine, an actress herself. MacLaine's whole New Age philosophy circles around the central concept of the Self, which creates life circumstances as a theatre for its personalities[29]. Most of her writings have to do with discovering the hidden meaning behind what happens in her life: trying to go beyond the "acting personality", as it were, in order to understand the deeper spiritual meaning of the script. MacLaine's description of the Higher Self amounts to a perfect summing-up of many central New Age beliefs:

---

[26] LL xvii.

[27] Marilyn Ferguson, for instance, describes the Higher Self as 'this invisible continent on which we all make our home', and concludes that 'the separate self is an illusion' (AC 106).

[28] OR 97.

[29] See about the "stage" analogy: OL 153; IAP 5-7, 119, 293, 300, 337; DWYC 142.

The higher unlimited superconsciousness can best be defined as one's eternal unlimited soul—the soul that is the real "you". The soul that has been through incarnation after incarnation and knows all there is to know about you because it *is* you. It is the repository of your experience. It is the totality of your soul memory and your soul energy. It is also the energy that interfaces with the energy we refer to as God. It knows and resonates to God because it is a part of God. As in the mind of man there are many thoughts, so in the mind of God there are many souls.

Our higher unlimited self, which has been a child of God from the beginning of time, is with us every instant, silently (and sometimes not so silently) guiding us through events and experiences which we elect to have for ourselves in order to learn more fully who we are *and* what the God energy is. That energy is *totally* aware and the more we listen to it, the more aware each of us can become.

The great spiritual masters such as Christ and Buddha were totally in touch with their higher unlimited selves and were therefore capable of accomplishing whatever they desired. They were fully realized human beings who understood all of their incarnational experiences and were able to incorporate their knowledge and understanding into lives of service for others. While the goal of realizing oneself is basically quite simple it is also awesome. It is to realize that we are part of God...which is to say, total love and light[30].

During acupuncture treatment administered by Chris Griscom, MacLaine had a vision in which she met her Higher Self face to face:

It took my breath away. I said nothing. ... It was a powerful form, quietly standing in the center of my inner space, looking at me with total love! The figure was very tall, an androgynous being with long arms and the kindest face I had ever seen. The hair was reddish gold and the features aquiline. The figure lifted its arms and welcomed me to recognize it, saying, "I am the real you!". I heard the words inside my heart and I *knew* they were true. Tears spilled down my cheeks as I proceeded to carry on an internal conversation with this being, who told me things about myself I had always wanted to know. I asked questions about people, my marriage, my family (what relation they had had to me previously), what to expect in my professional work, and so on[31].

After this session, MacLaine tried to connect with her Higher Self without the help of acupuncture, and 'It was there every time'[32]. Furthermore, it appeared able to exercise paranormal control over outside events, and to possess apparently unlimited knowledge[33]. Of course, because the Higher Self is MacLaine's own real being, the implication is that her *own* abilities proved to go beyond anything she had thought possible before. Most of the personal limitations she had supposed inevitable appeared to be only a matter of belief.

---

[30] DL 104.

[31] GW 87. The original description appears in DL 335ff.

[32] DL 349.

[33] Cf. DL 337-339, where MacLaine stops a tree from swaying in the wind, and 349, where her Higher Self locates missing objects, and appears to know who is at the other end of a ringing telephone.

The concept of the Higher Self evokes many questions. Of particular importance is the problem of *what* exactly is believed to be evolving through incarnations over time. When MacLaine describes the Higher Self as a "repository" of incarnational experience, this seems to suggest that, by voluntarily restricting itself to a limited personality in time/space, the Higher Self gathers the experiences needed for its own evolution. The Higher Self, on this premise, is in a process of learning and growth. On the other hand, the wisdom and knowledge of the Higher Self is very often emphasized to the point where it seems to become a perfect semidivine being. On this premise, the Higher Self does not need to learn anything: it is only the limited personality that is ignorant and in need of healing. In this case, one wonders what is the point of the whole process. The fact that most New Age sources emphasize both spiritual evolution as a universal dynamic *and* the boundless wisdom of the Higher Self results in a latent paradox which is seldom explicitly adressed in the sources. It does not seem to be a matter of much concern to most New Agers. What matters to them is the concept that whatever may befall the personality, the spiritual and moral integrity of the Higher Self remains unimpaired.

Nevertheless, it is important to look at those sources that do offer a theoretical solution[34]. The chief example is the Seth material. Seth's terminology has only partly been adopted by later authors[35], but his basic views have been extremely influential. Central to Seth's vision is the concept of the "multidimensional personality". This parallels what is mostly referred to as the Higher Self by later New Age authors. Seth himself uses a wide variety of terms ("entity", "whole self", "gestalt" or "(over)soul") to refer to this same concept.

> The soul *can* be considered as an electromagnetic energy field, of which you are part. It is a field of concentrated action when you consider it in this light—a powerhouse of probabilities or probable actions, seeking to be expressed; a grouping of nonphysical consciousness that nevertheless knows itself as an identity. ... The soul can be described ... as a multidimensional, infinite act, each minute probability being brought somewhere into actuality and existence; an infinite creative act that creates for itself infinite dimensions in which fulfillment is possible[36].

The essence of this soul is conscious, creative energy seeking to express itself. Each human being is a tiny part of such a greater soul or entity, and is therefore referred to as a "fragment personality". A fragment personality can be defined as a part of a soul which is focused more or less exclusively on one particular kind of reality. It can only do this by excluding other realities—all of which are in principle accessible to the soul—from conscious awareness. Now, these and all other realities do not exist apart from consciousness, but

---

[34] For the following paragraph cf. Hanegraaff, 'Channeling-literatuur'.
[35] PR 194; SoS 37.
[36] SS 93 & 256.

are directly *created* by it. In other words, it is not quite correct to say that part of the soul is incarnated on earth. Rather, part of the soul creates an experience of earth existence for itself, and it is only the focus on this particular reality (or maybe a series of realities: successive incarnations) which defines the individual identity of the fragment. When the experience ends, the fragment regains awareness of its wider soul perspective. The parallel with dreams is very close. All the time, the only "real" entity is the dreamer lying in his bed. This dreamer may experience all kinds of adventures in his dreams, which seem very real to him and during which the dream personality is unaware of its "real" personality (the sleeper). On one level, the dreamer remains who he is, regardless of what seems to happen to him in his dreams; on another level, he may learn from his dream experiences and be changed by them. In this way, the dream analogy illuminates the relation between Higher Self and personality: the former has perfect awareness (he has direct access to reality as it really is) as compared to the illusionary awareness of his dream self; nevertheless, he can learn and "evolve" through his dreams. In this way, the paradox mentioned above may be accounted for. The dream analogy breaks down only when we realize that, according to Seth's teachings, the Higher Self is and remains totally aware *during* the "incarnations" of its fragment personalities. In other words, the soul is able to dream many simultaneous dreams while being fully awake at the same time. This follows logically from Seth's basic assertion that time is an illusion. In the "spacious present" there can be no question of certain time periods during which the soul is awake to reality and others during which it is "dreaming" in its fragment personalities. Neither is it possible that the different fragments follow each other in sequential time order (i.e., in linear reincarnations): from the soul's perspective, all incarnations happen at the same time, or rather, out of time altogether. The picture becomes even more unusual when we realize that nothing then prevents different fragment personalities coming from the same soul to *meet* each other in their shared, intersubjective reality. In other words, there need not be a one-to-one relation between a human individual and his/her Higher Self. Many individual persons living at the same time may be part of one and the same soul[37]. Seth's teachings about the multi-dimensional personality, in the context of his holographic worldview, amount to a radical metaphysics which reminds one at every page that the medium in question started her career as a science-fiction writer.

The Unconscious

The Higher Self, or soul, can be regarded as the interface between the Universal Mind, or God, and the individual personality. According to New Age

---

[37] A prominent example mentioned by Seth is the soul of "The Christ", which included the three parallel personalities of John the Baptist, Jesus, and Paul (SM 271-272; Roberts, *God of Jane*, 211).

thinking, this is just another way of saying that it is the interface between a metaphysical and a psychological reality, on the tacit proviso that both alternatives are regarded as relative rather than absolute indications. In a holistic context as represented by Reed's star diagram, an absolute distinction between the Mind of God and the mind of man is impossible. A *relative* distinction, however, is necessary to allow for the fact that not everybody is aware of his/her oneness with God. The movement from the star's center to its periphery is seen as a movement from full universal consciousness to an ever narrower constriction of consciousness: from being fully "awake" and aware of one's real being to "falling asleep" and forgetting one's true origin. The state of mind which we usually regard as personal *consciousness* (the points of the star) is, therefore, not really "conscious" at all. If one's perception of reality is limited only to this narrow personal focus, one is, in fact, oblivious to one's real being.

Getting in touch with one's own unconscious is the first step towards a wider vision. The personal unconscious, however, is only a localized region of the *collective* unconscious which connects all individual human consciousnesses. This collective unconscious is a realm of the mind where we can get in touch with the universal archetypes. In Jungian fashion, the "gods" of traditional pantheons are often interpreted as archetypes, and reversely the archetypes of the collective unconscious are seen as powerful, numinous realities. In other words, traditional religious concepts are reinterpreted in psychological terms; but because psychology itself is embedded in an encompassing religious framework New Age authors can avoid the traditional reductionist conclusion that the gods are unreal because they exist "only in the mind". They *do* exist only in the mind, of course, but if God as well as all reality is ultimately mind, then where else could the gods be if not in the mind?

The concept of "inner worlds" is a key concept of New Age religion. Further discussion will be postponed to section 3C of the present chapter, where we will be able to take advantage of the wider context of "creating our own reality"-theories. In the next chapter we will encounter it again in the discussion of the "other worlds" entered by the soul after death.

New Age thinking is definitely post-Freudian in its awareness of the power of suppressed emotions and desires. However, it is not typical for New Age thinking to regard the power and influence of the *id* on human behaviour as a grave and pressing problem which can be relieved (if not fully solved) only at the price of long and arduous self-confrontation. In contrast to Freud's essentially tragic perspective on the human condition, New Agers typically take a rather optimistic view. First of all, it is frequently suggested that the human potential movement and transpersonal psychotherapy have now developed methods that can lead to a very quick and permanent solution of deep-seated traumas. In techniques like Orr & Ray's Rebirthing, Stanislav Grof's Holotropic Therapy and many similar practices, a strong emotional confrontation with the personal unconscious in therapeutically controlled Altered States of Consciousness allegedly leads to dramatic and lasting improvement[38]. The purported reason is that the direct experience induced by these techniques is far more effective than the indirect verbal interpretations relied upon by classical psychoanalysis: the former approach directly accesses the subconscious, while the latter only talks about it. Secondly, there is the not uncommon belief that the superconscious or Higher Self has the ability to "overrule" the subconscious. Aligning oneself with one's Higher Self will simply result in the disappearance of the negative, as light drives away darkness[39]. Thirdly, the unconscious can also be "reprogrammed" by conscious rather than superconscious intervention. It is believed that all suffering results from unconsciously-held beliefs; and these beliefs can be changed by suggestion, in particular with the help of so-called "affirmations". These last two beliefs are closely linked to the "creating our own reality" system which will be discussed in section 3B of the present chapter.

Finally, and perhaps most importantly, it must be emphasized that the New Age movement follows Jung, rather than Freud, in regarding the unconscious as much more than just a storehouse of repressed emotions. It has some remarkable "talents" of its own. Henry Reed points out that our unconscious notices everything which happens to us, down to the smallest details, but brings to conscious awareness only those sense impressions which are useful to us in a given situation. Without this unconscious selection process, normal functioning would be impossible: we would literally be bombarded by a chaos of impressions. Furthermore, the unconscious has perfect memory; all data stored in it over the years are in principle accessible to us, if only we know how to communicate with the unconscious[40]. Because unconscious impressions exist in a prereflective and nonverbal state, however, we have to translate them into words and images. This translation requires the use of the intuitive faculties. Both intuition and the unconscious are associated with the right brain hemisphere, which functions on holistic principles. The left hemisphere, in contrast, is analytic, intellectual, verbal. New Age sources do not tire to repeat that most of us rely heavily on the latter only, and neglect the former[41]. It is important to develop our "right-brain" faculties to an equal level as those of our "left brain". In this way we not only gain access to knowledge stored in the unconscious

---

[38] BB 385; AS 243-249; Cf. also Chris Griscom's acupuncture treatment as described by Shirley MacLaine.

[39] Some authors with a strong this-worldly orientation—neopagans in particular—have criticized New Age tendencies to emphasize only "light and love" and ignore (i.e., repress) the darker sides of life. Cf. W 201-202; OB 134-139, 154; DD *passim*. Somewhat unexpectedly, Shakti Gawain voices the same warning: RG 30.

[40] ECMM 31-48.

[41] See below.

(both personal and collective), but also to the superconscious or transpersonal realms. We may illustrate this with the case of Starhawk, who refers to the unconscious as "Younger Self", and contrasts this to the "Talking Self" of the conscious mind:

> Because they function through different modes of awareness, communication between the two is difficult. It is as if they speak different languages.
> It is Younger Self which directly experiences the world, through the holistic awareness of the right hemisphere. Sensations, emotions, basic drives, image memory, intuition, and diffuse perception are functions of Younger Self. Younger Self's verbal understanding is limited; it communicates through images, emotions, sensations, dreams, visions, and physical symptoms. Classical psychoanalysis developed from attempts to interpret the speech of Younger Self. Witchcraft not only interprets, but teaches us how to speak back to Younger Self.
> Talking Self organizes the impressions of Younger Self, gives them names, classifies them into systems. As its name implies, it functions through the verbal, analytic awareness of the left hemisphere. It also includes the set of verbally understood precepts that encourage us to make judgments about right or wrong. Talking Self speaks through words, abstract concepts, and numbers[42].

It is characteristic for Starhawk's neopagan immanentism that she does not use the term Higher Self, but prefers to speak of the *Deep* Self (or God Self). The basic connections, however, remain the same:

> ...the Deep Self is connected to Younger Self, and not directly linked to Talking Self. ... It is not the conscious mind, with its abstract concepts, that ever actually communicates with the Divine; it is the unconscious mind, the Younger Self that responds only to images, pictures, sensations, tangibles. To communicate with the Deep Self, the Goddess/God Within, we resort to symbols, to art, poetry, music, myth, and the actions of ritual that translate abstract concepts into the language of the unconscious.
> Younger Self—who can be as balky and stubborn as the most cantakerous three-year-old—is not impressed by words. Like a native of Missouri, it wants to be *shown*. To arouse its interest, we must seduce it with pretty pictures and pleasurable sensations—take it out dining and dancing, as it were. Only in this way can Deep Self be reached[43].

The emphasis on the unconscious world of symbols and archetypes as the *only* way to reach the divine (and the corresponding concentration on art, myth and ritual) is particularly characteristic for neopaganism; but the view of the unconscious as the connection between human and divine consciousness (via the Higher Self) is a general New Age tenet. There is wide agreement that the process of spiritual growth starts with confronting, exploring and cleaning up the unconscious realms of the psyche (both individual and collective), but ends in aligning with God by way of the Higher Self. This does not mean, however,

---

[42] SD 35.
[43] SD 36. Cf. Z Budapest's theory of "Slothwoman" (HBWM 8-9).

that the unconscious is left behind or transcended. It is true that a "fully real-ized being" would, presumably, no longer have a *"Freudian"* unconscious: he would no longer have to fear the contents of his own mind or need to repress part of it. The Freudian unconscious would, therefore, no longer be there; the person in question would have "become conscious", so to speak, of his uncon-scious, in the sense of his intuitive mind. He would have achieved a state of harmonious balance between the conscious and unconscious mind, i.e., between reason and intuition. Ideally, such a person would be able to maintain the con-nection to superconsciousness while living in the world of human conscious-ness.

Ego and Personality

We have now reached the most problematic level, according to New Age beliefs, of the human being. Although New Age sources seldom see the total dissolu-tion of individual consciousness (the separate personality) in the Universal Mind as a desirable goal, they do see individual "ego attachment" as the major stumbling block to enlightenment. The ego can be seen either as the result of alienation from the Higher Self, or as its cause. It is the *result* of a "false split" in consciousness, resulting from the illusion of total autonomy. As a "false self" that is constantly defending its autonomy, the ego is the *cause* of further illusion[44].

Ken Wilber has given a paradigmatic account of how a progressive series of ultimately illusory "splits" (or "dualism-repression-projections") occurring in absolute Mind, finally results in the appearance of the alienated ego (referred to by Wilber as "persona")[45]. The "primary dualism", in Wilber's view, takes place on the level of absolute Mind, and creates an apparent distinction between subject and object. This first split, by the way, occurs 'for no apparent rea-son—for reason itself does not exist here'[46]. A "secondary dualism" introduces the distinction between life and death. A "tertiary dualism" consists of the attempt on man's part to flee from death, by separating psyche from soma:

> ...man, not accepting death, abandons his mortal organism and escapes into some-thing much more "solid" and impervious than "mere" flesh—namely ideas. *Man, in fleeing death, flees his mutable body and identifies with the seemingly undy-ing idea of himself.* ... This "ideal image of himself", this "ego", seems to promise man something that his mutable flesh will not: immortality[47].

In a "quaternary dualism", finally, this ego disowns or alienates aspects of

---

[44] CiM:MfT 77; UM 149-151; ECRE 43-44; WW 158-159; BB 360-361; GMC 87; PST 142-144; AE 198-115; EiG 117-118.

[45] See SoC *passim*. The basic scheme is given as a diagram on page 143.

[46] SoC 109.

[47] SoC 125.

itself, which are then projected into the environment. The result is a distorted and impoverished self-image:

> a fraudulent self-image composed of only fragments of the true ego. In an attempt to make his self-image acceptable, the person renders it inaccurate. Now this inaccurate and impoverished self-image we will be calling the *Persona*; and the disowned, alienated, and projected facets of the ego which now appear to be external, we will call the *Shadow*[48].

The fact that Wilber speaks of "ego" where most New Agers will prefer terms like "personal self"[49], and of "Persona" where they may prefer "ego", is of minor importance. The important point is the view of common individual consciousness as an essentially limited and constricted state of being, resulting from the drive to defend the ego's autonomy against the rest of the world, and particularly against imagined threats that result from the projection of the inner "Shadow" into outer realities. This drive to be separate, to preserve its autonomy at all costs, betrays a fundamental lack of awareness of the actual unbroken wholeness of reality. The ego is fundamentally dualistic, fragmentary and based on estrangement; spiritual development accordingly means to overcome the split and regain consciousness of the whole. We already noted that wholeness in the New Age context does not have to imply (and actually seldom implies) total dissolution of individuality. More typical is the belief that different units of consciousness may ideally move and act "as one" and in harmony with the universal Mind. It is only the ego and its false attachments that prevent such a state of being, *not* as a result of its ability to act autonomously (the Higher Self has that same ability), but simply as a result of its "egoism". It is not the ego's autonomy, but its *attitude*, which is based on fear, that creates problems. We will return to this in detail in chapter ten, about New Age ethics.

   The ego's drive to assert itself against the rest of the world is counteracted by a drive toward wholeness. The discrepancy between the narrow interests of the ego and the individual's deep tendency to transcend that ego creates a tension that may translate into all kinds of problems. All human suffering may ultimately be reduced to this tension. Interestingly, physical and mental suffering may be regarded both as a direct negative result of egoic actions *and* as a basically positive force towards "healing". Symptoms of illness are actually symptoms of the individual's attempts to move towards "healing" of the split between ego and Mind. According to this perspective, illness is not correctly described as the disruption of a healthy organism, but must be seen as a signal that the natural movement towards *real* "healing"—healing of alienation

---

[48] SoC 142.
[49] Wilber himself mentions "self" as a synonym for "ego" (SoC 125).

from the whole—is being frustrated by the attitude of the ego. These symptoms should therefore be approached with a positive attitude, as reminders that one is not yet whole rather than as purely negative and unwelcome intrusions. New Age authors assert that the specific nature of the symptoms can teach us much about what parts of us require attention and healing. According to Stanislav Grof, this is the approach that characterizes all traditional healing methods.

> All these therapeutic strategies share the belief that, if the process behind the symptoms is supported, it will result in self-healing and consciousness expansion after a temporary accentuation of the discomfort. ... the driving force behind the symptoms seems to be, in the last analysis, the tendency of the organism to overcome its sense of separateness, or its exclusive identification with the body ego and the limitations of matter, three-dimensional space, and linear time. Although its ultimate objective is to connect with the cosmic field of consciousness and with a holonomic perception of the world, in a systematic process of self-exploration this final goal can take more limited forms. ... The major obstacle in the process of healing so understood is the resistance of the ego, which shows a tendency to defend its limited self-concept and world view, clings to the familiar and dreads the unknown, and resists the increase of emotional and physical pain. It is this determined effort of the ego to preserve the status quo that interferes with the spontaneous healing process and freezes it into a relatively stable form that we know as psychopathological symptoms[50].

The ego, according to the above view, is characterized by an attitude of aggressive self-assertion based ultimately on fear. This New Age belief has its background in psychoanalytic theories of repression and projection, adapted to a spiritual worldview. A further characteristic of the ego is based less on repression/projection theory than on the belief, outlined above, of a duality between rationality and intuition. The ego is commonly associated with "left-brained", narrow-minded rationality, and opposed to the "right-brained" intuitive and holistic faculties of the unconscious[51]. If both hemispheres are working in harmony, both the rational intellect and intuitive understanding complement each other and can function to their fullest potential. While the ego, as described above, is a fully negative concept in New Age thinking, the intellect is good and useful as long as it does not dominate its intuitive counterpart. New Age religion cannot consistently be characterized as anti-intellectual[52], though it might be labeled as "trans-intellectual".

Subtle Bodies
The distinctions between Higher Self, Unconscious and Ego all refer to the realm of the psyche *per se*. As exemplified in Henry Reed's star diagram, they

---

[50] BB 360-361.
[51] For instance ENF 9; OL 203, 208; DL 106; OR 13-14.
[52] Cf. WW 106; CCC 66.

are all part of a holistic continuum of Mind. A hierarchy of levels can be distinguished within this continuum, but these merge imperceptibly into each other. The same holistic concern with continuity characterizes the relation between the realms of the psyche and the realm of matter. Against the background of the discussions of chapter six it will be clear that the New Age cannot see the physical body as a "prison" from which the spirit must escape, or as a "substance" that differs radically from the substance of mind. Both "gnostic" and Cartesian dualism, in other words, are hard to combine with New Age holism. However, both spiritual and material monism are also problematic. The first tends towards a radical otherworldly "illusionism" which, as we saw, is not congenial to the spirit of most New Age thinking (*A Course in Miracles* being the main exception). The second seems to do away with the spiritual as such, which is also contrary to New Age thinking (even if there is reason to suspect that some theories, in fact, amount to this position). The favoured New Age solution is, again, a kind of "weak this-worldly illusionism". From the perspective of Mind, which is the only ultimate reality, the body is found to consist of a spiritual substance; but the "illusion" of matter is a *useful* illusion (although not necessarily a pleasant one[53]) on a given level of development, and meant to be taken quite seriously at that level. Although *A Course in Miracles* may exhort us to "awaken from the dream", the New Age in general suggests rather that we should first experience the dream and absorb what it has to teach us.

Against this background, the apparent gap between the physical body and spiritual reality is bridged by the concept of "subtle bodies", which in turn hinges on the concept of "subtle matter". The idea is an old one: it has found most cogent expression in neoplatonic traditions, and similar ideas may perhaps be found elsewhere[54]. The theories about a range of subtle bodies developed by modern Theosophy and Anthroposophy provide the direct literary source for New Age versions. In the New Age context, however, the traditional view (shared by Theosophy) of subtle bodies as mediating between *spirit and matter* receives a further, and highly characteristic elaboration: it now mediates between *objective and subjective* reality as well. It seems that this elaboration, admittedly "subtle" in itself, has not yet been sufficiently noticed by commentators on the New Age phenomenon. The background is, of course, the New Age tendency towards a "psychologizing of religion and sacralization

---

[53] In spite of the absence of "gnostic" or Cartesian types of dualism, New Agers may give expression to a feeling of being "weighed down" or constricted by the body. I refer to Sanaya Roman's comparison of physical incarnation with putting on many layers of clothes, which is strikingly similar to gnostic descriptions. Cf. also Shakti Gawain's remarks reproduced in chapter six, note 16.
[54] See chapter fifteen, section 1B.

of psychology" which we mentioned before and will discuss more fully below (section 3A).

Modern Theosophy and Anthroposophy have developed explicit theories about the precise number and nature of the subtle bodies. New Age authors, however, draw on these sources in a very eclectic manner. As a result, the details differ from author to author. Sanaya Roman talks quite unsystematically about the spiritual, emotional, mental and physical body, but also mentions a "desire body" and "body of the will", beside the "abstract mind"[55]. George Trevelyan distinguishes between the pure spirit, the astral body (also called the emotional body or soul) and the etheric body[56]. Starhawk discusses the subtle bodies in terms of "energies": the elemental, etheric or *raith* energy connected to Younger Self, the auric or astral energy connected with Talking Self and the finest and most powerful energy of the Deep Self[57]. All three appear as "bodies". Chris Griscom uses a particularly elaborate and idiosyncratic—but not exactly clear—system consisting of four bodies, each of which is said to have both a "manifest" and an "unmanifest" aspect: the physical body and its nonmanifest "light body", the mental body in its "finite" and its "higher" aspect, the emotional body which seems to be closely connected to the astral body, and the spiritual body associated with soul and higher self[58]. Many more examples could be given. The conclusion can only be that there is no perceptible agreement in New Age sources about the precise number, nature, interrelations and respective functions of the subtle bodies. The only thing about which the authors seem to agree is that subtle bodies exist. The concept of a subtle body is important to New Age religion because it gives a theoretical foundation, compatible with weak this-worldly holism, to the belief in out-of-body travelling (either through the normal world or on the "astral plane"), near-death-experiences, and reincarnation. Beyond the general belief that some sort of subtle body is required in all these cases, New Age consensus falls apart into a multitude of individual elaborations.

The Brain

Besides subtle bodies, there is one other obvious *locus* for an interface between spirit and matter: the human brain. In several New Age sources we find the conviction that *biological* evolution, having produced the human organism in its present form, is now making place for *consciousness* evolution. It is no longer the human organism as a whole, but the human brain which is the spearhead of evolution[59]. Several authors hasten to add that this must not be under-

---

[55] LJ 31, 104-108.
[56] VAA 6-7.
[57] SD 147-148.
[58] ENF 7-23.
[59] SOU 156; AE 57-58.

stood as physicalist reductionism: it is not the brain which "produces" consciousness, but the Mind which has quite literally produced the brain as a tool
for expression[60]. For the rest, we find several popular theories of brain functioning reflected in New Age literature. I already mentioned the theory of brain
hemispheres, which is found throughout the New Age corpus[61]. Robert Ornstein, in particular, has developed the experimental findings of split-brain
research into the well-known diagram of the verbal, analytic, sequential, rational left brain versus the nonverbal, holistic, synthetic, intuitive right brain[62].
As Nevill Drury notes in a popular exposition of the Human Potential Movement, 'It is a commonplace generalization among New Age devotees that in
modern Western society, which is dominated by scientific and technological
thinking, we have developed our left brain at the expense of the right. The criticism is that we rely too much on linear thought, on processing information
sequentially, and not enough on intuition'[63]. This criticism has remained as
strong as ever, but in more recent New Age sources we find a growing recognition that the popular left/right brain mystique is actually a rather crude generalization[64]. The most popular alternative is Karl Pribram's theory of the holographic brain, which was discussed in chapter six, section 2B. Another theory which enjoys some popularity is Paul D. MacLean's "triune brain", according to which our brain retains archaic parts representing earlier evolutionary
stages[65].

3. THE METAPHYSICS OF MIND

A. The Psychologization of Religion and Sacralization of Psychology

We are all familiar with the argument that traditional beliefs in "meta-empirical beings" can be explained as resulting from psychological mechanisms. The
gods that earlier generations believed in, as supernatural beings existing apart
from humanity, turn out to be mere projections of the human mind. It is humanity that creates gods instead of the opposite. Originally linked to the name of

---

[60] SOU 161; S 109; ECMM 45; GMC 55; cf. BQ 83-110.
[61] AC 81-88; OB 24; CCC 18-19; ENF 9; PR 6; PH 60-77; SD 33-34; OR 69-70; EiG 17,
131.
[62] Ornstein, *Psychology of Consciousness*.
[63] Drury, *Elements of Human Potential*.
[64] GMC 11 ('the "left-brain, right-brain" myth of pop psychology'); SD 215 (added commentary (1989) to the first edition of 1979: 'The left- and right-hemisphere brain research, so
exciting in the late seventies, today leaves me less enthusiastic'); HP:cht 138 (William Irwin
Thompson, 'Cautions': 'I hope the public will not do to the metaphor of the hologram what they
did to the model of the lateralization of the brain. Ornstein's ideas were overgeneralized *ad nau-
seum*'). Drury (*Elements of Human Potential*, 8-9) notes that Ornstein himself has in the meantime gone far beyond his original model (in *Multimind*).
[65] PH 96-113.

Feuerbach, this argument was adopted by Freudian psychology and, shocking as it may have been at the time of its inception, has now become almost a cliché. It has traditionally been regarded as an argument for atheism, because it implies that metaphysical realities can be reduced to "nothing but" the inner dynamics of the psyche. Now, an extremely important fact about the New Age movement is that it generally *accepts* the cogency of the argument, but nevertheless *rejects* the atheistic conclusion. This is accomplished simply by denying that the "human, all too human" God (or gods) rightly debunked by the projection argument have anything to do with *real* divine realities. The real God transcends not only the personal/impersonal framework, as we saw; it also transcends the ontological framework which distinguishes an objective metaphysical reality from merely subjective impressions belonging to the psyche. In other words, the atheist conclusion betrays a hidden dualistic premise, which takes it for granted that the distinction between objective reality and subjective experience is absolute and rooted in ultimate reality. Without this premise the relation between the psyche and God, but also the relation between the psyche and the world, is seen in a different light. It is no longer possible to take commonsense distinctions between reality and "mere imagination" (not to mention fantasy[66]) for granted. A new framework or paradigm is needed that overcomes this pervasive form of dualism.

Stanislav Grof, in *Beyond the Brain*, argues that the empirical results of Altered States of Consciousness research are incompatible with the Newtonian-Cartesian paradigm.

> The existence of transpersonal experiences violates some of the most basic assumptions and principles of mechanistic science. They imply such seemingly absurd notions as the relativity and arbitrary nature of all physical boundaries, nonlocal connections in the universe, communication through unknown means and channels, memory without a material substrate, nonlinearity of time, or consciousness associated with all living forms (including unicellular organisms and plants) and even inorganic matter.
>
> Many transpersonal experiences involve events from the microcosm and macrocosm—realms that cannot be directly reached by human senses—or from periods that historically precede the origin of the solar system, of planet Earth, of living organisms, of the nervous system, and of Homo Sapiens. These experiences clearly suggest that, in a yet unexplained way, each of us contains the information about the entire universe or all of existence, has potential experiential access to

---

[66] This distinction is sometimes made by authors who are included in my survey on the basis of my choice for an inclusive preliminary demarcation (cf. Introduction) but who turn out to be relative borderline cases. See esp. Caitlín and John Matthews: 'Pathworkings ... should not be confused with the kind of guided imagery techniques often used by the psychological schools' and is 'not a form of Dungeons and Dragons fantasy-gaming' (WW1 17); 'Your visualizations are not guided fantasy, as it is often called' (WW2 12). The term "pathworking" will be explained in section 3C of this chapter.

all its parts, and in a sense *is* the whole cosmic network, as much as he or she is just an infinitesimal part of it, a separate and insignificant biological entity[67].

Grof believes that transpersonal experiences empirically support a radically new, holographic paradigm: 'The universe is seen as an infinite web of adventures in consciousness, and the dichotomies between the experiencer and the experienced, form and emptiness, time and timelessness, determinism and free will, or existence and nonexistence have been transcended'[68]. However, the reader is left wondering what prevents us from interpreting all these experiences simply as intrapsychic phenomena reminiscent of dreams or hallucinations. Grof answers that

> it is not possible to interpret them simply as intrapsychic phenomena in the conventional sense. On the one hand, they form an experiential continuum with biographical and perinatal experiences. On the other hand, they frequently appear to be tapping directly, without the mediation of the sensory organs, sources of information that are clearly outside of the conventionally defined range of the individual[69].

The first argument does not seem very convincing: normal dreams also include biographical material, but we do not normally regard them as giving empirical access to "real worlds". The second argument is repeated throughout Grof's books; but he consistently fails to furnish hard, concrete evidence. It does not inspire confidence, furthermore, to find him mentioning '*genuine* ancestral, phylogenetic, racial, and past incarnation matrices, or ... *authentic* experiences of consciousness of other people, animals, or other aspects of the phenomenal world' (my emphases)[70]. How, one wonders, has Grof managed to check the "genuineness" or "authenticity" of such experiences?
It is not the purpose of this analysis to criticize Grof's scientific work, let alone his spiritual beliefs. It is extremely relevant, however, to realize that his argument for the necessity of a new paradigm rests *entirely* on his refusal to regard transpersonal experiences as intrapsychic, and that the only reasons he gives for this refusal are the meagre ones just summarized. The consistent treatment of transpersonal experiences, whatever their content, as furnishing empirical information about reality betrays an underlying belief that *anything that is subjectively experienced as real must therefore be regarded as real*[71]. On this basis any distinction between "reality" and "imagination" becomes untenable. Per-

---

[67] BB 44-45.

[68] BB 50-51.

[69] BB 127. The same passage is repeated almost verbatim in AS 161, only the confident 'frequently appear to be' has become 'seem to be'. Grof's conclusions, however, remain the same.

[70] BB 194-195.

[71] Cf. the quotation from Aldous Huxley in AS 37: 'Like the giraffe and the duck-billed platypus, the creatures inhabiting these remoter regions of the mind are exceedingly improbable. *Nevertheless they exist, they are facts of observation*; ...' (my emphasis).

sonal experience becomes the sole and exclusive yardstick for reality testing: "whatever I experience is real".

Grof is not alone in this belief. Michael Harner makes a fundamental distinction between the Ordinary State of Consciousness (OSC) and what he calls a Shamanic State of Consciousness (SSC). The latter is entirely consistent with Grof's transpersonal experiences. Harner concludes:

> Dragons, griffins, and other animals that would be considered "mythical" by us in the OSC are "real" in the SSC. The idea that there are "mythical" animals is a useful and valid construct in OSC life, but superfluous and irrelevant in SSC experience. "Fantasy" can be said to be a term applied by a person in the OSC to what is experienced in the SSC. Conversely, a person in the SSC may perceive the experiences of the OSC to be illusory in SSC terms. Both are right, as viewed from their own particular states of consciousness[72].

Harner quotes the definition in Webster's Dictionary, of empiricism as "the practice of emphasizing experience esp. of the senses" and concludes that the shaman is an empiricist. He adds, however, that the shaman is essentially humble: 'After all, none of us really knows what is going on'[73].

Similarly, Starhawk states that

> trance states are both subjective and objective. There is a continuum of experience, part of which is relevant only to the individual's interior world, and part of which can be shared and agreed on by others. What begins in the imagination becomes real—even though that reality is of a different order than the reality of the physical senses. ... whether those entities [experienced in trance states] are internal forces or external beings depends on how one defines the self. It is more romantic and exciting (and probably truer) to see them as at least partly external; it is psychologically healthier and probably wiser to see them as internal[74].

This use of transpersonal experiences (Altered States of Consciousness, trance states) as an empirical foundation for a spiritual worldview is a prominent example of the psychologizing of religion and sacralization of psychology. Defenders of the transpersonal perspective agree that religious entities are "all in the mind", but then go on to assert that whatever is in the mind is *real*. This belief is fully compatible with the holographic worldview of Seth, and its many New Age derivations, in which the essential distinction between "objective reality" and subjective realities (experienced in dreams, trance states, past life memories etc.) breaks down completely.

Harner's remark that 'none of us really knows what is going on' points to a possible elaboration of the view just outlined. Instead of saying that whatever is experienced is real, it may be said that we only have access to reality through the filter of our experiences. In this case, there is room for a distinc-

[72] WS xix. Cf. xxi, 50, 53.
[73] WS 45-46.
[74] SD 154-155. Cf. WW1 105.

tion between absolute and phenomenal reality. An example is Marian Green's discussion of elementals: 'we can't really be sure what they are like in their own realms, for like all beings that appear to our clouded vision, they tend to be shaped by our own imagination'[75]. Some authors employ Jung's theory of archetypes: universal psychological categories which are not limited to the precise form in which they appear in our mind. Others feel that the term archetype already implies psychological reductionism. Caitlín and John Matthews, for instance, discuss a book of Bob Stewart about other realities and their inhabitants:

> Stewart prefers not to call them 'archetypes', because that implies a set of psychological personae, implying unreality. Like the Gods ..., the Otherworlds and its inhabitants are real in their own worlds, in their own right, they are not the result of imaginative or mental states; for although ... their forms often vary between cultures, there is a close correspondence in the ways in which they are perceived[76].

In these cases, we may speak of a form of Kantian idealism: the *Ding an Sich* appears only as a phenomenon within the categories defined by our mind. Some New Agers will leave it at that, many others will say that we are able in principle to transcend appearances and apprehend the absolute. In this case too, personal experience is the sole and only touchstone for determining what is real; but, experience being bounded by one's personal level of spiritual evolution, one may, in the course of one's progress, learn to apprehend higher and higher realities, and ultimately absolute reality.

Finally, we should note the tendency to suggest that the "objective" realm investigated by (the New) Physics is in fact synonymous with the "subjective" realm of the mind. This idea is a spin-off from parallellism: if the human mind is part of the Universal Mind experienced by the mystics and now rediscovered by physics, then a distinction between psychology and physics seems untenable. Michael Talbot discusses John Lilly's experiments with Altered States of Consciousness in sensory isolation tanks:

> Are these other realities actually places as we conceive of them or do they exist within our head? In the paradigm of reality offered by both mysticism and the new physics, such a question becomes meaningless. ... In the words of Panchadasi, "A plane of being is not a place, but a state of being". The universe itself is not a *place* in the paradigm of the new physics. As Don Juan warns, there is no world

---

[75] WA 84. Elsewhere, Green even seems to espouse psychological reductionism: 'We now have the language of psychology to give us contemporary terms for what our ancestors spoke of as 'supernatural'. ... We talk about 'altered states of consciousness' whilst the priests of the past knew of visions and oracular messages' (EAM 7). It is probably this kind of reasoning which Matthew Fox is thinking of in his criticism, unusual in the New Age context, of "psychologism" as an example of "pseudo-mysticism": 'the Spirit is too vast to be restricted to psychology alone' (CCC 46).

[76] WW1 105.

"out there", only a description of the world. With the advent of the participator principle the entire matter-space-time continuum of the physical universe becomes merely a *state of being*[77].

Talbot's conclusion is that the New Physics offers a foundation for 'a religion based on the psychology of the human consciousness—indeed, on the psychology of the entire universe as a conscious force acting upon itself'[78]. Transpersonal psychologist Jean Houston similarly concludes that the realm of the psyche and the realm of higher physics 'may well be close neighborhoods, if not the same realm'[79]: 'Great nature is contained within and without, the planes of our inner life demanding differing frequencies of consciousness for nature's manifest forms, but offering perhaps equal ontological reality'[80]. In the end, according to Houston, all is "resonance", and we can become conscious and creative participants in the dance of frequency. 'In so doing', she concludes, 'we become world-makers'[81].

B. Creating Our Own Reality

This last quotation brings us to what was already identified as one of the most central concerns of the New Age movement: the belief that we create our own reality. In chapter six (section 2A) I discussed the role of this belief in the context of "Ultimate Source Holism" of the "generative" variety, where it functioned as a holistic explanatory principle for the nature of reality. However, the cluster of beliefs associated with the New Age slogan "we create our own reality" goes far beyond metaphysics or cosmology.

At first sight, New Age statements to the effect that we have created, are creating or may be able to create our own reality might easily be dismissed as suggestive rhetoric rather than serious convictions[82]. For instance when Marilyn Ferguson announces that 'if we realize that we are part of a dynamic system, one in which any action affects the whole, we are empowered to change it'[83], or when Erich Jantsch claims that in the self-reflexive human brain 'Mind becomes a creative factor not only in image-forming, but also in the active transformation of outer reality'[84], the theoretical or practical content of their statements seems negligible. One might conclude that it is merely the suggestive manner of formulating that makes for the excitement. However, closer

---

[77] MNP 164-165.
[78] MNP 161.
[79] PH 82.
[80] PH 164.
[81] PH 164.
[82] For instance AC 34, 118, 124, 134; OB 182, 202; SOU 161, 168, 176-177; RNA 52.
[83] AC 118.
[84] SOU 164.

scrutiny shows that if we would dismiss "creating our own reality" statements for these reasons, we would in fact be overlooking one of the most central concerns of New Age religion, the influence of which is indeed pervasive throughout our source material. There is a consistent belief system behind these statements.

The Law of Manifestation and its Implications
Two common meanings of the formula "creating our own reality" belong to other chapters, but should be mentioned briefly here. Both amount to the belief that we, as human beings, *have* created our present reality. Firstly, there is the belief that our world and/or our universe has not in fact been created by God but by *us*: in our original state, when we were still pure spiritual beings, we made the heavens and the earth. We got lost in our own creations, however, and are still struggling to find the way back to our original state. This New Age motive will be discussed in chapter eleven (section 2). Secondly, we find the very common belief that we have *chosen* our present life circumstances before being incarnated. Our life is, therefore, our own creation. This belief will be discussed in chapter nine (section 3).

More important in the present context is the view of "creating our own reality" as the general "natural law" underlying all manifestation. Seth, as we saw, teaches that we create reality as naturally as we breathe. We live our lives in "dreams" of our own making, which reflect our unconscious beliefs. By changing our beliefs, we automatically change our reality. This fundamental message of the Seth material is repeated over and over again in other sources[85]. Henry Reed, for example, describes all life experiences as 'projections of consciousness, like images on a screen' and assures his readers that they are 'as easy to change as it is to place a different film in the projector'[86]. What usually happens, however, is that 'we are hypnotized by the projection, and the dream becomes real'[87]. The central concern of New Age religion is therefore to "dehypnotize" consciousness, and to awaken to the realization that only we ourselves are responsible, from moment to moment, for creating our reality. Once we are aware of this underlying "law of manifestation", we can start to make active rather than passive use of it and change our reality for the better. Ramtha leaves us in no doubt that all this is meant just as radical as it sounds:

> How is your future created? Through thought. All of your tomorrows are designed by your thoughts this very day. For every thought you embrace, every fantasy you have, for whatever emotional purpose, creates a feeling within your body, which is recorded within your soul. That feeling then sets a precedent for the conditions

---

[85] DL 254; IAP 19; R 45-46, 95; ECMM 4, 7; TI 56-57; ENF 74; PH 199; PST 214; RS 102-103; SoC 70, 203, 336-337; CiM:T 14.
[86] ECMM 86-87.
[87] ECMM 88.

in your life, for it will draw to you circumstances that will create and match the same feeling that has been recorded in your soul. And know that every word you utter is creating your days to come ... Do you think that things happen to you simply by chance? There is no such thing as an accident or a coincidence in this kingdom—and no one is what is termed a "victim" of anyone else's will or designs. Everything that happens to you, you have thought and felt into your life. Either it has been fantasized in what-ifs or in fears, or someone has told you that something would be, and you accepted it as a truth. Everything that happens, happens as an intentional act that is ordained through thought and emotion. Everything! Every thought you have ever embraced, every fantasy you have ever allowed yourself to feel, all the words you have spoken, have all come to pass or are waiting to come to pass. For thought is the true giver of life that never dies, that never can be destroyed, and you have used it to create every moment of your life, for it is your link to the Mind of God[88].

In the large majority of cases, the belief in "creating our own reality" as the law of manifestation is part of a holographic worldview. Holography implies that each individual can be regarded as the creative source of the universe. In Jean Houston's words: '...the farthest star lives in you and you are the stargate through which the world is seeded with new forms. You are identity and holonomy, the One and the Many. You are ubiquitous through space-time, existent in the Ultimate, and uniquely yourself in local reality. You are the hologram knowing the Hologram'[89]. For all intents and purposes this means, of course, that "you are God". As MacLaine puts it: 'What is the center of the universe? Every place is the center. Who is the center? *Everyone* is the center'[90]. It is not difficult to see that this belief may naturally lead to a form of super-idealism or solipsism. Nevertheless, such a conclusion, if pronounced openly, may shock even a convinced New Age audience. Shirley MacLaine relates the following:

> Twenty of us sat around an oval table; a crystal was passed to each of us and we expressed in words what we would like to manifest in our lives for the following year. The open and direct honesty was heart-glowing to witness. But when the crystal came to me I found myself expressing an understanding that for me was true, but for some of the others seemed outlandish.
> I began by saying that since I realized I created my own reality in every way, I must therefore admit that, in essence, *I was the only person alive in my universe.* I could feel the instant shock waves undulate around the table. I went on to express my feeling of total responsibility *and power* for all events that occur in the world because the world is happening only in my reality. *And* human beings feeling pain, terror, depression, panic, and so forth, were really only aspects of pain, terror,

---

[88] R 45-46.
[89] PH 199. Cf. ECMM 270-273; TI 56-57; ENF 17, 74, 149; HP:npr 10; HP:cht (John Shimotsu, 'The Simplified and Revised Abridged Edition of Changing Reality by Marilyn Ferguson') 127; Cf. also RW 195-199. David Spangler sharply rejects the type of New Age thinking exemplified by Shirley MacLaine. Ironically, however, his speculations in this chapter come extremely close to hers.
[90] GW 315.

depression, panic, and so on, in *me*. If they were all characters in my reality, my dream, then of course they were only reflections of myself.

I was beginning to understand what the great masters had meant when they had said "you are the universe". If we each create our own reality, then of course we are everything that exists within it. Our reality is a reflection of us.

Now, that truth can be very humorous. I could legitimately say that I created the Statue of Liberty, chocolate chip cookies, the Beatles, terrorism, and the Vietnam War. I couldn't really say for sure whether anyone else in the world had actually experienced those things separately from me because these people existed as individuals only in my dream. I knew *I* had created the reality of the evening news at night. It was in my reality. But whether anyone else was experiencing the news *separately* from me was unclear, because *they* existed in my reality too. And if they reacted to world events, then I was creating them to react so I would have something to interact with, thereby enabling myself to know me better.

My purpose in mentioning this on New Year's Eve was to project a hope that if I changed *my* conception of reality for the better in the coming year, I would in effect be contributing to the advancement of the world. Therefore my New Year's resolution was to improve myself—which would in turn improve the world I lived in.

Most of the faces around the table looked scandalized. ... I had clearly gone too far. The discussion that ensued was a microcosm of the world itself. And while the others expressed their objections, I felt *I was creating them to object*, so that I could look at some things I hadn't resolved myself. In other words I *was* them. *They* were *me*. And all because I was creating them as characters in my play.

The classic question was asked: If what I was proposing was true, would it also be true that I did nothing for others, everything for myself?

And the answer was, essentially, yes. If I fed a starving child, and was honest about my motivation, I would have to say I did it for myself, because it made me feel better. Because the child was happier and more fulfilled, *I* would be. I was beginning to see that we each did whatever we did purely for self, and that was as it should be. Even if I had not created others in my reality and was therefore not responsible for them, I would feel responsible to my own feelings which desire to be positive and loving. Thus, in uplifting my own feelings I would uplift the feelings of my fellow human beings.

How do we change the world? By changing ourselves.

That was the gist of my New Year's projection[91].

The fact that this radical solipsism scandalized most of the people around the table[92] may throw doubt on whether it is typical for New Age thinking. Indeed, we may safely assume that only some of the authors who believe that we create our own reality would fully accept its radical consequences. Even so, however, solipsism must be seen as the logical outcome of the combination of "creating our own reality" with the holographic worldview which we found to be so prominent in the New Age. Furthermore, it is only a small and rather the-

---

[91] IAP 171-173.

[92] David Spangler might have been one of them. In RS 156 he recalls with obvious disgust how he has sat in groups 'where individuals have said they are not responsible for the suffering in the world since those who suffer have obviously chosen and created that experience'.

oretical step from this radical solipsism to the view that other people's realities, although they do exist "separately", are completely irrelevant to one's own reality. This attitude is found very prominently, for instance, in the work of Sanaya Roman: 'If you read something you don't like or don't agree with, don't accept it; it isn't true for you. It may be true for others, but you don't have to make it part of your reality'[93]. Henry Reed, although convinced that we create our own reality, has both variations in mind when he warns against narcissistic and egocentric interpretations: 'Those of us susceptible to the pitfalls of the "me generation" find creating our own reality leading us into a hall of mirrors. Everywhere we look, all we see is ourselves'[94]. Reed claims that the Cayce material avoids such pitfalls[95].

Although the internal logic of the belief inevitably leads to conclusions of the kind expressed by MacLaine or Roman, we should nevertheless not conclude too easily that *therefore* egocentricity, narcissism or solipsism is of the essence of "creating our own reality". Such a conclusion probably confuses the primary motivations for the belief, to be discussed below, with its possible theoretical outcomes. People who assert that they create their own reality do not necessarily pursue the logic of that belief all the way to its solipsistic or super-idealist conclusion. They may even abhor the idea when it is spelled out to them, as we saw in the MacLaine passage. The evidence strongly suggests that people come to believe that they create their own reality, not primarily for philosophical reasons, or out of a desire to emotionally seal themselves off from others (although that may certainly be a motive for some), but because they feel that it restores meaning to human existence.

Self-Responsibility
The belief that we create our own reality is fundamentally a reaction against the idea that life is random and meaningless, and that human beings are essentially passive victims of the impersonal forces of nature and society. For New Age believers, to say that "we create our own reality" is to affirm that everything in human life is deeply meaningful: everything happens for a reason, and we can learn to understand those reasons. Consider this passage from Shakti Gawain:

> The physical world is our creation: we each create our own version of the world, our particular reality, our unique life experience. Because my life is being created through my channel, I can look at my creation to get feedback about myself. Just as an artist looks at his latest creation to see what works well and what doesn't, we can look at the ongoing masterwork of our lives to appreciate who we are and to recognize what we still need to learn. ... In fact, the external world

---

[93] SG 124. Cf. also Louise L. Hay (YHL 7, *passim*).
[94] ECMM 7.
[95] ECMM 7, 96.

is like a giant mirror which reflects both our spirits and our forms clearly and accurately. ... Viewed in this way, the external world can teach us about hidden aspects
of ourselves that we can't see directly. The process is based on two premises:
1. I assume that *everything* in my life is my reflection, my creation; there are no
accidents or events that are unrelated to me. If I see or feel something, if it has
any impact on me, then my being has attracted or created it to show me something. If it didn't mirror some part of myself I wouldn't even be able to see it. All
the people in my life are reflections of the various characters and feelings that
live inside of me.
2. I try never to put myself down for the reflections I see. I know that nothing is
negative. Everything is a gift that brings me to self awareness; after all, I'm here
to learn[96].

The same view is defended by Louise L. Hay:

What we think about ourselves becomes the truth for us. I believe that everyone,
myself included, is 100% responsible for everything in our lives, the best and the
worst. Every thought we think is creating our future. Each one of us creates our
experiences by our thoughts and our feelings. ... We create the situations, and then
we give our power away by blaming the other person for our frustration. No person, no place, and no thing has any power over us, for "we" are the only thinkers
in our mind. We create our experiences, our reality and everyone in it. When we
create peace and harmony and balance in our minds, we will find it in our lives[97].

What both Gawain and Hay are saying is that we are *totally reponsible* for
whatever happens to us. Contrary to critics who argue that this will create
unbearable feelings of guilt, many New Agers see it as an "empowering"
belief[98]. It is an antidote, first of all, to the paralyzing notion that our lives are
steered by forces beyond our control. If we think that we are powerless to
change our situation, that not we ourselves but other people and circumstances
are responsible, we are in fact "giving our power away" to them and weaken
ourselves. The idea that we are powerless is just a *belief* masquerading as objective truth. This belief breeds passivity and is counterproductive; we use it as
an easy excuse for not having to change ourselves. Once we dare to believe
that our life can be changed, and we act on that belief, we will find that the
outside constraints are not as forbidding as they seemed. "Taking responsibility" for our life, according to New Age thinking, means a radical break with
the idea that we are dependent on others or on outside circumstances for our
happiness and success in life. Secondly, this attitude of self-responsibility is
"empowering" also because it restores meaning to our lives. That life is meaningless is just another limiting and paralyzing belief. If we have created our
reality ourselves, we can use it as a mirror. We can ask ourselves *why* certain
unpleasant and apparently meaningless or "unfair" things happen to us, instead

[96] LL 26-27.
[97] YHL 7.
[98] AC 117-119; CV 120; HHC 207; IAP 15, 214; DL 12; GW 32, 48-49; R 45; RI 151; NPR
27-28; SS 8; SG 119; PPA 119-120; PST 50, 54-55, 137, 211; VAA 82-85; SoS 138.

of choosing the easy way of blaming them on the rest of the world (or on its "absurdity"). We may then discover that, underneath the surface of apparently unconnected and meaningless events, there are deep-seated emotional patterns in our own thinking and behaviour that have worked to bring about these events. All circumstances in our life are thus not unrelated chance occurences, but are deeply meaningful lessons about ourselves.

It is easy to see that these beliefs have a core in plain commonsense psychology. It is a truism that pessimism about our own ability to accomplish something may actually prevent us from even trying; and it is a common experience that we are often conveniently blind to our own share in bringing about circumstances that we prefer to blame on others. As R.D. Rosen reminds us, 'in any remotely effective therapy, the individual is encouraged to assume responsibility for his distress and not perceive it as caused by a conspiracy or circumstance or other people'[99]. That we all "create" our own reality to some extent, and that we can learn from the results of our actions: these are clearly not beliefs but simple facts. What distinguishes the New Age belief is its radicality. We create *all* of our reality, and *everything* that happens to us has a deeper meaning with respect to ourselves. The only practical limits to our ability to create a perfect reality for ourselves are those imposed by the limits of our self-knowledge and understanding at any given moment. This does not mean that these limitations to total self-determination are easy to resolve. Negative situations in our lives reflect limiting beliefs or unresolved emotional patterns which may be quite stubborn. The removal of these "blocks" may involve hard work. For this reason, creating our own reality is indissolubly linked to inner psychological exploration. Spiritual growth in the New Age sense may well be characterized as an ongoing individual psychotherapy in which each of us is his/her own therapist, and unlimited freedom for creativity is the promised goal. Reincarnation is a necessary and integral part of this process. Obviously, New Age believers do not deny that many circumstances in life (sex, parents, country, social conditions, inborn abilities or disabilities, including inherited diseases, deformities etc.) are already present at birth. It is widely believed, however, that these circumstances were in fact consciously chosen by us before incarnation, as appropriate to our specific individual developmental needs. Again, we can blame neither God nor fate. "Taking responsibility" for our life means, in this case, no longer to rebel against any aspect of our lives, but to accept all of it as meaningful and to use it constructively as an offered opportunity for growth. Edgar Cayce referred to this general principle as "changing stumbling blocks into stepping stones". Commonly, and consistently given the basic premises, a similar argument is applied to such things as natural disasters, genocide etc.: the victims, we read, have purpose-

---

[99] Rosen, *Psychobabble*, 83.

ly chosen to "have the experience" of being killed in this way, for purposes that may not be apparent to their limited personality but are transparent to their Higher Self[100].

It goes without saying that the New Age doctrine of "self-responsibility" has little patience with its logical opposite, self-pity: 'You are not here to cry about the miseries of the human condition, but to change them'[101]. George Trevelyan speaks of a 'strong and courageous view': 'We will not whine or complain if we shoulder full responsibility for all we are and all that happens to us'[102]. Self-pity is a purely negative emotion without constructive value. It betrays a childish attitude of blaming the universe instead of making the best of one's situation. Critics argue that the doctrine of "self-responsibility" in fact engenders guilt complexes, but defenders have a different perspective. Guilt as such is a purely negative emotion: blaming oneself for having created one's reality is as detrimental as blaming anyone else. Self-responsibility is incompatible with the concept of guilt because it implies that everything that happens, happens for good reasons and is therefore ultimately meaningful and right. Blaming either ourselves or others for "negative" things that happen are both equally inappropriate responses. The only correct response is to take those negative things as welcome signals that there is something we do not yet see about ourselves: "what is the universe trying to teach me through this experience?". "The Universe", in this context, is regarded as a totally friendly, abundant, perfect, non-judgmental environment which enables all intelligent beings to learn their lessons in their own way and at their own pace. Sanaya Roman assures her readers that

> the universe is perfect and ... everything you do and everything that happens to you is perfect. As you grow spiritually, you will gain a greater understanding of why things are happening, and you will come to see the perfection in everything that occurs. From the higher perspective of today, you may be able to look back into the past and know that things you once interpreted as negative offered you growth and new beginnings[103].

Louise L. Hay similarly says that 'The universe is lavish and abundant and it is our birthright to be supplied with everything we need, unless we choose to believe it to the contrary'[104]. According to Shakti Gawain, there is 'no evil or limitation. There is only ignorance or misunderstanding ... combined with our

---

[100] Others, however, sharply reject such ideas. Starhawk criticizes the whole "creating our own reality" belief as an 'absolutist concept'. 'If my skin were another color, if I were mentally retarded because of early malnutrition, or disabled, I doubt that I would be quite so sublime about my ability to create reality. Does the rape victim create the assault? Did the children of Vietnam create napalm? Obviously, no' (SD 206).

[101] NPR 28.

[102] VAA 85.

[103] SG 101.

[104] YHL 120.

infinite creative abilities'[105]. Only ignorance and misunderstanding prevent us from creating a perfect reality, and greater insight can be gained only through learning from our experiences the hard way. This is where the New Age is not quite as "soft" as often portrayed.

The Mechanics of Changing Reality

Learning from one's experiences and resolving limiting emotional patterns is one prominent part of the process of creating a perfect reality. Because these patterns have been created over the course of many lives, the corresponding "therapy" is also supposed to require more than one life in most cases. We are told that in our present life, however, we can already dramatically improve our situation by systematically changing our beliefs and attitudes. What we think becomes real: our lives mirror our beliefs, and the way people react to us reflects our attitude towards them. In general terms, the process of changing our present reality involves two steps: de-constructing limiting beliefs, and replacing them by positive and constructive beliefs.

Many limiting beliefs are based on cultural conditioning: '...each of us, from infancy onward, is subjected to a complex set of suggestions from our social environment, which in effect teaches us how to perceive the world. ... and so each of us is literally *hypnotized* from infancy to perceive the world the way people in our culture perceive it'[106]. Prominent among these cultural suggestions is the belief that humans are essentially powerless and helpless victims at the mercy of circumstances. Another deep-seated belief, due largely to the western religious heritage, is that human beings are somehow flawed and guilty. Yet another belief, this time reflecting an outdated view of science, is that the world functions on the basis of impersonal, objective laws which the merely subjective mind cannot influence. The authors emphasized that these and other negative beliefs, which masquerade as "obvious" truths, are pervasive and quite stubborn. Breaking with them is difficult, both practically because their influence is often quite subtle, and psychologically because they destroy the safety of traditional certainties. This last point has been brought out very clearly by Shirley MacLaine. One of the main attractions of *Out on a Limb* is the convincing way she describes her gradual conversion to the "far out" New Age concepts as presented to her by David. She describes how she becomes more and more defensive and recalcitrant against the new ideas as it slowly becomes clear to her that she will really have to make a choice whether or not to commit herself to this whole "spirituality business". After a climactic inner struggle that lasts for days, she finally lets go of her scepticism, realizing that it

---

[105] CV 59.
[106] GMC 19.

was based on cultural conditioning rather than on her own deeper intuitions. She realizes that she has actually been afraid of the New Age ideas because they threatened her accepted values; she is now challenged to find her own truth even if it means rejecting the world view dominant in her social environment[107].

The principal complaint about the beliefs enforced by modern western culture is that they are negative, pessimistic and limiting to personal expansion. They suggest that there are limits and constraints where in reality there are none. The alternative beliefs must therefore be strongly positive, optimistic and expansive. Shirley MacLaine argues for the merits of positive thinking in a discussion with her sceptical friend, the politician Bella Abzug:

> "...now I don't see life as a battlefield. On the contrary, I believe it can be a paradise, and what's more, we should *expect* it to be. That is reality to me now. Dwelling on the negative simply contributes to its power".
> "But my darling, the negative exists. It has to be dealt with, doesn't it?"
> "Sure. What I'm saying is that a lot of it exists because we make it so. We *need* to believe in a positive reality right here on earth because the believing will help to make *it* so. That's the real power we have for change"[108].

Positive thinking may take different forms. Sanaya Roman's books are examples of a particularly radical variety. She argues simply that we must focus on the positive and avoid "negativity" everywhere and at all costs:

> You can tell everyone in your life how good they are, and help them recognize how much they are growing. Whenever they complain of problems or something wrong you can help them see how the situation is helping them, the positive changes it is giving them, and what it is teaching them. ... If you listen to people gripe, if you listen to their negativity, you are putting yourself in a position of being affected by their lower energy. You do not need to listen[109].

Put bluntly: 'If you hear people speaking of negative things immediately send them positive pictures and change the conversation'[110]. Admittedly, such an approach is considered extreme even by many other New Age authors. While Roman is convinced that positive thinking—the state of mind of the Higher Self—simply eliminates all conscious or unconscious negativity just as light drives away darkness, many others emphasize that positive thinking of and by itself is not enough. The belief that it is enough may even be dangerous. Shakti Gawain suggests that extremist views such as Roman's actually betray a deepseated fear of negativity and are therefore ultimately dualistic:

---

[107] OL 315-337.
[108] OL 364.
[109] LJ 38-39. Cf. YHL 110.
[110] PPA 63.

Many people, especially those in the spiritual and new age movements, believe that we can bring peace and light to the world by focusing on the light, trying to be unconditionally loving, visualizing peace, and so forth. There is a fundamental misunderstanding here. By trying to focus only on the things we deem "positive" and ignoring or repressing the rest, we are simply perpetuating the polarization of light and dark forces. Ironically, this further distorts and empowers the very energies we are trying to avoid

We must deeply realize that there is no split between "spiritual" and "unspiritual", good and bad. All aspects of life are elements of the life force and facets of the divine. True healing comes from owning and accepting all of life's energies within ourselves[111].

Apparently, the "negative energies" referred to by Gawain cannot be attributed to cultural conditioning alone, as authors like Roman or Hay often seem to suggest. The unconscious "shadow" is a reality, and it is dangerous to ignore it. It may be true that the shadow implies ignorance about our real being, reinforced by society, but it is psychologically naïve to expect that spiritual insight will simply make it vanish as clouds before the sun. On the contrary, deep-seated emotional patterns of our unconscious mind may simply make it impossible for us to be open to healthy positive beliefs. Many New Age sources therefore present the "healing" of such patterns and the "growth" of spiritual insight as a dialectical rather than a one-way process. Therapeutic healing and exposure to positive spiritual beliefs should mutually assist each other. The shadow must be confronted and dealt with in order to clear the way for positive alternatives[112]. Even Gary Zukav, whose emphasis on "love and light" is almost as strong as Roman's, suggests that we must take the "roots" of negativity seriously:

Each time you feel negative, stop, acknowledge that you are, and discharge it consciously. Ask what you are feeling and what is at the root of it. Go for the root of it in that instant and as you work to pull the root, simultaneously look at the positive side and remind yourself of the greater truth that there is something spiritually profound at work, that your life is no accident...[113].

According to Eva Pierrakos's *Pathwork*, the trick is to acknowledge that we have negative traits and yet not make ourselves feel guilty for having them: 'How can I acknowledge my negativity without either glossing over it or being devastated by it?'[114]. Feelings of guilt are unnecessary and counterproductive, but honest acceptance of our darker sides is necessary: 'This path demands from you that which people are least willing to give: truthfulness with the self,

---

[111] RG 30. Cf. Seth's ironic remark: 'If you find yourself running around in a spiritual frenzy, trying to repress every negative idea that comes into your head, then ask yourself why you believe so in the great destructive power of your slightest "negative" thought' (NPR 221).

[112] For instance NPR xx-xxii, 140-142, 206-207, 221; Cf. also OB 18-19.

[113] SoS 244.

[114] PST xv.

exposure of what exists now, elimination of masks and pretenses, and the experience of one's naked vulnerability'[115]. Pierrakos's "Introduction" actually criticizes "positive thinking" books for ignoring negativity instead of dealing with it, and recommends *Pathwork* as a better alternative[116]. We may conclude that New Age sources generally value positive thinking as essential, but that opinions about the extent of its power differ from author to author.

Louise L. Hay, reflecting a radicalism similar to Roman's, assures us that 'it is our natural birthright to go from success to success all our life'[117]. What, apart from cleaning up our limiting patterns and beliefs by therapeutic means, can we *do* to create the perfect reality promised to all of us in such statements? Obviously, our belief system must be changed. Many of our limiting beliefs are, however, unconscious or semi-conscious. This is why they are so difficult to change, and also why their influence is so strong: after all, the process of creating our own reality is largely an unconscious process. New Age sources claim that the unconscious belief structures that determine our reality can be changed by conscious intervention. The unconscious mind responds to verbal suggestions called "affirmations", as well as to nonverbal "visualisation" techniques.

Affirmations[118] are brief sentences with a strongly positive content. Willis Harman explains the underlying theory:

> Reprogramming the unconscious beliefs that block fuller awareness of our creative/intuitive capabilities depends upon a key characteristic of the unconscious mind, namely *that it responds to what is vividly imagined essentially as though it were real experience*. Thus, to revise the unconscious beliefs we need only vividly imagine new beliefs, and they tend to become "true"[119].

Affirmations must never be formulated as wishes (for instance "I want to be healthy and beautiful") but as statements of fact ("I am healthy and beautiful"). The reason given is that the unconscious takes the affirmations literally. If one affirms something to happen in the future, it will remain in the future. If one affirms it to be true already, the unconscious will start creating a reality which reflects that belief. Some random examples of affirmations recommended by Shakti Gawain:

> Every day in every way I'm getting better, better, and better
> I am naturally enlightened

[115] PST 9.
[116] PST xv.
[117] YHL 5.
[118] CV 21-26; YHL *passim*; PH 127-129; HHC 12-18; DL 111-113; R 190; ECMM 236-238; LJ 70; PPA 138; GMC 76-78; NB 128-129. According to PPA 138, even single words like "love, clarity, abundant" etc. are sufficient because they are 'the words of the soul' and stimulate corresponding vibrations.
[119] GMC 76-77.

My life is blossoming in total perfection
Perfect wisdom is in my heart
I am now attracting loving, satisfying, happy relationships into my life
I now have a perfect, satisfying, well paying job
I am always in the right place at the right time, successfully engaged in the right activity
It's okay for me to have everything I want!
Every day I am growing more financially prosperous[120].

With characteristic pragmatism, Gawain adds that 'affirmations are often most powerful and inspiring when they include references to spiritual sources. Mention of God, Christ, Buddha or any great master adds spiritual energy to your affirmation, and acknowledges the universal source of all things. You may prefer to use such phrases as divine love, the light within me, or universal intelligence'[121]. The result is affirmations such as these:

I am a radiant expression of God. My mind and body now manifest divine perfection
The Christ within me is creating miracles in my life here and now
My Higher Self is guiding me in everything that I do
Wherever I am, God is, and all is well![122]

It will come as no surprise that Shirley MacLaine especially recommends using the phrases "I am God" or "I am that I am", 'as Christ often did'[123] (suggesting that Jesus was already aware of the power of affirmations). Affirmations can be done silently, spoken aloud, written down, or sung or chanted. Their effect is amplified by a state of meditative relaxation. A typical New Age believer in affirmations may reserve some time each day for doing affirmations, for instance standing before the mirror or in the context of meditation exercises. It is also possible to use tape recordings. In that case, affirmations are often imperceptibly hidden in relaxing background music. These so-called self-help tapes claim even greater effectivity than normal affirmations because they rely on subliminal suggestion that bypasses the conscious mind altogether[124]. In a context such as Roman's refusal to acknowledge "negativity", *fighting* a problem is seen as counterproductive because it implicitly acknowledges the problem as real. Instead, affirmations can be used to convince oneself that the problem does not exist at all: 'If there is someone at work who bothers you, ... bless them with love every time you think of them. ... If this person is crit-

---

[120] CV 22-24. Notice the elements of "prosperity consciousness", prominently present in the more radical "creating our own reality" sources.

[121] CV 26.

[122] CV 26, 75.

[123] DL 112. In this context, MacLaine extends the "I am God" theme to affirmations such as 'I am God in health, I am God with ease, I am God in fun, I am God in humor, I am God in stamina, I am God in coolness, I am God in strength, I am God in light. She adds that 'the effect is stunning' (DL 112).

[124] Cf. ECMM 226-234 (critical).

ical, begin to affirm that he or she is loving and full of praise. If they are
grouchy, affirm that they are cheerful and fun to be around. If they are cruel,
affirm that they are gentle and compassionate'[125]. Hay relates anecdotes to
demonstrate the miraculous results of this strategy.

Starhawk, as we saw, suggests that "Younger Self" is largely non-verbal and
responds better to images than to words. The other prominent type of changing reality by self-suggestion makes use of visualisation techniques[126]. The
belief in the unlimited powers of the imagination naturally leads to the belief
that visualizing desires will make them happen: 'Creative visualization is the
technique of using your imagination to create what you want in your life. ... It
is your natural power of imagination, the basic creative energy of the universe,
which you use constantly, whether or not you are aware of it'[127]. We are told
that we can use this tool to create 'love, fulfillment, enjoyment, satisfying relationships, rewarding work, self-expression, health, beauty, prosperity, inner
peace and harmony'[128].

The basic rationale of visualization is similar to that of affirmation, only this
time the desired goal is visualized as lively as possible in the imagination. Of
particular importance in many such cases is the visualization of *light*. In the
following example, George Trevelyan uses the form of the Celtic Cross,
described as an 'archetypal symbol for the New Age' as a central focus for the
imagination.

> At first, our own heart is the crossing point where the light radiates as love. But
> the form can be enlarged indefinitely. Let it do so in the imagination until it stands
> like a great spherical temple with the altar and the six-pointed star shining in the
> centre. This temple can be thronged with beings of light; and from this great spir-
> itual lighthouse, we can beam out rays to link with other such centers. We can
> also direct the beams of light and love into the dark trouble spots of the world.
> Here, they will provide the substance which spiritual forces can use to penetrate
> the fog of psychic darkness which, quite objectively, lie over such areas as North-
> ern Ireland. Our image has a very real power, and we must accept that imagina-
> tion is a creative deed[129].

The visualizing of light, and "sending" this light in the imagination to places,
things or persons that need healing (including ourselves), is a common practice in New Age religion. Many variations are possible, for instance visualizing oneself inside a bubble of light, as protection against negative energies or
for enhancing one's rate of spiritual vibration[130].

---

[125] YHL 110.
[126] CV *passim*; EAM 14; MAA 43; PH *passim*; PR 231; ECMM 243-265.
[127] CV 2.
[128] CV 2.
[129] VAA 146.
[130] For instance OtC 138-139, 182; SG 18-27; DL 312, 333-334; SoS 91-104.

Creating Illness or Health

The most controversial part of the "creating our own reality" logic is the assertion that all illness is self-created. This belief has provoked vehement attacks
from health professionals and incurable patients[131]. The medical discussion
about psychosomatic factors in the emergence of illness and about the medical significance of the placebo effect is, of course, not limited to the New Age
movement. However, because New Age sources tend to be the most uncompromising in asserting that matter follows mind, and also because they often
show themselves extremely critical, even hostile, to the "medical establishment", the New Age has been singled out as the primary scapegoat for concerned doctors and patients. From the perspective of scholarly research, one
unfortunate side-effect of these heated controversies is that "New Age" is often
assumed to be almost synonymous with controversial therapies. The present
study argues, rather, that it is a far broader *religious* movement, which happens to include approaches to healing as an important part of its ideology.

The general reasoning behind the belief that illness is self-created should
be clear by now. Illnesses may be linked either to former incarnations or to
unhealthy beliefs and attitudes during the present life. In both cases, the authors
tell us, they do not strike at random and without a deeper reason. They have a
background in our own ways of thinking and acting, and should be understood,
not as purely negative intrusions, but as meaningful messages that some part
of our mind requires healing. At an unconscious or superconscious level (our
Higher Self) we have created these messages, and they can therefore be
approached as, perhaps painful, but ultimately meaningful learning tasks in the
context of personal evolution. Feeling guilty for having created one's own illness is an inappropriate response. New Age reasoning implies that not the "creating our own reality" belief as such is responsible for the engendering of guilt,
but the general belief structure of a society which has cultivated a detrimental ethics based on sin, guilt and punishment. The whole point of "creating our
own reality", so the argument goes, gets fatally distorted if we interpret it as
implying that our illness is a punishment for our faults. It should be understood only as implying that all things happen for a reason, and that we can find

---

[131] In the Netherlands, for instance, multiple sclerosis patient Karin Spaink published *Het
strafbare lichaam*. The book led to a lively discussion in the popular media, and enriched the
Dutch language with the term *orenmaffia* (the "mafia" which teaches that all illness originates
"between the ears"). It is interesting to compare the reactions of outsiders to those of insiders.
Ken Wilber, whose wife died of breast cancer, has documented their experiences with both regular and alternative healing methods (*Grace and Grit*). Wilber is known for his sharp criticism
of many "pop" New Age beliefs. His wife, nevertheless, practiced affirmations and visualizations (beside traditional approaches including chemotherapy), but these did not result in permanent healing. Wilber's views about having to deal with resulting feelings of guilt and inadequa-
cy add welcome nuance to the debate about self-healing.

that reason in ourselves if we take the trouble to look for it. Guilt does not
enter the picture at all unless we insist that it does so.

Indeed, the crux of the debate between defenders and opponents seems to lie
in a fundamental incompatibility of two worldviews, one of which has no place
for the concept of guilt, while the other one does. New Agers may legitimately claim that feelings of guilt result only from secondary interpretations, based
on cultural presuppositions, and that an alternative interpretation from a worldview that does not accept the concepts of sin, guilt and punishment is at least
theoretically possible. Critics, on the other hand, may as legitimately disagree,
and argue that guilt is an irreducible reality of life; and, even if they concede
that it is a cultural construct, they may still argue that it is psychologically
naïve to expect people moulded by western culture to be able to free themselves completely from its influence[132]. Briefly: either the engendering of guilt
is ascribed to indoctrination by New Age philosophies, or to indoctrination by
a western philosophy of sin and punishment. Neither party accepts the presuppositions on which the argument of the other part is based. We must conclude that if the debate about self-healing remains on the present superficial
level and fails to address the fundamental issues in terms of underlying worldviews, there is little hope that it will ever yield results other than increasing
polarization.

The debate over self-healing has been provoked mainly by extreme expo-
nents like Louise L. Hay[133]. Hay believes that the most fundamental limiting
belief leading to illness is "I am not good enough"[134]. The 'miracle cure'[135]
for all problems, then, is learning to love the Self unconditionally, and one of

---

[132] Ken Wilber suggests that this applies both to patients *and* to the sort of New Age believers who had the heart "compassionately" to ask his wife questions like 'why did you choose to
give yourself cancer?' (Wilber, *Grace and Grit*, 254). Underneath the surface, according to
Wilber, is thinly-concealed rage: "'I don't want to hurt you, I love you; but disagree with me
and you will get an illness that will kill you. Agree with me, agree that you can create your own
reality, and you will get better, you will live'" (266). Wilber does not hesitate to characterize
this as "borderline pathology". He adds that an article in which he expressed his opinion evoked
many reactions of people who shared his sense of moral outrage; but that it also evoked infuri-
ated reactions from "hard-core new agers", who said that 'if Treya and I thought that, she deserved
to get cancer. She was bringing it on herself with these thoughts' (266). Wilber's wife reacts
somewhat more mildly. She observes that the question "why did you give yourself cancer?"
betrays self-righteousness and is not constructive, but she can go along very well with questions
such as 'How are you choosing to use this cancer?': 'For me this question is exciting; it helps
me look at what I can do now, helps me feel empowered and supported and challenged in a positive way. Someone who asks this kind of question conveys that they see my illness not as a punishment for something I did wrong but as a difficult and challenging situation also potentially
full of opportunities for growth' (254).
[133] Some other examples include MAA 13; SoM 276-277 (illness is described as 'a state of
Mind' ultimately reflecting a lack of self-love).
[134] YHL 12.
[135] YHL 23.

the principal affirmations recommended by Hay is "I approve of myself"[136]. By instilling positive beliefs, she suggests, all illnesses can be cured[137]. Such beliefs are a prominent and important part of New Age thinking. However, it must be added that, while the radical approach of self-healing has inevitably attracted most of the popular attention, more moderate interpretations are at least as common. Marilyn Ferguson admirably summarizes all the basic beliefs in a few sentences, which may be interpreted radically but need not be:

> Health and disease don't just happen to us. They are active processes issuing from inner harmony or disharmony, profoundly affected by our states of consciousness, our ability or inability to flow with experience. This recognition carries with it implicit responsibility and opportunity. If we are participating, however unconsciously, in the process of disease, we can choose health instead. ... Illness ... is potentially transformative because it can cause a sudden shift in values, an awakening. If we have been keeping secrets from ourselves—unexamined conflicts, suppressed yearnings—illness may force them into awareness. ... Just as the search for self becomes a search for health, so the pursuit of health can lead to greater self-awareness. All wholeness is the same[138].

Fritjof Capra, in his influential chapters about healing in *The Turning Point*, concedes that any responsibility for illness can only be partial[139]. While applauding the cancer therapy developed by Carl Simonton, which is based on the principles of self-responsibility, Capra recognizes the emergence of countertherapeutic guilt feelings as a serious problem[140]. His exposition is representative for more moderate views of self-responsibility. The spectrum of self-healing in New Age terms therefore includes everything covered by Ferguson's description, but is not limited to the approach exemplified by Hay.

C. Inner Realms

In chapter eight (section 3A) we found that, in New Age religion, the fundamental distinction between objective reality and subjective experience is seri-

---

[136] YHL 84.

[137] This radical message pervades *You Can Heal Your Life*. Nevertheless, Hay does not directly adress the fact that her workshops with AIDS patients (known as the "Hay-rides"; cf. d'Antonio, *Heaven on Earth*, ch. 2) do not result in AIDS being cured. Dave Braun, in the foreword, relates how his 'respect and love for Louise grew as I observed my beloved AIDS people make their transitions enriched and at peace and complete ... and with a quiet respect for having created that precise learning experience'. In these cases, Hay's method apparently helps people accept AIDS, rather than cure it.

[138] AC 282. Most of what is said here seems not too unreasonable, except for the sudden overstatement 'we can choose health instead'. These kinds of rhetoric devices are responsible for much of the suggestive rather than precisely argumentative force of Ferguson's book (cf. beginning of chapter eight, section 3B).

[139] TP 329. Cf. UW 210, in which Capra discusses the problem of guilt with Carl Simonton.

[140] UW 210.

ously called into doubt, to say the least. A logical result is that religion is psychologized by discovering the psyche as the *locus* of the sacred. In section 3B of the same chapter we found that the so-called objective world is compared to a dream created by the mind: reality is explained in the terms of psychology; and this has consequences for the extent to which the mind can influence reality. We must now take a look at the complementary tendency to reify the realm of the psyche. First, we examine the so-called "cartographies of consciousness" developed by transpersonal psychology. Against that background we will discuss the concept of "inner space". In the next chapter, we will then be able to make a comparison with New Age ideas about survival after death.

Cartographies of Consciousness
Transpersonal psychology, as we saw, takes as its starting point the claim that consciousness is not limited to the dimensions recognized by traditional psychological schools. These schools are criticized for giving reductionistic accounts of "transpersonal" experiences, instead of taking these seriously as autonomous dimensions of the total psyche. A central concern of transpersonal psychology lies therefore in developing "maps" of the mind which explain the dynamics of consciousness within a comprehensive framework, encompassing the complete spectrum from unitive consciousness to the limited ego. Obviously, people will define "reality" very differently according to the level of consciousness to which they have access. In order to go beyond a level of pure phenomenological description (which can only support a stance of agnostic relativism with regard to the *meaning* of the data of consciousness) and develop a theoretical framework with explanatory value, transpersonal psychologists must adopt a clear position regarding the degree of "reality" that is to be accorded to each state of consciousness on the spectrum. While traditional psychological schools tend to regard "ordinary" personal consciousness as the norm (and must therefore see mystical states as—relatively or totally—illusionary), transpersonal psychologists do the opposite. The irreducibility of unitive consciousness is postulated, and individual consciousness must accordingly be regarded as based on the "illusion of separateness"[141].
Within the perimeters of this conviction, there is plenty of room for variations. Stanislav Grof's cartography of consciousness is developed to account for the

---

[141] This analysis does not contradict my above assessment of Stanislav Grof's work (section 3A in this chapter). Within the wider transpersonal framework, the statement "everything that is subjectively experienced as real, must be regarded as real" is equivalent to the statement "everything short of total unitive consciousness is equally illusionary". In other words: if Grof says that transpersonal experiences are "real", what he means is only that they have the same ontological status as everyday experience. Neither is my analysis incompatible with the hierarchical structure of transpersonal "consciousness maps". These hierarchies do not imply that the more encompassing our consciousness, the "more real" we are (although popular derivations may sometimes suggest this). They only imply that our mind drops more and more of its shutters as we come closer to the uniquely real.

findings of his empirical research, and Grof himself tends to interpret it within the framework of a holographic worldview based on universal interconnectedness. Ken Wilber, as we saw, sharply rejects that worldview in favour of the hierarchical ontology of perennial philosophy. His argument is theoretical rather than empirical: he starts from general metaphysical presuppositions rather than from experimental data, and develops a psychology that convinces first and foremost by its logical consistency and explanatory elegance. Furthermore, it can be doubted whether Grof's and Wilber's cartographies are really about the same terrain at all. Grof is basically concerned with systematizing Altered States of Consciousness (ASC's) only; Wilber's theory more ambitiously claims to adress *all* dimensions of the psyche and its basic dynamics.

A detailed exposition of Wilber's transpersonal psychology, and of the development of his thinking over the years, would take us far beyond the limits imposed by this study. We must restrict ourselves to a very brief overview. Wilber's early *Spectrum of Consciousness* is summarized in the following diagram:

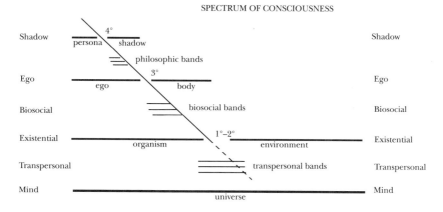

Figure C. The Spectrum of Consciousness. Courtesy of Quest Books, Wheaton, Ill., U.S.A.

Wilber emphasizes that the diagram is a simplification: 'the spectrum itself contains a vast number of bands and levels, but we have singled out a half dozen major ones since they are easily recognizable'[142]. Similar to a spectrum of broken light, the different "bands" of consciousness imperceptibly shade into one another[143].

As we move from Mind (bottom line) to the level of the individual persona (top), a progressive narrowing of consciousness occurs, in which large parts of mind are "split off" and rendered unconscious. This is indicated by the diag-

---

[142] SoC 107.
[143] SoC 144.

onal line. Everything to the left of the line is conscious, everything to the right
unconscious. While on the level of Mind there is perfect unlimited awareness
of all reality and therefore no unconscious, the diagonal line gradually starts
to appear when we move upward toward the existential level. This level is characterized by consciousness of oneself as an organism separate from the environment. The environment, in other words, is that aspect of Mind which has
become unconscious and therefore "alien". Next, within the organism, a split
occurs between ego and body. One experiences oneself as a conscious ego
which makes use of a bodily "vehicle" without consciousness. The body, in
other words, is now alienated from consciousness. The ego-body unity is disrupted; henceforth, consciousness seems to reside only in the ego. As a result,
the unconscious has expanded further, and consciousness has been further nar-
rowed. Finally, even the ego itself is disrupted. Large parts are disowned and
rendered unconscious. The parts which stay conscious are called the persona;
the rest is called the shadow. This, of course, is the psychological unconscious
as described in the psychoanalytic tradition. What the complete diagram intends
to demonstrate is that most people have alienated the largest part of their real
being and are out of touch with the whole. All this does *not* mean, Wilber
assures us, that a real split has occurred in the universe. The whole process of
progressive alienation is ultimately illusionary. No real division has ever
occurred from the perspective of Mind; it is only that certain aspects of Mind
experience themselves as separate. Accordingly, the healing of the split(s) is
not the healing of a flaw in the universe; it is only the removal of illusions[144].
Wilber therefore describes his model as

> a study in what Hindus and Buddhists call *maya*, a study in the distinctions "super-
> imposed" on Reality to apparently generate phenomena. Thus it would be useful
> to bear in mind the general nature of *maya* itself—namely the "magic" or "art"
> whereby we "create two worlds from one", a dualistic process that is very much
> a *creation* but an *illusory* creation, not real but "pretend", a make-believe mani-
> festation of the Absolute *appearing* as all phenomena. *Maya* is the Godhead's cre-
> ative power of emptying or reflecting itself into all things and thus *creating* all
> things, the power of Absolute Subjectivity to take an objective appearance. In
> reality the Godhead remains Void, but appears or takes form only as objects; and
> this power of phenomenal appearance-creation is called *maya*[145].

The diagram given in *The Spectrum of Consciousness* remains somewhat static. In *The Atman Project*, Wilber develops a dynamic theory of human development which is based on the groundwork laid down in his earlier work, but
goes considerably beyond it. Again, the basic framework is given in a diagram:

---

[144] This view is very similar to *A Course in Miracles*, which also emphasizes that no real separation between God and humanity has ever occurred. This basic tenet of the *Course* is implicit
in the opening statement "Nothing real can be threatened—Nothing unreal exists", and is repeated constantly throughout the material.
[145] SoC 107.

As the simple version [fig. D] shows, human development can be represented as a circular process consisting of two complementary halves. The development from the womb to self-consciousness is called the "outward arc", and the development beyond the personal self to superconsciousness is called the "inward arc". The circle is divided in three equal parts, representing subconsciousness, self-consciousness and superconsciousness. The more complicated

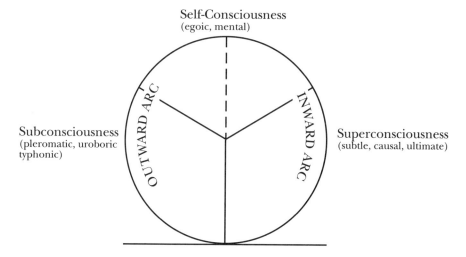

Figure D. The General Life Cycle. Courtesy of Quest Books, Wheaton, Ill., U.S.A.

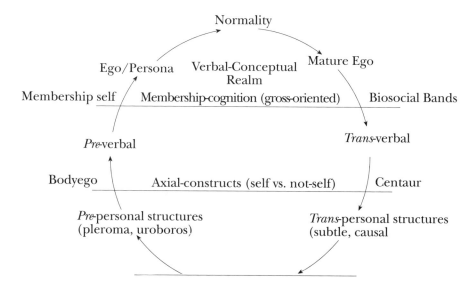

Figure E. Highlight of the Life Cycle: Pre- vs. Trans-. Courtesy of Quest Books, Wheaton, Ill., U.S.A.

shows a further development of Wilber's argument, showing that the outward and inward arc mirror each other. The development of the child from a *pre-personal* consciousness of oneness with the mother is mirrored by the *trans-personal* consciousness of oneness with the universe. This is Wilber's transpersonal answer to Freudian reductionism, which interprets mystical experience as a regressive state. According to Wilber, such an interpretation ignores the distinction between a consciousness that is *not yet* personal and one that is *beyond* the personal. The two look superficially similar only because both are, indeed, *not* personal. A similar parallellism exists between the *pre-verbal* stage of child development, and the *trans-verbal* stage in which experience moves beyond what can be expressed in discursive language. Of course, the diagram is again a simplified version, and each stage could be further subdivided in substages that imperceptibly shade into one another.

The distinction between pre- and trans- states has been of fundamental importance in Wilber's later work, as it allows a critical perspective on concrete religious phenomena. Among other things, Wilber has used it to distinguish between what he regards as genuine spirituality (based on the perennial philosophy) and pop mysticism. Wilber criticizes the New Age movement for confusing pre-states with genuine transcendence, and is clearly irritated by the fact that he himself is often associated with the New Age[146].

Stanislav Grof's cartography, as mentioned, differs strongly from Wilber's in being concerned almost exclusively with mapping Altered States of Consciousness. Grof labels normal, everyday experience of consensus reality as the *Hylotropic mode of consciousness* and nonordinary psychological states as the *Holotropic mode of consciousness*[147]. The transpersonal phenomena experienced in the holotropic mode show extreme variation but are all characterized by 'the subject's feeling that his or her consciousness has expanded beyond the usual ego boundaries and has transcended the limitations of time and space'[148]. In the holotropic mode, it is possible to obtain access to 'one's biological, psychological, social, racial, and spiritual history and the past, present, and future of the entire phenomenal world, [as well as] access to many other

---

[146] Cf. Wilber, *Sociable God*, esp. 91-110; *Grace and Grit*, 46 (New Age as 'A yuppified postmodern version of Christian Science'), and particularly 256-273. Wilber considers that probably about 20 % of the New Age movement is transpersonal (i.e., genuinely mystical), and 80 % prepersonal: 'You can usually find the transpersonal elements because they don't like to be called "new age"' (*Grace and Grit*, 268). This means that Wilber himself can hardly object to being included, as in this study, in the "New Age" in an inclusive sense.

[147] Grof emphasizes that this is *the* fundamental distinction to be made. The holotropic mode includes not only the transpersonal, but also biographical and perinatal experiences. The distinction between these categories was made 'primarily for didactic reasons' (AS 42). This fits precisely with Michael Harner's fundamental distinction between Ordinary State of Consciousness (OSC) and Shamanic State of Consciousness (SSC) (WS xix). Harner does not subdivide SSC into smaller categories: in his worldview, there are simply "two worlds".

[148] AS 38.

levels and domains of reality described by the great mystical traditions of the world'[149]. Grof refers to Wilber's spectrum model to summarize the hierarchy of these levels. Nevertheless, his own cartography is not ordered hierarchically but according to empirical criteria. Grof divides transpersonal experiences in three large groups: Experiential Extension *within* Consensus Reality and Space-Time, Experiential Extension *Beyond* Consensus Reality and Space-Time, and Transpersonal Experiences of Psychoid Nature. The first group is further subdivided in experiences transcending spatial boundaries; experiences transcending boundaries of linear time (i.e., these boundaries have not disappeared, but are no longer binding); and experiences of physical introversion and narrowing of consciousness. The first two subgroups are further subdivided in many smaller categories. The second group is split up into thirteen such smaller categories. The third group is concerned with the paranormal: synchronistic phenomena, spontaneous psychoid events, and intentional psychokinesis. Again, several smaller categories are distinguished. The detailed discussion of each of these categories (42 in all) results in a veritable gallery of the archetypal and psychedelic.

The most important implication of these cartographies of consciousness for New Age religion seem to be that the mind has many levels, and that the realities corresponding to these levels are ontologically on a continuum with everyday, consensus reality (i.e., distinctions between reality and mere fantasy are rejected). This view fits naturally with speculations about higher, "subtle" levels (with corresponding subtle bodies) of reality as developed in nineteenth-century occultism, particularly modern Theosophy. Depending on the particular author, the nature of these levels is described in relatively more "material" or psychological terms, but the common understanding is that such distinctions are of limited value. Although the precise details and the number of levels may vary somewhat from author to author[150], all these hierarchies exhibit a common structure. Invariably, the level of everyday consensus reality—the material reality of the "earth plane"—is located at the bottom. At the top of the spectrum is a reality of pure unbroken spirit. The gap between these two opposite poles is bridged by an intermediate realm which is neither matter nor pure spirit. This intermediate realm is most "dense" at the bottom, growing progressively more "subtle" and spiritual upwards. It is only with regard to the intermediate realm that different authors seem to contradict each other. It would be misleading, however, to put too much emphasis on these differences, because they all seem to agree that the intermediate realm is in fact an unbroken con-

---

[149] AS 39.
[150] Cf. WW 117 (7 levels, adopted from the influential occultist Dion Fortune); W 127-133 (4 levels, adopted from parapsychologist Lawrence LeShan); PH 145-147 (4 levels, developed by Houston and her husband, Robert Masters); RR 206 (7 levels, derived from Theosophy).

tinuum. The boundaries between different levels are therefore not absolute but approximate. In the end, all distinctions and levels are of an illusionary character compared with the ultimate reality of pure spirit.

It is almost superfluous to point out that the whole framework is modeled on the platonic "great chain of being" which we already encountered at the very beginning of our exposition. The distinctive trait of its New Age manifestation is the strong extent to which this traditional metaphysical framework is reinterpreted in psychological terms. The angelic and demonic realms that mediate between matter and spirit are identified as realms of the human unconscious[151], and this collective unconscious is in turn identified as an objective transpersonal realm accessed in the holotropic mode of consciousness. This is how the "gods" that seemed to have been banned from heaven reappear—without losing any of their power—from the depths of the human psyche.

Journeys through Inner Space

The sources tell us remarkably little about the ultimate realm of pure spirit. Most of the attention goes to the intermediate world(s). There is widespread agreement that we can "travel" through our own inner space in a very literal way. On these travels we may encounter all kinds of situations and entities that may help us in our quest for selfunderstanding, healing and growth.

Inner travels are made in an Altered State of Consciousness. This trance state may be induced in different ways. According to Starhawk, they all seem to function on four related principles: relaxation, sensory restriction, rhythm, and boredom[152]. Relaxation is fairly self-evident. Sensory restriction may involve simply closing one's eyes, or concentrating on one single unchanging source of sensory stimulation, such as a candle flame, a crystal ball or black mirror, and so on. Rhythm can be provided by music (holotropic therapy) or drumming (Harner's Shamanic trance), but also by the quiet recitation of words (guided visualization, "pathworkings"). That boredom induces trance is well known, 'as generations of daydreaming schoolchildren have discovered'[153]. Somewhat surprisingly, Starhawk does not mention breathing techniques, which are evidently a further prominent way of trance induction (for instance in holotropic therapy). Various authors may differ in their emphasis on this or that element, but usually they are all present in some form.

In Grof's holotropic therapy, the inner journeys are not prestructured. The "facilitator" who assists the process simply lets the experience unfold in its own way, trusting the wisdom of the psyche. In Harner's Shamanic sessions, a minimum structure is given beforehand. Typical shamanic journeys involve

---

[151] This is the title of an early work by Grof (*Realms of the Human Unconscious*).
[152] SD 162.
[153] SD 162.

entering some kind of opening in the ground (an imagined hole, cave, vortex, door etc.: anything that feels right and appropriate to the experiencing subject) which gives access to a tunnel leading to the "Lowerworld". The subject then travels freely wherever (s)he likes, and finally returns through the tunnel back to the normal world. Many guided imagination exercises follow a similar pattern, but may give more specific details. In that case, the subject is guided through inner space by spoken (or taped) instructions. Jean Houston, for instance, gives instructions for an inner journey that culminates in meeting a "Master Teacher" who will assist the subject to master a certain skill. The instructions start thus: 'Feel yourself lying alone in the bottom of a little row-boat. You are being carried out into the ocean by gentle rhythmic waves.'[154] The instructions then describe how the subject will feel him/herself going down into a vortex toward the bottom of the ocean (cf. the Shamanic pattern). Pulling a bronze handle, the subject finds a door opening to a stone stairwell leading to a realm underneath the ocean floor. In a cavern deep under the ocean floor, the subject comes to a large oak door, over which is written "The Room of the Skill". Behind the door, the subject meets a Master Teacher who gives instructions pertaining to the desired skill.

> in the room is a Master Teacher of the skill—perhaps someone you know or a historical figure or someone you have never seen or heard of before. Whichever it is, this person or being is your Master Teacher, and in the time that follows this teacher will give you deep and potent instructions to help you improve your skill. The Master Teacher may speak in words or not. Teachings may present themselves as feelings or as muscular sensations. The Master Teacher may have you practice old skills or learn new ones. The teacher may be solemn or quite comical. However this being works with you, the learning on your part will be effective and deep[155].

Five minutes of clock time are given for this learning process; but, in the altered time of trance experience, this may equal any necessary time period: hours, days, even weeks. Finally, the subject is instructed to thank the Teacher and return the way (s)he has come. This return journey is also described in detail. Houston suggests that this kind of trance exercise will produce real and lasting results, and adds a brief and suggestive discussion:

> The Master Teacher is a potent reminder of our inner "allies" and may often provide much more teaching and wisdom than we had intended when we set off on this journey. And the exercise may also lead you to the discovery that the inner realms have their own subtle machinations for guiding you. While we can use and orchestrate these inner realms, we must also listen to them, for they have urgent messages to send to us[156].

---

[154] PH 178.
[155] PH 178-179.
[156] PH 180.

The inner realms, in other words, have a life and reality of their own. Although we "orchestrate" them, they are more than just fantasy. While Houston does not press the issue of the "reality" of the inner planes, we have seen that other authors are much more definite in their assertions that the worlds of the mind are at least as real, if indeed not more real, than our world of space-time limitation. Both Shamanic journeys and Houston's exercises are similar to the practices known as "pathworking" among neopagans. As the name indicates, these guided imagery exercises describe a path to a goal and back. The goal may be anything representing wisdom, insight, understanding etc.: a wise teacher (human or animal), a god or goddess, perhaps a book, or simply a state of consciousness characterized by a deep sense of wholeness. The description of the path, as a slow approximation towards the goal, is a way to help the subject gradually to connect with his/her inner self "at the center" which may communicate through images or words[157].

The concern with inner journeys is yet another example of the New Age's high regard for the powers of the imagination. In fact, the imagination appears in New Age religion in two different roles, which are not unrelated but should be distinguished analytically. We already encountered it in the context of "creating our own reality". There it functioned as an essential *tool* for mobilizing and canalizing the creative powers of the mind: by cultivating inner images we make them become real in the outer world. In the present context, the imagination stands for the equally real *world(s)* we can "create": this time not in the outside world but in our own minds. According to Stewart Farrar,

> the imagination is not an enclave, but working territory ... Deliberately and methodically [the modern witch] explores this territory. He regards imagination not as an escape (however therapeutic) into illusion, but as a channel of communication with other levels of reality and the beings that inhabit them. He exercises and develops his imagination in exactly the same way that a professional traveller studies foreign languages, and for the same reason: so that he can understand, recognize, and communicate, beyond his 'normal' territory[158].

The primary example of entering "inner worlds" is, of course, dreaming. The common New Age view that reality is, in fact, a dream is complemented by the equally common view that dreams are reality. The connecting link is imaginative *consciousness*: all realities are just states of mind. By "altering" our state of consciousness we enter another reality: the question what is real and what illusion—when are we awake and when do we dream—depends on the

---

[157] For pathworkings, Marian Green is a good source. See MAA 44-48; EAM 26-29, 88-90; GAAM 96-111.
[158] WWD 144. This view of the imagination is particularly common in neopaganism and transpersonal psychology.

perspective taken, and is ultimately meaningless[159]. This argument is encountered particularly in connection with so-called *lucid dreams*: the extremely vivid and lively type in which the dreamer is aware that (s)he is dreaming, and is able to exercise active control over the dream. Lucid dreams, it is argued (and probably all dreams, it is added), are actually visits to parallel universes[160]. A variation on the theme of the "reality of dreams" is Reed's view— attributed, correctly or not, to Cayce—that dreams are a kind of preview of the likely outcome of our actions and attitudes: 'While we dream, the soul scans ahead to forecast the likely outcome of various attitudes and actions that are competing for our attention. It sorts through various mental patterns and selects new ones to place within the projector to be cast upon the screen of life. Dreams thus are like seeds of our future experiences. What we call real life is but the consequence of our dreams'[161]. Closely related is the view of dreams, particularly so-called "Big Dreams", as powerful messages from the unconscious about the dreamer's present condition and likely future[162]. The premise is that the unconscious holds the answers to all questions. It is characteristic, once more, for the New Age tendency of conflating metaphysics and psychology that this function of the unconscious is often explained with reference to the Theosophical concept of the "Akashic records": the universal memory of the Logos or world-soul which can be "tapped into" by psychics[163].

---

[159] SM 194-214.
[160] HU 65-66.
[161] ECMM 211.
[162] Cf. S 123-124; WS 99-101; CCC 13.
[163] WW 202; EAM 60 ('the Collective Unconscious of Jung, called the Akashic Records in past ages'); OL 104-105, 187; ECMM 60-61.

CHAPTER NINE

DEATH AND SURVIVAL

1. INTRODUCTION: THE EXPERIENCE OF DEATH

Existentialism has made us familiar with the notion that life is basically a meaningless and absurd spectacle of suffering and despair, leaving no other certainty than the final inevitability of death[1]. The human belief in immortality has been presented as a reaction—understandable, but ultimately futile—to this basic reality. The Dutch sociologist and philosopher Meerten ter Borg, for instance, starts a book about contemporary "immortality projects" by presenting the existentialist experience as an inescapable fact: 'How do we manage to endure life? For most of us there is quite a deal of misery in store. It may be that the cup happens to pass us by personally, but a moment of reflection teaches us that the chance for the opposite is greater. But even if we manage to avoid all misery, pain and grief, still at the end of everything death is waiting. The story ends badly for all of us, that much is certain'[2]. Religious beliefs in immortality are attempted answers to the absurdity of existence, or ways to avoid the necessity of facing it[3]. This reductionist position is theoretically unassailable but weak empirically. In the 1970s, Mircea Eliade analyzed the popularity of the French alternative journal *Planète* (which represents many of the concerns we now regard as "New Age") in terms which existentialists would certainly interpret as confirmation of their thesis, but which can equally well support the view that the New Age movement is a reaction not to the absurdity of existence but, rather, to the absurdity of existentialism:

> what was new and exhilarating to the French reader was the optimistic and holistic outlook which coupled science with esoterism and presented a living, fascinating, and mysterious cosmos, in which human life again became meaningful and promised an endless perfection. Man was no longer condemned to a rather dreary *condition humaine*; instead he was called both to conquer his physical universe and to unravel the other, enigmatic universes revealed by the occultists and gnostics[4].

New Age believers will often describe not suffering and death, but the won-

---

[1] A classic statement of the existentialist view of life is Camus, *Myth of Sisyphus*.

[2] Ter Borg, *Uitgewaaierde eeuwigheid*, 11. My translation.

[3] Ter Borg, *Uitgewaaierde eeuwigheid*, 11: 'People have always had a religion, by which the existential question could be answered, or—and that may be even more important—by which they could avoid having to pose it'.

[4] Eliade, 'Cultural Fashions', 10.

der and mystery of the universe as a basic, irreducible experience. The existentialist, with his *ennui*, has apparently lost the thrill of being alive; in his somewhat morbid overemphasis on suffering, he forgets to appreciate the gifts life has to offer. Like the existentialist position, this New Age perspective is theoretically unassailable but beyond empirical verification or falsification. Both reflect beliefs, not facts. Whether meaning is a human invention in the face of an absurd reality, or *ennui* a symptom of blindness towards a meaningful reality, cannot be decided with reference to human experience itself. We are thrown back, again, on the methodological agnosticism proper to empirical research.

From that perspective, we must conclude that New Age authors seldom or never present the human experience of death as an existential problem that requires an answer. It is true, however, that some of them report periods of hopelessness and loss of meaning in the face of death, followed by a kind of "healing" experience which restored meaning. Shakti Gawain, for instance, went through an existential crisis during adolescence: 'I could see that all the things that were supposed to provide significance in life—education, success, relationships, money—were in themselves ephemeral, meaningless, empty. There didn't seem to be anything else to fill the void'[5]. With hindsight, she interprets this as part of the educational process of 'piercing the veil of illusion'. She describes how, when she had reached the bottom of despair and expected to hit rock bottom, she found herself falling 'through a trap door into a bright new world—the realm of spiritual truth'[6]. Gawain thus interprets her crisis as a necessary part of the process of growth. In a structurally similar way, Ken Wilber, in his transpersonal theory of psychological development, assigns a crucial role to *thanatos*. Driven on by a metaphysical hunger (*eros*) which will only be satisfied by ultimate Wholeness (referred to by Wilber as *atman*), human beings try to satisfy this hunger by substitutes, such as money, power, knowledge etc. In the end, each atman substitute is bound to fail: 'the fearful background of death is still there to be thought of, and the skull will grin in at the banquet'[7]. This "existentialist" experience is referred to as *thanatos*; as a counterforce to *eros* it provides the dynamics behind spiritual growth. Only in the attainment of complete unity will *eros* find permanent satisfaction, which will leave no more opportunity for the skull to grin in. Wilber has developed a sophisticated theory, which takes the problem of death denial and "immortality projects" very seriously indeed, but from a general context based on the aprioristic certainty that the absolute finality of death is an illusion.

---

[5] LL xx-xi.
[6] LL xi.
[7] EfE 15. Wilber refers for this image to William James.

To the general rule that the New Age does not experience death as a pressing problem requiring an answer, we must note an occasional exception. The quest for "physical immortality", found in Rebirthing circles, is hard to interpret otherwise. When Leonard Orr and Sondra Ray claim that the necessity of death is no more than an ingrained belief, and that we can stay forever young and beautiful (provided, one assumes, that we are beautiful to begin with), they implicitly admit that they see death and aging as a threat[8]. The physical immortality movement is rather marginal, however, and has been criticized by others[9].

The only other place where the common *human experience* of death (as opposed to spiritual views or theories *about* death, or rather, about its absence) receives explicit attention is in neopaganism. Life and death belong together, as light and darkness, summer and winter[10]. The eternal life force expresses itself in cycles of growth and decay. Finite beings come to an end; and that is how it should be, for it is only thus that the infinite life stream can go on. The experience of death belongs to the darker, tragic side of nature; but this side should be revered as the necessary counterpart to its brighter, more joyful side. In the ongoing life process, death is never the final end, but is followed by rebirth. In spiritual development, and particularly in the ritual initiations of witchcraft, the experience of death is a necessary condition for regeneration and growth[11]. In other words, the experience of death again has the initiatic function of mediating between one state of consciousness and a higher one: it is a necessary part of evolution. The view is structurally identical to the one found in the work of Gawain and Wilber. In fact, this view that death is not an end but a mediation between life and rebirth turns out to be a constant factor in New Age thinking. While the *experiential encounter with death* (either as an existential sense of hopelessness and futility in individual consciousness, or as a symbolic encounter in neopagan rituals) functions to move an individual from one state of consciousness to a higher one, *actual physical death* functions to move him to an entirely new existence (reincarnation). The same principle can even be recognized in many views about the coming New Age: it is said that we are now witnessing the death of the old culture, but that this is a condition for the birth of the new one.

We may conclude that death and dying are consistently seen as passing but necessary experiences or stages in a larger development, *never* as a final end.

---

[8] See RNA ch. 6. The cause of physical immortality inspires slogans such as 'The alternative to aging is youthing' (RNA 63) and 'The truth is that all death is suicide' (i.e., because only the beliefs in our own mind create death).

[9] VS 12-13 ('It is only an unevolved soul who would seek to prolong life in order to avoid death').

[10] SD 41-47.

[11] SD 174-175.

This conclusion sums up all that is important about death in the New Age. The rest of the chapter will not be about death but about life, i.e., immortality.

2. OTHER REALITIES

A central aspect of New Age religion, as we saw, is the belief in "other realities" which can be freely accessed by human beings. This can be done in so-called Altered States of Consciousness (ASC's), either induced by certain spiritual techniques or appearing spontaneously. These other worlds were discussed in the previous chapter as an important aspect of the "psychologizing of religion and sacralization of psychology". In the present context, it is important to note the remarkable similarity between these "worlds of the mind" or "inner realms", on the one hand, and the realities which the soul is believed to enter after physical death, on the other. There is a very strong suggestion, to say the least, that they are one and the same. In describing the other realities to which the soul travels during ASC's, New Age authors constantly emphasize that these worlds are *not* merely subjective fantasy. They are as real as our world, although different. Particularly characteristic is the extent to which their appearance is influenced by the consciousness of the person who experiences them. We know that, in normal life, our perception of surrounding phenomena is partly determined by our individual perspective: the objects are there, but we do not all perceive them in exactly the same way. According to New Age thinking, this principle is strongly amplified in the other worlds. The influence of subjective perspectives is so strong that different persons may find themselves in completely different environments, which are ultimately self-created. Furthermore, these environments can be directly influenced and changed by the consciousness of the observer[12]. None of this means, however, that they are not real: they just appear differently to different persons. Again, we encounter the characteristic New Age strategy of making the very most of the distinction between the "real" and the "phenomenal".

If we compare these views about inner realities with descriptions of the worlds entered by the soul (either between incarnations or after having completed the incarnation cycle) we find that the differences are negligible. In the first case, it is asserted that what some would consider the product of fantasy is in fact real; in the second case, it is said that those who expect to enter a solid metaphysical world after death will find, instead, that their new environment reflects the movements of their own mind[13]. The resulting kind of reali-

---

[12] For instance WW 217.
[13] WW 120; VAA 45-55.

ty is often loosely referred to in theosophical terms as the "astral plane"[14]. George Trevelyan's description is characteristic:

> It appears that our friends are there to meet us in surroundings at first much like the world to which we are accustomed, though more beautiful. The explanation is simple enough. The 'next world' is composed from thought and imagination. It is a subtler plane of finer vibrations, and therefore 'substance' is immediately responsive to mentation and intention. ... Of course it is true that this is a plane of illusion; but that does not make the experience of it any less real, valid or important. It is, after all, no more illusory than our own earth plane. The 'Maya' of the material world is real and necessary enough for us while we are here. The crucial point to realise is that the genuine realms of spirit exist on far higher planes, attained only after long soul development and catharsis[15].

In traditional theosophy, the astral is only one level among others: there are higher levels, on which the individual creative freedom of the mind is progressively restricted. While it seldom follows the precise sevenfold schemes of Theosophical metaphysics, a comparable view is also found in the New Age. Just as the influence of mind on matter in our own physical world is relatively limited, so the malleability of reality decreases when higher and higher worlds are reached:

> When we become conscious on the astral plane, we find that in a sense we have more freedom of action on its 'middle reaches' than we do at either the lowest or the highest level of the spectrum. On the lowest plane ... the astral is very closely matched to the physical, and while projection can make our awareness of it more acute, and vastly increase our freedom of *movement* within it, our freedom of *action*—our ability to manipulate the 'astral counterparts' by which we are surrounded—is very limited indeed, because of their tight integration with their *physical* counterparts.
> The highest astral level, on the other hand, has close links with the mental and spiritual levels. The entities which people it tend to be of a higher order of being than ourselves. Conscious experience on that level, once we achieve it, is therefore likely to be receptive rather than active, and the environment to be awe-inspiring rather than malleable. ... The 'middle reaches' of the astral plane are much more of a free-for-all than either of these extremes. Experience here can be very rewarding—and it can also be dangerous[16].

Again, this view of a hierarchy of metaphysical worlds directly parallels a common hierarchy in ASC's. There, too, normal everyday consciousness and unitive consciousness are seen as the two extreme poles of a spectrum, with dreamlike states dominated by images and symbols occupying the gradations in

---

[14] WW 120; VAA 45-55. In this connection, both the Farrars and Trevelyan speak of the "summerland(s)" (also mentioned by Starhawk: SD 41) as a specific region of the astral plane. The term achieved popularity in 19th century spiritualism, and seems to have been invented by Andrew Jackson Davis (see Webb, *Occult Underground*, 31, 33).

[15] VAA 46-47.

[16] WW 216-217.

between. Such "cartographies of consciousness" have been discussed in chapter eight (section 3C). Their logic is derived from belief in a duality (*dualitudo*, not dualism) between matter and spirit; the "world(s) in between" bridge the gap because, in different gradations, they are more spiritual than matter and more material than spirit.

It should be noted that there is an implicit tension in New Age religion between these views, which regard unitive consciousness as the final goal of evolution, and those perspectives which emphasizes unlimited creative expansion. The distinction corresponds with a general distinction repeatedly encountered in the preceding discussions: i.e., the two contradictory Platonic strands, one of which emphasizes the return to unity, the other generativity, and their teleological and/or open-ended evolutionary implications. I will not repeat those discussions, but only remind the reader that alongside the "monistic pathos" we find the (at least as powerful) "evolutionary pathos" of unlimited cosmic expansion. A worldview based on the former asserts that individual creative freedom will be more and more restricted the closer one comes to the One. A worldview based on the latter, however, implies merely that the realities created by entities on higher and higher levels become progressively alien and unfathomable to us. A good example of this last possibility is Jane Roberts's discussions of "Seth Two". We remember that Seth regards time as nonexistent in the "spacious present". On that basis, it is not surprising that one day Jane Roberts found herself channeling a "future Seth", i.e., Seth on a far higher level of development. This entity no longer exhibited the "down-to-earth" personality traits of the normal Seth. His presence "felt" strange and unusual, and he sounded different: 'the voice became even more lilting and neuter. Finally it stabilized: high, clear, distant, and unemotional'[17]. This "Seth Two" described himself as 'more than the sum of what you will be when you are finished with the dimensions and times that I have known. For I have sprung entirely away from you and would be alien in your terms'[18]. Reversely, as the normal Seth explains later, for Seth Two 'physical reality is like a breath of smoke in air'[19]. Such entities, which inevitably remind one of science fiction, obviously do not fit well within traditional mystical cosmologies based on progressive reunion with the One. They can easily be accomodated, however, within a holographic universe. The conclusion must be that, apart from the "other realities" of an imaginative, symbolic or dreamlike character, on the one hand, and those higher realities characterized by unitive consciousness, on the other, we find a third category which might be labeled "transdimensional". Descriptions of such realities emphasize that they represent other dimensions

---

[17] SM 249.
[18] SM 251.
[19] SM 259.

which are far beyond the ability of our limited minds to grasp. Reports about entities living in these realities invariably emphasize that they, too, find it difficult to attune themselves to our vibrational level and make themselves understandable in our limited terms. While the first two categories mentioned above are associated with traditional cosmologies (platonic, theosophical, perennialist), transdimensional realities are typically connected with the holographic paradigm[20].

3. REINCARNATION AND BEYOND

New Age Reincarnationism and its Attractions
There is at least one fact about the New Age on which everyone seems to agree: New Agers answer the question of survival after death in terms of *reincarnation*. Obvious though it may seem at first sight, actually this assessment is fundamentally incomplete and therefore incorrect as a general statement. It is true that almost all New Agers believe in reincarnation. The sources make it quite clear, however, that the prospects for spiritual evolution beyond physical death are not at all limited to physical rebirth on our (or even on another) planet. Rather than reincarnation, the universal element in New Age ideas about survival is *progressive spiritual evolution* considered as a process which started before birth and will continue beyond death. Reincarnation is a crucial part, but nevertheless only a part, of this larger process. It is from this basic understanding that the subject of reincarnation must be considered.

Spiritual progress is made by learning from our ultimately self-created illusions, which are often referred to by New Agers as *maya*. However, the philosophical and religious context of New Age reincarnationism is of a weak thisworldly nature, in contrast to the otherworldliness officially taught by Hinduism and Buddhism[21]. The concept of *maya* is reinterpreted accordingly: *all* realities (including, usually, earthly reality) are regarded, not as misleading dreams or nightmares, but as deeply *meaningful illusions*. Although it is true that each illusion must ultimately be transcended, the point is that it should *first* be experienced to the fullest. This is because every reality one may find

---

[20] The development of David Spangler's ideas about the Christ, from theosophy to holography (see quotations at the end of chapter seven, section 2B) exemplify this difference very well.

[21] It is only occasionally that New Age believers themselves seem to realize (or, perhaps more accurate, show interest in) this difference. An example is George Trevelyan. His formulations characteristically avoid presenting the eastern and western perspectives as incompatible: '...because the West has always been more absorbed with individuality than the East, it is fitting for our western minds that evolutionary thinking should colour our understanding of reincarnation. ... Thus, the eastern "wheel of rebirth" is, in the West, transformed into a spiral staircase leading ultimately to "a new Heaven and a new earth"' (VAA 38).

oneself in constitutes a learning task, which serves the cosmic process of progressive spiritual education and evolution of consciousness. The general belief system implicit in this view of reincarnation was discussed in chapter six, section 1, and parts of chapter eight. I concluded that not reincarnation "as such", but only reincarnation as understood within this particular weak this-worldly framework is typical for New Age religion.

It is remarkable how seldom New Age sources take the trouble to explain their reasons for believing in reincarnation. Janet & Stewart Farrar are characteristic in this respect[22]. They start their chapter on reincarnation by stating that 'Almost all witches believe in reincarnation', and then immediately proceed to assure the reader that this belief is shared by the majority of the human race. Only the 'patriarchal monotheist religions of Judaism, Christianity and Islam' are exceptions, but even here only to a certain extent: belief in reincarnation can be found in Jewish Kabbalah, and was widespread among the early christians and gnostics until it was declared anathema in the sixth century. I will return to that last point in chapter eleven (section 4). The important thing to note here is that not the belief in reincarnation is apparently in need of explanation, but rather its *absence* in some (apparently "deviant") religions.

There are several reasons why New Agers generally regard reincarnation as too obvious to defend or argue for. First of all, in anything they say about the subject, the more general worldview of spiritual evolution by an "educational journey" through successive "realities" is already presupposed. Reincarnation is felt—correctly, it would seem—as a logical and natural implication of such a worldview. It is for this reason, incidentally, that critics of New Age reincarnationism can have little hope for succes if they focus only on questioning the empirical evidence often adduced in favour of reincarnation[23]. Such evidence is, predictably, welcomed by believers in reincarnation; but they clearly do not believe in reincarnation *because of* that evidence. In order to address the real reasons, one should begin with the underlying core of New Age reincarnationism: spiritual evolutionism as such, and its related metaphysical framework. The emic persuasiveness of these and other core New Age beliefs (holism and "creating our own reality", in particular) seems not ultimately to be based on (and therefore not dependent on) empirical or argumentative proof, but on the feeling that they invest human existence with *meaning*.

Nevertheless, we should mention very briefly what seem to be the main additional rationales for belief in reincarnation. It should be noted that, in contrast to the factor just mentioned, none of these has a privileged connection to *New*

---

[22] WW 115 and rest of chapter.

[23] Paradigmatic for empirical evidence of this kind is Stevenson, *Twenty Cases*; see also Stevenson, Pasricha & Samaratne, 'Deception and Self-Deception'.

Age reincarnationism. In principle they apply equally well to other belief systems, such as Hinduism and Buddhism, and it is therefore not surprising to encounter these or very similar arguments in contemporary philosophical or theological discussions from other than New Age perspectives. The New Age movement simply takes up certain reasonings which can also be encountered elsewhere today[24]. Firstly, it is commonly argued that reincarnation gives a logical and rationally consistent account of life after death. In this respect, it is held to be superior particularly to traditional Judaeo-Christian beliefs in the future reconstitution of dead bodies, which seem to fly in the face of common sense. Secondly, and more importantly, it is argued that reincarnation is morally superior because it provides the foundation for a rational ethics. The uneven distribution of earthly goods, talents, happiness or suffering, and so on, can be explained by assuming that they are "balanced out" in other lives; particularly in combination with the belief in karma (discussed in the next chapter), reincarnation can be seen as a mechanism which guarantees ultimate cosmic justice. Finally, traditional christian beliefs suggesting that one single life on earth—however brief, however miserable—is followed by an eternal life in heaven or hell, are becoming increasingly unacceptable to many modern westerners. Not only is the balance between one single life on earth and a possible eternity in hell felt to be out of all proportion, and therefore unfair; people in the modern west also frequently fail to see what is so attractive about eternal life in an apparently static and unchanging heaven. If nothing new and interesting can be expected to happen for the rest of eternity, heaven must be an extremely boring affair. Again, reincarnation seems to be highly *preferable*. We should take good notice of what this implies. The argument actually demonstrates that the reinterpretation of oriental reincarnationism in modern western evolutionist terms is not restricted to the New Age movement; rather, it is carried by a far more widespread search for reasonable alternatives to traditional western concepts. One particularly important aspect of "weak this-worldliness" is its concern that precisely those types of activities which invest our present life with human meaning should be *perpetuated* after our death (whereas from an otherworldly perspective, of course, the "things of this world" will pass away and whatever gives *real* and lasting meaning to existence must be different in its very essence). Perhaps nowhere is it more clear how strongly the

---

[24] For an example of attempts by modern theologians to incorporate reincarnation into Christianity, cf. McGregor, *Reincarnation in Christianity*. The contemporary discussion in philosophical theology about death and immortality is full of complications which cannot possibly be summarized here. Probably the most complete survey can be found in Hick, *Death & Eternal Life*. In the light of the present discussion of New Age religion, it is intriguing that Hick, in his final conclusions, suggests "many lives in many different worlds" as the most likely option, because it incorporates the philosophical and moral advantages of reincarnation while avoiding its disadvantages.

New Age movement is rooted in modern western presuppositions, and *rejects* the very foundations of oriental (as well as, we may add, gnostic) otherworld-liness.

The Process and "Mechanics" of Reincarnation

In a number of New Age sources we find detailed descriptions of the process of reincarnation, from death to rebirth, often with specific attention to the precise "mechanics" of this process. In spite of the fact that reincarnation is believed to be only part of a much larger process of spiritual education, little effort is usually made to theorize about the specifics of evolution through higher levels[25].

Noel Langley, in his volume *Edgar Cayce on Reincarnation*, gives us the general picture. The common idea that death is a tragedy is, according to this author, 'akin to throwing away the potato and glorifying the potato peel'. We have to look at it from a different perspective:

It is far simpler to think of the soul in terms of Telstar. It takes two booster-rockets to free it of gravity and set it in astral orbit. As soon as the rockets fulfill their function, they burn out and fall away, just as the flesh body—the earthly shell of the soul—burns out and falls away in death, to be followed by the expended "ego", the discarded conscious mind of the earth shell.

The soul is no longer entrapped in matter. It is free. All that it retains from its sojourn in its earth shell is the total recall of its worldly experiences, now safely stored in its "memory bank". But only the "conscious" mind has been discarded. The subconscious mind has survived because it neither consists of, nor depends on, matter. It now becomes the conscious mind of the soul, and will continue to function as such until the soul returns into the earth's dense matter to begin its next life.

Meanwhile, the superconscious mind assumes the functions relinquished by the subconscious mind, and the soul is now articulate as it could never be on earth. The "ecstasy" that certain Saints achieve is probably akin to a momentary recapturing of the exhilaration the soul enjoys at this level of existence.

When the time comes for the soul to return to earth and assume its next body, the process is quite simply reversed. The conscious mind returns to the subconscious level, and the subconscious mind returns to the superconscious level, where it subsides back into a womb-like sanctuary in the flesh body. It neither seeks nor desires emotional association with the pursuits of the subconscious mind and the new-born conscious mind, as they accustom themselves to their new ego. ...

The "new born" conscious mind, then, can never be older in age than the new body which is temporarily housing it. The new-born's accumulated store of wisdom, its caution and its intuitive appraisal of both itself and its fellow men all lie

---

[25] See for instance the Farrars: 'The immortal Individual, freed by its own efforts from the need for further incarnations on this plane, can then move on to the next stage. The nature of that stage we can only envisage dimly, at our present level of development; if we could grasp its essence and its detail, we should not still be here' (WW 121) The exception to this, the Farrars add, is the Bodhisattva.

at the subconscious level. Thus the only friend and counsellor to which it can turn is its own subconscious mind. Moreover, it can only make this contact while asleep in the "dream state", or by the enlightened process of meditation. Here, by dint of self-discipline, it trains itself to sit and listen for the "still small voice of conscience"[26].

This account may be summarized approximately as follows:

EARTH	ASTRAL
(Superconscious)	Superconscious
Subconscious	~~Sub~~conscious
Conscious	—

At death, the limited "ego" consciousness is discarded; the subconscious becomes conscious; and the superconscious "awakens" from a latent to an active state. The process is reversed during reincarnation. In chapter eight (section 2B) we saw that the psychological terminology used to distinguish between the various components of human beings is not completely fixed; accordingly, different New Age believers may give slightly different presentations depending on their favoured view of the human constitution[27]. The general outlines of Langley/Cayce's account are, however, representative of the mainstream New Age vision[28]. In all cases it is agreed that the human personality with which we identify during our life on earth is only part of a much larger spiritual "individuality" (or "soul", "spirit", "Higher Self"). At death one regains awareness of one's larger identity or "Higher Self"; the limited "ego" personality is in most cases believed to perish together with the physical body.

It is on this foundation that the New Age movement gives its own distinctive answer, as we saw in chapter eight (section 2B) to the theoretical question of "*what* exactly is it that (re)incarnates on earth?". In this regard, one may notice a remarkable incongruity between the way in which reincarnationism tends to function in popular New Age practice (regression therapies in particular), on the one hand, and how it is usually explained by theoreticians of the movement, on the other. Stated briefly: popular expressions to the effect that "I have been so-and-so in a former life" are difficult if not impossible to rec-

---

[26] ECRE 43-45.

[27] Compare in particular WW 118-121; LL 35-39; RR 1-21.

[28] Notice, however, the role accorded to the superconscious or Higher Self during the incarnated state. While Langley/Cayce claim that it remains latent (functioning, apparently, like the "inner spark" of divinity of traditional mysticism and gnosticism), we already saw that other New Age sources accord it a far more active role, emphasizing that it can be contacted (*via* the subconscious) in fully personalized form. Compare in this respect the dream analogy used in chapter eight (section 2B, last alinea of the paragraph about the Higher Self): does the Higher Self remain "awake" during incarnations or not? In Seth's exposition it does, and his explanation has been widely followed; Langley/Cayce's approach seems to be slightly more "traditional".

oncile with theories of identity as developed in New Age literature. The simple reason is that, by using the word "I", one is referring to one's "ego" personality which, according to theory, is quite literally mortal and knows only *one* single life[29]. Only one's "real" Individuality is believed to survive death, and it is only this True Individuality or Higher Self which provides the link of continuity between this life and former or future ones.

On closer analysis, it even appears doubtful whether the New Age perspective is rendered correctly by concluding that the Higher Self "transmigrates" from one human body to the next, by way of successive incarnations. The theories suggest that it does not "incarnate" at all, but only *creates* a succession of lives, or "realities" for itself, in order to further its own spiritual evolution. And even this formulation may be too inprecise: properly speaking, the Higher Self does not create a succession of lives/realities, but creates only the *illusion* of such a succession. All this brings us to two crucial, and closely related, aspects of New Age reincarnationism: the belief that we have created/chosen our own present life, and the even more radical belief that the succession of reincarnations takes place out of time. Both were already discussed above (chapter eight, section 2B, par. "The (Higher) Self"), and only some additions need to be made here.

The concept that we have *chosen* our present incarnation, as a learning task in our process of evolution, is extremely common in New Age thinking[30]. In chapter eight (section 3B) it was mentioned as one important aspect, among others, of the belief that we "create our own reality". One characteristic example is Louise L. Hay:

> Each one of us decides to incarnate upon this planet at particular points in time and space. We have chosen to come here to learn a particular lesson that will advance us upon our spiritual, evolutionary pathway. We choose our sex, our color, our country, and then we look around for the particular set of parents who will mirror the patterns we are bringing in to work on in this lifetime. Then, when we grow up, we usually point our finger accusingly at our parents and whimper, "You did it to me". But really, we chose them because they were perfect for what we wanted to work on overcoming[31].

---

[29] Cf. this passage from the Farrars, which points out that the personality is not preexistent: 'As the time for ... reincarnation approaches, the Individual starts to gather around itself the raw materials of the 'outer shells' required for a new Personality. They can only be the raw materials, because a fully developed Personality is the gradual creation of the circumstances of the new incarnation, and of one's reaction to it' (WW 121).

[30] HBWM , 97, 182; WW 120-121; LL 26-33; MAA 71; ENF 35; YHL 10; PR 163; DL 17, 259; IAP 5-7, 337; DWYC 142; RR 72; 167ff; HU 215; VAA 82-85; SoS 122. Cf. however SD 206, where Starhawk *rejects* the idea that we have created our own life circumstances; this is characteristic for Starhawk's social activism, but exceptional within the New Age movement as a whole.

[31] YHL 10.

The idea is that, in the period between death and a next incarnation, our Higher Self (perhaps assisted by other spiritual beings) evaluates what has been accomplished during the life that has just ended, and what kinds of experiences will be most needed in order to further the process of "education". Michael Talbot reports about the experiences of people who were hypnotically regressed to what they believed to be the interim between lives. They described this as

> a dazzling, light-filled realm in which there was "no such thing as time or space as we know it". According to [these hypnotized subjects], part of the purpose of this realm was to allow them *to plan their next life, to literally sketch out the important events and circumstances that would befall them in the future.* ...they entered an unusual state of consciousness in which they were acutely self-aware and had a heightened moral and ethical sense. In addition, they were no longer possessed of the ability to rationalize away any of their faults and misdeeds, and saw themselves with total honesty. ... Thus, when subjects planned their next life, they did so with a sense of moral obligation. They would choose to be reborn with people whom they had wronged in a previous life so they would have the opportunity to make amends for their actions. They planned pleasant encounters with "soul mates", individuals with whom they had built a loving and mutually beneficial relationship over many lifetimes; and they scheduled "accidental" events to fulfill still other lessons and purposes[32].

When planning its next incarnation, the Higher Self is no longer hindered by the ego-interests of the limited personality; this is necessary because, if left to its own devices, the latter would merely attempt to avoid all pain and suffering as much as possible. Our Higher Self, in contrast, knows that pain and suffering are often necessary parts of learning; accordingly, it devises a personal "learning program" which—like any "course" taken at school—does not have rest, harmony and happiness as its top priority, but is set up in order to provide the personality with the maximum opportunities for progress. The "teaching program" is highly personalized in the sense that the experiences which will be undergone by the incarnated personality are *exactly* the ones that this particular entity needs most in order to adress its "unsolved patterns". It is for this reason that we may find New Age believers using sentences like Shakti Gawain's affirmation: 'I am always in the right place at the right time, succesfully engaged in the right activity'[33]. What is meant is that nothing ever happens to anybody without a reason. "Meaningless suffering" or "injustice" are nonexistent: whatever happens to us can be welcomed as a learning task offered to us, for the very best of reasons, by our own Higher Self. However, it is added that everything that happens in our life is fully meaningful and right only *if* we react to the "lessons" in a positive way and absorb what they have to teach us. We are perfectly capable of missing the opportunities offered to us, or of reacting to them in a negative and non-constructive way. This hap-

---

[32] HU 215-216.
[33] CV 23.

pens especially when we complain about "injustices" done to us: by doing that, we are projecting guilt onto others and avoid taking responsibility for our own life. If this is the consistent pattern in our life, then after death we may find that we have led a meaningless life because we have let too many opportunities pass us by unnoticed. We have not "passed the exam", so to speak, and will have to try again in a next life.

It is easy to see why it makes sense, from this perspective, that during incarnation one should lose the exalted perspective of the Higher Self and forget one's former lives. Having access to the superior level of consciousness of the Higher Self would obviously rob our earthly life of most of its "pedagogical" value: from the very beginning we would know exactly why we are here, and what we are supposed to do in any given situation. There would no longer be any challenge. New Age evolutionism, in contrast, implies that we can only make spiritual progress along the hard road of experiential self-confrontation. Having free access to our former lives would, similarly, make it too easy for us to see where and why the lessons we failed to learn before are now being repeated in our present life. Again, we see that the inner logic of New Age reincarnationism is crucially based on its underlying "pedagogical" evolutionism.

At first sight, all this may seem to contradict the claims of New Age literature that we can learn to remember our former lives (see below) and contact our Higher Self (chapter eight, section 2B). It is clear from the sources, however, that conscious contact with the Higher Self is regarded as the ripe fruit of an already rather advanced development. Only those who have already come to the point where they consciously and purposely devote themselves to the spiritual path may eventually develop the ability to communicate with their Higher Self. But, even in such contacts, the distinction between personality and Higher Self remains very much intact. The establishment of such contact is a sign, in other words, that one is well on one's way in the right direction; but it does not imply that one has reached the goal. If that were the case, the distinction between personality and Higher Self would have ceased to be functional; in practice, this would mean that one no longer needed to be incarnated on earth. The function of past life memories will be dealt with later. Briefly: there is a common understanding in New Age literature that the unconscious will *select* only those past life memories which are useful to remember at any given moment. One is "given access" to episodes from former incarnations only insofar as recovery of them may assist the current process of growth. It is assumed that memories that would not serve any constructive educational purpose will remain blocked from conscious recovery.

A further important aspect of New Age reincarnationism is the common assertion that reincarnation does not involve time. I refer the reader once more to the paragraph about the "transcendence of space-time" in chapter 6 (section 4), and to the end of the paragraph about the Higher Self, in chapter eight (section 2B). Most that has to be said on the subject was already said there. From the perspective of the limited personality, which functions within the dimensions of space and time, reincarnation appears like a linear process; but from the perspective of the Higher Self, which exists in "the spacious present", such a linear view is 'a gross simplification'[34]. It is more correct to say that each separate life is the result of a limited *focus* of the Higher Self[35], in which it "temporarily" blocks out all realities which are not compatible with this focus. As Shirley MacLaine puts it:

> our experience of linear time is really an experience of focus that enables us to concentrate on that which interests and intrigues us for the limited moment. ... From this perspective, linear reincarnation ... is not a truth, but rather an experience of focus toward which we choose to direct our conscious attention. So, the present lifetime we are leading is simply a desired focus of our creation, which exists simultaneously with other created adventures that are occurring, but on which we are focusing "now"[36].

Essentially, MacLaine says that our personal lives are directly created by a "narrowing of consciousness" on the part of the Higher Self. This is not dissimilar, in principle, from the process by which a person in a crowded room may concentrate on one particular task to the point of becoming oblivious to the noise and confusion all around. The main limitation of that analogy is that the Higher Self has the ability to "focus" on *many* different realities at the same time (or rather, out of time). It is for this reason that Seth speaks of the Higher Self or soul in terms of a "multi-dimensional personality": a "group soul" which continuously splits off into multiple "fragment personalities".

This concept adds the finishing touch to a series of qualifications which had to be made about "reincarnation" in the New Age movement. We saw that, in contrast to common opinion, "reincarnation" in its strict sense is not the common denominator of New Age beliefs about survival; and that those beliefs, furthermore, do not actually imply that "we" have lived before. We may now add that, as Griscom puts it, even 'the term "past lives" is a misnomer'[37]. And this surprising statement is fully supported by the father of this whole line of

---

[34] SS 170.

[35] IAP 185: '...perhaps we weren't living linear incarnations one after the other; perhaps we were only *focusing* on one at a time'.

[36] GW 203. Note the significance of the assertion that we pick life experiences because they "interest" and "intrigue" us, and that our lives are essentially "adventures": this is another confirmation of my conclusions about the "this-worldly" character of New Age reincarnation and its distance from oriental otherworldliness.

[37] ENF 73. Griscom continues: 'We only use that term because it's a hook, a string people can pull. They can see it in a linear way. It's an experience of multidimensionality in a linear format'.

speculation, Seth. This foundational source of New Age religion states bluntly that reincarnation is a myth:

> The reincarnational structure is a psychological one. It cannot be understood in any other terms. ... The reality, the validity, the immediacy of those lives *do* exist simultaneously with your present life. The distance between one life and another exists psychologically, and not in terms of years or centuries. ... Reincarnation, as it is usually explained, in terms of one life before another, *is* a myth; but a myth enabling many to partially understand facts that they would otherwise dismiss—insisting as they do on the continuity of time[38].

Apparently, the meaning of "reincarnation" in the New Age context is often very different from what it is commonly assumed to be. Admittedly, these comparatively sophisticated views are not found in *all* New Age literature; especially in the sources with a more traditional theosophical background, such as Cayce or Ramala, we seldom find much emphasis on holographic multidimensionality, the transcendence of space-time, and the like[39]. Furthermore, the views just analyzed figure most prominently in the work of those authors who have a special fondness for theoretical speculation. However, it should be emphasized that several of these (Seth, Griscom, MacLaine) count among the most popular and influential authors of the whole movement. It would, therefore, be a grave mistake to dismiss their views as marginal. This is all the more so because such views of reincarnation are not isolated, but are intimately interwoven with other elements (universal interconnectedness, the holographic paradigm, creating our own reality, the psychologizing of religion/sacralization of psychology, etc.) which were identified as essential to New Age thinking.

Past-Life Recovery

"Reincarnation", as discussed so far, refers to New Age beliefs about a future life after death. "Past" lives, in contrast, obviously have to do with an individual's incarnational past[40]. They may be accomodated theoretically within one general worldview, but they must be distinguished nevertheless.

We have just seen how problematic the idea that "I have been so-and-so" is from a theoretical New Age point of view. The New Age concern with "past lives", however, is usually a very practical affair which need not be affected by theoretical debates[41]. Almost without exception, recovery of past lives takes

---

[38] SS 447/449.

[39] An interesting case is David Spangler, who started with a very "orthodox" theosophical/anthroposophical perspective, but apparently found it necessary to revise his views in favour of a non-linear holographic vision (RW 153-155).

[40] Actually, however, nothing is completely obvious within a context which denies the reality of time. For, as noted above, it is not considered impossible to "remember" one's future lives!

[41] Including the criticism of past-life regression which is sometimes voiced even by New Age authors who do believe in reincarnation. Neopagans and traditional occultists in particular are apt to suspect escapism, as in the case of Z Budapest: '...I am not surprised that people like to

place for broadly therapeutic reasons (therapy, as explained in chapter two, having always a spiritual aspect: healing *and* spiritual growth). It is regarded as an effective means to interpret the reasons and backgrounds of present problems, so as to assist in the resolution and healing of deep-seated negative patterns. Some New Age therapists claim to be able to find access to the past lives of their patients by clairvoyant means. Their classical inspiration in this regard is Edgard Cayce, who used to give descriptions of other people's past lives while he was "asleep". More usual in the New Age context is active past life regression, where the subjects *themselves* are stimulated (by various techniques, such as hypnosis, massage or acupuncture) to have subjective experiences which they may or may not interpret emically as "past lives". They may indeed interpret them otherwise: it is important to realize that, according to most regression therapists, the question whether or not the subject believes in reincarnation is irrelevant to the therapeutic efficacy of those experiences. In other words, memories of "past lives" are not necessarily connected with belief in immortality. It is for this reason that past-life regression must be regarded as a borderline case in the present chapter. One may well regard it as just one among many other human potential techniques (and I remind the reader that in Stanislav Grof's therapy, for instance, "past lives" fall under the general rubric of "transpersonal experiences").

Typically, while reincarnation gives an answer to the perennial question "where (if anywhere) do we go from here?", recovery of past lives is undertaken to answer another classical question: "who am I?". That question is usually answered, typically again, in genetic terms: "how have I come to be the person I am now?"[42]. While reincarnation adresses the question of the *continuation* of Self, past-life recovery adresses the search for a profounder *knowledge* of that Self[43].

---

spend someplace that's better and more decorative than our Here and Now. Still I resist the seduction. ... The Here and Now is our challenge, the only part in our lives where we are called upon to act as Goddess. Everything else has been done. We have the past for a reason: IT IS GONE. The Here and Now will soon become the past and while we dwelled in our fantasies we missed making our mark on the moment' (HBWM 197). The Matthews relate an ironic remark which also reminds us of the problem of identity, discussed above: 'Yes, I remember some incarnations, but are they *mine*?' (WW2 158).

[42] Incidentally, we should note the peculiarly modern character of this approach. It is only relatively recently that western people began to answer questions of "being" in genetic terms (cf. Lukacs, *Historical Consciousness*, 5-6).

[43] In other words, regression therapy is an important aspect of the search for *gnosis* in its New Age manifestation. It is suggestive to compare this with a passage in the *Corpus Hermeticum* (XI, 21), which states that the person who says 'I do not know what I was, I do not know what I will be' cannot attain *gnosis*. This translation by Brian Copenhaver (*Hermetica*) is not explicit on the point of reincarnation, in contrast to G. Quispel's Dutch translation, the English equivalent of which is 'I do not know who I was in a previous life, I do not know who I will be in a next life' (Van den Broek & Quispel, *Corpus Hermeticum*, 136).

Nowhere do we find this better demonstrated than in the autobiographies of Shirley MacLaine. The central theme in all her books is her quest for her inner "self": again and again we are reminded that learning to know the self is the essence of human existence and spiritual development. The regression sessions undergone with Chris Griscom (related in the last part of *Dancing in the Light*; continued in *It's All in the Playing*) play a pivotal role in that quest. Following these sessions, the concepts of reincarnation and karma (which will be further discussed in the next chapter) become crucial to MacLaine in understanding her present situation and her relations to other people (her family in particular). During regression sessions, MacLaine learns to interpret the complicated ways in which "she" has been involved, during many former incarnations, with the same group of individuals she now knows as her parents, her daughter, or her various lovers.

It is useful to compare this learning process with more traditional types of, mostly verbally-oriented, therapies. Such therapies usually concentrate on interpreting and dissolving constricting emotional patterns which have been produced in the relationship of, say, a daughter with her father. Regression therapy differs from such approaches in two crucial ways. Firstly, it does not rely only on verbal interpretation, but adds the dimension of direct experiential confrontation: the subject literally re-experiences episodes from his or her past. Secondly, of course, it expands the scope of this interpretation process by also considering the past-life relationships between these individuals. The goal is to find out what, exactly, are the unresolved patterns that have determined their choice to incarnate as father and daughter during this present life. During regression sessions, the daughter may discover that, for instance, in a former life *she* was the father and her present father was her son; in another life they may have been brother and sister; and in yet another life they may have had an unhappy love affair[44]. By reviewing what happened between them in this series of lives, she may discover that certain issues return again and again, which still haunt her present relationship with her father. Thus, she may learn (to give a simple example) to finally understand a deep-seated "irrational" feeling of distrust she has felt towards her father since childhood, and

---

[44] It is usually assumed that incarnating entities may switch gender between lives. The goal of evolution is not to create perfect men or women, but fully developed entities in which the masculine and feminine element are in perfect harmony; it is not surprising, therefore, that MacLaine describes her own Higher Self as androgynous. Obviously, both male and female incarnations are needed in order to reach a sufficient level of harmonious integration of opposites. One may encounter New Age authors who have definite views about the rules of gender change: whether the shift from male to female is regular or irregular, and so on. Reincarnation may also be used, for example, to explain homosexuality: i.e., by claiming that gay men have just completed a rather long string of female lives. Such speculations, however, do not form a consistent pattern in our corpus. When they occur, they can be regarded as expressing the personal preoccupations of some authors. They are of little significance for the New Age movement as a whole.

which used to make her feel guilty because she could find no reason for it; she now discovers that, in a former life, her present father was her lover, but betrayed her with another woman and left her behind in misery. Or, to take another simple example, she may discover that during many former lives she has missed golden opportunities because she always ran away from difficulties; and she may find that she is still repeating that same pattern now. And so on, and so forth: it is easy to see that the possibilities for emotional complications are literally unlimited. The essential premise of past-life recovery is that unravelling these complications assists self-knowledge: New Age authors tell us that with the help of past-life regression we will learn to see our present situation as a small part of a larger pattern, in which our own personal way of dealing with circumstances is the central, meaningful core. By learning to see how we reacted to circumstances and handled things in the past, and what resulted from our actions, we are stimulated to "take responsibility" for our behaviour in our present life. The net effect is, again, to perceive all reality as self-created. We are told that, although other people may have done things which hurt us, it is useless to put the blame on them. For in doing so we comfortably refuse to face our own share in creating the very circumstances that enabled them to hurt us in the first place. And furthermore, it is hardly necessary for us to try and "pay them back". For we may trust that they are not in any more privileged position than we are: like us, they are learning their own, often painful lessons from the experience. In the next chapter I will return to the question of the ethics involved in this perspective.

It was already observed that, in the practice of regression as a therapeutic technique, it is usually assumed that the spontaneous process of remembering can be fully trusted. This is because it is not random, but "steered" by an infallible inner wisdom, which ultimately derives from the Higher Self (who, of course, acts in perfect accordance with universal laws of spiritual evolution). Thus, MacLaine tells us:

> [Chris Griscom] explained that the higher unlimited self always puts the earth-plane self in touch with those memories that are the most beneficial in clearing problems one is experiencing in the present incarnation. Since we have all experienced many, many incarnations (in many forms from the beginning of time) the unlimited higher self scans the blueprint of the soul's history and chooses the emotional experiences which relate to karmic trouble spots. Rarely are the recalled experiences pleasant because there would be no point in going over territory that has already been resolved. The purpose of living is to clear the soul's conflict. The purpose of getting in touch with past-life experience, then, is to isolate the areas of emotional discord so that the conflict in relation to today's incarnation can be understood[45].

---

[45] DL 299.

This summarizes the essence of past-life recovery in the New Age context. MacLaine's mention of "karmic trouble spots" already suggests the importance of the concept of karma. This theme, although traditionally linked with reincarnation, is best discussed in the general context of "New Age ethics".

CHAPTER TEN

GOOD AND EVIL

1. INTRODUCTION: THE PARADOX OF ETHICAL HOLISM

In a previous section, we saw that New Age holism may be defined *indirect-ly*, i.e., by its rejection of various forms of dualism and reductionism[1]. Before investigating New Age conceptions of good and evil as expressed in our textual corpus, we should first ask to what extent a holistic framework can at all be extended to the sphere of morality. On the face of it, one might suspect that a consequent holism is incompatible with the very idea of a system of morality: the latter, after all, should be able to distinguish "good" from "evil", while the former cannot accept such distinctions as absolute. With respect to New Age religion, we should therefore consider two questions. Does New Age religion indeed expound a "holistic ethics"; and if so, how does it manage to reconcile holism with a duality of good vs. evil?

Before addressing these points, it is necessary to mention an objection that could be made *a priori*. Some might argue that such questions cannot even arise, because *any* so-called holism is necessarily based on dualistic presuppositions and is to that extent self-defeating. Holism, after all, cannot even be defined without reference to its opposite, i.e., dualism. Put differently: if "holism" is good and "dualism" is the root of evil, then obviously any so-called holism is implicitly dualistic. Whether this argument is convincing depends on what one wishes to demonstrate by it. It is correct, as we will see, as a theoretical prediction of how a "holistic ethics" will actually function within the New Age context. It is incorrect, however, as an *a priori* refutation of New Age claims. This is simply because, as we saw, New Age holism is not a theory or belief system but, rather, a guiding vision or ideal. Holistic theories or explicit belief systems are in principle vulnerable to criticisms which point out that they are not internally consistent. A religious vision or guiding ideal, however, does not crucially depend on logical consistency. The ideal vision of "wholeness" may well remain intact even if it is pointed out that such a vision cannot do without its opposite.

The first question mentioned above may simply be answered in the affirmative. That New Age religion does indeed expand its general holistic framework so as to defend a "holistic ethics" can hardly be doubted; with the pro-

---

[1] Chapter six, beginning of section 2.

viso, however, that this statement is taken as referring to the level of emic convictions. Etically, one may well question whether this conviction is supported by the evidence. For, with reference to the second question formulated above, we find that, in spite of this holistic ethics, many sources do actually make clear demarcations between "good" and "evil". On the other hand, we also find that several authors have recognized the problem, and have tried to solve it in various ways. It is in these cases that we are presented with attempts at developing holistic *theories* pertaining to the moral domain, the inner consistency of which is therefore important to investigate. In the next three sections I will discuss the general ethical framework on the basis of which the New Age movement answers questions of good and evil, and investigate what is considered as negative and as positive (or as conducive to negativity or positivity) from that framework. First of all, we should take a look at how and why New Age religion rejects traditional dualistic concepts of "good" versus "evil".

2. THE STRUCTURE OF COSMIC JUSTICE

Non-Dual Ethics and the Problem of Relativism
It is a common New Age assertion that the duality of "good versus evil" is ultimately illusory. "Evil", on this premise, does not really exist. The standard view is based on metaphysical presuppositions which should be familiar by now. I will first give an etic reconstruction of the general framework implicit in the material, and then illustrate this by emic statements from the sources.

On the foundational level of spiritual reality—the "spacious present" (or "implicate order", etc.) from which all phenomenal realities emerge and on which they depend—no duality exists. Good and evil, in other words, are not metaphysical realities. They are meaningless concepts from the viewpoint of the soul. It is only on the level of phenomena—the ultimately self-created "illusions" in which we live our lives—that a *duality* of opposing forces may come into existence. Just as our self-created illusions have to be valued positively, as tools for learning, so this duality also is not necessarily a negative thing. It only becomes negative when human beings misinterpret duality in terms of *dualism*. Such an interpretation means that "evil" is regarded as a metaphysical reality, fundamentally hostile to the "good". "Evil" becomes something that *should not be there* but unfortunately happens to exist nevertheless (for reasons which are not completely clear, and demand an explanation). From this perspective, it can only be perceived as some kind of cosmic accident: an unfortunate obstacle to happiness and peace, which must be fought in the name of the "good". It is precisely this dualistic idea that so-called "evil" (incl. suffering) should not be there which, according to a New Age perspective, *prevents* human beings from reacting to it in a constructive way. If, in contrast, everything that happens in our world is perceived as part of *one* ultimately benevolent cosmic design, the apparently "negative" may be approached as holding potential lessons which may assist human learning. From this perspective, it is taken as axiomatic that "whatever is, is right"; instead of fighting "evil", the task for human beings is to try to understand even evil and suffering as exemplifying that rightness.

In short: we have to distinguish between *ultimate wholeness*, *duality*, and *dualism*. From the rather straightforward logic just outlined, many New Age statements which may initially sound puzzling fall into place. The frequently-repeated statement that good and evil do not exist[2] has basically two aspects. It essentially refers to the "true" spiritual dimension of reality which is beyond duality; and it is repeated with such urgency in order to refute "judgmental" attitudes, which declare that this-or-that is "wrong" and should be fought against. Below, I will return to that last aspect in more detail. The distinction which, according to my analysis, can be defined etically as one between dualism and duality is repeatedly confirmed by emic statements. The following one by Shirley MacLaine is representative:

> ...we saw more clearly that all of life, technological or emotional, was a question of working with positive and negative energies and that *negative* didn't mean wrong. It simply meant the opposite polarity—the other end of the balance—of *positive*. Negative energy was as necessary as positive. It was the interacted combustion that produced and created life. The male energy (yang) was positive; the female energy (yin) negative. Science—and life—told us that. Life could not exist without both. Understanding the basic tenets of that principle was helpful then in extending our understanding that "evil" exists only in relation to the point of view: If a child steals to live, if a man kills to protect his family, if a woman aborts a fetus rather than give birth to an unwanted child, if a terrorist murders because he has been raised all his life to believe that killing is his right and proper duty—*who* is evil? And if a person kills "simply" out of hatred or greed, *he* perceives his motives as *his need*—others make the judgment that his act is "evil"[3].

The question to ask is whether this perspective implies ethical relativism. This problem is best divided into two different aspects. Firstly, one may wonder whether there are *any* kinds of action at all which these New Age theories identify as *un*desirable (I will avoid the word "wrong" here). The answer, as we will see, is that they do identify such kinds of action. Secondly, we need to make clear whether such undesirable action is ever rejected on *moral* grounds. We will see that the tendency in New Age religion to react to the "negative" with moral indignation is definitely weak; there are some exceptions, however,

---

[2] AC 419; ENF 105; PR 232-233; DL 246-247, 255-256, 299-300, 347, 350; IAP 144-145; RR 206; VR 23-34; R 195; SS 94-95; LJ 29; PPA 69, 74.

[3] IAP 144-145. Cf. about evil as "misdirected energy": PR 232-233; PST 211; SS 341.

which suggest that the ethical logic underlying that attitude is not always followed as strictly as one might perhaps expect.

With respect to the first question just mentioned: New Age sources *do* identify some kinds of action as undesirable. Characteristically, the most common distinction between what is and what is not desirable in human action is based upon whether or not such action assists the process of *evolution*. As the Farrars put it:

> ...self-development and the full realization of one's unique yet many-aspected potential are a moral duty. That which helps evolution forward is good; that which thwarts it is evil; and each of us is a factor in the cosmic evolutionary process. So one owes it not merely to oneself but to the rest of mankind and the world to look inside oneself and to discover and release that potential[4].

Because spiritual "evolution" in the New Age context is frequently associated with scientific theories of evolution, "evil" is sometimes presented in a way which makes it look like a purely physical phenomenon. David Spangler, for instance, defines evil as 'an unbalanced formative force that seeks to constrain the appearance of the higher dimensions or geometries'[5]. A particularly clear example of an "ethics of evolution", on Prigoginian foundations, is Erich Jantsch:

> Quite generally, we can define ethical behaviour as behaviour which enhances evolution. But this implies that ethics is not given a priori, but emerges with evolution and follows a development which, in principle, is wide open. ... As an integral aspect of evolution, ethics is not subject to revelation, as is the ethics of religions with a personal god. Rather, it may be experienced directly by way of the dynamics of self-organization and creative process. ... [an evolutionary ethics] would not only transcend the individual but all of mankind, and explicitly include the main principles of evolution, such as openness, non-equilibrium, the positive role of fluctuations, engagement and non-attachment[6]

Jantsch continues by defending an ethics based upon "responsibility" rather than upon human "rights". Not surprisingly, his cosmic ethics, which transcends both the individual and humanity as a whole, eventually leads to an unmistakably "Hegelian" conclusion:

> Perhaps, evolution will not be too deeply disturbed by a turbulent development possible in the near future, with the loss (or, to be precise, the premature loss) of many lives. An organism which has reproduced itself, may be spared by evolution. Perhaps the major catastrophes on the planet earth mean not much more to evolution than the weeding out of a garden which permits more beautiful flowers to grow. If, as Bertrand de Jouvenel ... holds, we are gardeners of the planet earth, we ought to understand this ambition of evolution[7].

---

[4] WW 136.
[5] RW 132.
[6] SOU 263-265.
[7] SOU 273.

Of particular significance in this quotation is its intentional shift in emphasis from the ethics of human life to the ethics of cosmic life. In this regard, it appears to be typical for New Age ethics generally. Human actions are regarded as undesirable to the extent that they run counter to the cosmic evolutionary process, or to one's own personal evolution which is part of that larger process; the extent to which they produce suffering, or are motivated by evil intentions, is *not* a primary criterion.

This conclusion goes a long way towards answering the second question, i.e., whether undesirable actions are ever defined on *moral* grounds. In order to understand New Age religion, it is of crucial importance to realize that *suffering is not valued negatively*. In order to demonstrate the existence of "evil" in the world, merely to point to the fact of suffering is therefore completely unconvincing to most New Age believers. Suffering is not felt to be a pressing problem requiring an explanation, but is accepted as a necessary aspect of life and evolution. Although it is quite possible to construct a rational New Age theodicy on the basis of reincarnation, cosmic evolution and karma, the truth is that the very questions in answer to which theodicies have traditionally been constructed do not even arise in the New Age context. In short: suffering is not regarded as a moral problem at all; if anything, it is a psychological problem (as we will see below). The mere fact of suffering does not produce doubts about cosmic justice (or at least, according to the sources, it *ought* not to produce such doubts). Paradoxically, as we will see in the discussion of karma, it is rather the other way around: New Age religion positively *needs* the fact of suffering in order to explain the nature of cosmic justice![8]

If this is the case, however, and if suffering is accepted as necessary to learning and growth, what about evil *intentions*? Arguably, the fundamental problem of morality lies not in the fact of suffering as such, but in the active intention to produce suffering in others. In this respect, it is crucial to understand that New Age ethics are *not formulated with reference to the will*. Undoubtedly, the striking absence in New Age religion of prescriptive moral injunctions ("thou shalt (not)...") is due partly to impatience with what it regards as religious authoritarianism; but it is also partly due to the influence of modern psychological theories. Freudian and neo-freudian psychologies have produced doubts about the autonomy of the conscious will by demonstrating that human behaviour and decision-making is profoundly influenced by unconscious motivations. This in itself may already have grave implications for a will-oriented morality. Those implications are even greater, however, once these traditional

---

[8] Cf. SS 341: 'Illness and suffering are the results of the misdirection of creative energy ... Suffering is not good for the soul, unless it teaches you how to stop suffering. That is its purpose'.

psychological frameworks are enlarged to include transpersonal dimensions. This is what has happened in New Age religion. If the conscious ego is defined primarily by its severely restricted understanding, it is obvious that its moral capacity must be equally restricted. Only the Higher Self is theoretically capable of making free moral choices, and may therefore be held fully responsible for them. About the extent to which it actually does make such choices, the sources leave us in some doubt: whether it naturally acts in accordance with "universal laws", or freely chooses to do so because it is aware of their wisdom, remains ambiguous. However that may be: it is clear that the will of the limited ego personality cannot possibly be condemned to bear the burden of full moral responsibility for its actions. It is for this reason that we mostly find a striking absence in New Age sources of moral indignation even in the face of overtly evil behaviour. Instead, we find an essentially "pedagogical" reaction: evil behaviour is regarded as the regrettable outcome of spiritual *ignorance* on the part of limited egos. If people behave aggressively towards others, it is only because their consciousness is so limited that they do not realize how their actions hinder their own evolution. It is only to be expected that people who are ignorant of their inner divinity—out of touch with their own Higher Self—should engage in negative behaviour. They should not be condemned for the products of their ignorance; for they literally "do not know what they are doing". It is in this context that we should interpret, for example, Kevin Ryerson's assertion, in his discussions with Shirley MacLaine and her lover, that 'there is no such thing as evil':

> "I think", said Kevin, "that what you are calling evil is really only the lack of consciousness of God. The question is lack of spiritual knowledge, not whether or not there is evil". ...
> "But where is the place of evil in this scheme then?"
> "It doesn't exist. That's the point. Everything in life is the result of either illumination or ignorance. Those are the two polarities. Not good and evil"[9].

We may conclude that New Age religion replaces a will-oriented ethics by an ethics which is oriented towards spiritual *gnosis*. According to this framework, the supreme moral task is not to do what is good and avoid evil but, rather, to develop one's inner divine potential. The assumption is that ethical behaviour, as normally understood, will naturally result from such inner development.

Although this conclusion summarizes the main thrust of New Age thinking, some nuance should be added. Evidently, a certain latent ambiguity may be perceived in the attitude of some New Age authors with regard to moral relativism. It is true that New Age ethics cannot accommodate the idea of radical—not to mention unforgivable—evil. That evil is a relative (and ultimately meaningless) concept might be taken to suggest that any kind of behaviour is

---

[9] DL 246-247. Cf. also DL 255-256, 347; IAP 144-145.

as good as any other. Such a conclusion, however, is usually rejected. Ramtha
is a particularly instructive example, because he preaches an extreme version
of the ethics just outlined *and* refuses to draw the conclusion that "anything
goes". The very reason why he bothers to speak through his channel J Z Knight
is to teach humanity that its present patterns of behaviour are destructive, and
that 'there is a better way'. But he immediately goes on to emphasize that this
better way is ultimately dependent upon the realization that evil does not exist.

> I have returned here simply to tell you that there is a better way. And also to tell
> you that you are already God. And that you've never failed. And you've never
> done anything wrong. And you're not miserable, wretched creatures. And you're
> not sinners. And there is no wonderful folly called a devil. When you realize these
> things, then you can get down to the business of being *happy*—which is what God
> is[10].

Apparently, everything is perfect; but some things are more perfect than others. The most probable solution to this paradox is that what Ramtha most deeply
objects to is attitudes of moral judgment, because *these* are at the root of suffering and prevent human beings from enjoying the "isness" of being. The conclusion must be that Ramtha rejects some kinds of action as undesirable
(although not "wrong") not on moral, but on essentially *pragmatic* grounds
(because they ultimately backfire on the acting subject). This attitude is qualitatively different from the one exemplified by another channeled entity, Seth.
During a group discussion under his supervision, Seth once intervened in
uncharacteristically authoritarian manner, in order to refute the idea that the
ultimate relativity of good versus evil implies moral relativism in daily practice:

> ...Sue said with some heat: "Well, I'am against violence, too. But sometimes it's
> justified -"
> She hardly got the words out of her mouth before Seth interrupted her. Everyone
> jumped. In the heat of the discussion, Seth and ESP in general had been forgot-
> ten. Now Seth's voice really boomed out. "There is never any justification for
> violence. There is no justification for hatred. There is no justification for murder.
> Those who indulge in violence for whatever reason are themselves changed, and
> the purity of their purpose adulterated, ...
> It is wrong to curse a flower and wrong to curse a man. It is wrong not to hold
> any man in honor, and it is wrong to ridicule any man. You must honor your-
> selves and see within yourselves the spirit of eternal validity. If you do not do
> this, then you destroy what you touch. And you must honor each other individ-
> ual also, because in him is the spark of eternal validity. ... And as long as one
> person commits acts of violence for the sake of peace, you will have war"[11].

---

[10] R 148.
[11] SM 273-274. Cf. SM 305: 'I am not condoning those violences that do occur. The fact is
that they can never be condoned, and yet they must be understood for what they are: man, learning through his own errors'.

Admittedly, even Seth's explanations may be interpreted as pragmatic: people who indulge in violence actually harm themselves the most, so it would be better for them not to do it. However, there is an unmistakable quality of moral indignation in his words, suggesting that violence is essentially *degrading* to the deeper self, and thus to "All That Is". To say that evil "offends" God would certainly be an overstatement; but that it is morally offensive to Seth seems fairly clear.

Evolutionist Karma
In chapter nine (section 3) I stated that not reincarnation proper but belief in spiritual evolution is the common denominator of New Age beliefs about survival. I argued that New Age reincarnationism is qualitatively different from views of reincarnation as found in the official teachings of Hinduism and Buddhism. The dominance of the evolutionist framework has a similar effect upon New Age interpretations of karma. The "law of karma" is commonly interpreted by New Age authors as the moral equivalent of the "universal law" of cosmic evolution. In order to understand how karma functions in New Age religion, I call attention once more to that larger context. A particularly eloquent description, given by Stanislav Grof, may be found in Fritjof Capra's autobiographical *Uncommon Wisdom*. Grof outlines a comprehensive metaphysical system, which he calls a 'psychedelic cosmology and ontology' (and which is labeled 'neo-gnostic' by R.D. Laing on the next page):

> It is based on the concept of a Universal Mind, or Cosmic Consciousness, which is the creative force behind the cosmic design. All the phenomena we experience are understood as experiments in consciousness performed by the Universal Mind in an infinitely ingenious creative play. The problems and baffling paradoxes associated with human existence are seen as intricately contrived deceptions invented by the Universal Mind and built into the cosmic game; and the ultimate meaning of human existence is to experience fully all the states of mind associated with this fascinating adventure in consciousness; to be an intelligent actor and playmate in the cosmic game. In this framework, consciousness is not something that can be derived from or explained in terms of something else. It is a primal fact of existence out of which everything else arises. This, very briefly, would be my credo. It is a framework into which I can really integrate all my observations and experiences[12].

One should note, in the context of what was said above, the significance of Grof's terminology. Speaking of what is traditionally described as "evil and suffering", he prefers to call them 'intricately contrived deceptions'. What is clearly meant is that evil and suffering are meaningful illusions, which are there in order to be experienced by human beings as part of the 'cosmic game'.

---

[12] UW 150.

The characteristic absence, noted above, of moral indignation in the face even
of abject evil and suffering is illustrated with particular clarity here. For, in
this case we are not dealing with a rational explanation in terms of "paedagogical" necessities or karmic dynamics (see below), but simply with a remarkably sunny, cosmic optimism. To be explicit, mentioning for instance the holocaust of World War II as an example of an "intricately contrived deception"
would certainly require a more than usual amount of nerve; more likely, however, when Grof discusses the 'problems and baffling paradoxes associated with
human existence', such pictures of horror do not enter his mind in the first
place.

The basic optimistic perspective on reality as a cosmic "adventure in consciousness" can be found throughout the New Age corpus. Thus, Shakti Gawain
says that 'we're here to master the process of creation'[13]. Louise L. Hay adds
that 'we're here to recognize our own magnificence and divinity'[14]. Both have
read Seth's *The Nature of Personal Reality*[15] which tells its readers that 'you
are here to use, enjoy, and express yourself through the body. You are here to
aid in the great expansion of consciousness'[16]. Roman's guides tell her 'you
are meant to live a joyful life. You are here to create your dreams'[17]. According to Jean Houston, 'The process of realization ... [aims at] raising the frequency and capacity of thought, evolving the self, and, finally, growing God-
in-us'[18]; whilst the Ramala messages speak of humanity as 'an experiment in
creation' and describe earth as 'a school for gods'[19]. Ramtha tells his audience: 'You are playing with creative thought ... for the purpose of gaining wisdom, understanding, and identifying the great mystery of yourself'[20].

This optimistic evolutionism may well be combined with a serious concern for
the way humanity presently misuses his creative abilities, as for instance in the
books of George Trevelyan[21]. But although this author concedes that 'man ...
has tragically abused the trust reposed in him'[22], he still believes that from the
cosmic perspective 'there are really no accidents' and accepts as axiomatic that
'we are where we are meant to be'[23]. Trevelyan's vision combines optimistic

---

[13] LL 35.
[14] YHL 37.
[15] See Gawain in LL xiv-xv: 'I read the Seth book, *The Nature of Personal Reality* by Jane
Roberts and was powerfully affected by the idea that we all create our own reality. Soon I began
to lead workshops and do private counseling and eventually I wrote *Creative Visualization*'. The
same Seth book is mentioned in Hay's YHL (209), which contains characteristic Seth-terminol-
ogy such as 'the point of power' (YHL 5).
[16] NPR 28.
[17] SG 46.
[18] PH 200.
[19] WR 193. Cf. VAA 34: 'experiment of God'.
[20] R 94.
[21] See for instance VAA 34-35, 82-85.
[22] VAA 35.
[23] VAA 82-83.

evolutionism with a sense of mission and unconditional trust in higher guidance:

> If we are striving for understanding of the spirit, we must assume we are now where 'they' want us. We are all volunteers in an army which takes no conscripts. If the 'High Command' wishes to post us somewhere else, our Higher Self—a part of that Command—will have no difficulty staging events and circumstances which transport us out of our present condition and into the one desired[24].

Even though he acknowledges that things have gone "wrong" on our planet, Trevelyan still believes that, from a higher perspective, "whatever is, is right".

This firm belief that we are living in the best of all possible worlds[25] is a further element (besides optimistic evolutionism, to which it is obviously closely related) which is crucially important in order to understand the New Age interpretation of karma. It should be analytically distinguished from the theoretical conviction, discussed above, that evil does not exist in an "ultimate" metaphysical sense. What we are dealing with here is the more practical belief that whatever happens could not possibly be better, because it perfectly serves the cosmic plan. Again, numerous examples could easily be given. Sanaya Roman emphasizes again and again that 'the universe is perfect and ... everything you do and everything that happens to you is perfect'[26]. According to Gary Zukav, 'an authentically empowered personality sees the perfection of each situation and each experience'[27]. He even goes so far as to say that 'you contribute appropriately and perfectly to your evolution and to the evolution of others no matter what you choose'[28]. One may well wonder why, if everything is already perfect, human beings should bother to change their spiritual perspective at all; but Zukav only emphasizes the other side of the coin: why not *consciously* devote ourselves to spiritual growth if we already do it unconsciously anyway? The Ramala masters, similarly, do not shrink from the impli-

---

[24] VAA 83-84. Cf. Gawain's move from a "magical" interpretation of "creating our own reality" towards an attitude of 'surrendering to the universe' and 'allowing the higher power to be in charge' (LL xvi-xvii).

[25] The references to eighteenth-century Enlightenment optimism are intentional, and will be returned to in Part Three of this study. At this point, it might be necessary to warn the reader against a common mistake. Lovejoy, discussing the doctrine of "the best of all possible worlds", explains that, although it is often assumed that 'the adherents of this doctrine must have been exuberantly cheerful persons, fatuously blind to the realities of human experience and human nature ... Yet there was in fact nothing in the optimist's creed which logically required him either to blink or to belittle the facts which we ordinarily call evil. So far from asserting the unreality of evils, the philosophical optimist in the eighteenth century was chiefly occupied in demonstrating their necessity. To assert that this is the best of possible worlds implies nothing as to the absolute goodness of this world; it implies only that any other world which is metaphysically capable of existence would be worse' (*Great Chain*, 208).

[26] SG 101.

[27] SoS 229.

[28] SoS 247. For other, similar statements about the perfection of reality, see for instance SoS 229, 240, 245-247.

cation that 'the most hideous atrocity, the most degrading disease, the most evil person to walk the face of this earth, all happen for a reason'[29].

The principal explanation adduced for these and similar views is the law of karma. Before moving on to that subject, we should mention that the general perspective just discussed has not remained unchallenged even in New Age circles. Starhawk and Matthew Fox have already been mentioned as dissident thinkers in this respect. Another example is David Spangler, who stresses that

> for the new age to prosper, it needs people willing to accept the reality of their creaturehood, the value of certain kinds of limits, the blessing of definition; it requires people who with loving and vigorous minds and hearts can exercise a rigorous and loving discrimination, who can call a fault a fault and a mistake a mistake, not just a "learning experience". It needs people who can shake off the mind-numbing effects of psychobabble and jargon ... and see and speak clearly, who can look evil in the eye and call it by its name[30].

Considering the prominence of Starhawk, Fox and Spangler, this perspective cannot simply be ignored as marginal. Nevertheless, it can hardly be called characteristic for the main thrust of New Age ethics.

New Age interpretations of karma can only be understood in the wider context outlined above. The "universal interconnectedness" of the cosmos; the universal process of consciousness evolution which is at work in that cosmos; and the optimistic conviction that in this "evolving whole" there are no mistakes or accidents, only benevolence and perfection: these three elements together constitute the background to how karma is believed to function. As remarked above, the (weak) this-worldly perspective, the optimistic attitude towards what happens in the universe, and the evolutionist framework are all qualitatively different from the official doctrines of Oriental religions (which are otherworldly; pessimistic about the order of this world; and not based on a progressive evolutionism).

In line with the tendency to relativize or deny the existence of moral evil, New Age authors often repeat that karma has no connection with punishment[31]. It is not a retribution in response to a moral transgression. As Roberts/Seth put it: 'Karma does not involve punishment. Karma presents the opportunity for development. It enables the individual to enlarge understanding through experience, to fill in gaps in ignorance, to do what should be done. Free will is always involved'[32]. Karma is the universal law of cause and effect, operating in an interconnected universe which has an inbuilt tendency towards moral balance. One of the Ramala masters gives a typical description:

---

[29] VR 27-28.
[30] RS 158.
[31] For instance: ECRE 51; DL 300; VAA 53.
[32] SM 151.

> Karma is the eastern name for the Law which you in the West call Cause and
> Effect and which I call Equalisation. What you have sown, what you have done
> in thought, word and deed has an effect and that effect will in turn be felt by you.
> It is as simple as that. What you have done not only in this life but also in your
> many previous lives has had an effect on the pool of life, and when you step into
> that pool you will be affected by the ripples that you have created both now and
> in the past.
> The essence of the Law of Karma is that everything in Creation is held in perfect
> balance. There is no such thing as inequality. ... Do not see karma only as a plus
> or minus column in a divine accountant's book in which is recorded what you
> owe to someone because of the wrong that you have done them! It does not work
> in that way. It is rather a teaching process in which you learn from what you have
> done. It is you that has created those ripples on the pond of life and they will in
> turn affect you. The purpose of karma is not punishment. It is rather a process of
> balance and education[33].

Universal interconnectedness ensures that any action ultimately rebounds upon
the actor: no one can escape having to experience, sooner or later, the equivalent of whatever action (s)he has done to others. Accordingly, New Agers quite
generally feel that judging other people's behaviour is not only unnecessary,
but may even be counterproductive. The cosmic law of cause and effect can
be trusted to be completely just and perfect; while human judgments are, by
definition, limited and imperfect. Attempts to interfere with cosmic law are
likely to produce more problems (i.e. new negative karma) than they solve: no
limited human personality, after all, is in a position which permits a complete
and unprejudiced perspective on the complete karmic pattern of another person. Only that complete pattern, which goes back over many lifetimes, explains
why another person has to do what (s)he has to do and to suffer what (s)he has
to suffer. The law of karma does take that whole pattern into account.

One question which is seldom addressed—and even less answered—is how
the belief in an "automatic feedback system" of karmic law relates to the belief
that we have freely chosen (created) our own incarnations before birth. In other words: what is the place of individual human freedom within the web of
karmic dynamics and pre-incarnational choices? In fact, this would seem to be
a major theoretical issue in New Age ethics; but, regrettably, it is almost never addressed by the authors themselves[34]. Seth may claim that 'free will is

---

[33] WR 90-91. The same image of "ripples in a pool" is used by the Farrars: WW 121Cf. Cf.
also LL 26ff (the world as our mirror, working like an automatic "feedback system"); TI 136;
OL 95, 98, 100, 228; VAA 52-53; SoS 33-46.

[34] An exception is the Ramala material, which severely limits human freedom: 'What is carried out on the surface of this Earth is the will, the power and the influence of the Beings who
are responsible for the Earth and, more especially, of our God, our Solar Logos, Who stands
above us all. Man might like to think that he has free will, but he does not. If he did but understand it, most things in his life are planned. Within the boundaries of his life Man has only a narrow choice to make, for he incarnates into a planned family, into a planned country, into a planned
way of life. He vibrates under a certain Ray, he is born under the specific influences of certain

always involved', but neither he nor others explain where its influence is to be located. Indeed, Seth's explicit mention of free will merely seems to betray his awareness of a problem to which no solution is readily present. We already encountered essentially the same problem when it was noted, above, that only the Higher Self is presumably capable of making free choices although the extent to which it actually does so is unclear. The reason for all this seems to be that in New Age religion we find a latent conflict between two different tendencies, which may be referred to as individualism and universalism. New Age religion is highly individualistic in its assertion that there are no limits to the capacity of human beings to create their own reality; but it is also highly universalistic in its assertion that the whole universe, including human beings, is inescapably subjected to a benevolent cosmic law. A convincing case could probably be made for relating the first strand to the predominantly American, "holographic" way of thinking which stresses unlimited creative expansion; and the second strand to the originally European, theosophical current which tends to emphasize the return of all beings to their ultimate source. However, these different models have so strongly intermingled in the work of many authors that the descriptive value of this distinction (in contrast to its heuristic value) is limited. For the purposes of analysing the structures of New Age religion, we can simply conclude that both tendencies are present side by side, in contexts which seldom make the latent tension between them explicit.

I return now to the New Age belief in a perfect and just law of karmic balance with which one should better not interfere from a limited personal perspective: it should be clear that this system in principle relieves New Age adherents from the task of judging other people's behaviour as "evil" or wrong. It is not difficult to see that this conflicts with attempts to actively reform the world, fight against injustice and, in Spangler's words, 'look evil in the eye and call it by its name'. Equally problematic is the question why, if everybody gets exactly what (s)he needs to get, one should try and relieve other people's suffering. As is well known, the Hindu doctrine of karma has often been criticized for promoting precisely this; and some New Age spokesmen draw the same conclusion:

> Since we cannot know what is being healed through each interaction—what karmic debts are coming to conclusion—we cannot judge what we see. For example, when we see a person sleeping in the gutter in the winter, we do not know what is being completed for that soul. ... It is appropriate that we respond to his or her circum-

---

planets. He has chosen to meet certain people in his earthly incarnation from which he will learn certain lessons. He has chosen many of the incidents that are to happen in his life: all this before he even incarnates into matter!' (RR 72). This approach may be compared to Trevelyan's statements, quoted above, about human beings as "volunteers" in an army under the "High Command" of spiritual beings and the Higher Self. Notice that both sources are strongly theosophical.

stance with compassion, but it is not appropriate that we perceive it as unfair, because it is not[35].

Why is it "appropriate" to react with compassion? The logic of New Age karma actually permits only one answer: it is appropriate because positive actions create positive karma and thus enhance evolution. But *whose* personal evolution, then, profits most from the action: that of the beggar or that of the "compassionate" helper? As usual, Shirley MacLaine is particularly honest: it is only the helper, not the beggar, who "profits". In a passage which has been quoted above (chapter eight, section 3B), she says:

> If what I was proposing was true, would it also be true that I did nothing for others, everything for myself?
> And the answer is, essentially, yes. If I fed a starving child, and was honest about my motivation, I would have to say I did it for myself, because it made me feel better. .. I was beginning to see that we each did whatever we did purely for self[36].

This is, undoubtedly, the inescapable *logic* of karmic ethics within the New Age context. Below, we will see how it relates to such "altruistic" virtues as love or compassion.

Finally, a few words should be said about the *moral motivations* underlying the New Age belief in karma. Among critics, there is a strong tendency to regard the implications of both "pre-incarnational choices" and karmic law as immoral or inducive to immorality. The background to this seems to be the feeling that, by giving a logical explanation for suffering, one is in fact *condoning* that suffering. The catalogues of human misery evoked to illustrate karmic law are indeed shocking enough:

> Under the negative emotional heading, we find such symptoms as incompatible marriage, alcoholism, impotence, neuroses such as manic depression and paranoia, mental perversions, and even possession in its medieval sense. On the physical side, it manifests itself in such defects as deafness, blindness, speech impediments, and the killer diseases such as leukemia and multiple sclerosis[37].

The criticism just mentioned is certainly not without justification. All these forms of human misery are, indeed, assumed to be ultimately meaningful, as means for "learning and growth"; though often painful, they are right and just from a larger "pedagogical" perspective. And, in relation to evil and destructive behaviour, we saw that New Age thinking implies that no human being has a right to judge the behaviour of others from his/her own limited perspective. From the larger cosmic perspective, '*tout comprendre c'est tout pardonner*'. It is true that New Age religion does distinguish between "positive" and

---

[35] SoS 43.
[36] IAP 173.
[37] ECRE 51-52.

"negative" actions; but this distinction is really synonymous with "desirable or undesirable from the perspective of evolution". The perfection of the evolutionary process itself is such that, in the end, even the "negative" produces fully "positive" results. From so-called evil, the process of karmic "equalization" produces a greater good. This brings us back to the paradox identified at the beginning of this chapter. A strict ethical distinction between good and evil is impossible to combine with the postulate of a consistent holism. Once holism is accepted as axiomatic, the only alternative to a radically evil world is a radically good one. Therefore if critics charge New Agers with immorality, they are in fact attacking holistic theories.

New Agers are likely to respond that, for *moral* reasons, all the alternative perspectives on evil are even less acceptable. That evil and suffering happens for no reason at all suggests that the very order of the universe—not to mention God—is wholly indifferent to it. That the holocaust of World War II can be explained from karmic dynamics and pre-incarnational choices may be hard to accept; but to New Agers it is even harder to accept that, from a "higher perspective", it must be concluded that six million Jews died a completely meaningless death. To ascribe evil and suffering, alternatively, to some cosmic "force of evil" is clearly unaccaptable both to New Agers and to their secular critics; and it is highly problematic to traditional theists, because they once again evoke all the traditional problems related to a rational theodicy. Evolutionary karma, in contrast, restores to New Age believers the traditional confidence in a divine, or at least "cosmic", moral order. Shirley MacLaine's reasoning is typical, when she blames the Christian church for leaving the basic problem of suffering unanswered:

> if the Church *had* been teaching that our souls were involved in a continual physical embodiment in order to work out Karmic Justice, I would have been interested in it from the time I was little. *That* would have made sense to me. ... And it also would have explained all the suffering and horror in the world which all my life had rendered me helplessly incapable of understanding or altering[38].

Undoubtedly, it is this essentially *moral* reasoning which explains much of the attraction karma has for New Age thinkers. And, by implication, it is a major factor in explaining the attraction New Age religion in general has for modern westerners who are trying to make sense of evil and suffering.

3. THE NEGATIVE

Against the background sketched above, it will be useful to look at what our source materials identify as "negative" and as conducive to "negativity" in the

---

[38] OL 235.

world. A general distinction can be made between negative *states of mind*; negative psychological *attitudes* which exemplify such states of mind; and negative *behaviour* which results from such attitudes. This sequence is significant in itself. Parallel to the minimizing of the factor of *will*, New Age sources hardly discuss the factor of *behaviour* other than as an inevitable outcome of more basic causes. Not *what* we do but *why* we do it is the fundamental issue. This question is answered in essentially psychological terms. These, in turn, ultimately refer to a negative "state of mind", which must therefore be identified as the ground of evil according to New Age religion.

Limited Consciousness
I observed that New Age religion replaces a will-oriented ethics by an ethics oriented towards spiritual *gnosis*. The fundamental duality is not between good and evil, but between spiritual insight and ignorance. Spiritual ignorance is the defining characteristic of the limited personality, dominated mainly by the narrow interests of the ego. Spiritual insight, in contrast, corresponds to the superior level of consciousness represented by the Higher Self. Put like this, it is clear that moral development must be equivalent to spiritual development: i.e., to a process of consciousness evolution which aims at overcoming an exclusive orientation on "earth plane" reality. Thus, it is also clear why whatever assists such evolution (including, at least potentially, the experience of suffering) is "good", while whatever goes against it is "bad".

The condition of "ignorance" consists, then, of a state of mind in which one is exclusively focused on "earth plane" reality, with its dualism and fragmentation, and oblivious of "higher" dimensions. It is often said by New Age authors that the mind in this state is "programmed" or "conditioned" by society. Louise L. Hay, for instance, states that at birth we were all perfect; but 'then we began to listen to adults around us who had learned to be fearful, and we began to deny our own magnificence'[39]; whilst MacLaine's entity "John" says 'Most people are suffering from *altered* egos. Altered by society, by the Church, and by education. Their true egos know the truth'[40]. Deprived of that knowledge, human beings (particularly in our own times) live in a state of alienation, as described by F. David Peat: 'self-divided, confused, out of touch with the body, and robbed of any meaning of the universe'[41]. This state, however, is not necessary; it only exists because humans have come to believe in

---

[39] YHL 25.

[40] OL 207. For more examples, cf. HHC xv, *passim* (see his metaphor of the "biocomputer" which has been programmed, and can be re-programmed); RNA ch. 6 (even physical mortality is merely a programmed belief); PST for instance 142; R 170-171 (about the "lower frequencies" created by social consciousness).

[41] S 227.

a "dream" (or nightmare) of their own making: 'We are hypnotized by the projection, and the dream becomes real. That life is like a dream is part of the
magic. That it becomes our reality is, however, somewhat of a problem'[42]. The
goal, then, is to "awaken" from the dream and "reprogram" our ingrained
beliefs and culturally-conditioned assumptions about reality. This basic message, repeated again and again in the sources[43], is summarized with particular
force by Ramtha:

> Once, you could create a flower. But what do you create for yourselves now?
> Your greatest creations are unhappiness, worry, pity, misery, hatred, dissension,
> self-denial, age, disease, and death. You create for yourselves a life of limitation
> by accepting limiting beliefs, which then become steadfast rules within your beings
> and thus the reality of your lives. ... You, the great creative gods who were once
> the winds of freedom, have become herd-like entities who cloister in great cities
> and live in fear behind locked doors. ... You have thought yourselves into despair.
> You have thought yourselves into unworthiness. You have thought yourselves into
> failure. You have thought yourselves into disease. You have thought yourselves
> into death. All of those things you have created. ...
> You have disbelieved in the greatest gifts of life; and because of that, you have
> not allowed a more unlimited understanding to occur. Life upon life, existence
> upon existence, you became so immersed in the illusions of this plane that you
> forgot the wonderful fire that flows through you. In ten and one-half years you
> have come from being sovereign and all-powerful entities, to where you are utter-
> ly lost in matter; enslaved by your own creations of dogma, law, fashion and tra-
> dition; separated by country, creed, sex and race; immersed in jealousy, bitter-
> ness, guilt and fear. You so identified yourselves with your bodies that you
> entrapped yourselves in survival and forgot the unseen essence that you truly are—
> the God within you that allows you to create your dreams however you choose.
> ...
> This life is all a game; it is an illusion. All of it is! But you, the players, have
> come to believe that it is the only reality. ... This life your are living is a *dream*,
> a *great* dream, a facade, if you will. It is thought playing with matter, and it cre-
> ates deep realities that bind your emotions to this plane until you, the dreamer,
> wake up[44].

I will return to the mytho-historical references in the next chapter. For the
moment, it is sufficient to point out that this neo-gnostic picture of the *condition humaine* perfectly summarizes the basic New Age perspective on "spiritual ignorance" and its alternative.

Psychological "Negativities": Sin, Guilt, Fear
We saw that terms such as "spiritual ignorance" or "restricted consciousness"
refer to a general condition of the mind which, in turn, is based on ingrained

---

[42] ECMM 86-88.
[43] Some random examples are CiM Introduction; CV 27; HHC 203; OL 207-208, 348; DL
396; PST 211; SG 172.
[44] R 47-50.

limiting *beliefs and assumptions*. This connection between psychological attitudes or states of mind, on the one hand, and more basic underlying beliefs or assumptions, on the other, is of fundamental importance. It implies that in order for any negative condition to be changed, what is needed is a restructuring of implicit beliefs. This is, of course, another aspect of "creating our own reality": we are never at the mercy of circumstances because, in principle, things are as they are only to the extent that we believe that they cannot be different. Any limiting condition can be changed by refusing to believe in it. As Louise L. Hay puts it: 'The Only Thing We are Ever Dealing With is a Thought, and a Thought can Be Changed'[45]. This principle has already been observed at work, for instance in the practice of creative visualisations and affirmations. We now encounter it again in the realm of morality.

The single most negative and destructive mental attitude, mentioned again and again in our sources, is that of *blaming and judging* either other people or oneself. New Age authors point out that this attitude is based on a set of fundamental beliefs: belief in the reality of *sin and guilt*, on the one hand, and a belief that we are at the mercy of "circumstances", on the other. Both are merely limiting assumptions, not objective truths. Once we start "taking responsibility" for whatever happens to us, by accepting that our circumstances are self-created, we naturally have to stop putting the blame on others[46]. And, once we accept that everything that happens is meaningful and right—that there are "no accidents in the universe"—we must stop being judgmental about the "faults" of other people or ourselves[47]. "Sin" is merely a word we use to project guilt upon others while conveniently absolving ourselves from it; and, when we project it upon ourselves (believing that we are inherently sinful beings) we are degrading our inner divinity while conveniently absolving ourselves, again, from having to take responsibility for our own actions. "Guilt", as well, is 'a totally useless emotion. It never makes anyone feel better nor does it change a situation'[48]. To believe that we are guilty is negative thinking; it sug-

---

[45] YHL 11.

[46] Cf. for instance IAP 15 'Blaming whatever happens to us on someone or something else went out with high-button shoes—it's old-fashioned'; GW 48-49; PPA 119-120.

[47] See for instance R 195ff; RI ch. 5.

[48] YHL 143. Cf. VR: 'Shame and guilt are wasted emotions and do nothing but drag the soul down'; and LJ 34: 'Every time you think of a bad memory that makes you feel sorry for yourself, bad about how you acted ... or makes you hold a negative picture of yourself, Stop! See what good you created from that experience'. Notice that Seth, as more often when he discusses ethics, is more moderate; he distinguishes "natural guilt" (a useful feeling which should serve to prevent us from repeating a wrong act) from "artificial guilt" (i.e., the "useless" or "wasted" emotion presently under discussion). The Ramala messages contain even more "traditional" passages, for example when they preach the virtue of humility and reproach their readers with the habit of not acknowledging one's faults: 'Above all, you must begin to act with humility. You must begin to realise that in every relationship that you encounter there is a lesson for you. When problems occur, why is it never your fault! Why is it always the fault of the other person in the

gests that we are "not good enough", and therefore have no right to create a better reality. By thinking low of ourselves, we prevent ourselves from changing our condition[49]. As a result, we remain trapped in negative patterns.

In addition to the active attitudes of judging, blaming and projecting guilt, mention must be made of their passive counterpart, which is *fear*. Fear is consistently described as a destructive emotion, which is the precise opposite of *love*. This is frequently expressed by the formula "Love is letting go of fear", which seems to have become almost a New Age cliché[50]. Ultimately, according to New Age thinking, *all* negative mental attitudes (including those of blaming, judging and guilt-projection) can be reduced to fear. Thus, Shirley MacLaine discovered that 'Fear was the root and circle around which our lives revolved'[51]. Ultimately, she tells us, the thing we all fear and try to escape from is the confrontation with our own Self. Fear and distrust of self is the root of suffering; restoring a healthy relation with it is, therefore, the cure. In books of a practical bent, such as Louise L. Hay's *You can Heal your Life*, this means primarily that we have to discard negative self-images and learn to love ourselves. In more theoretical terms, all reality can be represented as polarized between the extreme "frequencies" of love versus fear. According to Zukav,

> The human emotional spectrum can be broken down into two basic elements: love and fear. Anger, resentment, and vengeance are expressions of fear, as are guilt, regret, embarassment, shame, and sorrow. These are lower-frequency currents of energy. They produce feelings of depletion, weakness, inability to cope and exhaustion. The highest-frequency current, the highest energy current, is love. It produces buoyancy, radiance, lightness and joy[52].

Zukav adds that 'Love is of the soul. Fear is of the personality'[53]. This corresponds to the "neo-gnostic" association of earth-plane reality with negativity, and of the Higher Self (or soul) with positivity.

This whole line of reasoning is an exact reversal of traditional Christian

---

relationship?' (VR 6). It is hard to imagine Shirley MacLaine, Louise L. Hay or Sanaya Roman making such statements.

[49] This is the reason why discussions between defenders and opponents of "creating our own reality" generally remain fruitless. Opponents interpret the idea that we have created our own illnesses as meaning that we ourselves are to "blame" for them. This belief, they argue, adds psychological cruelty to misery: it makes people feel guilty merely because they are sick. Psychologically, this criticism probably makes sense. However, it can hardly be expected to convince the defenders, who will argue that this very interpretation in terms of guilt is destructive. Accepting that we "create our own reality" *without* discarding the belief in guilt means that one has missed the whole point. About the rejection of guilt, see for instance ECMM ch. 6; CiM 77-79 and *passim*; UM 63-71 (64: 'I think guilt is a very destructive idea. There is responsibility, which is correct, but guilt is a very destructive notion. That programs you in a very bad way'); PST *passim*; EiG 119 (guilt as "negative vibration").
[50] ECMM 155-156; Cf. CiM Introduction and *passim*; YHL 12-15; RI 123.
[51] OL 347; cf. OL 359.
[52] SoS 120.
[53] SoS 212.

ethics[54]. Human beings are not seen as fundamentally flawed by "sin and guilt", which makes salvation possible only by outside grace; rather, the belief in the existence of such flaws *is* the flaw[55]. Similarly, fear is not justified, by reference to a God who punishes transgressions: rather, it is this very belief which *produces* the problem in the first place. It is not surprising, therefore, that the most influential Christian theologian in the New Age movement, Matthew Fox, identifies the root of our present problems in the persistent influence of "fall/redemption" thinking based on the doctrine of original sin:

> A devastating psychological corollary of the fall/redemption tradition is that religion with original sin as its starting point and religion built exclusively around sin and redemption does not teach trust. Such religion does not teach trust of existence or of body or of society or of creativity or of cosmos. It teaches both consciously and unconsciously, verbally and non-verbally, *fear*. Fear of damnation; fear of nature—beginning with one's own; fear of others; fear of the cosmos. In fact, it teaches distrust beginning with distrusting of one's own existence, one's own originality, and one's own glorious entrance into this world of glory and of pain. ... What if, however, religion was not meant to be built on psychologies of fear but on their opposite—on psychologies of trust and of ever-growing expansion of the human person?[56].

In short: we saw that, according to New Age religion, evil does not exist but that the belief in its existence produces negative results; we now see that, similarly, sin and guilt do not exist but that it is the belief in their existence which produces negativity, especially because it legitimates and induces fear. As Shirley MacLaine puts it: 'we are not victims of the world we see. We are victims of the way we see the world. In truth, there are no victims'[57]. It is only by our judgmental attitudes, towards others and towards ourselves, and by psychological projection of sin and guilt upon others and ourselves, that we keep perpetuating the "circle of fear". In a way, it is by our ingrained belief in "original sin" that we needlessly increase suffering in the world and create "negative" karma.

---

[54] But, in line with their aversion to religious polemics, New Age authors seldom attack christianity explicitly for promoting a guilt-inducing ethics. An exception is Z Budapest, who emphasizes the need for woman to 'unburden herself of the crippling guilt, the morbid fears and the restrictive feelings of shame inherent in Judeo-Christian and other patrifocal traditions' (HBWM 63). More characteristic is an occasional sarcastic remark such as made by Louise L. Hay: 'There are so many different religions to choose from. If you have one now that tells you you are a sinner and a lowly worm, get another one' (YHL 136).

[55] Even David Bohm (not the most obvious person to come to mind in this connection) observes, as we saw in note 49, that guilt is a destructive notion and that '...man's misunderstanding of good and evil ... that metaphysical notion was one of the principal reasons for the propagation of evil. It got in the way of people seeing the real source of the trouble' (UM 65).

[56] OB 82.

[57] DL 114-115.

4. The Positive

Parallel to the discussion in the previous section, we can make a general distinction between positive *states of mind*; positive *attitudes*; and positive *behaviour*. Again, the last aspect remains largely implicit. It is simply assumed that once the attitude is right, right behaviour will naturally ensue.

Holistic Consciousness
I argued that "holism" is best defined indirectly, i.e., with reference to what it *rejects* rather than what it affirms. It is not surprising to find something similar in the case of "holistic consciousness": the exalted state of mind which is, presumably, the goal of spiritual evolution. Descriptions are scattered, fragmentary and generally vague. Most New Age authors are far more explicit about what is negative and should be left behind than about what will happen once this has occurred. Presumably, the great goal is a state of mind in which one is fully conscious of one's interconnection with the whole of the universe. Describing this "cosmic consciousness", Matthew Fox tells us that

> the more and more deeply one sinks into our cosmic existence the more fully one realizes the truth that there does not exist an inside and an outside cosmos but rather one cosmos: we are in the cosmos and the cosmos is in us. ... All things are interrelated because all things are microcosms of a macrocosm. And it is all in motion, it is all en route, it is all moving, vibrant, dancing, and full of surprises[58].

Chris Griscom speaks of 'cognition of ourselves as part of a cosmic, direct whole'[59], and often repeats that 'When people go into soul experiences; they have no body. They are total light, they are everything, they are God; there is total oneness, there is no separation'[60]. According to Ken Keyes, our goal is to become one with the 'vast Ocean of Oneness', also described as the 'Ocean of Living Love'[61].
Presumably, to attain complete holistic consciousness would imply that the limited personality has been left behind altogether, either temporarily (in "altered states" of ecstasy or bliss) or more permanently (after death). However, apart from such supreme states, it is also suggested that we can in any case learn to "think holistically" in our daily life. It is suggested that developing, on a day-to-day basis, our personal awareness of being interconnected with the whole will have profound practical, even political, consequences. David Bohm, whose

---

[58] OB 69.
[59] TI 49.
[60] ENF 147. Cf. ENF 5, 19-20, 132.
[61] HHC 200-201.

philosophical work is largely motivated by concern about the present world situation[62], expresses this hope in characteristically abstract fashion:

> What I am proposing here is that man's general way of thinking of the totality, i.e., his general world view, is crucial for overall order of the human mind itself. If he thinks of the totality as constituted of independent fragments, then that is how his mind will tend to operate, but if he can include everything coherently and harmoniously in an overall whole that is undivided, unbroken, and without a border (for every border is a division or break) then his mind will tend to move in a similar way, and from this will flow an orderly action within the whole[63].

What Bohm means to say is that holistic patterns of thinking will produce holistic patterns of action. Similar hopes are expressed by Shirley MacLaine, for instance[64]. In particular, it is frequently suggested that only by developing an "ecological consciousness" a solution can be found to the environmental crisis[65]. Typically, however, such expectations are not concretized. The unquestioned assumption is that the present situation of the world is a direct reflection of the dominating kind of consciousness. Therefore the necessity of a *Global Mind Change* (Willis Harman) is emphasized again and again as *the* solution for current world crises. Once humanity begins to think holistically, the world will change for the better. The practicalities involved are treated as of minor importance.

The Positive: Love, Surrender, Forgiveness
There is wide agreement in New Age sources that "love" is the supreme answer to negativity. We saw that it is the solvent of "fear", and of all the negative patterns associated with it. A closer analysis reveals, however, that the term "love" covers several meanings. It is of particular importance to notice that it is almost never defined with direct reference to human *actions*; in line with what was said above, it refers primarily to states of mind or mental attitudes[66]. Closest to traditional western perspectives are some sources with a theosophical background. The Ramala masters stress "sacrificial service in love" as *the* great moral imperative[67]. The channeled source of the early Spangler (which, we

---

[62] See the opening sentences of WIO. Cf. Bohm & Edwards, *Changing Consciousness.*
[63] WIO xi.
[64] GW 105, and compare especially MacLaine's revealing discussion with Stephen Hawking: GW 305-307.
[65] For instance PH 6; WS xiii.
[66] An exception, again, is Starhawk: 'The law of the Goddess is love: passionate sexual love, the warm affection of friends, the fierce protective love of mother for child, the deep comradeship of the coven. There is nothing amorphous or superficial about love in Goddess religion; it is always specific, directed toward real individuals, not vague concepts of humanity. Love includes animals, plants, the earth itself—"all beings", not just human beings. It includes ourselves and all our fallible human qualities' (SD 97).
[67] For instance RR 275-276. Cf. note 49.

remember, called itself "Limitless Love & Truth") explains:

> The greatest is the Law of Love. The presence of love within an individual is
> essential before he will be entrusted to receive true New Age energies. He must
> be able to think in terms of the whole as he plans his thoughts and actions. He
> must transcend a purely personal and selfish viewpoint and enter into a commu-
> nion of love and giving and receiving with the whole of which he is a part. His
> love must be without limit. He must become harmless, unable to will harm to
> another being deliberately and out of a spirit of fear, hatred or competition. He
> must be limitless love. ... Thus, he must love himself as well, not as a private,
> selfish entity but as a unique and meaningful expression and part of the whole[68].

Emphasis on concepts such as "service" or "sacrifice" seems to be largely limited to these theosophical/anthroposophical circles associated with the "New
Age *sensu stricto*"[69], but the difference with other and later New Age developments should not be overestimated. It is important to realize that, in these
"theosophical" New Age circles, love refers primarily to "the Christ"; accordingly, "sacrificial service in love" means that one partakes consciously of the
objectively existing "Christ energy". This tendency to describe love in terms
such as "energy", "frequency" or "level of vibration" is widespread. The basic
idea is that the energy of love is the energy of cosmic harmony and order[70];
accordingly, fear and other negative energies are essentially "disruptive",
unharmonious, chaotic. A characteristic discussion, in this respect, took place
between Shirley MacLaine and the physicist Stephen Hawking. MacLaine
writes:

> I thought I was beginning to understand something. "Would you call the universe
> a loving place?" I asked. "I mean, you said everything could be explained by well-
> defined laws".
> "Yes".
> "Well then, that means the universe operates within a harmony, doesn't it?"
> "Yes".
> "Well, isn't harmonic energy loving?"
> "I don't know", he answered, "that there is anything loving about energy. I don't
> think *loving* is a word I could ascribe to the universe".
> "What is a word you *could* use?"
> He thought for a moment. "Order", he said. "The universe is well-defined order"[71].

---

[68] RBNA 84.

[69] I further remind the reader of Trevelyan's statements to the effect that believers in the New
Age should see themselves as volunteers in an "army which takes no conscripts", and that they
should follow the "High Command" wherever it sends them; and compare this with what the
Ramala masters have to say about the "sacrifice of the will": 'That is the ultimate sacrifice, that
you are prepared to say and to mean 'Not my will, but Thy Will, be done, O Lord' and, what is
more, that you are prepared to accept that Will as and when it manifests' (VR 131). In addition,
some authors in the magical/neopagan tradition emphasize that 'the ultimate aim of all magical
work is SERVICE' (EAM 8; WA 70).

[70] Even David Bohm, as we saw above, is convinced that the ultimate "Ground" of Being, or
"order of orders", is characterized by such qualities as "love" and "compassion".

[71] GW 305.

MacLaine then goes on to explain, to Hawking's obvious puzzlement, her belief that the concept of an orderly universe would stimulate love and harmony in the world. Significant in this passage is how completely obvious it appears to be to MacLaine that "harmonic energy" must be "loving"[72]. It is precisely the ease and, indeed, naïvity[73] with which this inference is made, which makes the passage highly characteristic for New Age perspectives on "love".

Apart from love as unselfish service and as an "energy", there is a strong tendency to emphasize that all love must be grounded ultimately in *self-love*. The basic assumption is explained by MacLaine: 'If we didn't love ourselves, how could we really love anyone else? If we felt good about ourselves, we'd feel good about others'[74]. Of course, we have already encountered this kind of psychology above: if we see ourselves as "bad", we will project that "badness" on others; therefore, if we want to love others, we will have to love ourselves first. The frequent criticism that this reasoning leads to "narcistic" egoism seems to be justified only in part. To many New Agers, it merely functions to correct an over-emphasis on altruism. Nevertheless, there can be little doubt that in many New Age sources the balance tends to swing to the other side. This may easily happen when "love" is equated with "compassion", described as a "detached" state of mind in which one offers assistance without becoming emotionally involved oneself[75]. In this connection, I refer again to the statements, discussed above, of MacLaine and Zukav about how to react to the (karmically-induced) suffering of others. A particularly clear case is Sanaya Roman. This author speaks profusely about "sending love and light" to others; but she makes it very clear that everybody is responsible for his/her own problems, and that self-love should come first in all cases: 'Some of you believe you must be loving, supportive, and caring to everyone. Loving someone does not mean making their feelings more important than your own'[76]. Like MacLaine, Roman makes it clear that, in the end, one loves others not for their sake, but in order to further one's own growth:

> Giving opens your ability to see others and their systems of reality, and it most definitely enables you to see yourself in a higher and more loving way.
> You will automatically begin forgiving, supporting, acknowledging and appreciating yourself when you do so for others. Healing others is not just a gift you are giving to the world. It is also a gift to yourself[77].

---

[72] Cf. the words spoken by the entity "John": 'God is love—which is the highest vibrational frequency of all' (OL 202-203).

[73] MacLaine confirms this herself: 'I knew I was probably being simplistic in my assumptions, particularly where physics was concerned' (DL 329).

[74] DL 25.

[75] See for instance the discussion in HHC 34-36, based on the rule 'I feel with loving compassion the problems of others without getting caught up emotionally in their predicaments that are offering them messages they need for their growth'.

[76] PPA 33.

[77] PPA 49.

Apart from "love", many sources emphasize the necessity of an attitude of "trust" and "surrender" to the universe. This is, of course, hardly surprising. If "fear" is identified as the most fundamental negative attitude, based on false beliefs, then it is obvious that fear should be replaced by trust. This fits perfectly with the general New Age worldview. We are living in a perfect universe, steered by benevolent forces; the process of cosmic evolution can be fully trusted. A frequently encountered New Age slogan, put forward as an alternative to patterns of fear, is "letting go and letting God". Similarly, we can trust the inherent goodness and perfection of our own inner being; we can rely on the guidance of our Higher Self. Once we no longer feel that we need to remain "in control" all the time, we can relax and "go with the flow". Shakti Gawain relates how, after having discovered the "magic" of creative visualisation, she discovered its deeper dimension:

> As I explored the process of creating my own reality I gradually began to realize that the creative power I was feeling was coming from some other source than my personality/ego self. ... I began to realize that "it" (my higher self) seemed to know more than "I" (my personality self) did about a lot of things. I saw that it would probably be smart to try and find out what that inner guidance was telling me and follow it. Every time I did that it seemed to work.
> Eventually I lost interest in trying to control my life, to make things happen in a way that I thought I wanted them to be. I began to practice surrendering to the universe and finding out what "it" wanted me to do. I discovered that in the long run it really wasn't that different. The universe always seems to want me to have everything I want, and it seems to know how to guide me in creating it better than I would know how to do so myself. The emphasis is different though. Instead of figuring out what I want, setting goals, and trying to control what happens to me, I began to practice tuning in receptively to my intuition and acting on what it told me without always understanding why I was doing what I was doing. It was a feeling of letting go of control, surrendering, and allowing the higher power to be in charge[78].

Finally, there is the easily misunderstood New Age concept of *forgiveness*[79]. On the face of it, it may seem strange that New Age authors so often emphasize the necessity to forgive. One normally "forgives" people their sins or transgressions, so that they no longer have to feel guilty about what they have done. To use the concept of forgiveness therefore seems to entail that very *belief* in the reality of guilt which, as we saw, is rejected as the root of all negativity. The solution to this paradox lies in the new interpretation which New Agers

---

[78] LL xvi-xvii. About surrender, cf. also CiM *passim*; OB 82; YHL 99; HHC for instance 30-31; SoS 234-248.

[79] It is not impossible that the concept of "forgiveness" as used in the New Age context has originated in *A Course in Miracles* (see for instance CiM:WfS 391, in the characteristic style of the *Course*: 'Forgiveness recognizes what you thought your brother did to you has not occurred. It does not pardon sins and make them real. It sees there was no sin. And in that view were all our sins forgiven'; cf. also Wapnick, *Meaning of Forgiveness*). Some other references are OB 163; YHL 76; R 132; RI 102; RIC 58; ECMM 156-157; LJ 62; PPA 119-122.

give to the concept of "forgiveness". Essentially, forgiveness means the profound realization that the "other", whatever (s)he may have done, *has not sinned*. As a result, forgiveness means that one replaces former negative attitudes against others (i.e., resentment, anger, revenge etc.) by the positive attitude of love, understanding and acceptance. This ethical imperative, if it may be called such, is closely related to the New Age belief in "self-responsibility". If everybody creates his/her own reality, then one can no longer hold others reponsible for one's own problems; instead, one realizes that one can only be hurt by others to the extent that one allows them to do so. Nobody can ever be held responsible for the suffering of others. Of course, since "loving others presupposes that we love ourselves", forgiveness according to New Age parlance is possible only to the extent that one can first forgive *oneself*. One must profoundly realize that *nobody* is sinful or guilty, including oneself. Self-forgiveness, briefly, means to get rid of all negative, limiting self-images. "Forgiving", then, is ultimately done for one's own sake: it simply feels much better to love and forgive everybody including oneself, than it does to remain trapped in patterns of hate and resentment. New Age believers are convinced that, when more people discover this, it will have a profound impact on the world.

CHAPTER ELEVEN

VISIONS OF THE PAST

1. INTRODUCTION

In chapter five I mentioned the apparent discrepancy between New Age belief in large astrological cycles, on the one hand, and the almost exclusive focus on the arrival of the next age, on the other. Even though the belief in recurring cycles logically implies that the New Age will eventually be followed by yet another one, there seems to be practically no interest in such post-Aquarian ages. Likewise, the ages preceding the Piscean are seldom referred to by their astrological names, possible though this would be in theory[1]. While this situation seems rather strange from a strictly logical point of view, it makes sense if we interpret the New Age movement as a manifestation of popular *culture criticism*[2]. New Age thinking is essentially a reaction to the ideas and values which are perceived as having dominated western culture during the last two thousand years. I already made reference to this at the beginning of chapter six, section 2, and will return to it in Part Three of this study. At this point, it is important to emphasize that New Age visions of the past are strongly dominated by a systematic opposition of what might be called "Piscean" and "Aquarian" values. This corresponds to an opposition between the values of dominant Judaeo-Christian traditions and modern rationalism, on the one hand, and the values of New Age spirituality, on the other. The latter, however, are not emically regarded as new and unprecedented but as a revival of ancient wisdom traditions. Accordingly, we arrive at a circular vision which has *three* phases: an ancient period during which spiritual wisdom flourished (in some parts of the world at least); a period of spiritual decline (exemplified most clearly by the Piscean Age); and a hoped-for revival (the Age of Aquarius). As we will see, most New Age ideas about this cycle derive from modern Theosophical speculation which, in turn, is dependent upon older traditions in western esotericism. It is important to notice, however, the difference in emphasis

---

[1] The order of the astrological ages is the reverse of the order of the astrological year (where Aquarius *precedes* Pisces). This means that the Piscean Age was preceded by the Age of Aries (appr. 2000 B.C.), which was preceded by the Age of Taurus (appr. 4000-2000 B.C.), and so on; the coming Age of Aquarius will be followed by an Age of Capricorn (cf. Culver & Ianna, *Astrology*, ch. 6: 'The Age of Aquarius').

[2] Hanegraaff, 'New Age en cultuurkritiek'; id., 'Verschijnsel New Age'; id., 'New Age Movement'.

between the New Age movement and modern Theosophy. Theories of large cosmic cycles, successive "root races", ages of the world etcetera are a prominent and central part of traditional theosophical thought; in the New Age movement, however, these theories are used at most in a very eclectic manner. In general, "macrohistorical schemes" are loosely referred to when they come in convenient, but systematical expositions are scarce[3].

Special mention must me made of the fact that New Age visions of history are characterized by a remarkably exclusive concentration on *western* developments. Not the "spiritual" east, as one might expect, but the Christian west is consistently highlighted as the center stage for those historical events which have been essential to humanity's spiritual evolution. This "ethnocentric" focus betrays a latent ambivalence which I believe goes to the heart of New Age religion. The emergence of Christianity is generally believed to mark the beginning of the Piscean Age, and this might suggest that it should be valued negatively. However, a figure such as Z Budapest, who hates Christianity, is wholly uncharacteristic; her derisive remarks about Christianity's 'good guy, Jesus, in his long white nightgown'[4] would undoubtedly offend many New Age believers. It is true that New Agers are generally very critical of how the churches have ministered Jesus's message. Characteristically, however, rather than rejecting historical Christianity for that reason, they prefer to look for a hidden tradition of "esoteric Christianity" which is in fundamental agreement both with Jesus's message and with the esoteric core of other religions. New Age believers, then, although they proclaim the end of the Piscean Age, will seldom describe themselves as wholly hostile to the religion which dominated that age. This is not only for reasons of tolerance and "world ecumenism", although that is also involved. More importantly, it illustrates a thesis which will be put forward in Part Three of this study. We will see that New Age religion is rooted in complex post-Enlightenment developments of the western religious con-

---

[3] Fritjof Capra refers to the theories of Arnold Toynbee and Pitirim Sorokin about the rise and decline of cultures (TP 26-33). The Ramala masters present a revamped version of Joachim of Fiore's theories: the "Father aspect" of divine reality was grounded in Tibet or Northern Mongolia (but compare the accounts of RR and WR) at the beginning of the age of Aries (4000 years ago); the "Son aspect" in the Holy Land at the beginning of the age of Pisces; and the Age of Aquarius will complete the process by grounding the Holy Spirit in... Glastonbury (RR 270; WR 268. Cf. WR 269: the age that will begin two thousand years from now—presumably the age of Capricorn, cf. note 1—will begin in America. One cannot help wondering what "aspect" will be grounded on that occasion: the Father once again?); Ken Wilber's UfE presents a full-blown "neo-Hegelian" history of human evolution (UfE 314 about Hegel: 'Although I have not that often mentioned him in this book, his shadow falls on every page'), which is progressive rather than circular because it moves from the pre-personal to the personal to the trans-personal. Each of these theories stands isolated within our corpus as a whole. Only David Spangler's description of large astrological cycles (see his foundational text RBNA 92-97) seems to have found a wider echo.
[4] HBWM 162.

sciousness; and these have been crucially determined, not by a simple rejection of, but rather by a dialectic tension with traditional forms of Christianity.

2. BEGINNINGS

Cosmogonic Myths
Matthew Fox begins one of his books with "A New Creation Story" in the form of a poem. Modeled on the prologue of the Gospel of John, it also makes characteristic use of "Big Bang" cosmology and evolution theory along the lines of Erich Jantsch[5]:

> In the beginning was the gift.
> And the gift was with God and the gift was God.
> And the gift came and set its tent among us,
> first in the form of a fireball
> that burned unabated for 750,000 years
> and cooked in its immensely hot oven
> hadrons and leptons.
> These gifts found a modicum of stability,
> enough to give birth to the first atomic creatures,
> hydrogen and helium.
> ...[etc.][6]

Fox's "Christian science" is a case apart; but "creation stories" as such are common in New Age sources[7]. Shakti Gawain's version starts with 'original consciousness (which we can call Spirit, or God, or Source)' which 'while still remaining one, also created itself into two opposite energies which we can call yin and yang, or female and male, or dark and light, or spirit and form'[8]. This primal duality made possible the beginning of a process of progressive emanation and division. Starhawk begins with the Goddess; and, again, a primal oneness gives way to duality in order to make creation possible: 'She whose name cannot be spoken, floated in the abyss of the outer darkness, before the beginning of all things. And as She looked into the curved mirror of black space, She saw by her own light her radiant reflection, and fell in love with it'. The ecstasy of love-making which ensued 'burst forth in the single song of all that is, was, or ever shall be'[9]. The idea that creation begins when the primal deity "contemplates" itself and falls in love with its own image is also found in the messages of Ramtha: '...God always would have been Thought

---

[5] SOU is mentioned in the bibliography.
[6] CS 1.
[7] TiR 306ff; CS 1-4; RG 3ff; OL 145; S 190ff; R 79ff; SM 264ff; SD 31-32.
[8] RG 3.
[9] SD 31.

without form had he not contemplated himself—turned and bent inward unto himself the Thought that he was. When the Father contemplated the Thought that he was, he expanded himself into a unique form of himself. ... Thus the Father ... contemplated himself into a greateness'[10]. Like Starhawk, Ramtha goes on to emphasize that the love and desire of the deity for its mirror image stands at the beginning of creation and still remains its underlying essence: 'From that movement of love, all of you were born'[11]. While Ramtha describes how God "bent inward", the influential Edgar Cayce volume *There is a River* similarly describes how the original 'sea of spirit ... withdrew into itself, until all space was empty, and that which had filled it was shining from its center, a restless, seething mind. This was the individuality of the spirit; this was what it discovered itself to be when it awakened; this was God. God desired to express Himself, and He desired companionship. Therefore, He projected from Himself the cosmos and souls'[12]. And finally, I refer the reader to the long quotation given in chapter six (section 2A) from Seth's description of how All-That-Is created the cosmos.

Most New Age believers probably regard such creation myths as essentially poetical statements which can, at most, convey an intuitive grasp of a process which defies expression in human language. Therefore a detailed comparison would be rather pointless. The important thing is to notice the consistently holistic framework common to almost all of them[13]. They all describe how duality emerges within an original, primal oneness. This first "symmetry break"[14] is the beginning of a chain reaction, which over time brings into existence a world of infinite diversity. This process of emanation and diversification leaves the essential wholeness of the universe intact. It may be true that duality (or polarity: cf. chapter six, section 2C) is necessary to explain how the world could come into existence and maintain itself over time; but dual-*ism* is and remains an illusion. It is never more than a limiting belief, created by the mind.

The Descent of Man
According to Ramtha, the original burst of "Love" in God gave birth to a multiplicity of souls, or "gods": 'Your original heritage goes back to the birthing of Light; for each particum of light, born of the first contemplated thought,

---

[10] R 79.
[11] R 79.
[12] TiR 306-307.
[13] Fox's story is an exception, because it is in principle compatible with theism and traditional creationism. He evidently tries to remain just within the doctrinal borders of Catholic theology.
[14] Cf. SOU part II, titled 'Co-evolution of Macro- and Microcosmos: A History of Reality in Symmetry Breaks'.

became an individual, a god, a son. Thus, all became what is termed light-beings at the birthing of creation'[15]. These light-beings, participating in the primal creative power of God, proceeded to create the world. This is yet another aspect of the "creating our own reality" belief: we ourselves, when we were still "gods", literally created the very world which is now our home. Ramtha explains the process:

> Whenever you contemplate thought and emotionally embrace it, the thought expands into the vibratory frequency of light. If you slow the movement of the particles of light and condense it, you create electrum—an electromagnetic field that has positive and negative poles, which you call electricity. If you slow and condense the thought still further, beyond the electromagnetic fields, the electrum coagulates into gross matter. Gross matter then coagulates into the molecular and cellular structures called form. And the form is held together by the thought that the soul envisioned as an ideal of creation[16].
> All things are created by taking that which has no speed—thought—and expanding it into that which does—light—and then slowing the light down until you create this and that and all that is around you. ...
> In the beginning of created forms, the gods contemplated themselves (the lights that they were) and created the ideal of light into matter by creating what are called suns ... And from the great suns, the central sparks of life, rotating spheres called planets were created and thrust into their orbits. And upon the spheres, the gods created designs—and it took *eons* for you to learn design[17].

These "designs" included organisms: first very primitive ('a glob of something'[18]), later more refined in the forms of plants and animals.

> It was not until a food chain had been clearly established here that the gods decided to create a vehicle of matter through which they could experience their creations and continue to express their creativity—but as themselves rather than through their creations. And for that, they created the embodiment called man. ... Now, thought is a penetrating frequency, an essence that passes through matter. Thus the gods, who were thought in the form of light, could become the flower, yet they could never smell its aroma. ... In order for the gods to smell the flower, to hold the flower, to wear the flower, in order for them to know its beauty and experience its vividness, they had to create a vehicle of matter that vibrates at the same rate of speed that the flower is vibrating. Thus the embodiment called man was created, after all other things were created, so that the gods could experience their creations and express their creative ability through gross matter, or what is termed "solidity in mass"—Thought taken to its lowest form[19].

Ramtha describes this process as a conscious and purposive act, which was positive in principle because it widened the soul's possibilities of experience

---

[15] R 80.
[16] This doctrine of "Light" as the ultimate reality from which all else is created is also found in other sources. See especially SoS 96 and *passim*; RU 10-23.
[17] R 82-83.
[18] R 84.
[19] R 85.

and adventure. Other New Age authors interpret the same event more negatively as the "fall of man" into material consciousness. Shirley MacLaine's
Higher Self explains to her that

> individual souls became separated from the higher vibration in the process of cre-
> ating various life forms. Seduced by the beauty of their own creations they became
> entrapped in the physical, losing their connection with Divine Light. The panic
> was so severe that it created a battlefield known to you now as good and evil.
> Karma, that is, cause and effect, came into being as a path, a means, a method,
> to eventually eliminate the artificial concepts of good and evil. Eventually, too,
> souls lodged in evolved primates that later became Homo sapiens[20].

This basic theme of a "descent of man" is found in a range of New Age sources,
especially those with a broadly theosophical background. Probably the most
influential source is the Edgar Cayce material. This contains extended discussions that have enjoyed a wide influence in the New Age movement[21]. Cayce's
version contains numerous complications, however, which have seldom been
adopted by later New Age authors. He describes the descent into matter as taking place in two great waves, the first of which is an accident while the second one is best described as a rescue action. Originally, souls were "playing
at creating", in "imitation of God". This activity, however, interfered with the
divine plan and 'thus the stream of mind carrying out the plan for earth gradually drew souls into its current'[22]. The souls found themselves trapped in
'flesh prisons'. 'Hopelessly entangled in the procreative processes', they
became 'an anguished hybrid, neither human nor animal'[23]. Cayce refers to
these hybrid beings as the "sons of man". Other, wiser souls came to their rescue. As part of the plan to free their fellow souls, they selected a certain species
of ape and began to prepare it as a vehicle for incarnation:

> Souls descended on these apes—hovering above and about them rather than inhab-
> iting them—and influenced them to move toward a different goal from the sim-
> ple one they had been pursuing. ... All this was done by the souls, working through
> the glands, until the body of the ape was an objectification—in the third dimen-
> sion of the solar system—of the souls that hovered above it. Then the souls
> descended into the body and earth had a new inhabitant: man[24].

---

[20] DL 339-340.

[21] See for instance TiR 310-312; ECRE 133-134; ECMM 88-90 ('Souls at Play lose their Way
Home').

[22] TiR 311.

[23] ECRE 133.

[24] TiR 312. In several accounts it is added that "man" was originally androgynous (for instance
TiR 311; RR 194). In this connection it is not superfluous to call attention to the remarkably conservative opinions of the Ramala masters about women and sexuality (RR 194; WR 63, 72-73,
81; cf. Hanegraaff, 'Channeling-literatuur', 26). Ramtha, in contrast, says that 'at first only males
were created', and that '"womb of man" or woman was designed and created much later, as a
more perfected form of man' (R 86).

It is significant that this second wave, which consisted of genuinely *human* beings, is called the "Sons of God"[25]. I will return to their further story below.

We can conclude that, although the "descent of man" is mentioned in quite a number of sources (with an abundance of colourful details, which cannot be reproduced here[26]), explanations for this descent differ. On one side of the scale we find the cheerful vision of Ramtha, according to whom all incarnation is an adventurous play. More often, however, we find the descent described in relatively negative terms, as a "fall" (with Cayce's account as a more complicated variant). Other sources leave the issue somewhat vague; the early Spangler, for example, speaks of a "fall", and comments that it 'represented a sacrifice in some respects, yet it prepared the way for a more expanded expression of [man's] spirit'[27].

A comparison of these different accounts confirms the "weak this-worldly" character of most New Age literature. The prevailing attitude towards worldly existence is not fully positive or negative but *ambiguous*. The same ambiguity makes it rather difficult to determine what exactly is meant when the descent is described as a "fall". It is tempting to interpret some statements as gnostic dualism in the sense that *materialization as such* should never have occurred. However, it is more consistent with the sources and their underlying holism to say that not incarnation/materialization as such but the *exclusive identification of consciousness with the material plane* constituted the "fall"[28]. This, too, may be interpreted as gnostic dualism, but now it is the loss of *gnosis* due to "worldly influences" which is decisive. The "fall", in other words, is not a cosmological but a psychological event. The "limited consciousness" which charac-

---

[25] There is, however, some terminological confusion. Sometimes the term "sons of man" is used for the "sons of Belial", which is the name not of the hybrid beings of the first wave, but of renegade souls from the second wave.

[26] The Ramala material contains at least two mutually incompatible accounts. According to RR 193-194, humanity was 'created through the perfect breath according to the will of its Creator', and then placed upon the earth. According to WR 231-232 (and cf. VR 82, 318), however, the whole of humanity comes from Sirius. It had seriously misused its god-given talents there, finally endangering the whole planet on which it lived. To solve this problem, humanity was transported wholesale to our planet, intended to be a place where 'the wheat could be sorted from the chaff' (WR 232). Evidently, humanity has succeeded to mess up its second chance too. Sirius, as the origin of humanity, is also found elsewhere in the New Age, prominently for instance in Murry Hope's PR (16-19, 91, 201-202). It may be noted that much of the Sirius mystique in New Age religion, including Hope's, can be traced to the popular influence of the french anthropologist M. Griaule, who attracted much attention with his "discovery" that the African Dogon tribe knew that Sirius was a double star *before* modern astronomy discovered that fact. The implication was that Dogon culture must have derived that knowledge from ancient contacts with intelligent beings from Sirius. About this subject, cf. Van Beek, 'Dogon Restudied', 139-167; id., 'Dogon religie', 99-113.

[27] RBNA 101.

[28] Obviously, the difference between both options is minimized when it is assumed that materialization inevitably leads to "material consciousness".

terizes incarnated existence has been discussed already in chapter ten, section 3, and I especially refer the reader to the long quotation from Ramtha given there[29]. The Cayce material contains a brief characterization of the main idea:

> Though at first the souls but lightly inhabited bodies and remembered their identities, gradually, life after life, they descended into earthiness, into less mentality, less consciousness of the mind force. They remembered their true selves only in dreams, in stories and fables handed down from one generation to another. Religion came into being: a ritual of longing for lost memories[30]. ... Finally man was left with a conscious mind definitely separated from his own individuality. ... He built up theories for what he felt—but no longer knew—to be true. Philosophy and theology resulted. ... Downward he went from heavenly knowledge to mystical dreams, revealed religions, philosophy and theology, until the bottom was reached and he only believed what he could see and feel and prove in terms of his conscious mind. Then he began to fight his way upward, using the only tools he had left: suffering, patience, faith, and the power of mind[31].

Although it is assumed that the process of degeneration already began with the first generations of human beings, it is widely believed that the early civilizations retained a comparatively high level of spiritual insight. Subsequent developments increasingly forced the keepers of wisdom to withdraw in esoteric institutions.

3. FROM ATLANTIS TO THE HOLY LAND

Tales of lost continents, and of ancient civilizations which were superior to ours both in spiritual and in technological knowledge, belong to the stock-in-trade of western occultism. Modern theosophy and anthroposophy in particular have accommodated traditional stories and theories about the civilizations of Atlantis, Lemuria and Mu, and accorded them a central place in their visions of history[32]. Their literature is easily accessible in New Age bookstores. Most New Agers therefore pick up, somewhere along the line, at least some elements of this lore. The single most influential source is undoubtedly Edgar Cayce, with his frequent and detailed "eyewitness accounts" of his patients' past lives. On the basis of such accounts, Cayce describes a tradition of "perennial wisdom" that is passed on from Atlantis to Egypt, and from Egypt to the "great initiate" Jesus.

---

[29] Cf. also R chapter 15 for a detailed account of how the "gods" came to forget their divinity and developed into "herd-like entities" dominated by fear, hatred and self-denial.

[30] For a similar view of religion, cf. R 145.

[31] TiR 314-315.

[32] For a splendid history of the subject, see Sprague de Camp, *Lost Continents*.

Atlantis

The Edgar Cayce materials pick up the thread of humanity's evolution in Atlantis, which is said to have been located in what is now the Atlantic Ocean. In the period before 50.000 B.C., it had become the center of human civilization. A very high level of technological knowledge, equal or superior to our own, was attained. Humanity had discovered the powers of crystals, which were used for healing purposes but also to produce deadly weapons (death rays). It is assumed that the Atlanteans also knew how to use nuclear power. Irresponsible use of these powers ultimately brought about the destruction of their continent. As related above, humanity was constituted of two categories of incarnated souls. The hybrid beings referred to as the "sons of man" had, in the meantime, become enslaved to the so-called "Sons of Belial". The latter were renegade souls of the "second wave" (see above): although they had originally come to earth to free the sons of man from their entanglement in matter, they had forgotten their origin and had begun to misuse their power. They now looked upon the sons of man as soulless automatons, or "things", and treated them cruelly. The sons of Belial were opposed by the "Sons of the Law of One" (headed by the Christ soul), who had remained faithful to their original intention to liberate the souls that were lost in matter. The irresponsible behaviour of the Sons of Belial finally led to the destruction of the whole continent. This took place in three stages, approximately about 50.000, 28.000 and 10.000 B.C. During the second period of destruction, Atlantis was broken up into islands; during the final period those islands sank into the ocean[33].

Few accounts of comparable length and detail are found in other sources of our corpus. Atlantis is mentioned regularly, however, together with other, more shadowy civilizations: Lemuria, Mu, Cordemia and Lumania[34]. Lemuria, in particular, is important to the account given by Ramtha. Ramtha describes his single life lived on earth, 35.000 years ago, which was immediately 'before the continent broke up and great waters covered its land'[35]. Ramtha belonged to a group of exiles from Lemuria[36], and was born in poverty in the slums of

---

[33] See for all the details ECA *passim*.

[34] For references to various "lost continents", cf. WWD 26-27 (this book dates from 1971; notice that the Atlantis theme is almost completely absent in the later books by the Farrars); TI 78-79, 81, 145, 218; PR 16; WW2 4-5 (it is characteristic for the Matthews's comparatively scholarly attitude that they emphasize the mythic significance of Atlantis and downplay the importance of whether Atlantis really existed in space and time); RR 231-236 (notice the additional mention of the civilization of "Cordemia", 'the first great human civilisation on this Earth' (RR 232); I have not found this name mentioned by other authors); SS 240-254 (esp. about "Lumania", yet another civilization not mentioned elsewhere, which is said to have existed 'long before the time of Atlantis' (SS 254)).

[35] R 6. This does not accord with the three periods of destruction as given by Cayce.

[36] R 5: 'My people ... were a mixture of Lemurians, the people from Ionia (later to be termed Macedonia), and the tribes-people escaping from Atlatia, the land you call Atlantis. It is my

Onai, the greatest port city of Atlatia (his name for Atlantis). Like Cayce, Ramtha describes a social structure in which slaves were suppressed by cruel tyrants; but in his case these two groups are represented by the Lemurians and the Atlatians respectively. It is interesting to see how Ramtha characterizes their opposition:

> At that time, Atlatia was a civilization of people with great intellect, whose endow-ment for scientific understanding was superb. Their science was even greater than what you have at this time in your scientific community, for the Atlatians had begun to understand and use the principles of light. ... They even had aeroships that traveled on light, a science provided to them through an intercommunication with entities from other star systems. ... Because of the Atlatians' great involve-ment with technology, they worshiped the intellect. Thus, technological science became the religion of the Atlatians.
> The Lemurians were quite different from the Atlatians. Their social system was built upon communication through thought. They had not the advancement of technology, only a great spiritual understanding ... They *loved* an essence that could not be identified. It was a power they called the *Unknown God*. Because the Lemurians worshiped only this God, the Atlatians despised them, for they despised anything that was not "progressive". ...
> Under the abominable rule of these tyrants, the Lemurians were considered the dung of the earth, less than a dog in the street. ... we were considered stinking, wretched things. We were the no-things, the soulles, mindless wastes of intellect, because we were without the scientific understanding of such things as gases and light. ...
> That was my time. What sort of dream was I in? The beginning of man's advent into the arrogance and stupidity of intellect[37].

Obviously, this passage is intended to furnish a significant parallel to the pre-sent world situation: like the Atlatians opposed the Lemurians in the past, so the "Pisceans" oppose the "Aquarians" in contemporary society.

Ramtha's account refers to a period when Atlantis was already seriously degen-erated. Shirley MacLaine, on the other hand, during her regression sessions with Chris Griscom, has visions of Atlantis in its earlier period of glory. She describes a vision of a crystal pyramid, located 'off the east coast of what is now the United States, only it was on land'[38]; she discovers that this pyramid is somehow connected with weather control, a power she misused during her Atlantean lifetime; she sees strange-looking aircraft, and finally: 'lush, opu-lent green gardens with pink and turquoise water fountains. Gracefully lean people moved and walked along crystal walkways, They didn't talk. They com-municated telepathically. ... I saw one of the people walk to a tree, pick a piece

---

people's lineage that now makes up the populace of India, Tibet, Nepal, and Southern Mongo-lia'.
[37] R 6-7.
[38] DL 316.

of fruit, and materialize another in its place. There were buildings made of something white. ... The clothing was a crystal fabric of some kind and the same fabric was used as hair decoration'[39]. When MacLaine asks her Higher Self, the latter confirms that she has indeed seen Atlantis. Later on, Chris Griscom tells her that these pictures are the same with all her patients: 'They describe subdued colors of pink and violet and orange hues with fountains and crystal structures and many people wearing crystal headdresses. Atlantis is always described in the same way, even by people who never were aware they believed it existed'[40].

Egypt and the "Great White Brotherhood"
Because of the long periods between the three periods of destruction, Atlantians had many opportunities to emigrate. The sources are in general agreement that wherever the Atlantians went, the indigenous cultures were positively transformed by their superior culture. A fairly representative account[41] is given by Stewart Farrar[42]. The first emigration wave was dominated by what he calls the "Power Ray". It crossed northern Europe and Asia, 'contacting more primitive cultures as it went'. It produced cults of 'primitive power magic' and is described as 'a contaminated and dangerous stream'. The second emigration wave was dominated by the "Wisdom Ray"; via Central Europe and the Himalayas it reached India. To the extent that it remained uncontaminated by the first steam, it produced 'the great mind-mastering philosophies of the East'. The third emigration wave finally took place just before the final cataclysm and was dominated by the "Love Ray". Via North Africa it reached Egypt (although some Atlanteans went in the other direction, to Central America, whence the 'marked affinities' between ancient meso-american and Egyptian culture). From this impulse 'blossomed the Egyptian, Tyrian, Greek, Hebrew, Christian and Moslem spiritual achievements'. Significant in this account is not only its diffusionist view of religious history, but also its implicit religio-cultural hierarchy. It moves from "primitive magic" (power) to the more advanced level of Oriental religions (wisdom), finally to culminate in Middle-Eastern and Western religions (love). Egypt, the spiritual heir of Atlantis, is described as the fountain of wisdom from which have sprung the great monotheistic religions. About Egyptian culture, Farrar asserts that it was 'wholly occult-based. It was inspired and run by initiates'[43]. This perception of Egypt

---

[39] DL 318-319.
[40] DL 347.
[41] Again: representative only with respect to the main outlines. As regards details, *no* single New Age account of past history can be said to be representative.
[42] WD 26-27.
[43] WD 27.

as a culture of esoteric initiates is widely accepted in New Age circles[44].

Edgar Cayce's account of ancient Egypt is again exceptionally detailed, and introduces complications which have only partly been adopted by later authors[45]. The battle between the "Sons of the Law of One" and the "Sons of Belial" continues in Egypt. The central hero is a priest called Ra-Ta (actually: Cayce himself in a former incarnation), who is said to have come to Egypt from the Caucasian and Carpathian region during the period of the third and final Atlantean destruction. In Egypt, Ra-Ta 'concerned himself mainly with the setting up of spiritual codes for confirmity of worship of the One God and in building temples for physical and spiritual development of the masses'[46]. In order to deal with the inflow of Atlantean refugees, Ra-Ta visits Atlantis before its final destruction; he contacts the leader of the "Sons of the Law of One", who tells him about the battle with the "Sons of Belial". Back in Egypt he sets up "temples", meant as centers for the physical and spiritual development of the subhuman "sons of man":

> Combination hospital and educational institutions (called the Temple of Sacrifice and the Temple of Beauty) were set up, and probably functioned like the psychiatric wing of a modern hospital. There the masses flocked for mental as well as physical therapy. Evidently, besides low mental development and/or lack of moral judgment and self-control, some people classed as servants or 'things' or 'automatons' had physical deformities linking them to the animal world. They may have had tails, feathers, or scales. This was a holdover from the early projection of souls into materiality for selfish purposes at which time monstrosities as well as creatures of beauty were created[47].

Judging from the descriptions, these temples actually looked very much like present-day centers for holistic health: '...various forms of therapy were used in correcting both physical and mental deformities—Surgery, medicines, electrical therapy, diet, massage and manipulation. Vibrations of music and color, singing, chanting and dancing were also employed along with deep meditation. There was also a purification process involving the use of flames from the altar fires'[48]. Ra-Ta's succesful initiatives to liberate the "things" were opposed by his unrepentant enemies, the "sons of Belial". They succeeded in driving him into exile and temporarily threw Egypt into a chaos of rebellions and civil wars. Ra-Ta's victorious return, several years later, brought a new era of progress. In this period the Sphinx and the Pyramids were built, the Pyramid of Gizeh actually having been designed as the "Hall of the Initiates of the

---

[44] One should take notice of the influence of the romantic novels about former Egyptian lives written by Joan Grant (*Winged Pharaoh*) and Elisabeth Haich (*Initiation*).
[45] See especially ECA and ECSJ.
[46] ECSJ 89.
[47] ECA 121.
[48] ECSJ 94.

Great White Brotherhood". This last term returns frequently, and has survived in New Age parlance[49]. It is a general indication for the age-old tradition of the initiates in divine wisdom, from the earliest "Sons of God" via the "Sons of the Law of One" to the followers of Ra-Ta, the Egyptian mystery traditions and beyond. It is assumed to be still at work behind the scenes of world history.

Cayce's occultist vision of world history, dominated by the battle between the forces of good and evil, has been adopted only ambiguously by the New Age movement. Above, we saw that New Age religion speaks of a "fall of man", but tends to obscure or relativize its dualistic implications. Similarly, visions of world history may mention (most often vaguely and in passing) the existence of "dark forces" which oppose the forces of light, but the ethical dualism logically implied by this is usually not emphasized. Although these dark forces are given their due as representing whatever opposes the "light", their precise nature and origin are usually left unexplained. We may safely assume that "darkness", for most New Agers, stands simply for those tendencies to which they object, e.g. excessive rationalism, materialism, religious intolerance, or ... dualistic thinking. Descriptions of the "forces of darkness" in terms of stark contrasts, as an omnipresent demonic force that threatens "the forces of light", are far from unusual in various occultist traditions; but they are definitely not typical for New Age religion. For the latter, to believe in the "Great White Brotherhood is to believe that, since the beginnings of history, true spiritual wisdom has never been without its guardians and defenders. Its main function in the literature is to add a dimension of historical depth to contemporary spiritual beliefs. Although the concept of the "Great White Brotherhood" could easily have inspired heroic visions of quasi-metaphysical wars between good and evil, the holistic tendency of New Age religion all but neutralizes that potential.

The Essenes and Jesus[50]

I already noted that most New Agers are very positively inclined towards Jesus. When he is mentioned, it is almost without exception as a supreme example of spiritual wisdom: a "fully realized being", "great Master", or accomplished mystic or gnostic. He is often mentioned as one in a succession of "great initiates" who have periodically come down to earth in order to remind humani-

---

[49] Cf. for instance RI 1, 123.

[50] For obvious reasons, this subject has attracted much attention from Christian theologians and Christian authors generally. Several books exist which investigate the sources behind New Age claims about Jesus (cf. for instance Groothuis, *Revealing the New Age Jesus*; a very useful older study of these sources is Goodspeed, *Modern Apocrypha*. My discussion will inevitably be much briefer, and based only on what is found in the sources selected for the present study.

ty of its divine origin and give the impulse to a new spiritual awakening[51]. Among these divine "avatars" (to use another popular term) we find most of the great names of religious history and mythology: Buddha, Krishna, Lao-Tse, Zarathustra, Hermes, Moses etcetera. All are believed to have taught essentially the same message[52]. This, of course, reduces Jesus's religious status from God's only-begotten Son to just one among many "sons of God". Although that inference is indeed common, we saw (chapter seven, section 2B) that not all New Age authors agree on this point: some maintain that Jesus's union with "the Christ (Principle)" represents a unique historical event. As the Matthews put it: '...something changed direction from the point of the Incarnation: not just the birth of a tradition but the opportunity for consciousness to evolve, a necessary bridge between the impacted dualisms of the Classical world and the cosmic hope of the Mysteries'[53]. A more moderate version (which presents Jesus as unique, but without necessarily including belief in the incarnation of "the Christ" as a historical turning point) is that Jesus was just, as we read in MacLaine's work, 'the most advanced human ever to walk this planet'[54].

Regardless of their position on the uniqueness of Jesus, almost all New Age authors who describe his life seem to agree that he was an initiate in ancient esoteric wisdom. One popular version is that Jesus visited India. Kevin Ryerson tells Shirley MacLaine that 'The man Jesus studied for eighteen years in India before he returned to Jerusalem. He was studying the teaching of Buddha and became an adept yogi himself'[55]. Ramtha refers to Jesus as "Yeshua ben Joseph", and states quite generally that 'From the time he was 12 until he was 30, Yeshua traveled to many countries and studied under many great entities, who taught him and reminded him of the very same things I am teaching you'[56]. Of particular interest is the role accorded by various authors to the Jew-

---

[51] The direct source for this belief is Schuré, *Great Initiates*. This book had already gone through 220 editions in 1961.

[52] Some examples: CiM:MfT 83 ('The name of *Jesus* is the name of one who was a man but saw the face of Christ in all his brothers and remembered God. So he became identified with *Christ*, a man no longer, but at one with God. ... In his complete identification with the Christ ... Jesus became what all of you must be'); WW 177-179; OB 123, 239 (a special case: Jesus as 'a poet, a storyteller, an artist', who evidently exemplified Fox's ideal of the creation-centered mystic); DL 104 (a "fully realized human being"); RR 76ff (a "Master", one of many); ECMM 274-275 ('What was special about Jesus was that he was directly aware of his oneness with the Creator'); UfE 244-245 (Jesus as belonging to the "growing tip" of individuals who are ahead of the rest of humanity in any given period); RU 203-204 (one in a line of "highly advanced" beings); SoS 69 (one among many "beings of light").

[53] WW2 80.

[54] OL 91-92.

[55] OL 181. The idea of Jesus visiting India was first popularized at the end of the nineteenth century by Notovitch, *Vie inconnue de Jésus Christ*. Cf. Goodspeed, *Modern Apocrypha*, ch. 1.

[56] RI 124. According to the Ramala masters, Jesus also visited Glastonbury. In doing so, they follow an old legend (which inspired William Blake's famous lines in his poem "Jerusalem":

ish sect of the Essenes. It is widely believed that they provided Jesus with the link to Egyptian esotericism, and that it was under their supervision that Jesus made various "educational trips" to other countries before beginning his public ministry. Again, various accounts exist, which differ in many points of detail[57]. The Edgar Cayce material, being among the most influential sources of such information, is representative at least of the general idea. It presents a remarkable mixture of occultism, biblical literalism and traditional Christian elements.

According to Cayce's story, the Essenes were the representatives of the Great White Brotherhood active in Palestine at the time of Jesus. Their headquarters were not in Qumran[58] but on Mount Carmel. This site is associated with the prophet Elijah, and Cayce actually claims that the Essenes were the contemporary representatives of the same tradition which had originally been established at Mount Carmel by Elijah, and which was based on the teachings of the Great White Brotherhood. The Essenes believed in reincarnation (but referred to it as "resurrection"); and they were well versed in secret doctrines and sciences such as astrology, numerology and phrenology. Members of the "brotherhood" were disseminated all over Palestine, some living in monasteries such as Qumran and some as private persons. Contrary to current opinion, they accepted women as equal members in their ranks.

In the period before Jesus's birth, Essene activities were focused on the expected incarnation of the "Christ Soul", described as 'a soul which had completed its experience of creation and returned to God. ... This is the soul man knows as the Christ'[59]. Because the Christ Soul had been the first to finish the complete cycle of soul development, he is also referred to as humanity's "Elder Brother" (a title which suggests that Jesus is essentially a being like ourselves, only ahead of us in development). This same Christ Soul had already been incarnated repeatedly in the past: as 'Adam, Enoch, Melchizedek, Joseph,

---

'And did those feet in ancient time/ Walk upon England's mountains green? And was the Holy Lamb of God / On England's pleasant pastures seen'). Cf. Dobson, *Did our Lord visit Britain?*.

[57] The most important are those in the Cayce materials (esp. ECDS, ECJC and ECSJ), the Seth materials (for instance SS ch. 21; SM ch. 18; but cf. also many other Seth publications which have not been included in the present survey, for instance Roberts, *God of Jane*, ch. 20 & 21). Cf. also Ramtha's far less detailed story (RI ch. 16 'Yeshua'). Notice that Ramtha sharply opposes Jesus's teaching to that of the Old Testament: 'He taught them [the people and his disciples] the hypocrisy of the laws of Moses' (RI 127) and 'he did away with the laws of Jehovah and created the Law of One' (RI 129). While many New Age sources agree that Jesus's teachings were superior to the religions of his cultural environment, it is less usual to encounter such an open and sharply-worded rejection of Hebrew religion.

[58] However, the opening pages of ECDS make much of the claim that Cayce (who died before the discovery of the Dead Sea Scrolls) did identify the precise location of Qumran as the site of an Essenian settlement.

[59] TiR 314. In effect, the description makes of the Christ Soul a kind of Bodhisattva figure.

Joshua, Jeshua'[60]. The Essenes expected the Christ soul to incarnate once again at the beginning of the Piscean Age[61], and began to make preparations: 'it seemed the time had now come to choose and prepare ... a number of girls with the hope, the purpose, that from them one might be selected to become the mother of the messiah'[62]. The education of these selected girls took place at Mount Carmel and was supervised by a woman who was thoroughly learned in the secret teachings of India, Egypt and Persia. Mary, one of the girls, was finally elected by an angel who appeared at the temple steps[63]. She was married to Joseph after having been found pregnant. Jesus's birth, including the star of Bethlehem, choir of angels, and so on, took place exactly as recorded in the New Testament. During the flight to Egypt, Essenes were active in the background, travelling before and behind the family in order to secure safety. In Egypt, of course, Joseph and Mary used the opportunity to study esoteric sources in the library of Alexandria, which predicted the coming of the messiah. At a later stage, Jesus underwent a thorough occult training supervised by the Essenes and the Great White Brotherhood generally. He literally attended school, in preparation for his task:

> He was sent first again into Egypt for only a short period, then into India for three years, then into that later called Persia ... From Persia he was called to Judea at the death of Joseph, then went into Egypt for the completion of his preparation as a teacher. ...
> John, the messenger, the forerunner, was with Jesus during a portion of the period spent in Egypt, though John was in one class, Jesus in another. ... Jesus and John were in Heliopolis "for the periods of attaining to the priesthood, or the taking of examinations, passing the tests there. ... For ... the unifying of the teachings of many lands was brought together in Egypt, for that was the center from which there was to be the radical activity of influence in the earth ..."
> The Great Pyramid was built ... "to be the Hall of the Initiates of that sometimes referred to as the White Brotherhood. In that same pyramid did the Great Initiate, the Master, take those last of the Brotherhood degrees with John ...[64].

Thus Jesus emerges as the Great Initiate, and begins his appointed ministry. All his later actions must be interpreted within the framework of a large and international esoteric network, the teachings of which he presented to the world. The Cayce materials state that Jesus's ministry, crucifixion, resurrection and ascension took place essentially as recorded in the New Testament. Characteristically, however, this biblical literalism and, even more, the traditional

---

[60] ECJC 13.
[61] ECJC 22.
[62] ECJC 22.
[63] ECJC 29-30.
[64] ECJC 70-72. The sometimes strangely worded sentences between double quotation marks are literal quotations from the "readings", which are generally characterized by this language style.

Christian elements found in the Cayce messages have not been emphasized by his later New Age interpreters. In the end it was only the secret Essenic brotherhood, and its links to ancient esoteric traditions, which permanently captured their imagination. Cayce's conservative Christian ideas have never enjoyed a comparable popularity. This eclecticism on the part of his readership is highly characteristic for New Age "historiography" generally.

It is for this reason that, again, there would be little point in presenting here a detailed comparison of the rival accounts of Jesus's life. It seems that New Agers are not interested in incompatibilities between fine (and even less fine) points of historical detail; what matters to them is only the very general belief that Jesus was an Essene and a teacher of esotericism. Shirley MacLaine can serve as a good example of the memory residue that is left in the mind of most New Agers after an enthusiastic rather than critical reading of Cayce, Seth, Ramtha and others. Her account is bound either to shock or to exhilarate the historically-minded:

> The conventional story of the life of Christ is well known. Less well known is his connection to the Essene brotherhood. According to the Dead Sea Scrolls ... Christ was a member of the Essene brotherhood, which, among other things, believed in reincarnation. ... The Essene teachings appear in the Zend-Avesta of Zarathustra. They contain the concepts fundamental to Brahmanism, the Hindu Vedas, and the Upanishads. The tradition of yoga, including hatha and transcendental, all come from the same source as the Essene knowledge. Buddha taught the same principles of Essene knowledge and his sacred Bodhi tree is taken from the Essene tree of Life. And in Tibet the teachings once more found expression in the Tibetan Wheel of Life. ... Traces of Essene teachings appear in almost every culture and religion in the world. ... And of course, Jesus was an Essene teacher and healer. My reason for focusing so strongly on the Essenes ... is because their teachings, principles, values, and priorities in life were so similar to the so-called New Age today. ... Christ demonstrated what we would today call precognition, prophecy, levitation, telepathy, and occult healing. ... So Jesus and the Essenes, with their teachings of love and light and cosmic laws along with the Golden Rule of karma, sound very much like metaphysical seekers in the New Age today. These "new" systems of thought are rooted in ancient masteries and mysteries[65].

4. THE AGE OF PISCES

Christianity

New Age authors have made much of the New Testament passages according to which Jesus used parables when addressing the masses, but revealed the "secrets of the Kingdom of Heaven" only to his inner circle of disciples[66]. That Jesus apparently divulged "esoteric" teachings to his closest "initiates" obvi-

---

[65] GW 214-218.
[66] Matth. 13:10-17; Marc. 4:11-12; Luc. 8:9-10.

ously fits perfectly within the grand scheme that sees him as the Great Initiate who represents the Great White Brotherhood. Much has also been made of
the unexpected discoveries of ancient manuscripts shortly after World War II.
The mysterious sect of Qumran which produced the Dead Sea Scrolls, with
their references to an unidentified "Teacher of Righteousness", is obviously
highly suggestive. Inevitably, occultist authors would interpret the discovery
as a confirmation of their traditional beliefs: the "Teacher of Righteousness"
was, of course, Jesus, and the Essenes represented an esoteric tradition connected with Egypt[67]. To New Agers, the Qumran find was unmistakably providential: these scrolls had lain dormant throughout the Piscean Age, but now
that that age is ending and the world urgently needs a spiritual renewal, they
have "accidentally" been rediscovered. From the very beginning, the function
of the Dead Sea Scrolls within an occultist and New Age context has been to
throw doubt on "official" versions of Christianity, while at the same time adding
conviction to alternative Christian beliefs (or at least to general belief systems
which reserve at least a niche for Christian spirituality). Apparently, from this
perspective, the New Age should not bring the end of Christianity but, rather,
its transformation into a more spiritual and universal vision: more in line with
what are assumed to have been Jesus's original intentions than the dogmatic
faith of the churches. Very similar inferences have been drawn from the discovery of a "gnostic library" near Nag Hammadi in Egypt[68]. To the public at
large, the sudden emergence of a collection of forgotten "gospels" which offer
alternative accounts of Jesus's life and teachings suggests that the New Testament is little more than a thoroughly one-sided and therefore misleading selection. Many have concluded from popular Nag Hammadi literature that Jesus
must originally have been a teacher of *gnosis*, but that his true message was
purposely obscured and misrepresented by the early church fathers, who eventually replaced it by an anti-gnostic theology of their own fabrication[69].
The perspective just outlined might suggest that, from the perspective of New
Age religion, the rise of historical Christianity has been one big mistake, based
on regrettable misinterpretations and misrepresentations of Jesus's message and

---

[67] A perfect example is ECDS.

[68] See Robinson, *The Nag Hammadi Library*. Of the many publications which have appeared
about this "gnostic library", perhaps the most influential in New Age circles is Pagels, *Gnostic
Gospels*.

[69] If some readers expect a critical discussion at this point, I remind them that my concern is
with the *emic* beliefs of New Age religion, not with a comparison between these beliefs and
scholarly interpretations of the Dead Sea Scrolls and the Nag Hammadi library. It is true that
precise textual-historical criticism produces a very different, and certainly far more complicated
picture than the simple and straighforward one which dominates New Age literature. Scholarly
nuance in these matters is appreciated, by New Agers, only if it can be used to defend New Age
beliefs; whenever it undermines those beliefs it is rejected as exemplifying the rigid and dogmatic mindset of the religious and academic establishment.

intentions. Certainly, this interpretation is not alien to New Age thinking; at the very least, New Age thinkers regard it as obvious that the Christian church-es do not adequately reflect Jesus's original intentions. More representative for New Age thinking, however, is that the rise of Christianity should ultimately be valued positively, as a problematic historical phase through which "human-ity" (i.e., western humanity) had to pass: a collective "learning experience" which was necessary in terms of a more universal evolutionary process[70]. The original "theosophical" speculations about the Age of Aquarius, which char-acterize the New Age *sensu stricto*, certainly suggest this; and in the New Age *sensu lato*, as well, the belief that "whatever is, is right" suggests that although the Piscean Age represented a long period of spiritual ignorance, the passage through this "dark age" must have served a higher evolutionary purpose.

Now, if we search our corpus for general characterizations of the "Piscean Age", the results are surprisingly scanty. We find some *ad hoc* ideas, such as Marian Green's suggestion that this era 'encouraged people to act like fish'[71], i.e. collectively, while the Aquarian Age will encourage individuality. Or we may mention Chris Griscom's quite personal preoccupation with the Middle Ages as an age of supreme perversion, due not only to the activities of the inquisition but also because 'we became lost in the tyranny of alchemy'[72] (which to her seems to mean the misuse of sexual power). Furthermore, we should certainly mention the strong tendency in neopagan circles to see the Piscean Age as the logical result of the "great reversal" from matriarchy to patriarchy. The latter is seen as exemplified by religious exclusivism and intol-erance, reaching its culmination in Christianity: the "burning times" are empha-sized as the period in which patriarchy fully revealed its true face of terror and suppression[73]. Essentially the same perspective is found in the work of Matthew Fox: the Christian "fall/redemption" tradition has dominated Christianity, and is an exemplification of patriarchal patterns of thought[74]. In general, such quite general characterizations of the Piscean Age (as dominated by collectivism, patriarchy, intolerance, authoritarianism etc.) are seldom backed up by more concrete historical descriptions. New Agers seem to combine the conviction that the Piscean Age was generally ruled by "ignorance" with a marked lack of interest in the historical development of that age. As a rule, their percep-tion of western history is extremely sketchy, and can therefore be treated briefly here. Interest is restricted to a few key episodes only: the time of Jesus, which

---

[70] See for instance WW 159-160, which connects the Piscean Age with the "patriarchal takeover", but presents this as a necessary, if painful, evolutionary stage.

[71] MAA 8, 32-33.

[72] TI 78; cf. also 79-81.

[73] HBWM 4-7, 238-239, 293; W 29-34; WW 159; SD 18-22; DD 5, 183-219; TD 32-67. Cf. TP 29-30.

[74] See for instance OB 25, 75-77, *passim*.

has been discussed above; the falsification of his message by official Christianity; and the rise of the "Newtonian/Cartesian" paradigm. In other words: interest is focused almost exclusively on diagnosing *what has gone wrong*.

The Rejection of Reincarnation

If New Agers claim that official Christianity has falsified and obscured Jesus's message, this should not be understood as a claim about historical developments: the sources contain only the vaguest of notions about the actual course of events. The claim means simply that the Churches as they exist now are objectionable, but that Jesus himself is not held responsible because he was teaching something else. From these premises it follows that, somewhere along the line, the Church must have lost touch with the true message of Jesus. One specific episode in this process of decline merits special discussion, both because of its intrinsic relevance to New Age religion and because it provides an instructive illustration of the way New Age sources handle historical data.

It is a common assumption of New Age authors that Jesus himself taught reincarnation. Several New Testament passages (Matth. 16:13-14; 17:10-13; John 3:3; 9:1-4) are interpreted in this manner[75]. During the first centuries, it is further argued, reincarnation remained a common Christian belief. In the course of the establishment of the Biblical canon and the doctrinal consolidation of Christian theology, however, reincarnation was discarded. Explicit references by Jesus to reincarnation were removed from the Bible[76], and no efforts were spared to wipe out the traces of its existence in early Christianity. The final and decisive rejection of reincarnation was pronounced at the Fifth Ecumenical Council of Constantinople, in 553. This last motif returns in the work of several authors. Shirley MacLaine in particular has introduced confusion by mixing it up with the Council of Nicea. At one point, Kevin Ryerson tells her that 'The Council of Nicea altered many of the interpretations of the Bible'[77]; when the Council of Constantinople is mentioned, later in the book, as the occasion at which reincarnation was rejected, MacLaine apparently assumes that this must have been the same Council[78]. Actually, the Fifth Ecumenical Council, which was the second one to take place in Constantinople[79], formed

---

[75] For instance by Shirley MacLaine (IAP 217-219) and the Cayce material (TiR 220-221).

[76] See for instance Shirley MacLaine in IAP 217: 'I went into a quick silent meditation, got in touch with my higher self, and said, "Where can I find a reference by Christ to reincarnation in the Bible?" The answer came back: "Most of the references have been discarded, but several still remain. You will find it in the book of Matthew"'.

[77] OL 181.

[78] OL 234-235, 246.

[79] The Farrars are therefore correct to speak of the 'Second Council of Constantinople' (WW 115).

the culmination of controversies over Origen which dated from the late fourth century and were revived in the sixth[80]. It is a common assumption in occultist and New Age circles that, although this Council formally directed its anathemas against the doctrine of preexistence only, they 'also include subtle references to reincarnation'[81]. Very probably, the single most influential source of MacLaine's widely-disseminated belief is the eleventh chapter of Noel Langley's volume *Edgar Cayce on Reincarnation*, which dates from 1967. This chapter is titled 'Why isn't Reincarnation in the Bible? The Hidden History of Reincarnation', and explains the Council's anathemas with reference to political machinations by the emperor Justinian and his wife Theodora[82]. The chapter is backed up by a militantly-worded appendix about 'The Fifteen Anathemas Against Origen', which ridicules the 'idiocy' of these 'deranged' theological formulations[83]. In the context of Langley's account, Origen is depicted as the champion, not only of reincarnation, but of true spirituality in general. Very probably it is from this widely-disseminated source that we owe MacLaine's belief, further popularized by her, that "Nicea" symbolizes the momentous rejection by Christianity of reincarnation and of a whole spiritual worldview implied by it[84].

Cartesian/Newtonian Thinking

With only an occasional exception[85], New Age authors seem to take western history after "Nicea" for granted. What matters is only that, under the regime of an intolerant faith, spiritual wisdom declined. It is added that the flame was kept alive by heretics or secret societies; but details are seldom given. Marilyn Ferguson's approach is typical. She mentions 'alchemists, Gnostics, cabalists, and hermetics', and adds some great names: Meister Eckhart, Pico della Mirandola, Jacob Boehme, and Emanuel Swedenborg[86]. No details are given

---

[80] See for instance Jedin, *Handbuch der Kirchengeschichte*, 127-134.

[81] Head & Cranston, *Reincarnation*, 159. Cf. the discussion of Origen on pp. 144-148. A further influential source is MacGregor, *Reincarnation in Christianity*, of which a whole chapter is devoted to Origen.

[82] ECRE 179-201.

[83] ECRE 281-284.

[84] Ironically, Cayce himself did not share Langley's indignation about the decision of the church to "drop reincarnation". He seems to have regarded it as a wise choice: 'It was difficult to explain, for one thing, and it was difficult to swallow, for another. It made life more complex. It made virtue even more necessary. ... people who didn't examine the theory could easily say, 'Oh, well, we have other lives to live. We won't be sent to hell after this one. So let's enjoy it'. So they fought the Gnostics [sic] and won the battle. What they did was right, I suppose, because without a simplification of the faith it wouldn't have spread. It would have remained a small sect, for intellectuals and students of metaphysics' (TiR 219-220).

[85] WW2, in particular, presents a well-informed overview of western esotericism.

[86] AC 47.

about their teachings or about the historical relations between them; they are simply presupposed to have taught the very same truth which is proclaimed by Ferguson herself: 'We are spiritually free, they said, the stewards of our own evolution. Humankind has a choice. We can awaken to our true nature. Drawing fully from our inner resources we can achieve a new dimension of mind; we can see more'[87]. In Part Three of this study we will see that these traditions actually do form the main backgrounds to New Age thinking (though not for the reasons imagined by Ferguson). Most New Agers focus their attention on the first centuries (the time of Jesus, the gnostics after him), and are surprisingly ignorant about the actual historical roots of their beliefs.

We saw that the history of the Piscean Age, as described in New Age sources, is essentially an analysis of what has gone wrong with spirituality. If "Nicea" and the rise of dogmatic Christianity represented the first major disaster, the rise of "Cartesian/Newtonian" (or "mechanistic") thought represented the second. Again, we encounter a striking lack of precise historical interest. One searches in vain for detailed descriptions of the historical processes involved. What we do find is a series of very general "right-wrong" oppositions, with obvious polemical intentions. Most of these contrast the "new paradigm" favourably with the "Cartesian/Newtonian" paradigm, but one very seldom finds the latter discussed in connection with the preceding Christian worldviews. An exception can be found in the work of Ken Wilber, who describes the rise of modernity in terms of a dialectic between the "eyes" of flesh, reason, and contemplation:

> The point is that Buddhism and Christianity and other genuine religions contained, at their summit, ultimate insights into ultimate reality, but these transverbial insights were invariably mixed up with rational truths and empirical facts. Humanity had not, as it were, yet learned to differentiate and separate the eyes of flesh, reason, and contemplation. And because Revelation was confused with logic and with empirical fact, and all three were presented as *one truth*, then two things happened: the philosophers came in and destroyed the rational side of religion, and science came in and destroyed the empirical side. ... However, theology—which in the West had a somewhat weak eye of contemplation anyway—was so heavily dependent upon its rationalism and its empirical "facts" (the sun circles the earth as the Bible says), than when these two eyes were taken away by philosophy and science, Western spirituality all but went blind. It did not fall back on its eye of contemplation—but merely fell apart and spent its time in futile argument with the philosophers and scientists. From that point on, spirituality in the West was dismantled, and only philosophy and science seriously remained.
> Within a century, however, philosophy as a rational system—a system based on the eye of mind—was in its own turn decimated, and decimated by the new scientific empiricism. At that point, human knowledge was *reduced* to only the eye of flesh. Gone was the contemplative eye; gone the mental eye—and human beings had enough collective low self-esteem to restrict their means of valid knowledge

---

[87] AC 47.

to the eye of flesh—the eye we share with animals. Knowing became, in source
and referent, essentially subhuman[88].

Most New Agers will readily agree with such a conclusion, even if they do not
use Wilber's terminology. In the work of the major "new paradigm" authors,
who deplore the rise of mechanistic science and the worldview it implies, we
find little interest in its historical origins. Capra briefly describes the dominant worldview before 1500 as "organic", and quickly goes on to describe the
"mechanistic" paradigm which replaced it[89]. Ferguson and Grof display even
less interest: they altogether ignore Christianity and simply take the mechanistic paradigm as their point of departure.

The opposition between the "new paradigm" and "Cartesian/Newtonian"
thinking, and more generally between the New Age and the Age of Pisces, will
be taken up further in the next chapter. One final remark must be made here,
concerning a hiatus which may have important implications with respect to
common denunciations of New Age thinking as "irrational". While the rise of
mechanistic science is described again and again in strongly negative terms,
the authors do not usually make references to the eighteenth-century Enlightenment. Apparently, Enlightenment rationality as such does *not* present a grave
problem to New Age religion. It will prove important to ask why this is so, but
I will defer that discussion to Part Three of this study.

5. HISTORICAL RELIGIONS VERSUS UNIVERSAL SPIRITUALITY

It should be clear from the preceding sections that the New Age movement
does have "visions of the past", but displays little or no interest in historiography for its own sake. Instead, we find a conflation between history and myth,
which often makes it difficult to decide where one begins and the other ends.
Moreover, the New Age approach seems to exemplify a phenomenon known
as the "invention of tradition"[90]. Marian Bowman's observations, made in connection with New Age reconstructions of Celtic culture, apply to the New Age
movement generally. Bowman encountered '...a need to root present beliefs
and practices in the past, linking them with previous groups of enlightened
people. ... By sharing a particular view of the past, people belong to a com-

---

[88] EtE:ete 11-12.

[89] TP 53-54. He does not explain whether, and if so, how the New Paradigm is different from
the pre-scientific "organicism" of traditional Christian culture. Somewhat more interest in Christianity is displayed in Sheldrake's later work. RN locates the roots of the mechanistic worldview
in the protestant reformation. There seems to be a latent ambiguity here: Christianity may either
be interpreted as negative (because it is dogmatic, intolerant etcetera) or as positive (because it
had an "organic" worldview). It is not clear how the rejection of official Christianity as "dualistic" might be combined with Capra's emphasis on its "organicity".

[90] The expression derives from Hobsbawm & Ranger, *Invention of Tradition*.

munity, no matter how loosely constituted. The attraction of being heir to an esoteric tradition is immense. By knowing what 'really' happened, the past serves to justify one's present beliefs and practices'[91]. These beliefs and practices therefore constitute the foundation of New Age visions of the past. While the study of practices as such fall outside the scope of the present study, the beliefs in question are highly relevant here. The mytho-historical developments summarized in the preceding sections can be seen as a logical reflection of theoretical beliefs about the relation between historical religions on the one hand, and transhistorical or universal spiritual truth on the other. The religions as such are merely "exoteric", and are generally described in negative terms; the One Truth, however, surfaces again and again as the esoteric depth dimension behind merely outward forms and dogmas, or finds specific expression in more or less secret organizations.

Exoteric Religions

New Age literature contains harsh judgments on historical religions. When Shirley MacLaine asks her channel Kevin Ryerson whether he is religious, he almost chokes on his tea: 'Are you kidding? What church would have me? I'm treading on their territory. I say folks have God inside them. The Church says it has God inside of *it*'[92]. His attitude is confirmed by the channeled entity "John":

> There is much that I am saying that your worldly religions would take exception to. Your religions teach religion—not spirituality. Religion has exploited man for the most part. Your world religions are on the right track basically, but they do *not* teach that every individual is fundamentally the creator and controller of his own destiny. They teach that *God* assumes such a role. What I am endeavoring to explain is that each individual is a co-creator with God. This does not sit well with your churches and religions because they prefer to have control over mankind...[93].

Similarly, Stanislav Grof is at pains to point out the difference between spiritual experience and religion:

> Although we are still far from a comprehensive synthesis, significant elements of [the] emerging paradigm show far-reaching convergence with the worldview of the great mystical traditions.
> However, it is important to emphasize that this does not necessarily mean convergence of science and religion. The spirituality that emerges spontaneously at a certain stage of experiential self-exploration should not be confused with the mainstream religions and their beliefs, doctrines, dogmas, and rituals. Many of

---

[91] Bowman, 'Reinventing the Celts', 153.
[92] OL 181.
[93] OL 198.

them lost entirely the connection with their original source, which is a direct visionary experience of transpersonal realities. They are mainly concerned with such issues as power, money, hierarchies, and ethical, political, and social control. It is possible to have a religion with very little spirituality, complete absence thereof, or even one that interferes with genuine spiritual quest. ...
Spiritual experiences that become available in deep self-exploration typically do not bring the subject closer to the established church and do not inspire more frequent attendance of formalized divine service, whether the religion involved is Christianity, Judaism, or Islam. More frequently, it brings to a clear relief the problems and limitations of established churches and mediates understanding as to where and why religions went astray and lost contact with true spirituality. However, direct spiritual experiences are perfectly compatible with the mystical branches of the great religions of the world, such as the different varieties of Christian mysticism, Sufism, and Kabbalah or the Hasidic movements. ...
Mainstream religions typically advocate concepts of God where the divinity is a force that is outside of human beings and has to be contacted through the mediation of the church and the priesthood. ... In contrast, the spirituality revealed in the process of self-exploration sees God as the Divine Within. Here the individual uses various techniques that mediate direct experiential access to transpersonal realities and discovers his or her own divinity[94].

Similar opinions can be found in a number of other sources[95]. Evidently these ideas about "religions" in general are, actually, largely modeled on western examples. Established Christianity—definitely including its Old Testament heritage[96]—is regarded as the epitome of a non-spiritual religion. The status of oriental religions is left decidedly vague. Not surprisingly, if Judaeo-Christian traditions are specifically discussed, the criticism is even harsher. Examples are easy to find. Z Budapest's hatred of Christianity has already been mentioned, but remains exceptional in its vehemence[97]. Another neopagan, Vivianne Crowley, expresses the common neopagan opinion[98] in her account of the rise of Christianity: 'Christianity, true to its Judaic parent, was an intolerant masculine monotheism and there could be no question of co-existence alongside the older religions'[99]. Matthew Fox, himself a Christian, shares the neopagan criticism; however, he sees the suppression of a Judaeo-Christian tradition of "creation spirituality" by a patriarchal and intolerant "fall/redemp-

---

[94] AS 269-270.
[95] For instance R 35, 145ff; RIC 68, 89-91; SS 371; AE 146-147.
[96] Criticism of Judaism *per se* is, however, seldom. If it occurs at all, it usually concerns the Old Testament and the influence of the latter on Christianity. Statements such as made by Ramtha, about the 'hypocrisy of the laws of Moses' (RI 127; cf. 129), are uncommon.
[97] For instance HBWM 163-165, 235. See for the background of Budapest's hatred HBWM 239: 'My family has painful records of how my ancestors were tortured and killed: how they had to dig their own graves and lie in them, buried alive, only their faces showing, which the Christians then bashed in with iron rods. My heart is filled with eternal distrust towards a religion that sanctioned that genocide'.
[98] Note, however, an occasional exception such as the Matthews' WW1 131-158.
[99] W 29.

tion" theology as the reason for the degeneration of Christian culture. Michael Harner is relieved that 'thinking people have left the Age of Faith behind them. They no longer trust ecclesiastical dogma and authority ...'[100]. Similarly, the Ramala masters do not expect any good from the churches, which have perverted Jesus's message into 'a dogma which has limited the evolution of millions of souls'[101]. Louise L. Hay, finally, reacts to some of the crudest of Christian stereotypes when she ridicules the idea that the creator of the galaxies is nothing but a personal, wrathful deity interested in "sins of the flesh": 'an old man sitting on a cloud above the Planet Earth... watching my genitals!'[102].

In sum: the main complaint about religions is that they have degenerated into institutions of worldly power, which control and exploit the faithful, while denying them individual autonomy over their own lives; that they insist upon authoritarian doctrines, dogmas and rituals but belittle and deny the centrality of individual religious experience; and that they teach an external God rather than the inner divinity disclosed in such personal experiences. Individual freedom and autonomy in matters "spiritual" are apparently the yardstick against which religions are measured, and against which they fall short.

Perennial Wisdom

In spite of the degeneration of historical religions, and of Christianity in particular, New Agers usually believe that most, if not all, religions contain a hidden core of true spirituality. By going beyond the "exoteric" surface phenomena of established religions, one may discover a depth dimension of "esoteric" truth. This true essence of religions is not narrowly sectarian but universal, not exclusive but inclusive, and not dogmatic but experiential. Authoritarian religious structures do not promote a spirituality of inner freedom, but curtail and suppress it. Stanislav Grof quotes a pertinent remark by the psychologist of religion Walter Houston Clark: 'much of mainstream religion reminded him of vaccination. One goes to church and gets "a little something that then protects him or her against the real thing"'[103].

"The real thing" is described in various ways, but always has a holistic quality[104]. According to David Bohm, 'the basic feeling of religion is the yearning

---

[100] WS xi.

[101] RR 187; cf. VR 20-22, 161-162

[102] YHL 136. With relation to Christian asceticism, cf. Houston's PH 7 about the "body apocalypse" of Western culture.

[103] AS 269.

[104] It may be useful to distinguish between "introspective" and "extrovertive" experiences of wholeness (cf. Merkur, *Gnosis*, 16-17). I know of no clear examples in New Age religion of Merkur's third possibility, "communion"). Unambiguous examples of the former are scarce; *A Course in Miracles*, with its radical otherworldliness, is probably the best example (see for instance CiM:T 369, which must be read in context). Examples of the latter, not unusually con-

for wholeness'[105], and he immediately adds that historical religions sadly end up fragmenting that wholeness. Similarly, Matthew Fox states that 'mysticism is ... a common language, uttering a common experience. There is only one great underground river, though there are numerous wells into it—Buddhist wells and Taoist wells, Native American wells and Christian wells, Islamic wells and Judaic wells'[106]. Fox, therefore, emphasizes the positive side to "exoteric" religions: as long as they do not adopt an exclusivist stance, they can provide welcome entrances to the dimension of ultimate wholeness. He refers to that dimension as the "Cosmic Christ", but adds that this concept can be 'no particular tradition's private legacy'[107]: it is not specifically Christian, but pre-Christian and post-Christian as well. Fox specifically mentions Wilber's "isness" and Bohm's "whole" as equivalent terms for the 'living reality' that Christians may prefer to call the "Cosmic Christ"[108].

Neither Bohm nor Fox speak about "esoteric brotherhoods", as is done by Cayce and other theosophically-inspired authors, but they both believe in the existence of a "sophia perennis": a universal wisdom present, potentially at least, as the esoteric depth dimension *in* all great religions. New Agers generally fluctuate between two implications that may follow from such a belief. On the one hand, one may reject all exoteric religions, or take a stance of indifference towards them, because they all *fall short* of the universal esoteric wisdom. This is Bohm's attitude (and, *mutatis mutandis*, the attitude of those who believe in an esoteric "Great White Brotherhood"). On the other hand, one may welcome the plurality and diversity of religions because, although they are limited and culture-bound, they all *provide access* to that same wisdom. This is Fox's attitude, and it is probably more characteristic for New Age thinking than Bohm's. Both groups have in common their rejection of exoteric exclusivism and their belief that true spirituality transcends limited historical forms. New Age ideas about the relation between historical religions and universal spirituality generally fall within the parameters defined by these two positions. Depending on the perspective of the author in question, the perennial wisdom is described in various ways[109]. Whatever its description, however, it always

---

ceptualized as "cosmic feeling", abound: see for instance ToP 11; WA 36 (note that it is described as 'an altogether higher experience than those commonly undergone during rituals'! Although ritual magic is apparently "lower" in status, Green nevertheless focuses all her attention on it, and further ignores unitive experiences. Cf. W 126); GMC 87; PH 186-187; perhaps PST 51; RS 64.

[105] UM 148.
[106] CCC 230.
[107] CCC 241.
[108] CCC 241-242. Fox also mentions Paramahansa Yogananda, Rudolf Steiner and Carl Gustav Jung.
[109] Cf. for references to a "perennial wisdom" W 11-12; WWD 31; AS 265-273; GMC 81-89, 106-107; DL 350; WW1 3; WW2 65 (with criticism of common New Age beliefs: 'The

emphasizes ultimate wholeness and is polemically opposed to exclusivist exoteric religions in general and official Christianity in particular. Ken Wilber, who regards his whole oeuvre as grounded in the perennial philosophy, may serve as an example:

> The essence of the perennial philosophy can be put simply: it is true that there is some sort of Infinite, some type of Absolute Godhead, but it cannot properly be conceived as a colossal Being, a great Daddy, or a big Creator set apart from its creations, from things and events and human beings themselves. Rather, it is best conceived (metaphorically) as the ground or suchness or condition of all things and events. It is not a Big Thing set apart from finite things, but rather the reality or suchness or ground of all things[110].

The "wholeness" that New Agers consider basic to the tradition of "perennial wisdom" is grounded, according to them, not in dogma or rational speculation but in personal experience. The result is an ambiguity which is structurally similar to the one just encountered in relation to exoteric religions versus esoteric truth. On the one hand, the experience of ultimate wholeness must be *universal*, which suggests that all human beings have access to one and the same fundamental reality; on the other hand, the emphasis on the value of *individuality* combined with the irreducible character of individual experience means that *all* personal experiences must be fully honoured and respected. Nobody can be a judge of someone else's experience. Logically, the first option implies that only one kind of experience is "true" in an ultimate and absolute sense, while the second implies that many different kinds of experience are "true". Put differently, religious exclusivism is unacceptable to New Agers, but relativism is equally unacceptable: there must be one universal religious truth, and all religions must be allowed to participate in that oneness. The problem is, of course, what to do with religions which refuse to fit in this scheme because they do not share its premises. The New Age solution is as predictable as it is sobering: either such religions are "false" (dogmatic, exclusivist, merely exoteric etc.), which means that they only masquerade as "genuine" religion; or they represent "lower" levels in a hierarchy, or stages in a process of evolution towards genuine spiritual insight, which means that they are imperfect. Obviously, it is difficult to see how this should be distinguished from other forms of exclusivism or, in some cases, dogmatism. New Age "perennialism" suffers

---

Sophia Perennis is ... a bond between riven traditions. It can easily sink to an intellectual appreciation of comparative religion or a collection of woolly New Age aphorisms where one tradition can easily be substituted for another. Each tradition has its essential character ...'); RR 131-136; ECMM 96; AE 122-124, 146; VAA 23-27; OR 31 (with this both puzzling and characteristic passage: 'The great world religions need not merge and indeed should not merge, for each of them carries a tremendous facet of the Truth. But over all, a real and all-embracing world religion could begin to appear in recognition of the Lord of Light, overlighting all mankind'), 75, 87; UfE 4 and *passim*.
[110] UfE 4.

from the same inner conflict which haunts universalist schemes generally. It is meant to be tolerant and inclusive because it encompasses all religious traditions, claiming that they all contain at least a core of truth; but it qualifies the actual diversity of faiths by pointing out that, whatever the believers may say, there is only *one* fundamental spiritual truth. Only those religious expressions which accept the perennialist premises can be regarded as "genuine". All this can be reduced to two brief and paradoxical formulations: New Age "perennialism" (like perennialism generally) cannot tolerate religious intolerance; and it sharply excludes all exclusivism from its own spirituality. Specific authors may emphasize either one of these two concerns[111], but the conflict as such remains. Religious tolerance on a relativistic basis, which accepts other religious perspectives in their full "otherness", is unacceptable because it sacrifices the very idea that there is a fundamental "truth". It is against this background that we must interpret New Age statements about tolerance, religious diversity and the creative value of syncretism. The general presupposition is that there are many complementary paths which may lead to one goal[112]. Conversely, it is only the conviction that that universal goal is the final destination of all human beings, as well as of human history, which makes the fact of religious diversity acceptable.

---

[111] A particularly strong emphasis on diversity is found in many neopagan sources, for instance W 11, PR 194-195 or (very prominently) WW 175-176.

[112] See for instance W 11.

CHAPTER TWELVE

THE NEW AGE

1. INTRODUCTION

In the Introduction of chapter eleven, I argued that 'New Age thinking is essentially a reaction to the ideas and values which are perceived as having dominated western culture during the last two thousand years'. In this sense, New Age religion is a manifestation of popular culture criticism, defining itself primarily by its opposition to the values of the "old" culture. Accordingly, the "New Age" under the sign of Aquarius will presumably exemplify everything which has been neglected or missing during the Piscean Age. The New Age emerges as the positive mirror image of the Old Age. This is exemplified by the phenomenon of "diagrams of opposition", which may be found in a number of New Age sources. An occasional criticism of such diagrams, as voiced by David Spangler, indirectly testifies to their importance in New Age religion. Spangler points to the 'danger ... of applying the new paradigm in a non-holistic way':

> Often it is contrasted with the older, mechanistic paradigm, which appears to emphasize values of competition, exploitation, profit, centralization, and unlimited material growth at the expense of the environment. We should remember that industrial civilization has brought us many benefits, and that the mechanistic paradigm that supports it is not unrelievedly ugly. Both cultural views share values in common. Nor is the new paradigm absolutely pure and right. It will have its shadows, too. One can already see them in the form of groups that in the name of wholeness trample on individual rights, or individuals who, in the name of self-realization and growth, conveniently forget their accountability to others[1].

These remarks are characteristic of the later, "moderate" Spangler. Few other New Age authors are prepared to say something positive on behalf of the mechanistic paradigm. In *Original Blessing*, Matthew Fox includes a four-page appendix entitled "Fall/Redemption and Creation-Centered Spiritualities compared at a Glance"[2], a briefer version of which appears in *The Coming of the Cosmic Christ*:

from anthropocentrism	to a living cosmology
from Newton	to Einstein
from parts-mentality	to wholeness

---

[1] RS 105.
[2] OB 316-319.

from rationalism	to mysticism
from obedience as a prime moral virtue	to creativity as a prime moral virtue
from personal salvation	to communal healing, i.e., compassion as salvation
from theism (God outside us)	to panentheism (God in us and us in God)
from fall-redemption religion	to creation-centered spirituality
from the ascetic	to the aesthetic[3]

Some of these oppositions reflect Fox's personal "creation-centered" emphases, and many New Agers would replace Einstein by the proponents of quantum mechanics. In most respects, however, the list exemplifies common New Age beliefs about the kind of shift that will (or should) take place. Very elaborate opposition diagrams are to be found in several chapters of Marilyn Ferguson's *Aquarian Conspiracy*[4]. A particularly clear opposition is given by Stanislav Grof, who relates the two paradigms to his "hylotropic" and "holotropic" mode of consciousness respectively[5]. His oppositions are discussed one after the other, but may be schematically compared as follows:

In the hylotropic mode of consciousness, an individual experiences himself or herself as a solid physical entity with definite boundaries and with a limited sensory range. The world appears to be made of separate material objects and has distinctly Newtonian characteristics: time is linear, space is three-dimensional, and all events seem to be governed by chains of cause and effect. Experience in this mode supports systematically a number of basic assumptions about the world, such as: matter is solid; two objects cannot occupy the same space; past events are irretrievably lost; future events are not experientially available; one cannot be in more than one place at a time; one can exist in only one temporal framework at a time; a whole is larger than a part; or something cannot be true and untrue at the same time.

In contrast to the narrow and restricted hylotropic mode, the holotropic variety involves the experience of oneself as a potentially unlimited field of consciousness that has access to all aspects of reality without the mediation of senses. ... Experiences in this state of mind offer many interesting alternatives to the Newtonian world of matter with linear time and three-dimensional space. They support systematically a set of assumptions which are diametrically different from those characterizing the hylotropic mode: the solidity and discontinuity of matter is an illusion generated by a particular orchestration of events in consciousness; time and space are ultimately arbitrary; the same space can be simultaneously occupied by many objects; the past and the future are always available and can be brought experientially into the present moment;

---

[3] CCC 134-135. It is significant that Fox, as a Catholic Priest, does not say "from religion— to spirituality".
[4] AC 229-231 ("Power and Politics"), 270-271 ("Medicine and Health"), 317-319 ("Education and Learning"), 360-362 ("Economics").
[5] AS 239-240.

one can experience oneself in several
places at the same time; it is possible to
experience simultaneously more than
one temporal framework; being a part is
not incompatible with being the whole;
something can be true and untrue at the
same time; form and emptiness or existence and nonexistence are interchangeable; and others.

Although Grof's discussion reflects his own transpersonalist perspective, and
concerns the opposition between two states of consciousness, it amounts to an
overview of the old and the new paradigm as envisioned by him. Apparently,
he hopes for a world in which the validity of the holotropic mode will be generally accepted, so that reality will be perceived from a radically new "spiritual" perspective. Grof can therefore be regarded as a typical example of the
overlap between the concern with a new *scientific* paradigm and the hope for
a new age of *spirituality*.

2. THE AGE OF AQUARIUS

The Timing of the New Age
Like holism, the coming "New Age" is a vision rather than a theory. Talk about
the "Age of Aquarius" reflects the hope that the dominant culture of the present will change for the better. Beyond that shared wish for cultural and spiritual improvement, however, opinions are very diverse. This already begins
with the question of dates. It is not uncommon to encounter the statement that,
although we may not realize it, we have already entered the New Age[6]. In the
foundational work of the early David Spangler, which is devoted entirely to
the New Age theme, this is explained in anthroposophical terms (cf. chapter
seven, section 2B). The "Christ energy" has been impregnating the earth for
about two thousand years, and this process was recently completed. Accordingly, the whole earth has now been fully transmuted on the "etheric level":

It was as if an explosion of light ripped through the old etheric body, altering its
characteristics and raising it into a new level and form already prepared for it,
leaving behind only a memory, an etheric "shell", a corpse, a thought-form of
what it had been. Yet it was a thought-form with a residue of power, much of

---

[6] W 16: 'We have now entered the Age of Aquarius ...'; GW 189: 'We are now in the Aquarian Age, ...'; RBNA 51 (Limitless Love and Truth speaks): '...behold! I have placed my seal upon
this planet. ... I have transformed the planet'.

which came from the consciousness of mankind. Thus, there became two worlds, one of the old, one of the new[7].

The old world is the manifest one; the new one is as yet largely nonmanifest. In the manifest world, however, the Christ presence (Christ life, Christ energy, etc.) has now became fully available, and this is what is meant by the term "the second coming": 'he walks amongst us again, though clothed in etheric energy, and his presence quickens the etheric and spiritual life of all who can open in love and peace and, responding, arise to his level. More and more are becoming aware of his life with us'[8]. This reasonably clear picture is complicated by the fact that 'Limitless Love and Truth' (the channeled entity that dictated large parts of *Revelation*) seems to be the very same being as this Christ energy, but that the latter must not be confused with another, yet greater Being: the second coming of "The Christ"/Limitless Love and Truth is merely a preparation for the coming of the *Cosmic* (or Aquarian[9]) Christ. As stated by Limitless Love and Truth, with an obvious allusion to John the Baptist: 'I prepare the way for One greater than myself'[10]. Even this coming of the Cosmic Christ (cf. Matthew Fox's book of that title) has *already* occurred on the inner planes: 'This embrace has occurred. With the creation and activation of the new etheric body of Earth ... the Cosmic Christ has entered the auric field of the planet, bringing with him revelations without precedence, truly inaugurating a New Age of consciousness for Earth and all upon it'[11]. The crucial implication is that, although the old world is momentarily still dominated by a superseded level of human consciousness, its values are doomed. The old culture may be compared to 'a clock winding down'[12]; although it still exists, the life has gone out of it:

> Individuals who attune to the old will find themselves unable to be truly creative; what they build will not last. On the other hand, New Age individuals are attuned to the highly creative and magnetic energies which characterize this Aquarian cycle. What they put their hands to will prosper; what they build will last; what they create will grow. Thus, the objective world will increasingly take on New Age aspects and forms because only these forms will have the life and power and attunement to survive and prosper and develop[13].

In this way, the New Age has already arrived but will inevitably manifest itself more and more clearly over the years. The description of the process in *Revelation* is backed up with some precise dates[14]. In 1961 'a series of phenome-

---

[7] RBNA 119.
[8] RBNA 121.
[9] RBNA 161.
[10] RBNA 122.
[11] RBNA 123.
[12] RBNA 81.
[13] RBNA 145.
[14] RBNA 125.

na around the world, but centred in Britain, began to manifest'. One of them was the revelation of Limitless Love and Truth, who announced that he would reveal himself 'through the medium of nuclear evolution' on Christmas Day, 1967. Because 'again, man's consciousness tended to interpret this matter in physical objective terms', many expected a cataclysmic event to take place and were disappointed when nothing spectacular happened. However, the reason they did not notice the event was that they were too 'physically oriented':

> Thousands of other individuals around the world ... did experience a remarkable release of energy upon the Earth from higher dimensions. On 31st December, 1967, Limitless Love and Truth announced, 'My universal revelation, through the medium of nuclear evolution is complete ... The whole of nuclear energy is me and my whole power completely under my control ... The universal love flow is increasing. All is well'[15].

From this perspective, Spangler proclaimed the arrival of the New Age; and together with other representatives of what I have called the New Age *sensu stricto*, he endeavoured to hasten its outward manifestation. The later Spangler, as we saw, was to adapt his idea of the New Age to changing circumstances. He even appears to have changed his mind about its inevitability[16].

Spangler's identification of Christmas 1967 as the birth of the New Age is countered by alternative dates mentioned in other sources. Particularly well-known is the so-called "Harmonic Convergence" believed to have taken place on August 16-17, 1987[17]. In spite of such precise examples, we may safely conclude that most New Agers believe that the coming of the New Age roughly parallels the coming of the new millennium, without focusing too strongly on one particular date. Jean Houston, for instance, notes that 'we are clearly at the end of one age and not quite at the beginning of the new one'[18], but gives no dates. This seems to suggest, at least, that the New Age is not very far away. However, it is remarkable that several sources mention dates which are scarcely useful to inspire millennial enthusiasm because they are still hundreds of years in the future. Z Budapest includes an astrological calculation by Anna Kria, which times the beginning of the Aquarian Age in 2376[19]. This is consistent with Marian Green who, although most of her books have the word "Aquarian" in their titles, believes that the New Age will begin some-

---

[15] RBNA 125.

[16] RS 76: 'The new age is not guaranteed; an optimism based on a feeling of inevitability may only lessen our ability to enter into the work necessary to bring a different culture into being. The new age is, instead, an image that can motivate us to act and work for a transformated future ...'. To my knowledge, Spangler has not addressed the manifest incompatibility of this statement with his earlier vision.

[17] Cf. Melton, Clark & Kelly, *New Age Encyclopedia*, 145-146. The belief that 'a particularly powerful cosmic force peaked' at this date derives from the Mexican Jose Arguelles.

[18] PH 213.

[19] HBWM 193.

where 'in the next couple of hundred years'[20]. Murry Hope seems to think that a few hundred years more or less make little difference: 'The approximate date given by astrologers for the commencement of the Aquarian Age is around the year 2000, although by astronomical computation a more precise figure of 2740 is given'[21]. Seth, finally, links the coming of the New Age to a threefold incarnation of the Christ soul, whose mission will be completed by 2075[22].

The "Pathos of Change"

If there is no agreement between the authors about the precise timing of the New Age, neither do they describe its nature in the same way. What we find is a spectrum of opinions: at one extreme there are authors who merely predict a moderate change for the better, while on the other extreme some prophesy an Age of Light characterized by unimaginable splendor and bliss. Both will be discussed below. In addition, we may distinguish a category of New Age conceptions which are neither the one nor the other. They exemplify what I propose to call (with reference to Lovejoy's concept of metaphysical pathos) the "pathos of change". This concerns an essentially vague enthusiasm about the breaking down of traditional patterns and the opening up of new horizons. If anything, this important category of New Age statements gives expression to the sheer thrill of living in exciting times, marked by unprecedented changes and unheard-of opportunities. The character of this pathos of change is best conveyed by direct quotations. Jean Houston puts it like this:

> I see a change. It is vested in the greatest rise in expectations the world has ever seen. It is so far-reaching in its implications that one might call it evolution consciously entering into time, the evolutionary potential asserting itself. It needed a certain critical mass, a certain merging of complexity, crisis, and consciousness, to awaken. Now it is happening. ... And what is happening constellates around the idea of human freedom and human possibilities. The idea of freedom is expanding because the idea of what it is to be human is expanding[23].

Marian Green, also, speaks in very general terms of 'the way things are dying out and great changes taking place':

> A lot is happening, even in the political world ... This is only the start of the many changes the next couple of hundred years will bring. We could be on the verge of a true Golden Age, for the Water Bearer is the Grail Carrier who has found the vessel of rebirth and brought it into the world that its redeeming waters may be poured out for all in need. Also, the magical and supernatural arts will surely be allowed to take their place among the technologies of the future ... If we are strong

---

[20] GAAM 135.
[21] PR 193.
[22] SS 371.
[23] PH 212.

enough to be able to accept change and therefore the magic it brings, and to act with that change, in harmony with the Old Gods and Goddesses, whose being has always been immanent in some form, a wonderful future lies ahead for us[24].

A similar enthusiastic trust in the future expansion of human potential is expressed by Eva Pierrakos's channeled source:

> I am happy to say that quite a number of you are already part of this strong cosmic movement for which you have made yourself available. You experience hitherto undreamed-of expansion and joy, resolutions of problems that you never thought possible. And it continues. There are no limitations to your fulfillment, to the peace, to the productivity, to the creativity of living, to joy, love, and happiness, and to the meaning your life has acquired as you serve a greater cause. ... You are creating a new life for yourself and your environment, of a kind that humanity has not yet known. You are preparing for it, others are preparing for it, here and there, all over the world, quietly. These are the golden nuclei that spring up out of the gray, dark matter of untruthful thinking and living. ... Enter this new phase, my dearest friends, with courage and affirmation. Rise up and become who you truly are, and experience life at its best[25].

Finally, even David Spangler's work may be plausibly interpreted as primarily motivated by the pathos of change:

> The New Age is a concept that proclaims a new opportunity, a new level of growth attained, a new power released and at work in human affairs, a new manifestation of that evolutionary tide of events which, taken at the flood, does indeed lead on to greater things, in this case to a new heaven, a new earth and a new humanity[26].

The "Moderate" New Age
Not all New Agers believe in the advent of "a new heaven, a new earth and a new humanity". Seth, for instance, says that 'A new era will indeed begin—not, now, a heaven on earth, but a far more sane and just world, in which man is far more aware of his relationship with his planet and of his freedom within time'[27]. Matthew Fox hopes for a planetary "mystical awakening" which will stimulate peace, justice and wisdom in our treatment of the planet's resources[28]. The later, "moderate" David Spangler gives a rather detailed 'preview' of the emerging planetary culture. Some likely characteristics will be: an integration of planetary culture with regional cultures; some kind of political world agency, but not at the expense of local and regional bodies; more emphasis on communication, both in technological terms and in terms of inter-

[24] GAAM 211-212.
[25] PST 236-237.
[26] RBNA 91. For some further examples, cf. AC 30-31; SOU 307-311.
[27] SS 375. More information about the New Age is given on pp. 377-379.
[28] CCC 34.

cultural and interpersonal understanding; an emphasis on education as a life-long process; an economy based on the individual's creativity and production; larger economic entities with an accountability to society which transcends the economic sphere *per se*, and more participatory and democratic in character; a planetary spirituality that coexists side by side with separate religions and spiritual disciplines; existence of healing practices which combine techniques of medical intervention with stimulation of self-healing; a new interest in androgyny; and a deeper integration between science and mysticism, technology and ecology: 'In addition to traditional instrumentation and methods of experimentation, there will be added the intuitive capacities of the human mind and soul and its ability to gain information in altered states of consciousness through attunement to the "implicate order"'[29].

It is perhaps a telling fact that, seen within our corpus as a whole, this vision comes across as relatively "moderate" and down-to-earth. Yet, as soon as one attempts to imagine a world in which a planetary spirituality peacefully coexists with separate religions, and multinational corporations are prepared to sacrifice economic interest to the common good, it becomes evident that even this perspective looks like a dream. Spangler himself would probably not disagree but, rather, point out the importance of pursuing one's dreams. He ends RS with calling the New Age "a wild dream":

> I have a dream ... that one day we shall all walk this earth as if it were a new world—and in that time it will be new, for we will see it and ourselves with new eyes and touch each other with a new and gentle spirit. We will know the delight of the sacred within us and around us and the joy of being partners, cocreators, with the earth and with God. Whether my grandchild will witness the fulfillment of this dream is up to all of us[30].

Indeed, many speculations about the advent of the New Age are primarily expressions of the need for faith and optimism in the face of present crisis. Peter Russell draws a picture of what he calls the "high synergy society"[31]. It would be characterized by minimal conflict between the elements of the system and between the elements and the system as a whole; there would be a considerable reduction in crime, violence, international hostility and terrorism; once we would begin to realize that we are 'all of the same spirit, all human beings would become universally sacred'[32] so that war, murder or rape would become anathema; there would be real concern for the environment; we would cease to identify only with our narrow "skin-encapsulated ego", and spiritual values would be a universally accepted part of life; although we would live in

---

[29] RS 107-114.
[30] RS 163.
[31] AE 181-200. The chapter begins with a quotation from Buckminster Fuller: 'The world is now too dangerous for anything less than Utopia'.
[32] AE 182.

harmony, the values of diversity would be increased rather than diminished: 'Social synergy would not therefore imply any form of totalitarian world government'; the present preoccupation with economic growth would be rechanneled in the direction of inner rather than outer growth; attitudes to work and unemployment would change, as would attitudes to illness and health; the brain hemispheres would be more balanced, and in the relations between the sexes there would be a trend towards the ideal of androgyny; the principle of synchronicity would generally be accepted; finally, there would be an increase of ESP and other paranormal phenomena: '... a society of enlightened people could be a society in which we all had such faculties. Unbelievable? Impossible? Or are they an indication of just how profound the transformation could be ... ?[33]'. Like Spangler, Russell explicitly acknowledges the Utopian character of such future perspectives: 'Throughout this book I have been taking a very optimistic view of humanity and its future—and deliberately so. Why? ... because I believe that the image we hold of the future plays a role in helping that future to emerge'[34]. Unrealistic though it may seem, positive thinking about the future is necessary in order to create a more positive reality[35]. However, Russell is not oblivious to the risk of failure. The present world crisis is an "evolutionary test": if we pass the test we will move on to a higher level, but 'if we fail, we will probably be discarded as an evolutionary blind alley'[36]. In remarks like these it becomes obvious that New Age optimism is sometimes the mirror image of an acutely-felt sense of crisis, even despair.

Willis Harman, finally, discusses the New Age as follows:

> Surely it is not too idealistic to imagine a future global commonwealth in which each of Earth's citizens has a reasonable chance to create through his or her own efforts a decent life for self and family; in which men and women live in harmony with the Earth and its creatures, cooperating to create and maintain a wholesome environment for all; in which there is an ecology of different cultures, the diversity of which is appreciated and supported; in which war and flagrant violation of human rights in the name of the state has no legitimacy anywhere, and there is universal support of the rule of law throughout the world; in which throughout the entire human family there is a deep and shared sense of meaning in life itself[37].

We may conclude that "moderate" visions of a New Age combine specific New Age concerns (such as social acceptance of the transpersonal and of alternative healing approaches; convergence of science and mysticism; harmony of opposites such as the brain hemispheres or the sexes, etc.) with quite general

---

[33] AE 200.

[34] AE 201.

[35] Cf. the concept of affirmations discussed in chapter eight, section 3B (par. "The Mechanics of Changing Reality").

[36] AE 207.

[37] GMC 152.

ingredients of a "better world" (harmony and cooperation; reduction or abolition of war, violence and crime; a healthy environment, etc.). Of particular
importance is the oft-recurring emphasis on wholeness which *includes* diversity and individuality[38]. Humanity must become one large family, *but* one which
honours diversity among its members; global wholeness implies some kind of
world economy, *but* one which protects smaller regional economies; a global
spirituality is needed, *but* one which is compatible with a diversity of traditional religions; and some kind of world government may be needed, *but* not
a totalitarian world order which can overrule regional governments and individual freedom. It is only predictable that critics will accuse New Age authors
of wishing to have their cake and eat it too. Actually, this emphasis on unity-
which-includes-diversity is highly characteristic for New Age culture criticism.
Put in abstract terms, New Age authors, firstly, reject patterns of atomistic
"fragmentation": whenever and wherever parts become alienated from the
whole and forget the "higher good", a destructive war of all against all results.
This happens at all levels, whether the "parts" are individuals, economies, religious traditions, or countries. But, secondly, New Age authors also attach
supreme value to individualism at all levels, and reject authoritarianism and
the rule of external "power-over" (Starhawk). Whenever and wherever the
supreme value of "self-responsibility" is sacrificed, violence and oppression
results. Again, this happens on all levels: examples are suppression of individual freedom by church or state; suppression of small "green economies" by
powerful multinationals; or the totalitarian specter of Orwell's *1984*. Wholeness *and* diversity must, therefore, somehow be combined in the New Age. In
putting forward this ideal, New Age authors consistently follow the rule that
the *vision* must come first, and difficult questions of how to implement the
vision come second in line. This fits well with the further assumption that outer change, at all levels, must in principle be preceded by inner change. Critical objections to the effect that New Age authors do not prescribe concrete
measures or take a political stance will therefore fail to convince: New Agers
will regard that very question as reflecting the wrong premises. They are convinced that, in the end, the world will only change when people change first;
failing that, all discussions of practical policy are useless. Accordingly, the
goal of New Age authors is to encourage readers to change their perspective
on reality and thus to change reality itself.
Given the underlying belief-system analyzed in previous chapters, it is perhaps
understandable that even the apparent dilemma of wholeness versus diversity
outlined above is usually ignored on the *emic* level. The dominant assumption

---

[38] Cf. the primacy of "generative source" holism over the emphasis on a "self-sufficient
absolute" (chapter six, section 2A). This cosmological vision is perfectly in line with the social
vision.

is that the practice of "inner development" will resolve the problem. Having re-established contact with one's own higher self, one regains a proper perspective on how one's "separate" individuality is related to the greater whole within the larger perspective of evolution. The relationship of the incarnated and alienated personality to its universal soul, analyzed in chapter eight (section 2B), may be taken as paradigmatic of how the New Age movement looks at relationships between "parts and wholes" generally. Accordingly, only spiritual ignorance creates attitudes of "fragmentation" as well as attitudes of "power-over"; and only spiritual insight can heal dualism and fragmentation on all levels. Therefore the social and political dilemma of wholeness and diversity will only be solved—and the New Age will only be able to arrive—when the basics of New Age spirituality gain acceptance on a global scale.

The Age of Light

Alongside "moderate" visions of the New Age, we find those which describe an unprecedented revolution that will literally transform earth into heaven. The general vision of this "Age of Light" originated in the theosophically-inspired New Age *sensu stricto*, but has obviously influenced the New Age *sensu lato*. Shakti Gawain, for instance, is confident that 'Even the happiest of lives in the old world cannot compare to the depth of fullness and bliss that will be possible at the higher levels of consciousness available in the new world'[39]. Ramtha is similarly optimistic. The 'Age of Flesh' is ending, and we are at the beginning of 'the Age of Light, the Age of Pure Spirit, the *Age of God*', in which humanity regains an 'unlimited' consciousness[40]. Ramtha announces a 'utopia called Superconsciousness, a collective whose social order will differ drastically from what you know it to be now'[41]:

> All of you have been promised for e'er so long that you would see God in your lifetime. Yet lifetime after lifetime you never allowed yourself to see it. In this lifetime, most of you will indeed. You will live to see a magnificent kingdom emerge here, and civilizations will come forth that you had not even the slightest notion existed. And a new wind will blow. And love, peace, and joy in being will grace this blessed place, the emerald of your universe and the home of God[42].

The Ramala masters, too, assert that 'all things will be possible in the New Age'[43]. The changes will be so momentous that human beings will be able to survive them only if they themselves undergo radical change:

> You will not be able to survive the changes that are to come simply by adapting

---

[39] LL 4.
[40] R 150.
[41] RIC 145.
[42] RI 6-7.
[43] WR 117.

physically, for the physical body that you are seeking to protect will not exist in the New Age. The physical structure of the human beings that will dwell in the New Age will have changed radically. Whereas, now, a large percentage of your body is water, in the New Age it will be air. ... The human form will be different and will vibrate to a different note. The physical nature of the Earth will be very different. The angels and the great Masters will actually be present on Earth, in physical appearance, and will walk and talk with you. The whole structure of matter, the frequency range in which you live, vibrate and have your being will have been altered. Therefore only one thing, only one factor, can guarantee your survival, if that is indeed your concern, in the natural cycle of this change and that is consciousness, your soul consciousness. For it is your soul that will build the body that you require, that will change the atomic structure of your being and so prepare you for the life of the millennium which is to come—the Golden Age of Aquarius[44].

Sanaya Roman's description is apparently indebted to a vision similar to Spangler's coming of the "Cosmic Christ". She speaks of the advent of a cosmic 'wave of energy passing through your galaxy that is altering the course of all life it touches. This wave affects the very nature of energy and matter, bringing all matter into a higher vibration'[45]. Initially, this energy-wave seems to have surprised even Roman's channeled source Orin: he describes how he and his fellow-entities "investigated" the wave and discovered that 'it is light and it is conscious'[46], and that it assists evolution and growth. As a result of its influence, humanity is 'rapidly evolving into a new race of beings ... a telepathic race'[47]. The new human will have a 'body of light that is able to vibrate at a higher frequency and radiate light'[48]. As a result:

> What you struggle so intently with now—to be more loving, to believe in yourself, to forgive, to have compassion, and to release pain and negativity, will be easier in future times as human energy systems become more evolved. Humanity will have a more fully formed body of light and will become a radiating source of light[49].

As the New Age comes, many "high guides" make themselves available for channeled advice. Even the very nature of time is changing: we move from linear time to 'a more intuitive time'[50]. Earth gravity will be altered slightly, and changes will occur in the electromagnetic frequencies of the earth. The influence of the wave of light will be particularly strong at so-called 'power spots'[51]: energy centers on the earth surface comparable to acupuncture points

---

[44] VR 63.
[45] SG 1.
[46] SG 1.
[47] SG 2-3.
[48] SG 155.
[49] SG 155.
[50] OtC 218.
[51] See OtC 165, 167; SG 5.

on the human body. Between these points all over the earth, a network of light will spread which encompasses the earth.

Probably the single best source for descriptions of the "Age of Light" is the work of George Trevelyan. The cover of *Operation Redemption* shows an angelic being, complete with large wings, standing over the earth. Its arms are outstretched to a source of white light above it, the light of which enters its head from above, and is apparently received in its heart. From its feet extend a kind of tentacles which encompass the earth globe. The angelic being apparently acts as a mediating figure, "channeling" the light from above to the earth below, thus assisting "Operation Redemption" which brings in the New Age. Trevelyan speaks of a 'Second Coming' which brings in 'a New Birth on a planetary and cosmic scale'[52]. Humanity will evolve to 'fourth and fifth dimensional awareness'[53]. The release of 'powerfully creative and uplifting energies' will result in 'a new civilization based upon enduring values of love, truth, joy, peace and the ideal of service ...'[54]. The people and the governments of the world can choose either to resist or to recognize the 'higher wisdom and intelligence which is being made available to us'[55]. Only the last option will prove effective in the end, and will result in 'a universal civilization—a true brotherhood of Man upon Earth'[56]. In this new civilization, people will no longer be able to kill; cruelty to animals will be intolerable; war will cease and non-violence will be the rule: 'The basic values of tolerance, honesty, respect for truth, cooperation and compassion will become ever more manifest, while the very capacity to deceive another, to bear false witness, steal or murder will be eradicated from the patterns of human behaviour'[57]. Long descriptions of the blessings of the Age of Light may be found throughout Trevelyan's oeuvre. They all amount to the same thing: a momentous "cleansing of the planet" will result in radically positive change, unlimited "light and love", bliss, happiness, peace and plenty. Before his mind's eye, Trevelyan sees how 'an etheric mantle of light is gathering around the earth'[58]; this 'redemptive flow' will lift the consciousness of humanity towards a higher dimension, and then all will be well.

Trevelyan assures his readers that 'we are not talking about naive optimism, pious hopes or airy idealism', but adds that 'The New Age is not a social plan based on intellectual concepts'[59]. It should certainly be clear from the above that radical visions of the "Age of Light" are qualitatively different from the more moderate visions of an improved society. Only the former can be regard-

---

[52] VAA 22.
[53] VAA 77.
[54] VAA 63.
[55] VAA 64.
[56] VAA 64.
[57] VAA 69.
[58] VAA 114.
[59] VAA 69.

ed as an unambiguous case of New Age millenarianism. The coming of the Aquarian Age conceived as a religio-spiritual rather than a socio-political event is heavily indebted to the theosophically-inspired New Age *sensu stricto*. If the vision of an improved future dominated by a new paradigm/vision of reality constitutes one extreme on a scale of New Age visions, then the vision of the millenarian "Age of Light" constitutes its logical opposite. The middle range between both extremes provides room for a variety of more ambiguous visions, in which elements of both may be combined in various ways.

3. THE SHIFT FROM OLD TO NEW

It can roughly be said that "moderate" approaches to the New Age mostly call on human beings to accomplish a spiritual reorientation, while visions of the "Age of Light" mostly emphasize some kind of outside intervention. Accordingly, the first vision takes the possibility of failure more seriously than the second. Within these parameters, various ideas are in circulation about how the shift from the old to the new culture will or should take place. In all cases, the background to New Age visions is an acute sense of crisis, and of humanity having arrived at a crucial "turning point" situation. This is most often explained in the context of a larger process of evolution. Believing that we have arrived at a turning point in evolutionary history, some New Age authors call on humanity to take the right steps in order to fulfil the evolutionary purpose. A distinct minority believes that, whatever steps we take, the great reversal will come in any case.

The Potentials of Crisis
The starting point of the hoped-for transformation lies in an acutely-felt sense of crisis. New Age literature is pervaded with assertions to the effect that the development of western culture has now brought us to a point of extreme danger to humanity and the planet as a whole. Fritjof Capra begins *The Turning Point* as follows:

> At the beginning of the last two decades of our century, we find ourselves in a state of profound, world-wide crisis. It is a complex, multidimensional crisis whose facets touch every aspect of our lives—our health and livelihood, the quality of our environment and our social relationships, our economy, technology, and politics. It is a crisis of intellectual, moral, and spiritual dimensions; a crisis of a scale and urgency unprecedented in recorded human history. For the first time we have to face the very real threat of extinction of the human race and of all life on this planet[60].

---

[60] TP 21.

Capra goes on to discuss some examples: nuclear catastrophe, mass starvation in many parts of the world, the environmental crisis, a corresponding crisis in health care, widespread social and psychological disintegration, and a malfunctioning economy. He argues that the root of all these problems is a crisis of *perception* due to an outdated mechanistic worldview, and proceeds to outline the characteristics of the "rising culture" which will be based on an alternative paradigm and a corresponding view of reality. Similary, Willis Harman describes the various aspects of the crisis as 'interconnected components of what we might call the one world macroproblem', and argues that 'they are consequences of a mind-set and the behaviors and institutions associated with it ... which brought great benefits in the past but now creates problems faster than it solves them. The world macroproblem will be satisfactorily resolved only through fundamental change of that mind-set'[61].

A sense of crisis and potential doom is evident in the work of many other authors. Marilyn Ferguson refers to the literary device of the "Black Moment" (the point at which all seems lost just before the final rescue) and its counterpart in tragedy known as the "White Moment" (a sudden rush of hope for salvation just before the final inevitable disaster): 'Some might speculate that the Aquarian Conspiracy, with its hope of a last-minute turnabout, is only a White Moment in Earth's story; a brave, desperate try that will be eclipsed by tragedy—ecological, totalitarian, nuclear. *Exeunt* humankind. Curtain'[62]. Such examples suggest how seriously the crisis is experienced. Expressions of deeply-felt concern, sometimes of evident despair, about the world situation may be found in the works of very different authors. Matthew Fox has nightmares about the dying of the earth and of all human and spiritual values[63]; Shirley MacLaine describes a rapidly deteriorating culture[64]; Starhawk is haunted by visions of a nuclear holocaust, ecological disaster and general decline of human values[65]; Peter Russell compares humanity to a sort of 'plan-

---

[61] GMC 111-112.

[62] AC 45.

[63] OB 12-15; CCC 11-34 is based on a dream of despair. Fox describes the crisis under these headings: 'Mother Earth Is Dying; The Mystical Brain is Dying; Creativity is Dying; Wisdom is Dying; The Youth are Dying; Native Peoples, Their Religions, and Cultures Are Dying; Mother Church is Dying; Mother Love (Compassion) is Dying'. Fox ends, however, with a reminder to his reader that 'Our Mother is Dying, but Not Dead'.

[64] OL 7; DWYC 12. MacLaine's entity "John" speaks of 'progressive insanity, depression, confusion of purpose, and total human inequality and despair' (OL 198). MacLaine feels that the world is heading for disaster: 'time is running out' (OL 327).

[65] DD was written as an attempt to exorcize fears of nuclear holocaust: 'For me, the journey began in a place of despair. During the writing of the early versions of this book's first chapter, I was haunted by visions of annihilation. Images of the city destroyed, of curling flesh, of the sudden flash in the sky—then nothing. I could not look at a friend, at my family, at children, without picturing them gone. Or worse, the long, slow deterioration of everything we love. ...

etary cancer' constituting a deadly threat to Gaia's survival[66]; and even such a
convinced believer in the Age of Light as George Trevelyan does not always
succeed in concealing his moments of despair: 'It is likely that we have gone
so far in our evil and ignorant ways that repentance ... cannot in itself repair
the damage. We need ... the aid of higher power. That power *does* exist and *is*
alert to the crisis. In this fact lies our hope. ... The Creative Intelligence perhaps revels in games of brinkmanship. But there is still time, if only just enough
...'[67].

Trevelyan is one prominent example among several New Age authors who
speculate that the outbreak of nuclear war might actually be the signal for the
Age of Light to begin. In a highly characteristic passage (which also exemplifies the British chauvinism of many New Agers *sensu stricto*) Trevelyan
announces that if only the "Folk-Soul" of Britain would allow itself to be
impregnated with the Christ power, it would be protected from nuclear attack:
'Then (O science fiction!) the Russian rockets fired at our unresisting land,
would, when they reached the protective barrier, simply disappear! The situation would be so dramatic, so totally contrary to rational and logical thinking,
that the Divine Power could no longer be ignored and would have to be admitted'[68]. Some pages later, Trevelyan asserts that full-scale nuclear war will not
be allowed by the powers of Light: 'Is it not more probable that the pressing
of the button will be the signal for a controlled and vast demonstration of light
filling the heavens?'[69]. The same idea appears in the work of the early Spangler: if 'a human press-button device would be used ... simultaneously with the
pressing of the button, instead of disaster, the universal Revelation would
occur'[70]. And a similar line of reasoning is found in the work of Chris Griscom,
who suggest that our evolution into "light beings" will render nuclear radiation harmless: 'Radiation is light. We are in the evolutionary process of becoming light bodies. ... One word describes our choice: *adapt*'[71]. Actually, Griscom
is saying that the spiritual evolution of humans into "light beings" has become
a necessity of survival[72].

Despair pushed me into an obsession with history, in particular, the crucial sixteenth and seventeenth centuries. I had to know how we got into our present predicament'.
   [66] AE 19-20.
   [67] VAA 108. Latent feelings of despair may also be suspected behind an occasional almost
suicidal remark: 'Let us admit that a great tidal wave would be the quickest way to the New
Jerusalem!' (OR 181).
   [68] OR 189.
   [69] OR 194.
   [70] RBNA 63. Cf RBNA 64: ("Limitless Love and Truth" speaking) 'Should nuclear devices
be used, the energies will be the revelation of me. All that will remain is what I am and all that
is not of me shall disappear ...'.
   [71] ENF 78.
   [72] ENF 128: 'We just did something we can't fix, like Chernobyl. What are we going to do

Many more examples of the sense of crisis, impending doom and the consequent necessity of radical change may easily be found[73]. The examples just given already suggest that the occurrence of a "crisis" need not be evaluated negatively in all cases. Often, it is conceptualized as a necessary and therefore healthy aspect of *evolution*. Thus, Shakti Gawain seems to welcome the crisis as a decisive step towards "world healing":

> People frequently talk about what terrible shape the world is in. In many ways, things seem to be going from bad to worse, and this can be very frightening. It has helped me considerably to recognize that the world is currently going through a major healing crisis, very similar in form to what individuals are experiencing. When we as individuals begin to wake up to the light, we also begin to become aware of the darkness in which we have been living. ... Fears and distortions which have been denied and ignored because they were too painful to look at begin to come into our consciousness in order to be released. Problems that were "swept under the rug" come forth to be solved.
> This is what I see happening on a worldwide level today. If we recognize the seeming chaos and pain in the world as a giant manifestation of our individual healing process, we can see that it's a very positive step[74].

According to another frequent belief, the current crisis constitutes a major "bifurcation point" in evolution. This idea is an application of Prigogine's theory of dissipative structures: if the condition of such a system is "far from equilibrium", small fluctuations are sufficient to suddenly drive the whole system over a critical threshold and to an entirely new and higher level of complexity. Thus, Marilyn Ferguson suggests that the current "disequilibrium" of society provides the appropriate conditions of heightened stress in which a 'dissident minority like the Aquarian Conspiracy'[75] may effect a complete social transformation[76]. The main attraction of Prigogine's theory seems to have been that it allowed Ferguson to entertain hope rather than feel passively powerless in the face of overwhelming global problems. Ferguson conveniently chose not to emphasize the fact, noted above, that Prigogine actually depicts a 'dangerous and uncertain world'[77], in which no happy ending is guaranteed because tiny random events may have unpredictable consequences. Peter Rus-

---

now? Dematerialize it, because that's the only choice we have. The threshold between the manifest and the unmanifest worlds allows matter to pass both ways. We are now in a place where if we do not use the higher mind that we have, we will not survive. We all know that'.

[73] For some further relevant statements, including extensive listings of the vices of modern society, see WW 159; WR 193; SOC 207; LL 183-184; BB 429; PH xiv-xv; SOU 73-74;

[74] LL 183; cf. RG 23-24.

[75] AC 180.

[76] For Ferguson's complete argument, see AC 170-181. Cf. Prigogine's statement in OC 176: 'Under certain circumstances ... the role played by individual behavior can be decisive. ... We expect that near a bifurcation, fluctuations or random elements would play an important role, while between bifurcations the deterministic aspects would become dominant'.

[77] OC 313.

sell, in contrast, openly includes the possibility of failure in his Prigoginean account of the world crisis:

> ...extreme fluctuations within dissipative structures can lead to the emergence of new levels of organization. In evolutionary terms the fluctuations appear at periods of instability, or crises, in which organisms are forced either to adapt to the changed environment—perhaps moving on to higher levels of organization—or be extinguished ...
> In the present day it is readily apparent that society is also going through some major crises. Looking at humanity from the perspective of dissipative systems, we can see that the two principal characteristics of a major fluctuation are present: increasing throughflow of energy and matter, combined with high entropy. ... This is apparent as increasing disorder both within society (e.g. rising social unrest, increased crime and growing economic chaos), and in the surroundings (e.g. increasing despoliation of the environment and rising pollution).
> We would seem to be rapidly approaching the breaking point. And there are two possible outcomes—breakdown or breakthrough[78].

Evolution of Consciousness
Whether or not they regard a crisis to be necessary, New Agers generally believe that we are living at a crucial "turning point" in the evolution of consciousness. Critics might comment on an apparent discrepancy between belief in an Aquarian Age of limited duration, on the one hand, and belief in a decisive evolutionary advance, on the other. The first option suggests a vision of recurring cycles; the second one suggests a scheme of linear progression. Although it would probably not be impossible to integrate both options within one macrohistorical model, New Agers typically do not address this problem at all[79]. This marked absence of interest once more confirms the interpretation of the New Age movement as based primarily on a popular criticism of modern western culture. Accordingly, the all-important point for New Agers is to emphasize the urgent necessity of *change*. The precise function of the hoped-for New Age in the larger scheme of things is felt to be a merely theoretical problem of minor interest. For this reason, it is pointless to require too much precision about the evolutionary significance of the "new consciousness" that New Agers associate with the coming of the New Age. Whether it will be a temporary phenomenon (ending together with the Age of Aquarius, i.e., in circa 2000 years) or a permanent acquisition; whether in this last case it represents a stage which will be followed by yet higher developments, or the final consummation of all evolution (as seems to be suggested by the perfect bliss of the "Age of Light"); and how this latter vision of earthly perfection relates to the vision

---

[78] AE 52-53.
[79] I noted something similar at the beginning of chapter eleven, section 1.

of unlimited cosmic expansion in ever "higher dimensions": all these questions remain wide open. New Agers simply focus their attention on one aspect or another, but seldom on the relatedness of the aspects.

The all-important point, as was noted, is the need for *change*. Since the world situation is moving from bad to worse, and since reality is created by consciousness, it is human consciousness that must change radically in order to reverse the tide. This is the simple foundation of the New Age belief in an imminent "evolution of consciousness". Many descriptions of the new consciousness follow directly from their function as an expression of culture criticism and a sense of crisis. David Bohm and F.David Peat argue that humanity is caught up in a 'destructive generative order' which may well produce a 'cataclysmic failure of the human race'; they therefore call for a 'new creative surge' (and even 'a *new order* of creative surge') which should produce a new way of doing science, a new society and a new kind of consciousness[80]. The Farrars likewise assert that 'homo sapiens is on the threshold of an evolutionary leap in his psychic functioning', immediately after a discussion of the world crisis[81]. Jean Houston reminds her readers that 'we find ourselves in a time in which extremely limited consciousness has the powers once accorded to the gods', and infers from this that now must be the time for a decisive evolutionary breakthrough to multidimensional consciousness[82]. David Spangler prophesies the 'emergence of a new kind of consciousness, an intuitive-mental awareness, attuned to a level of knowing and power unlimited by space and time', opposing it to the old consciousness which is bounded by concepts of separation, space and time[83]. George Trevelyan, in the same context, speaks of a 'new type or species of humanity', called 'Homo sapiens noeticus'[84] and elsewhere referred to as 'a superior race'[85]. This selection could easily be expanded further. Although there is general agreement that humanity has now arrived at an evolutionary crisis or turning point, and can progress towards a new and higher consciousness, opinions differ with regard to the role human beings play in this process.

---

[80] SOC 207-209.

[81] WW 279.

[82] PH 213.

[83] RBNA 99-100.

[84] OR 69-70; EiG 21. Vgl. EiG 31, 146.

[85] EiG 21. In speaking of a new man, a superior race etcetera, readers will inevitably be reminded of Nietzsche's *Übermensch* including its fascist associations. Trevelyan seems to share in a certain naivity with which many adherents of modern theosophy still speak of human "races" but, like the large majority of theosophists, he does not use the term in a fascist sense (about the oft-recurring idea that the New Age movement is (quasi-)fascist, see Hanegraaff, 'Verschijnsel New Age', 94-96).

The Human Contribution: Creating Critical Mass

Many New Age authors are decidedly ambivalent about the role played by human action in the coming of the New Age. Visions of 2000-year cycles, a progressive evolution of consciousness, or the coming of the Cosmic Christ all suggest that the New Age is inevitable; many New Agers, however, apparently realize that this view may easily breed passivity, and therefore emphasize the importance of the human contribution. We have already seen that David Spangler moved from his early "interventionist" perspective to the conviction that the New Age will have to be created by human action. However, although a figure such as Starhawk may strongly promote social and political action, the overwhelming majority of authors emphasize "inner work". Shakti Gawain is a typical example:

> Some ... become angry because they believe I am endorsing a narcissistic self-absorption that denies the problems of the world and negates the necessity of social and political action. Upon further discussion I am usually (though not always!) able to make them understand that this is not the case. Being willing to deal internally and individually with the original source of the problem is simply the most practical and powerful way to effect real change. ... The underlying cause of world problems is the pain, fear, and ignorance we experience from being disconnected from the power of the universe. If we continue to project our problems outside of ourselves and fail to recognize the inner power we actually have, I believe we will support the very evils we are fighting. On the other hand, if we are willing to take responsibility for our fears and deal with them, we will clear the way for being able to hear the voice of the universe within us. If it tells us to take action, we can be sure the action will be powerful and truly effective[86].

On the basis of such a perspective, many authors do emphasize that, although the opportunities may be particularly favourable at the present historical moment, the decisive shift to the New Age must still be accomplished by human beings[87].

The most typical and widespread expression of the belief that a transformed minority may effect world-wide change is known as the theory of *critical mass*. This theory can be traced to the story of the so-called "Hundredth Monkey Phenomenon" told in Lyall Watson's book *Lifetide* (1979)[88]. According to Watson, primatologists studying the behaviour of wild macaques on the islands off the coast of Japan noticed a baffling phenomenon in the fall of 1958. The researchers observed how a female monkey washed a potato in order to remove sand and grit from it. She taught the trick to other members of the group, and

---

[86] LL 184.
[87] For instance MAA 11; GMC 157; OL 364; WR 193.
[88] Watson, *Lifetide*. For the dissemination of the story to a wide New Age audience, see Clark, 'Hundredth Monkey'. For a critical review, see O'Hara, 'Of Myths and Monkeys, 61-78.

soon all the monkeys were cleaning potatoes in the same way. At that point, something extraordinary happened:

> Let us say, for argument's sake, that the number (of potato washers) was 99 and that at 11 o'clock on a Tuesday morning, one further convert was added to the fold in the usual way. But the addition of the hundredth monkey apparently carried the number across some sort of threshold, pushing it through a kind of critical mass, because by that evening almost everyone in the colony was doing it. Not only that, but the habit seems to have jumped natural barriers and to have appeared spontaneously, like glycerine crystals in sealed laboratory jars, in colonies on other islands and on the mainland in a troop at Takasakiyama[89].

Watson himself seems to have scarcely believed his eyes but, as noted by a historian of New Age religion, 'the story was quickly seized upon by those who thought they had found a way the human race might avert nuclear war'[90]. Ken Keyes published a bestselling book *The Hundredth Monkey* in 1982[91], and a movie about the subject was produced by Elda Hartley[92]. To Peter Russell, as to many other New Agers, the theory implies that once the number of people who have achieved "higher consciousness" will have reached a certain "critical mass", enlightenment will suddenly spread as a chain-reaction throughout society. Russell quotes several authorities (Teilhard de Chardin, G.I. Gurdjieff, and the Maharishi Mahesh Yogi[93]) as having suggested the same. Explicit or veiled references to the theory of critical mass, either with or without reference to the "hundredth monkey", may be found throughout our corpus[94]. David Bohm believes that even a group of ten fully committed persons, having achieved a higher consciousness, could effect a decisive change: 'Even one man like Hitler who had a great passion, had a tremendous effect, though for destruction. If there had been ten people with Hitler's passion, all working together, nobody could have resisted them'[95]. It seems somewhat bizarre that while the scientist Bohm believes a number of ten people to be sufficient, an "extreme" believer in the Age of Light such as George Trevelyan mentions a far "safer" number: 'We are told that if fifty million people will simultaneously think and pray Peace for an hour in meditative stillness, then it will suf-

---

[89] Watson as quoted by Clark, 'Hundredth Monkey', 226. The same quotation appears in AE 176, but Russell leaves out the reference to glycerine crystals.

[90] Clark, 'Hundredth Monkey', 226.

[91] Keyes, *Hundredth Monkey*. 300.000 copies were distributed during the first year. It was translated into nine languages and reached a sale of more than a million copies within a few years (Clark, 'Hundredth Monkey', 226).

[92] Clark, 'Hundredth Monkey', 226.

[93] Essentially the same theory is indeed strongly promoted by the Maharishi's Transcendental Meditation movement. As noted in chapter five, TM is a major influence on Russell's worldview.

[94] Apart from the sources quoted in the main text: TP 418-419; AC 26; LL 178-179; PH 212

[95] HP:euu 79. Cf. mf 86.

fice to start such a chain reaction, such 'morphogenic resonance'"[96]. This last term refers to the obvious resemblance between the theory of critical mass and the theory of morphic resonance developed by Rupert Sheldrake. Since his theory looks as though it was devised especially in order to solve the Hundredth Monkey enigma, it has generally been assumed that Sheldrake is a defender of the hundredth-monkey theory[97]. Actually, the story as told by Watson is conspicuously absent from Sheldrake's work. Since it is hard to believe that he would not be aware of it, this is most likely a deliberate choice. Sheldrake probably realized that the scientific credibility of his already "heretical" theory could only be adversely affected by association with a doubtful popular legend. Particularly revealing is *The Rebirth of Nature*, in which Sheldrake explicitly discusses the hope for a 'new millennium' and asserts the real power of group prayers for world peace[98]. One might expect morphic resonance to be mentioned here as a scientific explanation of the efficacy of prayer, but that connection, so obvious to Trevelyan and many other New Agers, is not made by Sheldrake himself. This leads to a remarkable conclusion. Sheldrake is admired by many New Agers because they believe him to have given scientific credibility to the theory of critical mass and thus to the idea of a sudden transformation of society. The connection made by his followers is, however, not shared by Sheldrake himself. With respect to popular New Age theories of critical mass, he seems to be a sceptic rather than a believer.

Images of Intervention
The theory of critical mass may be interpreted in several ways. Many New Agers will argue that, while the sheer enormity of the world crisis tends to paralyze people, the theory of critical mass is "empowering". By suggesting that even individuals can make a real difference, it stimulates people to pursue inner transformation. David Spangler, on the other hand, suspects that the theory may breed passivity: 'people are simply waiting for this quantum leap that will make the world right again'[99]. Indeed, it seems that this latter attitude is as widespread as its opposite. A strong belief in the ultimate perfection of the cosmic process may easily be felt to imply that the coming of the New Age is an inevitable evolutionary event. Examples involving superhuman cosmic processes, such as waves of energy or an "accaleration of frequency", as

---

[96] EiG 157.
[97] Clark, 'Hundredth Monkey', 226 incorrectly states that 'The political and scientific implications of the phenomenon are examined in Rupert Sheldrake's *A New Science of Life*'. Lyall Watson or the hundredth monkey appear neither in NSL nor in PP or RN.
[98] RN 221-223.
[99] RS 97.

described by the early Spangler or Sanaya Roman, have already been discussed above[100]. In addition, it is not unusual to find the belief that the late 20th century is a time in which many souls are incarnating with the specific intention of helping to bring in the New Age[101]. The consistent theme is that the decisive shift towards a New Age is steered not primarily by human action, but by the higher powers of Light which operate from invisible levels of reality. This belief does not necessarily imply that a happy ending is guaranteed, for humanity may still frustrate the process by stubbornly refusing to cooperate. However, the interventionist perspective does strongly suggest that if only we let "operation redemption" run its course, the world will be saved.

In chapter five I noted that, with few exceptions[102], only the New Age *sensu stricto* can properly be called millenarian or apocalyptic. It seems that strong interventionist beliefs are based almost entirely on the theosophical frameworks which are characteristic for this group. Accordingly, the clearest examples of apocalypticism are found in the work of the early Spangler, Trevelyan and the Ramala masters; and to these must be added the Cayce material, which is also strongly influenced by modern theosophy. The only New Age apocalypticist without an overt theosophical background is Ramtha[103].

Edgar Cayce predicted that momentous "earth changes" would take place in the period between 1958 and 1998[104]. He mentioned a shifting of the earth's gravity poles accompanied by great upheavals such as earthquakes and floods. These cataclysms would be accompanied by the reappearance of Atlantis[105], which would rise from the sea in a period which would see the simultaneous rediscovery of Atlantic historical records hidden in the vicinity of the great pyramids.

A very similar picture is presented by the Ramala masters. Due to the ongoing process of evolution, the "vibration" of the other planets of our "Solar Body" is gradually quickening. Our earth, however, is falling behind: at the moment, it is 'toppling, or swaying, almost like a spinning top which is about to stop'. In order to prevent that, the Great Beings are now artificially quickening the earth's vibration. This process is accompanied by 'great confusion

---

[100] Cf. also Capra's belief in the inevitable decline of the old cycle and rise of the new, in TP 418-419; or Gawain's emphasis on the evolutionary necessity of the current crisis: RG 23-24.

[101] TI 200-201; PR 193.

[102] One might think of Erich Jantsch, although his case is somewhat ambiguous. He seems to welcome the possibility of a worldwide catastrophe from an evolutionary perspective which reminds one of Hegel's "cunning of reason". See the quotation in chapter ten, section 2 (par. "Non-Dual Ethics and the Problem of Relativism").

[103] Which does not necessarily mean, of course, that this source was not influenced by theosophical thinking at all.

[104] The best source is SP, which is presented as an overview of "The life, the prophecies and readings of America's most famous psychic" but concentrates very strongly of the prophecies.

[105] Actually, Atlantis should have appeared already in 1968 or 1969 (SP 229).

and disruption'[106]. According to *The Revelation of Ramala* (published in 1978), the last years of the twentieth century will be characterized by earthquakes, heavy rains and floods, droughts, famines and plagues. Among other thing, the 'Insect Kingdom' will cover the earth[107]. There will be seven great plagues, the first of which is AIDS: an epidemic that is due to humanity's abuse of sexuality[108]. A much worse disease is in the making[109]. In the course of events, old structures will be wiped out and the world will be totally transformed. The Ramala masters, also, say that Atlantis will reappear, and they add that space beings will contact humanity[110].

Ramtha's apocalypticism surfaced strongly in a controversial channeled address on May 17-18, 1986[111]. His predictions for the near future included the appearance of sun spots resulting in great droughts on earth, followed by famine; an unprecedented increase in earthquakes, in connection with what Ramtha refers to as the "zippers" on the earth crust; pestilentious diseases and widespread violence (but *no* nuclear war[112]). Although Ramtha was sometimes explicit about the years and dates of the events[113], he also hinted that the events might happen at a later date or even not at all[114].

Spangler's *Revelation* is a special case. Although it must certainly be regarded as an "interventionist" text, it is less specific about coming cataclysms and adds some elements not found elsewhere. Ideas of a "final judgment" are explicitly rejected by Limitless Love and Truth:

> I have not come to sift the good from the bad. I am not the judge. I simply am what I am. If you are that I am, then you are of me. If you are not, then you come under a different law and must obey it before its cup can pass from your lips. ... None are saved. None are lost. There is always only what I am, but I have revealed myself in new life and new light and new truth. Those who attune to that will not

---

[106] RR 163.

[107] WR 129.

[108] WR 272. In WR 206, AIDS is called 'but a warning to Humanity to show it what lies ahead': it is the precursor of a far worse disease which will afflict the whole planet (repeated in VR 274). VR 93-94 and 274 tell the reader that AIDS can be healed by inner transformation and removing 'the psychological blockage that is causing the disease'. Only a few people will heal themselves in this way, however, 'because only a very few people have either the power or the will to do so' (VR 94).

[109] VR 274.

[110] RR 231-236.

[111] It was a particularly clear example of the shift from the early to the later Ramtha to which I referred in the introduction to his messages in chapter one.

[112] RIC 35, 54. Neither will there be a shift of the earth's axis. This explicit rejection of Cayce's prediction is found in RIC 35.

[113] For instance RIC 22, 54.

[114] RIC 22: 'The time of the drough *can* change. It can be at a later time. But it *is* coming'. On RIC 106 Ramtha reminds his audience that 'time is an illusion ... To predict an exact time frame is the greatest speculation there is...'. In RIC 141ff Ramtha even suggests that the cataclysms may not take place after all, and J Z Knight suggests that humanity may still prevent the apocalypse by taking control of their lives and changing their reality (RIC 7, 11).

be saved. They will only be attuned to what I am in my new revelation. And those who heed me not, but follow the downward course as human level consciousness unwinds itself and enters a new cycle, they are not lost[115].

Somehow, the "two worlds" will come to be separated. Those who attune to Limitless Love and Truth will enter the New Age, and those who do not will be 'shepherded' to their own proper place or dimension of further evolution. *Revelation* is concerned to explain that the New Age is not to be associated with "destruction" but only with creativity and "uplifting" energies[116]. However, there is more than a hint that this may be so only for those with the right "attunement", while those who remain locked in limited patterns of thought may well experience real cataclysms: 'When the energies of atomic power are released, they will be of me and revelation will occur. But heed this: I am not prophesying war. ... Let no man think I have placed upon him through Truth the inevitability of destruction, disaster and death. These are all illusions save to those who are not of me. What the old invokes that it may disappear need not disturb the new'[117]. Apparently, this means that the "pushing of the button" may trigger world-wide revelation from the perspective of those with the right "attunement", while *simultaneously* bringing real death and destruction to unenlightened souls. The very same event will be experienced in radically different ways depending on what "world" one belongs to. Spangler, in his commentary on the revelations, seems to be determined to play down this vision of real nuclear holocaust (for the unenlightened) by discussing it only in the vaguest of terms: 'It is in the second world, the world of man's consciousness, that the true cataclysms may be felt. ... Thus, the first impact of Aquarius was the introduction of interim energies designed to shatter the outdated thought-forms and creations ... Such energies may express destructively ...'[118].

If *Revelation* is characterized by a certain ambiguity towards the "harder" aspects of apocalypse (an ambiguity shared by George Trevelyan[119]), no such ambiguity is evident in the Ramala materials. According to this source, 'all the events that are prophesied in the Bible will come to pass', including the appearance of an Antichrist[120] and a veritable day of judgment: 'This is the time of Armageddon. This is the time of the sorting of the wheat from the chaff. If you are wheat, do not take heed for the chaff for the wind of evolution will blow it away. Only the wheat will remain, but that wheat must be pure, must be healthy, must be strong'[121]. Like *Revelation*, the Ramala masters assure their

---

[115] RBNA 64-65.
[116] RBNA 140.
[117] RBNA 65.
[118] RBNA 141.
[119] Cf. for instance VAA 109-110; OR 27, 181, 187, 194.
[120] VR 69 & 331.
[121] WR 261.

readers that the "chaff" will not be exterminated but will receive new chances to fulfil their evolutionary potential[122]. For the time being, however, the prospects are decidedly grim. As noted in *The Vision of Ramala* (the last and most apocalyptic of the Ramala books) the end of the Piscean age will mirror its beginning: '...the fact that Jesus died a violent death on the cross indicates a violent end to the Age'[123].

We may conclude that belief in an outside intervention is widespread in the theosphically-inspired sources, most of which belong to the New Age *sensu stricto*, and that apocalyptic visions of worldwide disaster are common. These visions stand side by side with images of a gradual and nonviolent shift to a better society. Roughly it may be said that there is a correlation between the nature of the shift, on the one hand, and the nature of the expected outcome, on the other. Whenever the New Age is regarded as a perfect Age of Light, it is coupled with (mostly apocalyptic) interventionism. For, evidently, only higher powers can effect such a change; mere human beings are not capable of doing so, although they *are* able (according to most sources) to frustrate "operation redemption". Reversely, to the extent that the New Age is depicted as the product of a global change of mind or paradigm shift (i.e., as something accomplished by human beings), it is consistently described in more moderate—although still highly optimistic—terms.

4. EPILOGUE: CONTROVERSIES OVER THE NEW AGE *SENSU LATO*

Finally, one should note that not only the "New Age" in the sense of an imminent new era is a frequent subject for discussion, but the "New Age" in the sense of the movement of that name as well. New Agers often reflect on the nature of their own "movement", and a few words must be said about what they say about it. Marilyn Ferguson, in her early "manifesto" of what would come to be known as the New Age movement, describes how she came to choose the name "Aquarian Conspiracy": 'I was drawn to the symbolic power of the pervasive dream in our popular culture: that after a dark, violent age, the Piscean, we are entering a millennium of love and light—in the words of the popular song, *The Age of Aquarius*, the time of "the mind's true liberation"'[124]. Ferguson described the emerging new movement in terms of "universal connectedness", with reference to the concept of "Segmented Polycen-

---

[122] WR 234. They will return to a 'Group Energy', and once they have 'earned the right to individuality' they will once more take the path of spiritual progress.

[123] VR 73.

[124] AC 19. Actually, the use of the term "Aquarian Age" does not necessarily include any dogmatic conviction about astrological inevitabilities. My research suggests strongly that, in spite of the term, astrology plays only a minor part in New Age expectations.

tric Integrated Networks", or SPINs[125]. Her description of a SPIN shows the concern, commented upon above, for a non-hierarchical holistic structure which does not threaten individual freedom: 'Whereas a conventional organization chart would show neatly linked boxes, the organization chart of a SPIN would look like 'a badly knotted fishnet with a multitude of nodes of varying sizes, each linked to all the others, directly or indirectly'[126]. The similarity to Ferguson's other favourite concept, the holographic paradigm, is evident. Applying the SPIN concept to the Aquarian Conspiracy, Ferguson suggested that the latter could be regarded as 'in effect, a SPIN of SPINs, a network of many networks aimed at social transformation. The Aquarian Conspiracy is indeed loose, segmented, evolutionary, redundant. Its centre is everywhere'[127]. Ferguson's conceptualization of the Aquarian network has been adopted by many later authors[128]. Capra describes essentially the same process of various "countercultural" networks linking and joining forces in order to form the vanguard of the "rising culture"[129]. Harman sees the same countercultural movements coming together as 'different drops in a single wave of transformative change'[130]. At the very beginning of her first New Age book, Shirley MacLaine describes how she discovered Ferguson's SPIN of SPINs. Having travelled all her life, she could not but notice a gradual but frightening deterioration of the world's condition[131]. However, at a certain moment she noticed that a quiet change was taking place: 'People I talked to began to speculate on what it was that was missing. The tone of our conversations shifted from dismay and confusion to a consideration that the answers might lie within ourselves ... I found myself in touch with a network of friends all over the world who were involved with their own spiritual search'[132]. This discovery, partly documented in *Out on a Limb*, was a source of hope. At the very end of the book, MacLaine repeats the theme of the emerging SPIN of SPINs: '...everywhere I went, I continually encountered a deep need for spirituality and expanded consciousness, a need for people to come together to share their energies in *something* that worked'[133].

Ferguson and MacLaine may perhaps be taken as representative for the vision and the reality respectively: as I noted in chapter five, 'If the Aquarian Conspiracy is the manifesto of a hoped-for new culture, MacLaine's bestselling

---

[125] The concept was proposed, according to Ferguson, by the anthropologists Luther Gerlach and Virginia Hine, in order to account for the structure of social-protest networks since the 1960s.
[126] AC 235.
[127] AC 236.
[128] Apart from those discussed in the text, cf. also PH 214; WW1 12-14; AE 70-77 (in terms of the "Information Age"); RS 88.
[129] TP 46.
[130] GMC 117.
[131] OL 7.
[132] AC 7-8.
[133] OL 352. Cf. also DL 305; GW 8.

autobiographies represent the subculture which actually emerged'. The every-day reality of the New Age movement *sensu lato* has provoked criticism even from within the movement itself. Fritjof Capra attempts to steer a middle course:

> The shift to the value system that the holistic health movement, the human poten-tial movement, and the ecology movement advocate is further supported by a num-ber of spiritual movements that reemphasize the quest for meaning and the spir-itual dimension of life. Some individuals and organizations among the "New Age" movements[134] have shown clear signs of exploitation, fraud, sexism, and exces-sive economic expansion, quite similar to those observed in the corporate world, but these aberrations are transitory manifestations of our cultural transformation and should not prevent us from appreciating the genuine nature of the current shift of values. As Roszak has pointed out, one must distinguish between the authen-ticity of people's needs and the inadequacy of the approaches that may be offered to meet those needs[135].

Others have been more outspokenly critical[136]. Matthew Fox regards parts of "New Ageism" as examples of 'the rise of pseudo-mysticism', which runs the risk of forgetting social justice and a real compassion for the suffering[137]. The kind of criticism which accuses the New Age movement of "narcissism" has found its most explicit spokesman in the man who might be called the found-ing father of the New Age *sensu stricto*, David Spangler.

Spangler distinguishes four levels of meaning that may be attached to the term "New Age": 1. New Age as merely a superficial label, usually in a com-mercial setting; 2. New Age as "glamour":

> This is the context in which individuals and groups are living out their own fan-tasies of adventure and power, usually of an occult or millenarian form. ... The principal characteristic of this level is attachment to a private world of ego ful-

---

[134] This implies a definition which limits the term "New Age" only to these explicitly spiri-tual groups. In practice such a distinction is impossible to maintain, and subsequent develop-ments have demonstrated Capra's apparent concern to distinguish his own "rising culture" from the "New Age" to be illusory.

[135] TP 415.

[136] Critical remarks are particularly common in neopagan and some traditional occultist cir-cles; cf. for instance HBWM xvii (rejection of 'safe, New Age-ish words that don't threaten any-body'), 296-297; WW2 75-76.

[137] "New Ageism" must be condemned as pseudo-mysticism to the extent that is shows: exces-sively literal interpretations of past-life experiences without regard for their metaphorical mean-ing; underestimation of people's present responsibilities and opportunities; excessive preoccu-pation with altered states of consciousness; a neglect of commitment to healing society (CCC 45-46). Notice that Fox also rejects "psychologism" (i.e., the reduction of spirituality to psy-chological categories): 'an entire generation of would-be spiritual leaders is often forfeited to the god of counseling' (CCC 46). In CCC 141 he adds that a certain kind of 'distortion occurs in certain trends in the New Age movement which are all space and no time; all consciousness and no conscience; all mysticism and no prophecy; all past life experiences, angelic encounters, untold bliss, and no critique of injustice or acknowledgment of the suffering and death that the toll of time takes. In short, no body'.

filment and a consequent (though not always apparent) withdrawal from the world. On this level, the new age has become populated with strange and exotic beings, masters, adepts, extraterrestrials; it is a place of psychic powers and occult mysteries, of conspiracies and hidden teachings[138].

Spangler adds that this is what is most popularly regarded as "new age". He himself, however, wishes to be associated only with the third and especially the fourth category. 3. New Age as an image of change, usually thought of as a paradigm shift: 'In this context the idea of an emerging new culture is usually seen in social, economic, and technological terms rather than spiritual ones, and the term *new age* itself is rarely used'[139]. 4. The New Age as the incarnation of the sacred, described as

> a spiritual event, the birth of a new consciousness, a new awareness and experience of life ... a deepening into the sacramental nature of everyday life ... the new age as a state of being, a mode of relationship with others that is mutually empowering and enriching. Rather than spiritual *experience*, which is the focus one is more apt to find in the second level ... this level centers upon the spiritual *function*, which is service: the giving of life, the nourishing of life, the upholding of life in its desire to unfold[140].

Although Spangler's distinctions are helpful, from the perspective of the present study they can be used only as subdivisions within one multifarious movement, not as tools to separate the "true" from the "false" New Age movement. In any case, while Spangler himself in his younger years must, in terms of his own categories, be relegated to the "glamour" category, his mature understanding of New Age as "incarnation of the sacred" seems to be largely a private concern. If this is the real "new age", then most of what usually goes under the name is not; it is therefore more reasonable to conclude that Spangler's fourth category (but certainly not Spangler himself[141]) is a borderline case. His later criticism of New Age "narcissism" seems to have resulted from his horror at seeing how the movement he himself had helped to found got out of hand during the 1980s. Having started as an idealistic world-reformer, Spangler has continued to emphasize the importance of social responsibility and active this-worldliness, while the New Age movement in general increasingly moved away from these concerns[142]. In 1988, his frustration at being asso-

---

[138] RS 78-79. Spangler says that he 'encountered this world during the early days' but not that he was actually involved in it himself. He does not address the status of his own early "theosophical" work, which seems to fit this second category very well.

[139] RS 80.

[140] RS 81.

[141] RS and RW demonstrate abundantly that Spangler by no means restricts himself to his own categories. At the very least, the third category is a prominent part of his later concerns, and several discussions in RW (such as about "the Christ", analyzed in chapter seven, section 2B) would still be regarded by many as belonging to the second category.

[142] A similar development may be noted in the case of Matthew Fox. Positive statements about

ciated with the wrong kind of New Age led to his publication of The New Age, a small booklet which amounts to a frontal attack on New Age "glamour". The New Age is described as 'a myth, a metaphor, a metamorphosis, and a menace'[143]. While the first three meanings are positive, most of Spangler's attention is focused upon the "menace". His criticism is summarized by him as follows:

> The shadows of the New Age are alienation from the past in the name of the future; attachment to novelty for its own sake without a proper alignment to history and tradition; indiscriminateness and lack of discernment in the name of wholeness and communion, hence the failure to understand or respect the role of boundaries and limits; selfishness arising from misplaced self-development; a subtle surrender to powerlessness and irresponsibility in the name of waiting for the New Age to come rather than being an active creator of wholeness in one's own life; identifying the New Age primarily as an event rather than as a process; confusion of psychic phenomena with wisdom, of channeling with spirituality, and of the New Age perspective with ultimate truth[144].

Spangler's discussion makes clear that the critique of the New Age movement as "narcissistic" is certainly not voiced only by outsiders, but it should be added that in the end he wishes to emphasize the positive. Even with respect to the movement of the 1980s and 1990s, he rejects the popular idea that 'the New Age is simply an expression of yuppie narcissism'[145]. The really selfish, irrational or narcissistic New Agers are a 'small minority': 'Far and away the great majority of folk I have known have been very serious seekers after truth'[146]. Therefore, Spangler ends by calling for discernment:

> Is there a valid spirituality within the New Age movement? I feel there is, and it is not always apparent on the surface. Here is where the glamor of channels, crystals, and past lives may hinder us; if the surface sparkles too much, we may fail to look beneath it, either in disgust or because we are too dazzled. Yet, if we are to gain the benefits that I feel the New Age has to offer to us, then we must go beneath this surface. We must learn to separate the real from the unreal, the meaningless from the meaningful[147].

This same conclusion is drawn by other New Age authors who take the trouble to address the "shadow sides" of the movement. It is perhaps appropriate to end this analysis with an observation by Peter Russell, which is certainly applicable to the New Age movement generally: '...at least these people are

---

the New Age movement occur in OB 16, 251, 255, 315. In his later work, however, he speaks of the need for a "global renaissance" (and equivalent terms) but avoids the term "New Age" in that connection (CCC 5, 34, 160, 200, 240ff).
    [143] NA 7.
    [144] NA 13-14.
    [145] NA 28.
    [146] NA 27.
    [147] NA 28-29.

putting their energies in the direction of furthering inner growth, rather than hunting whales, strip-mining, building arsenals of nuclear weapons or pursuing any other potentially life-destroying activity'[148].

---

[148] AE 161.

PART THREE

INTERPRETATION:
NEW AGE RELIGION AND TRADITIONAL ESOTERICISM

CHAPTER THIRTEEN

TOWARDS A HISTORICAL PERSPECTIVE ON NEW AGE RELIGION

1. A SHORT EVALUATION

Having outlined the major trends of New Age religion in Part One of this study, I concentrated on the variability of its beliefs in Part Two. Before proceeding to an interpretation of this material from the perspective of the history of religions, it will be useful to summarize the central themes that have emerged. In doing so, I will assume that they are understood as broad generalizations only, which neither can nor should make superfluous or diminish in importance the distinctions and nuances discussed in Part Two. By the same token, the common tendency of reifying or "hypostatizing" such generalizations must be regarded as contrary to the intentions of this study[1].

I suggest that, on these premises, the results of the analysis can be summarized in terms of five basic tendencies. These may, accordingly, be regarded as constitutive for New Age religion as it is expressed in the primary source material.

(1) *This-worldliness, particularly of the weak variety*, characterizes the attitude of New Age believers to experiential reality. In this respect, a text such as *A Course in Miracles*, although often regarded as belonging to the New Age domain, is decidedly atypical. The somewhat problematic status of neopaganism within the New Age movement (cf. chapter four) is confirmed by the fact that the former tends towards a strong this-worldliness, while weak this-worldliness is the rule in most other expressions of New Age religion.

(2) *Holism* is pervasive in all forms of New Age thinking. In accordance with (1), it is seldom of a "transcendent absolute" variety; instead, New Age holism emphasizes the universal interrelatedness of all things, either or not based upon a common creative Source of Being. These kinds of holism are equally central to New Age views about the nature of the cosmos and to New Age beliefs

---

[1] For this point, see the debate about "unit ideas", *sensu* Lovejoy, summarized in Wilson, 'Lovejoy's *The Great Chain of Being*' (and note especially the pertinent criticisms formulated by Louis Mink and Quentin Skinner); and Hanegraaff, 'Empirical Method', which contains an extensive discussion of the methodology followed in the present study, with special attention to the "Lovejovian" approach to the history of ideas. Lovejoy himself has repeatedly warned that the history of ideas 'may easily degenerate into a species of merely imaginative historical generalization' (*Great Chain*, 21). Cf. also note 13.

about the relationship of human individuals to the universe and to God (cf. the "star diagram" discussed in chapter eight, section 2A).

(3) *Evolutionism* is equally pervasive. In accordance with the "generative" tendency of (2), New Age believers do not regard evolution as random, but as teleological and/or creative. The idea of a universal process of evolution of consciousness, in which souls learn to evolve by learning self-designed lessons, is central to New Age beliefs about the meaning of existence, life beyond death, and ethics. Furthermore, evolutionism is central to discussions of the universe, the world, and human society.

(4) What I referred to as *the psychologization of religion and sacralization of psychology*, in its various dimensions, is highly characteristic of New Age religion. In the context of (3) it implies that the evolution of consciousness leads to a perfect gnosis or illumination, in which Self-realization and God-realization are one and the same. In order to assist its own evolution, the mind creates "meaningful illusions" (cf. (1)) which hold spiritual lessons. Ultimately, all realities (inner realms, "higher" realms, as well as "normal" reality) are created by "mind". The fundamental New Age tenet that we "create our own reality" (a tenet, again, with various dimensions) is directly based on this fourth tendency.

(5) *Expectations of a coming New Age*, ranging from moderate improvement to total bliss, are the most direct expression of the movement's criticism of the worldviews dominant in western culture generally, and modern western culture particularly. This expectation may or may not be expressed with reference to mytho-historical frameworks based on belief in a "perennial wisdom" at the core of all religions.

Once again, it must be emphasized that a brief summary can only provide a bare skeleton. The "flesh" on the skeleton consists of *specific* ideas (as analyzed in Part Two of this study) which reflect the personal perspectives and idiosyncracies of the various authors who have formulated them. Terms such as "holism" or "evolutionism", even if further specified as "generative" or "creative", are extremely vague and general umbrella terms; as such, they are insufficient for defining *any* concrete historical movement. Accordingly, the central problem of defining a phenomenon such as the New Age movement is to find a way not to sacrifice historical contingency to the demand for theoretical abstraction[2]. I will attempt to do so by investigating, in this third and final part, *the historical processes by which the conditions were created that made it possible for the New Age movement to appear in the later twentieth century*. This formulation was chosen carefully. Notice that it explicitly minimizes the factor of causal determinism. Although (as will be demonstrated) certain

---

[2] As concluded also by Bochinger, "*New Age*", 515.

historical developments in modern western culture have indeed "caused" a reaction of dissatisfaction among part of the populace, the actual forms in which that reaction was embodied might have developed very differently. The specific constellation of New Age religion has depended in crucial respects upon the personal contributions of influential authors as well as on various other historical contingencies which could not possibly have been predicted beforehand[3]. What *can* be done, however, is describe how various traditions have come into existence, and how their convergence created conditions which made the emergence of the New Age movement possible. It is for this reason that the question of the historical "roots of the New Age movement" is discussed at the *end*, rather than at the beginning of this study. The New Age movement is not to be seen as a logical (hence predictable) outcome of earlier traditions: from the perspective of the past, it would have been impossible to say whether, and if so, how existing traditions would come to be adopted (and in the process reinterpreted) by future generations. Accordingly, to investigate the historical roots of New Age thinking at the end of this study means to emphasize the fact that these roots can only be decided upon *post factum*. With hindsight, one can see how certain historical developments have made it possible for the New Age movement to become what it has become. Accordingly, the historical interpretation of New Age religion offered here has two dimensions: (a) we use its empirical manifestations, analyzed in Part Two, as a *heuristic tool* for probing the past; and (b) we use the results to create a framework for interpreting the material. This is not a circular procedure but a dialectical one[4]. I suggest that, with respect to an elusive movement such as the New Age, this is the only historically valid approach.

The final outcome of the following discussions will be a threefold characterization of the nature of New Age religion (assuming, of course, its initial

---

[3] Cf. the discussion of Joseph Dan's "contingental" approach to the study of mysticism, in Hanegraaff, 'Empirical Method', 124: '... the contingent, historical and philological approach ... seeks the creative and the individual aspects, as opposed to the eternity of absolute, unchanging truth, which negates all possibility of creativity and annihilates the position of the mystic as a unique contributor, as an individual, to the history of human spirituality' (see Dan, 'In Quest', 58-90). Dan's formulations are put in opposition to the 'mystical unifying attitude' which assumes that mystical truth must be universal because it is beyond time and history; they are equally applicable, however, to the tendency of some secular scholars to impose "immutable" laws and principles on their materials (Hanegraaff, 'Empirical Method', 104). As for historical contingencies other than the influence of individual creativity, see for instance the fact that if the United States had not rescinded the Asian Exclusion Act in 1965 (which had kept Asians out of the country for forty years), America would not have been flooded by Asian missionaries during the later 1960s. The development of the cultic milieu from which the New Age emerged would have been incalculably different from what it is now (see Melton, 'New Thought and the New Age', 20).

[4] I refer once more to Snoek's argumentation with respect to definitions (see Introduction), which is, *mutatis mutandis*, equally applicable to the historical interpretation of New Age religion.

demarcation outlined in the Introduction as a starting point): (1) in terms of the detailed empirical description of beliefs offered in Part Two and summarized above; (2) by outlining how these beliefs represent a systematic counterreaction to existing cultural forms; (3) by outlining how and why specific historical traditions were reinterpreted under modern conditions, in order to formulate such a reaction.

2. PERSPECTIVES ON THE NEW AGE

Before embarking upon the project just outlined, it will be useful to give a brief critical summary of the main scholarly interpretations of the New Age phenomenon that have been offered thus far. This will enable us to assess the current "state of research", with a view to formulating desiderata for the present study and future research.

It would be impossible as well as pointless to strive for completeness in this regard. An incredible amount of publications, varying strongly in quality and scope, has been published in reaction to the emergence of the New Age movement, and this stream is still growing daily[5]. However, the number of serious scholarly contributions to understanding the New Age phenomenon is remarkably small, and I will restrict myself to a necessary minimum here. The work of Hans Sebald, although comprising only a few articles, is interesting because it is one of the earliest attempts, and still an interesting one, to come to terms with the New Age phenomenon; Christof Schorsch and Christoph Bochinger merit attention for having written the only two book-length studies to date which are both serious and not inspired by overt polemical or apologetical considerations; and J. Gordon Melton *cum suis* have unquestionably been responsible for the best-informed studies of New Age religion in the English-speaking world. Although, in addition, some sociological interpretations could have been included, it was found that these either suffer from fundamental methodological shortcomings which are characteristic of a certain type of "sociology of the occult"[6], or were simply concerned with questions which, although important in themselves, are irrelevant to the more limited goals of this study[7]. However, sociological methodologies are in themselves, not only a legitimate,

---

[5] See the ca. 120 pages of bibliographical material appended to Bochinger, *"New Age"*, 535-659.

[6] See Hanegraaff, 'Empirical Method', 119-121, and below (chapter fourteen, section 3).

[7] Cf. my Introduction, where I suggested that a complete perspective on the New Age movement will ultimately require a combination of sociological research with the type of historical research undertaken here. For a strictly sociological approach, I refer to York, *Emerging Network*, and Heelas, *New Age Movement*.

but an important ingredient of the empirical and historically-oriented study of religion[8]; limited use was therefore made of them in my own initial demarcation (see Introduction) and will be made again in what follows.

Hans Sebald

An early attempt at a serious analysis of the New Age movement as understood in the present study[9] was published in 1984 by the sociologist Hans Sebald. In two articles published in 1985 and 1989 he further developed his thesis that the New Age movement is basically a "romantic movement"[10]. Sebald begins with the observation that 'The sociocultural dynamics of late-20-century America involve the interaction of three social movements: the Moral Majority, secular humanism, and the New Age. Clamor of battle between the former two has obscured awareness of the significant growth of the latter'[11]. As will be seen, this distinction between the Christian Right, its secularist opponent, and the New Age movement, as a phenomenon different from both, is significant. Focusing attention on the New Age movement, Sebald proceeds to characterize its essence as 'a nouveau romanticism'[12]. Romanticism is presented not primarily as a historical movement but, rather, as a universal tendency of the human mind[13], described pejoratively as a way of looking at the world which substitutes fantasy and imagination for facts and objectivity,

---

[8] Cf. Hanegraaff, 'Empirical Method', 105, 119.

[9] In view of my demarcation of the New Age movement (see Introduction) I will disregard the oft-quoted book by Roszak, *Unfinished Animal*. Apart from the question whether Roszak is to be taken as a primary or a secondary source (he has been understood in both senses by different authors; cf. Bochinger, *"New Age"*, 77 nt 173), not a few later commentators have ignored the fact that a book published in 1975 cannot possibly be used as an authoritative account of the 1980s. In this respect, its status is similar to Ferguson's *Aquarian Conspiracy* (cf. my comments in chapter five).

[10] Sebald, 'New Age Romanticism', 106-127; id., 'Romantik des "New Age"', 215-237; id., 'New-Age-Spiritualität', 313-341. Cf. the criticism in Lewis, 'Approaches', 9-10.

[11] Sebald, 'New Age Romanticism', 106.

[12] Sebald, 'New Age Romanticism', 108.

[13] Sebald, 'New Age Romanticism', 108: 'Romanticism is always in easy reach of human longing, and there is hardly an epoch that is free of it'. This universalist approach to Romanticism, found in the work of many older specialists but still far from extinct today, was the object of attack in A.O. Lovejoy's foundational article 'On the Discrimination of Romanticisms', 235: 'There is no hope of clear thinking on the part of the student of modern literature, if—as, alas! has been repeatedly done by eminent writers—he vaguely hypostatizes the term, and starts with the presumption that "Romanticism" is the heaven-appointed designation of some single real entity, or type of entities, to be found in nature. He must set out from the simple and obvious fact that there are various historic episodes or movements to which different historians of our own or other periods have, for one reason or another, given the name'. A "nominalist" approach, as defended by Lovejoy, is fundamental to the present study (cf. his warnings about "imaginative historical generalization", note 1 above). Cf. Hanegraaff, 'Romanticism'.

and 'thrives on the childlike, hedonistic, picturesque, bizarre, unknown, and mystical'[14].

As for the demarcation of "New Age", Sebald consistently distinguishes between the counterculture of the 1960s and the New Age movement, describing the latter as a less conspicuous outgrowth of the former[15]. However, Sebald's actual view of the movement still betrays an overemphasis on its older "countercultural" side. This is illustrated by his enumeration of characteristics, where we read for instance that most New Agers live in small groups, communes, or small communities; that they emphasize dietary principles (mostly vegetarianism) and "appropriate technology"; that they long for a more simple and natural lifestyle characterized by simplicity in dress, diet, housing, transportation etcetera; and that their speech is characterized by a shared lingo[16]. Not surprisingly, Sebald's descriptions are based on fieldwork conducted in a New Age commune during the 1970s[17]; and a continued emphasis on the youth culture resulted from his later emphasis on research amongst university student populations. Therefore, although his studies appeared during the 1980s and correctly present the New Age as a transformation rather than a continuation of the counterculture, they nevertheless perpetuate a disproportionate emphasis on elements which are most typical for the 1960s and 1970s (and, it should be added, to which the label "romanticism" is most readily applicable).

Finally, Sebald recognizes that the New Age movement should be viewed in the context of the history of religions. He describes it as a product of religious syncretism, rejecting the negative connotations adhering to the term[18]. After all, he reminds the reader, most religions have originally been the product of "syncretism". There is no historical justification for seeing the syncretistic character of New Age religion as a sign of superficiality or decadence; in fact, the current alternative scene might well herald the birth of a new world religion[19]. However, Sebald does not delve into the historical roots of this new syncretism; and, actually, his matter-of-fact assumption that "Romanticism" and "mysticism" are more or less synonymous with the "childlike, hedonistic,

---

[14] Sebald, 'New Age Romanticism', 108.

[15] Sebald, 'New Age Romanticism', 108-109: '...the romanticism germinated in the anti-war counterculture has now blossomed as New-Age Romanticism. The New Age, less raucous and conspicuous than its progenitorial counterculture, is an amorphous movement that teaches and spreads the romantic attributes'.

[16] Sebald's characteristics mentioned in 1984 were retained in 1989 ('New-Age-Spiritualität', 316-317) plus an added element ('Von besonderer Bedeutung'), i.e., the "Institutionalization of Vital Functions" by way of Ashrams, bookshops, organizations, expositions, meetings, communes, healing centres, media networks and workshops.

[17] Sebald, 'New Age Romanticism', 112.

[18] Cf. next chapter, nt 55.

[19] Sebald, 'New-Age-Spiritualität', 319.

picturesque, bizarre and unknown" hardly suggests a profound familiarity with the history of these two phenomena.

Christof Schorsch

In 1988, the philosopher and sociologist Christof Schorsch published a monograph which still counts among the few serious book-length attempts at a comprehensive interpretation[20]. Schorsch's main interest is the *Weltanschauung* of the New Age[21], which he investigates on the basis of primary source materials. A fundamental problem with his study as a whole is that his initial demarcation of the field and his choice of sources is purely "essential-intuitional" (see Introduction). Schorsch seems to assume that, since the New Age movement derives its name from the expectation of a radical transformation of society, the movement as a whole may be studied with reference to a limited number of sources which express that expectation. As a result, his textual corpus consists of two undisputed "classics" (Ferguson's *Aquarian Conspiracy* and Capra's *Turning Point*) plus the work of Spangler, Trevelyan, Russell, Wilber, Theodore Roszak, and a few additional (mainly German) authors[22]. Almost all of these belong to the fifth and final category distinguished in Part One, above (chapter five). As a result, Schorsch's book should be seen as a study of explicit *programmatic statements* formulated by a limited category of influential New Age thinkers, rather than of its actual historical manifestations. The choice of sources results in an overemphasis on the millenarian and utopian side of the movement, at the expense of aspects such as channeling, alternative therapies or neopaganism.

With reference to these source materials, Schorsch characterizes the New Age movement in terms of twelve basic concepts: New Age, Paradigm, Wholeness, New Consciousness, Expansion of Consciousness, Self-realization (or Self-actualization), Spirituality, Androgyny, Network, Self-organization, Transformation, and Planetary Consciousness[23]. Further on, he adds that of these twelve, self-realization is the central concept around which the others revolve[24]. His extensive discussions of these twelve concepts consist essentially of a nar-

---

[20] Schorsch, *New Age Bewegung*; see also id., 'Versöhnung', 342-354; id., 'Utopie und Mythos', 315-330. Cf. the criticism in Bochinger, *"New Age"*, 58-61.

[21] Schorsch, *New Age Bewegung*, 11.

[22] Schorsch, *New Age Bewegung*, 17. Notice that Schorsch seems nevertheless to have rather definitive opinions about demarcation criteria. In 'Utopie und Mythos', 317 nt 1, he claims that Sheldrake, Bohm and Grof play a role in theoretical discussions within the New Age movement, but do not themselves belong to that movement. No arguments are given.

[23] Schorsch, *New Age Bewegung*, 17-92.

[24] Schorsch, *New Age Bewegung*, 177: '*Selbstverwirklichung* als zentralen Begriff der Bewegung ... um den sich alle anderen Begriffe und Prämissen gruppieren'.

rative commentary on quotations from his source materials. Unfortunately, Schorsch's assumption that his sources are representative of "the" New Age movement repeatedly leads him to suggest a far stronger agreement between different authors than actually exists[25]. Thus, for instance, a series of quotations presented out of context suggests that Wilber, Ferguson, Roszak and Spangler have the same idea about "illusion"[26]; or, when Spangler defines the ("real"!) New Age as "incarnation of the Sacred", Schorsch assumes that he is speaking on behalf of the New Age Movement as a whole: 'therefore the New Age Movement is about the promise of a global sacred civilization'[27]. In short: Schorsch ignores the importance of distinguishing carefully who is saying what, and in which context; the result is an image of inner coherence which may be welcome to New Age believers but does not adequately reflect reality[28].

In addition to his twelve concepts, Schorsch emphasizes the importance of two 'hidden premises and deep theories'[29] underlying explicit New Age beliefs: (1) the "primacy accorded to mind/spirit"[30] and (2) the "primacy accorded to the individual"[31], suggesting that the first logically entails the second[32]. Against this background, he argues (with almost exclusive reference to Capra) that the New Age movement is based upon an *idealistic* epistemology which, however, is often incongruently combined with realist and intuitionist tendencies[33].

It seems that Schorsch's motivation to study the New Age movement has derived primarily from his personal concern about the ecological crisis[34] and

---

[25] Bochinger (*"New Age"*, 132) is therefore correct in observing that Schorsch's "basic concepts" describe not a *Weltanschauung* but merely a thematic catalogue.

[26] Schorsch, *New Age Bewegung*, 60.

[27] 'Es geht damit der NAB um die *Verheißung* einer globalen *sakralen* Zivilization' (Schorsch, *New Age Bewegung*, 101. Cf. my discussion in chapter twelve, section 4).

[28] Schorsch's approach exemplifies the tendency, mentioned above, to "reify" generalizations at the expense of historical contingency. Cf. the correct evaluation by Christoph Bochinger, *"New Age"*, 59.

[29] 'Verschwiegene Prämissen und tiefe Theorien' (Schorsch, *New Age Bewegung*, 93ff).

[30] Schorsch, *New Age Bewegung*, 93-101. Orig.: *'Primat des Geistes'*. The German *Geist* may be translated either by mind or by spirit.

[31] Schorsch, *New Age Bewegung*, 101-120.

[32] Schorsch, *New Age Bewegung*, 102: *'Aus dem Primat des Geistes folgt der Primat des Individuums'* (italicized in the original).

[33] Schorsch, *New Age Bewegung*, 128-133, esp. 130. In demonstrating the covert reductionism in Capra's thinking, Schorsch ignores Capra's development between *Tao of Physics* and *Turning Point*

[34] See especially his earlier work *Die große Vernetzung*. In his Introduction, Schorsch says that he regards himself neither as a protagonist nor a critic of the New Age movement. He adds that, from that perspective his own earlier works, including the one just mentioned, require a critical re-evaluation. Presumably this means that Schorsch was originally closer to the New Age movement, due to a shared concern with the ecological problem. According to Christoph Bochinger (*"New Age"*, 58) Schorsch originally regarded himself as a New Ager.

his professional interest in the role of utopianism and mythology in contemporary society. In the second and third parts of his book, New Age beliefs are interpreted from a combined sociological and philosophical perspective, and increasingly used by Schorsch as a foil for formulating his own ideas. Although interesting in themselves, these discussions are of limited interest for our concerns. More important is his characterization of the New Age movement as a reaction to the crisis of modernity[35]. Schorsch is sympathetic to its attempts to create a counterforce against the dangers of extreme rationalization, secularization, disenchantment of the world and mechanization[36]. In spite of this sympathy, however, he finally comes out on the side of "reason" against what he sees as the New Age's naïve belief in the veracity of myth[37]. Revealingly, he does this on the basis of a quasi-Hegelian theory of cultural evolution which is strikingly similar to the one proposed by Ken Wilber![38] Like Wilber, Schorsch argues that New Agers, in their concern for a re-enchantment of the world, *regress* to a mythical stage of consciousness. The New Age movement falls prey to what Wilber has labeled the "pre/trans-fallacy":

> The result is that one speaks of super-consciousness whereas one is moving merely in the regions of the deceptive unconscious, and confuses transformation with regression, mysticism with myth. Not the intended clarity of expanded consciousness is attained, but the return to the darkness of restricted consciousness, to the musty darkness of spiritistic ratifications and the impenetrable night in which the phantoms roam[39].

In spite of this attempt to situate the New Age Movement in a hypothetical history of human consciousness, and of his concern with the conditions for its emergence (*Entstehungsbedingungen*), Schorsch does not present a properly historical perspective. He mentions that the New Age 'largely falls back on concepts and images of Christianity'[40], and highlights the apocalyptic and millenarian currents in Western history; but these indications remain general and abstract, and no attempt is made to outline any specific historical connection. The New Age movement is presented as essentially a product of contemporary social conditions, and analyzed in terms of supposedly "universal", trans-historical constants (in this case, *mythos* and *logos*)[41].

---

[35] Schorsch, *New Age Bewegung*, 146-155, esp. 146.
[36] Schorsch, *New Age Bewegung*, 154-155.
[37] Schorsch, *New Age Bewegung*, 224
[38] Both Wilber and Schorsch have been profoundly influenced by the work of Gebser, *Ursprung und Gegenwart*. In addition, both are highly positive about the work of mythographer Joseph Campbell.
[39] Schorsch, *New Age Bewegung*, 223.
[40] Schorsch, *New Age Bewegung*, 136.
[41] Cf. my criticism of the "sociology of the occult" in Hanegraaff, 'Empirical Method', 119-121.

J. Gordon Melton (cum suis)

The serious academic investigation of the New Age Movement in the U.S.A. has been dominated by J. Gordon Melton and a number of scholars loosely associated with the Institute for the Study of American Religion (Santa Barbara). Melton has published no book-length study of the subject but has edited several collective works, all of which contain articles by his hand as well as by others[42].

Melton presents the New Age Movement as a contemporary manifestation of what he refers to as "occult/metaphysical religion": 'a persistent tradition that has been the constant companion of Christianity through the centuries and has blossomed heartily as a product of eighteenth-century scientific enlightenment'[43]. This formulation is mildly puzzling, but Melton apparently means that the tradition as such has accompanied Christianity since its early beginnings, but took on new forms under the impact of the Enlightenment. This is confirmed by his important statement that, during the last two centuries, the tradition in question has 'jettisoned most of its older supernatural trappings and wed itself to newer models derived from science'[44]. Thus, Melton presents New Age religion as a manifestation of older traditions while emphasizing that it represents not a simple continuity but a *reinterpretation* of traditional tenets under the impact of modern developments. Such an approach is obvious to the historian. Actually, however, many writings about the New Age movement are methodologically flawed because they operate with vaguely defined and covertly ideological ideal types such as "the occult" versus "rationality" or "the mystical worldview" versus "the scientific worldview", ignoring the fact that mysticism and "the occult" *have a history*[45]. Melton does not dwell further on the premodern phases of that history, but presents New Age religion as deriving from the combined 18th/19th century traditions of Swedenborgianism, Mesmerism, Transcendentalism, Spiritualism, New Thought and modern Theosophy, duly noting the reception of Oriental thought in these currents[46].

---

[42] Melton, 'History of the New Age Movement'; Melton, Clark & Kelly, *New Age Encyclopedia*; id., *New Age Almanac*; Melton, 'New Age Movement'; Lewis & Melton, *Perspectives*.

[43] Melton, 'Introductory Essay', xxii; cf. id., 'History of the New Age Movement', 36.

[44] Melton, 'History of the New Age Movement', 35. Cf. 'Introductory Essay', xxii: 'one cannot understand the New Age Movement without some understanding of its full acceptance of science and its subsequent use of science as a major vehicle for expressing its perspective'.

[45] Cf. Dan, 'In Quest', 58-90; cf. my discussion in 'Empirical Method', 124-125. In view of the persistent tendency to treat the "irrational" as non-historical, cf. also the brilliant study by Biale, *Gershom Scholem*, for instance 23-24 (about Heinrich Graetz' view of Jewish mysticism).

[46] Melton, 'History of the New Age Movement', 37-41; 'Introductory Essay', xxii-xxvii. Swedenborgianism is not mentioned in 'New Age Movement', 165-168. Several other contributions in the section 'Historical Roots' of Lewis & Melton, *Perspectives* further investigate the role of these traditions (Melton, 'New Thought and the New Age'; Alexander, 'Roots of the New Age'; Diem & Lewis, 'Imagining India'; Ellwood, 'How New is the New Age?'; Albanese, 'Magical Staff').

In his earlier articles, Melton states that 'The New Age Movement can best be dated from around 1971'[47], mentioning the publication of the periodical *East-West Journal*, the public appearance of Baba Ram Dass (Richard Alpert) and the emergence of New Age network directories as his main arguments. Subsequently, he seems to have concluded that this was true only of the United States. He now added that 'The original stirrings which became the New Age Movement can be traced to Great Britain', mentioning the appearance during the 1960s of what he calls "Light Groups" (Findhorn being an especially prominent example): 'independent Theosophical groups which began to "network" around a common vision of a coming New Age and their role of facilitating the coming of the New Age by acting as channels of spiritual light'[48]. This accords very well with my distinction between an original New Age *sensu stricto* (originally English, theosophical, focused on the expectation of the coming New Age) and a subsequent New Age *sensu lato* (especially American, transcendentalist/metaphysical, with the coming New Age as only one of its concerns). For the reasons outlined in the Introduction, however, I would argue that the New Age *sensu lato* did not emerge clearly before the second half of the 1970s.

As for the essence of this New Age phenomenon, Melton has consistently claimed that the movement is held together by a generally shared concern with *transformation*:

> The central vision and experience of the New Age is one of radical transformation. On an individual level that experience is very personal and mystical. It involves an awakening to a new reality of self—such as a discovery of psychic abilities, the experience of a physical or psychological healing, the emergence of new potentials within oneself, an intimate experience within a community, or the acceptance of a new picture of the universe. However, the essence of the New Age is the imposition of that vision of personal transformation onto society and the world. Thus the New Age is ultimately a *social* vision of a world transformed, a heaven on earth, a society in which the problems of today are overcome and a new existence emerges[49].

This definition is problematic for several reasons[50]. Melton's "personal transformation" is difficult if not impossible to distinguish from the general phenomenon of religious *conversion*[51]; as such it can hardly be seen as charac-

---

[47] Melton, 'History of the New Age Movement', 36; 'Introductory Essay', xxii.

[48] Melton, 'New Age Movement', 164-165; cf. Melton, 'New Thought and the New Age', 20. Note that with regard to the date of 1971, Melton now writes that 'The New Age Movement *in the United States* can best be dated from 1971' (165; my emphasis).

[49] Melton, 'History of the New Age Movement', 46; cf. 'Introductory Essay', xiii-xiv; 'New Age Movement', 172.

[50] Cf. also the doubts expressed by Melton's colleague Lewis ('Approaches', 3).

[51] Cf. for instance the well-known cases described in James, *Varieties of Religious Experience*, lectures IX & X. The study of conversion is a major concern of the sociological study of New Religious Movements; see for instance Robbins, *Cults, Converts & Charisma*, ch. 3.

teristic for the New Age vision specifically. Although Melton's emphasis on "transformation" in a social sense is certainly applicable to the New Age movement, it seems questionable whether a movement of such obvious diversity, and with such vague boundaries, may be defined on the basis of one single tendency, however important in itself. This is connected with a further problem of Melton's approach in general: i.e., the fact that (in spite of statements to the contrary[52]) he tends to treat the New Age movement more or less as a discrete New Religious Movement, which may be distinguished rather unambiguously from other movements. This is demonstrated most clearly by Melton's repeated predictions about the future of the New Age. He correctly notes that 'Insofar as the New Age Movement represents primarily an updating of the long-standing occult and metaphysical tradition in American life, it has a bright future'[53]. However, his actual view of "the Movement" seems to be more specific, which explains why in an early statement he says that 'as a movement ... the days of the New Age are numbered'[54]. This prediction was later replaced by the more cautious observation that, with respect to the future, the New Age 'is facing some immense obstacles'[55]. Finally, Melton came to replace prediction by observation, announcing as a fact the 'decline of the New Age'[56]. It should be noted that his explanation of this decline is no longer the same as the one he originally used in order to predict it[57]: Melton now observes that the New Age movement has fallen prey to negative media coverage (so that many original adherents have come to reject the label "New Age") combined with disappointment among its adherents when the hoped-for "transformation" failed to occur. These two developments are indeed quite evident. The question is, however, whether the mere label "New Age" and the expectation of social transformation are sufficient, first to define "the movement", and then to announce its demise when these two elements are no longer prominent. At the time of writing (1995), I see no evidence that the New Age *sensu lato* is in decline. Melton himself concludes, finally, that 'as the New Age as a movement fades through the 1990s ... the substance of the New Age will continue into the indefinite future'[58]. I will return to such distinctions between a

---

[52] Melton, 'New Age Movement', 163 (introductory Note).

[53] Melton, 'History of the New Age Movement', 50; 'Introductory Essay', xxx.

[54] Melton, 'History of the New Age Movement', 51.

[55] 'Introductory Essay', xxx. This article is largely a revision of 'History of the New Age Movement'; Melton's reformulation may therefore be interpreted as a correction.

[56] Melton, 'New Age Movement', 177.

[57] Cf. 'History of the New Age Movement', 51-52 and 'Introductory Essay', xxx-xxxi, with 'New Age Movement', 177.

[58] Melton, 'New Age Movement', 178. Cf. Melton, 'New Thought and the New Age', 29: Melton expects that channelers are most likely to survive as remnants of the New Age Movement, and 'These groups will in turn settle into the landscape of the larger esoteric world as variations of Theosophical and Spiritualist religions, while the esoteric community prepares itself for the next "movement" which will offer to revitalize its life'.

New Age "movement" and its "substance" in the conclusions of this study. At this point, I suggest that there is indeed a historical beginning to the New Age Movement, but no presently foreseeable end. If the New Age *sensu lato* is, as I suggested, 'the cultic milieu having become conscious of itself as constituting a more or less unified "movement"' (see Introduction) (rather than a movement dependent for its existence on being labeled "New Age" or on the centrality of millenarian hopes for all its adherents) then that milieu will probably continue under one name or another regardless of whether the millennium arrives[59]. When new advocates come to the fore, the movement's present ideas (i.e. its substance) will gradually be transformed; but, I suggest, within the broad perimeters outlined above (section one).

Christoph Bochinger
Christoph Bochinger's substantial dissertation, published in 1994, is doubtless the most ambitious study of the New Age Movement so far. Although explicitly restricted to the German domain, its discussions are highly relevant to the New Age as an international phenomenon.

According to Bochinger, the term "New Age" (consistently written by him between quotation marks) is, at least in Germany, 'nothing but a label, which was "pasted on" the new religious scene by the publishers, the secondary literature and a few protagonists: in the German-speaking domain, "New Age" has never lived, and even less is it a social movement which might be described in the singular'[60]. Briefly: there is no such thing as a "New Age Movement". Furthermore, and contrary to popular assumptions, 'at the beginning of the developments stood, not the much-read books by Capra or Ferguson ... but congresses, experimental meetings, pioneering book projects, symposia and bookseries, which attempted to bring divergent themes together under one common name ...'[61]. In support of this thesis, Bochinger describes in great and interesting detail the emergence into public consciousness of the *label* "New Age", with special attention to the history of "New Age" bookseries that were developed by several of the leading German publishing houses in the 1980s[62]. Thus, while many observers have described New Age as a religious (super)market, Bochinger takes the idea seriously and suggests that "New Age" was actually produced by the application of marketing principles to the religious domain[63].

---

[59] See again my closing observation on the initial demarcation in the Introduction: the components of the New Age movement as understood by me are associated by contiguity, not necessarily by similarity (as in Melton's definition); to speak of the New Age as one "movement" in this sense does not necessarily imply coherence in terms of beliefs.

[60] Bochinger, *"New Age"*, 35. Cf. also 103, 129, 137, 183.

[61] Bochinger, *"New Age"*, 39.

[62] Bochinger, *"New Age"*, ch. 3.

[63] But see his qualification in *"New Age"*, 40. Of course, "New Age" was not simply invented one-sidedly by image-specialists, publishers and other "information-sellers"; rather, it emerged in a complex process of interaction with the "market".

As such, "New Age" is a characteristic exponent of "modern religion" in a general sense[64].

Bochinger denies that the phenomena covered by the label "New Age" display a deeper coherence in terms of an underlying *Weltanschauung*. However, there are grounds for the suspicion that that absence is a premise of his research rather than its result. Initially, Bochinger observes (correctly) that the peculiar speech jargon of the "New Age" scene does not necessarily reflect a consistent intellectual system; he adds that his initial goal will not be to establish such a *Weltanschauung* but to investigate the processes which have led to the creation of the "New Age" *syndrome*[65]. Later, he states that the search for a 'systematic center' is impossible to realize, because the New Age syndrome is 'in reality composed of many heterogeneous elements'[66]. However, since he has (by his own admission) not investigated the idea structure of "New Age", it seems that Bochinger merely presents an assumption as if it were a conclusion. Further on again, he simply states that in the case of "New Age" we are not dealing with a *Weltanschauung* but merely with a "heuristic field" consisting of questions and possible answers[67]. Finally, this statement is presented as a conclusion: 'it was found that "New Age" is not an even remotely homogeneous "Weltanschauung" or "Ideology"'[68]. Actually, no such thing was "found", because Bochinger never attempted to investigate the amount of coherence of New Age ideas.

It might be concluded that, if "New Age" is merely an artificially-created contemporary 'phantom'[69], a search for "its" historical context and backgrounds is impossible. However, the second (and largest) part of Bochinger's study is entirely devoted to an analysis of "New Age" from the perspective of the history of ideas and concepts[70]. Bochinger's solution to this apparent paradox is to concentrate entirely on the history of the relevant covering *labels*: "New Age" and "Aquarian Age", as well as "Esotericism" and "Spirituality". Thus, the reader is presented with extraordinarily detailed discussions of occidental theories of the "Ages of the world", the varieties of millenarianism in western history, and astrological traditions, as well as with long chapters about the two thinkers highlighted by Bochinger as "key figures" for understanding the origins of "New Age": Emanuel Swedenborg and William Blake[71]. These

---

[64] Bochinger, "*New Age*", 402.
[65] Bochinger, "*New Age*", 24. Cf. 27.
[66] Bochinger, "*New Age*", 105.
[67] Bochinger, "*New Age*", 129.
[68] Bochinger, "*New Age*", 135.
[69] Bochinger, "*New Age*", 35: '"New Age" as currently used is a phantom—but the phantom has left traces in reality!'
[70] '*Begriffs- und Ideengeschichtliche Zugänge*' (Bochinger, "*New Age*", Part Two).
[71] I fully agree with Bochinger about Swedenborg's importance with respect to New

highly erudite discussions are among the most interesting of the book; but, for all their brilliance, they demonstrate an ambivalence which is fundamental to Bochinger's total approach. If "New Age" is not more than a label, then what is the relevance of the fact that some *other* historical traditions also happen to have used that label (or similar ones)? When Bochinger warns against the suggestion of "unity" and coherence falsely created by a mere label, then why is it that, when it comes to investigating the past, the label is suddenly taken so seriously? If the current "New Age" is really a phantom, then Bochinger's historical analyses amount to a heaping of spectral evidence; *if*, on the other hand, they are to be taken as referring to traditions in western religious history which are in some sense "real" (and his discussions strongly suggest that he does) then, in order for them to be relevant at all, the current New Age Movement also must be more "real" than Bochinger suggests. To be precise: if the label "New Age" can be used to construct a historical framework for interpreting what nowadays goes under that name, then (contrary to Bochinger' statements) the label *does* provide a measure of coherence.

The conclusions arrived at in the present study differ strongly from Bochinger's[72]. (1) With respect to what I proposed to refer to as the New Age *sensu lato* (and in contrast to the original New Age *sensu stricto*), "New Age" is indeed a mere label. Attempts to define New Age religion (or to demarcate the New Age Movement) on the basis of the label are bound to fail: ultimately, they all lead to an overestimation of the "millenarian" component which is really applicable only to the New Age *sensu stricto*. Accordingly, the term "New Age" can be used *neither* (*pro* Bochinger) to suggest an inner coherence *nor* (*contra* Bochinger) to provide a heuristic instrument to probe the past. In short: the implications of Bochinger's thesis that "New Age" is nothing but a label seriously threaten his own historical approach. (2) While Bochinger assumes beforehand that the phenomena popularly covered by the label "New Age" reveal no coherence, the present study is an attempt to investigate *whether or not* this is the case. The presupposition of that project is that there are crite-

---

Age religion (see below), but Bochinger's focus on Blake seems disproportionate. Cf. chapter five nt 6.

[72] The differences between Bochinger's approach and mine are probably better described in terms of incommensurability than in terms of incompatibility. Discussions with Dr. Bochinger based on the manuscript of the present study have taught me that our methodological presuppositions differ on a very basic level; and for my part I freely admit that Bochinger's way of approaching the problem of "New Age" is so different from my own that we tend to talk at cross-purpose. Since a fundamental discussion about methodology is out of the question here, I must restrict myself to pointing out that I consider my central criticism (i.e., of how Bochinger relates his historical analysis to his approach of "New Age" as only a label) to remain valid *on the basis of the methodological assumptions which underly the present study*—which I am prepared to defend—while granting that these assumptions in turn are bound to be called into doubt from the perspective of Bochinger's methodology.

ria other than the "New Age" label which make it possible to provisionally demarcate the domain and thus make it available for study. These criteria were presented in the Introduction. At this point, no final conclusion with respect to the amount of coherence has been arrived at yet. As Bochinger correctly observes (with reference to Schorsch) a mere thematic catalogue should not be confused with a *Weltanschauung*; similarly, the five basic tendencies mentioned at the beginning of this chapter are no more than rough generalizations, which provide a measure of orientation but little more. (3) In order to provide a context for interpreting "the varieties of New Age experience" (Part Two), the ideas of the movement must be placed in a historical framework. Such a framework must rest on foundations other than the mere use of the label "New Age" or equivalent concepts. It should certainly allow for the presence of "millenarian" elements; but it cannot be based on the latter, any more than the New Age *sensu lato* is based on it.

In fairness to Bochinger, it should be added that his study provides much valuable material for the construction of such a framework. Departing from the archimedean point of "New Age" (and equivalent or related concepts), his discussions frequently (and fortunately) digress to general religious traditions in which speculations about the millennium, the "Ages of the World" or of astrological cycles were at home. Most of these traditions have emerged as centrally important in my own research as well. As a result, Bochinger's conclusions and mine finally converge much more strongly than one might otherwise assume, although the emphases are inevitably different.

3. DESIDERATA FOR ACADEMIC RESEARCH

In the volume *Perspectives on the New Age*, published in 1992, James R. Lewis notes that 'much remains to be done in every area of research on the New Age'[73], and proceeds to highlight the need for quantitative research and the application of already existing theoretical perspectives to the New Age phenomenon. As I have pointed out in the Introduction, the present study rests on the assumption that, apart from an in-depth analysis of New Age ideas, study of the historical backgrounds to New Age is another urgently-needed desideratum. That Lewis & Melton do not especially call attention to this is understandable, since they may legitimately claim that their book is the first one to contain serious historical contributions. Nevertheless, they would probably agree that much still needs to be done in this area too. In attempting to place the New Age movement in its historical context, however, one is confronted with a peculiar problematique.

---

[73] Lewis, 'Approaches', 11.

With respect to what Melton calls the "occult-metaphysical" tradition (but for which I will use the term "Western Esotericism"; see below), the current state of academic research is still very inadequate. Although the number of serious studies belonging to this field is considerable[74], they are easily over-looked because they are not perceived as contributions to a generally-recognized and clearly demarcated field of academic research. That scholars so often display acute signs of helplessness and loss of orientation when confronted with the New Age phenomenon is largely a result of the neglect of esotericism by generations of academic research. The reasons for such neglect are complicated. One reason has to do with the fact that the academic study of religion, in the course of emancipating itself from Christian theology, has tended to neglect the domain of Christian culture as a domain for study. As observed by Bochinger,

> To date, the academic study of religion has ... not developed adequate models for the scientific understanding of the new religious scene. Partly due to the brack-eting of aspects pertaining to the Christian churches and theology out of its work-ing domain, it lacks the conceptual framework which would be needed in order to describe non-church phenomena in occidental religious history[75].

Church history, even if conceived as a historical and impartial discipline, has largely concentrated either on the Church or on the well-known Christian here-sies which have historically threatened its hegemony. The common assumption on the part of the academic study of religion that the Christian domain can be left to Church historians betrays (apart from a questionable lack of concern with the *systematic* rather than merely historical *raison d'être* of the study of religion) a neglect of the distinction between a history of the Christian church-es and a history of Christianity[76]. The result is a deficient state of academic knowledge about important parts of the western religious heritage.

The academic marginalization of western esotericism has been further stimu-lated by ideological factors. As is also the case in the new discipline of women's history, the modern historical study of western esotericism entails a profound correction of the way in which the scholarly "construction of tradition" has tended to be steered by ideological mechanisms[77]. It is useful here to compare academic approaches to ancient gnosticism, on the one hand, and to modern (i.e., post-Renaissance) esotericism, on the other. The remarkable contrast between the two fields in terms of academic recognition can be explained as an outcome of the battle between doctrinal Christian theology and Enlighten-ment rationality which began about two centuries ago. An impartial, instead

---

[74] See 'A Bibliographical Guide to Research' in Faivre, *Access*.

[75] Bochinger, *"New Age"*, 84.

[76] In illustration of this point, it is instructive to compare, for instance, Smart, *Phenomenon of Christianity* with a standard Church history.

[77] Cf. Hanegraaff, 'On the Construction'.

of polemical, historical study of gnosticism was potentially dangerous to the
self-understanding of traditional Christianity and its 18th/19th century representatives, but held little threat to the liberal theologians, Bible critics and historians of religion who increasingly came to dominate the academic study of
Christianity[78]. On the contrary: the historical study of gnosticism was useful
to these scholars because it helped them to undermine the claims of their more
conservative colleagues. With respect to modern esoteric traditions, the situation was different. Not only were these less distant in a strictly chronological
sense, they were also much closer in spirit. Having flowered in the same period which saw the emergence of modern science and rationality (and, as we
now know, crucially involved in that emergence[79]) they evidently touched upon
the very roots of modernity itself. If gnosticism had traditionally been perceived as the enemy of established Christianity—exemplifying what were
essentially regarded as pagan temptations—modern esotericism held a comparable position in relation to the newly-established rationalist worldview. To
the intellectual heirs of the Enlightenment, it appeared very much as gnosticism had appeared to the early Church fathers: as a collection of superseded
but potentially dangerous superstitions. They were regarded as the epitome, to
be precise, of those kinds of error from which human Reason had now finally managed to emancipate itself. It is essentially in this spirit that Christof
Schorsch deplores the tendency of New Age religion to return to 'the musty
darkness of spiritistic ratifications and the impenetrable night in which the
phantoms roam' (see above), or the sociologist Küenzlen characterizes New
Age as 'a gnostic-esoteric amalgam, occultism, yes: obscurantism, ... pagan-
magical pieces of scenery, ... fluttering mythologisms ...'[80]. Such statements
hardly qualify as scholarly interpretations. They are expressions of a secularized heresiology which can flourish in the space left vacant by serious research.
An additional problem of studying the New Age from a historical perspective
has to do with a complementary pro-esoteric approach to "esotericism" on the
part of many of its present students. At present, most students in the field
approach it with "religionist" presuppositions. Many of them have become
interested in traditional forms of esotericism primarily as a result of their personal search for alternatives to modern secular rationalism. From this perspective they are often particularly hostile to what they regard as the superficial pseudo-esotericism of New Age religion. What worries them is the popular tendency to understand "esotericism" and "New Age" as almost or com-

---

[78] About the history of the study of gnosticism, cf. Rudolph, *Gnosis*, 30-52; Van den Broek,
'Present State of Gnostic Studies', 41-71.
[79] The literature on this subject is rapidly expanding. See for instance Yates, 'The Hermetic
Tradition in Renaissance Science'; Righini Bonelli & Shea (eds.), *Reason, Experiment, and Mysticism*; part 2 of Merkel & Debus, *Hermeticism and the Renaissance*.
[80] Küenzlen, 'New Age', 38.

pletely synonymous terms. In an understandable attempt to protect their own already vulnerable subject, they tend to deny *any* connection between what they see as "real" esotericism, on the one hand, and New Age religion, on the other. I will argue, in contrast, that New Age religion unquestionably emerged from esoteric traditions in western culture; but I will add that historical processes of creative *reinterpretation* of traditional esotericism under the impact of modernity are crucial for a correct understanding of New Age religion. Thus, the similarities and the differences between traditional esotericism and New Age religion must both be taken into account.

The inadequate state of research into western esotericism imposes severe limits on what can be done here. Since I cannot assume a general "working knowledge" of western esotericism, some kind of overview of that field has to be included; but since our subject is not western esotericism but the New Age movement, such an overview must be strictly subordinate to the specific aims of this study. Any attempt to do justice to all the complexities of western esotericism would take so much space that the result would be a highly unbalanced book: one which would no longer be about the New Age movement but about esotericism as such. The only alternative is a highly condensed discussion, which cannot but fall short of the nuance that I have called for in my Part Two. Since I have consistently warned against the tendency to generalize about the "basic concepts" of New Age religion, a similar warning is appropriate with respect to the extremely complicated processes by which the elements of New Age religion have emerged in the context of western esotericism and under the impact of processes of secularization. Although I will attempt to trace those developments, it should be understood that my discussion will necessarily be of an *exploratory* nature. During the last decades, and with increasing speed during recent years, the field of "western esotericism" is being rediscovered as a subject for serious study[81]. This allows us to perceive at least the main lines of development, and to formulate the most important problems connected with the historical emergence of New Age religion. In so doing, I hope to develop a general framework for interpretation which, however, will do no more than provide a general orientation for future research. Much further work, and more space than is available here, is necessary in order to "fill in" this framework with historical detail; and in the course of such research the framework itself will need to be nuanced and, probably, adapted.

---

[81] Faivre & Voss, 'Western Esotericism'; Faivre, 'Avant-Propos'.

CHAPTER FOURTEEN

A HISTORICAL FRAMEWORK

1. The Modern Hermeticist Revival and the Emergence of Western Esotericism

The study of western esotericism is strongly indebted to the contributions of French research. In France, more than in other countries, a modest but important academic tradition has developed with respect to this field. In developing a historical framework for interpreting New Age religion, I will take as my point of departure the work of Antoine Faivre, whose chair for "History of Esoteric and Mystical Currents in Modern and Contemporary Europe" (Sorbonne, Paris) is unique in the world. Faivre's work, and his more recent publications in particular, provides us with a reliable means of "Access to Western Esotericism"[1].

A. "Esotericism" as Technical Terminology

The adjective "esoteric" dates back to antiquity. While Aristotle is often credited with having invented the term, it was first introduced around 166 C.E. by Lucian of Samosata[2]. "Esotericism" as a substantive, however, is a relatively recent invention. It was popularized by Eliphas Lévi since 1856[3], and was subsequently introduced into the English language by the theosophist A.D. Sinnet in 1883[4]. Lévi himself may well have derived the term *l'ésotérisme* from Jacques Matter's *Histoire du gnosticisme* (1828)[5]. In the same book which pop-

---

[1] Faivre, *Access to Western Esotericism*. This English translation contains most of the materials from the French original *Accès de l'ésotérisme occidental*, and Faivre's small introduction *L'ésotérisme*. The substantial essay on 'Ancient and Medieval Sources' (published originally in *Accès*, but not included in the English *Access*) is included in Faivre & Needleman, *Modern Esoteric Spirituality*. The French *Accès* was recently expanded into a two-volume work.

[2] For an extended discussion, see Riffard, *L'ésotérisme*, ch. V. A brief overview is included in Corsetti, *Histoire de l'ésotérisme*, 7-11.

[3] Eliphas Lévi, *Dogme et rituel*. Eliphas Lévi was the pseudonym of Alphonse-Louis Constant (1810-1875), a key figure in 19th-century occultism (cf. McIntosh, *Eliphas Lévi*). In Faivre's earlier works one still finds Lévi mentioned as not just the main popularizer but the inventor of the neologism (*Accès*, 13; id., 'Esotericism', 38). This is corrected in Faivre, *Access*, 86, where Jean-Pierre Laurant is credited with discovering an earlier reference in the work of Jacques Matter (see text; cf. Laurant, *L'ésotérisme*, 40-41).

[4] Eliade, 'The Occult and the Modern World', 49. Eliade mentions not 1883 but 1881 as the year in which Sinnett's *Esoteric Buddhism* was published; Riffard, *L'ésotérisme*, 78-79.

[5] According to Laurant, *L'ésotérisme*, 40-41, followed by Faivre, *Access*, 86, and Faivre &

ularized the term *l'ésotérisme*, Lévi also introduced *l'occultisme*. This latter term was most probably invented by Lévi himself, inspired by Cornelius Agrippa's *De Occulta Philosophia* (1533). Although the terms "esotericism" and "occultism" have often been regarded as equivalent[6], especially in older studies[7], I will proceed to argue that occultism is better used to denote a specific development *within* esotericism. For the moment, it suffies to observe that, in Lévi's usage, the two terms roughly covered the traditional "occult sciences" and a wide range of religious phenomena connected or loosely associated with it. Thus, he provided useful generic labels for a large and complicated group of historical phenomena that had long been perceived as sharing an *air de famille*[8]. This is the sense in which Faivre, too, understands the term "esotericism". Accordingly, he explicitly distinguishes it from two other commonly-encountered meanings. To define "esotericism" with direct reference to "secrecy" or a "discipline of the arcane" is overly restrictive: many manifestations of alchemy or Christian theosophy, for instance, have never been secret but were widely disseminated[9]. To define esoteri(ci)sm as the "spiritual center" or transcendent unity common to all particular religious traditions (as done in the so-called "perennialist" school of Comparative Religion) implies that one subscribes to a religious doctrine which is more properly regarded as an *object* of study[10].

As a technical term in the study of religion, esotericism *sensu* Faivre must further be distinguished from its popular usage in the current New Age context. Christoph Bochinger describes how a new meaning of the term has emerged in addition to the more traditional ones. In current New Age parlance, the concept of "esotericism" does not primarily refer to a historical tradition or cluster of traditions, but is

> ... first and foremost a concept referring to *Individualkultur* according to the motto: "You have it all inside yourself, check it out!" ... Thus Esotericism changed

---

Voss, 'Western Esotericism', 56, Matter is the earliest reference known to scholarship. According to Riffard, however, the English equivalent *esotery* is attested as early as 1763, while *esoterism* and *esotericism* appeared only after 1828 (Riffard, *L'ésotérisme*, 77). Unfortunately, Riffard's source reference in this case is unclear.

[6] Thus, for instance, in Amadou, *L'occultisme*, or Copenhaver, *Symphorien Champier and the Reception of the Occultist Tradition*.

[7] Cf. also Bochinger, "*New Age*", 371 nt 2.

[8] Faivre & Voss, 'Western Esotericism', 49.

[9] Faivre, *Access*, 5.

[10] Cf. Faivre, *Access*, 5; and Hanegraaff, 'Empirical Method', 110. Faivre does not explicitly mention perennialism, but this is clearly the perspective he is referring to (cf. his observation that perennialists usually speak of *esoterism* rather than esotericism; cf. Hanegraaff, 'Empirical Method', 110 nt 24). For introductions to perennialism, see Nasr, 'Introduction'; Smith, 'Introduction to the Revised Edition'. For a critical discussion, see the Dossier "Pérennialisme" published in *ARIES* (Association pour la Recherche et l'Information sur L'Ésotérisme) 11 (1990), 5-45, and subsequent contributions in *ARIES* 12-14 (1990-1991).

... from a special tradition of knowledge into a special type of "religion", the "journey within". ... Similar to the word "spirituality", "Esotericism" thus became a
surrogate word for "religion", which accentuates its subjective element focused
on inner experience[11].

This observation is confirmed by my own research. With reference to the rest
of this discussion it will be essential to understand that, although Western Esotericism will be presented as a framework for interpreting New Age religion,
I will consistently be referring to the technical meaning of esotericism *sensu*
Faivre, *not* to the popular meaning *sensu* New Age!

B. The Origins of Western Esotericism

As presented by Faivre, the foundations of western esotericism can be traced
back at least as far as antiquity. In a long essay about the 'Ancient and Medieval
Sources of Modern Esoteric Movements', he discusses the contributions of
neo-pythagoreanism, stoicism, hermetism, gnosticism, neoplatonism and
Christianity[12]. It is only with hindsight, however, that these various traditions
are perceived as having contributed to the emergence of a new, semi-auto-
nomous domain. Faivre dates the beginnings of the process of autonomization
to the 12th century, but mentions the 14th century as the decisive turning point.
It is in the 12th century, with the development of the *artes mechanicae* at the
expense of the *artes liberales*, that he sees the first signs of a 'secularization
of space and time that entailed a "mechanization" of the image of the world'[13].
The "discovery of nature", as an organic and lawful domain worthy of attention in its own right, produced a twofold result: on the one hand, a secularization of the cosmos at the expense of the sense of the sacred and, on the other hand, a revival of *magia* in the sense of a participatory philosophy of nature[14].
The first development would eventually lead to the mechanization of the world
picture, the second to the *magia naturalis* fundamental to Renaissance esotericism. Faivre describes this process as coming to a head during the 14th century, under the dual impact of Averroism and nominalism. The acceptance of
Averroes's Aristotelian cosmology destroyed the intermediate angelic realms

---

[11] Bochinger, "*New Age*", 376.

[12] See nt 1. Notice that the following discussion will be restricted to the development of western esotericism in the Christian context: this is the area covered by Faivre's oeuvre, and the one
with direct relevance to our concerns. Actually, however, such a limitation is articifial. As I have
argued elsewhere ('Empirical Method', 122-123) esotericism must be seen as a domain of study
within all three great scriptural traditions, which means that esotericism *sensu* Faivre would have
to be regarded as a historically and culturally demarcated subdomain. A similar approach is found
in an important recent contribution to the subject: Merkur, *Gnosis*.

[13] Faivre, 'Esotericism', 43; cf. id., 'Renaissance Hermeticism'.

[14] Faivre, 'Ancient and Medieval Sources', 26.

of neoplatonic cosmology; and the triumph of nominalism destroyed the traditional assumption that the laws and realities of the sensory world stand in an analogical and homological relationship to higher celestial or divine worlds[15]. Accordingly, there was no longer a continuity between a spiritually structured universe, on the one hand, and physical and self-sufficient laws, on the other. This opened the way for the development of modern science, but it had other results as well. Paradoxically, it was precisely the destruction of traditional cosmology that made possible its eventual reconstitution as an autonomous domain. As formulated by Faivre & Voss, 'When theology cast off what had been formerly part of itself, the result was an enormous abandoned field. This field was quickly reconstituted, "reinterpreted" from the outside (i.e., from outside theology) by humanists with esoteric leanings'[16]. This reconstitution of a traditional cosmology took place under the impact of the neoplatonic and hermetic revival of the later 15th century, and marks the proper beginning of western esotericism in a precise sense.

It is important not to misconstrue the nature of the connection between the "discovery of nature" and the emergence of esotericism. Christoph Bochinger mistakenly concludes that Faivre's description of esotericism, as a historical counter-current against the secularization of the cosmos, implies a dichotomization which diametrically opposes "esotericism" and "science". He argues that

> the close interconnections between "esoteric" and "natural scientific" traditions of knowledge from the Renaissance to the 17th and 18th centuries make the dichotomy observed by [Faivre] appear as a later construct, which does not do full justice to the development of the tradition. Actually it is only in modernity that this split—and a corresponding amalgamation of various "esoteric" alternative proposals—can be observed[17].

Actually, however, the close interconnection correctly observed by Bochinger confirms Faivre's account. Modern[18] western esotericism is a product of the

---

[15] Faivre, 'Ancient and Medieval Sources', 52-54. Faivre's account of Averroism is dependent on the work of Henry Corbin (see his *Creative Imagination*, 10-13), whose analyses with reference to a *Mundus Imaginalis* are a subject of controversy in Islamic studies. Incidentally, for a correct understanding of Faivre's account, a serious mistake in the English translation of his article should be noted. The line 'Their disappearance [i.e., of the *animae coelestes*], in Averroes and his followers, is found in the "Imaginal" ...' makes no sense in the context. The original reads *'Leur disparition, chez Averroès et dans l'averroïsme, est celle de l'Imaginal ...'* (Faivre, *Accès*, 115), i.e., the disappearance of the *animae coelestes* means the disappearance of the "Imaginal".

[16] Faivre & Voss, 'Western Esotericism', 51.

[17] Bochinger, *"New Age"*, 373 nt 8.

[18] Note that Bochinger uses the term "modern" in a more restricted sense than Faivre. For Faivre, it covers the period since the Renaissance, and esotericism *sensu* Faivre is therefore a tradition belonging to modernity; Bochinger, according to a tradition dominant in German research, uses the term "modernity" for the period roughly since 1750 (personal communication, 25.2.1996).

"discovery of nature" and has, from the very beginning, displayed a strong interest in understanding the secrets of the natural world. This is the reason for its persistent liaisons with natural science and *Naturphilosophie* (cf. chapter three)[19]. Therefore Faivre's presentation of esotericism as a "counter-current" to the "secularization of the cosmos" cannot simply be equated with an "esotericism-science" dichotomy. Esotericism formed a counter-force against a mechanistic worldview and against a science based on wholly secular principles; its alternative was an "organic" worldview, and a science based on religious assumptions. It is this vision which created a first condition for the emergence of New Age religion in the later 20th century.

C. The Components of Western Esotericism

There can be no question here of relating in sufficient detail the history of western esotericism as it developed since the second half of the 15th century. It is not insignificant that even Faivre's fairly comprehensive overview modestly claims no more than to provide an *Access to Western Esotericism*[20]. Since, moreover, the subject of this study is not western esotericism as such but the New Age Movement, I will restrict myself to sketching the main components that went into the new synthesis and became fundamental to "the formation of a Referential Esoteric Corpus in the Renaissance"[21]. In doing so, I will approach the historical materials from a systematic rather than a strictly diachronic perspective, and will highlight those elements which will later prove significant for understanding our main subject, New Age religion. One may roughly distinguish two philosophical traditions (neoplatonism and hermeticism), three "traditional sciences" (astrology, *magia*, and alchemy), and one current of theosophical speculation (kabbalah). The status within esotericism of Christian mysticism and Reformation "spiritualism" is problematic, for reasons that will be discussed separately.

Philosophical Frameworks: Neoplatonism and Hermeticism
The influence of neoplatonism upon the esoteric tradition is so pervasive that it is often not even explicitly mentioned[22]. The beginnings of modern esotericism are generally located in the Florentine Platonic Academy founded by Cosi-

---

[19] See especially Faivre & Zimmermann, *Epochen der Naturmystik*.

[20] Cf. Faivre's remark that a real *History of Esotericism in the West* would be premature (*Access*, x). Other comprehensive overviews include Frick, *Erleuchteten*; id., *Licht und Finsternis*; Corsetti, *Histoire de l'Ésoterisme*; Van den Broek & Hanegraaff, *Gnosis & Hermeticism*.

[21] Faivre, *Access*, 6.

[22] The Index to Faivre, *Access* has no special entries for "neoplatonism" or "platonism", and gives only four references to "Plato". Similarly, Yates, *Giordano Bruno* only has an entry for "Plato".

mo de' Medici in the second half of the 15th century and entrusted to the care of the young scholar Marsilio Ficino[23]. It is true, as we will see presently, that 'Ficino can be called a Platonist only with reservations'[24]; nevertheless, it was in a thoroughly neoplatonist (and anti-aristotelian/averroist[25]) atmosphere that modern esotericism was born, and this philosophical orientation has remained dominant ever since. It is this fact which explains the direct applicability, which might seem surprising at first sight, of A.O. Lovejoy's *Great Chain of Being* to New Age religion. Lovejoy worked too early to be influenced by the rediscovery of Renaissance hermeticism (see below) under the impact of Frances A. Yates and other scholars associated with the London Warburg Institute. As a result, the phenomenon of a hermetic neoplatonism (or neoplatonic hermeticism; see below), which is central to the emergence of Western esotericism, still lay beyond his horizon. One may assume that Lovejoy would have followed the common opinion of his day and disregarded Renaissance "occult philosophy" as marginal to the true history of thought[26]. With hindsight, however, his study of the fundamental dynamics of Platonism reveals itself as highly relevant to the study of esotericism. I suggest that the importance in New Age religion of "ultimate source holism", especially of the "generative" variety, is based on a neoplatonic cosmology inherited from esoteric sources.

The influence of the philosophical *Hermetica*[27], ever since Ficino, is largely responsible for the fact that these esoteric sources seldom contain a "pure" philosophical Platonism. About 1460, a Greek manuscript of the *Corpus Hermeticum* was brought from Macedonia to Florence by a monk, Leonardo da Pistoia. Apart from the *Asclepius*, these texts had never been available in the Christian west. Anxious to read them before dying, Cosimo de' Medici instructed Ficino to interrupt his translations of Plato and give first priority to the new find. Ficino's translation was finished by the end of 1462 and published under the title *Pimander* (an adaptation of the title of the first treatise, *Poimandres*) in 1471. It went through many editions during the 16th century, and must be regarded as a "classic" of the period[28]. Mainly responsible for this popularity

<hr/>

[23] Kristeller, *Philosophy of Marsilio Ficino*; id., *Eight Philosophers*, ch. 3; Yates, *Giordano Bruno*, chs. I-IV; Boer, 'Translator's Introduction'; Hankins, *Plato in the Italian Renaissance*, Part IV.
[24] Schmitt, 'Perennial Philosophy', 507.
[25] About Ficino's rejection of Aristotelianism and Averroism see Hankins, *Plato in the Italian Renaissance*, 269-278.
[26] This neglect has led to a somewhat bizarre situation for instance with respect to the study of German Idealism and Romanticism, where scholars have often vaguely referred to "neoplatonic" influences where actually the influences in question were often at least as much hermetic as neoplatonic, and should be regarded as aspects of the esoteric tradition. See for instance the important study of De Deugd, *Metafysisch grondpatroon*. Cf. my discussion in chapter fifteen, section 1A; and Hanegraaff, 'Romanticism'.
[27] For the distinction between the philosophical and the "magical" *Hermetica*, see below.
[28] Relevant sources are Bonardel, *L'hermétisme*; Merkel & Debus, *Hermeticism and the*

was the generally-shared belief that the mythical author of the *Corpus Hermeticum*, Hermes Trismegistus, had been a contemporary of Moses and the fountainhead of a primordial wisdom which united the two "sister streams" of Theology and Philosophy[29]. True theology was, of course, Christian; and true philosophy was Platonic[30]. Ultimately, it was argued, they were one: both were expressions of the primordial wisdom tradition known as *prisca theologia*, which derived from Hermes and Zoroaster and led up to Plato[31]. Reconceptualized in the 16th century as *philosophia perennis*, this theme of an ancient genealogy of divinely inspired philosopher-sages became centrally important to the esoteric tradition; reconstructed by nineteenth-century occultists under the influence of the "oriental renaissance" and comparative religion, it was finally adopted in the New Age movement[32]. Since the *Pimander* was believed to derive from Hermes himself (the source of Moses and Plato), it was perceived as not just a collection of interesting discourses, but as a principal source of wisdom which contained the essence of religious and philosophical truth. This explains its authority among Platonizing intellectuals in Renaissance culture. Before 1614, no one doubted that the *Corpus Hermeticum* was written by Hermes in a period long before the advent of Christianity. In that year, the Greek scholar Isaac Casaubon published a large-scale criticism of Cesare Baronius's *Annales Ecclesiastici* (1588-1607), a church history in Counter Reformation style. Included in Casaubon's book was a demonstration, on the basis of internal and stylistic evidence, that the hermetic writings could not possibly have been written before the advent of Christianity[33]. Casaubon's argu-

---

Renaissance; Anonymus (ed.), *Présence d'Hermes Trismégiste*; Faivre, *Eternal Hermes*; a textual history with illustrations was published as Anonymus (ed.), *Hermes Trismegistus: Pater Philosophorum*.

[29] For overviews see Walker, *Ancient Theology*; Schmitt, 'Perennial Philosophy', 505-532; Yates, *Giordano Bruno*, ch. I.

[30] Schmitt, 'Perennial Philosophy', 508.

[31] For a good overview of beliefs about Hermes, see Yates, *Giordano Bruno*, ch. I. In the *Theologia Platonica*, Ficino gives the genealogy as (1) Zoroaster; (2) Mercurius Trismegistus; (3) Orpheus; (4) Aglaophemus; (5) Pythagoras; (6) Plato. But, in the preface to his Plotinus commentaries, he states that the *prisca theologia* began simultaneously in Persia and Egypt, represented by Zoroaster and Hermes respectively. Mercurius Trismegistus is a common synonym for Hermes. About the obscure Aglaophemus, presumably an Orphic teacher of Pythagoras, see Schmitt, 'Perennial Philosophy', 510 nt 36.

[32] The term *philosophia perennis* was invented by Agostino Steuco (1497-1548). About the development from the *prisca theologia* espoused by Ficino, Pico della Mirandola and others, to Steuco's *philosophia perennis*, up to Leibniz, see Schmitt, 'Perennial Philosophy'. The esoteric idea of a primordial but largely hidden wisdom tradition is central to modern Theosophical doctrine as expounded by H.P. Blavatsky in *Isis Unveiled* (1877) and *The Secret Doctrine* (1888). Particularly important with respect to the New Age movement is the immensely popular book by Schuré, *Great Initiates*, which went through hundreds of editions since its first publication in French in 1889. Schuré's genealogy consists of Rama, Krishna, Hermes, Moses, Orpheus, Pythagoras, Plato and Jesus.

[33] Casaubon, *De rebus sacris et ecclesiasticis exercitationes XVI*. See the summary in Yates, *Giordano Bruno*, 398-403.

ments have never been refuted, and modern scholarship generally assumes the *Corpus Hermeticum* to have originated somewhere between the first and third century C.E.[34]. Casaubon's criticism amounted to a bomb-shell under the whole edifice of Renaissance Hermeticism but, as it turned out, it did not mean the end of the tradition. The effect of Casaubon's argument was delayed by the fact that it was "hidden away" in his large polemic against Baronius; and many Hermeticists, when they came to hear of it, either ignored it or refused to believe it[35]. In the long run, however, Casaubon's rebuttal could not fail to undermine the intellectual respectability of Renaissance hermeticism, and to contribute seriously to its eventual decline.

Apart from having a key function within the context of the *philosophia perennis*, the *Corpus Hermeticum* contains ideas which would become of crucial importance to Western esotericism. Most important in this respect is its combination of an emphasis on intuitive *gnosis* and a positive attitude towards the cosmos and to man's role in it. A famous passage from C.H. XI contains all these themes, and illustrates the fascination that hermeticism was bound to hold for Renaissance Humanists such as the author of the *Oratio on the Dignity of Man*, Pico della Mirandola:

> ... you must think of god in this way, as having everything—the cosmos, himself, <the> universe—like thoughts within himself. Thus, unless you make yourself equal to god, you cannot understand god; like is understood by like. Make yourself grow to immeasurable immensity, outleap all body, outstrip all time, become eternity and you will understand god. Having conceived that nothing is impossible to you, consider yourself immortal and able to understand everything, all art, all learning, the temper of every living thing. Go higher than every height and lower than every depth. Collect in yourself all the sensations of what has been made, of fire and water, dry and wet; be everywhere at once, on land, in the sea, in heaven; be not yet born, be in the womb, be young, old, dead, beyond death. And when you have understood all these at once—times, places, things, qualities, quantities—then you can understand god.
> But if you shut your soul up in the body and abase it and say 'I understand nothing, I can do nothing; I fear the sea, I cannot go up to heaven; I do not know what I was, I do not know what I will be', then what have you to do with god? ...
> And do you say, 'god is unseen'? Hold your tongue! Who is more visible than god? This is why he made all things: so that through them all you might look on him. This is the goodness of god, this is his excellence: that he is visible through all things. For nothing is unseen, not even among the incorporeals. Mind is seen in the act of understanding, god in the act of making[36].

---

[34] About Hermetism in antiquity, see the classic studies by Festugière, *Révélation d'Hermès Trismégiste*, and id., *Hermétisme et mystique païenne*. A more recent study is Fowden, *Egyptian Hermes*. Notice that, according to Van den Broek & Quispel (*Corpus Hermeticum*, 24-25, 188 nt 2), the fact that the *Corpus Hermeticum* was written in the first centuries C.E. does not exclude the possibility that it may contain much older Egyptian traditions.

[35] Yates, *Giordano Bruno*, 398, 402.

[36] *Corpus Hermeticum* XI: 20-22 (quoted according to Copenhaver, *Hermetica*). Notice that according to a passage of C.H. XI: 21 not included in my quotation, "love of the

Apart from being congenial to the high-minded aspirations of Renaissance humanists such as Pico della Mirandola, this passage is also obviously suggestive with respect to New Age religion. Its basic themes are strikingly similar to the worldview of contemporary authors such as Jane Roberts/Seth, Shirley MacLaine, or Stanislav Grof, as analyzed in Part Two of this study. I am definitely not suggesting that these authors should simply be seen as latter-day hermeticists, much less that they have been influenced directly by the hermetic writings; rather, both the *Hermetica* and these contemporary authors must, each for themselves, be seen in their own context. What I do suggest is that the hermetic writings decisively contributed to, and that New Age religion has in turn emerged from, a religious tradition which strongly stimulates expressions of "cosmic religiosity".

The "Occult Sciences": Magic, Astrology, Alchemy
It has sometimes been argued that a sharp distinction should be made between the "philosophical" Hermetica (*Corpus Hermeticum* and the *Asclepius*), on the one hand, and a wide array of astrological, alchemical and magical sources, many of which were ascribed to Hermes Trismegistus, on the other. This distinction was at least partly inspired by a desire to demonstrate the superiority of the former category compared to what was regarded as the "masses of rubbish" belonging to the latter[37]. However, as pointed out by Yates, the "philosophical" *Asclepius* admiringly describes the magical practices by which the Egyptians "drew down" the gods into statues, and even the loftiest and most mystical of the philosophical *Hermetica* presuppose an astrological pattern in the cosmos[38]. In any case, the fact that the "occult sciences" were apparently legitimated by Hermes Trismegistus himself rehabilitated them in the eyes of Renaissance hermeticists. What resulted was the characteristic phenomenon of the *occulta philosophia* of the Renaissance period, pioneered by Marsilio Ficino and provided with a standard textbook by Cornelius Agrippa in 1533[39]. Predictably, this Christian appropriation of magic was controversial already in its own time. The irony of the situation has been expressed well by Frances Yates:

---

body" is evil, and incompatible with true understanding of the beautiful and the good. Although the *Corpus Hermeticum* exalts the beauty and perfection of the cosmos, the sphere of earthly existence is evaluated less positively (Van den Broek & Quispel, *Corpus Hermeticum*, 21); about the relation between gnosticism and hermetism, esp. with regard to dualism, world-rejection and asceticism, cf. Van den Broek, 'Gnosticism and Hermetism in Antiquity'.

[37] Yates, *Giordano Bruno*, 44, with reference to W. Scott.

[38] Yates, *Giordano Bruno*, 44.

[39] See the new critical edition: Perrone Compagni (ed.), Cornelius Agrippa: *De occulta philosophia*. The work was written in 1510. Cf. the well-known study of Yates, *Occult Philosophy*. An interesting, well-informed study of the occult sciences was published by an author under the pseudonym Alexandrian, *Histoire de la philosophie occulte*.

Believing in the immense antiquity of the *Corpus Hermeticum* and the *Asclepius*, and following Lactantius' estimate of their holy and divine character, the pious Christian, Ficino, returns in his study of them, not, as he thinks, to the antiquity of a *priscus theologus* who prophetically saw into Christian truth (and authorized the practice of magic), but to the type of pagan philosophical gnosis with Egyptianizing and magical tendencies, which characterised the anti-Christian reaction under Julian the Apostate[40].

Magia in the Renaissance sense of the word refers to a highly complicated area which, in spite of several solid studies, remains elusive in many respects[41]. Part of this complexity is conveyed by Faivre when he refers to the differences, far from clear-cut, between demonic, natural, and celestial/astronomical magic:

> Witchcraft and its spells, black magic, pacts with the Devil, and incantations are not directly linked to the concept of esotericism as we have defined it, but represent the black side of Philosophia occulta and an important part of the collective imaginary[42] of the time. There was here a great deal of *magia naturalis*, a premodern type of natural science. *Magia naturalis* is the knowledge and use of occult powers and properties that are considered "natural" because they are objectively present in nature ... This type of magic is hardly distinguishable from the tentative beginnings of modern science and often looked like a form of naturalism colored by atheism. But this ambiguous expression could also refer to *magia* in the esoteric sense, seen as an attempt to unify Nature and religion ... To *Magia* belongs white magic or theurgy, which uses names, rites, and incantations with the aim of establishing a personal link with entities that are not part of the world of physical creation. These two aspects of *magia naturalis* ... sometimes mingle, as in "celestial" or "astronomical" magic, where the stars can in fact be considered simultaneously from the point of view of the influence they are supposed to exert physically and of the influence exerted by their "will"[43].

As illustrated by the category last mentioned, it is often impossible to separate the domains of magic and astrology. "Spiritual" or "celestial" magic, as practiced for instance by Marsilio Ficino, can be understood only within an astrological context; and the third book of his classic treatise on magic explicitly instructs the reader 'On Making Your Life Agree With the Heavens'[44]. More-

---

[40] Yates, *Giordano Bruno*, 60.

[41] See especially Walker, *Spiritual and Demonic Magic*; Schumaker, *Occult Sciences*; Couliano, *Eros and Magic*. A look at my discussion of magic in chapter four of this study will suggest the theoretical problems involved, especially with respect to the question of whether magic is to be seen primarily as a practice or as a worldview.

[42] Faivre & Voss, 'Western Esotericism', 72 nt 3, explain this gallicism as follows: 'In the sense that the term ... has acquired in the humanities, mostly in France ("*l'imaginaire*" "*un imaginaire*"), this noun refers to the images, symbols, and myths which underlie and/or permeate a discourse, a conversation, a literary or artistic work, a current of thought, an artistic or political trend, etc. (whether consciously or not). In this sense, the word should not of course be understood to mean "unreal", nor should it be confused with the term "imagination" which is used to refer to a faculty of the mind'.

[43] Faivre, *Access*, 66.

[44] Ficino, *De Triplici Vita* part 3: *De Vita Coelitus Comparanda*. Title as rendered in the translation by Boer, *Marsilio Ficino's Book of Life*. Cf. however, the new translation with Latin

over, not only are magic and astrology difficult to distinguish in the context of esotericism; it could even be argued that, within the boundaries of the Renaissance period, esotericism and *Magia* are almost equivalent terms. Renaissance esotericism is epitomized by the characteristic type of the Renaissance *magus*, incarnated in such figures as Cornelius Agrippa, Giordano Bruno or John Dee; and, of course, the *prisci theologi* such as Zoroaster, Hermes or Orpheus were considered to have been divinely-inspired *magi*. With respect to New Age religion, the implications of this close association of Renaissance esotericism and *magia* are far-reaching. Renaissance magic (including its Christian kabbalistic element, on which see below) is undisputably fundamental to the ceremonial magic of 19th century occultism and has thus provided the historical conditions for the emergence of its contemporary descendant, New Age Neopaganism (which, as I argued, can be regarded as magic both in an emic and an etic sense). In addition, however, the "magical worldview" of Renaissance esotericism is also the model *par excellence* for the "re-enchantment of the world" that provides orientation to the New Age quest for a new paradigm[45]. In this case, "magic" is understood as referring, not primarily to magical practices or rituals, but to a "participatory" holistic *worldview* which re-unites the spiritual and the material dimension. Even in this case, however, the practical application of its hidden laws and forces is never far behind, as illustrated by the New Age concern with "creating our own reality" by means of visualizations and affirmations.

Magic and astrology are theoretically two distinct streams, but in the context of Renaissance esotericism it is perhaps more correct to say that astrology is implicit in the very concept (however unclearly defined) of *magia*. Alchemy, on the other hand, although merging in various ways with the other components of esotericism, remains a somewhat more clearly demarcated pursuit. Again, its hermetic character was obvious: the foundational *Tabula smaragdina* was one among the many ancient texts ascribed to Hermes[46], and alchemy was generally regarded as the hermetic science *par excellence*. Whether or not *spiritual* alchemy in a strict sense existed before the Renaissance period is a subject for debate[47], but in the context of Renaissance alchemy, at least, alchemy was unquestionably a spiritual pursuit[48]. The perspective of

---

original: Kaske & Clark, *Marsilio Ficino*, with the more prosaic translation "On Obtaining Life from the Heavens".

[45] Cf. Berman, *Reenchantment of the World*. This book, which is popular in New Age circles, focuses especially on alchemy as a paradigm for the "enchanted" world and on Gregory Bateson's systems theory as the foundation of a hoped-for re-enchantment.

[46] See Holmyard, *Alchemy*, 97-100; Faivre, *Eternal Hermes*, 19-20, 91-92.

[47] Merkur (*Gnosis*, chs. 2-4) argues that "spiritual alchemy" did not exist before the Renaissance period, as assumed by C.G. Jung and his followers.

[48] About alchemy in general and spiritual alchemy in particular, see Holmyard, *Alchemy*; Hutin, *Histoire de l'alchimie*; id., *L'alchimie*; Coudert, *Alchemy*; id., 'Renaissance Alchemy'; Bonardel, *Philosophie de l'alchimie*; id., 'Alchemical Esotericism'.

the spiritual alchemist is summarized by Allison Coudert:

> All the ingredients mentioned in alchemical recipes—the minerals, metals, acids, compounds, and mixtures—were in truth only one, the alchemist himself. He was the base matter in need of purification by the fire; and the acid needed to accomplish this transformation came from his own spiritual malaise and longing for wholeness and peace. The various alchemical processes ... were steps in the mysterious process of spiritual regeneration[49].

The interconnectedness of esotericism, *Naturphilosophie* and natural science is perhaps nowhere as evident as in Renaissance alchemy; in that context, Isaac Newton's well-documented fascination for the subject is less surprising than it may seem at first sight[50]. With reference to New Age religion, it may be argued that traditional alchemy is relevant primarily because of its occultist interpretations in the context of the 19th century and their influence on the work of Carl Gustav Jung, the most popularly influential interpreter of alchemy of this century. On the other hand, Jung himself (as will be demonstrated) was essentially an esotericist; his theories have deep roots in the German tradition of Romantic *Naturphilosophie*, which itself goes in an unbroken line back to Renaissance esotericism. We will return to that subject later. For the moment, the main thing to notice is that "transmutation" was interpreted as referring to an essentially religious process of spiritual regeneration and purification.

The Theosophical Component: Christian Kabbalah

The Christian interpretation of Jewish Kabbalah, in the general context of hermetic *magia*, has proved to be of momentous importance to the emergence of western esotericism[51]. The Florentine humanist Giovanni Pico della Mirandola, a close associate of Ficino, is usually mentioned as the first Christian kabbalist. It is likely that, even before him, Jewish converts to Christianity sometimes legitimated their conversion by using kabbalistic arguments[52]; but Pico was undoubtedly the first non-Jewish Christian kabbalist, as well as the most influential one. Pico's collection of nine hundred theses about the concordance of all philosophies, which he took with him to Rome in 1486 and offered to defend in public debate, contained seventy-two Kabbalistic *Conclusiones*. Within his

---

[49] Coudert, 'Renaissance Alchemy', 279. That the alchemical processes had 'nothing to do with chemical change', as stated by Coudert, seems to be an overstatement probably influenced by Jungian theory. Actually, the alchemical process was believed to take place simultaneously both on the material and the spiritual level.

[50] Dobbs, *Foundations of Newton's Alchemy*; several contribution to Righini Bonelli & Shea, *Reason, Experiment, and Mysticism*.

[51] On this subject, see Blau, *Christian Interpretation of the Cabala*; Secret, *Kabbalistes Chrétiens*; id., *Hermétisme et Kabbale*; Wirszubski, *Pico della Mirandola's Encounter*; Scholem, 'Zur Geschichte der Anfänge' (and cf. revised edition in French: Scholem, 'Considérations'); Masters, 'Renaissance Kabbalah'.

[52] Scholem, 'Zur Geschichte der Anfänge', 170.

larger framework of a hermetic *prisca theologia*, they purported to prove the
superiority of the Christian religion on the basis of Hebrew wisdom. When
they were first published, Pico's theses met with considerable disapproval from
orthodox quarters. He reacted with a public apology for his views, which
included his now-famous *Oration on the Dignity of Man*. Here, he repeats his
assertion that 'the ancient mysteries of the Hebrews [serve as] ... the confirmation of the inviolable Catholic faith'[53]. His argument is a perfect example
of the hermetic creed of a *concordia Mosis et Platonis*:

> When I purchased these [kabbalistic] books at no small cost to myself, when I
> had read them through with the greatest diligence and with unwearying toil, I saw
> in them (as God is my witness) not so much the Mosaic as the Christian religion.
> There is the mystery of the Trinity, there the Incarnation of the Word, there the
> divinity of the Messiah; there I have read about original sin, its expiation through
> Christ, the heavenly Jerusalem, the fall of the devils, the orders of the angels, pur-
> gatory, and the punishments of hell, the same things we read daily in Paul and
> Dionysius, in Jerome and Augustine. But in those parts which concern philoso-
> phy you really seem to hear Pythagoras and Plato, whose principles are so close-
> ly related to the Christian faith ...[54]

Pico's Christian Kabbalah was adopted and further developed by Johannes
Reuchlin, Francesco Giorgi, Cornelius Agrippa, Guillaume Postel, and others.
The study of kabbalistic sources provided western esotericism with a rich reser-
voir of theosophical speculations which, not least due to a common neoplatonic background, could be syncretized with hermeticism and the occult sciences.

We will see later that the Western process of secularization affected esotericism as strongly as it affected more orthodox forms of Christianity. As a result,
Christian kabbalism eventually survived in occultist forms which are more
properly called post-Christian. As such, they have most strongly affected the
contemporary "magical" scene from which neopaganism emerged. However,
in sharp contrast to the contemporary current mostly referred to as "High Magic", neopaganism tends to disemphasize precisely the "kabbalist" element in
occultist magic. The *specific* contribution of (Christian and post-Christian) kabbalah to New Age religion must therefore be regarded as rather insignificant.

D. *The Worldview of Western Esotericism*

Renaissance Hermeticism may be described as the manifestation of a religious
syncretism[55], based on the desire for a new cosmology that can assimilate the

---

[53] Pico della Mirandola, 'Oration on the Dignity of Man', 249.

[54] Pico della Mirandola, 'Oration', 252.

[55] I am aware of the problematic status of the term "syncretism". According to Leertouwer,
'Regardless of how syncretism is defined, it always refers to the situation in which two configurations of religious phenomena which could originally be distinguished with precision have

philosophical and scientific "discovery of nature" without sacrificing the dimension of the sacred. This concern with synthesizing religion and science has remained characteristic of esotericism right up to the present day, and is the foundation of an ever-present ambiguity. It explains the shifting allegiances of esotericism with respect to modern processes of secularization and rationalization, and often makes it impossible to classify its representatives according to a dichotomy of "progress" versus "reaction". We will return to this important point later. In order to establish a systematic foothold for our further discussion, it is useful to conclude this discussion of Renaissance esotericism with a summary of the general definition of "esotericism" recently developed by Faivre[56].

In several publications[57], Faivre has described esotericism as a distinct "form of thought", in terms of six characteristics. The first four are presented as intrinsic to the definition of esotericism, which means that they all have to be pre-

---

melted together completely' (Leertouwer, 'Syncretisme', 17). The core of Leertouwer's argument is that, since "coherence" and "distinctiveness" are relative concepts, syncretism in this strict sense cannot possibly exist in reality. This argument is logical rather than empirical. One might argue that the concept of syncretism need not be discarded as long as it is stated explicitly that, since monolithic and strictly separated religious configurations do not exist in reality, it is obvious *a priori* that the term syncretism cannot possibly be intended to convey such a notion. Such an approach seems to be reflected in Michael Pye's distinction between syncretism as a dynamic process and synthesis as a resolution of syncretistic patterns (Pye, 'Syncretism versus Synthesis', 222). Leertouwer's description of syncretism as the end result of a process would seem to refer to synthesis in Pye's sense. However, this means that Leertouwer's criticism can now be applied to Pye's concept of synthesis. By arguing that a dynamic process (syncretism) can be resolved in a static unity (synthesis), Pye seems to ignore the fact that *all* religious systems are dynamic. I concur with Leertouwer that a static religious synthesis is a non-existent phenomenon; but I would follow Pye in retaining the term "sycretism" as referring to dynamic processes. Still, it might be argued that, on that foundation, *all* religions are syncretistic so that the term syncretism becomes superfluous. However, it seems more helpful to retain the term in order to distinguish between periods characterized by a state of heightened religious ferment and periods of comparative stability. Accordingly, the term "syncretism" could be applied to all situations which (from an observer's perspective) are characterized by widespread *attempts* at creating a new synthesis, in contrast to situations which are characterized by the widespread *assumption* that a consensus already exists. It is undoubtedly true that, in any strict sense, these attempts are bound for failure and the assumption is mistaken; but it is also true that the former situation reflects emic motivations and aspirations which are no longer characteristic of the latter. It must be noted that this means that "syncretism" is defined with reference to such emic beliefs and motivations, and no longer with reference to observed processes of interaction and reinterpretation; and it implies that we should speak of "syncretistic periods" rather than of "syncretistic phenomena". My suggestion here is that such an approach enables us to apply the term syncretism to phenomena such as early Christianity or Renaissance hermeticism, as distinguished from later developments such as medieval Catholicism or Christian theosophy.

[56] One may observe the development of Faivre's thinking in this respect by comparing his discussion in *L'ésoterisme au XVIIIe siècle* with, for instance, his article 'Théosophie', 548-562 (discussion of the "constitutive elements of esotericism" on pp. 549-551) and his recent work (see text). The significance of this development will be returned to below.

[57] Faivre, *L'ésotérisme*, 14-22; id., 'Introduction I', xv-xx; id., *Access*, 10-15; Faivre & Voss, 'Western Esotericism', 60-62. Cf. my discussion in Hanegraaff, 'Empirical Method', 111-112.

sent in order for a certain movement or oeuvre to qualify as "esoteric"; accordingly, although they may be distinguished for analytical purposes, they are more or less inseparable. The last two characteristics are called relative or non-intrinsic: they are frequently present, but need not be. I will outline them briefly here:

a. *Correspondences*, symbolic or actual, are believed to exist between all parts of the visible and the invisible universe. As explained by Faivre, 'These correspondences, considered more or less veiled at first sight, are ... intended to be read and deciphered. The entire universe is a huge theater of mirrors, an ensemble of hieroglyphs to be decoded. Everything is a sign; everything conceals and exudes mystery; every object hides a secret'[58]. A distinction may be made between two possible applications. Correspondences may exist between visible and invisible levels of reality, following the well-known scheme of macrocosmos/microcosmos; accordingly, occult relations may be assumed to exist between the seven metals and the seven planets, between these and the parts of the human body, between the observable cosmos and the (super)celestial levels of the universe, and so on. Furthermore, correspondences may exist between nature (the cosmos), history, and revealed texts. Nature and scripture are believed to be in harmony; the "Book of Nature" contains the same truths as revealed in the Bible, and this correspondence may be brought to light by a visionary hermeneutics.

b. *Living nature.* The vision of a complex, plural, hierarchical cosmos permeated by spiritual forces is fundamental to the Renaissance understanding of *magia*. In this context, nature is perceived as a living *milieu*, a dynamic network of sympathies and antipathies, 'traversed by a light or a hidden fire circulating through it'[59]. In combination with (a), this furnishes the theoretical foundations for concrete implementation: various kinds of magical practice, "occult medicine", theosophical soteriologies based on the framework of alchemy, and so on, are based on it. One might add (although Faivre himself does not use the term) that, since it is the force of divinity which "enlivens" Nature, the concept is most properly described as a form of panentheism[60].

c. *Imagination and Mediations.* The idea of correspondences implies the possibility of mediation between the higher and the lower world(s), by way of rituals, symbols, angels, intermediate spirits, etcetera. *Imaginatio*, far from being mere fantasy, is regarded as an 'organ of the soul, thanks to which humanity

---

[58] Faivre, *Access*, 10.
[59] Faivre, *Access*, 11.
[60] The term panentheism was introduced by the German Idealist philosopher, Freemason and Swedenborgian K.C.F. Krause (1781-1832). The applicability of the term to western esotericism is confirmed by Frick, *Erleuchteten*, 115-116. About Krause's masonic background, cf. Miers, *Lexikon des Geheimwissens*, 237-238. About Krause's Swedenborgianism, see Kirven, 'Swedenborg and Kant Revisited', 106-107.

can establish a cognitive and visionary relationship with an intermediate world, with a mesocosm—what Henry Corbin proposed calling a *mundus imaginalis*[61]. *Imaginatio* in this sense is the main instrument for attaining *gnosis*: it is regarded as 'a tool for the knowledge of the self, of the world, of myth; it is the eye of fire penetrating the surface of appearances in order to make meanings, "connections", burst forth, to render the invisible visible ...'[62].

Faivre adds, with notes of caution, that the element of mediations is perhaps most useful for demarcating esotericism from mysticism:

> In somewhat oversimplified terms, we could say that the mystic—in the strictly classical sense—aspires to the more or less complete suppression of images and intermediaries because for him they become obstacles to the union with God. While the esotericist appears to take more interest in the intermediaries revealed to his inner eye through the power of his creative imagination than to extend himself essentially toward the union with the divine. He prefers to sojourn on Jacob's ladder where angels (and doubtless other entities as well) climb up and down, rather than to climb to the top and beyond[63].

Faivre leaves no doubt that this distinction should be understood as merely heuristic and ideal-typical. That reality is not always so clear-cut is illustrated by what might be called the "esoteric mysticism" of Hildegard of Bingen, or the "mystical esotericism" of Louis-Claude de Saint-Martin[64]. Actually, Faivre's discussion has the effect of pointing to the demarcation between "esotericism" and "mysticism" as a potentially problematic point. Below, this will occupy us in relation with the status of Reformation "spiritualism"[65].

d. *Experience of Transmutation*. As pointed out by Faivre, without this fourth component the concept of esotericism 'would hardly exceed the limits of a form of speculative spirituality'[66]. The terminology of alchemy is used here to convey the notion of an inner process or mystical "path" of regeneration and purification. Since its function is to "initiate" the esotericist into the hidden mysteries of the cosmos, God, and his own self, the experience of transmutation is most properly regarded as pertaining to the salvific quest for a perfect

---

[61] Cf. Corbin, '*Mundus Imaginalis*', 1-19. About *Imaginatio* in the context of esotericism, see Couliano, *Eros and Magic*; and in particular Godet, "*Nun was ist die Imagination...*". Notice Faivre's mention (*Access*, 13) of the connection with the celebrated "Art of Memory" (cf. Yates, *Art of Memory*).

[62] Faivre, 'Introduction I', xvii-xviii.

[63] Faivre, *Access*, 12.

[64] Faivre, *Acces*, 12.

[65] In my 'Empirical Method', 122, I argued that, particularly if one compares the Christian with the Jewish and Islamic domains, conventional distinctions between "gnosticism", "mysticism" and "esotericism" appear to 'amount to little more than Christian polemics in a secularized garb'. If this is correct, then it is no longer evident that a more inclusive domain should be called "esotericism" rather than "mysticism" (or "gnosis"). This has implications for the status of esotericism *sensu* Faivre.

[66] Faivre, *Acces*, 13.

gnosis. As pointed out under (c), the principal tool to this end is the *imaginatio*, which gives access to the intermediate realms between spirit and matter.

e. *The praxis of Concordance*. This additional component refers to 'a marked tendency to seek to establish commonalities between two or more different traditions, sometimes even between all traditions, with a view to gaining illumination, a gnosis of superior quality'[67]. Prominent examples are the belief in a *prisca theologia* or a *philosophia perennis*, as in the medieval and Renaissance periods, and the concern with a primordial "Secret Doctrine" or wisdom tradition considered as the key to all "exoteric" religious traditions, as in the Theosophical Movement of the 19th century.

f. A final component concerns the *transmission* of esoteric teachings from master to disciple, by way of preestablished channels of initiation. It includes both the idea of a historical genealogy of "authentic" spiritual knowledge (a "tradition" of esoteric truth), and the element of esoteric initiations in which sacred knowledge is transmitted directly from master to disciple.

The worldview of esotericism *sensu* Faivre can be characterized as "holistic", and it displays a highly suggestive similarity to basic elements of New Age religion. It would not be difficult to put forward an argument to the effect that New Age religion is therefore an expression of western esotericism[68]. The holographic paradigm, according to which the whole cosmos is reflected even in its smallest components, looks as if it is designed as a modern formulation of the correspondence between macrocosmos and microcosmos. That the cosmos is permeated by divine spirit, or "energy", is a commonplace of New Age thinking. A belief in "mediations" is evident in the cosmic hierarchy of spiritual levels, inhabited by spiritual entities; and the role of *imaginatio* is demonstrated by the exploration of transpersonal realities. The importance attached to "individuation", and the arduous ascent of human souls upwards through the spheres, seem to exemplify the elements of spiritual transmutation. Furthermore, New Age adherents strongly believe in a "perennial wisdom" which is the enduring core of all religious traditions. The non-intrinsic element of initiatic "transmission" seems somewhat less prominently displayed. Although New Age adherents tend to have a positive view of enlightened "masters" or gurus who impart insight to their pupils, the idea of being dependent on somebody else (rather than on one's own inner self) for spiritual illumination is not congenial to New Age individualism.

Such argumentation could easily be expanded with further examples. However, the quick and easy conclusion that New Age = esotericism must be regard-

---

[67] Faivre, 'Introduction I', xix.
[68] As has indeed been done by Kranenborg, *Andere weg van Jezus*.

ed as superficial and misleading. It exemplifies the ever-present tendency of the History of Ideas to degenerate into a species of merely 'imaginative historical generalization' (Lovejoy)[69]. To avoid this pitfall, it is vitally important to explore the historical developments under the impact of which the integral worldview of Renaissance esotericism developed into *new* directions. Thus, it will be possible to illustrate, on the one hand, the historical connection which indeed exists between traditional esotericism and New Age religion *and*, on the other, the historical/cultural distance which separates the two.

2. ESOTERICISM BETWEEN RENAISSANCE AND ENLIGHTENMENT

A. The "Inner Church" and Esotericism

According to Faivre's characterization, the "referential corpus" created in the Renaissance contained all the essential elements of esotericism. Accordingly, 'studying the history of Western currents of esotericism ... means first of all identifying the simultaneous presence of the four intrinsic components, and possibly also the two relative components, in the works in which they may be found'[70]. It must be admitted that, from a methodological perspective, this is potentially problematic. It would seem to imply that, in principle, no new development of the tradition which began in the Renaissance period can possibly lead to the emergence of *new* characteristics. A 16th-century worldview is presented as the defining norm; and any further development can never lead to more than the addition, at the very most, of further *non*-intrinsic elements. However, one might object that such new additions might eventually become so important that they must be regarded as *intrinsic* elements of the new development.

It seems to me that this problem becomes acutely important when we consider the tradition known as Christian Theosophy, which emerged in the 17th century on the foundation of older currents. As it happens, Christian Theosophy in general and, even more particularly, its later developments in 18th century Illuminism have been a subject of preference in Faivre's research[71]. In this context, it is interesting to examine the definition of "esotericism" included in his earlier work, which reflects a strong focus on Christian Theosophy and Illuminism. In his introductory study of 18th century esotericism, which was published in 1973, Faivre states that the adjective "esoteric" applies to thinkers,

---

[69] See chapter thirteen, nt 1.

[70] Faivre & Voss, 'Western Esotericism', 62.

[71] See especially Faivre, 'Courant théosophique' (& enlarged version in *Travaux de la Loge Nationale de Recherches Villard d'Honnecourt* 29, 119-176; and his two large studies of the 1960s: *Kirchberger*; and *Eckartshausen*.

Christian or not, who emphasize three points: Analogy, the Inner Church, and Theosophy[72]. Furthermore, he explicitly excludes 'witchcraft, magic, astrology, mantic arts'[73], noting that he will mention them only to the extent that a certain thinker happens to use them in a theosophical context. Apparently, he regards the "occult sciences" and Christian esotericism/theosophy as neighboring but distinct fields.

How to explain this shift of opinion? Obviously, it is natural and legitimate for a scholar to change his mind over the years. More to the point, definitions are always *etic* constructs, guided by the specific interests of the scholar in question. The early Faivre was first and foremost a specialized historian concerned with German and French movements of the 18th and early 19th century; it is only after he was appointed to the chair of "History of Esoteric and Mystical Currents in Modern and Contemporary Europe" in 1979 that the demarcation of "western esotericism" as a distinct area of academic research seems to have moved into the center of his attention. The differences between his earlier and more recent definitions reflect that change[74].

For us, the relevance of Faivre's intellectual development lies in the fact that his earlier definition explicitly allows for what might roughly be called the "spiritualist"/pietist element in 17th/18th century esotericism, while this element seems to have vanished from his later definition. This may be demonstrated with reference to Jacob Böhme, highlighted by Faivre and others as the principal fountain from which Christian theosophy has emerged[75]. As pointed out by Pierre Deghaye, Böhme's oeuvre is fed by two streams. One of these consists of a Hermetic-alchemistic *Naturphilosophie* in the Paracelsian tradition; the other consists of the tradition of German mysticism associated with Eckhart, Tauler and Suso. This second tradition was transmitted to Böhme via the "spiritualist" current of Reformation Germany, represented by the famous *Theologia Deutsch* which inspired the young Luther, and by a range of dissenters such as Sebastian Franck, Caspar Schwenckfeld, Valentin Weigel and others. The "spiritualist" tradition, with its emphasis on *Gelassenheit* and *Wiedergeburt*, became essential to the Pietistic traditions of the 17th and 18th century. Not only Böhme and the tradition of Christian theosophy but these Pietistic traditions as well have, in turn, been influenced by esotericism and

---

[72] Faivre, *L'ésotérisme au XVIIIe siècle*, 7-9.

[73] Faivre, *L'ésotérisme au XVIIIe siècle*, 13.

[74] Still, it might be argued that the surprisingly marginal position in Faivre's presentations of figures such as Sebastian Franck or Caspar Schwenckfeld (the former does not appear in the index of *Access*; the latter appears once in a special essay about Franz von Baader, but not in Faivre's historical overview) points to an emphasis on the *Naturphilosophische* aspects of Theosophy at the expense of their "mystical/spiritualist" side.

[75] See Faivre, 'Courant théosophique', 6-41. About Böhme specifically, cf. Deghaye, *Naissance de Dieu*.

were instrumental in disseminating elements of it[76]. Both currents have assimilated speculations in the tradition of Renaissance hermeticism, including the alchemy, Christian kabbalism and *magia* syncretized in that period[77].

As a result of these developments, a definition of "esotericism" with primary reference to the 17th/18th century situation is likely to be different from a definition based on the original "referential corpus" of Renaissance hermeticism. The fact that elements of the latter have been assimilated by Christian theosophy, Illuminism and various currents within Pietism is not the issue. The problem is, rather, that the tradition of Reformation "spiritualism" (with its further roots in medieval German mysticism) eventually became so influential in the esoteric tradition that, already in the case of Böhme, it can hardly be called "non-intrinsic" anymore. This problem is closely connected with the question (already mentioned with reference to Faivre's concepts of imagination/mediations) of the relationship between mysticism and esotericism (an adequate discussion of which, as I have argued elsewhere[78], will have to consider the status of "gnosticism" as yet a third variable). Although clarity about these issues will be of major importance to the future academic study of esotericism, this is obviously not the place to discuss them in detail. It suffices for the moment to take proper notice of the problem. Faivre's characterization of western esotericism in terms of four/six components remains valid and useful as a point of departure; but in my further discussion I will introduce Reformation "spiritualism" as an additional factor, essential to create a framework for the interpretation of New Age religion.

B. The Factor of Reformation "Spiritualism"

Christoph Bochinger is to be credited with having first called attention to the relevance of Reformation "spiritualism" for the interpretation of New Age religion[79]. As pointed out by him, it is crucial to distinguish the term "spiritualism" (*Spiritualismus*) as it has been used by Church historians since the end of the 19th century from other meanings. Apart from its philosophical sense (as a term closely associated with Idealism), the term is frequently used as a near synonym for 19th century spiritism. Since that movement, too, will prove

---

[76] Wehr, *Esoterisches Christentum*, or the large monograph by Deghaye, *Doctrine ésoterique de Zinzendorf*.

[77] Illustrative for this point is the fact that Goethe could derive the thoroughly hermeticist elements for his early *Privatreligion* from books circulating in Pietist circles. See the foundational study of Zimmermann, *Weltbild des jungen Goethe*.

[78] Hanegraaff, 'Empirical Method', 122-123.

[79] Bochinger, *"New Age"*, 244-257. Bochinger himself relies on the classic studies of Troeltsch, *Soziallehren*, esp. 848-940; and Hegler, *Geist und Schrift*. Further useful studies pertaining to Reformation "spiritualism" include Koyré, *Mystiques, spirituels, alchimistes*; Lindeboom, *Stiefkinderen*; Weeks, *German Mysticism*.

to be important for our concerns, I will adopt the convention of writing the term in quotation marks whenever the Church-historical usage is meant. Thus, our present subject is "spiritualism"; and the 19th century phenomenon will be referred to as spiritualism.

There can be no doubt that when Faivre, in his early publications, highlights the belief in an "inner church" as constitutive for Christian Theosophy and Illuminism, he is referring to the "spiritualist" tradition. Decried by the Reformers as *Schwärmgeister* or *Enthusiasts*, the "spiritualists" represent the Reformation current of radical religious subjectivism which, as one author has put it, 'aimed less at the synthesis of diverse sources of authority than at dissent from doctrinal authoritarianism'[80]. With reference to the classic studies of Hegler and Troeltsch, Christoph Bochinger analyzes the "spiritualist" perspective in terms of twelve closely interrelated aspects: 1. Interiorization of the expectation of a New Era and the return of Christ; 2. Spiritual hermeneutics and reliance on the "Inner Word"; 3. Opposition between religious experience and "external" knowledge; 4. Certainty about spiritual things; 5. Interconnection of God-knowledge and self-knowledge; 6. Systematic criticism or reconceptualization of traditional Church dogma; 7. Criticism of the doctrine of justification and its practical/ethical results; 8. Religious freedom and personal responsibility; 9. Religious tolerance and criticism of Church intolerance: complete rejection of violence in matters of religion; 10. Criticism of the mediation of salvation by the Church and by external cultic ceremonies; 11. Affinity with rationalism; 12. Cosmological foundation of hermeneutics and doctrine of salvation.

Since Reformation "spiritualism" is a well-known topic of Church history and the sociology of religion, little more need be said about it here. I will adopt Bochinger's analysis, but with the proviso that the "spiritualist" element will be discussed, more explicitly than he does, in close connection with western esotericism. Even with respect to the 16th century, it would be artificial to insist upon a too strict separation of the hermetic/alchemistic tradition of *Naturphilosophie*, on the one hand, and a tradition of mystical piety relying on the "inner word", on the other[81]. The "cosmological" dimension of "spiritualism"

---

[80] Weeks, *German Mysticism*, 143.

[81] Cf. Goeters, 'Spiritualisten, religiöse', 255, where the movement is described as 'fed by medieval mysticism, neoplatonism and humanism, augustinian influences and the renaissance of Naturphilosophie'. Thomas Müntzer had read Plato and humanistic authors including Pico della Mirandola; Hans Denck was indebted to neoplatonism (Weeks, *German Mysticism*, 152, 155); Sebastian Franck mentions Hermes Trismegistus in connection with Pythagoras, Socrates, Plato, Plotinus, and others (Hegler, *Geist und Schrift*, as quoted in Bochinger, "*New Age*", 256 nt 54). A figure such as Valentin Weigel, belonging to a younger generation, was strongly influenced by Paracelsian *Naturphilosophie* especially in his later life (see for instance Weeks, *German Mysticism*, 162-167; Koyré, *Mystiques, spirituels, alchimistes*, 131-184; Gorceix, *Mystique de Valentin Weigel*; his blend of "spiritual-ism" and Paracelsianism prefigures Böhme.

(nr. 12) is a reflection of this. Actually, the relevance of hermeticism to Reformation "spiritualism" seems to have been underestimated, probably due to its minimal treatment in Troeltsch's standard work. On the other hand, as illustrated by Deghaye's discussion of Böhme mentioned earlier, the two streams should be distinguished at least typologically.

As demonstrated by Bochinger, the "spiritualist" element is important because of its general relevance to the emergence of characteristically modern types of religious sensitivity and, by implication, of New Age religion as one characteristic expression of "modern religion"[82]. New Age believers share with many of their contemporaries what may be called a "spiritualist" criticism of the Christianity of the established Churches: the latter are perceived as narrowly dogmatic, unduly preoccupied with sin, intolerant, and apt to encroach upon an individual's right of autonomy in religious matters (nrs. 6-10). Characteristic for New Age religion specifically are the expectation of a New Age, return of the Christ (often perceived as a purely spiritual event), an intuitive approach to sacred texts, reliance on "inner experience" as the foundation for spiritual insight, *gnosis* as entailing both self-knowledge and God-knowledge, and a cosmic religiosity (nrs. 1-5; 12). Of special interest is the affinity between "spiritualism" and rationality (nr. 11)[83]. Troeltsch is at pains to point out that this affinity is highly ambiguous, and argues that modern rationalism is in many respects closer to scholasticism than to "spiritualism"[84]. Nevertheless, the latter's rationalistic side, inherited from humanism, is evident. It is demonstrated with particular clarity in its religious tolerance, based on a religious universalism which may easily lead to religious relativism, since the Absolute is believed to be present in all its more limited expressions. Troeltsch concludes:

> ... the toleration preached by "spiritual reformers" did gain ground, because it everywhere recognized Truth and Revelation in every relative approach to the one Truth, which, ultimately, could only be experienced in the present. Only among the "spiritual reformers" was there liberty of conscience within the religious community ... But in this respect also this "spiritual" movement differs from strict rationalism, which, with its absolute demand for the truth of its ideas, tends rather towards intolerance, like the churches, and is only ready to tolerate the opinions of others out of contempt and opportunism. Real toleration was and is found only among those rationalists who have steeped themselves at the same time in mystical and "spiritual" ideas[85].

Surely this conclusion would be applauded by any New Ager today.

---

[82] Bochinger, *"New Age"*, 256.
[83] Troeltsch, *Soziallehren*, 870-872.
[84] Troeltsch, *Soziallehren*, 871.
[85] Troeltsch, *Soziallehren*, 872. Translation according to the English edition by Olive Wyon (Troeltsch, *Social Teaching*, 750-751).

3. A Clash of Worldviews

The quotation from Troeltsch suggests an affinity between "spiritualist" esotericism and Enlightenment rationalism. After the concept of western esotericism *sensu* Faivre (chapter fourteen, section 1), and the additional factor of
"spiritualism" (section 2), the impact of Enlightenment and post-Enlightenment developments on western esotericism will be our next focus of attention.
This, however, implies a jump from Renaissance esotericism and Reformation
"spiritualism", with only passing reference to Christian Theosophy, directly to
the 18th and 19th century. Any reader even remotely familiar with Western
esotericism will realize how much is being passed over in this. Two examples
must suffice: the phenomenon which Frances Yates has referred to as the "Rosicrucian Enlightenment" of the early 17th century is passed over in silence[86],
and the relevance of esotericism to the thinking of a range of influential philosophers, such as the Cambridge Platonists, is equally ignored. At this point, I
wish to repeat once more that my intention is not to write a brief history of
Western esotericism, but to highlight only those historical developments which
seem to have been crucial factors in creating conditions for the emergence of
New Age religion. I do believe that a detailed study of the movements just
mentioned would reveal that they are not wholly irrelevant to that concern,
since they contributed to weaving the complex tissue of latter-day esotericism
and created vehicles for its transmission. Nevertheless, their specific contributions seem not to have been such that the New Age movement as we now
know it could not have come into existence without them.

The impact of Western processes of rationalization and secularization, on
the other hand, is of an importance which can scarcely be overestimated. My
central thesis on the following pages will be that it represents *the* decisive
watershed in the history of western esotericism. The survival of esotericism
under the conditions of post-Enlightenment processes of secularization produced new and unprecedented phenomena. I will argue that, in spite of their
diversity, they have emerged essentially from two broad movements, both of
which are rooted in the late 18th century and have flourished in the 19th. The
first of these is *Romanticism*: a movement with deep roots in the esoteric tradition, but shaped decisively by the Enlightenment and, especially, the Counter-
Enlightenment. The second is most properly referred to as *occultism* (and
should not be confused with the "occult sciences" or "the occult"[87]). Both
movements, I will argue, can be defined as the products of a clash of worldviews. Romanticism emerged from a momentous event: the reinterpretation of
esoteric cosmology under the impact of the new evolutionism. This changed

---

[86] Yates, *Rosicrucian Enlightenment*.
[87] See Hanegraaff, 'Esoterie, occultisme en (neo)gnostiek', 11-12.

the nature of esotericism forever, but left the internal consistency of its world-view essentially intact. Occultism, in contrast, came into existence when the esoteric cosmology (based on universal correspondences) increasingly came to be understood in term of the new scientific cosmologies (based on instrumental causality). As a result, the internally consistent worldview of traditional eso-tericism gave way to an unstable mixture of logically incompatible elements. In both streams (and in the various hybrid combinations that emerged) tradi-tional esoteric ideas and concepts continued to be used under the new condi-tions but, since meaning and function depend on context, they inevitably under-went subtle but important changes. I submit that investigation of precisely these transformations—broadly put: the secularization of esotericism—should be a top priority of the academic study of esotericism and of New Religious Move-ments. Unfortunately, however, such research has hardly begun yet.

It is as a result of that hiatus that erroneous theories based on unhistorical presuppositions remain largely unchallenged. This can be demonstrated with reference to both streams distinguished above, but the case of occultism is per-haps most illustrative. The common perception, firstly, of "the occult" as a col-lection of "survivals", 'the ghosts of old forgotten creeds'[88], suggests that con-tinued adherence to it means regression to a superseded stage of cultural and religious development. This is the assumption behind descriptions of New Age religion as 'a gnostic-esoteric amalgam, occultism, yes: obscurantism, ... pagan-magical pieces of scenery, ... fluttering mythologisms ...'[89]. Such "inter-pretations" descend directly from a discredited 19th-century evolutionism which treated the "magical worldview" of the "primitive mind" as an essen-tially "pre-historical" syndrome in the literal sense of the word[90]. This approach is now widely regarded as incorrect with respect to the religions of tradition-al societies, and is equally unwarranted with respect to our subject. Esoteri-cism, as should be evident by now, *has a history*. Contrary to assumptions which are common among adherents as well as critics, it does not survive unchanged but is continually reinterpreted in the light of new social and cul-tural circumstances, including those of secular society.

A second frequent error, different in theory but related in practice, is to regard "the occult" as an anomaly of the human mind in general, or of modern soci-ety in particular. Thus, Marcello Truzzi has defined "the occult" as

> a residual category, a wastebasket, for knowledge claims that are deviant in some way, that do not fit the established claims of science or religion ... a common denominator for most (if not all) perspectives labelled occult (by anyone) is that they have in some way concerned themselves with things anomalous to our gen-erally accepted cultural-storehouse of "truths". That is, we are here dealing with

---

[88] Bateson & Bateson, *Angels Fear*, 6.
[89] Küenzlen, 'New Age', 38.
[90] As pointed out, for example, in Ter Haar, 'Gemeenschapsgodsdiensten', 11-13.

claims that contradict common-sense or institutionalized (scientific or religious) knowledge. This contradiction of accepted beliefs is the very thing which makes the occult somehow strange, mysterious and inexplicable. It is the very character of the occult that it deals with dissonant or contradicting knowledge claims[91].

A "sociology of the occult" on these premises is defective in several respects. It makes the very definition of "the occult" dependent on the values of modern secular rationality[92], thus precluding in advance the very possibility of investigating it in a historical framework. Its barely hidden assumption is that the occult is merely another word for "the irrational": a term which is used (again) in such a way as to denote not a historical tradition, but a recurrent temptation of the human mind[93]. Once again, this approach tells us more about its underlying secularist ideologies than about "the occult".

Both approaches are incompatible with an historical approach. The popular attraction of occultism during the 19th century was due, not to regression or a "disease of reason", but to its attempt to reformulate traditional beliefs in modern terms, and thus to present them as eminently reasonable. As noticed by Antoine Faivre, 'Generally occultists do not condemn scientific progress or modernity. Rather, they try to integrate it within a global vision that will serve to make the vacuousness of materialism more apparent'[94]. As in the case of Christian theology, we are dealing not with a simple pattern of total rejection of modernity but with a dialectical process of qualified acceptance. Both Christianity and esotericism have been profoundly affected by the process of secularization, and have attempted in various ways to update traditional tenets and present them as relevant to the secular world. In so doing, both developed religious theories, speculations and practices of a new, in-between type: bound to be still too "religious" for fully secular mentalities, yet too "secular" for those who wish to defend tradition against latter-day contaminations. Thus, both Christian theology and esotericism have their traditionalist conservatives and their liberal-minded modernists. In the case of esotericism specifically, the former group rejects occultism as a perversion[95]. It is only the second group,

---

[91] Truzzi, 'Definition and Dimensions', 245-246. Cf. the criticism of Galbreath, 'Explaining Modern Occultism', 15-16; cf. Hanegraaff, 'Empirical Method', 119-121; id., 'Esoterie, occultisme en (neo)gnostiek', 1, 17-18, 23-24 nt 1.

[92] It is true that Truzzi speaks of "anomalies" in relation to generally scientific *and* religious knowledge ('Definitions and Dimensions', 246). This was to be expected, however, for doing otherwise would lead to the absurd conclusion that large segments of modern Christianity have to be called "occult". In practice, Truzzi concentrates entirely on the contrast between occultism and modern science, as demonstrated by his discussion of the "authority of occult claims" (o.c., 249-250 & closing paragraph).

[93] For a more extended discussion of this persistent tendency, cf. Hanegraaff, 'On the Construction'.

[94] Faivre, *Access*, 88.

[95] See for instance Guénon, *L'erreur spirite*; id., *Le théosophisme*.

i.e. occultism, which is relevant with respect to New Age religion.

"Esotericism", on the one hand, and "secularization", on the other (combined in the concept of occultism) thus emerge as the two key concepts in my following interpretation of New Age religion. The concept of secularization is, however, elusive in the extreme. It refers not to a clear and simple proposition, but to an highly complicated series of historical processes[96]. In the discussion which follows, I will highlight four of them as particularly important to the emergence of New Age religion. I put them forward as aspects of "secularization" simply in the sense that all of them have been important factors in the historical processes which have led to a decline of Christian authority since the 18th century. They are not necessarily expressions of *secularism*, in the sense of an anti-religious ideology. A "secularized religion" may well be precisely that: secularized and religious. The only thing it is not is "traditional", in the sense of resting on presuppositions which are uninfluenced by secularization. My following account, in the next four sections, of the secularization of esotericism can be summarized in terms of two parallel developments.

(1) The transformation of esotericism into *occultism* is a clear manifestation of what Max Weber once called the "disenchantment" of the world. Contrary to common opinion, I will claim that, although New Age religion calls for a "re-enchantment", its own foundations consist of an already thoroughly secularized esotericism. The development from an internally consistent worldview of correspondences to an ambivalent worldview, consisting of intermingled elements of correspondences and causality, constitutes the first step of the secularization of esotericism and marks the birth of occultism as such (chapter fifteen, section 1B). However, three further aspects of the general secularization process have influenced *further* developments and have become decisive, together with the first one, for the emergence of New Age religion. These are the modern study of religions (including the so-called "oriental Renaissance" and the rise of Comparative Religion)(chapter fifteen, section 2); the rise of popular evolutionism (section three); and the popular impact of religious types of psychology (section four).

(2) The *Romantic* stream is distinguished from the occultist stream initially by its more consistent defense of a worldview of correspondences against a worldview of causality. Its specific character as "secularized esotericism" is derived, instead, from its combination of that traditional worldview with the innovative element of evolutionism (chapter fifteen, section 1A & 3). The two other elements (the study of religions; and popular religious psychologies) have exerted an influence at least as strong as in the case of occultism (chapter fifteen, section 2 & 4).

It should be superfluous to add that this general typology does have its lim-

---

[96] See the brilliant discussion by Chadwick, *Secularization of the European Mind*, ch. 1.

itations. Any attempt to reduce historical processes to rigid schemes is bound ultimately to suffer shipwreck on the unpredictable factor of human creativity. However, I do not believe that these distinctions have merely heuristic value. In proposing them, my intention is first and foremost to provide a framework for interpreting New Age religion; but, beyond that, I also hope to demonstrate that the study of religions in secular modernity might do better than continue to rely on meaningless expressions such as "the occult", "the irrational" or, even, "mysticism"[97].

---

[97] About the ideological backgrounds to usage of the term "mysticism" as a generalized category, cf. Merkur, *Gnosis*, 3-4, and *passim*.

CHAPTER FIFTEEN

THE MIRROR OF SECULAR THOUGHT

1. Esotericism Between Enlightenment and Counter-Enlightenment

It is a common assumption that traditions and phenomena referred to as "mystical" or "occult" are not only opposed to, but *incompatible* with the values of the Enlightenment. Accordingly, they are usually associated with Counter-Enlightenment and Romanticism. This assumption is understandable, but in need of modification.

I will take as my point of departure Isaiah Berlin's classic article on 'The Counter-Enlightenment'[1]. With respect to the 'central ideas of the French Enlightenment', Berlin makes two points. First of all, the Enlightenment was based upon

> The proclamation of the autonomy of reason and the methods of the natural sciences, based on observation as the sole reliable method of knowledge, and the consequent rejection of the authority of revelation, sacred writings and their accepted interpreters, tradition, prescription, and every form of non-rational and transcendent source of knowledge ...'[2]

This is the familiar picture of the Enlightenment as the arch-enemy of traditional religious authorities. To the extent that it emphasized reason as the *exclusive* foundation for reliable knowledge and the pursuit of a just society, these tenets are clearly incompatible with all varieties of esotericism (including occultism and New Age). However, Berlin continues by arguing that underlying the doctrines of the Enlightenment there was an unshaken belief in the reality of natural law and of eternal principles which apply to humanity in all times and places. The Enlightenment thinkers opposed these eternal principles to what they regarded as the 'chaotic amalgam of ignorance, mental laziness, guesswork, superstition, prejudice, dogma, fantasy'[3] characteristic of traditional Christianity. In other words, Enlightenment thinkers still shared with most of their contemporaries

> a wide area of agreement about fundamental points: the reality of natural law ..., of eternal principles by following which alone men could become wise, happy, virtuous, and free. One set of universal and unalterable principles governed the

---

[1] Berlin, 'Counter-Enlightenment'. For further discussion of the Enlightenment specifically, see especially Cassirer, *Philosophie der Aufklärung*. Cassirer is a principal pillar of Gay, *Enlightenment* (2 vols.). Gay's study was conceived as a reaction to the older study by Becker, *Heavenly City*. For recent overviews, cf. Porter, *Enlightenment*, and Outram, *Enlightenment*.

[2] Berlin, 'Counter-Enlightenment', 1.

[3] Berlin, 'Counter-Enlightenment', 1. He adds the 'interested error' maintained by rulers, held responsible for most of the 'blunders, vices and misfortunes' of the history of humanity.

world for theists, deists and atheists, for optimists and pessimists, puritans, prim-
itivists and believers in progress and the richest fruits of science and culture; these
laws governed inanimate and animate nature, facts and events, means and ends,
private life and public, all societies, epochs and civilisations; it was solely by
departing from them that men fell into crime, vice, misery. Thinkers might differ
about what these laws were, or how to discover them, or who were qualified to
expound them; that these laws were real, and could be known, whether with certainty, or only probability, remained the central dogma of the entire Enlightenment'[4].

There are several reasons why the addition of this factor makes the question
of the relationship between esotericism and the Enlightenment considerably
more complicated. First, as we will see, 19th century occultists generally adopted the characteristic arguments of the Enlightenment to attack conventional
Christianity. In so doing, they frequently presented themselves as defending a
reasonable religion (based on eternal principles of cosmic law, and compatible with science) against what they saw as the irrational dogmas preached by
the Churches. Like Enlightenment thinkers, they were especially averse to the
doctrine of original sin[5]. It can be noted in passing that these "enlightened"
opinions display suggestive similarities to several tenets of humanist esotericism and Reformation "spiritualism"; they gained decisive momentum in the
post-Enlightenment climate, and would eventually be adopted by the New Age
movement.
A second complication has to do with Berlin's concept of the "Counter-
Enlightenment" itself. It is defined by him in terms of its attack on the belief
of the Enlightenment in eternal principles of natural law accessible to human
reason. The Counter-Enlightenment is described as rooted in ancient traditions
of scepticism and relativism, reasserting itself strongly in 16th century figures
such as Agrippa (sic), Montaigne and Charron, and finally coming to the fore-
front in Vico, Hamann, Herder, Schelling, and a range of other thinkers associated with Romanticism and German Idealism[6]. Rejecting the Enlightenment
principles of universality, objectivity and rationality, they emphasized contingency, unicity, subjectivity, and the irrational instead. It is clear from Berlin's
account that this counterreaction must not be misunderstood as a simple
reassertion of traditional religious values in the face of Enlightenment criticism. Rather, in its very reaction against Enlightenment tenets it was yet deeply
influenced by it. Both Enlightenment *and* Counter-Enlightenment have, in different ways, contributed to the process of secularization. For our concerns, it
is important to note an element of ambivalence in Berlin's concept of the
Counter-Enlightenment. It throws doubt, first, on whether the latter's internal

[4] Berlin, 'Counter-Enlightenment', 3-4.
[5] Berlin, 'Counter-Enlightenment', 20: 'What the entire Enlightenment has in common is denial
of the central Christian doctrine of original sin ...'.
[6] Berlin, 'Counter-Enlightenment', 1, 2, and *passim*.

coherence goes any further than a common opposition of various movements to the Enlightenment; and, secondly, on whether the phenomenon of occultism can be interpreted in terms of the Enlightenment/Counter-Enlightenment dichotomy. I suggest that, on closer scrutiny, Berlin's concept of the Counter-Enlightenment appears to be made up of two disparate and only superficially connected elements.

(1) The rise of "historical consciousness" took its inspiration from the Counter-Enlightenment rejection of "universal" laws and principles and its corresponding emphasis on (historical and personal) unicity, contingency and creative innovation. The relativism implicit in the new historiography, resulting in scepticism with regard to claims of universal and absolute truth (whether religious or rationalistic), eventually proved to be a force for secularization at least as powerful as Enlightenment rationalism. For us, the essential thing to notice is that neither occultism nor New Age have much affinity with the Counter-Enlightenment in this sense: they combine a firm belief in universal cosmic laws and universal principles with a decidedly non-historical attitude. The characteristic concern of historians with the unique and contingent, and their emphasis on detailed analysis rather than holistic synthesis, are generally rejected as conducive to fragmentation. However, both occultism and New Age *are* highly interested in large-scale theories of the evolution of humanity and of consciousness, of the general type exemplified by German Idealist philosophers such as Herder, Schelling and Hegel. We saw that these, too, are regarded by Berlin as representatives of the Counter-Enlightenment. Apparently, we are dealing with two different approaches to history, both of which are presented by Berlin as products of a single phenomenon called the Counter-Enlightenment. The first approach is best referred to as "historism", the second as "historicism": two perspectives which are generally regarded as incompatible[7]. Put briefly, historicism attempts to overcome the relativism implicit in historism, and to save the "universal laws" believed in by the Enlightenment by reinterpreting them in evolutionist terms. In a sense, its position is therefore intermediate between Enlightenment and the more radical types of Counter-Enlightenment. The same holds true for the "historicist" schemes of occultism and New Age.

(2) Berlin presents the sceptic/relativist attitude of the Counter-Enlightenment as its central defining characteristic and convincingly explains the rise of historical consciousness as one of its outcomes. Far less convincing is the connection suggested between relativism/scepticism and "irrationalism". It is true that scepticism about the Enlightenment belief in universal laws accessible to

---

[7] Ankersmit, *Denken over geschiedenis*, 172-173. Unfortunately, the English term "historicism" is usually applied to both, with predictably confusing results. For an unpretentious but clarifying discussion, see Seiffert, *Einführung*, 45-55. Cf. Rand, 'Two Meanings of Historicism'.

human reason may (and actually did) lead some thinkers to embrace "the irrational" in some sense of the word. It does not follow, however, that people who are perceived as holding "irrationalist" beliefs must therefore be sceptics or relativists in the sense that they do not believe in eternal laws or principles! On the contrary, they are quite likely to argue that the true and eternal nature of reality can only be understood by some kind of supra-rational faculty, and to reject scepticism and relativism as the mirror image of rationalism. This is certainly the position most characteristic of esotericism, inherited by occultism and New Age[8], and presented by them as a "reasonable" alternative to what they see as the "irrational dogma" of Christianity, on the one hand, and the "dogmatic rationality" of the Enlightenment, on the other.

All this adds up to a surprising conclusion. If any impassable barrier must be drawn, it does not divide a rational Enlightenment from an irrational Counter-Enlightenment, but cuts right through the Counter-Enlightenment itself. With reference to Berlin's *own* central criterion of universalism versus relativism, the relativist strand which became fundamental to the rise of "historical consciousness" must be distinguished clearly from a second, non-relativistic strand in 18th century culture which, as will be seen, is permeated by elements of the esoteric tradition. It is only in the "historicist" strand that the two come together, but this happens by sacrificing most of the relativist potential in the interest of a *rapprochement* to Enlightenment universalism.

In conclusion, it should be remarked that the very terminology of Enlightenment/Counter-Enlightenment has the unfortunate effect of detracting attention from the fact that Berlin's argument is based primarily on the dichotomy relativism/scepticism versus universalism. Instead, it has popularly been understood as implying primarily a dichotomy of rationalism versus irrationalism; and this in turn made it possible for the terms "Enlightenment" and "Counter-Enlightenment" to be generalized as applicable, in retrospect, to all periods of history[9]. Both in its original version and in its popular derivations, however, the attempt to interpret esotericism and occultism as exemplifying one or the other alternative in these dichotomies results in historical simplification. The common perception of these movements as Counter-Enlightenment forces is

---

[8] I would deny that this is incompatible with Troeltsch's argument, mentioned at the end of chapter fourteen, section 2B, that "spiritualist" rationalism contains a tendency towards relativism. Troeltsch is referring merely to relativism *with respect to worldly institutions*, not with respect to ultimate reality. At this point in my argument I will ignore the fact that New Age religion, in *contrast* with both esotericism and occultism, does contain tendencies of radical relativism. One can think of neopagan pragmatism with respect to the nature of the "gods"; or of Shirley MacLaine's solipsistic utterances. I regard these as expressions of the psychologization of occultism, i.e. the fourth dimension of secularization (to be discussed in section 4 of the present chapter).

[9] As done for instance in Schmidt, *Aufklärung und Gegenaufklärung*. In fairness to the editor, it must be said that he does recognize the problem ('Einleitung', 1ff).

gratifying to pro-Enlightenment sentiments but finds little support either in theory or in reality[10]. This does not necessarily imply that the Enlightenment/Counter-Enlightenment framework as such must be discarded. It does imply that the concept of the "Counter-Enlightenment" must be applied in a nuanced fashion, and that the general distinction must be used as a heuristic tool rather than as a description of historical movements.

A. The Emergence of Romanticism

Above, I made a sharp distinction between what I referred to as the "historist" stream, on the one hand, and a largely "esoteric" stream, on the other; but I argued that basic elements of the two come together in a third, "historicist" stream. This stream consists of attempts to synthesize elements of Enlightenment, historism and esotericism: it is characterized by a concern with universal laws; an emphasis on historical process; and a positive appreciation of the non-rational or supra-rational. Neither this last element nor the intrinsic nature of the universal laws were emically regarded as *ir*rational, although Enlightenment critics have, of course, preferred to present them as such. This is illustrated in the description given by Isaiah Berlin, with primary reference to Schelling:

> ... the universe [was seen] as the self-development of a primal, non-rational force that can be grasped only by the intuitive powers of men of imaginative genius— poets, philosophers, theologians or statesmen. Nature, a living organism, responds to questions put by the man of genius, while the man of genius responds to the questions put by nature, for they conspire with each other; imaginative insight alone ... becomes conscious of the contours of the future, of which the mere calculating intellect and analytic capacity of the natural scientist or the politician, or any other earthbound empiricist, has no conception. This faith in a peculiar, intuitive, spiritual faculty which goes by various names—reason, understanding, primary imagination—but is always differentiated from the critical analytic intellect favoured by the Enlightenment, the contrast between it and the analytic faculty or method that collects, classifies, experiments, takes to pieces, reassembles, defines, deduces, and establishes probabilities, becomes a commonplace used thereafter by Fichte, Hegel, Wordsworth, Coleridge, Goethe, Carlyle, Schopenhauer and other anti-rationalist thinkers of the nineteenth century, culminating in Bergson and later anti-positivist schools'[11].

Notice that the cosmic life force is "non-rational", but that "reason" is one of the names given to the faculty which may access it. On one level, this suggests the ambivalence characteristic of a movement influenced by, yet dissatisfied

---

[10] The same conclusion is arrived at in a recent attempt to apply the Enlightenment/Counter-Enlightenment dichotomy to an 18th-century esoteric movement. See McIntosh, *Rose Cross and the Age of Reason*, 21, 179-183.

[11] Berlin, 'Counter-Enlightenment', 17.

with, Enlightenment rationality. But it is also reminiscent of Platonic conceptions of pure intellectual vision: a "higher reason" considered to be as different from a merely analytical Enlightenment rationality as it is from an irrational obscurantism.

What I have referred to as the "historicist" strand of the so-called Counter-
Enlightenment is synonymous with the Romantic movement (assuming that
German Idealism is understood not as a discrete phenomenon but as the philo-
sophical wing of Romanticism). Since I have elsewhere investigated in detail
to what extent and in what sense Romanticism is connected with esotericism,
I will restrict myself to a summary here[12].

The background to my interpretation of Romanticism as a "historicist" mix of
18th-century esotericism and the new temporalism consists of a series of
detailed studies which have demonstrated the great importance of esoteric traditions for the Romantics and the Idealist Philosophers[13]. Because most of
these studies are in French or German, their influence on English research has
remained limited. It is precisely for this reason (apart from the fact that even
a summary treatment of detailed connections is out of the question here) that
I will investigate the "esoteric connection" of Romanticism with reference not
to these French and German studies but with reference to English and American publications. The fact that the "esoteric connection" suggested by French
and German research is confirmed (as will be seen) by the conclusions arrived
at by English and American scholars, *even* though their familiarity with the
former is superficial, in effect strengthens my argument.

A review of the secondary literature in the English language about the nature
of Romanticism reveals an interesting development. Arthur O. Lovejoy published an oft-quoted article in 1924, in which he argued that there is no such
thing as "Romanticism" in the singular[14]; but this did not prevent him from
developing, in his later work, a systematic perspective on the characteristics
of "the romantic period"[15]. In 1949, René Wellek launched a frontal attack
against Lovejoy's early article, arguing that Romanticism was a coherent unity[16]. In the context of an attempt to reconcile Lovejoy and Wellek, Morse Peck-

---

[12] Hanegraaff, 'Romanticism'.

[13] Viatte, *Sources occultes* (2 vols.); id., *Victor Hugo*; Benz, *Sources mystiques*; id., 'Mystik';
Guinet, *Zacharias Werner*; Faivre, *Kirchberger*; id., *Eckartshausen*; id., *Mystiques, théosophes...*;
Ayrault, *Genèse du romantisme allemand*; Graßl, *Aufbruch zur Romantik*; Zimmermann, *Welt-
bild des jungen Goethe*, vol. I; Lütgert, *Religion des deutschen Idealismus*; Gode-von Aesch,
Natural Science in German Romanticism; Sladek, *Fragmente*; several contributions to Faivre &
Zimmermann, *Epochen der Naturmystik*.

[14] Lovejoy, 'On the Discrimination'.

[15] Lovejoy, 'Bergson'; id., 'Meaning of 'Romantic''; id., 'Schiller and the Genesis'; id., 'Optimism and Romanticism'; id., *Great Chain*, chs. IX-XI; id., 'Meaning of Romanticism'.

[16] Wellek, 'Concept of "Romanticism"', 1-23 & 147-172.

ham argued two years later that the typical development of the Romantic psyche entailed a process of death and rebirth, or secular conversion[17]. This dynamic or developmental element was adopted by M.H. Abrams in 1971, in an impressive synthesis governed by the dynamic image of the "circuitous journey" or educational spiral[18]. His presentation of Romanticism as dependent on a paradigm of "separation and return" originally derived from neoplatonic sources was countered by Ernest Lee Tuveson in 1982. Tuveson explained Romanticism entirely as a modern form of Hermeticist panentheism, and completely denied any substantial Neoplatonic influence[19]. Although these proposals vary strongly in quality and profundity, a discussion of their stronger and weaker points need not detain us here[20]. Important for our concerns is that three elements emerge from this ongoing debate as centrally important to the nature of Romanticism. I have proposed to call them *organicism, imagination,* and *temporalism.*

(1) Romantic organicism as described by Lovejoy may be defined more precisely as a "diversitarian holism": the belief in an organic cosmos which presents the triumphant unfolding of the divine creative power, in a dazzling spectacle of infinite diversity. As such, it is a modern manifestation of the Platonic Great Chain of Being in its "generative" manifestation. Lovejoy's diversitarian holism is fully compatible with Berlin's concept of the Counter-Enlightenment; for, as emphasized by Lovejoy, Romantic "diversitarianism" was intended precisely as a reversion of Enlightenment "uniformitarianism". Romanticism asserted 'the value of diversity in human opinions, characters, tastes, arts and cultures'[21]; according to Enlightenment assumptions, in contrast, 'what is rational is uniform; and what is not uniform is *eo ipso* not rational; and diversity is therefore the easily recognizable mark of error'[22]. The emphasis on diversitarianism is especially pronounced in Lovejoy's discussions but, as I have argued, his description of an organicist universe is compatible

---

[17] The original article appeared in 1951, and Peckham added a substantial part in 1961. Both parts are reproduced as 'Toward a Theory of Romanticism'.

[18] Abrams, *Natural Supernaturalism.*

[19] Tuveson, *Avatars.*

[20] Lovejoy ignores the importance of the Romantic Imagination correctly emphasized by Wellek. The contributions of Wellek and Peckham do not really contain a rejection of Lovejoy's "nominalism" but demonstrate merely that they misunderstand his point; as a result, they make the very methodological mistakes which Lovejoy had warned against. Wellek, moreover, ignores the temporalist/evolutionist element of Romanticism correctly emphasized by Lovejoy. Abrams's presentation is the most complete and convincing of all, but misconstrues the connection between neoplatonism and hermeticism in the esoteric tradition that influenced Romanticism. Tuveson explains Romanticism with reference to a "pure hermeticism" without any neoplatonic contaminations: a hermeticism which exists in his imagination rather than in the cultural milieu since the late 15th century.

[21] Lovejoy, 'Meaning of Romanticism', 275.

[22] Lovejoy, 'Meaning of Romanticism', 276.

with Wellek's emphasis on an organic nature[23] or Peckham's "dynamic organicism"[24]. Abrams describes the organicist worldview with reference to systems theory[25], and Tuveson does the same in terms of panentheism[26].

(2) The element of the Romantic Imagination plays no role in Lovejoy's work and only ambiguously in Peckham's, but it is central to Wellek's account. Wellek describes the "unity of Romanticism" in terms of three criteria: 'imagination for the view of poetry, nature for the view of the world, and symbol and myth for poetic style'[27]. Actually, the faculty for the understanding of symbols is the imagination, and Wellek's element of "nature" is really about nature *as perceived by* the Romantic imagination. The imagination therefore emerges as the central element in Wellek's view of Romanticism. This centrality of the imagination is confirmed by Abrams[28] and Tuveson; the latter draws connections with the Renaissance concept of *Imaginatio* in the context of a cosmic religiosity on hermeticist foundations.

(3) Finally, all authors except Wellek and Tuveson emphasize the importance of Romantic temporalism, exemplified most clearly in evolutionary theories. Central to Lovejoy's account is what he refers to as the "temporalizing of the Chain of Being"[29]. The Platonic Chain, pictured as the fullness of creation (or emanation) ordered in a graded hierarchy, had traditionally been conceived as the *perfect and complete* unfoldment of divine creativity. As such, it excluded the very possibility of change, progress and the emergence of novelty. In the 18th century, however, as brilliantly formulated by Lovejoy, 'The *plenum formarum* came to be conceived by some, not as the inventory but as the program of nature, which is being carried out gradually and exceedingly slowly in the cosmic history'[30]. In this momentous development, he argues, we have the origins of Romantic evolutionism as well as of the Romantic aspiration towards the "infinite". This combination of a "diversitarian holism" with the new temporalism is obviously compatible with Berlin's concept of the Counter-Enlightenment. It is also found in the accounts of Peckham and Abrams, who give added emphasis to what might be called the "educational" dimension of the process. The typical Romantic as described by Peckham undergoes an experience of spiritual death and rebirth: 'A man moves from a trust in the universe to a period of doubt and despair of any meaning in the universe, and then to a re-affirmation of faith in the cosmic meaning and goodness, or at least mean-

[23] Wellek, 'Concept of "Romanticism"', 161.
[24] Peckham, 'Toward a Theory of Romanticism', 240-241.
[25] Abrams, *Natural Supernaturalism*, 172-177.
[26] Tuveson, *Avatars*, 4.
[27] Wellek, 'Concept of Romanticism', 147.
[28] Abrams, *Natural Supernaturalism*, 117-122.
[29] Lovejoy, *Great Chain*, ch. IX.
[30] Lovejoy, *Great Chain*, 24

ing'[31]. This same process is replicated on a cosmic scale in the evolution of the universe from unity through alienation back to a higher unity. Similarly, Abrams speaks of the "circuitous journey" as an educational process: when the Platonic idea of circular return was fused with the idea of linear progress, the result was 'a distinctive figure of Romantic thought and imagination—the ascending circle, or spiral'[32]. Again, this process took place at both levels: the macrocosmos as well as the human microcosmos.

I already mentioned the basic compatibility of these accounts of Romanticism with Berlin's concept of the Counter-Enlightenment. Against this background, the differences between Enlightenment and Romanticism may be summarized in terms of an opposition between mechanicism—organicism; uniformitarianism—diversitarianism; reason—imagination; and static universalism—evolutionist temporalism. This makes it possible to establish the contribution of esotericism to the emergence of Romanticism with greater precision. The historical connection between Neoplatonism and Romanticism has been recognized for a long time, and was strongly confirmed especially by Lovejoy and Abrams. But the relevance of Hermeticism, and its close historical association with Neoplatonism, has been recognized only recently. Abrams made an important step by discussing Romanticism with primary reference to Neoplatonism, on the one hand, and "the esoteric tradition", on the other[33]. However, he still presented them as separate strands; and, in the end, the "esoteric" element remains of only marginal importance to his interpretation of Romanticism. Tuveson made a similarly articificial distinction by, conversely, presenting Romanticism as a revival of Hermeticism without any debt to Neoplatonism. Actually, Neoplatonism and Hermeticism were inextricably interwoven in the popular religious eclecticism of the second half of the 18th century[34], and it should be recognized that much of what the Romantics called "neoplatonism" either belonged to or was perceived in close connection with the domain of esotericism *sensu* Faivre. This throws a new light on the conclusions drawn, apparently independently of each other, by Wellek and Abrams. Wellek says that he is aware that his three elements of Romanticism

> have their historical ancestry before the age of Enlightenment and in undercurrents during the eighteenth century. The view of an organic nature descends from Neoplatonism through Giordano Bruno, Böhme, the Cambridge Platonists, and some passages in Shaftesbury. The view of imagination as creative and of poetry as prophecy has a similar ancestry. A symbolist, and even mythic, conception of poetry is frequent in history, e.g., in the baroque age with its emblematic art,

---

[31] Peckham, 'Toward a Theory of Romanticism', 242. Cf. Cellier, *L'épopée*.

[32] Abrams, *Natural Supernaturalism*, 184.

[33] Abrams, *Natural Supernaturalism*, 154-169.

[34] For the German-speaking domain, see in particular the introductory chapter of Zimmermann, *Weltbild des jungen Goethe* I, 11-43.

its view of nature as hieroglyphics which man and especially the poet is destined to read. In a sense, romanticism is the revival of something old, but it is a revival with a difference; these ideas were translated into terms acceptable to men who had undergone the experience of the Enlightenment[35].

And Abrams concludes:

> Renaissance vitalism had envisioned an integral universe without absolute divisions, in which everything is interrelated by a system of correspondences, and the living is continuous with the inanimate, nature with man, and matter with mind; a universe ... activated throughout by a dynamism of opposing forces ... In this way of thinking some Romantic philosophers detected intimations of a viable counter-metaphysic to contemporary mechanicism, elementarism, and dualism; provided that ... the mythical elements are translated into philosophical concepts, and these are ordered into a "scientific", that is, a coherent conceptual system[36].

The connection with what we have referred to as the "esoteric" worldview, described by Faivre in terms of correspondences and living nature is, therefore, confirmed by two of the most authoritative modern scholars of Romanticism. As noted above, this connection is actually what could have been expected in view of the continuity of esoteric traditions in late 18th century "hermeticism" documented by French and German researchers. Moreover, with respect to Faivre's third element (imagination/mediations), the connection is further confirmed by Wellek's and Abrams's emphasis on the Romantic imagination. However, Wellek correctly remarks that Romanticism is a revival *with a difference*. Although I fully concur with his suggestion that the esoteric worldview was translated into terms acceptable to those 'who had undergone the experience of the Enlightenment', it seems that Wellek's neglect (see above) of the "temporalist" element made him overlook the crux of the matter. An esoteric, Neoplatonist-Hermetic worldview constitutes the traditional background of Romanticism; but it is the *temporalist* framework—a product, not of the original Enlightenment, but of its Counter-Enlightenment reaction—which constitutes the truly innovative element. This has consequences particularly with respect to Faivre's fourth and final intrinsic characteristic of esotericism. As I have argued elsewhere[37], "transmutation" was not originally an evolutionist concept; this is, however, how it has been represented almost universally since the 18th century[38].

Thus, it is in modern evolutionist garb that the esoteric tradition has entered the 19th and 20th centuries, whether in the form of Romantic religion and its later derivations, or in the form of occultism. Historically, there are close inter-

---

[35] Wellek, 'Concept of "Romanticism"', 171.

[36] Abrams, *Natural Supernaturalism*, 171.

[37] Hanegraaff, 'Romanticism'.

[38] This reinterpretation (more precisely: misrepresentation) can be studied with particular clarity with reference to the interpretation by Schelling and Hegel of Jacob Böhme's theosophical system. See the discussion at the beginning of section 3 of the present chapter (below).

connections between these two strands, but they should not be confused. There is a Romantic religiosity which, while a product of traditional esotericism and post-Enlightenment Evolutionism, remains rooted in a worldview of correspondences. I have defined occultism, on the other hand, as based on a mixture of correspondences and causality: it is, therefore, doubly secularized. It is to this development that we must now turn.

B. The Emergence of Occultism

In an article published in 1987, Antoine Faivre makes these remarks:

> The industrial revolution naturally gave rise to an increasingly marked interest in the "miracles" of science. ... Along with smoking factory chimneys came both the literature of the fantastic and the new phenomenon of spiritualism. These two possess a common characteristic: each takes the real world in its most concrete form as its point of departure, and then postulates the existence of another, supernatural world, separated from the first by a more or less impermeable partition. Fantasy literature then plays upon the effect of surprise that is provided by the irruption of the supernatural into the daily life, which it describes in a realistic fashion. Spiritualism, both as a belief and as a practice, follows the inverse procedure, teaching how to pass from this world of the living to the world of the dead, through séances of spirit rappings and table tippings, the table playing a role analogous to that of the traditional magic circle. It is interesting that occultism in its modern form—that of the nineteenth century—appeared at the same time as fantastic literature and spiritualism.[39]

Although Faivre distinguishes here not only between fantastic literature and spiritualism but also between the latter and occultism (demarcated as a predominantly French phenomenon of the later 19th century), his statements are highly suggestive with respect to occultism as such. Firstly, the close connection between the literature of "gothic" fantasy, modern spiritualism and the French occultist movement of the late 19th century makes sense in view of their well-documented influence on the art and literature of that period[40]. Secondly, and of greater importance here: Faivre's remarks provide us with important clues about the impact on esotericism of the "brave new world" which took shape most decisively during the 19th century. A profound analysis would have to take into account the relevance to the emergence of occultism not only of new ideas, but of social and political changes as well. For our more limited concerns, most important is the increasing prestige of modern science and the positivist-materialist philosophies which flourished in its wake. Faivre explicitly mentions a "disenchanted" world as the context of the emergence of

---

[39] Antoine Faivre, 'What is Occultism?', 7. Cf. Faivre, *Access*, 88; and id., 'Genèse d'un genre narratif'.

[40] See Mercier, *Sources ésotériques et occultes*; Senior, *Way down and Out*; several contributions in the exhibition catalogue *Spiritual in Art*.

occultism[41]. This is what makes for the importance of his statement that both fantastic literature and spiritualism 'take[s] the real world in its most concrete form as its point of departure' in order to postulate the existence of the supernatural. Below, I will return on several occasions to Faivre's suggestion and its implications.

In order to account for the emergence of New Age religion, we need to define with precision the difference between esotericism and occultism, and construe the latter (on a par with the former, *sensu* Faivre) as an etic category in the study of Western religions. Occultism, I suggest, can be defined as a category in the study of religions, which comprises *all attempts by esotericists to come to terms with a disenchanted world or, alternatively, by people in general to make sense of esotericism from the perspective of a disenchanted secular world*. This definition contains several assumptions which need to be made explicit.

(1) It obviously presupposes that the term "esotericism" has already been defined. Since my account is based upon the concept of esotericism *sensu* Faivre (with added emphasis upon the "spiritualist" element, see chapter fourteen, section 2), occultism must be seen as an subcategory useful within the study of esotericism in general. It describes neither a new phenomenon, nor the survival of an old one, but the emergence of a new development in the history of esotericism. This new development became decisive for the emergence of several movements in the 19th century, including modern Spiritualism, occultist ritual magic, and modern Theosophy (with its offsprings). (2) My definition rejects the idea, originally suggested by Tiryakian and widely followed by others, that a theoretical dimension ("esotericism") can be demarcated from a practical one ("occultism")[42]. Robert Galbreath has correctly remarked about so-called "esotericists" and "occultists" that 'the notion of a purely abstract knowledge divorced from personal development and personal participation is alien to them. It is a nonexistent distinction'[43]. I suggest that this approach to occultism is analogous with (and has probably been influenced by) a quasi-apologetic tendency of separating "mere magic" from "real" religion. (3) My definition implies that the 19th century controversies between spiritualists and "occultists" (especially those of the French school of Papus; and the Theosophical Society, see below) must be regarded as a controversy *within* occultism. In other words, my definition of occultism as an etic category is independent of emic usages of the term. (4) The definition allows us to spec-

---

[41] Faivre, *Access*, 88.

[42] Tiryakian, 'Toward the Sociology, 265. The distinction is quoted favourably for example by Mircea Eliade, 'Occult and the Modern World', 48; and, somewhat surprisingly, by Faivre, 'What is Occultism?', 3.

[43] Galbreath, 'Explaining Modern Occultism', 17-18.

ify the essential distinction between the two major 19th century developments historically dependent upon esoteric traditions: Romantic religiosity (chapter fifteen, section 1A) and occultism. Occultism, I suggest, is essentially an attempt to adapt esotericism to a disenchanted world: a world which no longer harbours a dimension of irreducible mystery (see chapter four, with reference to Van Baal[44]) based upon an experience of the sacred as present in the daily world[45]. To the extent that it makes such an attempt, it *accepts* that world (consciously or unconsciously; in a spirit of resignation or with enthusiasm). The irony is that, by so doing, it cannot but distance itself from the "enchanted" world of traditional esotericism. Romanticism, on the other hand, rejects such compromises; it attempts to re-enchant the world and bring back the mystery driven away by the "coldness" of the new science and its attendant worldview. (5) The definition obviously assumes the validity of distinctions between an "enchanted" and a "disenchanted" worldview. Following recent proposals by Tambiah and others, I suggest that the essence of the distinction may profitably be defined in terms of "participation" versus "(instrumental) causality"[46]. I already discussed this distinction in chapter four, with reference to the problem of "magic"; and the connection proposed here would confirm my earlier suggestion (chapter fourteen, section 1C) that, at least in its original Renaissance manifestation, esotericism and *magia* are closely equivalent. The implication of my present discussion is, then, that occultism is the product of a syncretism between *magia* and science, correspondences and causality.

I will attempt to demonstrate the transformation of esotericism into occultism as exemplified by three crucial historical phenomena. The teachings of Emanuel Swedenborg, on the one hand, and the phenomenon of Mesmerism, on the other, can be seen as two early manifestations of the process of secularization. But it is in 19th-century spiritualism (crucially influenced by both Swedenborgianism and Mesmerism) that occultism finally emerges in fully-developed form.

---

[44] Van Baal himself has, towards the end of his life, departed from a strict empirical perspective towards a perspective which seems closer to religionism and affirms the centrality of "mystery as revelation" (Van Baal, *Boodschap uit de stilte*, 81-130). In contrast to the perspective of van Baal or, more pronouncedly, Rudolf Otto in his discussion of the numinous as *mysterium tremendum ac fascinans* (*Das Heilige*), my use of the term "mystery" does not entail the religionist assumption that it can only be understood by means of a privileged "intuitive" faculty.

[45] See Faivre, 'Genèse d'un genre narratif', 33: 'in both cases [i.e. spiritualism and fantastic literature] a normally impermeable barrier separated nature from the supernatural; and the fact that this barrier is solid presupposes that the supernatural has been driven from our daily reality, and no longer is an integral part of it'.

[46] Apart from Tambiah and other theoreticians who describe a "magical worldview" in terms of "participation" (see chapter four), see also Albanese, *Corresponding Motion*, ch. 1.

Emanuel Swedenborg

Figures who have one foot in the scientific and the other in the religious domain
risk losing their foothold in both. The case of Emanuel Swedenborg (1688-
1772) illustrates this point with particular clarity[47]. Nowadays, he is mostly
remembered as a somewhat obscure clairvoyant who was exposed by the young
Immanuel Kant in the latter's *Träume eines Geistersehers*[48]. Actually, Kant's
attack succeeded in putting an abrupt end to the intellectual respectability of
a man who had been known for most of his life not as a visionary but, rather,
as an esteemed scientist of the modern post-Cartesian school[49]. Inge Jonsson
has demonstrated that Swedenborg's visionary works, which began to appear
after his spiritual crisis in 1745, do not constitute a radical break with the past
but largely consist of an application of his early scientific and philosophical
theories to the supernatural domain[50]: 'In order to explain rationally his continuous experiences with spirits and angels during and after the great spiritual crisis around the middle of the 1740s, Swedenborg needed to make only
small changes in his psycho-physical theorizing, mainly simplifications'[51]. Jonsson backs up his argument by expert analyses of Swedenborg's scientific
development in the context of the scientific debates of his time, and convincingly demonstrates the basic continuity between the "scientific" and the
"visionary" Swedenborg. Moreover, Jonsson is at pains to minimize the influence on Swedenborg of Renaissance "neoplatonism", the Cambridge Platonists, the mystical *Naturphilosophie* associated with Paracelsus and Johann Baptist van Helmont, and similar "esoteric" currents[52]. As a result, Swedenborg
emerges from his discussion as essentially a scientific mind, whose visionary
experiences caused him to be wrongly stigmatized by posterity as an "esotericist". This interpretation is congenial to the tendency among Swedenborg scholars to present Swedenborg's visions as direct and unmediated revelations. Asked
about his familiarity with the Christian theosophers Jacob Böhme and William
Law, Swedenborg himself wrote in 1767: 'I have never read them, and I was
forbidden to read authors on dogmatic and systematic theology, before heav-
en was opened to me; because unfounded opinions and fictions might have

[47] For Swedenborg's development, see Sigstedt, *Swedenborg Epic*.
[48] Kant, *Träume eines Geistersehers*.
[49] About Kant's criticism and its results, see Benz, 'Immanuel Swedenborg', 8-13; id., *Swedenborg in Deutschland*, 233-285; Kirven, 'Swedenborg and Kant Revisited'; Florschütz, *Swedenborgs verborgene Wirkung*; Gerding, *Kant en het paranormale*.
[50] Jonsson, *Emanuel Swedenborg*; id., 'Emanuel Swedenborgs Naturphilosophie'; id., 'Swedenborg and his Influence'.
[51] Jonsson, 'Emanuel Swedenborgs Naturphilosophie', 251.
[52] See for example Jonsson, *Emanuel Swedenborg*, 17, 61-62, 81-82, 85; id., 'Emanuel Swedenborg's Naturphilosophie', 235-236, 249-250. See also Swedenborg's attempts to replace the
Cartesian hypothesis of *spiritus animales*, regarded by him as occult assumptions, by a thoroughly mechanistic alternative (Jonsson, *Emanuel Swedenborg* , 47, 58-60).

easily insinuated themselves thereby, which afterwards could only have been removed with difficulty'[53].

In accordance with this, Swedenborg's religious writings contain no references to religious sources, esoteric or otherwise; and this makes the question of his position in the context of esotericism less easy to determine than might be expected[54]. It is true that his father was a Lutheran bishop with pietistic leanings, and that "spiritualist" elements are quite evident in his later doctrine[55], but this is not sufficient to make him an heir of esoteric traditions. Apart from some speculations about a possible familarity with figures such as the Christian kabbalist Knorr von Rosenroth[56], Swedenborg has long been presented as an essentially isolated figure whose visions were subsequently assimilated into theosophical and illuminist traditions, rather than as a product of the esoteric tradition itself[57]. This has been changed by the research of Marsha Keith Schuchard[58]. Schuchard uncovered hitherto unsuspected connections, beginning with Gottfried Wilhelm Leibniz's interest in Rosicrucianism and Christian kabbalah; his influence on Swedenborg's brother-in-law Eric Benzelius; the latter's visit (instigated by Leibniz) to the alchemist and Christian kabbalist Francis Mercurius van Helmont; and Benzelius's profound influence on the young Swedenborg, beginning when the latter moved into his house at the age of fifteen. Tracing Swedenborg's subsequent development, Schuchard reveals a consistent pattern of fascination for esoteric subjects, and for Christian kabbalah in particular. In the light of this evidence, Swedenborg's contribution seems to consist essentially in his synthesis of esoteric speculation, on the one hand, and post-Cartesian science and natural philosophy, on the other. Not surprisingly, his perspective defies neat categorization in terms of Enlightenment versus Counter-Enlightenment[59].

---

[53] Tafel, *Documents*, 650.

[54] Williams-Hogan, 'Place of Emanuel Swedenborg'.

[55] See for this point the analysis of Bochinger, *"New Age"*, 257ff.

[56] Viatte, *Sources occultes*, 73; Faivre, *L'ésotérisme au XVIIIe siècle*, 104.

[57] The acceptance of Swedenborg in esoteric circles was, however, ambiguous. See Viatte, *Sources Occultes* I, 85.

[58] Schuchard, 'Swedenborg, Jacobitism, and Freemasonry'; id., *Freemasonry, Secret Societies...*. Cf. Godwin, *Theosophical Enlightenment*, 95-103.

[59] See the opening remarks of Garrett, 'Swedenborg and the Mystical Enlightenment'; Jonsson suggests that Swedenborg may be a link between 17th-century rationalism and the natural philosophy of Romanticism (Jonsson, *Emanuel Swedenborg*, 66-67), but also mentions the 'deeply rationalist' orientation of his worldview ('Emanuel Swedenborgs Naturphilosophie', 254: '...die tief rationalistische Prägung, die seiner durchsystematisierten Vorstellungswelt aufgedrückt ist'); Colleen McDannell and Bernhard Lang have called attention to his typical Enlightenment conviction 'that humankind was fundamentally good and, given proper education in a wholesome environment, would freely progress toward the good' (*Heaven*, 226; this interpretation is however challenged by other specialists [Jane Williams-Hogan, personal communication 26.11.1995]), but they also observe that Swedenborg's picture of heaven 'defied the traditional preference for stasis over motion, sameness over variety, and contemplation over activity', which

The relevance of Swedenborg to New Age religion has been highlighted by several authors[60]. Bochinger has given particular emphasis to his function in the transmission of "spiritualist" ideas, his prediction of the "New Church" as an intermediate concept between Joachim of Fiore's Kingdom of the Spirit and contemporary "New Age", and his paradigmatic status with respect to modern attempts at reconciling religion and science[61]. It is this last aspect which is of immediate importance for the argument put forward here.

The Swedenborgian specialist Jane Williams-Hogan has recently applied Faivre's conceptualization of western esotericism to Swedenborg's worldview, with interesting results. She concludes that Faivre's intrinsic characteristics 1, 3 and 4 (Correspondences, Imagination/Mediations, Transmutation) are also found in Swedenborg, but that the second one (living nature) is absent. For Swedenborg, the post-Cartesian scientist, nature and the natural 'has no life of its own, even though it mirrors and can reveal the spiritual, and corresponds to it'[62]. In other words: the constellation of a "higher" spiritual world of Life is mirrored by a lower material world, which is dead. This is illustrated by Swedenborg's discussion of the spiritual versus the natural sun:

> Creation itself cannot be ascribed in the least to the sun of the natural world, but must be wholly ascribed to the sun of the spiritual world; because the sun of the natural world is altogether dead; but the sun of the spiritual world is living; for it is the first proceeding of Divine Love and Divine Wisdom; and what is dead does not act at all from itself, but is acted upon; consequently to ascribe to it anything of creation would be like ascribing the work of an artificer to the tool which is moved by his hands[63].

---

would seem to bring him closer to the Counter-Enlightenment (o.c., 199). See also their comparison with Rousseau's noble savage: 'the soul does not become more sophisticated as it progresses, but more childlike' (o.c., 202).

[60] Melton, 'Introductory Essay', xxii-xxiii; Bochinger, *"New Age"*, 257-280; Ruppert, 'Swedenborg und New Age', 353-363. Cf. also the several relevant articles in Larsen e.o., *Emanuel Swedenborg* (esp. Martin, 'Swedenborg, Transpersonal Psychology, and Wholeness'; Stanley, 'Relevance'; Talbot, 'Swedenborg and the Holographic Paradigm').

[61] In addition, several of the specific New Age ideas encountered in Part Two may well have their historical origin in Swedenborg. Some examples would be Ramala's description of God as "the sun of this universe", understood not in a metaphorical but in a quite literal sense (cf. Viatte, *Sources occultes* I, 82); the crucial concept that the angels are actually highly-developed human souls (cf. Faivre, *L'ésotérisme au XVIIIe siècle*, 103); and the no less crucial idea that the after-death environment is essentially self-create (McDannell & Lang, *Heaven*, 193). One might also point out such elements as Swedenborg's "spiritualist" belief that God enjoys religious pluralism (Viatte, *Sources occultes* I, 83: 'la variété du culte plaît à Dieu'), or his pronounced anti-ascetic this-worldliness (hence his belief that sexuality continues in the higher worlds, see for this element and its continuation by William Blake and other Romantics, McDannell & Lang, *Heaven*, 226ff). A detailed comparative and historical study would be necessary in order to determine the actual extent of Swedenborgianism in New Age religion.

[62] Williams-Hogan, 'Place of Emanuel Swedenborg'.

[63] Swedenborg, *Divine Love and Wisdom*, # 157, as quoted in Williams-Hogan, 'Place of Emanuel Swedenborg'.

It seems evident that, for Swedenborg, his celebrated doctrine of correspondences provided the long-sought solution of the Cartesian dilemma[64]. His scientific work had convinced him, as observed by Williams-Hogan, that 'nature can be penetrated to its smallest elements without discovering the eternal, the spiritual, and the divine. This truth, Swedenborg discover[ed] himself, when his own philosophical quest to find traces of the divine in nature brought him to an intellectual dead end, or in Swedenborg's own words "an abyss"'[65]. This profound crisis was resolved, for him, not by a new scientific or philosophical insight but by divine revelation.

It is of crucial importance to recognize the full extent of Swedenborg's innovation. If Faivre is correct in stating that his four intrinsic characteristics of traditional esotericism mutually imply each other in the context of one integral worldview of correspondences, then Swedenborg's understanding of the natural world in terms of a Cartesian *res extensa* must have disruptive effects. In traditional esotericism, *all* parts of the universe were alive, and it was the universal law of correspondences which guaranteed the essential wholeness of reality. The small corresponded with the large (as microcosmos versus macrocosmos), the lower world with the higher ("as above, so below"), and the visible with the invisible; but all phenomena in the visible world *as well*, both spatially and temporally, were conceived as held together not by causal relations but by non-causal correspondences. Accordingly, the meaning of correspondences in esotericism is not adequately expressed by stating only that natural phenomena correspond to heavenly phenomena. Essential to the character of esotericism as a modern *Naturphilosophie* is the additional perception that divinity is immanent in nature itself. Accordingly, a salvational gnosis is obtained not just by using natural phenomena as a springboard for gaining insight into their eternal archetypes (a conception with evident "otherworldly" implications); rather, the same insight is obtained in the very perception of the natural world as a living and mysterious whole, permeated by a secret "fire" and held together by a web of correspondences. This "pansophical" dimension necessarily vanishes when a panentheistic *Naturphilosophie* is replaced by a mechanistic science resting on Cartesian premises. From this perspective, Swedenborg's doctrine of correspondences emerges as an impoverished version of the esoteric original, in the sense that it retains only the "vertical" dimension

---

[64] The Cartesian dilemma, as is well known, consists in the problem of how a strict dualism of *res cogitans* versus *res extensa* is to be reconciled with the fact that the former is able to act upon the latter. Explanations in terms of instrumental causality have to make assumptions which are all *a priori* incompatible with the basic dualism: i.e., they must assume that the two substances can make contact with each other, or that one can be reduced to the other, or that there is a third substance of some kind which mediates between the two (in which case the problem shifts to the question of how *this* substance relates to the two others).

[65] Williams-Hogan, 'Place of Emanuel Swedenborg'.

of heavenly archetype versus natural reflection and, as a result, re-introduces
an element of dualism which posits the superiority of spirit over matter. Actually, one suspects that for Swedenborg the doctrine of correspondences was
attractive, *not* because it unites mind and nature, but for precisely the *contrary*
reason: because it solved (for him) the Cartesian dilemma[66]. It enabled him to
retain a fundamental distinction between spirit and nature (modeled upon the
distinction between *res cogitans* and *res extensa*)[67]; to continue seeing spirit
as the active cause and nature as passive substance "acted upon" by spirit[68];
but to explain that relationship *without* having to assume the existence of mechanisms of instrumental causality. The law of correspondences, which had been
an expression of the experienced wholeness of being in traditional esotericism,
is essentially reduced to the status of a scientific hypothesis by Swedenborg.
It should be noted that Cartesian dualism is combined in Swedenborg's mind
with a traditional Christian emphasis on renouncing the things of this world
for the sake of heaven: '...man has withdrawn himself from heaven by the love
of self and love of the world. For he that loves self and the world above all
things gives heed only to worldly things, since these appeal to the external
senses and gratify the mind'[69]. Not matter as such is responsible for evil (as
in the typical case of gnostic dualism) but the mental orientation or state of
consciousness of human beings. Williams-Hogan's description of Swedenborg's
perspective reveals a striking similarity to New Age concepts of the Self:

> every human being lives in the natural and the spiritual world simultaneously. ...
> However, we are conscious of living in only one. Death is the common doorway
> from one world to the other; or from one form of consciousness to another. Pri-
> or to death we live consciously in this world, and inwardly or unconsciously in
> the spiritual world. After death, we live consciously in the spiritual world, while
> remaining in unconscious connection with this one[70].

I conclude that a combined Cartesian and Christian dualism (the latter quite
compatible with Swedenborg's native "spiritualist" Christianity), not an esoteric *Naturphilosophie*, forms the cosmological framework of Swedenborg's
doctrine of correspondences. The frameworks he inherited from esoteric traditions were changed by him into something new. The innovation has impli-

---

[66] This crucial difference is easily missed. Thus, for instance, in the statement of McDannell
& Lang that 'Underneath the appearances was a spiritual reality. Matter was not alienated or separated from spirit, but essentially one with it' (*Heaven*, 192).
[67] Cf. these lines in Swedenborg, *Divine Love and Wisdom*, #83 (as quoted in Williams-Hogan,
'Place of Emanuel Swedenborg'): 'There are two worlds, the spiritual and the natural. The spiritual world does not draw anything from the natural, nor the natural world from the spiritual. The
two are totally distinct, and communicate only by correspondences ...'
[68] Cf. also Judah, *Metaphysical Movements*, 37.
[69] Swedenborg, *Heaven and Hell*, #87, as quoted in Williams-Hogan, 'Place of Emanuel Swedenborg'.
[70] Williams-Hogan, 'Place of Emanuel Swedenborg'.

cations for the meaning of "imagination/mediations" as well. As presented by Faivre, the *imaginatio* in esotericism was the fundamental faculty of a symbolical hermeneutics. It claimed to reveal deeper levels of meaning hidden in revealed Scripture and the Book of Nature, and to give access to an "intermediate world" of myth and symbol[71]. In Swedenborg's writings, the concept is understood in a far more literal sense: as a term for the mental process which enables the human soul to "create its own reality" after death. As expressed by Williams-Hogan: 'the natural world is the world of appearances, and the spiritual world is the world of the real. Throughout one's life, the inner self of each person builds for themselves their own real world, which they bring with them after death to create their own heaven'[72]. This view is obviously very close to New Age religion. Here, it is important to notice that, as several commentators have observed, in Swedenborg's interpretation the poetic and symbolic dimension of imaginative vision is largely or completely lost, in favour of a dry literalism more congenial to physics than to art[73].

I suggest that, in the context of esotericism, Swedenborg's reconceptualization of nature as not living but dead represents not just a minor modification which leaves the other aspects more or less intact. It signals a momentous shift in perspective which touches the heart of the esoteric worldview and is essential for understanding the nature of occultism. I am not suggesting that occultism was created by Swedenborg, although his contribution was highly significant and widely influential. More importantly, Swedenborg exemplifies with particular clarity a shift of perspective which would become increasingly natural as "science" gained in popularity during the nineteenth century. Swedenborg's teachings announce the emergence of a *nouveau* esotericism (i.e., occultism) which indeed, in Faivre's words, 'take[s] the real world in its most concrete form as its point of departure' for exploring the world of the supernatural.

---

[71] Actually, these are two different meanings. I have noticed elsewhere that the concept of *imaginatio* in esotericism is in urgent need of further clarification. An incomplete list of meanings includes (1) the power of visualizing images for magical purposes; (2) the faculty by which images and symbols (for instance in alchemy) may become vehicles of inner transmutation; (3) the faculty which gives access to a "mesocosmos" or *mundus imaginalis*; (4) the process of "internalizing the cosmos", closely connected to the so-called "Art of Memory" (Hanegraaff, 'Romanticism'). The fact that these meanings are not distinguished in Faivre's third characteristic of esotericism makes it difficult to assess the differences between the role of the imagination in traditional esotericism, on the one hand, and in romanticism and occultism, on the other.

[72] Williams-Hogan, 'Place of Emanuel Swedenborg'.

[73] See for instance the ironic comments made by Viatte, *Sources occultes*, 78, 81; cf. Faivre, *L'ésotérisme au XVIIIe siècle*, 104. Cf. Croce, 'Scientific Spiritualism', 253: Henry James Sr. was an enthusiastic admirer of Swedenborg, even though he admitted that he found his books "tedious" and "artless": 'James actually found the scientific mystic's artlessness an indication of his spiritual authenticity, an authenticity based on the scientific quality and accuracy of his spirituality'.

Franz Anton Mesmer

For the scientist Swedenborg, traditional notions of a "subtle matter" inter-mediate between the spiritual and the material, or of "occult forces" operative in nature were highly problematic. It is revealing that, early in his scientific period, he opposed the traditional concept of *spiritus animales* (mediating organs between body and soul) primarily for *religious* reasons: acceptance of these intermediate forces might tempt modern scientists to deny the independent existence of the spiritual![74] Considering his convictions about nature and its correspondence with the spiritual, it is unlikely that he would have accepted Franz Anton Mesmer's doctrine of a subtle invisible fluid, which was to achieve an enormous popularity within a decade after Swedenborg's death; and one can only try to imagine his reaction, had he known that mesmerism and his own teachings would eventually be presented as fully compatible by occultists during the course of the century which followed. Mesmer's doctrine reflects the belief in a living nature permeated by an "occult" force, and is certainly closer to esoteric and Romantic *Naturphilosophie* than Swedenborg's system. Unlike Swedenborg, however, Mesmer and his followers could point to empirical phenomena as furnishing experimental proof for their beliefs. This aspect turned out to be highly congenial to 19th century projects of a "scientific religion". Just as Mesmer's invisible fluid was intermediate between spirit and matter, so his system could be regarded as mediating between religion and science. As a result, it led some of his followers to spiritualism, others to materialism, but most of them to a mixture of both[75].

The remarkable story of Mesmerism has often been told[76], and need not be repeated in detail here. Having practiced for some years as a physician in Vienna, Mesmer moved to Paris in 1778, where he rapidly achieved fame with his new method of treatment called "animal magnetism"[77]. Henri Ellenberger has summarized his theory in terms of four basic principles:

> (1) A subtle physical fluid fills the universe and forms a connecting medium between man, the earth, and the heavenly bodies, and also between man and man. (2) Disease originates from the unequal distribution of this fluid in the human body; recovery is achieved when the equilibrium is restored. (3) With the help of

---

[74] Jonsson, *Emanuel Swedenborg*, 48.

[75] Cf. Turner, *Between Science and Religion*, 81.

[76] Most widely known is Darnton, *Mesmerism*. This smoothly-written book is less original than has sometimes been assumed, as it replicates information that can already be found in older studies such as Podmore, *Mesmerism and Christian Science*, or Viatte, *Sources occultes* I, esp. 223-231, and id., *Victor Hugo*, ch. I. Some other reliable discussions include Ellenberger, *Discovery of the Unconscious*, chs. 2-4; Benz, *Franz Anton Mesmer*; Fuller, *Mesmerism*; Gauld, *History of Hypnotism*, 1-270; Godwin, *Theosophical Enlightenment*, ch. 8.

[77] According to Benz (*Franz Anton Mesmer*, 21), Mesmer had hesitated for a long time whether to call his basic force magnetism or electricity. Both of these invisible and apparently "occult" forces fascinated thinkers of the time (cf. Benz, *Theologie der Elektrizität*; Faivre, 'Magia Naturalis (1765)'.

certain techniques, this fluid can be channeled, stored, and conveyed to other persons. (4) In this manner, "crises" can be provoked in patients and diseases cured[78].

The theory implied that "there is only one illness and one healing"[79], and has been controversial from the very beginning; but its suggestion of a universal panacea combined with the spectacular aspects of the trance states induced by the new method created a veritable "mesmeric mania", which ensured that the subject was discussed by all levels of society. For a long time, the more bizarre aspects of the popular craze have caused mesmerism to be dismissed as not worthy of serious attention[80]; but, with hindsight, the historical importance of Mesmer's discovery can hardly be overestimated. Ellenberger, in his monumental history of dynamic psychiatry, does not hesitate to compare Mesmer with Columbus: both discovered a new world although both, also, 'remained in error for the remainder of their lives about the real nature of their discoveries'[81]. Ellenberger is referring to the split which eventually occurred in mesmerism between those who followed Mesmer in ascribing the effect of mesmeric treatment to an invisible fluid of "subtle matter" (the magnetic force), manipulated by the healer; and those who explained the same effects in psychological terms[82]. This second interpretation led from mesmerism to hypnosis and became crucially important for the development of modern psychiatry, on the one hand, and of new forms of "religious psychology", on the other. That line of development will be examined in due course. It is the discredited "fluidic" theory which is of immediate interest here, because it became fundamental to occultist projects of a scientific religion.

Important for understanding the popular perception of mesmerism is Mesmer's role in the famous controversy over the Bavarian exorcist Johann Joseph Gaßner (1727-1779), who healed patients by casting out demons in the name of Jesus. As noted by Ernst Benz, the significance of Gaßner's popular success is 'that exorcism is powerfully confirmed by him during a period in which the scientific Enlightenment and the philosophy of rationalism had got a hold even on the leading circles of the Church, and in which the movement created by him brought forth a kind of demonological mass hysteria'[83]. It is in this

---

[78] Ellenberger, *Discovery of the Unconscious*, 62.

[79] Ellenberger, *Discovery of the Unconcious*, 63.

[80] See for example Darnton, *Mesmerism*, 4-10 (with contemporary illustrations).

[81] Ellenberger, *Discovery of the Unconscious*, 57. Likewise, Gauld's no less authoritative *History of Hypnotism* begins with Mesmer.

[82] Kaplan, "'Mesmeric Mania'", 699; Podmore, *Mesmerism and Christian Science*, 75-77, 83-86, 91; Fuller, *Mesmerism*, 10-15; Ellenberger, *Discovery of the Unconscious*, 72. Ellenberger makes a further distinction, arriving at three theories: the "fluidists" believed in Mesmer's physical fluid, the "animists" in psychological phenomena, and an intermediate theory believed that a physical fluid was directed by the will of the healer (o.c., 75).

[83] Benz, *Franz Anton Mesmer*, 26. Cf. Graßl, *Aufbruch zur Romantik*, 8, who describes Gaßner as the instigator of a 'mass psychosis which affected the whole of Germany', and was a matter of concern both for the Emperor and the Pope.

specific cultural constellation that Mesmer was invited by the Church authorities, in 1775, to come to Munich and clear up the real nature of Gaßner's healing practice. His intervention was succesful. He rapidly convinced not only the
Cardinal, but the Munich Academy of Sciences as well, 'that such experiments
should be ascribed neither to deception, nor to supernatural miracles, but to
nature'[84]. The diseases cured by Gaßner were caused, not by the influence of
demons, but by a disharmony in the body which hindered the flow of the invisible fluid[85]; if Gaßner was a succesful healer, this was simply because he happened to possess an excess of animal magnetism, which enabled him to restore
the balance in his patients and thus to heal them[86]. In short: without knowing
it, Gaßner was really a mesmerist who mistakenly attributed illnesses to demons
and healings to Jesus. Notice that Mesmer's argument implied *not* that
Gaßner's healing method was ineffective but only that his explanation was
unscientific and wrong; it is significant that this was sufficient ground for the
authorities to resort to practical measures. Gaßner was forbidden to continue
his healing practice, while Mesmer was made a member of the Bavarian Academy of Sciences. Several authors have emphasized the significance of the
Gaßner-Mesmer episode with respect to the complicated relations between
Enlightenment and Counter-Enlightenment currents during the later 18th century[87]. In Germany in 1775 Mesmer was fully acceptable, even to the Church
authorities, as representing the voice of science and reason against the mass
hysteria provoked by Gaßner's "superstitious" practice. Within a few years,
however, the same Mesmer had created his own mass hysteria in Paris, comparable to Gaßner's not only in popularity but also because of the striking similarity between the outward phenomena of exorcism and of mesmeric trance.
This time, it was Mesmer's turn to be denounced as a fraud by the scientific
and medical authorities. In both cases, the controversy raged less over the effectivity of the treatment than over the question of whether the phenomena should
be explained by natural or supernatural influences.

The discrepancy between Mesmer's reception in Bavaria and in Paris can
partly be explained by differences between the German *Aufklärung* and the
more radical French Enlightenment[88]. More important here is that it was the
inherently ambiguous nature of Mesmer's theory which made such radically
opposed evaluations possible. The same ambiguity explains why representa-

---

[84] Wolfahrt, *Erläuterungen zum Mesmerismus*, Berlin 1815, as quoted in Benz, *Franz Anton Mesmer*, 30. For an extensive discussion of the Gaßner controversy and Mesmer's role in it, see Graßl, *Aufbruch zur Romantik*, esp. 131-171 and 424-429.

[85] Cf. the distinction between personalistic and naturalistic healing systems, discussed in chapter two.

[86] Graßl, *Aufbruch zur Romantik*, 156.

[87] Graßl, *Aufbruch zur Romantik*, esp. 131-171, 424-429; McIntosh, *Rose Cross and the Age of Reason*, 98-101.

[88] See for this point the discussion of McIntosh, *Rose Cross and the Age of Reason*, ch. 1.

tives of the medical and scientific establishment could distrust mesmerism for its "mystical" connotations, while others distrusted it for its "materialism". The influential French esotericist Louis-Claude de Saint-Martin already seems to have been puzzled by the fact that, of all people, it had to be a person such as 'Mesmer, the disbeliever, this man who is nothing but matter' who 'opened the door to sensory demonstrations of the spirit'[89]. Indeed, Mesmer himself has correctly been described as 'a son of the Enlightenment [who] was seeking a "rational" explanation and rejected any kind of mystical theory'[90]. Nevertheless, that his theory is largely rooted in esoteric traditions is beyond doubt[91]. Mesmer's fluid is a modern manifestation of long-standing speculations about a "subtle" agent, deriving ultimately from the Aristotelian and Stoic concepts of *pneuma* and the Platonic *ochèma*. These ancient authorities became foundational for a complicated cluster of traditions, which include the medieval theory of medical spirits (natural, vital and animal) and the neoplatonic concept of the astral body[92]. These theories of subtle matter are prominently represented in western esotericism (which is, of course, not surprising given its many expressions of *Naturphilosophie* on a neoplatonic/hermetic foundation), and Mesmer's indebtedness to the occult sciences has been recognized by his enemies and defenders alike.

The continuity between esotericism, Mesmerism and occultism is therefore not in any doubt, and Mesmer's theory may legitimately be regarded as a modern presentation of *magia naturalis*. More important here is the question of what happened to these kinds of ideas in the scientistic climate of the 19th century. According to Frank Podmore,

> ... the whole of the Viennese physician's doctrine is implicitly contained in the writings of his predecessors. But there is one subtle difference. To Van Helmont the Magnetic system is still primarily a spiritual affair, a link between the heavens and the earth. Man can only obtain a complete mastery over the powers which sleep in his own nature by assimilating his will to the Divine Will. In the writ-

---

[89] Saint-Martin, *Oeuvres posthumes* I, 251, as quoted in Viatte, *Sources occultes* I, 223. About Saint-Martin's attitude towards Mesmer, cf. also Darnton, *Mesmerism*, 68-69.

[90] Ellenberger, *Discovery of the Unconscious*, 62. Cf. Fuller, *Mesmerism*, 4-5. But for the "romantic" side of his character, see his own description of the period of depression between his years as a physician in Vienna and his move to Paris: Benz, *Franz Anton Mesmer*, 23-24.

[91] The most important representatives are Paracelsus, Rudolf Goclenius the younger, Athanasius Kircher, Johann Baptist van Helmont, Robert Fludd, William Maxwell, Procop Divisch, Friedrich Christian Oetinger. See Podmore, *Mesmerism and Christian Science*, 29-38; Benz, *Franz Anton Mesmer*, 12-21; Viatte, *Sources occultes* I, 225; Graßl, *Aufbruch zur Romantik*, 158-159; Kiefer, 'Goethe und der Magnetismus', 267ff; Faivre, *L'ésotérisme au XVIIIe siècle*, 140; id., *Access*, 76-77.

[92] See Dodds, 'Astral Body in Neoplatonism', 313-321; Schlichting, 'Leer der spiritus', 41-54; Walker, 'Astral Body in Renaissance Medicine', 119-133; Hunter, 'Seventeenth Century Doctrine', 197-213. Probably the most complete historical overview is Poortman, *Vehicles of Consciousness*. Some blank spaces in Poortman's historical exposition are filled in by Van Dongen & Gerding, *Voertuig van de ziel*.

ings of Maxwell and Fludd greater stress is laid upon the material operations of
the fluid; the theory tends to become less mystical and more scientific. But neither quite loses sight of the spiritual aspect of the matter. It is not the starry light,
says Fludd, "which operateth so universally, but the Eternal Centrall Spirit". And
Maxwell gives an even more emphatic expression to the Spiritualist view. ... But
in Mesmer's exposition this spiritual aspect of the doctrine has entirely disappeared. For him the Magnetic system is purely a question of matter and motion'[93].

Since the same "fluid" could be interpreted as either spiritual or material, it is
not surprising that elements of mesmerism were adopted by various individuals and movements for very different reasons. Mesmerism was embraced by a
whole range of illuminist and occultist movements (including 19th century
spiritualism) as a theory which could serve to unify esotericism and modern
science. But there were also figures such as the influential English physician
John Elliotson (1791-1868). This enthusiastic defender of Mesmerism espoused a philosophy of materialism for reasons similar to the early Swedenborg: not out of atheism but out of a concern with keeping science and religion from interfering with one another[94]. To many of its defenders who were
influenced by Enlightenment ideas of progress, mesmerism was just one more
exponent of the triumph of science over nature. As such, it could lead to a millenarianism reminiscent of the New Age:

> "While the entire globe seems to prepare itself, by a remarkable revolution in the
> movement of the seasons, for physical changes on the surface of its atmosphere,
> natural science and philosophy make the greatest of efforts in order to spread and
> propagate everywhere their beneficial lights ... Above all, the end of this century
> represents an historically highly interesting epoch, marked by a sudden, and almost
> general fermentation of the spirit. This fermentation is produced by two singular
> circumstances, the aerostatic experiences and animal magnetism".
> "Behold a general revolution ... Men of a new kind will inhabit the earth; they
> will make it more beautiful by their virtues and their works; they will not be held
> back by their careers, or by ailments; they will know of our evils only from his-
> tory"[95].

Like George Trevelyan or Marilyn Ferguson in our time, enthusiasts of scientific progress in the decades before and after 1800 were dazzled by the prospect
of a radical new age: 'Who knows how far we can go? What mortal would dare
set limits to the human mind ...?'[96]. And in both periods, the concept of a unification of spirit and matter was easily linked to a non-political utopianism:
'It is necessary to throw all political, moral and economic theories into the fire
and to prepare for the most astonishing event ... FOR THE SUDDEN TRAN-

---

[93] Podmore, *Mesmerism and Christian Science*, 39-40. Cf. 26-27.

[94] Godwin, *Theosophical Enlightenment*, 159; Kaplan, "'Mesmeric Mania'", 700-701.

[95] Quotations from J.L. Carra, *Examen physique du magnétisme*, and P. Hervier, *Lettre sur le magnétisme animal*, in Viatte, *Sources occultes* I, 224. For the reference to aerostatic experiences, cf. Darnton, *Mesmerism*, 18ff, on the popular enthusiasm for balloon flights.

[96] *Journal de Bruxelles*, May 29, 1784, 226-27; as quoted in Darnton, *Mesmerism*, 23.

SITION FROM SOCIAL CHAOS TO UNIVERSAL HARMONY'[97]. One is tempted to conclude that, if contemporary authors such as George Trevelyan announce the "Age of Light", that age may well be rooted in the Age of the Enlightenment.

It is hardly possible to overestimate the relevance of Mesmerism for religious and cultural history after the end of the 18th century. It seems probable that its wide dissemination was due in large part to its essential simplicity: an invisible fluid connects all parts of the universe, whether "spiritual" or "material", and this fluid is the universal key to health and harmony. Scientists, physicians, psychologists, philosophers, or occultists could all adapt such a proposition to their own purposes, and draw from it implications undreamt-of by its originator[98]. In all cases, the theory suggested (even if it did not prove) a unification of opposites: religion and science, mind and matter, even God and the universe; and to many people such a unification held the promise of a new society, in which humanity would have progressed from fragmentation to wholeness.

Modern Spiritualism

At the origins of occultism we have found ideas and concepts derived from the esoteric tradition, adopted and reinterpreted by a scientist of the mechanistic school and an essentially pragmatic physician. This remarkable constellation prefigures the development of the spiritualist movement, which derived its essential impulses from Swedenborg and Mesmer.

The beginnings of modern spiritualism are usually dated from March 31, 1848, the day on which the sisters Margaret and Kate Fox professed to have found a way of communicating with a spirit which had been producing mysterious rappings in their Hydesville home for several months. The case was widely publicized in the press, and within a few years spirit communication had become a popular pastime throughout the United States and elsewhere. Reliable studies are available about the various stages in the development of the craze; the emergence of spiritualism as a religious movement, including the establishment of spiritualist churches; its importance for the emergence of "psychical research"; its relevance to progressive causes such as women's emancipation; the problematic connections between spiritualism and other "occultist" movements; the influence of spiritualism on the established Church-

---

[97] Charles Fourier, as quoted in Darnton, *Mesmerism*, 143. Darnton notes that the mesmerist influence is evident in many of Fourier's works, although he assimilated it 'as one of many foreign elements ... in a vision that was ultimately his own' (o.c. 144). Fourier's followers were profoundly involved in Mesmerism, which inspires Darnton to speak of a "mesmero-fourierism" (o.c., 145).
[98] Viatte, *Sources occultes* I, 224-225.

es and Christian theology, and so on[99]. For us it is important to recognize that, although the activities of the Fox sisters certainly marked the beginning of spiritualism as a mass movement, in most other respects its antecedents can be traced at least as far back as the illuminist movements of the second half of the 18th century. Communication with "elevated beings" is a feature frequently reported from illuminist orders such as Martinez de Pasqually's *Elus-Cohens*, Dom Antoine-Joseph Pernety's *Illuminés d'Avignon*, Jean-Baptiste Willermoz's *Chevaliers Bienfaisants de la Cité Sainte*, and similar religious orders closely connected to or derived from them[100]. These spirit communications could still be interpreted as examples of "articulated revelations" from higher beings, similar to channeling in the New Age context (see chapter one). But communication specifically with the (recently) departed, accompanied by empirical "phenomena" similar to those of 19th century spiritualism, are attested as well. Such examples of spiritualism avant-la-lettre seem to have flourished especially in the many societies which were more or less strongly influenced by Swedenborgianism[101]. Thus, one reads about a seance at which a human head appeared to be floating in mid-air and refused to disappear, to the distress of the participants: 'it responded to questions, and when they wished to put an end to the apparition, the two evocators became very frightened at seeing this unhappy head floating around them for three hours more; and it was only with extreme difficulty that they could finally make it disappear'[102]. During meetings of the so-called *École du Nord* (Copenhagen) of Duke Karl von Hessen-Kassel, a light used to appear, 'with a phosphorous appearance, which [gave] precise answers to questions posed to it, by two signs, one of which meant *yes* and the other *no*'[103]. Johann Caspar Lavater has left us a detailed account of

---

[99] For the history of spiritualism and its various aspects, see Nelson, *Spiritualism and Society*; Webb, *Occult Underground*, ch. 1; Moore, 'Spiritualism'; id., *White Crows*; id., 'Occult Connection?'; Isaacs, 'Fox Sisters'; Brandon, *Spiritualists*; Oppenheim, *Other World*; Owen, *Darkened Room*; Braude, *Radical Spirits*; Godwin, *Theosophical Enlightenment*, chs. 10; Jansen, *Op zoek naar nieuwe zekerheid*.

[100] See the descriptions of Viatte, *Sources occultes* I, 52 (Pasqually), 96-97 (Pernety), 143-144 (Willermoz). Notice that the first example (Pasqually) relies on a description given by the French "Martinist" Papus (pseudonym of Gérard Encausse) long after Pasqually's death. Papus's description of Pasqually's Christian theurgy (involving the appearance, 'in the full light of day' and 'without sleeping mediums, without ecstasies or morbid hallucination', of invisible beings who gave elevated lectures and called for prayer and meditation) seems inspired by an apologetic concern with demarcating "true occultism" from the popular spiritualism of his own day.

[101] Cf. Benz, 'Reinkarnationslehre', 150-175 (repr. in Resch, *Fortleben*, 346-347). Benz mentions Tardy de Montravel as the originator of modern spiritualism in 1787, and mentions a Swedenborgian "Exegetical and philantropical society of Stockholm" as the first group to organize spiritualist sessions with somnambulist mediums (also in 1787). "Empirical phenomena" of a spiritualist kind seem, however, to have occurred at least as early as 1776 (see text).

[102] Reported by Marie-Daniel Bourrée de Corberon in his journal on May 1, 1776 (Viatte, *Sources occultes* I, 109).

[103] Reported by Kirchberger to Eckartshausen, april 4, 1795 (Viatte, *Sources occultes*, 132).

these seances, which should be recognized as an important document for the early history of spiritualism[104]. To my knowledge, the possible connections between these illuminist seances and the later spiritualist movement have not yet been sufficiently explored. More attention has been given to some other pre-1848 manifestations of spiritualism. For example, the German Friederike Hauffe (1801-1829) achieved fame as the "Seeress of Prevorst" after being magnetized by the doctor-poet Justinus Kerner in 1826. She communicated with spirits of the dead, was the focus of poltergeist activities (knocks, raps, flying furniture), and gave inspired teachings "channeled" from a higher source[105]. Moreover, as pointed out by Joscelyn Godwin, historians have neglected the widespread occult practice of scrying (crystal-gazing): another technique which resulted in communications with the dead and messages from higher beings[106].

Such examples demonstrate that it is indeed quite arbitrary to begin a history of spiritualism with the Fox sisters: as noted by Godwin, the only thing that was novel about the 1848 phenomena was the publicity[107]. The impression of a "sudden outbreak" easily obscures the fact that the dissemination of Swedenborgian ideas, on the one hand, and the practice of Mesmerism, on the other, had quietly been preparing the ground for several decades. Robert S. Ellwood is essentially correct in stating that 'spiritualism is Swedenborgian ideology, mixed with an experimentation with transic states inspired by mesmerism'[108]. A crucial role in this respect was played by Andrew Jackson Davis, the so-called "Poughkeepsie seer", who has been referred to as '*the* spiritualist theologian if the movement had one'[109]. Davis's clairvoyant abilities were discovered when he was mesmerized as a teenager, but he eventually learned how to enter an "illuminated state" without the help of magnetism. He claimed that, in such a state, he was able to converse with the spirits of such famous personalities as the Greek physician Galen and Emanuel Swedenborg himself. Davis's huge and immensely popular volume of inspired lectures called *The Principles of Nature, Her Divine Revelations, and a Voice to Mankind* was published one year before the Hydesville phenomena, and was followed by a number of other books over the next couple of decades. Just as Swedenborg denied

---

[104] Lavater, *Nachtrag zu dem Resultate meiner Reise oder Verschiedenes zur Erläuterung und Bestätigung des Nordischen Sache*, february 9-12, 1794. Reproduced in French by Viatte, *Sources occultes* I, 132-135, and in the German original in Faivre, 'J.C.Lavater, Charles de Hesse...', 37-52. Cf. also Faivre, *Kirchberger*, 140-147.

[105] See for example Godwin, *Theosophical Enlightenment*, 161-162.

[106] Godwin, *Theosophical Enlightenment*, ch. 9.

[107] Godwin, *Theosophical Enlightenment*, 187-188.

[108] Ellwood, 'American Theosophical Synthesis', 126. Whether the additional 'backdrop of Native American shamanism' was as important as Ellwood believes is a question which deserves further study.

[109] Albanese, 'On the Matter of Spirit', 4; cf. id., 'Magical Staff'.

having read esoteric authors such as Böhme, Davis denied ever having read Swedenborg. Both claimed to have received their knowledge directly from heaven; but this cannot prevent us from observing that Davis's worldview is essentially Swedenborgianism in 19th-century garb.

That Swedenborgianism became popular among spiritualists is not surprising: it provided a convenient theoretical background for the practice of communicating with "the other world". The fact that the official Swedenborgian "Church of the New Jerusalem" 'spent more energy assailing Spiritualism than any group except the adventists'[110] could not prevent an eclectic spread of Swedenborgianism. The New Church accused spiritualists of espousing materialism; of denying the existence of a personal God and the divinity of Christ; and of ignoring both Swedenborg's claim to uniqueness as a chosen vessel of divine revelation and his warnings against casual spirit communication. As it happens, they were right on all counts, but their protests did little to prevent an eclectic adoption of Swedenborgian ideas in spiritualist circles[111]. While Swedenborgianism provided spiritualism with a theoretical framework, including descriptions of the other world sufficiently 'graphic and literal'[112] for the matter-of-fact attitude of the time, it was Mesmerism which stood at the foundation of spiritualist *practice*. I mentioned the fact that Mesmeric treatment had the effect of inducing a trance state in the patient, which typically culminated in a violent "crisis". This Mesmeric trance was developed by Amand-Marie-Jacques de Chastenet, Marquis de Puységur (1751-1825), into a less violent type of trance. Originally referred to as "induced somnambulism", today it is known as hypnosis[113]. It is not necessary here to discuss the many remarkable

---

[110] Moore, 'Spiritualism', 94.

[111] For the influence of Swedenborgianism on spiritualism, see Swatos, 'Spiritualism', 472-473; Moore, 'Spiritualism', 87, 94; id., *White Crows*, 9-10, 56, 232; Isaacs, 'Fox Sisters', 80; Ellwood, 'American Theosophical Synthesis', 126; Cross, *Burned-over District*, ch. 19; Oppenheim, *Other World*, 233-235; Nelson, *Spiritualism and Society*, 53-54.

[112] Moore, 'Spiritualism', 96. See especially the similarity between Swedenborgian and spiritualist perceptions of the "other world". 'No other American religion in the nineteenth century had more concrete and individualized notions of the afterlife. Spirits retained all the discrete characteristics of their earthly personalities. Their astral bodies looked very much like their earthly bodies. Spirit babies grew up into men and women as they would have done on earth. The spirit realms presented landscapes very similar to those on earth' (o.c., 89). Actually, Swedenborgian and spiritualist conceptions are perfect examples of Lovejoy's characterization of this-worldliness as 'a prolongation of the mode of being which we know ... with merely the omission of the trivial or painful features of terrestrial existence, the heightening of its finer pleasures, the compensation of some of earth's frustrations' (see beginning of chapter six, section 1). Having described the splendour of the celestial landscapes reported by spiritualists, Moore concludes that 'such messages contained the comforting assurance that the departing spirit lauching itself into the next world, say, from Kansas, would be leaving behind a good bit that was drab but not all that was familiar'.

[113] About de Puységur's discoveries see, for example, Podmore, *Mesmerism and Christian Science*, 70ff; Ellenberger, *Discovery of the Unconscious*, 70-74; Gauld, *History of Hypnotism*, 39-52; Godwin, *Theosophical Enlightenment*, 153-154. The term "hypnosis" was introduced by

abilities of a "paranormal" nature displayed by subjects under hypnosis, or their importance for the early development of psychiatry. Important for us is that subjects in a somnambulic state induced by mesmerism frequently displayed mediumistic abilities. The implications, given the cultural climate of the times, were far-reaching. For large numbers of people the discovery of somnambulism made it possible, not only to *believe* in a spiritual world, but to make the attempt at convincing themselves and others of its existence by "experimental" means. In principle, such proof did not require expert scientific knowledge: all that one needed was a sufficiently suggestible person willing to act as a medium. Spiritualism, in other words, was a religion perfectly suited to modern secular democracies: not only did it promise "scientific" proof of the supernatural, but its science was non-elitist as well. In principle, every civilian could now investigate the supernatural for him/herself, without the need to rely on religious or scientific authorities[114].

As a religious movement, spiritualism was characterized by a pronounced scientistic attitude combined with a vehement opposition to institutionalized Christianity. Here, it is important to notice that this combination, which has been discussed *in extenso* by R. Laurence Moore[115], led to a belief system which, while continuing the Enlightenment *critique* of Christianity, displays striking similarities with New Age religion. Moore remarks that many adherents of the new faith made a point of referring to themselves as "Christian spiritualists"[116], while strongly objecting to the faith of the established Churches. Spiritualists 'shared an aversion to what they called Christian orthodoxy (meaning, as a minimum, a belief in the Trinity, human depravity, predestination, vicarious atonement, and a final judgment). They moved in the direction of theological liberalism'[117]. Most spiritualists accepted the Transcendentalist perception of divinity as dwelling in the human soul and/or permeating nature as a nonpersonal "principle", and consciously opposed this to traditional Christian beliefs. As one author put it, 'A belief in a personal God, as above Nature, is the cause of all error'[118]. At the same time, they firmly insisted on the uniqueness of the individual soul before and after death; like Seth in the New Age context, they affirmed that 'You will never lose your identity. If God designed

---

James Braid around 1843 (see Podmore, *Mesmerism and Christian Science*, 146; Kaplan, '"Mesmeric Mania"', 702; Gauld, *History of Hypnotism*, 279-288). Podmore notices that de Puységur 'viewed with dislike and suspicion the crisis attended with violent convulsions which he had witnessed at Mesmer's establishment, and deplored the discredit which the spectacle of this *enfer à convulsions*, as he calls it, had brought upon the practice of Animal Magnetism'.

[114] *Contra* Zinser, 'Moderner Okkultismus', 290-291. It is inconceivable to me how Zinser can claim that not only the new discoveries of the natural sciences, but also those of spiritualism, required from the general public a blind reliance on the authority of "specialists".

[115] See Moore, 'Spiritualism'; and id., *White Crows*, ch. 1.

[116] Moore, 'Spiritualism', 82.

[117] Moore, 'Spiritualism', 83.

[118] Moore, 'Spiritualism', 88.

to absorb all souls into himself, there would have been no necessity at first to give off from himself distinct identical germs, possessing all the characteristics of independence'[119]. Moreover, spiritualist ideas about morality are essentially similar to those of the New Age movement. The doctrine of vicarious atonement was seen as 'an insult to morality in the suggestion that a man could win salvation through someone else's effort or someone else's sacrifice'[120]. The underlying belief in spiritual progress based on an individual's own efforts was combined with a marked tendency to dismiss evil as a cosmic category and affirm that "Whatever is, is right"[121]. Moore's discussions should be studied for a complete overview, but these examples will suffice to illustrate my conclusion that New Age religion is close to spiritualism in many important respects.

Spiritualists not only objected to what they perceived as "dogmatic Christianity", but were also emically opposed to "materialism". With hindsight, however, it is clear that they were profoundly influenced by the enemy. Moore has argued convincingly that spiritualism was both a reaction to materialist science *and* an extreme product of positivism[122]:

> Against the belief that nothing existed in the universe but matter, spiritualists waged a steady, though confused, battle. ... In major spiritualist publications the rescued spirit looked suspiciously like the matter out of whose jaws it presumably had been wrested. ... Spiritualists had some difficulty clarifying their views about the nature of spirit. Most agreed that "immaterial substance" could not exist. ... The spirit teachers seemed to concur that soul and spirit should not be considered something discontinuous from matter, but rather a higher, perfected form of matter. ... In trying to convince science to apply its instruments of measurement to things that lay beyond earthly horizons, spiritualists wound up reinvesting spirits with all the qualities of matter. [the psychologist Wilhelm Wundt concluded:] "From early times ... materialism has had two forms: the one denies the spiritual, the other transforms it into matter". Modern spiritualism, according to Wundt, had fallen into the latter trap'[123].

For a full discussion, I refer again to Moore's publications. His analysis is confirmed by other students of the subject[124]. Catherine L. Albanese concludes that 'Spiritualism ... brought together a theology of materialism ... with an empiricism that insisted on the tangibility of scientific "proof" of spirit visi-

[119] Spirit message published in Edmonds & Dexter, *Spiritualism*, 360, as quoted in Moore, 'Spiritualism', 89.

[120] Moore, 'Spiritualism', 90.

[121] See Moore's quotation from Child's, *Whatever Is, Is Right*, 2: 'Every law of Nature ... is a law of God, every jot and tittle of which must be fulfilled. God being infinite, there can be no nature or law outside of infinitude. God being good, all that is in God is good. So every deed of human life is good—not one is evil' (Moore, 'Spiritualism', 91).

[122] Moore, *White Crows*, 38.

[123] Moore, *White Crows*, 23-24.

[124] See for example Swatos, 'Spiritualism', 473-476; Nelson, *Spiritualism and Society*, 136-143; Oppenheim, *Other World*, 199ff.

tation and a new social program that would translate the experience of spiritualism into a new science of the perfect society'[125]. She has highlighted the case of Andrew Jackson Davis, mentioned above as the "theologian of spiritualism", as particularly illustrative. A fundamental aspect of Davis's so-called "Harmonial Philosophy" was the material being of spirit and of God: 'Inasmuch as God is a Fact, a Reality, a Principle, it is agreeable with science to suppose that He is Substance—is Matter'[126]. Albanese demonstrates that Davis not only went beyond Swedenborg by interpreting the latter's cosmology in the terms of 19th-century materialism, but that he also consistently relied on the scientific language and metaphors of magnetism and electricity[127].

In closing: perhaps most remarkable about the nature of spiritualism as a typical 19th-century scientistic (although not scientific) religion is the fact that its essentially positivistic and materialist philosophies were apparently widely understood as "spiritual", and were defended as viable alternatives to the very worldview of which they were an expression.

Conclusion

My general argument in Part Three of this study is that New Age religion emerged from traditions of western esotericism, as reflected "in the mirror of secular thought". Actually, however, we are dealing with a whole series of mirrors (i.e., different factors which have contributed to the secularization process), under the impact of which traditional esotericism was gradually transformed into new manifestations. I have argued that Romanticism emerged from a combination of traditional esotericism and the new "Counter-Enlightenment" temporalism; and I suggested that the new evolutionism, although a significant innovation, did not completely disrupt the internal consistency of Renaissance esotericism. Next, I argued that occultism, as the second major modern heir of esotericism, emerged from the interaction of an esoteric worldview of "correspondences" with a new worldview of "causality". This combination did disrupt the original coherence; it produced what may be described as hybrid forms, bound to be as unacceptable to scientific rationalism as they would have been unacceptable to Renaissance esotericists.

Spiritualism is of crucial importance to the emergence of occultism because it exemplifies occultism at its most extreme. However, although occultism would continue to be characterized by ambivalent worldviews halfway between

---

[125] Albanese, 'On the Matter of Spirit', 3.

[126] Andrew Jackson Davis, *The Great Harmonia*, vol. 2: *Being a Philosophical Revelation of the Natural, Spiritual, and Celestial Universe* (1851), 266, as quoted in Albanese, 'On the Matter of Spirit', 1.

[127] However, in line with my previous discussion, I would contest Albanese's statement that it was already Swedenborg who 'collapsed the distinction between matter and spirit' (Albanese, 'On the Matter of Spirit', 6).

traditional esotericism and modern "scientific" worldviews, not all its later manifestations are as radical as spiritualism. One reason is the assimilation of Romantic perspectives within occultism; another has to do with the revival of the traditional "occult sciences", disseminated by authors such as Éliphas Lévi, an influence which has been important to modern Theosophy and the various manifestations of occultist ritual magic but is marginal with respect to spiritualism specifically. Both factors will be discussed in the sections below. Yet another crucial factor is that scientific thinking itself moved beyond the types of positivism and materialism typical of the 19th century. Actually, the relation between 19th-century spiritualism and occultism in general is similar to the relation between 19th century positivism and modern science in general. The positivistic/materialistic ideology of the 19th century is now widely rejected as crude and naive; but it created basic paradigms for scientific thinking and practice, which continue to influence even its most outspoken critics. Similarly, the spiritualist ideology is a product of the 19th century and is no longer representative of present-day occultism; but I suggest that it created a paradigm for occultist thought and practice which continues to influence even its most outspokenly critical insiders up to the present day. Occultists may proclaim a primordial wisdom which goes back to Atlantis and beyond, and they may reject "Cartesian/Newtonian" thought as detrimental; but in doing so they have not been able to free themselves from their own history and return to a perspective innocent of "causality". Perhaps the most profound irony of "esotericism in the mirror of secular thought" consists in the fact that the evolution of consciousness proclaimed by occultists (and New Agers) requires them to embrace the very innovations which undermine their claim to represent "ancient wisdom".

The new worldview of "causality" represents one mirror, or prism, by which traditional esotericism is reflected so as to produce a new development called occultism. The three other "mirrors" of secularization have led to subsequent developments *within* the newly-constituted field of occultism. While the first "mirror" has a special status because it constitutes a momentous break with the past, the three others represent highly important additional factors in the process of secularization. In order to understand the emergence of New Age religion out of occultism, they now have to be discussed.

2. THE IMPACT OF THE STUDY OF RELIGIONS

It would be interesting to investigate the influence of western esotericism on the emergence of the study of religions. The interest of the Renaissance Platonists for the religions of antiquity has been mentioned as an important episode in the pre-history of the discipline, although that significance has been denied by others[128]. An almost entirely neglected question concerns the extent to which the Romantic scholars and philosophers who first "discovered" India may have been inspired by intuitions of an affinity between Oriental religions and their own backgrounds in (mostly German) esotericism[129]. I will restrict myself here to less controversial issues. There is no doubt that the so-called "oriental renaissance"[130], the gradual academic emancipation of the study of religions, and the emergence of the comparative study of religions have been closely interwoven with the Enlightenment criticism of Christianity and the emergence of a relativistic "historical consciousness" associated with its "Counter-Enlightenment" reaction[131]. The modern study of religion can be seen both as a product of the secularization process[132] and as an important factor in its success. Once again, we find that esotericists and occultists were profoundly involved in that process, and that their motivations were inspired at least as profoundly by Enlightenment as by Counter-Enlightenment concerns. H.P. Blavatsky's modern theosophy is an example of Comparative Religion on occultist premises, developed with the express intention of undermining established Christianity. A somewhat different picture is presented by the impact of Oriental religions (Hinduism in particular) on American Transcendentalism, which is the offshoot of Romanticism most important in creating conditions for New Age religion. Our second "mirror" of secular thought is therefore relevant to both major heirs of esotericism (i.e., occultism and Romanticism) in the 19th century.

A. The Theosophical Synthesis

The title of a recent landmark study by Joscelyn Godwin, *The Theosophical Enlightenment*, summarizes the author's central thesis that Blavatsky's theosophy 'owed as much to the skeptical Enlightenment of the eighteenth century as it did to the concept of spiritual enlightenment with which it is more readily associated'[133]. On the basis of little-known source materials, Godwin has

---

[128] See Kohl, 'Geschichte der Religionswissenschaft', 227-229. For a contrary assessment, see Eliade, 'Quest for the "Origins" of Religion', 39.

[129] Some suggestions in that direction can be found in Gérard, *L'Orient et la pensée romantique allemande*, esp. 77-83. Cf. Versluis, *American Transcendentalism*, 20-23

[130] Schwab, *Oriental Renaissance*.

[131] For historical overviews of the historical, anthropological and comparative study of religions, see for example Kohl, 'Geschichte der Religionswissenschaft'; Morris, *Anthropological Studies of Religion*; Van Baal & Van Beek, *Symbols for Communication*; Sharpe, *Comparative Religion*.

[132] See for example Jackson, *Oriental Religions*: '... the Enlightenment's emphasis on religious toleration, the influence of the environment in the formation of one's ideas, and the basic oneness of human nature all contributed to a more sympathetic attitude toward Asian thought'.

[133] Godwin, *Theosophical Enlightenment*, xi. Although Godwin is modest enough not to

uncovered developments in the 19th-century history of religious ideas which
add new meaning to Peter Gay's characterization of the Enlightenment as "the
rise of modern paganism"[134]. Since Godwin's study is virtually unique in its
expert discussion of precisely those interactions between the study of religion
and occultism which concern us here, my following discussion is profoundly
indebted to his researches.

Proto-Theosophical Perspectives
One important factor in the development of occultism was the emergence, during the last decades of the 18th century, of new speculative theories of myth
and the origin of religion. Many of these theories suggested that all ancient
mythology, as well as the newly discovered religions of India, could be interpreted in terms of sexual symbolism. One of the authors who put forward this
theory was the still-famous Sir William Jones; but other authors who have now
largely been forgotten, such as Richard Payne Knight (1751-1824), were hardly less influential in their own times. Godwin demonstrates convincingly that
these theories were largely the product of Enlightenment "neopaganism": 'A
handful of erudite libertines, taking advantage of a climate which allowed them
to advertise their nonbelief in Christianity, fastened on sex as the universal
explanation of mythology and religious origins'[135]. A second influential theory explained ancient religions, and ultimately religions in general, as origi-
nating in sun worship. Christianity was no exception. According to Charles-
Francois Dupuis, for example, 'Jesus Christ ... is the sun, and his life is nothing but an allegory of the sun's course through the Zodiac, from birth, through
crucifixion on the cross of the solstices and equinoxes, to resurrection. Thus
the Christian religion is just another distorted representative of the great, original religion of Nature'[136]. Such arguments obviously assisted in the hoped-
for overthrow of Christianity, and it does not surprise that the author of a similar work, Dupuis's friend Constantin Francois de Volney (1757-1820), used to
be mentioned in one breath with Voltaire. Godwin discusses leading proponents of these theories and a number of other freethinkers who took up their
line of thinking, and demonstrates that such deliberately anti-orthodox theories of religion were widely disseminated on a popular level. Of particular interest is the case of Godfrey Higgins (1772-1833), who had no interest in esotericism or occultism, but whose *Anacalypsis* (2 vols., 1833 and 1836) in particular prefigures Blavatsky's work in many respects[137]. It is not insignificant

---

emphasize it, no student of esotericism can fail to recognize the additional reference to Frances
A. Yates's *The Rosicrucian Enlightenment*.
  [134] Gay, *Enlightenment* I.
  [135] Godwin, *Theosophical Enlightenment*, 24.
  [136] Godwin, *Theosophical Enlightenment*, 34.
  [137] Among many other things, Higgins discussed the shift from the Piscean to the Aquar-

that the ties between these freethinkers and the esoteric tradition were tenuous or non-existent in most cases, although their theories about religion and its mythical origins were to be adopted later in occultist circles. Implicit in Godwin's account is the conclusion that many of the beliefs which are generally regarded as "occultist" today did *not* originate in esotericism, but in early theories in the study of religion; it was only when the professionalization of the discipline caused such theories to fall into discredit that they became the sole possession of occultists[138].

A pivotal role in the assimilation of Enlightenment mythography by occultism was played by the spiritualist Emma Hardinge-Britten (1823-1899). As a trance medium, she received messages on "the origin of all religious faiths" in 1858, which were published as *Six Lectures on Theology and Nature* in 1860. Godwin concludes that it was Hardinge-Britten who 'achieved the marriage of spiritualism with the mythography of the Enlightenment'. Indeed, his summary of her lectures demonstrates perfectly how the anti-Christian sentiments of the Enlightenment mythographers could be used to strengthen those of spiritualism:

> She told her audience that the world was not thousands but millions of years old, and that the cradle of civilization was in the East. It was there that the first worship had arisen, that of the powers of nature. This developed into cults of the sun and of its passage through the zodiac, creating an astronomical religion whose vestiges survive throughout the known world, and which is the origin of all known religions, including Christianity. The priests of every nation exploited the mysterious side of religion, encouraging cults of celestial and natural objects without telling the people that these were all subordinate to the one God. It was the priests, too, who in every religion instituted sacrifices in order to sustain their own power and splendor.
>
> Emma, or her guide, praised the founders of religions—Christ, Moses, Osiris, Buddha, and Zoroaster—for breaking the chains of priestcraft; but every time, the priests forged them the stronger. She railed at the dogmas of Nicea and the Thirty-Nine Articles of the Anglicans; she told the Christians that their denial of all other religions was atrocious; and she urged her listeners to go and read the Book

---

ian Age. His discussion implies that the latter began in 1810 (Godwin, *Theosophical Enlightenment*, 84).

[138] Godwin, *Theosophical Enlightenment*, 311-312: '... when the *Asiatic Researches* resumed publication in 1816 ... there were no more of the delightful, speculative articles such as Jones had written on the Greek and Hindu gods, or Wilford on the Sacred Isles of the West, which brought India, via comparative mythography, into the family of nations. The time of the gentleman amateur was passing. Whereas formerly an educated man could read the whole journal with pleasure and understand most of it, now it was a vehicle for conversations among a handful of scholars. ... A similar change was taking place in the field of mythography. No longer could one man pretend to take all the world's myths and religions as his topic, and propose some all-embracing theory to explain them, but the work had to be done piecemeal by specialists. Consequently, the only people who persisted with universal theories were the occultists or esotericists who felt themselves exempted, by the possession of special knowledge, from the impossible burden of becoming adept in a dozen Western and Eastern languages'.

of Nature if they wanted to know the true God. As the lecture course proceeded, she expounded the doctrine of the macrocosm and the microcosm (the sun corresponding to the human heart), and the new theory of evolution. She praised death as the necessary transformational agent of nature, without which there could be no development, and refused its identification with sin, which has no part in nature but what humans have given it. She told of how death leads us on to the spirit world, whence we become the guardians of those we loved on earth. Finally, she gave a series of gruesome quotations taken from Christian writers who exulted in the prospect of eternal torment, especially of unbaptized infants[139].

It should be evident that we have here another crucial precedent for the emergence of New Age religion. The "science" which spiritualism opposed to Christianity now included not only the natural sciences, but the history of religions as well, within a larger framework which was evidently dependent on esoteric traditions.

Apart from spiritualism, on the one hand, and the sexual and solar theories of religion, on the other, a third crucial factor in the development of occultism consisted in the revival of the traditional occult sciences. Godwin mentions the importance in this respect of Francis Barret's *The Magus* (1801), which consists of plagiarized materials of famous esoteric authors such as Cornelius Agrippa, Peter of Abano, J.B. van Helmont and Giambattista Porta; and he puts particular emphasis on the pivotal role of the well-known writer Edward Bulwer-Lytton (1803-1873) and his highly influential occult novel *Zanoni* (1842). Although Éliphas Lévi has often been mentioned as the principal source of the French occult revival of the later 19th century[140], it is likely that Lévi himself was indebted to Bulwer-Lytton for introducing him to magic[141]. *Zanoni* is a veritable 'encyclopedia of ideas about the occult sciences'[142] and reveals deep roots in the illuminism of later 18th century France. Books such as *The Magus* and *Zanoni* provided interested readers with easily accessible manuals of traditional esotericism and the occult sciences.

A perfect illustration of how these materials could be syncretized with the new study of myth and religion, so as to produce an occultist mixture, is found in the work of Hargrave Jennings (1817?-1890): yet another forgotten but important figure uncovered by Godwin's researches[143]. In the same year that Emma Hardinge-Britten received her spirit messages on the "origin of all faiths", Jennings published a book called *The Indian Religions*, in response to an essay on Buddhism published by F. Max Müller in April 1857. In order to estimate the significance of this publication, it should be remembered that, at

---

[139] Godwin, *Theosophical Enlightenment*, 203.
[140] McIntosh, *Eliphas Lévi*.
[141] Godwin, *Theosophical Enlightenment*, 196.
[142] Godwin, *Theosophical Enlightenment*, 126.
[143] Apart from the discussion in *Theosophical Enlightenment*, see also Godwin, 'Hargrave Jennings'. Jennings is briefly mentioned in Webb, *Occult Establishment*, 380-381, 391, 399.

the time, most Europeans and Americans experienced 'a deep distaste for Buddhism's negations'[144]; as formulated by Godwin:

> At mid-century, knowledge of Buddhism in Europe and America was slight, and enthusiasm for it nil. The American Transcendentalists, whose admiration for Hindu doctrines was based on the ample source material of the Asiatic Researches, found Buddhism chilly and negative by comparison. Academic experts such as Burnouf, Müller, and Barthélemy Saint-Hilaire painted Buddhism as a gloomy religion of negation, and Nirvana as nothing more or less than extinction[145].

This perception remained dominant until the popular success of Sir Edwin Arnold's *The Light from Asia* in 1879[146]. In this context, Jennings's defense of "Buddhism" more than twenty years earlier must (in spite of its incoherent presentation) be recognized as highly original[147]. Like most of his contemporaries, Jennings assumed that the Buddha was not the founder of Buddhism but merely its most famous proponent, and that his religion was *more ancient* than the Brahmanism of the Hindus. This made sense from the perspective of an Enlightenment belief in progress: if the simple preceded the complex, then the supposedly atheistic and nihilistic doctrines of Buddhism had to be more primitive than the colourful polytheism of India[148]. Contrary to such negative evaluations, however, Jennings claimed that 'the original, pre-Gautama Buddhism was the primordial wisdom of mankind'[149], from which the other religions, including those of India, had descended. He argued that the mistaken perception of Buddhism as atheistic was based on the inability of westerners to conceive of God other than as a being; the Ultimate in Buddhism, however, should not be understood as nothingness but as a "sublime Non-Being". In an attempt to further explain this concept, Jennings argued that the objectors to Buddhism mistakenly start from the assumption that "life is real", whereas it is actually illusory in the face of Nirvana. On this basis, he came to an Idealistic conclusion: 'Ideas ... are all which we have. And these are not real things, but mere delusive lights of the master phantom-light of intelligence'[150]. Elsewhere, he associated this latter concept with Nature or with the "soul of the world", which works through complementary opposites such as Light and Darkness, Life and Death. At this point it becomes clear, as noted by Godwin, that Jennings perceived Buddhism as closely related to a Hermetic worldview. And this is hardly surprising, for Jennings himself mentioned among his principal sources not

---

[144] Jackson, *Oriental Religions*, 142, cf. 56; see also Godwin, *Theosophical Enlightenment*, 322-326; Arthur Versluis, *American Transcendentalism*, 20, 23, 72. Cf. Robinson & Johnson, *Buddhist Religion*, ch. 11.
[145] Godwin, *Theosophical Enlightenment*, 266.
[146] Jackson, *Oriental Religions*, 143.
[147] Godwin, *Theosophical Enlightenment*, 266.
[148] Godwin, *Theosophical Enlightenment*, 264.
[149] Godwin, *Theosophical Enlightenment*, 264.
[150] Jennings, *Indian Religions*, 32, as quoted in Godwin, *Theosophical Enlightenment*, 265.

only William Jones's *Asiatic Researches* and William Ward's now largely forgotten *Religion of the Hindoos*[151]; but also Cornelius Agrippa, Paracelsus, J.B.
van Helmont, Swedenborg, books on magnetism and spiritualism, and works
of Romantic *Naturphilosophie* such as Catherine Crowe's *The Night-Side of
Nature* and Ennemoser's *History of Magic*[152]. Jennings's later works would be
marked by an increasing influence of Rosicrucianism and related traditions,
connected by him with an obscure late-16th century sect of "Fire-philoso-
phers". Fire, or Light, was described by Jennings as the central agent both of
annihilation into Non-Being (Nirvana) and of cosmic creativity[153]. This emphasis on Fire as the first principle of religion and mythology, together with an
emphasis on polarities of Light/Darkness, Life/Death, Creation/Destruction,
was obviously congenial to the solar and sexual theories mentioned above,
which became increasingly important in Jenning's later publications.

   We saw that Hardinge-Britten proclaimed a mixture of spiritualism and the
sexual/solar theories of religion, opposing both to the dogmatism of traditional Christianity. Jennings's combination of the same theories of religion with
traditional esotericism, occult sciences and Romantic *Naturphilosophie* now
proceeded to present Buddhism as the "primordial wisdom" at the root of all
true religion. We thus witness a characteristic transformation of the traditional esoteric concern with a "concordance" of religions (i.e., Faivre's fifth element). Originally, esotericists had pointed to Hermes or Zoroaster as the fountains of a perennial wisdom which had attained to full flower in Christianity.
Now, in a secularized climate and under the impact of the new knowledge about
Oriental religions, the sources of wisdom were moved increasingly eastward
and Christianity was believed not to have fulfilled but to have corrupted them.

The New Theosophy

It was Helena Petrowna Blavatsky (1831-1891) who brought the various elements mentioned above together into an occultist synthesis which became the
foundation of modern theosophy. It is useful here to recall the official objectives of the Theosophical Society, which finally came to be formulated as follows[154]:

   1. To form a nucleus of the Universal Brotherhood of Humanity, without distinction of race, creed, sex, caste or colour.
   2. To encourage the study of comparative religion, philosophy and science.
   3. To investigate unexplained laws of Nature and the powers latent in man.

---

[151] Ward, *View of the History*, mentioned briefly in Schwab, *Oriental Renaissance*.
[152] Godwin, *Theosophical Enlightenment*, 262.
[153] Godwin, *Theosophical Enlightenment*, 267-268.
[154] I quote the final version of 1896. In the context of the argument put forward here, the
development of the stated objectives between 1875 and this year is highly interesting. See the
overview in Ransom, *Short History*, 545-553.

The significance of these objectives in the context of the previous discussions should be clear. The first objective implicitly rejects the "irrational bigotry" and "sectarianism" of traditional Christianity as perceived by spiritualists and theosophists[155]. The second and third objectives point to the study of science, philosophy and Comparative Religion as, apparently, of crucial importance for the creation of a "Universal Brotherhood of Humanity". It is not immediately obvious from the objectives themselves that, for theosophists, "science" meant the occult sciences and philosophy the *occulta philosophia*, that the laws of nature were of an occult or psychic nature, and that comparative religion was expected to unveil a "primordial tradition" ultimately modeled on a Hermeticist *philosophia perennis*.

For the argument put forward here, it is not necessary to trace the historical development of the Theosophical Society and its many offshoots, although this constitutes a fascinating subject in itself[156]. I will argue that the fundamental contribution of modern theosophy to the history of occultism consists in its assimilation, by the early founders, of elements of Oriental religions and a perspective of "Comparative Religion" in an already existing western occultist framework. Later developments of modern theosophy under the influence of Charles Webster Leadbeater, Annie Besant, and others are far from insignificant; but they amount to shifts of emphasis within an already existing framework rather than to fundamental innovations.

Blavatsky's early involvement in spiritualism, as a medium and a defender of the authenticity of spiritualist phenomena[157], is not in any doubt. It is a matter of debate, however, to what extent she ever accepted spiritualist teachings. Important for the later development of modern theosophy is that the later Blavatsky demarcated "true occultism" from spiritualism, arguing that the spiritualist phenomena were genuine in themselves, but were caused not by the spirits of the dead but by "elementals" (cf. chapter seven, section 3B) or by

---

[155] Cf. an earlier version of the objectives (1879): '(b) To oppose and counteract—after due investigation and proof of its irrational nature—bigotry in every form ... (f) To promote in every practicable way non-sectarian education ...' (Ransom, *Short History*, 547).

[156] There is an extensive literature on Blavatsky and the Theosophical Society. A history from a theosophical perspective is Ransom, *Short History*. A useful overview by an outsider is Campbell, *Ancient Wisdom Revived*. Joscelyn Godwin's *Theosophical Enlightenment* contains fundamental new insights in early theosophical history. Of the many biographies of Blavatsky, usually written by admirers, one of the more interesting ones is Fuller, *Blavatsky and her Teachers*. Blavatsky's successor Annie Besant is the subject of an extensive biography in two volumes by Nethercot, *First Five Lives of Annie Besant* & *Last Four Lives of Annie Besant*; for a brief biography, see Dinnage, *Annie Besant*. A biography of the most influential "second generation" theosophist, as well as the best history of the Theosophical Society between Blavatsky's death and the early 1930s, is Tillett, *Elder Brother*. For a brief but solid study of theosophical beliefs, see Ellwood, *Theosophy*. Finally, mention should be made of the journal *Theosophical History*, published since 1985, which has developed into a good resource for study.

[157] See for example Bevir, 'West turns Eastward', 750.

so-called "astral shells"[158]. The meaning of this latter concept and the implications with respect to spiritualism are summarized by Godwin. Astral shells were

> psychic detritus left behind by human beings who had passed beyond the possibility of communication. Just as a corpse looks for a while like a living body, so the shells could supposedly imitate, up to a point, the individual who had sloughed them off. Thus the spiritualists who thought that they were talking to Socrates, Ben Franklin, or their grandmothers, were told bluntly that they were being bamboozled. As an alternative to this profitable farce, Blavatsky urged the study of Hermeticism and the occult sciences ...
> Occultism taught one not just to sit back and exchange sentimentalities with the "spirits", but to *try*: that is, to cultivate one's will, increase one's knowledge, and eventually to master the higher powers and faculties that lie latent in everyone'[159].

As noted by Bevir, Blavatsky did not repudiate spiritualism, but reinterpreted it as a subordinate element within a larger occultist framework[160]. This framework was based on the revival of the occult sciences combined with popular theories of religion, and can be seen as a further development of prior trends as exemplified with particular clarity by Hardinge-Britten and Jennings. It retained the innovative elements of earlier forms of occultism: an obsessive anti-Christianity (which suggests, as one critic has noticed, that Blavatsky's *Isis Unveiled* would have been more appropriately entitled *The Horrors of Christianity Unveiled and the Excellencies of Hinduism Praised*[161]), and a strong colouring by the positivistic *Zeitgeist*[162]. However, the important point here is that it now claimed scientific legitimacy in a double sense: with reference not only to the natural sciences, but also to the newly-emerging discipline of Comparative Religion.

To begin with the former: Blavatsky presented occultism as a form of *magia naturalis*. It 'did not contradict the laws of nature, but rather used natural powers that scientists did not yet acknowledge: thus, "magic is but a *science*, a profound knowledge of the Occult forces in Nature, and of the laws govern-

---

[158] From the perspective of the present study, the controversy between spiritualists and occultists must be seen as internal to "occultism" in an etic sense. See for the development of this debate Godwin, *Theosophical Enlightenment*, esp. 206, 210, 216, 243, 282. Yet a third occultist explanation consisted in an influence of living adepts or "masters" who were able to cause physical events at a distance (see for this explanation o.c., 291, and the connection to the "provocation theory" of the Hydesville phenomena (o.c. 196-200): a characteristic occult conspiracy theory according to which spiritualism was provoked by living persons with the intention of changing western civilization).

[159] Godwin, *Theosophical Enlightenment*, 282 & 292. The motto TRY was derived from Paschal Beverly Randolph (1825-1875). For this neglected pioneer of American occultism, see Godwin, *Theosophical Enlightenment*, 348-261; and cf. Melton, 'Paschal Beverly Randolph'.

[160] Bevir, 'West turns Eastward', 751.

[161] Jackson, *Oriental Religions*, 160.

[162] Eliade, 'Quest for the "Origins" of Religion', 42-43.

ing the visible or invisible world"'[163]. Her characteristically 19th-century understanding of natural magic as natural science is demonstrated clearly by statements such as the following:

> Nothing can be more easily accounted for than the highest possiblities of magic. By the radiant light of the universal magnetic ocean, whose electric waves bind the cosmos together, and in their ceaseless motion penetrate every atom and molecule of the boundless creation, the disciples of mesmerism—howbeit insufficient their various experiments—intuitionally perceive the alpha and omega of the great mystery. Alone, the study of this agent, which is the divine breath, can unlock the secrets of psychology and physiology, of cosmical and spiritual phenomena[164].

The mesmeric fluid is here presented as synonymous to the "divine breath", and Blavatsky argues that this occult unifying agent can be studied in a scientific manner.

Blavatsky's use of popular theories of religion, in the context of an anti-Christian polemic in the spiritualist tradition, is prefigured in several occultist works appearing in roughly the same period. In 1873, William Stainton Moses received messages from an entity named "Imperator+"; an anonymous book entitled *Art Magic* was edited by Emma Hardinge-Britten and published in 1876; and the Countess of Caithness published *Old Truths in a New Light*, also in 1876. Blavatsky's *Isis Unveiled*, published one year later, seems to have been the culmination in what Godwin refers to as 'a concerted effort in the early 1870s to give out fresh doctrines to a world already familiar with spiritualistic ideas of occult phenomena and the afterlife. The new doctrines would be known collectively as "occultism", and for some years the relative merits and meanings of occultism and spiritualism would be debated'[165]. Godwin's comparison of the teachings of these sources is highly interesting, and can be summarized in terms of the following elements. 1. The rise of spiritualism, even if its explanation is controversial, is described as 'a great spiritual outpouring' which heralds a new dispensation. 2. The bible, including the description of Jesus's life, must be understood in a symbolic rather than literal fashion. 3. Modern Christianity is a degenerate offspring of Jesus's original teachings; the errors of Christianity and crimes of the Church are described in great detail. 4. Humanity must turn from Christianity to the "primordial wisdom". Each religion is 'a ray of truth from the Central Sun'. All religions are valid, because they all worship the same divinity revealed in Nature, as confirmed by the sexual and solar theories. The ultimate source of primordial wisdom is India; but it was continued by the ancient Egyptians, whose knowledge was superior to modern science, and by the Mysteries of antiquity. 5. Jesus was one among

---

[163] Bevir, 'West turns Eastward', 751.
[164] Blavatsky, *Isis Unveiled*, 282, as quoted in Bevir, 'West turns Eastward', 754-755.
[165] Godwin, *Theosophical Enlightenment*, 302-303.

many messiahs; he was educated by the Egyptians. 6. Man is not in need of vicarious atonement: instead, he 'makes his own future, stamps his own character, suffers for his own sins, and must work out his own salvation'. 7. Evil consists in ignorance and opposition to the Divine plan; there are no devils other than those we create for ourselves. 8. Mankind, together with the whole universe, is in a process of continuous evolution, which is conceptualized either as eternal or as culminating in a reunion with divinity. 9. Reincarnation is mostly regarded as an error. 10. Spiritualist phenomena are caused by elementals or astral shells; they must be welcomed, however, because they refute materialism.

Most of these elements speak for themselves. Spiritualism is evidently seen as a mixed blessing: welcomed as the beginning of a new "outpouring", but easily misinterpreted. The rejection of reincarnation by most of these authors (with the exception of Countess Caithness), as well as the evolutionist element, will be returned to below. Especially evident from the summaries provided by Godwin is that the idea of a "primordial wisdom", with Egypt and India as the primary centers, has definitely moved into the center of attention. That these two countries are mentioned side by side is highly significant. It points to a tension between the original roots of occultism in Hermeticist traditions, on the one hand, and the profound impression that was made on occultists by the newly-discovered Orient, on the other. Sooner or later, the question had to be asked whether "Egypt" or "India" should be given precedence. Blavatsky's solution to this discrepancy resulted in a shift of emphasis which divides her career into an early "hermeticist" period (epitomized by *Isis Unveiled*) and a second "Oriental" one (the manifesto of which is *The Secret Doctrine*)[166].

In spite of her later protestations to the contrary, Blavatsky's early roots are not in the far East but in western occultist movements. She was profoundly involved, not only in spiritualism but also in various types of secret societies rooted in 18th-century esotericism[167]. Up to the publication of her first major work, *Isis Unveiled* (1877), it was not an Indian but an "Egyptian" atmosphere which prevailed in the Theosophical Society[168]. As Carl T. Jackson has noted,

> When Olcott delivered his inaugural presidential address to the new society in November 1875, he devoted much more attention to the organization's spiritualistic goals than to Eastern religions. India and Oriental religion are mentioned, but most of the references are to Neo-Platonists, Kabbalists, and Hermeticists, suggesting a dominantly Western viewpoint. His statement of the society's future work also suggests spiritualist preoccupations: "Mesmerism, Spiritualism, Od, the astral light of the ancients (now called the universal ether) and its currents—all

---

[166] Notice, however, Neufeldt's correct observation that, to be precise, 'never does Blavatsky view her own teaching as Eastern. Clearly she views it as universal ...' (Neufeldt, 'In Search of Utopia', 235).
[167] Godwin, *Theosophical Enlightenment*, 277-281.
[168] Godwin, *Theosophical Enlightenment*, 286.

these offer us the widest and most fascinating fields of exploration". Until 1878, psychic phenomena and mediums were much more central in Theosophy than Oriental religion[169].

The evolution of modern theosophy from a "hermeticist" to an "orientalist" perspective is illustrated by the likely backgrounds to the mysterious book of Dzyan on which *The Secret Doctrine* (1888) claims to be a commentary, and the no less mysterious book to which Blavatsky referred eleven years earlier, in *Isis Unveiled*. Gershom Scholem has suggested that behind the so-called Stanza's of Dzyan stands the Zoharic text *Sifra Di-Tseniutah*[170], which she probably knew from the Latin translation in Knorr von Rosenroth's famous *Kabbala Denudata* (1677-1684). Scholem's suggestion is based on Blavatsky's words on the first page of *Isis Unveiled*: 'There exists somewhere in this wide world an old Book ... It is the only original copy now in existence. The most ancient Hebrew document on occult learning—the Siphra Dzeniouta—was compiled from it ...'[171]. Scholem seems to have been too quick, however, in concluding that 'The Book Dzyan is therefore nothing but an occultistic hypostasy of the Zoharic title'. Karl R.H. Frick has called attention to an article by the sinologist Giovanni Hoffmann, who points to the teachings of a Taoist of the fourth century named Ly-tzyn, or Dzyan in Tibetan[172]. His book, Yu-Fu-King or "The Book of Secret Correspondences", was published in Florence in 1878. It seems probable that Blavatsky knew this book but incorrectly interpreted its contents as Vedic. If these suggestions are correct, *Isis Unveiled* was inspired by a kabbalistic source transmitted to Blavatsky in the context of Knorr von Rosenroth's Christian kabbalah; and *The Secret Doctrine* by a Taoist treatise interpreted as Vedic.

This shift from one "authoritative scripture" to another has symbolical significance. However, in spite of Blavatsky's increasing oriental contacts after her travel to India in 1868, it is extremely doubtful whether it also reflects a profound change of mind. I will not discuss here the complicated story of Blavatsky's (and Olcott's) involvement with Ceylonese Buddhism, her relations with the neo-hinduistic movement (Rammohun Roy's *Brahmo Samaj*, Keshub Chunder Sen, Ramakrishna, and Dayananda Saraswati's *Arya Samaj*), and the influence on her work of the non-dualist Vedanta as explained to her by T. Sub-

---

[169] Jackson, *Oriental Religions*, 161. The western esoteric and occultist background of *Isis Unveiled* is abundantly demonstrated by Blavatsky's (unacknowledged) sources, which were the subject of an extensive investigation by Emmette Coleman in the late 1880s. See Emmette Coleman, 'The Sources of Madame Blavatsky's Writings', published as an appendix in: Solovyoff, *Modern Priestes of Isis*; and the discussion in Campbell, *Ancient Wisdom Revived*, 32ff.

[170] Scholem, *Major Trends*, 398-399 nt 2.

[171] Blavatsky, *Isis Unveiled* I, 1.

[172] Frick, *Licht und Finsternis* II, 280-281. Giovanni Hoffmann's article appeared in *The Theosophist*, October 1908, and was reissued in German translation in *Neue Metaphysische Rundschau* 17 (1909).

ba Row (1856-1890)[173]. All these factors are significant, but an attempt to
reduce Blavatsky's later synthesis of western occultism and "Oriential wisdom"
to specific sources is likely to suffer shipwreck on the capacity of her 'omniv-
orous mind'[174] to assimilate whatever she found useful. I will restrict myself
to the question how her mature theosophical system, as expounded in *The
Secret Doctrine* and taken further by her successors, relates to the teachings
of the Oriental religions of which it claims to represent the esoteric core. Helmut Glasenapp has investigated this question in 1960, and Jörg Wichmann has
done the same in 1983[175]. Glasenapp recognizes that the theosophical motto
"No Religion Higher than Truth" is derived from the Mahârâja of Benares,
although he doubts whether the translation is correct[176]. The theosophical belief
in enlightened Mahatmas or Masters living in the Himalayas indeed has an
Indian background. The description of the emanation of the world as well as
the individual souls out of the divine Absolute may have been inspired by the
Vishnu-Purâna or Nepalese Buddhism[177] (although, one is inclined to add, it
would hardly be difficult for Blavatsky to find parallels in western Gnostic and
Platonic sources); and the doctrine of karma is of course a standard component of Hinduism and Buddhism. Glasenapp adds, however, that these ideas
are developed into entirely new directions under the influence of modern scientific thinking. He especially calls attention to the influence of modern evolutionism, to which I will return below. In addition, Glasenapp mentions a
range of theosophical concepts which have no Oriental parallels, such as trini-
tarian conceptions, Logos-speculation, the idea of a spiritual hierarchy, and the
theory of root races. As a representative example, Glasenapp discusses the
characteristic theosophical doctrines of the sevenfold constitution of human
beings and of the Akashic records (the universal cosmic "memory bank" which
can be tapped into by clairvoyant means). He concludes that both concepts are
dependent on authors such as Agrippa or Paracelsus rather than on Oriental
sources (and one is inclined to add that the vogue of mesmerism will have been
important as well). The subtle bodies as described in theosophy do not correspond with similar concepts in Hinduism; and although âkâsha is sanskrit for
ether, the theosophical idea of a cosmic memory is alien to Indian thought[178].
Similar conclusions are arrived at by Wichmann, who concentrates on the relation between theosophy and Advaita-Vedanta and Sankhya philosophy. Wich-

---

[173] See Godwin, *Theosophical Enlightenment*, 312-331.

[174] Godwin, *Theosophical Enlightenment*, 292.

[175] Von Glasenapp, *Indienbild deutscher Denker*, 196-202; Wichmann, 'Theosophische Menschenbild', 12-33.

[176] Glasenapp, *Indienbild*, 196. The Sanskrit original is *satyân nâsti paro dharmah*.

[177] The Visna-Purâna was translated by H.H. Wilson in 1840 and B.H. Hodgson first presented Nepalese Buddhism in his *Essays* of 1841 (Glasenapp, *Indienbild*, 198).

[178] Glasenapp, *Indienbild*, 199-200.

mann, too, emphasizes the impact of the new evolutionist framework, and his conclusions about the sevenfold constitution of human beings are similar to those arrived at by Glasenapp. With respect to karma, Wichmann notes that 'Theosophy understands karma as a kind of natural law (in a 19th-century sense) ... The idea of a purely spiritual causal law first emerged in the west, although it must be noted that in India, too, the concept of karma was eventually more and more spiritualized'[179].

The analyses of both authors lead to the conclusion that Blavatsky's shift from a "Hermetic" to an "Oriental" perspective is more apparent than real. Her theosophical synthesis is constituted of three basic components: esoteric traditions in general and the occult sciences in particular; 19th century science; and the new mythography. It is from these perspectives that theosophists have perceived the oriental religions. To my knowledge, there is no evidence to support the opposite idea that modern theosophy eventually came to interpret esotericism, occultism or western science from perspectives which are distinctly oriental and have no precedent in the west. The theosophical approach is basically eclectic: selected concepts of Hinduism and Buddhism were adopted in sofar as it seemed that they could be assimilated; if not, they were either ignored or given a new meaning. This does not mean, of course, that theosophy owes nothing to the Orient. It seems evident that karma, in particular, became of central importance only after Blavatsky's travel to India in 1878. However, I will suggest below that it was embraced essentially because it provided a solution to problems connected with typical modern western concepts of spiritual and moral evolution. As such, it does not refute but confirm my thesis that theosophy—although it has been instrumental in stimulating popular interest for Indian religions—is not only rooted in western esotericism, but has remained an essentially western movement.

B. The Orient and American Transcendentalism

When J. Gordon Melton describes New Age religion as rooted in the "occult-metaphysical" tradition, his terminology refers to two strands: occultism, on the one hand, and the so-called "metaphysical movements", on the other. This last term was coined by J. Stillson Judah in his standard work on the subject published in 1967[180]. Judah points out that the term "metaphysical movements" refers primarily to the New Thought groups (see below), but can be used in a more comprehensive sense to include spiritualism and theosophy[181]. Occultism could thus be seen as an aspect of the metaphysical movements; but since, as

---

[179] Wichmann, 'Das theosophische Menschenbild', 25-26.
[180] Judah, *Metaphysical Movements*.
[181] Judah, *Metaphysical Movements*, 11.

I will argue, the latter were crucially dependent on esoteric traditions and saw themselves as 'both scientific and religious'[182] they can also be seen as aspects of occultism according to my definition (chapter fifteen, section 1B). Here, I will use the term "metaphysical movements" in the stricter sense, as referring only to the various New Thought groups[183]. These groups are occultist in the technical sense employed here, but if theosophy is characterized by a background in *magia naturalis* and an emphasis on comparative religion, the typical metaphysical movements are characterized by their debt to American Transcendentalism and their concern with psychological healing. I will return to them in section 4A of this chapter, but the function of transcendentalism (as a mediating link between the Romantic stream, including some of its esoteric elements, and the occultism of the metaphysical movements) must be discussed in the present section. If modern theosophy was one major factor in the western occultist reception of Oriental religions, transcendentalism was the other.

The reception of Oriental religions by transcendentalism is the subject of several older studies, of which those of Arthur Christy and Frederick I. Carpenter (written in the early 1930s) are the most important[184]. Recently Arthur Versluis has published a new monograph, which is considerably more comprehensive in scope than its predecessors and has replaced them as the standard work on the subject[185]. From the perspective of this study, the existence of Versluis's book is particularly fortunate because its author is also well known as a specialist of esotericism, and is therefore able to point out connections which would be missed by others.

A first observation which is suggestive with respect to New Age religion is the millenarianism of the transcendentalists and its connection with comparative religion:

> All believed in the intuitive human ability to grasp the essences of all the world's religions, and all ... believed that humanity was on the verge of a new religious understanding, one that could make sense of all traditions at once, an "age of the spirit" as Frothingham said, citing Joachim of Fiore. Most of the Transcendentalists expected a coming "golden age", a reign of the Spirit, a unity of all the world's religions through intuitive insight and scholarship'[186].

---

[182] Judah, *Metaphysical Movements*, 11.

[183] Notice that the term "metaphysical movements" has also been applied to post-war movements which evidently stand in the New Thought tradition but would nowadays be referred to as "New Age". Thus, for example, in an interesting study of the so-called "Spiritual Frontiers Fellowship" from 1975-1976, Wagner, *Metaphysics in Midwestern America*.

[184] Christy, *Orient in American Transcendentalism*; Carpenter, *Emerson and Asia*. See further Goodman, 'East-West Philosophy', 625-645; Jackson, *Oriental Religions*; and id., 'Oriental Ideas'.

[185] Versluis, *American Transcendentalism*.

[186] Versluis, *American Transcendentalism*, 307. Cf. the opening line of Versluis's book: 'To study nineteenth-century American Transcendentalist Orientalism is to study variants in American millennialism' (o.c., 3).

If the spiritualists and theosophists perceived a "great outpouring" which would lead from materialism and dogmatic Christianity to a new spirituality compatible with science, a similar concern inspired the transcendentalists: they, too, sought to overcome both materialism and orthodox Christianity by an alternative vision based on the new science, comparative religion, and a belief in "progress"[187]. Like theosophy, they approached the religions of the world in an eclectic manner: abstracting from the original religious context whatever element they could use, while disregarding or reinterpreting whatever did not attract them[188]. However, there were differences as well. One of these has to do with my general distinction between Romanticism and occultism, to which I will return below; another is the absence in Transcendentalism (with the notable exception of Alcott) of an "esoteric" emphasis, understood here in the restricted sense of a concern with a secret wisdom tradition passed on by initiates[189].

The transcendentalists were certainly not of one mind in their attitude to Oriental religions; but it is evident that they were almost all fascinated by them, and contributed strongly to popular American conceptions of the Orient. James Freeman Clarke's *Ten Great Religions* (1871) counts as one of the century's most popular American treatments of Oriental religions[190]; Samuel Johnson's *Oriental Religions and their Relation to Universal Religion* (1872) interpreted all religions as stages in the evolution of Infinite Mind[191]; and Moncure Conway's *My Pilgrimage to the Wise Men of the East* (1906) is suggestive by its very title, which could easily be (mis)understood as corroboration of the theosophical Mahatmas[192]. Conway actually visited India and, other than most of his transcendentalist predecessors, eventually came to recognize the 'great difference between the Western idea of the East and the observable reality, between the literary conception and the complex reality'[193]. Indeed, the Orientalism of the transcendentalists was essentially what Versluis has called a "literary religion". We can best see this in the work of Ralph Waldo Emerson, on whom I will further concentrate. Although the transcendentalist movement as a whole contributed to the creation of a cultural *milieu* which encouraged a positive reception of Oriental ideas, it was Emerson who is generally regarded as the epitome of transcendentalism[194]. He can be regarded as a *pars pro*

---

[187] Versluis, *American Transcendentalism*, 8.
[188] Versluis, *American Transcendentalism*, 5, 62.
[189] Versluis, *American Transcendentalism*, 307.
[190] Jackson, *Oriental Religions*, 125.
[191] Jackson, *Oriental Religions*, 130.
[192] Actually, Conway visited Blavatsky but found her mahatmas fraudulent (Jackson, *Oriental Religions*, 136).
[193] Jackson, *Oriental Religions*, 136.
[194] However, mention should at least be made of the importance of the more practically-oriented Henry Thoreau. His Walden experiment is important with respect to 20t-century trends of

toto in estimating the importance of transcendentalism for the metaphysical movements[195] and, by implication, for the New Age movement.

Emerson's debt to Plato and Plotinus is well known[196], and there is little doubt that he regarded Platonism essentially as 'an introduction and corroboration of the Hindus'[197]. Versluis observes that Emersons's Neoplatonic readings increasingly gave way to Oriental ones[198], but adds that 'finally, Emerson was using the Neoplatonic tradition to transcend it—the gods in question are, ultimately, neither Neoplatonic nor Indian but just the gods, beyond such contingent distinctions'[199]. Less attention has been given, at least before Versluis's study, to the interconnection in the mind of the transcendentalists between platonism and hermeticism: an interconnection which, as I argued above, is actually not too surprising. A good illustration is provided by an entry in Alcott's *Journal* (1839):

> Emerson passed the afternoon with me. We had desultory conversation on Swedenbourg, Bruno, Behmen [Boehme], and others of this sublime school. I proposed that some measures should be taken to put English readers in possession of the works of these great minds. Confucius, Zoroaster, Paracelsus, Galen, Plato, Bruno, Behmen, Plotinus, More, Swedenbourg, etc., should be in the hands of every earnest student of the soul. ... We should have access to the fountains of truth through the purest channels[200].

This passage certainly reflects the personal preferences of Alcott himself, who was more attracted to western esotericism than to Oriental religions[201]. But Emerson, too, saw Plato together with a range of neoplatonists, esotericists (Böhme in particular), and legendary sages from East and West, as so many aspects of the tradition of perennial wisdom[202] which he himself was pro-

---

"back to nature" and communal living, including those of the post-war counterculture.

[195] Judah, *Metaphysical Movements*, emphasizes the importance of the transcendentalists to the metaphysical movements, but Emerson is the only major transcendentalist mentioned in the index. A similar emphasis is found in Parker, *Mind Cure in New England*.

[196] The best references for this influence are Harrison, *Teachers of Emerson*; and Carpenter, *Emerson and Asia*. See further Emerson's two essays on Plato in *Representative Men*, 39-89.

[197] Christy, *Orient in American Transcendentalism*, 50.

[198] Versluis, *American Transcendentalism*, 54. Cf. 63: 'for the last fourteen years of his life—except for an occasional return to Proclus or Plotinus—he read primarily Eastern works when concerning himself with religious matters'.

[199] Versluis, *American Transcendentalism*, 64.

[200] Shepard, *Journals of Bronson Alcott*, 136-137, as quoted in Jackson, *Oriental Religions*, 71.

[201] Versluis, *American Transcendentalism*, 104

[202] Jackson, *Oriental Religions*, 53; cf. Versluis, *American Transcendentalism*, 55 (Emerson's reading list contains Plotinus, Hermes Trismegistus, Porphyry, Iamblichus, Synesius, Proclus, and Olympiadorus), 57 (he compares the experiences of Socrates, Plotinus, Porphyry, St. Paul, Boehme, George Fox and the Quakers, and Swedenborg), 74 (the figure of the inspired poet is exemplified by "the Bramins", Pythagoras, Socrates, Plato, Orpheus, Proclus, Chaucer, St.John, Aesop, Jacob Boehme), 75 (in 1867 he still mentions in one breath Homer, Menu, Viasa, Daedalus,

claiming in his literary work. The function of comparative religion was to demonstrate that the same universal truths had found expression in all of these traditions, in other words: to demonstrate the "concordance" of traditions. Special mention must be made of the role in this context of Swedenborg[203]. In an early letter to Carlyle, Emerson expressed his expectation that Swedenborgianism would contribute more than any of the other sects to the "new faith which must arise out of all"[204]. This might be taken as an accurate prediction of the New Thought movement (see below), but Emerson was eventually to grow more critical himself. His essay "Swedenborg: or, the Mystic" in *Representative Men*[205] combines admiration with criticism, and is illustrative with regard to my distinction between romanticism and occultism. Discussing Swedenborg's doctrine of correspondences, Emerson notes:

> This design of exhibiting such correspondences, which, if adequately executed, would be the poem of the world, in which all history and science would play an essential part, was narrowed and defeated by the exclusively theologic direction which his inquiries took. ... He fastens each natural object to a theologic notion;—a horse signifies carnal understanding; a tree, perception; the moon, faith; a cat means this; an ostrich that; and artichoke this other;—and poorly tethers every symbol to a several ecclesiastic sense. The slippery Proteus is not so easily caught. In nature, each individual symbol plays innumerable parts, as each particle of matter circulates in turn through every system. The central identity enables any one symbol to express successively all the qualities and shades of real being. In the transmission of the heavenly waters, every hose fits every hydrant. Nature avenges herself speedily on the hard pedantry that would chain her waves. She is no literalist[206].

Thus, Emerson rejects Swedenborg's doctrine of correspondences in the name of what he regards as the *true* doctrine, and which is indeed much closer to the original esoteric view. The latter is expressed by him in statements as the following: 'The entire system of things gets represented in every particle. There is something that resembles the ebb and flow of the sea, day and night, man and woman, in a single needle of the pine, in a kernel of corn, in each individual of every animal tribe. The reaction, so grand in the elements, is repeated within these small boundaries ...[207]'. Catharine Albanese observes that this type of correspondence theory 'exceed[s] the scientific canons of cause and

---

Hermes, Zoroaster, Swedenborg and Shakespeare), 76 (a continuity of wisdom which includes Plato and Proclus, Hermes Trismegistus and Manu).

[203] About Emerson and Swedenborg, see Hallengren, 'Importance of Swedenborg'; Taylor, 'Emerson'. See further the bibliography on Emerson and Swedenborg as given in Hallengren, 'Importance of Swedenborg', 243 nt 7.

[204] Judah, *Metaphysical Movements*, 33.

[205] Emerson, *Representative Men*, 93-146.

[206] Emerson, *Representative Men*, 121.

[207] Emerson, *Essays*, first series (1841), par. 7.

effect and fit[s] instead the definition of magic'[208]. Provided that magic is understood in the Renaissance sense of *magia*, this conclusion seems correct. Emerson's criticism of Swedenborg amounts to a romantic defense of the traditional esoteric view of correspondences, against the proto-occultist view of Swedenborg.

It was from a western romantic viewpoint, informed by the "esoteric" belief in a perennial wisdom tradition, that Emerson understood those Oriental religions which he found congenial. Buddhism remained alien to him, as to many of his contemporaries[209], and the same goes for Taoism. Confucianism, in contrast, was admired by Emerson for its ethical concern and common sense. But his deepest appreciation was for hinduism, which he perceived (partly under the influence of the reform-hinduism of Rammohun Roy's *Brahmo Samaj*, which had fascinated European and American Unitarians since the early 19th century[210]) largely in terms of Advaita Vedanta. Like the other Transcendentalists, he ignored the ritualistic aspects[211] and cultural context of hinduism in order to focus on those "universal" aspects which were congenial to his own idealistic viewpoint. His view of "comparative religion" was informed by an enthusiastic belief that the convergence of the religions of the world was leading to a new synthesis and a new world: 'Every nation of the globe is in our day, whether willingly or reluctantly, holding up its sacred books and traditions to our eyes, and we find in our mythology a key to theirs, and in our experience a key to their experience'[212]. Such statements suggest that, his admiration for the Orient notwithstanding, Emerson essentially borrowed from it only what he needed in order to create a vision which remained essentially occidental[213]: 'Hindu philosophy widened and deepened his thought rather than formed it'[214]. He was more outspoken about this than the theosophists, and even went so far as to emphasize the ultimate superiority of the West. Thus, the "Oriental mind" is described as marked by fatalism and resignation, while the West stands for activity, creativity, freedom and will; therefore, 'We read

---

[208] Albanese, *Corresponding Motion*, 7.

[209] Jackson, 'Oriental Ideas', 431; id., *Oriental Religions*, 56. Typical for Emerson's confused perception of Buddhism are his references to the Bhagavad Gita as the 'much renowned book of Buddhism' or to the 'Hindoo Buddhism' represented in the 'prayers of the Bhagavata Purana'.

[210] Jackson, 'Oriental Ideas', 429.

[211] Versluis, *American Transcendentalism*, 52, 80.

[212] Emerson, inaugural essay of the Chestnut Street Club (1867), in: Sargent, *Sketches and Reminiscences*, 3-4, as quoted in Versluis, *American Transcendentalism*, 309.

[213] Cf. Jackson, 'Oriental Ideas': 'The close resemblances of his concept of the "Over-Soul" to the Hindu concept of Brahman, of his "Compensation" to karma, and of his "Illusions" to maya are striking. Of course, he had already arrived at these concepts before developing a wide and sympathetic interest in the Orient, but it is evident that he quickly assimilated the Hindu formulations into his thought'.

[214] Jackson, 'Oriental Ideas', 430.

the Orientals, but remain Occidental'[215]. Versluis concludes that Emerson's orientalism is essentially a "literary religion" created in the study:

> ...Emerson's reproducing of Hindu scriptures was a literary, not a religious, manifestation. His emphasis was on self-transcendence; he was interested in divine inspiration, not in ritual, in the blasting light of mysticism, not in form, in ethical responsibility, not in adherence to any particular religion. ... When religion is stripped of its cultural and practical implications, rendered as merely ethical strictures and "abandonment to the Invisible", it becomes "literary religion". This, I believe, is the heart of Emersonian Orientalism[216].

Similar conclusions can be drawn about the orientalism of the "metaphysical movements", which is indebted both to transcendentalism and theosophy[217]. Mention should be made, moreover, of the impact of Swami Vivekanda's famous appearance at the World Parliament of Religions in Chicago in 1893; and of his Ramakrishna mission and the Vedanta society founded in the years that followed[218]. Vivekananda's religion was a typical product of the Hindu reform movements which had begun about a century earlier and are characterized by a confluence of hinduism and western Enlightenment ideals[219]. Hinduism as presented by Vivekananda consisted essentially of an abstract philosophical version of Advaita Vedanta, perfectly adapted to modern western tastes. It confirmed Transcendentalist universalism; it claimed that hinduism was fully compatible with Western science; it criticized "dogmatic Christianity"; but it did not require of its admirers to look at themselves as pagans: Vivekananda could reassure his audience that, rumours to the contrary notwithstanding, 'there is no polytheism in India'[220]. The neo-hinduistic pattern as exemplified by Vivekananda would become typical of orientalism in the metaphysical movements. Oriental doctrines were 'trimmed and refashioned'[221] to make them fit with New Thought philosophies; and the general approach to "the Orient" was marked by a pragmatic eclecticism. As Carl T. Jackson has shown, the metaphysical movements felt attracted primarily by the doctrines of karma and reincarnation, and by the practice of yoga[222]. Arthur Versluis, as well, describes the popular reception of transcendentalism by New Thought,

---

[215] Emerson & Forbes, *Journals of Ralph Waldo Emerson*, 116, as quoted in Jackson, *Oriental Religions*, 58.

[216] Versluis, *American Transcendentalism*, 78.

[217] See Jackson, 'New Thought Movement', 523-548.

[218] Jackson, 'New Thought Movement', 529; see the relevant parts in Hummel, *Indische Mission*; Finger, *Gurus, Ashrams und der Westen*.

[219] See for example Smart, 'Asian Cultures'; Godwin, *Theosophical Enlightenment*, 312ff; Diem & Lewis, 'Imagining India'.

[220] Vivekananda, *Complete Works*, 15, as quoted in Diem & Lewis, 'Imagining India', 55.

[221] Jackson, 'New Thought Movement', 532.

[222] Jackson, 'New Thought Movement', 529-535, 543.

and makes no attempt to hide his aversion against this 'Transcendentalism of the masses'[223]:

> ... diluted Asian religion—much in the manner of twentieth-century "New Age" dilettantism—did permeate American society in the late nineteenth century via an amalgam of diluted Buddhism and Swedenborgianism, spiritualism, and Emersonian Transcendentalism that came to be called "New Thought" or "mind-cure". New Thought preceded Theosophy—the other bastard form in which Asian religious traditions came to be known in America—but coincided with it principally in that both presented elements of Buddhism, Hinduism, and Taoism in popularized and distorted form. ...
> The pseudoreligious potpourri found in Boston and across much of America during the late nineteenth century is clearly a predecessor of the "New Age" movement during the late twentieth century. Just as the New Thought movement represented diluted Emersonian Transcendentalism for the masses, the New Age movement pandered to a materialist interpretation of what originally were authentic traditional teachings[224].

In spite of widespread interest in the Orient, it remained difficult for westerners living in the late 19th century to achieve an adequate and balanced perspective on Hinduism or Buddhism as they actually functioned in their own cultural context. Oriental religions were consistently idealized and adapted to Western conditions. One particularly important factor in this process was repeatedly alluded to already, in the context both of theosophy and of transcendentalism, and will be the center of attention in the next section. Arthur Versluis states that the western 'belief in progress ... is both the reason that Transcendentalist Orientalism came into being and its greatest obstacle to actually understanding Asian religions'[225]. Indeed, modern theories of secular progress and of evolution are as alien to the Orient as they originally were to western esotericism. They represent a third "mirror of secular thought" through which esotericism—already profoundly affected by "causality" and the new study of religions—had to be reflected in order to be acceptable to 19th and 20th-century mentalities.

3. EVOLUTION AS RELIGION

To discuss popular evolutionism separately from the emergence of the new scientific worldview (section 1, above) and the study of religions (section 2), as done here, is admittedly somewhat artificial. At least since the end of the 18th century, both developments were strongly informed by a belief in evolution and its close cognate, progress[226]. These two terms, by the way, should not be

---

[223] Versluis, *American Transcendentalism*, 316.
[224] Versluis, *American Transcendentalism*, 314 & 316.
[225] Versluis, *American Transcendentalism*, 3.
[226] The Enlightenment's belief in modern science as a principal instrument for secular progress

seen as strictly synonymous: most theories of evolution have nothing to say of values, and one does not have to believe in progress in order to accept evolutionary theory. As one author has put it, "evolution is a fact, but progress is a myth"[227]. However, even though evolution does not have to imply progress, to most people in the 19th century the suggestion of a movement from worse to better was the heart of the theory[228]; and it is as such that popular evolutionism is important to our subject. Evolutionism understood as historical progress is found neither in traditional esotericism, nor in the Oriental religions which were assimilated by Romanticism and occultism; but before the century was over, this occidental innovation had been assimilated so profoundly that it could seem as though it had never been absent.

I already referred to the modern tendency to misunderstand traditional esoteric speculations about creation, fall and reintegration as historical processes. In a study of French Romantic philosophies and their relation to illuminism, Arthur McCalla points out that, for Christian theosophers and illuminists such as Jacob Böhme, Louis-Claude de Saint-Martin or Antoine Fabre d'Olivet, the creation, fall and reintegration of humanity were purely spiritual processes which (with the notable exception of the Incarnation) did not refer to historical events[229]. For Böhme, events such as the Thirty Years' War do mark the stages of the rehabiliatory process, but in no way effect them: 'History is merely the arena in which the forces of the eternal world operate; historical time is utterly overwhelmed by the eternally present drama of fall and redemption'[230]. Similarly, for Saint-Martin, 'historical events are symbolic of, not instrumental to, the reintegration of humanity'[231]. And in 1813 Fabre d'Olivet explicitly warned against the increasing tendency to look at illuminist speculation through "historicist" glasses; he distinguishes between "allegorical" and "positive" history:

> In allegorical history, actions and events, including fictional or mythological ones, stand for the extra-historical spiritual progress of the human race toward reintegration. Positive history merely offers a scrupulous record of dates and events.

---

is, of course, well known. As Peter Gay puts it, 'there were two things of which the philosophes remained confident: if there was one area of human experience in which progress was reliable it was science, and if there was any real hope for man, it was science that would realize it' (*Enlightenment* II, 124). For the study of religion, see Brian Morris's historical overview which significantly begins with Hegel (*Anthropological Studies of Religion*, ch. 1), Eric Sharpe's statement that comparative religion, as originally conceived, 'rested squarely on the evolutionary hypothesis' (*Comparative Religion*, 28); or the discussions of Trompf, *In Search of Origins*; and Waller & Edwardsen, 'Evolutionism'.

[227] Inge, 'Idea of Progress', as quoted in Conner, *Cosmic Optimism*, 4. For standard discussions of evolutionism, see for example Goudge, 'Evolutionism', 178; Roszak, 'Evolution'.

[228] Conner, *Cosmic Optimism*, 4-5.

[229] McCalla, 'Illuminism'.

[230] McCalla, 'Illuminism'.

[231] McCalla, 'Illuminism'.

There is an unbridgeable gap between positive history, which chronicles events that happened but that have no spiritual significance, and allegorical history, which arranges events that may never have happened into a dramatization of the spiritual destiny of humanity. Allegorical history alone, Fabre declares, is worthy of study[232].

As McCalla puts it, for illuminist authors 'Reintegration does not redeem history, it is a redemption from history'[233]. Such a perspective was to become increasingly alien to the emerging historical consciousness of the 18th and 19th centuries, as illustrated by Fabre d'Olivet's very concern with refuting it. The anachronistic procedure of reading evolutionist histories back into esotericism affects the heart of its approach to reality. I have addressed this point in a discussion of Jacob Böhme's cosmogony:

> The incarnation of God in "eternal nature" occurs in a sevenfold cycle. If we imagine this process as unfolding in time—which is almost impossible to avoid -, strictly speaking we commit a category error. The sevenfold "succession" in eternal nature must be understood as the original *archetype of time* as we know it from our own, material world. From the perspective of the completed cycle, i.e. from its seventh stage, all earlier stages are one. Thus, the succession of the first six stages is a prefiguration of time, and the completion in the seventh is a prefiguration of eternity. Time is therefore not a primary category, but a secondary derivative from a primal reality which can not be described in terms of its derivatives. The modern tendency to understand the Hermetic dictum "as above so below" (which is fundamental to Böhme as well) in terms of *identity* is among the primary sources of misunderstanding with respect to esoteric speculation. Böhme thinks in terms of a symbolic doctrine of correspondences according to which the "lower" reflects the "higher". The Feuerbachian reversal of this idea, which turns the higher into a reflection of the lower, is alien to Böhme's thought. For this reason it is misleading, with respect to his sevenfold succession, to use a term such as "evolution"[234].

That traditional esotericists such as Böhme were not evolutionists is one thing; that evolutionism has been adopted by almost all esotericists since the 18th century is another. McCalla documents the reinterpretation of illuminist speculation by Romantic philosophies of history, with the French authors Ballanche, Lamartine and Quinet as examples. His conclusions confirm my interpretation of Romanticism (including German Idealism) as a modern evolutionist reinterpretation of traditions which largely fall within the domain of esotericism. It was an essentially romantic evolutionism, as well, which would become important both to the American metaphysical movements and to modern theosophy. These movements developed in the period after the publication of Darwin's *Origin of Species* in 1859, when evolution had become one of the hot

---

[232] McCalla, 'Illuminism'.
[233] McCalla, 'Illuminism'.
[234] Hanegraaff, 'In den beginne was de toorn', 46-47. See for a detailed analysis of Böhme's cosmogony, Deghaye, *Naissance de Dieu*; id., 'Jacob Boehme and his followers'.

issues of the day. With respect to Darwinism, again, occultists generally sided with "science" against "dogmatic Christianity". Nevertheless, the scientific evolutionism associated with Darwin seems to have served less as a direct source for occultist theories than as a welcome instrument for the "scientific" legitimation of philosophical or religious theories.

The importance of evolutionism (especially since Darwin) for the culture of the 19th century is a commonplace of historiography; but if one attempts to gain a clearer perspective on how the new evolutionism was popularly understood by non-scientists, one finds that most references are frustratingly vague. This observation prompted the historian of literature Frederick William Conner to investigate the reception of evolutionism by American poets. His valuable but somewhat neglected study of 1949 bears the (for us) suggestive title *Cosmic Optimism*[235]. Conner notes that, in what the poets did with evolutionary theories, their debt to science was very slight. They had little interest in detailed evidence or the question of evolutionary mechanisms: 'What interested them rather was how the new theories could be related to deeply rooted and persistent convictions concerning the benevolence and efficacy of God and the spiritual nature of man'[236]. Their enthusiasm for "evolution" rested on their interpretation of it as a scientific concept which could replace traditional Christian notions of history but did not necessarily threaten religion as such. On the contrary: evolution could be seen as 'a progress that is inevitable because in some sense it is divinely motivated'[237]. Although Conner's study is about American literature rather than religion, his discussion is highly relevant, not only to "literary religion" in the Emersonian tradition, but to occultism as well. Both traditions were profoundly affected by the idea of evolution as the key to a unification of science and religion.

Conner discusses the "temporalization of the chain of being" with reference to Lovejoy[238]; and he adds that it gained additional impetus from discussions about the progress of civilization which had been going on since the seventeenth century[239]. A particularly crucial factor in the emergence of evolutionary thought consisted of theories developed by the German idealists, Schelling and Hegel in particular[240]. The formulation of such philosophical frameworks converged with scientific developments in cosmology, embryology and geology. This last discipline was particularly influential in creating the ground-

[235] Conner, *Cosmic Optimism*. I also call attention to a thorough criticism of popular contemporary evolutionism: Midgley, *Evolution as Religion*.
[236] Conner, *Cosmic Optimism*, vii.
[237] Conner, *Cosmic Optimism*, viii.
[238] Cf. also Goudge, 'Evolutionism', 178.
[239] Conner, *Cosmic Optimism*, 6-10.
[240] Conner, *Cosmic Optimism*, 11-17.

works for the Darwinian revolution. Geology divided the world's past into well-defined epochs, most of which had been inhabited by living beings; and it demonstrated that new and progressively more complex forms of life had appeared, culminating in humanity: 'The invitation to a theory of the evolution of species seems obvious now, and it was plain to some even then'[241]. It is therefore not surprising that doubts about the traditional assumption of the immutability of species (including the inference that, if species were mutable, man might have descended from the apes) were expressed already in the early 19th century[242], not only by scientists but also by poets such as Tennyson, Emerson and Whitman. Conner suggests that, although Darwin's theory was revolutionary from a strictly scientific point of view, on a popular level it merely served to give scientific legitimacy to ideas that had been in the air for decades.

The theological controversy caused by Darwin's *Origin of Species* is well known[243]. But, although Darwinism was evidently incompatible with a literal understanding of *Genesis*, those who took a liberal attitude to the scriptural canon could reconcile religion with science by reinterpreting the natural theology of the 18th century in immanentist terms. Deistic conceptions of God as the great Artificer were clearly incompatible with evolutionism; but there seemed to be no objection to conceiving God as a force of creativity which works from within, bringing forth the world by means of a gradual process in time[244]. Such theories were teleological rather than mechanical[245], and more congenial to the vitalism of *Naturphilosophie* than to Darwin's theory of evolution by natural selection; but this was of minor interest to those who were impressed more by the *idea* of evolution than interested in the scientific or conceptual problems connected with it. However, if an immanentist teleology seemed to solve part of the religious problem, it still left open the question of how an apparently material world could bring forth a spiritual being such as man[246]. As long as it was assumed that an effect cannot contain more than its cause, evolution seemed to imply that either mind was a mere appearance of matter or matter a mere appearance behind which lies Mind[247]. Conner con-

---

[241] Conner, *Cosmic Optimism*, 23. Conner mentions Jean Baptiste Lamarck and Geoffrey Saint-Hilaire.

[242] Conner, *Cosmic Optimism*, 25. Already in 1809, Washington Irving ridicules the conjecture 'that the whole human species are accidentally descended from a remarkable family of monkies!'.

[243] See for example Kent, 'Religion and Science'.

[244] Conner, *Cosmic Optimism*, 27-28.

[245] For a nuanced discussion of the concept, see Mayr, 'Idea of Teleology', 117-135.

[246] Conner, *Cosmic Optimism*, 28.

[247] Conner, *Cosmic Optimism*, 28. Conner mentions more recent theories of "emergent evolution", which claim to solve the dilemma by denying the prior assumption. New Age evolutionism is strongly influenced by this trend. With Conner, I doubt whether emergent evolution really solves the dilemma.

cludes that, for most of the poets who are the focus of his study, the choice was an easy one: 'Accepting evolution and convinced beyond question of the independent reality of the spiritual life known inwardly, they came ... to the conclusion that somehow mind is the reality and matter the appearance. However loosely interpreted by the poets, this of course was metaphysical idealism'[248]. The type of idealism which proved most congenial to the new evolutionism saw the "external world" as depending upon 'an Absolute Mind which was at once the type, sum, and ground of all individual minds—the individual soul universalized'[249]. This type of "transcendental evolutionism" was obviously very different from the biological theory, but whether or not the two theories are compatible in theory, it is certain that they were somehow combined in practice. Conner's conclusion is highly suggestive with respect to our subject:

> ... the scientific account was regarded as the "phenomenal outer aspect" of an ultimate spiritual being that was good, true, and beautiful and must therefore operate to good, true, and beautiful ends. In the apt simplification of Oliver Wendell Holmes, physical processes like evolution were "simply God himself in action". Thus was the theoretical basis of an evolutionary cosmic optimism established. In the words of Professor Randall: "On one point all the romantic and idealistic philosophers agreed: they rejected the traditional dualism of the natural and the supernatural, and united in the monistic belief that the world is the expression of one great principle permeating all its parts and including all events in its cosmic process. Man is one with nature, and man and nature are one with God—not, perhaps, the whole expression of the divine life, but existing as essential parts of it. It was easy for religious souls to see in the whole long story of evolution itself the unfolding of the hand of Providence, and in its goal of a perfected human society "the one far-off divine event to which the whole creation moves""[250].

Seen against the background of Part Two of this study, the relevance with respect to New Age religion should be clear. Interpretations of evolutionism in terms of "cosmic optimism" have been particularly typical of the specifically American context, and were to flourish in the "positive thinking" of the metaphysical movements[251]. The optimistic element is less pronounced in modern theosophy, but the basic frameworks are essential similar in both strands.

A. The "Metaphysical" Context

I argued that Romanticism represents a "historicist" reinterpretation of Platonic and Hermetic traditions which either exemplify or are closely connected

---

[248] Conner, *Cosmic Optimism*, 33.
[249] Conner, *Cosmic Optimism*, 33.
[250] Conner, *Cosmic Optimism*, 35-36. The quotations are from Holmes, 'Agassiz's Natural History', 333; and Randall, *Making of the Modern Mind*, 555.
[251] See Fuller, *Americans and the Unconscious*, 22-27 and *passim*.

with esotericism. The Romanticism American-style known as Transcendentalism is a good illustration. I already mentioned the enduring influence of Platonic traditions on Emerson's thinking, and the fact that he was strongly dis-
posed to perceive Platonism as part of a "golden chain" of philosopher-sages
modeled upon the Renaissance idea of a *philosophia perennis*. I also mentioned his fascination with Swedenborg, which was sufficiently strong to select
the latter, together with Plato, Montaigne, Shakespeare, Napoleon and Goethe,
as one of the six "representative men" discussed in his essays of that title. In
Emerson's Swedenborg essay, the Swedish seer was repeatedly compared
(unfavourably) with Jacob Böhme[252]. The interest in Böhme as well as the new
temporalism seems to have been conveyed to Emerson largely by the literature
of German idealism and *Naturphilosophie*. The writings of authors such as
Schelling, Hegel, Goethe, Novalis, Oken and Oerstedt were either available in
translation or known to Emerson from his contacts with other Romantics,
Coleridge in particular[253]. The scientific evolutionists, including Darwin, seem
to have been a minor influence. Frederick Conner has documented the development of Emerson's thinking from his early years, when he was still critical
not only of evolution but of the Orient as well[254], to his eventual acceptance
of evolution[255]. He characterizes Emerson's mature position as follows:

> ... Emerson's evolutionism was as remote as possible from that of the scientists.
> Not only was his idealism the polar opposite of their materialism and mechanism,
> but he was utterly unconcerned about the question of greatest importance to them,
> the immediate causes of transformation. Never once did he mention natural selec-
> tion or the inheritance of acquired characteristics, and ... he saw no essential
> advance in Darwin over Stallo. The sciences, Emerson felt, dealt only with sur-
> faces and were to be valued only for the light that, often in spite of themselves,
> they shed beyond. They were a kind of half-knowledge, not wrong but incom-
> plete. Or, as he most liked to express it, they were "false by being unpoetical".
> The scientist thought in terms of parts, while the poet and philosopher, taking a
> broader view, recognized that the parts make up a whole that has a unitary sig-
> nificance superior not only to each of its constituents but to the sum of all. In this
> view, the parts of nature exhibited an ordered interrelationship that corresponded
> perfectly with the categories of the individual mind and bodied forth the phases
> of that Over-Mind which is the ultimate reality. That this supreme One is truly
> all-encompassing and all-dissolving was Emerson's basic belief, and any inter-
> pretation of his thinking that disregarded it would be false to him. Consequently,

---

[252] See Emerson, 'Swedenborg', 142-143: 'How different is Jacob Behmen! *He* is tremulous
with emotion and listens awe-struck, with the gentlest humanity, to the Teacher whose lessons
he conveys; and when he asserts that, "in some sort, love is greater than God", his heart beats
so high that the thumping against his leathern coat is audible across the centuries'.

[253] See Conner, *Cosmic Optimism*, 17-20. For a complete discussion, see Vogel, *German Literary Influences*.

[254] For his early criticism of evolution, see Conner, *Cosmic Optimism*, 40ff; with respect to
the Orient, see Jackson, *Oriental Religions*, 48; Versluis, *American Transcendentalism*, 51-52.
Significantly, Emerson's first poem about the Orient was entitled "Indian Superstition".

[255] Conner, *Cosmic Optimism*, 37-66.

in the matter of evolution ... Emerson saw only the phenomenal manifestation of a Creative Mind[256].

The similarity of this viewpoint to much of New Age evolutionism is evident. Emerson's explicit concern with demarcating his "poetical" evolutionism from the literalism of science is shared neither by the more "occultist" metaphysical movements nor by the contemporary New Age movement. However, although New Agers like to present their theories of evolution as scientific, they are in fact very close to this transcendentalist vision; and the latter, in turn, is clearly indebted to the platonic "great chain" and evolutionist conceptions pioneered by German Idealism.

The Emersonian tradition is highly important to the "metaphysical movements" and, through them, to the emergence of New Age religion. Nevertheless, it must be emphasized that it represents only one among many expressions of romantic evolutionism. The complexity of the subject (both from a philosophical and from a historical perspective) is demonstrated with particular force in an important early article by Lovejoy, which takes Henri Bergson as the point of departure for a general discussion of the Romantic types of evolutionism deriving from the *Naturphilosophie* of Schelling and others[257]. Most important here is Lovejoy's distinction between what seems to be a sort of pre-Teilhardianism, and a further development of it which he calls "radical temporalism". The former

> affirms the existence of a perfect and supratemporal Reality, a Being whose existence is immutably and eternally complete, with respect to every metaphysical and every moral attribute. But it conceives this Being neither as the efficient cause of the imperfect and temporal, nor yet as an all-inclusive unity in which the imperfect and temporal are contained. The relation of the Perfect Reality to all the beings that change and develop in time is translated ... from the terms of efficient to terms of final causality. In other words, God is declared to be, not the source from which finite being emanates, not the Creator who calls it into existence by his volition, not the Whole of which it is a part,—but the realized ideal which draws all less complete existences onward towards fuller likeness with itself[258].

This conception is much closer to Platonism than to the Darwinian conception of evolution as a blind mechanicism ruled by chance. In contrast with the latter, it suggests 'a tendency which is within things as if it were an inner spring that pushes them onward in a movement that is without end'[259]. Actually, this last point already suggests a further theoretical option, referred to by Lovejoy as "radical temporalism" and introduced by him (in 1913) as 'a natural, not to say an inevitable, outcome of the reflective movement of the past half-centu-

---

[256] Conner, *Cosmic Optimism*, 58-59.
[257] Lovejoy, 'Bergson', 429-487.
[258] Lovejoy, 'Bergson', 468-469.
[259] Lovejoy, 'Bergson', 471-472.

ry'[260]. This option no longer assumes the existence of a perfect or eternal Being, not even as final cause of the upward-reaching activity of imperfect beings. The only God it knows is 'a God in the making'[261]. Lovejoy argues that such a radical temporalism is implied by Bergson's theory, and that the latter's own attempts to reserve a niche for an "absolute Being" which is not affected by time are inconsistent with it. Whether or not Lovejoy is right in this, his discussion demonstrates the importance of distinguishing between explicit evolutionist *statements*, on the one hand, and the inner logic of evolutionist *theories*, on the other. We have seen on several occasions in Part Two of this study that, in a New Age context, the holistic concept of a timeless "absolute reality" is frequently combined with evolutionist theories even though the two do not imply each other and may even be incompatible. The inevitable tension between temporalism and a concentration on "the Absolute" (i.e., between basically dynamic and static conceptions) leads to various attempts at reconciliation, some of which are more convincing than others. In assessing the traditions which lead up to New Age religion, romantic evolutionism must therefore be seen (like "holism") as a general vision rather than as a specific theory. As different thinkers attempt to express such a vision, the theories they come up with may differ strongly. A detailed investigation of such theories (including those of Bergson or Teilhard de Chardin), and of their specific contributions to New Age evolutionism are beyond the scope of this study. Here we can restrict ourselves to the following conclusions. (1) New Age evolutionism is rooted less in Darwinism than in romanticism; (2) As such, it continues a general tendency to adopt scientific theories only to the extent that these can be used to add an appearance of scientific respectability to various types of romantic evolutionism. I suggest that this is what happened with Darwin during the nineteenth century, and has happened again with Prigogine during the twentieth (as demonstrated by a comparison between Prigogine and Jantsch); (3) Emersonian Transcendentalism has a special importance for us, but not because its expression of romantic evolutionism is particularly remarkable in itself. Its importance lies in the fact that it became fundamental to a characteristically American cultural tradition, which was congenial both to romantic evolutionism as such and to an eclectic and pragmatic attitude toward scientific theories of evolution.

B. *The Theosophical Context*

The foundations of theosophical and of transcendentalist evolutionism are essentially similar: both are rooted in the types of romantic evolutionism

---

[260] Lovejoy, 'Bergson', 476.
[261] Lovejoy, 'Bergson', 477.

referred to above. However, in the case of modern theosophy, the theory of evolutionism came to serve new ends which went beyond those of authors inspired by transcendentalism. In Blavatsky's synthesis, progressive evolution functions as *the* great Law of Nature: 'Nature must always progress, and each fresh attempt is more succesful than the previous one'[262]. Since everything (both visible and invisible) is seen as part of Nature and subject to its universal laws, the theory of evolution emerges as fundamental to all aspects of Blavatsky's thought, whether pertaining to the "physical" or the spiritual domains. It accounts for the development of the universe and of the planet; for the history of humanity and of religious consciousness; and for the development of the human soul before birth and after death. I will concentrate on this last point, because it is essential to the question of how relevant the oriental religions are to Blavatsky's occultism and because it is this point which has created essential (but largely neglected) conditions for the emergence of New Age religion. Moreover, it was arguably the most central aspect for Blavatsky herself as well; as Ronald Neufeldt remarks:

> The emphasis is ... on spiritual rather than physical evolution, although the physical is not forgotten. Purely physical evolution, however, is rejected. Constant reference is made by Blavatsky to materialists, whom she finds as sinister as misguided Christians and spiritists, and who are viewed as the offspring of Charles Darwin. It is the search for man's divine self which is significant although the material is transformed through such a search or more correctly, through such an evolution. The goal in other words is to become a new and more perfect man whose "capabilities and faculties will receive a corresponding increase in range and power, just as in the visible world ... each stage in the evolutionary scale is marked by an increase of capacity"[263].

Before proceeding further, I recall my thesis central to chapter nine, section 3. I argued that, contrary to popular assumptions, reincarnation as such is *not* the central New Age belief with respect to survival after death: 'Rather than reincarnation, the universal element in New Age ideas about survival is *progressive spiritual evolution* considered as a process which started before birth and will continue beyond death. Reincarnation is a crucial part, but nevertheless only a part, of this larger process'. This applies fully to modern theosophy too. We will see that, for Blavatsky, progressive spiritual evolutionism was far more central than the belief in reincarnation *per se*. She certainly did not adopt evolutionism in order to explain the reincarnation process for a modern western audience; what she did was to assimilate the theory of *karma* within an already-existing western framework of spiritual progress. This has implications for the question of her "orientalism". It is not the case that she moved from an occi-

---

[262] Blavatsky, *Collected Writings*, vol. 4, 572, as quoted in Neufeldt, 'In Search of Utopia', 248.

[263] Neufeldt, 'In Search of Utopia', 248.

dental to an oriental perspective and abandoned western beliefs in favour of
oriental ones. Her fundamental belief system was an occultist version of romantic evolutionism from beginning to end; and karma was adopted in order to
provide this evolutionism with a theory of "scientific" causality.

Above, we noted Godwin's suggestion that *Isis Unveiled* (1877) seems to have
been the culmination of a series of publications which appeared in the 1870s,
most of which regarded reincarnation as an error. The discrepancy between the
absence or near-absence of reincarnation in *Isis Unveiled* and its affirmation
in *The Secret Doctrine* (1888) has elicited much discussion[264]. I will not enter
into this controversy, which is more complicated than it seems at first sight.
In her later attempts at explanation, Blavatsky claimed that 'From the more
exoteric point of view given in *Isis Unveiled*, it was correct to say that a *person* is never reincarnated. Yet from a higher point of view, an *individuality*
is'[265]. This is explained with reference to her theory of the sevenfold constitution of human beings, according to which only the spiritual soul or intelligence (*buddhi*) and the pure spirit (*atman*) are eternal and indestructible, and
reincarnate as long as is necessary for their evolution. During incarnation, they
manifest under the cloak of ego personalities which consist of the five other
elements, none of which is immortal. This perspective is broadly compatible
with that of the New Age, which distinguishes between the immortal Higher
Self and the mortal personality and limited ego. As I noted in chapter nine,
section 3, the ego personality is, according to New Age theory, 'quite literally mortal and knows only *one* single life'. As far as Blavatsky is concerned, it
is significant that when reincarnation (or its cognates, transmigration and
metempsychosis) is discussed in *Isis Unveiled*, this is done as frequently with
reference to occidental as to oriental traditions. Most important here is to take
notice of the close association in Blavatsky's mind—at least in her later work—
between reincarnation and evolution. It is not unusual to find the terms mentioned as synonyms: 'Theosophy believes ... in the *Anastasis* or continued existence, and in transmigration (evolution) or a series of changes in the soul'[266].
This association becomes understandable if we investigate the *western* roots
of what is (imprecisely, as I argued) called "reincarnation" in occultist and
New Age contexts. We then discover that these roots are the *same* as those of
modern evolutionism: theosophical "reincarnationism" *and* evolutionism both
have their origins in the "temporalization of the Great Chain of Being" during
the 18th century. Taking that phenomenon as a starting point, the modern theo-

---

[264] Summarized very briefly in Godwin, *Theosophical Enlightenment*, 340-342. See the appendix 'Theories about Reincarnation and Spirits' (1886) added by Blavatsky to later editions of *Isis
Unveiled*, in which she denies that there is a discrepancy.
[265] Godwin, *Theosophical Enlightenment*, 341.
[266] Blavatsky, *Collected Writings* II, 91-92, quoted in Neufeldt, 'In Search of Utopia', 234.

sophical and New Age doctrine of immortality can be described as the product of a convergence of three distinct elements: (1) the idea of spiritual progress after death; (2) the idea of reincarnation on this earth; (3) "scientific" evolutionism as popularly understood in the 19th century. I will discuss the development in that order.

Spiritual Progress after Death

Lovejoy has demonstrated how a reaction began, at the beginning of the 18th century, against the static conception of the Great Chain as traditionally understood. Increasingly, it came to be

> reinterpreted so as to admit of progress in general, and of a progress of the individual not counterbalanced by deterioration elsewhere. And ... the traditional conception, when so reinterpreted, suggested a new eschatology, or rather the revival of an old one. Since the scale was still assumed to be minutely graduated, since nature makes no leaps, the future life must be conceived to be—at least for those who use their freedom rightly—a gradual ascent, stage after stage, through all the levels above that reached by man here ...[267]

One of the authors who explained the concept of an open-ended creative "evolution of consciousness" was Joseph Addison. His reflections, in 1711, on the idea of a progressive advance through stages of increasing spiritual perfection are strikingly similar to what would be proclaimed by the New Age movement (for example, by Seth) more than two centuries and a half later:

> ... the several generations of rational creatures, which rise up and disappear in such quick successions, are only to receive their first rudiments of existence here, and afterwards to be transplanted into a more friendly climate, where they may spread and flourish to all eternity. There is not, in my opinion, a more pleasing and triumphant consideration in religion than this of the perpetual progress which the soul makes towards the perfection of its nature, without ever arriving at a period in it. To look upon the soul as going on from strength to strength, to consider that she is to shine forever with new accessions of glory, and brighten to all eternity, that she will be still adding virtue to virtue and knowledge to knowledge, carries with it something that is wonderfully agreeable to that ambition which is natural to the mind of man. Nay, it must be a prospect pleasing to God himself, to see his Creation ever beautifying in his eyes, and drawing nearer to him, by greater degrees of resemblance[268].

This idea of a spiritual ascent through higher realities after death is commonly encountered in 18th century Christian theosophy and illuminism, and has remained a part of the esoteric tradition ever since. From a Christian esoteric perspective, it could be understood as an exemplification of purgatory. It is in this sense that Saint-Martin, for example, explicitly *opposed* it to the idea of

---

[267] Lovejoy, *Great Chain*, 246.

[268] Joseph Addison (in the *Spectator*, 1711), as quoted in Lovejoy, *Great Chain*, 247.

earthly reincarnation[269]. Similarly, Karl von Eckartshausen (1752-1803) believed in an "ascendant metempsychosis" but not in reincarnation. Faivre's observations are highly relevant to our concerns: they confirm both the connection between "ascendant metempsychosis" and the Great Chain of Being and the original difference between the former and reincarnation.

> [Eckartshausen] understands too well the essence and the originality of the Christian message to accept the idea of reincarnation, a doctrine which is incompatible with the teaching of Christ[270] ... Ascendant metempsychosis, i.e. the successive purifications which the spirit undergoes after death, is a manner of conceiving of purgatory; it accords perfectly with Eckartshausen's ruling idea concerning the uninterrupted chain of beings "from the polyp to the cherub" right up to God. The theosopher writes that the spirit of man does not move backwards after death but passes on to the world of spirits, in the same manner as the caterpillar becomes a butterfly ... Our physical death is undoubtedly not the only death which awaits us. Each of our demises will be a leap into a new light, a new life, until the moment when, having moved through the successive existences, we will finally have understood their meaning. Therefore it is important to purify ourselves already in this world in order to be able to live in the higher spheres. Heaven is nothing but the *Ähnlichwerdung*, the union of our spirit with God[271].

We must take good notice of the fact that this 18th-century theory of immortality entailed the idea of a spiritual *progress* through higher worlds (which might even include a succession of distinct "existences" separated by "deaths" equivalent to earthly death), in the course of which the human spirit gained a deeper understanding (or "gnosis") of the meaning of existence. This is already the basic framework of New Age ideas of immortality, with the sole difference that the whole process does not yet include a phase consisting of earthly reincarnations. It is this framework, too, which we encounter in the teachings of Emanuel Swedenborg[272]. Swedenborg is not only important as one of the principal links by which these conceptions of after-death progress influenced occultism, but he also provides a good illustration of the idea of the afterlife as a continuing process of *education*. In the Swedenborgian heaven(s), human souls are not punished for their transgressions but are confronted with the reality which they have "created" for themselves by their spiritual attitudes. Their environment serves as a mirror for their own state of mind; and thus, to the extent that the environment is less than perfect, they are stimulated to "change

---

[269] Viatte, *Sources occultes* I, 278; Faivre, *Kirchberger*, 146.

[270] In a footnote, Faivre deplores the 'regrettable confusions which have not stopped to multiply up to our own days in theosophical works and environments' with respect to the concept of reincarnation. The latter is incompatible with Christianity in any sense of the word: 'Without risking to be mistaken, one can say that any "Christian" esotericist who professes this doctrine has understood nothing of Christianity ...'

[271] Faivre, *Eckartshausen*, 542.

[272] See McDannell & Lang, *Heaven*, 183, 188ff. Cf. Horn, 'Reinkarnation und christlicher Glaube'.

their mind" and improve it. In this way, they continue to learn from experience the hard way, in an educational process which has perfect spiritual understanding as its goal.

The idea that the soul progresses through a series of "existences" after death makes it hardly surprising that the doctrines of "ascendant metempsychosis" and of reincarnation have frequently been confused[273]. The distinction became even more subtle and theoretical when the "higher worlds" came to be associated with the *planets*. This post-Copernican option, also, became increasingly popular during the 18th century. One of those who seriously considered the possibility of transmigration to other planets was Immanuel Kant[274]. His *Allgemeine Naturgeschichte und Theorie des Himmels* of 1755 contains these speculations:

> Should the immortal soul in all its future eternity, which even the grave not interrupts but only changes, remain attached to this point of space, our earth? Should she never gain a closer familiarity with the other *Wonders of Creation*? Who knows?—she may be destined to get to know from nearby, one day, those distant globes and the excellency of their design, which already from afar stimulate the curiosity so profoundly. Perhaps, therefore, some globes of the planet system fashion themselves so as to prepare new places of residence for us, when the time period which has been prescribed for our sojourn here has been completed. Who knows, might perhaps those moons circle round Jupiter, *in order to illuminate us one day*?[275]

In these speculations, the young Kant was close to his opponent Swedenborg (who has left detailed descriptions of his visionary travels to other planets[276]), and to other thinkers influenced to various extents by esotericism, such as Oetinger, Jung-Stilling, Lavater, and even Goethe[277]. The doctrine of reincarnation on other planets is also found in one of the most influential defenders of reincarnation in 19th-century occultism, the French spiritualist Allan Kardec[278].

Reincarnation

Most Christian theosophers and illuminists regarded reincarnation in the strict sense (i.e., being born again in the flesh on this same planet) as incompatible with Christianity. Nevertheless, the doctrine seems to have been a popular top-

---

[273] The standard work of Viatte (*Sources occultes* I & II), too, unfortunately does not distinguish carefully between the possible meanings of the term metempsychosis. Although he frequently mentions it, it is often unclear whether it refers to an actual belief in reincarnation.

[274] Benz, 'Reinkarnationslehre' (in Resch, *Fortleben*), 323-326; and id., *Kosmische Bruderschaft*, 37-44.

[275] Kant, *Allgemeine Naturgeschichte und Theorie des Himmels*, vol. I, Preussische Akademie der Wissenschaften 1755, 366, as quoted in Benz, 'Reinkarnationslehre', 325.

[276] Benz, *Kosmische Bruderschaft*, 57-71.

[277] Benz, *Kosmische Bruderschaft*, 73-100. Cf. Viatte, *Sources occultes* II, 119.

[278] Benz, *Kosmische Bruderschaft*, 101-108; id., 'Reinkarnationslehre', 348-352.

ic of discussion in illuminist circles during the second half of the 18th century; and, as "pagan" tendencies became more prominent during that period, it was bound to increase in popularity. Thus, for example, the members of the neo-pythagorean *École du Nord*, which we already encountered in connection with spiritualism, not only firmly believed in reincarnation, but also indulged themselves in speculations about their former lives[279]. The "neopagan" esotericist Restif de la Bretonne not only believed in reincarnation but even anticipates the New Age idea that (at least, in his case, if one has lived a virtuous life) one can choose one's own incarnation[280]; a doubtful privilege, since (as Viatte concludes from Restif's descriptions) souls often seem to have made stupid choices[281]. Claude-Julien Bredin, in the 1820s, was convinced that we are reincarnated several times in order to be tested and purified[282]; and Charles Fourier knew with precision that he had lived 801 lives[283]. The sources of this increasing popularity of reincarnation are complex. The dissemination of new knowledge about Hinduism undoubtedly contributed to the vogue of reincarnation; but esotericists could as easily derive the idea from the platonic, pythagorean and kabbalistic strands of western esotericism, or from the discussions of philosophers such as Henry More or Leibniz[284].

Of particular interest is the case of Charles Bonnet (1720-1793). This pioneer of biological evolutionism developed a theory of "palingenesis" which has been described as 'a "classic internalist theory" of development: a program placed in the germs at the Creation unfolds in its divinely preordained pattern'[285]. At the same time, it provided a naturalistic explanation of resurrection: 'In place of a radical difference between this life and the next, between this life as a sojourn in the physical world followed by eternity in a spiritual realm, Bonnet offers an innumerable series of terrestrial lives in which there is no other reward than the progress effected from life to life'[286]. Bonnet's theorie of palingenesis was adopted by Pierre-Simon Ballanche, and once again we see that terrestrial reincarnation is understood within the wider framework of evolution through higher worlds. McCalla notes:

[279] Viatte, *Sources occultes* I, 135. Viatte suggests that after his journey to Copenhagen Lavater tended towards a belief in reincarnation, which to him suggested "progress" (o.c., 136). Faivre (*Kirchberger*, 145-146) denies that he accepted reincarnation.
[280] This somewhat neglected figure seems quite important to the emergence of occultism. A comparison between the relevant discussions in Viatte (see index to both his volumes) and Part Two of the present study will reveal that he anticipates a remarkable number of New Age themes.
[281] Viatte, *Sources occultes* I, 259.
[282] Viatte, *Sources occultes* II, 228.
[283] Des Georges, *Réincarnation des âmes*, 205.
[284] Des Georges, *Réincarnation des âmes*, 196-202.
[285] McCalla, '*Palingénésie philosophique*', 427.
[286] McCalla, '*Palingénésie philosophique*', 427; and id., 'Illuminism'; Des Georges, *Réincarnation des âmes*, 203.

For Ballanche as for Bonnet, human destiny extends beyond a single terrestrial existence: "The appearance of humanity on earth is only one phase of its existence". Indeed, at present, the human race, though lord of the earth, occupies a relatively modest position in the chain of being: "Humanity is at the head of this world in order to admire it and enjoy it. Other intelligences exist in order to admire and enjoy the whole of creation". As humanity progresses first on earth and then through the celestial hierarchies, it undergoes progressive spiritualization. Eventually, the physical body and the entire physical world will disappear as the terrestrial phase of the rehabilitation of humanity culminates in freedom from the universe of space and time[287].

I mention in passing that this last element (transcendence of space and time), which is so congenial to New Age reincarnationism, seems to constitute a distinctly western theme. A further important aspect of Bonnet's and Ballanche's theories of palingenesis is their emphasis on the evolutionary necessity of suffering. McCalla notes that, in Bonnet's theory, 'all suffering is part of the unfolding of progressively greater happiness as planned by God from the beginning'[288]. When humanity has reached the culmination of its evolution, it will be able to look back on its history and understand that all suffering happened for a reason: 'we will comprehend [moral and physical evil] distinctly in their strength and most distant effects: and we will acknowledge proof *that everything that God made was good*'[289]. The influence of Leibniz's *Theodicy*, to which Bonnet refers, is evident. Bonnet affirms that we are living in the "best of all possible worlds" because any suffering permitted by God is necessary from a higher point of view; Ballanche goes one step further in affirming that suffering is a condition of the very operation of evolution[290].

This view of reincarnation as an often painful but necessary 'initiation through the body'[291] is close to another important source of western reincarnationism: Gotthold Ephraim Lessing's *Die Erziehung des Menschengeschlechts* (1780), which was influenced by Bonnet's work[292]. There is not much in Lessing's view of reincarnation which would suggest a significant debt to oriental religions. Firstly, like most other modern western reincarnationists[293], Lessing concentrates on humanity alone: transmigration into animals is not an option[294]. Sec-

---

[287] McCalla, '*Palingénésie philosophique*', 435-436 (quotations in the text are from Ballanche). Cf. Viatte, *Sources occultes* II, 239-240. See further McCalla, *Expiation, Progress, and Revolution*.

[288] McCalla, '*Palingénésie philosophique*', 428.

[289] Bonnet, *Oeuvres*, vol. 7, 667, as quoted in McCalla, '*Palingénésie philosophique*', 428.

[290] McCalla, '*Palingénésie philosophique*', 438.

[291] Pierre-Simon Ballanche, *Ville des expiations*, 107 & *Palingénésie sociale* I, 63, as quoted in Viatte, *Sources occultes* II, 239.

[292] That Lessing had read Bonnet's *Idées sur l'état futur des êtres vivants ou Palingénésie philosophique* is clear from his conversations with Jacobi in 1780 (Sperna Weiland, note to his edition of Lessing, *Opvoeding van de mensheid*, 114).

[293] There are exceptions. See for example Viatte, *Sources occultes* II, 35.

[294] Cf. Benz, 'Reinkarnationslehre', 320-321.

ondly, he assumes that reincarnation is not a more or less random succession of sometimes higher, sometimes lower existences, but a continuous "upward" progress[295]. Finally, reincarnation is not interpreted in a negative and otherworldly sense (as the "wheel of rebirth" which chains the soul to a world of suffering), but as a wholly positive, this-worldly process of learning and growth[296]. For Lessing, reincarnation is not a cycle of necessity from which human souls should try to escape, but a process of education by which God patiently leads the human race to maturity. If we ignore the theistic element for a moment, it is evident that this is precisely equivalent to the New Age idea of the universe as a learning environment or "school", in which every incarnation is equivalent to a "class" in which certain tasks have to be mastered. In contrast to the oriental context, reincarnation in the later 18th and early 19th century is simply one possible explanation (competing with others, such as exclusive "ascendant metempsychosis" in other worlds) of how spiritual evolution takes place. Not reincarnation *per se* but progress or evolution is therefore the heart of the theory. This is demonstrated by the fact that reincarnation is discussed as one possible elaboration of the more general idea of progressive ascent through the chain of being; and that the latter was indeed a concept originally independent of reincarnation is further suggested by the centrality to romanticism of what M.H. Abrams has called the "educational spiral". That reincarnation implied progress is illustrated by the fact that for late 18th-century reincarnationists (as for late 20th-century New Agers), the prospect of many more lives after this one did not inspire dread but exhilaration[297]. It could be experienced as a romantic concept which filled the heart with a 'wondrous happiness'[298]. Reversely, the idea of having lived many *previous* lives was congenial to the emerging historical consciousness. Thus, Johann Georg Schlosser, who defended reincarnation against Herder, relates a dream which anticipates New Age attitudes:

[The dream] leads me through all the worlds, and leads all nations to me. I like to think that perhaps in another body I was Socrates' friend or one dear to Rousseau; the idea makes me happy that the deceased who were dear to me still roam the earth and will perhaps be connected with me again in a hundred ways, more closely than ever: that they will perhaps be my parents, my children, my brothers or sisters; I am happy that when I will perhaps die soon, I will come among wiser, better, nobler people than those among whom I live already; that I

[295] Cf. Wichmann, 'Theosophische Menschenbild', 25, about the theosophical view of reincarnation in contrast with Indian views: '*Es ist ... hier die Entwicklungsrichtung der Reinkarnationsfolge eher vektoriell verstanden, während nach dem indischen Modell ziemlich munter "durcheinanderinkarniert" wird, d.h. ein Mensch kann auch wieder auf das tierische Niveau herabsinken, kann eine Weile ein Gott, dann wieder Mensch werden usw.*'.
[296] Benz, 'Reinkarnationslehre', 321, 344.
[297] Benz, 'Reinkarnationslehre', 321.
[298] Benz, 'Reinkarnationslehre', 335 (with reference to Peter Hebel).

myself, in another body, will become wiser, better, nobler! I enjoy the happiness which I experience because, when I have to leave it, another awaits me at death; I use my happiness and my misfortune as states of experience, which will make my soul better, more independent, and which will heighten my ability to enjoy my better Self[299].

I have suggested that the kind of "cosmic religiosity" which inspired the Romantic aspiration to experience in one's own mind all aspects of the universe, from the highest being to the lowest and from the ancient past to the distant future, was already anticipated by Renaissance humanists such as Pico della Mirandola. The passage from *Corpus Hermeticum* XI quoted in that connection in chapter fourteen, section 1C (par. "Philosophical Frameworks: Neoplatonism and Hermeticism"), is highly congenial to central aspects of Romanticism[300], and is equally reminiscent of New Age descriptions of transpersonal consciousness. *Corpus Hermeticum* XI 20-22 states that an understanding of God can only be attained by those who have experienced to the fullest all aspects of the universe; and under the impact of the "temporalization of the Great Chain of Being", the conclusion was drawn that such understanding would require many lifetimes. Thus, romantic minds could come to conceptualize the supreme fulfillment as that point at which 'man, at the end of his pilgrimages, consciously perceives its chain in its entirety'[301]. Perfect gnosis would thus imply the attainment of a fully-conscious understanding of one's whole reincarnational history, and a contemplation of the ultimate perfection of the intricate pattern of experienced events. Thus, as in the case of Bonnet, even pain and suffering would be perceived with hindsight as part of the divine plan. This is the essence of that type of romantic evolutionism discussed by Conner as "Cosmic Optimism".

The Law of Evolution

The whole conceptual structure of progressive "reincarnation" (actually: spiritual progress by learning from experience, during many lives in this *and* other worlds) which would be adopted by modern theosophy, and ultimately by the New Age movement, already existed by the end of the 18th century. Not only did it emerge together with modern concepts of evolution; it is most plausibly interpreted as a direct inference from them. It was during the 19th century that evolution was developed from a philosophical and religious concept into a scientific one, and I have summarized that development above. When applied

---

[299] Schlosser, 'Über die Seelenwanderung', as quoted in Benz, 'Reinkarnationserfahrung', 334.

[300] Regardless of my criticism formulated in chapter fifteen, section 1A, such similarities between hermeticism and romanticism have been demonstrated convincingly by Tuveson, *Avatars*.

[301] Benz, 'Reinkarnationslehre', 336.

to "reincarnation", this resulted in a distinct shift of emphasis. While evolution had originally been conceived in terms of divine providence it now came to be understood as a law of nature. I have mentioned the shift from a deistic to an immanentist theology, which conceptualized God not as an "external" artificer but as a creative force working from within. But once a traditional theism had been replaced by such an "occult" force of nature, it was easy to take one further step and conceive of the latter as a natural force pure and simple. Similar to what happened with Mesmer's "fluid", it made not too much difference whether or not the force of evolution was called "divine". It is in this context that Blavatsky's views of evolution and reincarnation must be understood. Blavatsky inherited theories of evolution rooted in romantic *Naturphilosophie* but, as part of her effort to present theosophy as a "scientific religion" superior both to Christianity and to materialism, she frequently described them in the terminology of modern science. Evolution was presented as the great Law of Nature which governs the natural as well as the supernatural (material and spiritual) levels of existence. Accordingly, the 18th-century theory of spiritual evolution—through many lives in this world, on other planets, and in higher worlds—was adopted by Blavatsky, but it was reconceptualized by her as based on Natural Law rather than divine providence.

Now, it is highly characteristic for the occultist rather than traditional esoteric nature of Blavatsky's theosophy that this universal law of nature had to be based not on correspondences but on *causality*. Paradoxically, what she seems to have derived from Hinduism and Buddhism is *not* reincarnation, but the idea of an impersonal "causal law" which could serve as a "scientific" alternative to Christian morality! This is how she describes the concept of karma:

> Karma thus, is simply *action*, a concatenation of *causes* and *effects*. That which adjusts each effect to its direct cause; that which guides invisibly and as unerringly these effects to choose, as the field of their operation, the *right person in the right place*, is what we call *Karmic Law*. What is it? Shall we call it the hand of providence? We cannot do so, especially in Christian lands, because the term has been connected with, and interpreted theologically as, the *foresight* and *personal design* of a personal god; and because in the active laws of Karma—*absolute Equity*—based on the Universal Harmony, there is neither foresight nor desire; and because again, it is our own actions, thoughts and deeds which *guide that law*, instead of being guided by it[302].

This really says it all. Most theories of "ascendant metempsychosis" of the 18th and early 19th century conceived of the process as providential, and largely assumed a system of morality based on traditional Christian principles. These were unacceptable to Blavatsky. What she needed was to ground western conceptions of spiritual progress in an alternative system of morality, with refer-

---

[302] Blavatsky, *Collected Writings*, vol. X, 144-145, as quoted in Neufeldt, 'In Search of Utopia', 237-238.

THE MIRROR OF SECULAR THOUGHT

ence to a universal causal law that could be presented as "scientific". For her, the oriental concept of karma did just that. Whether or not it is adequate to understand karma in terms of western concepts of instrumental causality is less important here than the fact that this is how Blavatsky understood it. While the idea of "ascendant metempsychosis" (with or without reincarnation) is of western origin and was derived by Blavatsky from traditions connected with esotericism, the doctrine of karma was undoubtedly derived from the East. Its interpretation in terms of causality strengthened Blavatsky's conviction that true religion was compatible with true science, and that both were opposed to dogmatic Christianity. By pointing to karma as the great Natural Law of spiritual progress, Blavatsky achieved the combination of "ascendant metempsychosis" (1) including reincarnation (2), and (what she regarded as) a scientific rather than a religious account of its underlying process (3).

This leads me to the following conclusions. Whether or not Blavatsky believed in reincarnation already during the early phase of her development, her eventual emphasis on it is certainly not based on a "discovery of the east" beginning with her trip to India. Considering her intense and lifelong involvement in occultist movements, and her profound familiarity with esoteric literature, she was certainly aware of the western tradition of "ascendant metempsychosis" and reincarnation and did not need the Orient to learn about it. Reversely, she already discussed oriental religious ideas in *Isis Unveiled*, and even if she did reject reincarnation in her early work, she cannot have done so because she was unaware of it before her trip to India. Her mature doctrine displays all the characteristics (progress by "education"; optimistic this-worldliness; exclusion of animal incarnations etc.) which we noticed as typical for western reincarnationism and atypical for oriental religions. It gives an evolutionist account of the "Education of the Human Race" which is much closer to Lessing than to either Hinduism or Buddhism. The absence or near-absence of reincarnation in Blavatsky's early period can plausibly be explained in terms of "occultist politics". The most explicit and influential defenders of reincarnation were the French spiritualists in the tradition of Allan Kardec, who combined two things resented by Blavatsky: popular spiritualism (see above) and a pronounced Christian emphasis[303]. Considering the competition between Kardecism and theosophy, it would make sense for Blavatsky to denounce "vulgar" doctrines of reincarnation in favour of a more sophisticated esoteric doctrine of "ascendant metempsychosis"[304]. I suggest, however, that the crucial question for

---

[303] See for example Kardec's *Book of the Spirits*, which is written in the form of a catechism. Some characteristic passages are reproduced in Benz, 'Reinkarnationslehre', 350-352.
    [304] Cf. Godwin, *Theosophical Enlightenment*, 258: '... although every being passes through multiple lives, it only incarnates once on earth as a human. This was ... the doctrine of Ghost Land ..., of Emma Hardinge Britten, and of Blavatsky's "Hermetic" phase'.

Blavatsky was *not* whether or not "ascendant metempsychosis" also included reincarnation but, rather, *how to account for the process of spiritual evolution*. All things considered, the first problem concerned only a detail in the already-established framework of "progressive rebirths"; the second, however, concerned the very foundations of the whole occultist edifice. If souls progressed through many lives (whether on earth or not), then how could that process be explained in "scientific" terms acceptable to a modern audience? I suggest that Blavatsky had not yet solved this problem when she wrote *Isis Unveiled*, but subsequently realized that karma provided the long sought-for answer. The index to *Isis Unveiled* lists a considerable number of references to metempsychosis, reincarnation and transmigration, but only three to karma (plus a fourth to the appendix added in 1886; see above). In *The Secret Doctrine*, on the other hand, karma has definitely moved to center stage, while reincarnation and its cognates are mentioned far less often[305]. Blavatsky had to convince herself that karma did not imply something reminiscent of the hated concept of predestination, i.e., that it was not a blind force of necessity which would undermine her "Enlightenment" values of individual autonomy and personal responsibility[306]. Once she had done that, she could present it as the universal Law of Nature which safeguards cosmic justice within an encompassing evolutionary framework. Blavatsky's interpretation of karma may or may not be compatible with oriental conceptions. The important point here is that she assimilated the concept within a thoroughly occidental framework: as *the* fundamental "causal law" which should lend scientific credibility to the belief in spiritual progress.

4. THE PSYCHOLOGIZATION OF ESOTERICISM

In Part Two of this study I have called attention to a process which I defined as "the psychologization of religion and sacralization of psychology" in New Age religion. As a background to the following discussions I refer the reader particularly to the first paragraph of chapter eight, section 3A. The popular impact of psychology represents our fourth and final "mirror of secular thought", which completes the series of transformations by which an esoteric religious worldview was gradually adapted to contemporary society. We will see that this final factor lands us, with a suddenness that may be surprising, right in the middle of New Age religion. Most of the beliefs which character-

---

[305] Actually, the original Index mentions metempsychosis, reincarnation and transmigration not once (Blavatsky, *Secret Doctrine*). Compare, however, the more comprehensive new Index separately published in 1939 (Anonymous, *Index to the Secret Doctrine*), which does contain references to these subjects, although far less than to karma.
[306] See the end of the quotation about karma (text).

ize the New Age were already present by the end of the 19th century, even to such an extent that one may legitimately wonder whether the New Age brings anything new at all. I will return to that question in the concluding chapter. Here, as in the previous sections, I will make a distinction between two main strands: the so-called metaphysical movements of the "New Thought" variety, and the tradition of Carl Gustav Jung.

A. Harmonial Religion

Fortunately, the traditions which are the subject of this section have been discussed in several solid studies. Most recently, Robert C. Fuller has traced in detail the development from mesmerism to New Thought, and from the latter to the New Age movement, in three interesting studies published in 1982, 1986 and 1989[309]. Fuller demonstrates that both the New Thought movement of the late 19th century and large parts of the New Age movement of the late 20th century exemplify typically American types of religious psychology, or psychological religion. Like Ellenberger in his historical study of dynamic psychiatry, Fuller observes that psychological theories and schools are determined less by empirical "facts" than by philosophical and cultural factors. They reflect basic assumptions and presuppositions of researchers, which can be studied as "belief systems" by the historian of ideas[310]. In his study of American concepts of the unconscious (which, like Ellenberger's book, amounts to a history of psychology in general), Fuller thus notices that

> American psychologies of the unconscious mind represent structural replays of indigeneous American religious and cultural traditions. The "American" unconscious has displayed an enduring tendency to symbolize harmony, restoration, and revitalization. In sharp contrast to those European psychologists who saw in the unconscious a symbol of rift, alienation, and inner division, Americans have imbued the unconscious with the function of restoring harmony between the individual and an immanent spiritual power[311].

In tracing the sources of "American psychology", Fuller begins with Mesmerism: 'the nation's first popular psychology'[312]. We saw that Mesmer's healing method was developed into new directions by the founder of hypnosis de Puységur, and it was mainly in this form that mesmerism would reach the

---

[309] Fuller, *Mesmerism*; id., *Americans and the Unconscious*; id., *Alternative Medicine*. The connections between New Thought and New Age are explicit in the work of Albanese as well. See for example her *Nature Religion*; and cf. id., 'Physic and Metaphysic', 489-502. Important older studies include Podmore, *Mesmerism and Christian Science*; Judah, *Metaphysical Movements*; Braden, *Spirits in Rebellion*; Parker, *Mind Cure in New England*; Meyer, *Positive Thinkers*. A classic discussion is contained in James, *Varieties of Religious Experience*, lectures IV & V.
[310] Fuller, *Americans and the Unconscious*, 4-5, 61, 165.
[311] Fuller, *Americans and the Unconscious*, 5-6.
[312] Fuller, *Mesmerism*, x, 181.

United States[313]. Of great importance for subsequent developments was the fact that de Puységur gave less emphasis to the idea of an invisible "fluid" than to the special *rapport* established between the healer and the entranced patient. He believed that trance healings were effected primarily by the action of the healer's *will* upon the vital principle of the patient's body, and suggested to his audience that the whole secret of animal magnetism lay in the two words *Croyez et Veuillez*: Believe and Will[314]. Thus, he shifted attention away from physical to psychological causality, and paved the way for an acceptance of healing by "suggestion".

American Mesmerism and the Rise of New Thought
When the French mesmerist Charles Poyen embarked upon a lecture tour through New England in 1836, he discovered to his surprise that the subject which had been occupying his countrymen for decades was still virtually unknown to his American audience[315]. Poyen staged public platform demonstrations during which he brought volunteers under hypnosis, and this new sensation ensured him wide publicity. Poyen himself saw animal magnetism as a purely natural science, and proclaimed it to his audience as a force of progress which would make America into "the most perfect nation on earth"[316]. However, already for many of his earliest followers, animal magnetism proved not only the power of mind over matter but the truth of a spiritual worldview and the immortality of the soul as well[317]. After Poyen's return to France in 1839, his work was continued by Robert Collyer, who popularized mesmerism not only in New England but all along the American eastcoast. By that time, the first do-it-yourself manual of animal magnetism (Thomas C. Harthorn's translation of the French mesmerist J.P.F. Deleuze, entitled *Practical Instructions in Animal Magnetism*) was already available to an American audience, and scores of similar books or pamphlets would flood the market in the decades to follow[318]. When the Fox sisters launched the popular vogue of spiritualism in 1848, mesmerism was well established in popular American culture. This is also reflected in the literature of the period. Edgar Allen Poe's famous horror story "The Facts in the Case of M. Valdemar" (originally called "Mesmerism

---

[313] Fuller, *Mesmerism*, 10. About the reception of mesmerism in the U.S.A., cf. Benz, *Franz Anton Mesmer*, 34-42, and see the extensive bibliography in his note 66.
[314] Podmore, *Mesmerism and Christian Science*, 77; Fuller, *Mesmerism*, 11; Ellenberger, *Discovery of the Unconscious*, 72; Gauld, *History of Hypnotism*, 47.
[315] About Poyen, see Fuller, *Mesmerism*, 17-23; Gauld, *History of Hypnotism*, 180ff; Benz, *Franz Anton Mesmer*, 40.
[316] Poyen, *Progress of Animal Magnetism*, 55, as quoted in Fuller, *Mesmerism*, 21.
[317] See for example a letter in the *Boston Recorder* of February 1837 (reproduced in Fuller, *Mesmerism*, 22), about a conversion 'from materialism to Christianity' by the facts of animal magnetism.
[318] Fuller, *Mesmerism*, 29-30.

in Articulo Mortis"), which was circulated in literary magazines during the mid-1840s, describes how a decaying corpse is artificially kept alive by trance induction. The story created a heated controversy, as newspapers and magazines were inundated with letters from readers who wished to know whether such a thing was really possible[319]. Incidentally, Poe's story and its notoriety illustrate the range of interpretations which could be given to mesmerism: it suggested a spiritual worldview to some, materialism to others, and a sinister diabolism to still others.

Among Poyen's audience in 1838 was the young Phineas Parkhurst Quimby (1802-1866), whose novel interpretation of mesmerism was to create the foundations of the New Thought movement[320]. Impressed by Poyen, Quimby established himself as a mesmeric healer and, like many of his colleagues, he used an assistant (named Lucius Burkmar) who acted as a medium during healing sessions. In a trance state, Burkmar displayed clairvoyant and telepathic abilities, which enabled him to diagnose people's illnesses and prescribe a cure which would harmonize their vital fluids. All this was standard practice in mesmeric healing. However, on some occasions Quimby dispensed with the medium's help and proceeded directly to influence his patients by psychic means. Both methods proved equally succesful. Reflecting on this, Quimby noted that the common factor in both methods was the *belief* of his patients that healing had to do with magnetic or "electric" phenomena which influenced their vital fluids. As a result, Quimby eventually grew sceptical of whether the healings really had to do with animal magnetism alone. He concluded that what actually might be happening was that Lucius used his telepathic abilities to find out what the patients *already* believed was the cause of their troubles; and that his "accurate" diagnoses impressed the patients so much that they put their full confidence in whatever cure he prescribed. From this, Quimby drew a radical conclusion: it was the *beliefs and expectations* of the patient which were *fully* responsible for his/her illness or health. The source of all illness and all healing was the mind. Fuller notes that this did not mean that Quimby discarded the idea of the mesmeric fluid, although he has later been interpreted as such. He still believed that the source of health was the magnetic fluid or vital force, but he added that beliefs functioned as a sort of "control valves or floodgates" which were able to interrupt the flow[321]. Even so, it is evident, with hindsight, that Quimby had laid the foundations for the new mind-cure philosophy later known as New Thought, and must be recognized as the father of that influen-

---

[319] Fuller, *Mesmerism*, 36-38.
[320] About Quimby, see Podmore, *Mesmerism and Christian Science*, 250-255; Fuller, *Mesmerism*, 118-136; Braden, *Spirits in Rebellion*, 47-88; Albanese, *Nature Religion*, 107-115; Judah, *Metaphysical Movements*, 146-168; Parker, *Mind Cure, passim*.
[321] Fuller, *Mesmerism*, 122; id., *Americans and the Unconscious*, 46-47.

tial New Age belief which holds that we create our own reality, including our own illness or health.

> Quimby's gospel of mind cure had a beautiful simplicity about it. Right beliefs channel health, happiness, and wisdom out of the cosmic ethers and into persons' mental atmospheres. By controlling our beliefs we control the shunting valve connecting us with psychological abundance. The key element, Quimby counseled, was to identify ourselves in terms of internal rather than external reference points. So long as persons believe that the external environment is the only source from which to derive measures of self-worth they will lose contact with their inner, spiritual selves. ... Human misery, then, is the lawful consequence of allowing other persons and outer events to supply us with our sense of self-worth. Or, in Quimby's own words, "disease is something made by belief or forced upon us by our parents or public opinion ..."[322].

There are many other aspects to Quimby's healing practice which remind one of the New Age "healing & growth" movement. From the French mesmerist Deleuze he adopted the idea of magnetizing bottles of water and prescribing that water as medicine, a procedure which is still widely practiced. Having entered a self-induced trance state, he claimed to "see" a psychic atmosphere which enveloped the body of his patient and which contained the traces of his/her past experience and present beliefs and opinions. Thus, he not only seems to have practiced what is nowadays known as "aura reading"; he also claimed to be able to implant images of health directly into his patient's subconscious minds, from where they would materialize in the physical body by mediation of the psychic atmosphere. This picture was obviously congenial to the theosophical doctrine of "subtle bodies" intermediate between the pure self and the material body; and, indeed, both the metaphysical movements and the New Age movement have commonly assumed that the "aura" is simply the manifestation of that subtle vehicle on which the physical body depends for living[323]. Robert C. Fuller compares Quimby's method of clairvoyant diagnosis by self-induced trance with shamanistic procedures, and adds that Quimby actually claimed to travel to the 'land of darkness with the light of liberty, [to] search out the dungeons where the lives of the sick are bound, enter them and set the prisoners free'[324].

---

[322] Fuller, *Mesmerism*, 128.

[323] Judah, *Metaphysical Movements*, 149ff, suggests that Andrew Jackson Davis may be a common source for the ideas of theosophy and of Quimby about a "psychic atmosphere", and that his influence upon the healing movements has been underestimated. Davis's *Great Harmonia* (1850) and *Harbinger of Health* (1861) contain a philosophy of healing.

[324] Quimby, *Quimby Manuscripts*, 52, as quoted in Fuller, *Mesmerism*, 125. Fuller calls it 'a difficult hermeneutic issue whether this is to be taken literally or figuratively', but I see no reason not to assume that Quimby meant what he said. Nowadays, it is still far from unusual for healers in the alternative scene to describe travels to "the astral plane" with the purpose of leading souls "from the darkness back to the light". See for example the Dutch "healing medium" Jomanda, who has become a media celebrity in the Netherlands (Van de Wetering & Onder-

Quimby stands squarely in the tradition of Swedenborgianism and spiritual-ism[325]. Like occultists before and after him, he acknowledged that his healing method had a religious or spiritual dimension, but insisted that his was a "scientific religion": 'what distinguished irrational faith from true religion was that the latter demonstrated itself as a science of cause and effect'[326]. In this "true religion", the ultimate cause was "mind", and its effect could be either health and harmony or illness and misery. The result, as Fuller notices, was a psychologized theology:

> [Quimby] taught his patients to recognize God as "invisible wisdom which fills all space, and whose attributes are all light, all wisdom, all guidance and love". Reconciling ourselves with God's emanative spirit is a function of psychological self-adjustment. No other mediator is needed. The doctrine of Christ was thus both a folly and a stumbling block. The Christ "is the God in us all ... the Christ or God in us is the same that was in Jesus, only in greater degree in Him". Jesus himself predicted that greater things than these we shall do also; Mind Cure Science would instruct us how[327].

Even more specifically, Quimby psychologized the Protestant ethic and came up with a doctrine which was peculiarly well-suited to a country raised in the Puritan tradition. His doctrine implied that God 'sanctions men's acts according to their beliefs, and holds them responsible for their beliefs right or wrong without respect to persons'[328]; and it confirmed that "right belief" and material prosperity are intimately connected. At the same time, Quimby built a bridge between the romantic religiosity of Emersonian Transcendentalism and a worldview which is more properly referred to as occultism. As Fuller puts it, he managed 'to translate the rather vague metaphysical language of an Edwards or Emerson into the semblance of an empirically-based science', with 'a reified version of Transcendentalism' as the result[329]. I would suggest that this tendency toward reification (which changes an essentially poetical worldview into a worldview which claims to be "scientific" and lends itself to utilitarian purposes) catches the essence of the process which (as we saw) was denounced by Arthur Versluis as a trivialization by New Thought of the original Transcendentalist perspective.

The historical stages in the development of New Thought need not be summarized here. Mary Baker Eddy's church of Christian Science is based on New Thought principles, but only remotely relevant to the emergence of New Age

---

water, *Jomanda*, 73, cf. 120). For a more extensive interpretation of Quimby in terms of shamanic healing, see Porterfield, 'Native American Shamanism', 276-289, esp. 283-287.

[325] About the influence of Swedenborg and Andrew Jackson Davis on Quimby's thinking, see Judah, *Metaphysical Movements*, 146-159.

[326] Fuller, *Mesmerism*, 127.

[327] Fuller, *Mesmerism*, 129.

[328] Quimby, *Quimby Manuscripts*, 327, as quoted in Fuller, *Mesmerism*, 131.

[329] Fuller, *Americans and the Unconscious*, 48.

religion[330]. More important is the role played in the dissemination of Quimby's teachings by his pupils Julius and Anetta Dresser and, particularly, Warren Felt Evans. They were instrumental in developing Quimby's mind cure into a full-blown philosophy of "positive thinking", which could be applied not only to the healing of illness but to routine affairs of everyday life as well. As Fuller observes, the result was

> an uncritical use of mind cure psychology for deriving surefire solutions to difficulties arising in home life, interpersonal relationships, and business. Books like *Thought is Power*, *How to Use New Thought in Home Life*, *How to Get What You Want*, and *Making Money: How to Grow Success* turned belief in the powers of the mind into a full-blown ideology. In other words, mesmerism eventually evaporated into a fairly uncritical cult of the power of positive thinking[331].

The same type of self-help books is still being widely disseminated in New Age circles; New Age authors such as Sanaya Roman, Louise L. Hay or Sondra Ray are typical contemporary examples of the tradition. If we compare their ideas with those of the New Thought pioneer Warren Felt Evans, it is remarkable how little seems to have changed. Like other New Thought authors, Evans connected Quimby's mind cure with elements of German Idealism, Emersonian Transcendentalism and Swedenborgianism[332], and presented the result as a form of "esoteric" Christianity[333] which prefigures New Age religion. It must be somewhat sobering for present-day New Age believers to read these words, written over a hundred and twenty years ago: 'We live in one of those mighty transitory epochs of human history, when old things are becoming new. We are realizing the fulfillment of the prophetic announcement of ages ago, that God would pour out his spirit upon all flesh'[334]. Evans suggested that the secrets of mental healing were as old as Christianity but, 'had long been occult and withheld from the multitude'[335]. Among these secrets was the idea of using positive verbal formulas or "affirmations": a technique apparently invented by Evans, although he himself (like Shirley MacLaine in our times) attributed them to Jesus[336]. Like Quimby, Evans anticipates many characteristic elements of New Age religion as well, some of which would be pre-

---

[330] About Christian Science and its place within the New Thought movement, see Podmore, *Mesmerism and Christian Science*, 262-299; Judah, *Metaphysical Movements*, 256-289; Parker, *Mind Cure*, 129-129; Moore, *Religious Outsiders*, 105-127.

[331] Fuller, *Mesmerism*, 146.

[332] See esp. Fuller, *Mesmerism*, 151; Judah, *Metaphysical Movements*, 160ff. The pervasive influence of Emerson and Swedenborg is attested to again and again in the literature on the subject. Particularly illustrative are the two chapters about their influence on New Thought in Parker, *Mind Cure*, ch. 2 & 3. Cf. also James, *Varieties*, 106; Podmore, *Mesmerism and Christian Science*, 256.

[333] Fuller, *Mesmerism*, 147.

[334] Evans, *Mental Medicine*, 16, as quoted in Fuller, *Mesmerism*, 147.

[335] Evans, *Esoteric Christianity*, 5, as quoted in Fuller, *Mesmerism*, 147.

[336] Judah, *Metaphysical Movements*, 162, 167.

THE MIRROR OF SECULAR THOUGHT

sented in the later 20th century as "new" discoveries. Thus, for example, far before Robert Ornstein was even born[337], Evans speculated about the brain hemispheres as the seats of our voluntary and involuntary nature, the latter being the conduit of divine wisdom[338]. Restoring the relationship with the immortal Self would lead the brain hemispheres to be united and would restore 'the right relationship of mind to the potent active forces of the universe'[339]. People got alienated from that inward connection with the divine (also referred to as one's "Christ Nature"[340]) because they identified themselves exclusively with social roles and identities, and because they were indoctrinated by the limiting beliefs which society constantly imposes on its members. Positive thinking implied a process of "reprogramming" by which negative beliefs were replaced by positive ones, so that reality would change accordingly.

The core of the New Thought message was that individuals could "take responsibility" for their situation: it told them that the only reason why external circumstances seemed to have any power over them was because they *believed* that to be the case. The breakthrough to this realization was equivalent to a religious conversion:

> Before the cure they had believed that matter (i.e., large government, crowded streets, social mores, unloving spouses) had the power to inflict emotional damage. It was as though matter had an intelligence and causal force of its own. Mental healing proved these assumptions false. Their cures convinced these patients that their troubles had quite literally been all in their heads. Since happiness and misery proved to be governed by intrapsychic laws of cause and effect, they at last found themselves always in a position to take control of their lives. The moment they overcame the illusion of the outer senses and began to shift their identities inward, they no longer felt so weak and vulnerable[341].

In contemporary New Age parlance: they realized that they had been "giving their power away" to others. That the New Age doctrine of "Creating our own Reality" and the complete attendant philosophy is directly derived from New Thought could be illustrated with an abundance of quotations, but for an extensive discussion I refer to the publications of Fuller. I will restrict myself to one by Ralph Waldo Trine, an author whose work has been characterized as 'a *Reader's Digest* condensed and Bowdlerized Emerson'[342] and is still being reprinted today to serve a New Age readership[343]:

> In just the degree that we come into a conscious realization of our oneness with the Infinite Life, and open ourselves to the Divine inflow, do we actualize in our-

---

[337] Cf. chapter eight, section 2B, paragraph on "The Brain".
[338] Fuller, *Mesmerism*, 147.
[339] Evans, *Mental Medicine*, 53, as quoted in Fuller, *Mesmerism*, 149.
[340] Judah, *Metaphysical Movements*, 166.
[341] Fuller, *Mesmerism*, 142-143.
[342] Versluis, *American Transcendentalism*, 315.
[343] Trine, *In Tune with the Infinite*.

selves the qualities and powers of the Infinite Life, do we make ourselves channels through which the Infinite Intelligence and Power can work. In just the degree
in which you realize your oneness with the Infinite Spirit, you will exchange disease for ease, inharmony for harmony, suffering and pain for abounding health
and strength[344]

The same lines could have been taken right out of a book by Gary Zukav or
George Trevelyan.

Functionalist Psychology
The popular cult of "positive thinking" in the New Thought context is not the
only factor in creating an American context for the New Age's psychologization of religion and sacralization of psychology. It is important to emphasize
the extent to which it converged with dominant traditions of indigenous academic psychology. We will see that William James's chapters about "The Religion of Healthy-Mindedness" in his *Varieties of Religious Experience* are not
accidental. They represent his attempt to come to terms with a popular religious psychology which showed more than superficial resemblances to his own
viewpoint. James's *Varieties* has been highlighted as the most representative
text of the functionalist school in American psychology which, in turn, has
been presented as the beginning of the so-called "Psychology and Religion
Movement"[345]. This whole movement, which can be traced from the 1880s to
today's Human Potential movement, is a distinctly American phenomenon: no
European nation has displayed a similar fascination with uniting religion and
psychology as is found in the United States since the late 19th century[346]. Here,
I will concentrate on the first phase, which has tended to be neglected by historians of academic psychology although it has actually provided the later
movement with most of its central ideas[347].

Once again, the story begins with Emerson[348]. Sydney E. Ahlstrom, in his
authoritative *Religious History of the American People*, not only refers to him

---

[344] Trine, *In Tune with the Infinite*, 16, as quoted in Fuller, *Americans and the Unconscious*,
181.
[345] A good overview is Peter Homans, 'Psychology and Religion Movement'. Cf. also Beit-
Hallahmini, 'Psychology of Religion, 1880-1930', 84-90; and Fuller, *Americans and the Unconscious*, 65ff. According to Homans, the functionalist phase (1885-1930) was succeeded by a period of dialogue with theology (1930-1960), in which psychoanalysis was dominant and Paul Tillich
was the most dominant figure; a period of "breakdown of the dialogue" after 1960, dominated
by Eliade, Altizer, humanistic psychology, and a tendency to return once more to Freud; and a
period of "segmentation" during the 1970s and 1980s. This distinction looks somewhat artificial,
but the important point here is that it suggests, among other things, a continuity between the early functionalist school and the humanistic psychology which became so central to the Human
Potential movement and Transpersonal psychology.
[346] Homans, 'Psychology and Religion Movement', 67.
[347] Homans, 'Psychology and Religion Movement', 68.
[348] Fuller, *Americans and the Unconscious*, 14-17.

as, together with William James, 'peculiarly America's own philosopher' but
continues with calling him 'the theologian of something we may almost term
"the American religion"'[349]. Indeed, as Robert C. Fuller demonstrates, the influence of Emersonian transcendentalism has been so important in creating a cultural background to psychological theorizing that it can be seen as providing
a link of continuity between Emerson and James right up to the humanistic
psychologist Carl Rogers[350]. It was largely on the basis of Emersonian idealism that the functionalist school reacted to the positivistic tenets of academic
psychology in its early phase. The so-called "New Psychology" began to
emerge between 1885 and 1890, and can be regarded as the beginning of the
search for a "psychology without a soul" which would inspire Behaviorism
after the first decade of the next century[351]. Functionalism emerged slightly
later, from about 1890. Fuller emphasizes that it is not to be understood as a
distinct school or theory, but rather as a general outlook or epistemological
attitude which was loosely structured around certain universities and individuals[352]. Functionalism derives its name from the major tenet in which it dif-
fered from a rival approach known as structuralism. Structuralism held that the
object of psychology is "consciousness", and that the unconscious therefore
falls outside its domain; functionalism, on the other hand, held that psychology must not be concerned with what consciousness *is* but with what it *does*
(i.e., with its functioning). Beyond that, however, functionalist theories typically adopted the more specific premises of "romantic evolutionism" within a
broadly Transcendentalist framework:

> Approaching Darwin's developmental-evolutionary theory armed with the roman-
> tic philosophies of Hegel, Schelling, and eventually Bergson, the functionalists
> robbed Darwinian biology of its reductionistic sting. Henceforth all discussions
> of nature—even when couched in scientific terms—could be interpreted as
> descriptions of the concrete processes whereby an immanent divine force pro-
> gressively unfolds its creative potential. By implication, psychology is essential-
> ly a special instance of a distinct metaphysical interpretation of reality. Psycho-
> logical descriptions of human nature, though framed in the language of secular
> science, could yet be understood as defining the structures that allow us to par-
> ticipate in nature's upward surge[353].

Functionalist approaches are central to many authors of the period but, as I
noted, William James is generally regarded as the central figure[354]. It seems
evident that he is a major source for the "psychologization of religion and

---

[349] Ahlstrom, *Religious History of the American People*, 605.
[350] Fuller, *Americans and the Unconscious*, 164ff.
[351] Fuller, *Americans and the Unconscious*, 54-55.
[352] Fuller, *Americans and the Unconscious*, 55.
[353] Fuller, *Americans and the Unconscious*, 62-63.
[354] Homans, 'Psychology and Religion Movement', 68; Fuller, *Americans and the Unconscious*, 98-99 & ch. 4.

sacralization of psychology" which characterizes the New Age movement, and indeed New Age authors see him (together with C.G. Jung) as a pioneer of Transpersonal Psychology[355]. This relevance is explicitly confirmed by Robert C. Fuller:

> When William James interpreted the unconscious as humankind's link with a spiritual "more", he gave shape to a peculiarly modern spirituality. James's vision of the unconscious depths of human personality as at once psychological and spiritual made it possible for modern Americans to view self-exploration as spiritually significant and religious experience as psychologically profound[356].

Here, indeed, is a major source for the perspective represented perhaps most clearly by Henry Reed's "star diagram" of the mind (see chapter eight, section 2A). In addition, I call attention to the relevance of James's "radical empiricism" to the underlying epistemological assumptions of transpersonal psychologists such as Stanislav Grof. In chapter eight (section 3A) I noted that Grof's argument rests on the assumption that 'anything that is subjectively experienced as real must therefore be regarded as real'. Similarly, James's radical empiricism 'concedes no a priori or preconceived limits to what constitutes a "fact"'[357]. On such a foundation, he concluded that the basic datum of psychological science was 'the entire field of consciousness including its margins or fringes'[358]. Acknowledging his indebtedness to the psychic researcher F.W. Myers[359], James compared this field of consciousness to a light spectrum, of which we ordinarily perceive only small fractions while the rest remains "unconscious". The upper or higher reaches of the unconscious could, however, be studied in such phenomena as telepathy, clairvoyance, religious experience or trance states. These assumptions (which are, of course, the foundation of transpersonal psychology) originated neither with Myers nor with James: theories about a hierarchy of "levels of consciousness" had been proposed by mesmerists at least since the beginning of the 19th century[360]. Finally, I call

---

[355] Apart from Fuller, *Americans and the Unconscious*, which traces the connection in detail, cf. also Alexander, 'William James', 191-205. Notice that, according to Fuller, *Americans and the Unconscious*, 153, 'the approach to psychological science which is now being labeled as phenomenological and existential is ... virtually the same as that taken by William James, G. Stanley Hall, and other early functionalists. Humanistic psychology to a large extent represents the resurgence of the indigenous American functionalist orientation'.

[356] Fuller, *Americans and the Unconscious*, 79.

[357] Fuller, *Americans and the Unconscious*, 85.

[358] Fuller, *Americans and the Unconscious*, 85.

[359] About Myers, see chapter 5 of Turner, *Between Science and Religion*.

[360] Fuller, *Mesmerism*, 41, describes Chauncy Townshend (*Facts in Mesmerism*, 1844) as presenting 'a technique for moving awareness along a continuum which began with ordinary sense perception and led toward a point where entirely new ranges of experience emerged into consciousness'. Fuller describes how this continuum came to be interpreted as a "hierarchy", and notices that American mesmerists used to distinguish at least sixlevels. The sixth and highest seems to be synonymous with Grof's transpersonal level: it is described as a stage of 'lucidity

attention to James's notion of a "subliminal self", another concept he took over from Myers. Myers' description, replicated in James's *Varieties of Religious Experience*, precisely matches Seth's concept of the Higher Self: 'Each of us is in reality an abiding psychical entity far more extensive than he knows—an individuality which can never express itself completely through any corporeal manifestation'[361].

The immediate sources of James's psychological synthesis are complex, but it is evident that most of the traditions which have been discussed in previous sections of this chapter had a lasting impact on his thinking. James's father, Henry James Sr., was a confirmed Swedenborgian[362]; and although William attempted to free himself from the near-suffocating influence of his father and his beliefs, there is much that speaks in favour of Fuller's conclusion that his functionalist psychology brought him, ironically, back to a worldview close to Swedenborgianism[363]. It is perhaps an overstatement that 'it is possible to construe each one of James's major works as an addition, a qualification, or a rejoinder to Henry James Sr.'s Swedenborgian metaphysics'[364]; but, taking into account that Henry James Sr.'s Swedenborgianism significantly influenced William James's co-founder of pragmatism, C.S. Peirce, as well[365], it seems certain that the Swedenborgian factor should be taken very seriously indeed. To this should be added the obvious factor of psychical research into mesmerism and spiritualist phenomena, the importance of which for the history of psychology and psychiatry in the late 19th century is beyond doubt[366], and

---

or clairvoyant wisdom' where the subjects 'feel themselves to be united with the creative principle of the universe (animal magnetism). There is a mystical sense of intimate rapport with the cosmos. Subjects feel that they are in possession of knowledge which transcends that of physical, space-time reality. ... Telepathy, cosmic consciousness, and mystical wisdom, all belong to this deepest level of consciousness discovered in the mesmerists' experiments' (Fuller, *Mesmerism*, 46). Strongly similar typologies of consciousness were proposed as early as 1811 by the German mesmerist Karl Kluge (o.c., 192 nt 49).

[361] James, *Varieties of Religious Experience*, 487, and cf. 490, about 'the fact that the conscious person is continuous with a wider self through which saving experiences come' (italics in original).

[362] Hoover, 'Influence of Swedenborg'; Croce, 'Scientific Spiritualism'.

[363] Fuller, *Americans and the Unconscious*, 88.

[364] Taylor, 'Appearance of Swedenborg', 159.

[365] Taylor, 'Appearance of Swedenborg', 160-161.

[366] See for example Ellenberger, *Discovery of the Unconscious*, 85. Here, it is useful to reproduce the suggestion by Swatos, 'Spiritualism as a Religion of Science', 474-475: 'A simple exercise can ... be performed in America to demonstrate the extent to which the phenomena of spiritualism were associated with developments in psychology that would still be considered scientifically credible today (e.g. Pavlov, Wundt). This is accomplished by going to any library whose collection dates from at least the 1890s, has not had titles officially deacquisitioned, and continues to use the Dewey system of classification. Integrated with monographs and texts that would appear part of the standard history of "legitimate" psychology will be works on spiritualism and other psychic phenomena, the core text of which is F.W.H. Myers's *Human Personality and Its Survival of Bodily Death* (1903). Freud's work of dreams, for example, also appears as part of this literature'.

which caused not a few psychologists to take into serious consideration the worldviews of spiritualism. Taking these historical contexts into account, James's interest in "The Religion of Healthy-Mindedness" and the convergences between his views and those of the New Thought movement are not at all surprising. Both New Thought and functionalist psychology can be seen as parallel and partly overlapping manifestations of a distinctly American tradition which seeks to combine psychology and religion on the basis of premises which are derived largely from a combination of romantic and occultist traditions. By continuing that tradition from the late 19th up to the late 20th century, popular self-help philosophies and academic psychology have both contributed to the emergence of New Age religion.

Harmonial Religion and the Sacralization of the Psyche
We already saw that Arthur Versluis described Emerson as the founder of a "literary religion". Robert C. Fuller has called attention to William Clebsch's notion of "esthetic spirituality", described by him as a spirituality based upon 'a consciousness of the beauty of living in harmony with divine things—in a word, being at home in the universe'[367]. Esthetic spirituality in this sense is characteristic for the American mixture of Transcendentalist universalism, Swedenborgianism, Mesmerism and spiritualism under discussion here, and Clebsch discusses Jonathan Edwards, Ralph Waldo Emerson and William James as its most characteristic representatives. That they are of central importance is certainly correct, but it must be added that they are only the most famous names connected with a religious approach which was widely disseminated at a popular level. Another name for essentially the same type of religiosity is "Harmonial Religion"[368]. This term was introduced by Sydney Ahlstrom in his study of American religion, and defined by him as encompassing 'those forms of piety and belief in which spiritual composure, physical health, and even economic well-being are understood to flow from a person's rapport with the cosmos. Human beatitude and immortality are believed to depend to a great degree on one's being "in tune with the infinite"'[369]. Evidently, "harmonial religion" in this sense is still an essential component of the American manifestations of New Age religion.

Representative figures such as Quimby, Evans and James demonstrate the characteristic tendency of "Harmonial Religion" to understand "the cosmos", "the universe", or "the infinite" in psychological terms. The cosmos depends upon, or is even more or less synonymous with, an immanent divine "Mind"

---

[367] Clebsch, *American Religious Thought*, xvi. Fuller refers to Clebsch in *Mesmerism*, 83-84.
[368] Fuller, *Mesmerism*, 196-197 nt 29.
[369] Ahlstrom, *Religious History of the American People*, 1019. Notice that the term "rapport" is typical of Mesmerist terminology; and "In Tune with the Infinite" is, of course, a reference to R.W. Trine's book of that title.

which is the source and foundation of finite minds. Health and harmony on the level of human existence is achieved by replicating in one's own mind the harmonious perfection of the cosmic whole. Since the universe is flawless, the individual soul is flawless as well; it is only by *believing* otherwise (i.e., by creating an illusion of imperfection) that one disturbs the harmony and interrupts the continuity between the outer and the inner universe. These basic assumptions of "cosmic optimism" become evident already in the work of early American mesmerist authors, such as John Dods[370], and had become of central importance by the end of the century. This psychologizing tendency of Harmonial Religion is clearly another product of secularization processes, motivated by the search for a "scientific religion". R. Laurence Moore's analysis of spiritualism (discussed in section 1B of this chapter) is echoed by Robert C. Fuller's analysis of early mesmerist psychology:

> Unable to decide whether psychology should be considered an extension of physiology or metaphysics, the mesmerists chose to blur the distinctions between the two. ... it was their very reluctance to make hard and fast distinctions between sacred and secular which enabled them to investigate psychological issues without thinking themselves to be undermining traditional religious values. Mesmerism's location midway between the religious and scientific paradigms competing for the allegiance of nineteenth-century Americans made psychological ideas appear as a way of shifting, not eradicating, traditional categories of self-understanding[371].

Increasingly, "spiritual" and "psychological" became interchangeable terms[372]. With a characteristic faith in scientific progress, it was believed that empirical investigation of the psyche would eventually verify religious belief; and to those who believed so, it seldom seems to have occurred that something might be lost in that process[373]. There is certainly reason enough to attribute this (as does Fuller) at least partly to "fuzzy thinking" on the part of Mesmerists and New Thought enthusiasts[374]; but I suggest that, in addition, the phenomenon is highly significant with respect to the very meaning of "religion" or "spirituality" as understood by the groups and individuals discussed here. It seems that in Harmonial Religion of the late 19th century, secular assumptions had become assimilated to such an extent that explanations of religion in psychological terms (i.e., psychologization of religion) were not even experienced as "reductive" anymore. The reverse process of explaining psychology in religious terms (sacralization of psychology), however, which invested the science of psychology with a spiritual dimension, was definitely welcomed as an

---

[370] Fuller, *Mesmerism*, 85-89.
[371] Fuller, *Mesmerism*, 49-50, cf. 54, 64-68.
[372] Fuller, *Mesmerism*, 59.
[373] Fuller, *Mesmerism*, 66-68.
[374] Fuller, *Mesmerism*, 49.

enrichment. More than anything else, this illustrates the extent to which secular assumptions had become natural and "obvious" to those who wished to preserve a spiritual worldview in modern society. Indeed, it was on the foundation of secular assumptions that such a spiritual worldview was developed.

B. Carl Gustav Jung

Above, I referred to William James's conviction that the human unconscious is both psychological *and* spiritual, and it may be useful to add how this could lead to inferences about social "conditioning" which are essentially similar to those of the New Thought movement. Fuller remarks with reference to James: 'The "fact" that God can be approached through our own unconscious minds suggests that only a self-imposed, psychological barrier separates us from an immanent divinity. The cultivation of receptivity to the unconscious is thus a spiritually as well as psychologically regenerative act of the whole personality'[375]. Significantly, these lines would be equally applicable to the perspective of Carl Gustav Jung. However, while James and other representatives of Harmonial Religion emphasized harmony between the human mind and the cosmos, we will see that Jung described the Self as a spiritual sun. It is not without interest that both psychologists resorted to models derived from cosmology when speaking about the human psyche: both interpreted an esoteric doctrine of macrocosmos versus microcosmos in psychological terms.

The importance of Carl Gustav Jung in the history both of psychology and of esotericism cannot be evaluated without confronting the public *legend* of Jung. Generations of Jungians have cultivated an ideal image of the Swiss psychiatrist which he consciously helped to manufacture himself. This ideal image paradoxically combines two claims. Firstly, Jung and his followers have never tired to emphasize that he was essentially a doctor and an empirical scientist. Thus, for example, Gerhard Wehr: 'It is beyond doubt ... that Jung has always considered himself first and foremost as a *medical* psychologist, not as a philosophizing one, or one who surrounds himself with mysticism. ... Jung stepped forward as a doctor and a natural scientist, and he has always held on to the principle of empiricism implied by this'[376]. This image of Jung as the strict scientist is popularly combined (secondly) with the mysterious and romantic image conveyed by his autobiographical volume *Memories, Dreams, Reflections*, which presents him rather as a sort of modern shaman or an initiate into numinous mysteries. Both images are fundamental to understanding the contemporary fascination with Jung: the former suggests that his work lends sci-

---

[375] Fuller, *Americans and the Unconscious*, 95.
[376] Wehr, *Esoterisches Christentum*, 261; cf. id., 'C.G. Jung', 381. See also Wehr's valuable biography, *Carl Gustav Jung*.

entific legitimacy to religious beliefs, and the latter seems to demonstrate how a "sacred" dimension can be restored to the cold world of science. In short: Jung seems to exemplify, in his own person, the possibility of unifying science and religion by means of psychology. The question of whether or not Jungian psychology can indeed effect such a unification falls beyond the scope of the present discussion. For us it is important to notice that, as demonstrated by recent research, the ideal image of Jung does not stand up to historical scrutiny. With primary reference to the groundbreaking analyses of Richard Noll, in his book *The Jung Cult*[377], I will argue that Jung is essentially a modern esotericist, who represents a crucial link between traditional (i.e., pre-occultist) esoteric worldviews and the New Age movement[378].

Jung and German Romanticism
A first observation is that Jung, who was Swiss by birth, was essentially a product of German cultural traditions of the late 19th century and must be understood from that context[379]. Of particular importance is the profound influence on his thinking of Romantic *Naturphilosophie* and the so-called *Lebensphilosophie* which had gained ascendancy in German culture since the last decades of the 19th century[380]. Jung was exposed at an early age to the *Naturphilosophie* (including its profound interest in medical theory and practice) of Romantics such as Schelling, Goethe, Lorenz Oken and Carl Gustav Carus, and he has often been characterized as a late representative of this tradition[381]. That Romantic *Naturphilosophie* is rooted in esoteric speculation is a commonplace in the study of esotericism[382], and is confirmed by Jung himself in

---

[377] Noll, *Jung Cult*.

[378] Perhaps it should be added that, in my estimation, the interpretation of Jung as an esotericist does not at all imply that his achievements are therefore discredited. I have consistently described western esotericism as a religious tradition which, like other religious traditions, has its superficial and its profound representatives. Admirers of Jung have good reason to value him as a profound esotericist, and to appreciate the significance of his work. Moreover, that Jung was an esotericist does not imply that he was "therefore" not a doctor. Like Paracelsus in the 16th century, Jung was both; and in both cases there is no disgrace in the fact that they approached the art of healing from the perspective of their esoteric beliefs. As I noted above (beginning of section 4A), with reference to the work of Ellenberger and Fuller, *all* psychological schools are rooted in prior belief systems and assumption. All of them have to be judged, not on the basis of what they believe, but on the basis of whether or not these beliefs have led them to develop medical approaches which can be empirically demonstrated to be effective.

[379] Noll, *Jung Cult*, 19-22.

[380] Noll, *Jung Cult*, 38-39 and *passim*.

[381] Noll, *Jung Cult*, 41; Faivre, 'Esotericism', 47; Ellenberger, *Discovery of the Unconscious*, 657.

[382] See esp. Faivre & Zimmermann, *Epochen der Naturmystik*, which discusses Ficino, Agrippa, Paracelsus, Weigel, Böhme, Christian kabbala, J.B. van Helmont, Daniel Czepko, Catharina Regina von Greiffenberg, Swedenborg, Oetinger, Martinez de Pasqually, Saint-Martin, Goethe, Blake, von Baader and Schelling under the general heading of *Naturmystik*. The connection is also noted in Ellenberger, *Discovery of the Unconscious*, 730.

his later work: '...the psychology of the unconscious that began with C.G. Carus took up the trail that had been lost by the alchemists. This happened, remarkably enough, at a moment in history when the apparitions of the alchemists had found their highest poetic expression in Goethe's *Faust*. At the time Carus wrote, he certainly could not have guessed that he was building the philosophical bridge to an empirical psychology of the future'[383]. Below, I will have more to say about how Jung conceived this continuity between alchemy, *Naturphilosophie* and analytical psychology. For the moment, it is sufficient to point out his close familiarity with these types of German Romanticism.

As far as I know, there is still no major historical and comparative treatment of the connection between Romantic *Naturphilosophie* and fin-de-siècle *Lebensphilosophie*, or of the latter's debt to esoteric traditions in general[384]. It is evident, however, that *Lebensphilosophie*—which emphasized the importance of direct experience and intuition over rationality—had strong affinities, at the very least, with earlier traditions of German *Naturphilosophie*. Of particular importance in this respect is the impact of the publisher Eugen Diederichs (1867-1930), who was 'perhaps the most important disseminator of *Lebensphilosophie* in central Europe from 1896 to 1930'[385]. Richard Noll observes that

> Due to his keenly felt calling to resurrect German culture through publishing German mystics such as Meister Eckhart, Angelus Silesius, and Jacob Böhme, works on Germanic folklore (including fairy tales and mythology), and a wide variety of theosophical, anthroposophical, and mystical "nature religion" or pantheistic tracts, after establishing the Eugen Diederichs Verlag in 1896 he became perhaps the most highly influential aristocratic patron of the neo-Romantic and völkisch pantheistic elements in Central Europe. To be published by the Eugen Diederichs Verlag was to be accepted in intellectual circles in a way that publishing perhaps the same occultist material by the Theosophical Society would not be, although the publications of the Theosophical Society were nonetheless also widely read[386].

Noll observes that Jung's personal library contained many volumes published by the Eugen Diederichs Verlag, and calls attention to the multivolume series *Gott-Natur*, which reissued the works of Giordano Bruno, Paracelsus, Lamarck, Goethe, Carus and various lesser-known proponents of Romantic *Naturphilosophie*[387]. It is significant that traditional esotericism and *Naturphilosophie* were disseminated in close association with typical occultist literature. Jung, too, was familiar with the whole range of esoteric traditions, from Paracelsus to Swedenborg to modern theosophy[388].

---

[383] Jung, *Mysterium Coniunctionis*, para. 791, as quoted in Noll, *Jung Cult*, 42.

[384] One may at least gain an impression, however, from Webb, *Occult Establishment*.

[385] Noll, *Jung Cult*, 87.

[386] Noll, *Jung Cult*, 86.

[387] Noll, *Jung Cult*, 87.

[388] For Jung's familiarity with Swedenborg, see Eugene Taylor, 'Appearance of Swedenborg',

Of particular importance for Jung's *Lebensphilosophie* is the enormously influential evolutionistic monism of Ernst Haeckel (1834-1919), who dominated discussions of evolutionary theory in the German-speaking world during the second half of the nineteenth and beginning of the 20th century. Darwin himself remarked that Haeckel's books confirmed almost all his own conclusions, and that if one of them had appeared before *The Descent of Man* (1871), he would probably never have completed it[389]. Haeckel's views were spread by his bestselling books (in particular *Die Welträtsel* of 1899) but also by the *Monistenbund*, an influential organization devoted to furthering Haeckel's new "scientific religion". Haeckel's Monistic Religion developed by various stages 'from its inception as an obscure part of the young Haeckel's materialistic-mechanistic view of Darwinism to its distinct emergence, near the end of his life, as an idealistic and semivitalistic version of the Darwinian theory of evolution'[390]. Characteristically, it was often not easy to determine whether Haeckel's monism amounted to materialism or idealism, and whether it intended to replace religion by science, or to invest science with a religious dimension, or both. It is certain that Haeckel's theories were yet another example of the widespread attempt to replace traditional Christianity by a "scientific religion". What such otherwise different movements as modern theosophy, Haeckelian monism and Jungism have in common is a vehement opposition against the personal God of Christianity[391] and the attempt to replace him by an impersonal, indwelling divine "force" that could be presented as compatible with science. Not accidentally, Haeckel's final published statement on God was entitled *Gott-Natur* (1914): the same title as Eugen Diederichs' series on *Naturphilosophie*[392]. Richard Noll demonstrates in detail Jung's debt to Haeckel's evolutionary monism. Having read *Die Welträtsel* in 1899, Jung took up Haeckel's suggestion of a "phylogeny of the soul", and developed it into an evolutionary theory of human consciousness. As Noll notes, 'Jung's deliberate use of Haeckelian evolutionary biology in *Wandlungen* [und Symbole der Libido] implies the possibility that one day, through the historical science of psychoanalysis, biology and psychology would converge via the principle that ontoge-

---

163-166. For modern theosophy, see in particular his familiarity with G.R.S. Mead (see text, below).

[389] Holt, 'Ernst Haeckel's Monistic Religion', 265.

[390] Holt, 'Ernst Haeckel's Monistic Religion', 267.

[391] For Haeckel, see for example Holt, 'Ernst Haeckel's Monistic Religion', 274: 'We know no personal God, but we do know a religion'; 277: God as the 'unknowable cause of all thoughts, the conscious and theoretical Basis of Substance'; for Blavatsky, see Godwin, *Theosophical Enlightenment*, 328: '... her personal animus against Judeo-Christianity made her prefer to be seen as an atheist than as a believer in the hated "P.G.", or Personal God'.

[392] Holt, 'Ernst Haeckel's Monistic Religion', 278-279. Note that the fascination of the New Age movement for crystals is prefigured in Haeckel's last book, called *Kristallseelen* (1917), which discusses the "interior qualities" and "atomic souls" in crystals (Holt, o.c., 279).

ny recapitulates phylogeny'[393]. It is clear from Noll's discussions that Jung's *Naturphilosophie* passed through the evolutionist "mirror of secular thought".

I have already mentioned the interest of the German Romantics for the so-called "occult phenomena", including those which would later come to be central to modern spiritualism. That Jung inherited this interest is evident from his early fascination, which would continue throughout his life, for spiritualism and psychical research[394]. Since this interest was common among psychologists of his time, it is not a sufficient argument in itself for making Jung into an esotericist. Far more important is the general perspective from which Jung perceived psychic phenomena. Most psychic researchers (like the spiritualists themselves) approached the subject on the basis of assumptions which may roughly be characterized as "positivistic". Jung, however,

> rejected the science of the early twentieth century and instead embraced the world-view and methodologies of early nineteenth-century romantic conceptions of science. ... in 1916 Jung had already left the scientific world and academia, never to really return (despite later pleas for the scientific nature of his analytical psychology). The adoption of the ... theory of dominants or archetypes completed this break and formally allied Jung with Goethe, Carus, and the morphological idealists of the romantic or metaphysical schools of Naturphilosophie that reigned supreme between 1790 and 1830 in German scientific circles.
> This rejection of twentieth-century science had its roots in Jung's medical-school days, where he preferred the vital materialism of nineteenth-century German biology over mechanistic materialism in his study of evolutionary biology and comparative anatomy. ... By 1916, in "The Structure of the Unconscious", Jung attacks the scientific worldview and defends the validity of occult movements like Theosophy, Christian Science, the Rosicrucians, and those who practice "folk magic" and astrology by arguing that, "No one who is concerned with psychology should blind himself to the fact that besides the relatively small number of those who pay homage to scientific principles and techniques, humanity fairly swarms with adherents of quite another principle"[395].

Noll notes that Jung, characteristically, removed his attacks on the scientific establishment in later editions of his essay. That Jung's view of science is rooted in Romantic *Naturphilosophie* has interesting implications. I argued that the principal difference between the two major 19th-century heirs of esotericism (i.e., Romanticism and occultism) consists in the fact that the former retains a worldview of "correspondences" opposed to scientific "causality", while the latter produces hybrid mixtures of the two. From this perspective, Jung is definitely not an occultist. If the American New Thought movement contributed to the "psychologization of religion and sacralization of psychology" within an occultist framework (in spite of the Transcendentalist factor),

---

[393] Noll, *Jung Cult*, 115.

[394] Wehr, *Carl Gustav Jung*, 67-73 and *passim*; Noll, *Jung Cult*, 144-146 and *passim*.

[395] Noll, *Jung Cult*, 269-270. For Nolls's reference to the roots of the theory of dominants or archetypes in Romantic *Naturphilosophie*, cf. o.c., 40-41, 270-271.

Jung's contribution is distinctly Romantic and consciously opposed to "causality". This is demonstrated with particular clarity by his theory of Synchronicity, which is a restatement in psychological terminology of the esoteric world-view of "correspondences" (as explicitly confirmed by Jung, and illustrated by his discussion of "forerunners", among whom one finds Pico della Mirandola, Agrippa, Paracelsus, Kepler and Leibniz)[396]. Its opposition to "causality" is demonstrated by the very title of Jung's essay on the subject: *Synchronicity: An Acausal Connecting Principle*. Jung begins this essay by stating that the philosophical principle of causality is 'only statistically valid and only relatively true', and concludes that only the alternative hypothesis of synchronicity gives an adequate explanation of facts such as ESP phenomena[397].

The Cult of the Interior Sun
Jung was, according to my definitions, not an occultist but a German Romantic esotericist: he defended "correspondences" against "causality" rather than attempting to synthesize the two, and reinterpreted traditional esotericism from a "temporalistic" framework exemplified most clearly by a Haeckelian evolutionism. The two remaining "mirrors" of secular thought (the study of religions and, of course, psychology) are strongly evident in his thought as well. I have already referred to the work of Joscelyn Godwin, who demonstrates the importance to occultism of the new speculative theories of myth and the origins of religion. His discussion of the English-speaking domain is closely paralleled by Noll's discussion of German culture; for, as it turns out, precisely the same types of theories became crucial to Jung's worldview. Noll gives special emphasis to the theories of Max Müller, and mentions German Romantics such as Friedrich von Schlegel, Joseph von Görres, Schelling, Hegel, Jacob Grimm and Friedrich Creuzer as predecessors[398]. Jung's pivotal *Wandlungen und Symbole der Libido* (1912) was the first major product of his mythological studies; and it is significant that it also exemplifies a renewed study of occult phenomena[399]. That it was precisely this work which marks the break with Freud is hardly surprising. In a well-known anecdote, Jung relates how Freud implored him that the sexual theory of psychoanalysis should be made into a 'bulwark' against 'the black tide of mud—of occultism'[400]: something which Jung evidently had no intention of doing. But Noll also notes that Freud could not possibly ignore that precisely the type of mythography which permeated *Wandlungen* was common in the *völkisch* movement, which presented "Aryan" paganism as superior to Judaic and Christian traditions. Freud must

---

[396] Jung, 'Synchronicity', 485-504.
[397] Jung, 'Synchronicity', 421 & 505.
[398] Noll, *Jung Cult*, 80-86. Cf. Wehr, *Carl Gustav Jung*, 118ff.
[399] Wehr, *Carl Gustav Jung*, 124.
[400] Jung, *Memories, Dreams, Reflections*, 173.

have been particularly shocked by finding that Jung uncritically cited major *völkisch* figures, such as Houston Stewart Chamberlain, known for their racism and antisemitism[401]. The evidence indeed leaves no doubt that Jung was essentially a *völkisch* intellectual[402]. That he was therefore a fascist, as has been inferred[403], does not automatically follow. Noll correctly notes that the *völkisch* movement of the pre-Nazi era was a complex phenomenon, and that not all its representatives can be characterized with fairness as "pre-fascist" or "pre-Nazi"[404]. With respect to Jung, he concludes (perhaps too leniently) that 'the best that can be said is that the evidence is compelling that Jung's work arose from the same Central European cauldron of neopagan, Nietzschean, mystical, hereditarian, völkisch utopianism out of which National Socialism arose'[405].

Noll describes *Wandlungen und Symbole der Libido* as based on a 'relentless syncretism of solar mythology and psychoanalysis' which, if examined outside the context of psychoanalytical literature, might well be regarded as 'an eccentric work of Müllerian solar mythology'[406]. The sexual theories of myth evidently lent themselves well to a treatment in terms of psychoanalysis[407]; but it was the solar theory, interpreted in a context of Romantic vitalism, which appears to be most central to Jung's mature vision. Richard Noll notes that, throughout his book, 'Jung dizzyingly unites the following in an associative chain of equivalences: the sun—the phallus—brightness—god—father—fire—libido—fructifying strength and heat—hero'[408]. Jung points out his conviction that God, the sun or fire, is synonymous with a person's own vital force, or libido: an argument typical for Romantic vitalism, and obviously reminiscent of the "vital fluid" of mesmerism. The argument culminates in an explicit proclamation of solar worship as the only reasonable and scientific religion:

> The sun is, as Renan remarked, really the only rational representation of god, whether we take the point of view of the barbarians of other ages or that of the modern physical sciences ... the sun is adapted as nothing else to represent the

---

[401] See esp. Noll, *Jung Cult*, 103, 129-135, 198, 259-260.
[402] Noll, *Jung Cult*, 103.
[403] Noll, *Jung Cult*, 102-103.
[404] Noll, *Jung Cult*, 102-103, 130, 135.
[405] Noll, *Jung Cult*, 135. Actually, something more can be said. Several of Jung's essays written during the 1930s contain passages which can only be interpreted as support for National Socialism (Wehr, *Carl Gustav Jung*, 284-286); and, according to Gershom Scholem, briefly after World War II Jung admitted to Leo Baeck that he had indeed suffered himself to be deluded by Nazism (o.c., 291). The vexed question of Jung's alleged antisemitism is important, but marginal to our concerns here. I restrict myself to Noll's plausible conclusion (based on recently-discovered evidence) that, although Jung may never have been openly antisemitic, a tendency of covert antisemitism is hard to deny (Noll, *Jung Cult*, 133 & 259-260).
[406] Noll, *Jung Cult*, 111, 116.
[407] See for example the quotation in Noll, *Jung Cult*, 118.
[408] Noll, *Jung Cult*, 121.

visible god of this world. That is to say, that driving strength of our own soul, which we call libido ... That this comparison is no mere play of words is taught to us by the mystics. When by looking inwards (introversion) and going down into the depths of their own being they find "in their heart" the image of the Sun, they find their own love or libido, which with reason, I might say with physical reason, is called the Sun: for our source of energy and life is the Sun. Thus our life substance, as an energic process, is entirely Sun[409].

It is from this context that one should interpret Jung's references to "the God within". In the last of the *VII Sermones ad Mortuos*, written down in the middle of Jung's existential crisis four years after the publication of *Wandlungen*, one reads this impressive passage:

> —Man is a gateway, through which one enters from the outer world of the gods, demons and souls, into the inner world, from the greater world into the smaller world. Small and insignificant is man; one leaves him soon behind, and once again one finds oneself in infinite space, in the smaller or innermost infinity.
> In immeasurable distance there glimmers a solitary star in the zenith. This is the one God of this one man. This is his world, his Pleroma, his divinity.
> In this world, man is Abraxas, who gives birth to or devours his own world. This star is man's God and goal[410].

It is interesting that, according to G. Quispel, who is otherwise very much inclined to interpreting Jung as a gnostic[411], this has *no* parallel in ancient gnosticism[412]. In the context of our general discussion and of Noll's interpretation of Jung, this is hardly surprising. Actually, Jung's idea of the "God within" is not modeled upon ancient gnosticism but upon a combination of modern esoteric and occultist speculations (in which the sun was commonly used as a symbol for God or Christ[413]) and the new solar mythology. What Jung does is to interpret the doctrine of the correspondence of macrocosmos and microcosmos in a radical psychological fashion. It is through the human unconscious that one passes from the "greater world" to the "smaller world" of the interior universe. The God of the "exterior" universe is the sun; and the interior world is, accordingly, illuminated by the sun of man's personal inner divinity. Dan Merkur has correctly concluded that Jung generally understands the archetypes of the collective unconscious as 'psychic phenomena simultaneously of the macrocosm and the microcosm'[414]. From the perspective of a psychologist, this meant that the world of the psyche and the world of "outer"

---

[409] Jung in *Wandlungen*, as quoted in Noll, *Jung Cult*, 122.

[410] Jaffé, *Erinnerungen, Träume, Gedanken von C.G. Jung*, 397 (my translation). Cf. two other English translations: Hoeller, *Gnostic Jung*, 57-58; Segal, *Gnostic Jung*, 193. Hoeller is slightly more poetic, Segal more literal, but both have their merits. I have adopted Hoeller's decision to change '*ihr*' (2nd person, plur.) into 'one'; Segal chooses to archaize the German ('ye').

[411] Quispel, 'How Jung Became a Gnostic', 47-50; cf. id., 'Gnosis and Psychology', 17-31.

[412] Quispel, 'Hesse, Jung und die Gnosis', 257.

[413] Cf. Viatte, *Sources occultes* I, 82, 254-255, 265; id., *Sources occultes* II, 54, 156.

[414] Merkur, *Gnosis*, 66.

reality were just different reflections of the *unus mundus*; thus, Jung describes the "inner planes" in terms which are a perfect illustration of the "psychologization of religion and sacralization of psychology": 'This region, if still seen as a spectral "land beyond", appears to be a whole world in itself, a macrocosm. If, on the other hand, it is felt as "psychic" and "inside", it seems like a microcosm'[415].

The vision of the interior sun seems to have been induced by a spiritual technique which Jung refers to as "active imagination", and which resulted in vivid visionary experiences[416]. The "alternate reality" to which this technique gave access was interpreted by Jung in psychological terms, but he indicated clearly that he regarded it as "real" in every sense of the word[417]; this suggests that he subscribed to a "radical empiricism" as understood by William James before him (see above) and continued by New Age adherents such as Stanislav Grof after him. Jung described this alternate reality as a realm of the unconscious, and referred to it as "the land of the Dead". He makes abundantly clear that it is a world of symbols and archetypes by means of which a person is initiated into the mysteries of the psyche, finally to encounter his/her divine Self. It is evident that this "intermediate reality", to which one gains access by active imagination, is an example of the "imagination/mediations" element central to Faivre's definition of esotericism; and what Jung refers to as the initiatic process of individuation, based on such experiences, is a clear example of "transmutation" *sensu* Faivre[418]. Moreover (although one should beware of hasty conclusions) there is a close similarity at the very least between Jung's "land of the dead" and what the theosophists refer to as the "astral plane". Jung's sensitivity to myth and symbolism is much closer to the poetic conception of a Romantic mythographer such as Friedrich Creuzer (and to traditional esotericism in general)[419] than to the literalist tendency of occultism. Although both realms are (according to the respective theories) accessible by means of the active imagination, the insufficient conceptual clarity of that concept[420] precludes a quick and easy identification. Nevertheless, Noll is certainly not very far from the truth when he concludes that 'from 1916 onward, in practice, Jung

---

[415] Jung, *Mysterium Coniunctionis*, 300-301, as quoted in Merkur, *Gnosis*, 66.

[416] For a highly interesting critical discussion, see Merkur, *Gnosis*, ch. 2.

[417] Noll, *Jung Cult*, 209-210.

[418] I refer to Noll, *Jung Cult*, 209ff, for an extensive discussion of how Jung modeled the initiatic process of individuation (understood as deification) on his understanding of the Mithraic mysteries.

[419] See Ellenberger, *Discovery of the Unconscious*, 729: 'Jung himself recalls that he had devoured his works with passionate interest. In Creuzer's works Jung found a rich mine of myths and symbols with their interpretations, and also a specific conception of myths and symbols. They are neither historical nor literary material, but specific realities intermediate between abstraction and life'.

[420] Cf. nt 71 of this chapter.

probably had far more in common with figures such as Blavatsky, List, and Steiner than he did with Freud, Adler, or even Gross'[421]. The only difference, I would add, is that Jung was not an occultist. The significance of his psychological approach to esotericism is that it enabled him to appear "scientific" while *avoiding* the necessity of compromising with the worldview of "causality". It is by building his psychology on a concept of science derived from Romantic *Naturphilosophie* (and opposed to modern "causality") that Jung may have succeeded in finding a way to "up-date" traditional esotericism without disrupting its inner consistency. From the perspective of the historical study of esotericism, this makes him a unique figure.

Jung gave a psychological twist to solar mythology by moving from the sun as divinity to its microcosmic "correspondence": the "solitary star" which illuminates the interior universe of the individual psyche. But, of course, Jung is particulary well-known for his theory of the *collective* unconscious. Having first proposed that theory in 1916, he returned to it in an essay of 1918 published in a popular Swiss monthly[422]. Richard Noll calls it 'perhaps the most nakedly völkisch essay Jung ever wrote'[423], and mentions the significant fact that Jung here referred to the collective unconscious as the "*supra*personal unconscious" as well. In this essay, Jung shows himself to be profoundly indebted to *völkisch* theories of *Bodenbeschaffenheit*: the idea that the human soul is decisively shaped by the environment. On this foundation, Jung suggested that there is a fundamental difference between the Jewish and the Germanic psyche. Taking up the characteristic line of argument used by *völkisch* antisemites for excluding Jews from the Germanic *Gemeinschaft* and *Vaterland*, Jung argued that Jews were not "rooted" to the earth and the land as the Germans were[424]. One implication of this difference, he suggested, was that Freud and Adler's psychoanalytic theories were applicable mainly to Jews[425]. Jung's own theories, in contrast, were presented by him as eminently applicable to the Germanic soul, for analytic psychology could heal the split in the German psy-

---

[421] Noll, *Jung Cult*, 230, cf. 178, 238. About the "ariosophist" Guido von List, see Goodrick-Clarke, *Occult Roots of Nazism*. About the crucial importance to Jung's development of the Nietzsche-admirer, physician, psychoanalyst and eventual anarchist Otto Gross (1877-1920), see Noll, *Jung Cult*, esp. 151-176.

[422] *Schweitzerland: Monatshefte für Schweitzer Art und Arbeit* 4 (1918), 464-472, 548-558. I have not seen the original. Noll quotes the title as 'Über den Unbewusste' in his main text (*Jung Cult*, 97), and as 'Über des Unbewusste' in a note (o.c., 338 nt 80). Both titles are grammatically impossible. The first title, corrected as 'Über den Unbewussten', would have to be translated as "About the one who is unconscious". I assume that the title should be 'Über das Unbewusste'; the case is characteristic of Noll's far from perfect command of German as demonstrated in other parts of his book as well.

[423] Noll, *Jung Cult*, 97.

[424] See Noll's reference (*Jung Cult*, 98) to Mosse, *Crisis of German Ideology*, 16, about the concept of "rootedness" in *völkisch* ideology.

[425] Noll, *Jung Cult*, 98.

che which had been caused by Christianity: 'Christianity split the Germanic barbarian into an upper and a lower half, and enabled him, by repressing the dark side, to domesticate the brighter half and fit it for civilization'[426]. Here it becomes evident that the experience of the inner sun, which has been interpreted as "gnostic" by most of Jung's later followers, is actually something very different: it is the discovery by the "Germanic soul" that, deep down inside, his allegiance is not to the alien faith of Christianity but to pagan solar worship. The goal of analysis was to break through to an early, pre-Christian stage in the phylogenetic development of human consciousness. In this context, the primary cause of neurosis in the case of the "German soul" consisted of a conflict between the pagan core of the German psyche, on the one hand, and the values of Christian civilization, on the other. This is the conflict which had plagued Jung himself and led to his psychic breakdown in 1913; a crisis which culminated in the "gnostic" *Septem Sermones ad mortuos* (1916) which begins with the return of the dead from Jerusalem, 'where they did not find what they were seeking'. As Noll concludes:

> In light of the historical method of psychoanalysis offered by Jung for uncovering evidence for the phylogeny of the human soul, his geophysically informed vision is plain: in the individual psyche there are strata that comprise the sediment of two thousand years of Christianity. Two thousand years of Christianity makes us strangers to ourselves. In the individual, the internalization of bourgeois-Christian civilization is a mask that covers the true Aryan god within, a natural god, a sun god, perhaps even Mithras himself. This is as true as the scientific fact that within the earth is glowing sun-matter that is hidden by thousands of years of sediment as well[427]. In society, too, Christianity is an alien mask that covers our biologically true religion, a natural religion of the sun and the sky. The scientific proof are the cases of patients with dementia praecox documented by Jung and his Zurich School assistants (Honegger, Nelken, and Spielrein) that demonstrate that there is a pre-christian, mythological layer of the unconscious mind. It is archaic and corresponds to the thought and especially to the souls of our ancestors. It does not produce purely Christian symbols, but instead it offers images of the sun as god[428].

The detailed evidence must be studied in Noll's original. Here, it suffices to point out its fundamental significance for understanding the nature of Jung's worldview. It will come as a shock to Jung's present-day admirers to learn from Noll that, moreover, the empirical foundation of the collective unconscious is

---

[426] Jung, 'Über das Unbewusste', as quoted in Noll, *Jung Cult*, 97.

[427] See, with respect to this element, Jung's diagram of the "geology of the personality", reproduced in Noll, *Jung Cult*, 100. Noll calls attention to the similarity with Jung's frequent references to the sun as the core of the human personality; and in the present context I refer the reader especially to the structural similarity with Henry Reed's "star diagram" discussed in chapter eight, section 2A). Notice in particular Jung's reference to 'the central fire, with which ... we are still in connection', and compare this with "the one mind" in Reed's diagram.

[428] Noll, *Jung Cult*, 128.

by no means so secure as it might seem. Richard Noll has proved conclusively that the notorious case of the so-called "Solar Phallus Man", which has carried the weight of the theory of the collective unconscious, is a fabrication[429]. To what extent this affects the credibility of Jung's theory of the archetypes should be investigated further[430].

With respect to our more limited concerns, the conclusion seems evident: Jung attempted to obscure the fact that his collective unconscious is not a conclusion from empirical research but part of a religious belief system. Jung's personal religious synthesis, presented by him as scientific psychology, combined esoteric traditions, Romantic *Naturphilosophie*, evolutionist vitalism, "neopagan" solar worship, *völkisch* mythology and a considerable dose of occultism. In itself, this mixture was not at all uncommon at the time. Jung's particular genius probably consists less in the originality of his basic worldview than in his remarkable ability to present it to his readers in the termi-

---

[429] Noll, *Jung Cult*, 181-184. According to the official version, this (anonymous) inmate of the Burghölzli clinic had a hallucination in 1906 that the sun had a phallic tube hanging from it that produced the wind. Jung did not know what to make of this, until he discovered precisely the same motives four years later, in Albrecht Dieterich, *Eine Mithrasliturgie*, of 1910. This reference could not possibly have been known to the patient, because (still according to the official version) prior to Dieterich's publication it existed only in an obscure unpublished manuscript, which was inaccessible to this patient. Therefore, his hallucination could only be explained by assuming the existence of a collective unconscious. Noll demonstrates that this story is a fabrication. The first edition of Dieterich's *Mithrasliturgie* appeared already in 1903; and the title page of the 1910 edition, used by Jung, says clearly that it is the second edition. Moreover, the Mithras liturgy was also included in a theosophical publication by G.R.S. Mead, published in 1907. The "Solar Phallus Man" himself was not a patient of Jung's but of his colleague Honegger; a fact which is still mentioned in the German *Wandlungen* but was removed from the English revision of 1952. Since Honegger started working with psychiatric patients in 1909, he could not have treated this particular person in 1906. Honegger's own personal papers were rediscovered in 1993 and indeed contain a written case history of the patient, whose name appears to have been E. Schwyzer. All this suggests that the motif of the solar phallus could well have been known to Schwyzer either from Dieterich's first edition of 1903 or from Mead's of 1907. A footnote in Jung's *Collected Works* admits the existence of Dieterich's first edition but claims that the patient had been committed already some years before 1903. This, of course, invites the question why Jung nevertheless stuck to the false story even as late as 1959. Finally, even if Schwyzer was indeed committed already before 1903, it appears that he could have found the motif of the solar phallus in Creuzer's *Symbolik und Mythologie der alten Völker* (1810-1812) or in Bachofens *Das Mutterrecht* (1861). At first sight it might seem somewhat far-fetched to assume that a regular patient of a mental asylum would have read authors such as Creuzer, Bachofen or Dieterich; but Noll demonstrates that at least a part of the institutionalized Burghölzli population consisted of people who had been thoroughly exposed to occultist and mythological materials (Noll, *Jung Cult*, 184-185; cf. 107-108, 176).

[430] The difference in Jung's theory between "archetypes" proper and "archetypal images" has often been misconstrued, as explained by Ellenberger, *Discovery of the Unconscious*, 706. Since the hallucinations of the "Solar Phallus Man" were highly culture-specific, they would seem to be archetypal images rather than archetypes. The falsification of the "Solar Phallus Man" story would then affect only the assumption that specific archetypal *images* can be stored in the collective unconscious. That the symbolic contents of the unconscious are structured according to universal archetypes would still remain a viable hypothesis, although not an established fact.

nology of modern psychoanalysis. Psychology made it possible to present esotericism (once again) as a "scientific religion" but, this time, so as to avoid
the positivistic "causality" characteristic of 19th-century science. In this way,
Jung had found a "scientific" alternative to occultism. It is remarkable that an
essentially esoteric worldview with deep roots in German culture could become
immensely successful particularly in the United States. It is from these same
roots (rather than from some sort of "universal" gnosis) that one may interpret
the peculiar religious atmosphere which pervaded the Eranos conferences organized by Olga Froebe-Kapteyn since 1933, of which Jung was the central inspiring figure[431]. It is significant that many of the lecturers of the Eranos conferences had originally been associated with a similar forum: Graf Hermann Keyserling's *Schule der Weisheit*, which operated in Darmstadt from 1920 to 1927.
The continuity between the meetings of Keyserling's circle and those of the
Eranos conferences is underlined by a similar continuity between Keyserling's
views and those of contemporary American Jungism, which is strongly associated with New Age religiosity. In 1918, Keyserling remarked that

> Theo- and Anthro-posophy, New Thought, Christian Science, the New Gnosis,
> Vivekananda's Vedanta, the Neo-Persian and Indo-Islamic Esotericism, not to
> mention those of the Hindus and the Buddhists, the Bahai system, the professed
> faith of the various spiritualistic and occult circles, and even the Freemasons all
> start from essentially the same basis, and their movements are certain to have a
> greater future than official Christianity[432].

Thus, we encounter an interest for the American "metaphysical movements"
even in the midst of German culture; and, reversely, the German perspective
of Jung, similar to Keyserling's, would be assimilated with enthusiasm in American culture after World War II[433].

Gnosticism, Alchemy, and Jungian Psychology

It is evident that contemporary adherents of Jung's theories have a hard time
reconciling Jung's own references to a continuity between ancient gnosticism,
alchemy and analytic psychology with his insistence that his theories were
based not on religious speculation but on empirical facts. Thus, one reads with

---

[431] Cf. Holz, 'ERANOS'. It should be noted, however, that many scholars who were invited
to the Eranos conferences did not share the religious attitude exemplified by Jung. Looking back
on his participation in the conferences, Gershom Scholem admits that many of the lecturers opt-
ed for a somewhat uneasy compromise between their own scholarly approach and the appearance of religious commitment expected of them by Olga Froebe. As Scholem notes, *'Es war
sozusagen ein bißchen Schwindel dabei'* (Scholem in *Neue Zürcher Zeitung* 1.3.1980, quoted in
Holz, 'ERANOS', 252).
[432] Keyserling, *Reisetagebuch eines Philosophen* (1918) as quoted from the English translation (1925) in Webb, *Occult Establishment*, 183.
[433] Jung's impact on American psychology began in the late 1950s and early 1960s (Fuller,
Americans and the Unconscious, 152).

amazement how Gerhard Wehr, an otherwise very reliable specialist who is well aware of the cultural backgrounds of Jung's thinking, claims that 'Jung's analytical psychology does not raise any kind of religious claims, not even claims that might be interpreted as the rivalry of one esoteric movement or another. Indeed, simply to preserve its scientific character, it must be concerned to keep clear of any influence stemming from a religion or worldview'[434]. When the same author nevertheless describes Jung as an "esoteric Christian"[435] it becomes clear that he does not understand esotericism as a "religion or world-view" at all. Rather, he seems to understand it as a "universal" experience of the human mind, which must be distinguished from the phenomenon of "exo-teric" religion (such as established Christianity)[436] and which has been for-mulated in scientific terms by Jung. It should be evident that this view of eso-tericism is incompatible with the historical approach of the present study, and that it rests not on empirical foundations but on Jung's personal religious beliefs. As I remarked above (nt 378), this does not necessarily discredit the validity of Jungism *as a religious worldview*, but it certainly throws doubt upon its validity as a scientific theory which may be used as a key to understand-ing religious phenomena in general. However, like almost all the thinkers and traditions discussed in this chapter (and, indeed, in this study), Jung and his followers seem to assume as self-evident that religion needs to be "scientific" in order to be credible.

I suggest that it is from the understanding of Jungism as an essentially eso-teric religious worldview that one should interpret Jung's claims about the con-tinuity between gnosticism, alchemy and analytical psychology[437]. These claims are not based on historical considerations, nor on empirical research, but on theoretical assumptions which only make sense in the context of Jung's own worldview.

I already referred to Jung's interpretation of gnosticism, which has pro-foundly affected several specialists of ancient gnosticism as well. Thus, G. Quispel has characterized the essence of gnosis as 'mythical expression of the experience of the Self'[438]. This interpretation may or may not be correct; but the methodological problem involved in this interpretation is that it *starts* from the assumption that "the experience of the Self" is a universal constant of the human mind which finds mythical expression in specific cultural contexts. Such an assumption is beyond empirical proof[439], and ultimately rests upon

---

[434] Wehr, 'C.G. Jung', 385-386.

[435] Wehr, 'C.G. Jung', 386, 394.

[436] Cf. Wehr, 'C.G. Jung', 388.

[437] For this claim, see for example the quotation in Wehr, 'C.G. Jung', 385.

[438] '*Mythischer Ausdruck der Selbsterfahrung*'. Quispel, *Gnosis als Weltreligion*, 37.

[439] See the discussion of "religionist" approaches to the study of religions, in Hanegraaff, 'Empirical Method'; and cf. the discussion of Quispel in id., 'On the Construction'.

the personal beliefs and/or experiences of the person who proposes the interpretation. In this case, that person is Jung; and whether or not one accepts his
interpretation of gnosticism will depend on whether or not one agrees with
him that his particular worldview (i.e., a mixture of esotericism, *Naturphilosophie*, 19th-century vitalism, and elements of occultism) is a correct
expression of a "universal" experience of the Self. In other words: accepting
Jung's interpretation of ancient gnosticism means accepting Jung's religious
worldview. From a historical perspective, far more significant than Jung's
alleged encounter with his own self is his encounter with the writings of G.R.S.
Mead. Mead was a theosophist and a prolific scholar of gnosticism, hermeticism, orphism and early Christianity; and he is identified by Noll as 'an enormous—but still unacknowledged—influence on Jung'[440]. Jung's personal library
contained no less than eighteen books written by Mead, including his well-
known study of gnosticism entitled *Fragments of a Faith Forgotten* (1906),
books with titles such as *The Gnostic Crucifixion* (1907), *The Gnostic John
the Baptizer* (1924), *Simon Magus: An Essay* (1892), *Pistis Sophia: A Gnostic Miscellany* (1921), and the 3-volume *Thrice-Greatest Hermes* (1906)[441].
Mead seems to have been responsible, more than anybody else, for introducing
Jung to gnosticism and hermeticism; and Jung has continued to quote Mead's
publications from 1911 until the end of his life. Noll is right when he expresses surprise that 'Most scholars who analyze the Gnostic elements in Jung's
work ignore the materials that initially attracted Jung to Gnosticism—Mead's
"occult" writings—and instead focus on mainstream academic scholars of
Gnosticism (such as Gilles Quispel) who entered Jung's life much later. Despite
his importance, Mead is not even mentioned, for example, in Robert Segal,
The Gnostic Jung'[442]. A profound analysis, both of Jung's interpretation of
gnosticism and of the question in what sense he was himself a "gnostic", certainly cannot ignore the relationship between Mead and Jung; and such a study
will have to take the cultural impact of 19th-century occultism more seriously than has been done in the past.

There is strong evidence to suggest that Jung's interpretation of alchemy has
a similar background as his interpretation of gnosticism. Dan Merkur has
recently attempted to prove that spiritual alchemy did not exist before the 16th
century, thus attacking Jung's assumption that medieval alchemy built a historical bridge between ancient gnosticism and his own analytical psychology[443]. Although early alchemists did use religious symbolism, there is no evidence, according to Merkur, that they understood the alchemical process as

---

[440] Noll, *Jung Cult*, 69.
[441] Noll, *Jung Cult*, 326 nt 28.
[442] Noll, *Jung Cult*, 326 nt 28.
[443] Merkur, *Gnosis*, chs. 2-4.

taking place simultaneously on a material and a spiritual level. Thus, the spiritual alchemy which Jung saw as a perfect exemplification of the psychological process of individuation was an "esoteric" innovation of the 16th century. Whether or not Merkur's arguments are fully convincing is less important here than his highlighting of Mary Ann Atwood, *née* South (1817-1910) as the author who laid the earliest foundations for Jung's theory, in her influential *A Suggestive Inquiry into "The Hermetic Mystery"*, published anonymously in 1850[444]. Joscelyn Godwin connects Mary Ann Atwood with the circle of James Pierrepont Greaves (1777-1842), an English Behmenist[445] who, incidentally, seems to have been an important source for Emerson's knowledge of Böhme[446]. She was especially influenced by Lorenz Oken's *Elements of Physio-philosophy*, a characteristic work of German *Naturphilosophie* available to her in the English translation of 1847[447]. During the 1840s, Atwood fell under the spell of popular mesmerism and began to experiment with trance states. She and her father, who shared her interests, concluded that mesmeric trance states could provide 'a short cut to mystical experience'. Given a context dominated by German esotericism (Böhmian theosophy, Romantic *Naturphilosophie*, Mesmerism) it is not surprising that they saw the alchemists and hermetic philosophers as the primary examples of true mysticism. Jung knew Atwood's book, but refers to it in disparaging terms which are interesting for us in more than one sense: 'a thoroughly medieval production garnished with would-be theosophical explanations as a sop to the syncretism of the new age'[448]. Certainly, it was to be the fate of *A Suggestive Inquiry* to appeal less to scholars than to occultists[449]. A second early precedent of Jung's approach to alchemy was Ethan Allen Hitchcock (1798-1870), an enthusiast of Hermeticism, Swedenborg and Masonry, whose *Remarks upon Alchemy and the Alchemists* appeared seven years after Atwood's book[450]. Hitchcock's thesis was 'that *Man* was the *subject* of Alchemy; and that the object of the Art was the perfection, or at least the improvement, of Man. The salvation of man ... was symbolized under the figure of the transmutation of metals'[451]. The psychoanalyst Herbert Silberer (1881-1923) acknowledged Hitchcock's merit of having been the first to rediscover that the value of alchemy went beyond chemistry and physics[452]. Sil-

---

[444] Merkur, *Gnosis*, 56-58.

[445] Böhme has often been referred to as "Behmen" in the English-speaking world, whence the common indication "Behmenism".

[446] See the discussion in Versluis, *Hermetic Book of Nature*.

[447] Godwin, *Theosophical Enlightenment*, 232-234.

[448] Jung, *Practice of Psychotherapy*, 297, as quoted in Merkur, *Gnosis*, 56.

[449] Merkur, *Gnosis*, 56.

[450] Martin, 'A History', 10-12. It is strange that Merkur refers to Martin's article but does not mention Hitchcock; Martin, in turn, does not mention Atwood.

[451] Hitchcock, *Remarks upon Alchemy and the Alchemists*, iv-v, as quoted in Martin, 'A History', 12.

[452] Martin, 'A History', 12.

berer's *Probleme der Mystik und ihrer Symbolik* (1914) is the first major psychoanalytic study of alchemy, and the English edition is known today under
the more appropriate title *Hidden Symbolism of Alchemy and the Occult Arts*[453].
Jung's reactions to Silberer's work are somewhat puzzling. Although the two
psychoanalysts corresponded about Silberer's book, Jung showed little interest in the latter's views about alchemy. It was only after reading the Chinese
alchemical text *The Secret of the Golden Flower* in 1928 that Jung allegedly
realized what Silberer had already understood seventeen years before: 'Finally, I realized that the alchemists were talking in symbols—those old acquain-
tances of mine'[454]. It is hard to believe that this had not occurred to Jung before;
one suspects, rather, that he wanted to claim the credit of having first discovered the true significance of alchemy. In any case, it is certain that Silberer's
approach to the subject was different from Jung's. Silberer tended to reduce
the meaning of alchemical symbols to psychoanalytical categories; and one is
not surprised to read that, when he had taken his life in 1923, Jung expressed
the opinion that this was the result of his overly rationalistic psychologism[455].
According to Merkur, Jung's approach was the opposite of Silberer's: 'Jung
did not apply clinical theories to alchemical data. He expressed Atwood's theories of alchemy in psychological terms and called them scientific'[456]. Whether
it were really Atwood's theories or Hitchcock's requires further investigation.
More important is the fact that *both* had come to the subject from firmly committed esoteric or occultist perspectives. The same is true, as we have seen, for
Jung himself. Although the history of spiritual and psychological interpretations of alchemy prior to Jung is in urgent need of further investigation, what
is known at present confirms my previous conclusions. Jung's view of spiritual alchemy, like his view of gnosticism, was rooted in 19th-century eso-
teric/Romantic and occultist worldviews. There is, however, an important difference between the cases of gnosticism and of alchemy. The connections
between ancient gnosticism and modern esotericism are far too tenuous to permit the claim that Jung "descended" from ancient gnosticism in a historical-
genetic sense. That a spiritual alchemy existed at least since the 16th century
is, however, undisputed; and we have seen that this tradition is an important
part of traditional esotericism. It is beyond doubt that, as such, spiritual alchemy has profoundly contributed to the emergence of the very same worldviews
from the perspective of which it has eventually come to be interpreted by Jung.
In other words: Jung's interpretation of spiritual alchemy is, in the end, essentially an esotericist's interpretation of esotericism.

---

[453] Silberer, *Hidden Symbolism*.
[454] Jung, *Memories, Dreams, Reflections*, as quoted in Martin, 'A History', 16.
[455] Martin, 'A History', 16.
[456] Merkur, *Gnosis*, 69.

Carl Gustav Jung turns out to be a direct link between the esoteric traditions in German Romantic *Naturphilosophie* and the contemporary New Age movement. His contribution consisted in his ability to present an esoteric worldview in psychological terms, thereby providing a "scientific" alternative to occultism. More importantly, he not only psychologized esotericism but he also sacralized psychology, by filling it with the contents of esoteric speculation. The result was a body of theories which enabled people to talk about God while really meaning their own psyche, and about their own psyche while really meaning the divine. If the psyche is "mind", and God is "mind" as well, then to discuss one must mean to discuss the other. Whether the ancient gnostics thought in this way must be doubted; but that the New Age movement does so is certain.

CHAPTER SIXTEEN

CONCLUSIONS:
THE NEW AGE MOVEMENT AND THE NATURE OF
NEW AGE RELIGION

> So much of twentieth century thought seems a long series of footnotes
> on last century's grand themes. Putting this with more dejection, we all
> suffer from a series of nineteenth century 'hang-overs', and whether it is
> the strange creatures called 'evolutionism', or 'romanticism', or 'Marx-
> ism', even 'psycho-analysis' (from the turn of the century), with which
> we wrestle, it is essential for the sake of our own self-knowledge to apprise
> the great trajectories of thought which lie behind our own consciousness,
> and behind the stresses and strains of our contemporary society[1].

In the three Parts of this study I have been building up a cumulative argument,
not only about the nature of New Age religion, but also about the manner in
which I believe it can most fruitfully be approached by scholars. Most of the
conclusions which have been arrived at were already formulated at various
points in the text. It is now time to see whether they can help us reach a final
conclusion about the nature of New Age religion. As announced at the end of
chapter thirteen, section 1, I suggest that the discussions contained in this study
lend support to a threefold characterization: (1) in terms of the detailed empirical description of beliefs offered in Part Two; (2) in terms of how these beliefs
represent a systematic counterreaction to existing cultural forms; (3) in terms
of how and why specific historical traditions were reinterpreted under modern
conditions, in order to formulate such a reaction.

  For the first of these, I can refer the reader to the whole of Part Two and to
the brief evaluation in chapter thirteen, section 1. Having first discussed the
ideas of the New Age movement in thematic order (Nature of Reality; Meta-
empirical and Human Beings; Matters of the Mind; Death and Survival; Good
and Evil; Visions of the Past; The New Age), I summarized the results of the
analysis in terms of five basic elements which may be regarded as constitutive
for New Age religion. They are: (1) This-worldliness, particularly of the weak
variety; (2) Holism; (3) Evolutionism; (4) Psychologization of religion and
sacralization of psychology; (5) Expectations of a coming New Age. As I pointed out, each of these five elements is far too general in itself to provide much
more than a very rough and preliminary orientation. Although all New Age
religion is (at least from the emic perspective of its adherents) "holistic" in

---

[1] Trompf, *In Search of Origins*, 16.

some sense, a variety of holistic theories exists; although New Agers share a belief in "evolution", they have different ideas about what it is, how it works and where it is going; and similar conclusions can be drawn about the other elements. With respect to the emic level of explicit ideas alone, one can certainly agree with Christoph Bochinger that '"New Age" is not an even remotely homogeneous "Weltanschauung" or Ideology'[2], and is 'composed of many heterogeneous elements'[3]. The question remains, however, what it is that nevertheless conveys the suggestion of a "movement" with common goals and aspirations. Is this just an illusion created by marketing and publishing strategies, as one may conclude from Bochinger's account? I believe that, its evident heterogeneity notwithstanding, a measure of coherence can be demonstrated even on the level of New Age beliefs. This brings me to my second and third approach to characterizing the nature of New Age religion. Firstly, the New Age movement as a whole can be defined *indirectly* as based on a common pattern of criticism directed against dominant cultural trends. Secondly, New Age religion formulates such criticism not at random, but falls back on a specific tradition: western esotericism.

New Age as Culture Criticism

Although New Age religion is not a unified ideology or *Weltanschauung*, the suggestion of common goals and aspirations can be explained by the fact that *all* New Age trends, without exception, are intended as alternatives to currently dominant religious and cultural trends. There is a persistent pattern of New Age *culture criticism*, directed against what are perceived as the dominant values of western culture in general, and of modern western society in particular. In this sense, the label "New Age" is highly appropriate, since the very aspiration to a new age implies that the old age is objected to. At the beginning of chapter six, section 2, I suggested that 'the only thing which demonstrably unites the many expressions of "holism" is their common opposition to what are perceived as *non*-holistic views, associated with the old culture which the New Age seeks to replace or transform'. I argued that all forms of New Age holism have in common a rejection of *dualism* and *reductionism*:

> The main forms of dualism for which the New Age movement tries to develop holistic alternatives are: 1. The fundamental distinction between Creator and creation, i.e. between God and nature and between God and man; 2. The distinction between man and nature, which has traditionally been conceived as a relation based on domination of the latter by the former; 3. The dualism between spirit and matter in its various derivations, from Christian asceticism to Cartesian dualism. It is generally assumed in the New Age movement that such dualistic tendencies are ultimately based on the Judaeo-Christian roots of western civilization.

---

[2] Bochinger, *"New Age"*, 135.
[3] Bochinger, *"New Age"*, 105.

Reductionism is a more recent development, associated with the scientific revolution and the spirit of modern rationalism. Its main forms are: 1. The tendency
to fragmentation, which treats organic wholes as mechanisms that can be reduced
to their smallest components and then explained in terms of the latter; 2. The tendency to reduce spirit to matter, so that spirit becomes merely a contingent
"epiphenomenon" of essentially material processes. In all these five domains, the
New Age alternatives are called "holistic". The only common characteristic of
these alternatives is that they systematically attempt—with varying degrees of
success—to avoid and replace dualism and reductionism.

It may be noted that the rejection of dualism, in all its forms, is directed prin-
cipally against dominant forms of Christianity, while the rejection of reductionism is directed specifically against modern scientific rationalism. Thus,
New Age holism emerges as a reaction to established Christianity, on the one
hand, and to rationalistic ideologies, on the other. The fact that it has to fight
on two fronts creates a certain amount of ambiguity. As a religious reaction to
rationalism and scientism, it has to demarcate itself from its principal religious
rival, Christianity; but in its reaction to traditional Christianity it frequently
allies itself with reason and science, and therefore has to demarcate itself from
rationalist and scientistic ideologies. The solution to this dilemma is, of course,
the affirmation of a "higher perspective" in which religion and science are one.
"Holism" may thus be regarded as the central core of New Age religion, *not*
in the sense that it refers to a consistent and generally-shared theory, *Weltanschauung* or ideology (which it does not), but in the sense that it is an appropriate label for a generally-shared pattern of culture criticism. To defend
"holism" in a New Age context is a short way of saying what one *rejects*. It
means that one is *against* a radically transcendent and anthropomorphic deity,
separated from human beings and from the rest of his creation, who can only
be blindly believed in but not experienced; *against* the belief that human beings
are dependent for salvation on this divine "other", and are therefore essentially powerless to create their own destiny; *against* the idea that human beings
are alienated from nature and strangers in the cosmos; *against* human attitudes
of domination and exploitation of this alienated nature; *against* the idea that
spirit and matter are separate realities, so that spirituality implies an otherworldly transcendence of matter, nature, and the cosmos; *against* religious attitudes of otherworldly asceticism suggested by such ideals of transcendence;
against the overly rationalistic "parts mentality" of traditional science, which
"murders to dissect"; *against* the denial of spirit by materialist ideologies. This
pattern of criticism, directed against what are perceived as the dominant traditions of western culture, is found throughout the materials analyzed in Part
Two of this study. It confirms that the New Age movement is indeed a heir of
the "counterculture" of the 1960s, and allows us to characterize the nature and
demarcation of New Age religion as follows:

NEW AGE AS CULTURE CRITICISM:
All New Age religion is characterized by a criticism of dualistic and reduction-
istic tendencies in (modern) western culture, as exemplified by (what is emically
perceived as) dogmatic Christianity, on the one hand, and rationalistic/scien-
tistic ideologies, on the other. It believes that there is a "third option" which
rejects neither religion and spirituality nor science and rationality, but com-
bines them in a higher synthesis. It claims that the two trends which have hit-
herto dominated western culture (dogmatic Christianity and an equally dog-
matic rationalistic/scientistic ideology) have been responsible for the current
world crisis, and that the latter will only be resolved if and when this third option
becomes dominant in society.

This first characterization of the nature of New Age religion also provides us
with initial criteria for demarcation. It implies that no group or invididual which
does not accept this core of cultural criticism, at least implicitly, can legitimately be referred to by the label "New Age".

Nevertheless, although all New Age religion falls within the perimeters
defined above, one might argue that not everything which falls within those
perimeters is necessarily "New Age". The nature of New Age religion can be
circumscribed further with reference to the *specific* traditions on which it relies
for formulating its criticism of western culture and for presenting alternatives.

New Age as Secularized Esotericism
My discussions in Part Three imply that New Age religion is not, as popularly assumed, a product of the "oriental renaissance". Oriental ideas and concepts have, almost without exception, been adopted only in sofar as they could
be assimilated into already-existing western frameworks. This has been the pattern in western esotericism since the beginning, and I know of no evidence
which suggests that the New Age movement has brought a fundamental change.
Oriental religious ideas have been adapted to a modern occidental context, and
in that process their meanings underwent subtle (and sometimes not-so-sub-
tle) changes. Both in esotericism generally and in the New Age movement particularly, the Orient has functioned mainly as a *symbol* of "true spirituality"
and as a repository of exotic terminology; its *ideas* have not fundamentally
changed those of western recipients. The basic structures of New Age religion
have emerged, practically without exception, from long-standing occidental traditions which either belong to, or are closely connected with western esotericism (*sensu* Faivre). The foundations of New Age religion were created during the late 18th and the 19th century, in the course of a process which I have
referred to as the secularization of esotericism. I have described how the new
streams of Romanticism and occultism emerged from esoteric backgrounds,
and how certain romantic and occultist traditions have been affected further
by subsequent aspects of the secularization process. Those traditions on which
the New Age movement has drawn can be characterized as western esotericism

reflected in four "mirrors of secular thought": the new worldview of "causality", the new study of religions, the new evolutionism, and the new psychologies. As far as the conditions for the emergence of New Age religion are concerned, this process was completed during the decades around 1900. Between this period and the 1970s there has certainly been as much esoteric activity as before, but I have encountered no evidence to suggest that this has resulted in more than the addition of 'footnotes on last century's grand themes'.

In chapter five I included a brief historical sketch of the period between the 1950s and the 1980s, and in that context I distinguished between a New Age *sensu stricto* and a New Age *sensu lato*. From the perspective of Part Three, it may now be added that the New Age *sensu stricto* has its principal roots in the characteristic occultist worldview of modern theosophy (particularly as presented by two of its later offshoots: the movements of Alice Bailey and Rudolf Steiner), which has not significantly been affected by the trend of "psychologization". The New Age *sensu lato*, on the other hand, is rooted first and foremost in the typically American Harmonial Religion of the New Thought variety, in which the psychological component is of fundamental importance. The former is therefore affected by three aspects of secular thought, the latter by four. Both in the New Age *sensu stricto* and *sensu lato*, the occultist element is dominant. The specifically Romantic component (exemplified by conceptions derived for example from American transcendentalism, Jungian psychology or, to some extent, Anthroposophy[4]) has contributed to New Age religion in important ways, as we have seen, but to an overriding extent it loses its specificity by being assimilated in an occultist context.

If the New Age movement is based on a popular culture criticism, as I argued, then it is important to understand why it has found these western esoteric (Romantic and occultist) traditions so especially congenial as a foundation for formulating alternatives to established Christianity and dogmatic rationalism. I suggest this may be explained by the fact that western esotericism, too, can typologically be described as an alternative "third option" in western culture. In an article entitled 'A Dynamic Typological Approach to the Problem of "Post-Gnostic" Gnosticism'[5], I argued for a general idealtypological distinction between *reason*, *faith*, and *gnosis*:

---

[4] In spite of the importance of anthroposophical Christology to the New Age *sensu stricto*, I have estimated the specific influence of anthroposophy on New Age religion as not decisive enough to necessitate a separate discussion in the previous chapter. Anthroposophy is interesting, however, because it is an occultist movement which explicitly emphasizes the western esoteric tradition and is strongly indebted to Romantic *Naturphilosophie*. Rudolf Steiner's work would be a particularly interesting case for testing my distinction between Romanticism and occultism.

[5] Hanegraaff, 'Dynamic Typological Approach', 5-43; cf. the brief version: 'Problem of "Post-Gnostic" Gnosticism'. The idea of "gnosis" as a third component of western culture was originally derived from Quispel, *Gnosis*, but I do not share Quispel's religionist presuppositions.

Reason. According to this, truth—if attainable at all—can only be discovered by making use of the human rational faculties, whether or not in combination with the evidence of the senses. In principle, knowledge based on *reason* is accessible to all human beings, and its findings can be expressed in discursive language, which makes mutual communication, and therefore discussion possible.

Faith. According to this, human reason does *not* in itself have the power to discover the basic truths about existence. The ultimate truth must be revealed to man from some transcendental sphere. This revelation can be found in traditional stories, dogmas or creeds, the pronouncements of authoritative figures, holy scriptures, etc. The common characteristic is that one has to *believe* (or "have faith") in the authority of these as means of revelation.

Gnosis. According to this, truth can only be found by personal, inner revelation, insight or "enlightenment". Truth can only be personally experienced: in contrast with the knowledge of *reason* or *faith*, it is in principle not generally accessible. This "inner knowing" cannot be transmitted by discursive language (this would reduce it to rational knowledge). Nor can it be the subject of *faith* (in the above sense) because there is in the last resort no other authority than personal, inner experience[6].

It should be emphasized that these are *ideal types*, intended as heuristic tools rather than as a description of actual historical movements. Although, in a western context, *reason* is roughly equivalent with philosophical and scientific rationalism, and *faith* with institutional Christianity, it is obvious that there have been strong rationalistic traditions in Christianity and that a reliance on authority rather than reason and observation is far from unusual in philosophy and science. Similarly, the third component of *gnosis* has been combined with *reason* and *faith* in many ways. It is therefore essential to emphasize that the three components of this typology refer not to actual historical movements, but to theoretically conceivable avenues to the attainment of truth[7]. Provided that the heuristic rather than descriptive function of the typology is perceived correctly, it can be concluded that *gnosis* has been central not only to ancient gnosticism but to western esotericism as well, in a similar manner as *reason* and *faith* have been central to philosophical and scientific rationalism and established Christianity respectively.

The importance of this typological distinction lies in the fact that the attitudes of *reason* and *faith* have generally been dominant in western culture to a much larger extent than the attitude of *gnosis*. One should be careful with referring to it as a marginal "undercurrent": an indication which is not uncommonly inspired by apologetic or polemical concerns rather than by a sober investigation of the facts (western esotericism was anything but marginal in the Renaissance period, and its academic neglect until comparatively recent times reflects mainly the fact that scholars tended to emphasize those aspects of Renaissance culture which they found congenial to their own beliefs). Nev-

---

[6] Hanegraaff, 'Dynamic Typological Approach', 10.
[7] See my later reflections on my typology: Hanegraaff, 'On the Construction'.

ertheless, the epistemological attitude of *gnosis* has certainly not determined the course of western cultural and religious history to the extent that *faith* and *reason* have. We thus get the picture of a culture dominated by the two pillars of Christianity and rationalism, plus a sort of counter-current which emphasizes inner knowledge expressed in non-discursive ways (myth, symbolism etc.). Again, it must be emphasized that the perception of this third stream as anti- or irrationalistic and vehemently opposed to Christianity is a caricature: in many cases it was a matter of emphasis rather than of a radical choice for *gnosis* and against *reason* and *faith*. The very fact that representatives of this third component were themselves products of a general culture dominated by *reason* and *faith* had as a result that they frequently defended their beliefs as eminently "reasonable" or as exemplifying the true essence of Christianity, or both. Clean and unambiguous distinctions between the three components exist in theory but not in historical reality.

The traditions based on *gnosis* can be seen as a sort of traditional western counter-culture, and this goes a long way to explaining why New Age religion expresses its own criticism of dominant western culture by formulating alternatives derived from esotericism. Like the New Age movement, western esotericism has from the beginning been characterized by an ambiguous position "in between" official religion and science. Like the New Age movement, it is critical of dualism and reductionism (even if not all its alternatives are equally succesful in avoiding it), and strives for a "higher synthesis" most congenial to the epistemological attitude of *gnosis*. The fundamental complaints of New Age religion about modern western culture are similar to those of western esotericism generally; in fact, all the elements of New Age culture criticism listed above would be quite acceptable to western esotericists in earlier periods. There is, however, one fundamental distinction: traditional esoteric alternatives to dominant cultural and religious trends were formulated in the context of an "enchanted" worldview, while the New Age movement has adopted that worldview in a thoroughly secularized fashion. This, I suggest, is the second decisive characteristic of New Age religion (apart from its nature as a popular movement of culture criticism): a characteristic which, from different perspectives, might be seen as its basic irony by some, and as its principal strength by others:

NEW AGE AS SECULARIZED ESOTERICISM
All New Age religion is characterized by the fact that it expresses its criticism of modern western culture by presenting alternatives derived from a secularized esotericism. It adopts from traditional esotericism an emphasis on the primacy of personal religious experience and on this-worldly types of holism (as alternatives to dualism and reductionism), but generally reinterprets esoteric tenets from secularized perspectives. Since the new elements of "causality", the study of religions, evolutionism, and psychology are fundamental components,

New Age religion cannot be characterized as a return to pre-Enlightenment worldviews but is to be seen as a qualitatively new syncretism of esoteric and secular elements. Paradoxically, New Age criticism of modern western culture is expressed to a considerable extent on the premises of that same culture.

The addition of this element makes it possible to summarize my conclusions about the nature of the New Age movement in a brief formula:

The New Age movement is characterized by a popular western culture criticism expressed in terms of a secularized esotericism.

Thus, in spite of the extreme variation of New Age beliefs, the central question of this study (see Introduction) has been answered affirmatively: it is possible to speak of *one* New Age movement not only on the basis of "association by contiguity" but also on the basis of "association by similarity" (of beliefs). New Age beliefs are similar not because they have the same positive contents but because they are opposed to the same things.

A Final Problem: The Demarcation in Time

It seems to me that, in terms of the *beliefs* of the New Age movement (which have been the focus of this study), the definition just given is as far as one can go. However, it still leaves one highly important question unanswered. It defines the nature of New Age religion and enables us to demarcate it from other phenomena (i.e. movements which are not a reflection of popular culture criticism; or, if they are, do not fall back on secularized esotericism); but, once again, although it defines the perimeters within which all New Age religion falls, one may still legitimately object that, reversely, not everything which falls within those perimeters should be referred to as "New Age". The reason is that the definition contains insufficient criteria for demarcating the New Age movement in *time*. According to my analysis, the process of the secularization of esotericism was completed not later than the early decades of the 20th century; and I have observed that, by this time, the elements of New Age religion were already so fully present that one may wonder whether the New Age movement since the later 1970s has brought anything new at all. Indeed, I have encountered no evidence that it did bring something *essentially* new. This has, of course, far-reaching implications. It would seem to imply that what is called New Age religion has actually been with us during most of this century. And, even more serious: the definition would seem to imply that movements such as (for example) anthroposophy, which emerged far before the term "New Age" became current, can legitimately be referred to as "New Age" movements. I have, however, rejected such a use of the term in the Introduction of this study.

The dilemma can be resolved with reference to my discussions in the Introduction, combined with the review (chapter thirteen, section 2) of J. Gordon Melton's distinction between the "substance" of the New Age and New Age as a "movement". The subject of this study, and the final definition given above, concern the "substance" of New Age religion (i.e., its belief structure). My findings leave no other option than to conclude that the perspective which we have referred to as "New Age religion" was born in the 19th century and had reached maturity not later than the beginning of the 20th[8]. The "cultic milieu" described by Colin Campbell continued this same perspective. In the Introduction I have argued that it was only in the second half of the 1970 that this cultic milieu "became conscious of itself as constituting a more or less unified movement", and I proposed to take this phenomenon as the beginning of the New Age movement in a precise sense. If this is to be combined with the definition given above, we have no other option than making a distinction between *New Age religion* (i.e., the general type of culture criticism based on a foundation of secularized esotericism) and the *New Age movement* specifically. Although the "substance" of New Age religion has long been present, those who adhered to it clearly began to perceive themselves as being part of a "movement" approximately in the second half of the 1970s. This distinction is compatible with my repeated emphasis in the Introduction that the analysis of the present study concerns only the level of New Age *ideas*, on the understanding that 'a definitive and complete view of the New Age movement would require the combination of several methodologies, focusing on different dimensions of the New Age'. Indeed, we find that a study of New Age ideas allows us to define the essential nature of the New Age movement, but gives us no convincing arguments to demarcate that movement from other movements which fall under the definition. The question now arises whether, under these conditions, one should continue referring to the whole field falling under the definition by the name "New Age religion". I have consistently used that indication because it is, indeed, the type of religion characteristic of the New Age movement; but since it has turned out to be characteristic not of that movement only but of other movements as well, I suggest that the term "secularized esotericism" may ultimately be more appropriate.

This combination of the analysis of New Age *religion*, on the one hand, and the additional demarcation of the New Age *movement*, on the other, makes possible a final further development of my definition:

The New Age movement is the cultic milieu having become conscious of itself, in the later 1970s, as constituting a more or less unified "movement". All manifestations of this movement are characterized by a popular western culture criticism expressed in terms of a secularized esotericism.

---

[8] *Contra* Heelas, *New Age Movement*, ch. 2. One is surprised to read that, according to Heelas, 'the New Age ... has been around for a very long time indeed. The Upanishads, for example, include much the same kind of spirituality as that which is in evidence today'.

Postscript

In 1976, the sociologist Robert N. Bellah speculated about the future. Concentrating on American culture, he perceived three possible options: a "liberal" scenario according to which society 'would continue as in the past to devote itself to the accumulation of wealth and power. The mindless rationalization of means and the lack of concern with ends would only increase as biblical religion and morality continue to erode'[9]; a "neo-fundamentalist" scenario according to which a complete breakdown of society would be followed by a 'relapse into traditional authoritarianism'[10], most probably dominated by Right-wing protestantism; and an unlikely but perhaps not impossible "revolutionary" scenario according to which the alternative movement would succeed in renewing society and actually bring in a new age[11]. Almost twenty years later, we can conclude that western culture is still unfolding in accordance with the "liberal" scenario, and that Bellah's neo-fundamentalist backlash remains a distinct possibility. The New Age has not arrived, but the alternative movement increasingly shows symptoms of being annexed by liberal utilitarian culture (a possibility which was astutely recognized by Bellah[12]). Given the extent to which western esotericism has allowed itself to be affected by the general secularization process during the 19th century, there is little reason to expect that its contemporary occultist heirs will prove invulnerable to contemporary forces such as the ethos of commerce which is dominating western society in the mid-1990s. The New Age started out as an idealistic movement, inspired by deeply-felt concern about the world situation, and firmly committed to change. This idealism still survives in some quarters; but now, in the mid-1990s, it may legitimately be doubted whether a New Age movement which has become increasingly subservient to the laws of the marketplace is likely to provide a viable alternative to a culture of liberal utilitarianism. No student of the New Age can fail to ask himself, sooner or later, whether the movement is a force for better or worse, but in attempting to answer such questions one will move beyond the confines of the present study. The historian's concern is with interpreting the past and the present, not with predicting the future; and it is certainly not the business of the scholar of religions to adjudicate the ultimate validity of contemporary religious beliefs, whether commercialized or not. What he can and should do, however, is indicate what has been lost in the course of the processes by which modern movements and individuals have attempted to preserve the "wisdom of the past". With respect to that question, I find it appropriate to step aside and leave the final word to

---

[9] Bellah, 'New Religious Consciousness', 349.
[10] Bellah, 'New Religious Consciousness', 350.
[11] Bellah, 'New Religious Consciousness', 351-352.
[12] Bellah, 'New Religious Consciousness', 345-346.

the person who must be recognized as this century's greatest scholar of eso-tericism (in an inclusive sense[13]). In an interview of 1975, Gershom Scholem demarcated the Kabbalistic viewpoint from the perspective which has become common to modern secular society; and he did this in terms which are equal-ly applicable to Christian (and Islamic) esotericism. It seems to me that his remarks catch the essence of what threatens to be lost in the process of secu-larization:

> Modern man lives in a private world of his own, enclosed within himself, and modern symbolism is not objective: it is private; it does not obligate. The sym-bols of the kabbalists, on the other hand, did not speak only to the private indi-vidual—they displayed a symbolic dimension to the whole world.
> The question is whether in the reality in which today's secular person lives, this dimension will be revealed again.
> I was strongly criticized when I dared to say that Walt Whitman's writings con-tain something like this. Walt Whitman revealed in an utterly naturalistic world what kabbalists and other mystics revealed in their world.
> Today we are living in an altogether different time. Technology is proceeding—leaping—forward with giant strides, but the problem remains.
> If humanity should ever lose the feeling that there is mystery—a secret—in the world, then it's all over with us[14].

Private symbolism and the dissipation of mystery are indeed connected. The New Age movement tends to make each private individual into the center of his or her symbolic world; and it tends to seek salvation in universal explana-tory systems which will leave no single question of human existence unan-swered, and will replace mystery by the certainty of perfect knowledge. The reader of this study will have to make up his or her mind about whether the attainment of such knowledge would save the world or, instead, deprive it of all meaning.

---

[13] See the possibility of understanding the term "esotericism" as referring to all three scrip-tural traditions (Judaism, Christianity, Islam), as explained in chapter fourteen nt 12. For Scholem as a scholar of Jewish esotericism, rather than Jewish mysticism, see Dan, 'In Quest', 62-63; Hanegraaff, 'Empirical Method'; id., 'On the Construction'.

[14] Scholem, 'With Gershom Scholem', 48.

APPENDIX

Primary New Age Sources (in alphabetical order)

AC Marilyn Ferguson, *The Aquarian Conspiracy: Personal and Social Transformation in the 1980s* (1980), Paladin. Grafton Books: London etc. London 1982.

AE Peter Russell, *The Awakening Earth: The Global Brain* (1982), Ark: London etc. 1984.

AP Ken Wilber, *The Atman Project: A Transpersonal View of Human Development*, The Theosophical Publishing House: Wheaton/ Madras/London 1980.

AS Stanislav Grof, *The Adventure of Self-Discovery: Dimensions of Consciousness and New Perspectives in Psychotherapy and Inner Exploration*, State Univ. of New York Press: Albany 1988.

BB Stanislav Grof, *Beyond the Brain: Birth, Death and Transcendence in Psychotherapy*, State Univ. of New York Press: Albany 1985.

BQ Michael Talbot, *Beyond the Quantum* (1987), Bantam Books: Toronto etc. 1988

CCC Matthew Fox, *The Coming of the Cosmic Christ: The Healing of Mother Earth and the Birth of a Global Renaissance*, Harper: San Francisco 1988.

cht (Div. authors), 'Commentaries on the Holographic Paradigm', in: HP

CiM (Anonymous), *A Course in Miracles: The Text, Workbook for Students and Manual for Teachers* (1975), Arkana 1985.
  CiM:T Text
  CiM:WfS Workbook for Students
  CiM:MfT Manual for Teachers

CNA David Spangler, *Channeling in the New Age*, Morningtown Press: Issaquah 1988.

cr Marilyn Ferguson, 'Karl Pribram's Changing Reality', in: HP

CS Matthew Fox, *Creation Spirituality: Liberating Gifts for the Peoples of the Earth*, Harper: San Francisco 1991.

CV Shakti Gawain, *Creative Visualization* (1979), Bantam Books: Toronto etc. 1982.

DD Starhawk, *Dreaming the Dark: Magic, Sex and Politics* (1982), new ed. Beacon Press: Boston 1988.

DL Shirley MacLaine, *Dancing in the Light*, Bantam Books: Toronto etc. 1985.

DWYC Shirley MacLaine, *Dance While You Can*, Bantam Books: New York etc. 1991.

EAM Marian Green, *Experiments in Aquarian Magic: A Guide to the Mag-*

ical Arts and Skills that will unlock the Secrets of the 'Gods for the Future', Aquarian Press: Wellingborough 1985.

ECA Edgar Evans Cayce, *Edgar Cayce on Atlantis*, Warner Books: New York 1968.

ECDS Glenn D. Kittler, *Edgar Cayce on the Dead Sea Scrolls*, Warner Books: New York 1970.

ECJC Anne Read, *Edgar Cayce on Jesus and his Church*, Warner Books: New York 1970.

ECMM Henry Reed, *Edgar Cayce on Mysteries of the Mind* (1989), Aquarian Press 1990.

ECR Hugh Lynn Cayce, *The Edgar Cayce Reader*, Warner Books: New York 1969.

ECRe Noel Langley, *Edgar Cayce on Reincarnation* (1967), Aquarian Press: Wellingborough 1989.

ECSJ Jeffrey Furst, *Edgar Cayce's Story of Jesus*, Berkley Publ.: New York 1968.

ECSU Lin Cochran, *Edgar Cayce on Secrets of the Universe* (1989), Aquarian Press 1990.

EiG George Trevelyan, *Exploration into God*, Gateway Books: Bath 1991.

ENF Chris Griscom, *Ecstasy is a New Frequency: Teachings of the Light Institute*, Simon & Schuster: New York etc. 1987.

EtE Ken Wilber, *Eye to Eye: The Quest for the New Paradigm*, Expanded ed. Shambhala: Boston & Shaftesbury 1990

euu David Bohm & Renée Weber, 'The Enfolding-Unfolding Universe', in: HP.

f Karl Pribram, 'What the Fuss is all about', in: HP

GAAM Marian Green, *The Gentle Arts of Aquarian Magic: Magical Techniques to help you master the Crafts of the Wise*, Aquarian Press: Wellingborough 1987.

GMC Willis Harman, *Global Mind Change: The Promise of the Last Years of the Twentieth Century*, Knowledge Systems: Indianapolis 1988.

GW Shirley MacLaine, *Going Within: A Guide for Inner Transformation*, Bantam Books: New York etc. 1989.

HBWM Zsuzsanna Budapest, *The Holy Book of Women's Mysteries* (1980), repr. (in one volume) Wingbow Press: Berkeley 1989.

HHC Ken Keyes, *Handbook to Higher Consciousness*, Love Line Books: Coos Bay 1975.

HP Ken Wilber (ed.), *The Holographic Paradigm and other Paradoxes: Exploring the Leading Edge of Science*, Shambhala: Boston & London 1985.

HU Michael Talbot, *The Holographic Universe*, Grafton Books: London 1991.

IAP Shirley MacLaine, *It's All in the Playing*, Bantam Books: Toronto etc. 1987.

isio David Bohm & Renée Weber, 'The Implicate and the Super-Implicate Order', in: Renée Weber (ed.), *Dialogues with Scientists and Sages: The Search for Unity*, Routledge & Kegan Paul: London & New York 1986.

LJ   Sanaya Roman, *Living with Joy: Keys to Personal Power & Spiritual Transformation*, H.J.Kramer: Tiburon 1986.

LL   Shakti Gawain (with Laurel King), *Living in the Light: A Guide to Personal and Planetary Transformation* (1986), repr. Eden Grove Editions: London 1988.

LTMW   Janet & Stewart Farrar, *The Life and Times of a Modern Witch* (1987), repr. Phoenix Publ. Inc.: Custer 1988.

MAA   Marian Green, *Magic for the Aquarian Age: A Contemporary Textbook of Practical Magical Techniques*, Aquarian Press: Wellingborough 1983.

mf   Rupert Sheldrake, 'Morphogenetic Fields: Nature's Habits', in: Renée Weber (ed.), *Dialogues with Scientists and Sages: The Search for Unity*, Routledge & Kegan Paul: London & New York 1986.

mmc   David Bohm & Renée Weber, 'Mathematics: The Scientist's Mystic Crystal', in: Renée Weber (ed.), *Dialogues with Scientists and Sages: The Search for Unity*, Routledge & Kegan Paul: London & New York 1986.

mmf   Rupert Sheldrake & David Bohm, 'Matter as a Meaning Field', in: Renée Weber (ed.), *Dialogues with Scientists and Sages: The Search for Unity*, Routledge & Kegan Paul: London & New York 1986.

MNP   Michael Talbot, *Mysticism and the New Physics* (1980), Routledge & Kegan Paul: London 1981.

NA   David Spangler, *The New Age*, Morningtown Press: Issaquah 1988.

NB   Ken Wilber, *No Boundary: Eastern and Western Approaches to Personal Growth*, Shambhala: Boston & London 1985.

NPR   Jane Roberts, *The Nature of Personal Reality: A Seth Book*, Bantam Books: New York etc. 1978.

npr   (Anonymous), 'A New Perspective on Reality', in: HP

NSL   Rupert Sheldrake, *A New Science of Life: The Hypothesis of Formative Causation* (1981), Paladin Grafton Books: London etc. 1987.

OB   Matthew Fox, *Original Blessing: A Primer in Creation Spirituality, Presented in Four Paths, Twenty-Six Themes, and Two Questions*, Bear & Co.: Santa Fe 1983.

OC   Ilya Prigogine & Isabelle Stengers, *Order out of Chaos: Man's New Dialogue with Nature* (1984), Fontana: London 1985.

OL   Shirley MacLaine, *Out on a Limb*, Bantam Books: Toronto etc. 1983.

OR   George Trevelyan, *Operation Redemption: A Vision of Hope in an Age of Turmoil* (1981), Stillpoint Publ.: Walpole 1985

OtC   Sanaya Roman & Duane Packer, *Opening to Channel: How to Connect with your Guide*, H.J.Kramer: Tiburon 1987.

PH   Jean Houston, *The Possible Human: A Course in Extending your Physical, Mental, and Creative Abilities*, J.P.Tarcher Inc.: Los Angeles 1982.

pm   David Bohm & Renée Weber, 'The Physicist and the Mystic', in: HP

PP   Rupert Sheldrake, *The Presence of the Past: Morphic Resonance and the Habits of Nature* (1988), Vintage Books. Random House: New York 1989.

PPA   Sanaya Roman, *Personal Power through Awareness: A Guidebook for Sensitive People*, H.J.Kramer: Tiburon 1986.

PR   Murry Hope, *The Psychology of Ritual*, Element Books: Longmead 1988.

PST   Eva Pierrakos, *The Pathwork of Self-Transformation*, Bantam Books: New York etc. 1990.

QQ   Ken Wilber, *Quantum Questions: Mystical Writings of the World's Great Physicists*, Shambhala: Boston & London 1985.

R   (Anonymous), *Ramtha* (Steven Lee Weinberg, ed.), Sovereignty: Eastsound 1986.

RBNA   David Spangler, *Revelation: The Birth of a New Age* (1976), Findhorn Foundation: The Park, Forres 1977.

RG   Shakti Gawain, *Return to the Garden: A Journey of Discovery*, New World Library: San Rafael 1989.

RI   (Anonymous), *Ramtha: An Introduction* (Steven Lee Weinberg, ed.), Sovereignty: Eastsound 1988.

RIC   (Anonymous), *Ramtha Intensive: Change, The Days to Come*, Sovereignty: Eastsound 1987.

RN   Rupert Sheldrake, *The Rebirth of Nature: The Greening of Science and God*, Bantam Books: New York etc. 1991.

rn   Ilya Prigogine, 'The Reenchantment of Nature', in: Renée Weber (ed.), *Dialogues with Scientists and Sages: The Search for Unity*, Routledge & Kegan Paul: London & New York 1986.

RNA   Leonard Orr & Sondra Ray, *Rebirthing in the New Age* (1977), repr. Celestial Arts: Berkeley 1983.

RR   (Anonymous), *The Revelation of Ramala*, C.W.Daniel Co.: Saffron Walden 1978.

RS   David Spangler, *The Rebirth of the Sacred*, Gateway Books: London 1984.

RU   Arthur M. Young, *The Reflexive Universe: Evolution of Consciousness*, Robert Briggs Ass.: Lake Oswego 1976.

RW   David Spangler & William Irwin Thompson, *Reimagination of the World: A Critique of the New Age, Science, and Popular Culture*, Bear & Co.: Santa Fe 1991.

S   F. David Peat, *Synchronicity: The Bridge between Matter and Mind*, Bantam Books: Toronto etc. 1987.

SD   Starhawk, *The Spiral Dance: A Rebirth of the Ancient Religion of the Great Goddess* (1979), 2nd ed. Harper: San Francisco 1989.

SG   Sanaya Roman, *Spiritual Growth: Being your Higher Self*, H.J.Kramer: Tiburon 1989.

SM   Jane Roberts, *The Seth Material*, Bantam Books: Toronto etc. 1970.

smdm   David Bohm & the Dalai Lama, 'Subtle Matter, Dense Matter', in: Renée Weber (ed.), *Dialogues with Scientists and Sages: The Search for Unity*, Routledge & Kegan Paul: London & New York 1986.

SOC   David Bohm & F. David Peat, *Science, Order, and Creativity*, Bantam Books: Toronto etc. 1987.

SoC   Ken Wilber, *The Spectrum of Consciousness*, The Theosophical Publishing House: Wheaton/Madras/London 1977.

SoM   J Z Knight, *A State of Mind: My Story—Ramtha: The Adventure Begins*, Warner Books: New York 1987.

SOS   Harmon Hartzell Bro, *Edgar Cayce: A Seer out of Season*, Aquarian Press: Wellingborough 1989.

SoS   Gary Zukav, *The Seat of the Soul*, Simon & Schuster: New York etc. 1989.

SOU   Erich Jantsch, *The Self-Organizing Universe: Scientific and Human Implications of the Emerging Paradigm of Evolution*, Pergamon Press: Oxford etc. 1980.

SP   Jess Stearn, *Edgar Cayce: The Sleeping Prophet* (1967), Bantam Books: New York etc. 1968.

SS   Jane Roberts, *Seth Speaks: The Eternal Validity of the Soul* (1972), Bantam Books: Toronto etc. 1974.

SSh   Roger Walsh, *The Spirit of Shamanism*, J.P.Tarcher: Los Angeles 1990.

TD   Starhawk, *Truth or Dare: Encounters with Power, Authority, and Mystery*, Harper & Row: San Francisco 1987.

TI   Chris Griscom (with Wulfing von Rohr), *Time is an Illusion* (1986), Simon & Schuster: New York 1988.

TiR   Thomas Sugrue, *There is a River: The Story of Edgar Cayce* (1942), Dell Publ.: New York 1970.

ToP   Fritjof Capra, *The Tao of Physics: An Exploration of the Parallels between Modern Physics and Eastern Mysticism* (1975), Flamingo. Fontana: Glasgow 1983.

topr   Fritjof Capra & Renée Weber, 'The Tao of Physics Revisited', in: HP.

TP   Fritjof Capra, *The Turning Point: Science, Society, and the Rising Culture* (1982), Bantam Books: Toronto etc. 1983

UfE   Ken Wilber, *Up from Eden: A Transpersonal View of Human Evolution*, Routledge & Kegan Paul: London/Henley/Melbourne 1981.

UM   David Bohm, *Unfolding Meaning: A Weekend of Dialogue with David Bohm* (1985), Ark: London & New York 1987.

UW   Fritjof Capra, *Uncommon Wisdom: Conversations with Remarkable People* (1988), Flamingo. Fontana: London 1989.

VAA   George Trevelyan, *A Vision of the Aquarian Age* (1977), Coventure: London 1979.

VR   (Anonymous), *The Vision of Ramala*, C.W.Daniel Co.: Saffron Walden 1991.

W   Vivianne Crowley, *Wicca: The Old Religion in the New Age*, Aquar-
         ian Press: London 1989.
WA   Marian Green, *A Witch Alone: Thirteen Moons to Master Natural
         Magic*, Aquarian Press: Wellingborough 1991.
WIO   David Bohm, *Wholeness and the Implicate Order* (1980), Ark: Lon-
         don & New York 1983.
WR   (Anonymous), *The Wisdom of Ramala*, C.W.Daniel Co.: Saffron
         Walden 1986.
WS   Michael Harner, *The Way of the Shaman* (1980), repr. Harper: San
         Francisco 1990.
WW   Janet & Stewart Farrar, *The Witches' Way: Principles, Rituals and
         Beliefs of Modern Witchcraft* (1984), repr. Phoenix Publ. Inc.: Custer
         1988.
WWD   Stewart Farrar, *What Witches Do: A Modern Coven Revealed* (1983),
         repr. Phoenix Publ. Inc.: Custer 1989.
WW1   Caitlín and John Matthews, *The Western Way: A Practical Guide to
         the Western Mystery Tradition I: The Native Tradition*, Arkana: Lon-
         don 1985.
WW2   Caitlín and John Matthews, *The Western Way: A Practical Guide to
         the Western Mystery Tradition II: The Hermetic Tradition*, Arkana:
         London 1986.
YHL   Louise L. Hay, *You can Heal your Life* (1984), repr. Eden Grove
         Editions: London 1988.

BIBLIOGRAPHY

* The bibliography contains all primary and secondary source materials mentioned in the text and footnotes, with the exception of the primary New Age sources which formed the basis of the analysis in Part Two and which are referred to by abbreviations. For these: see the Appendix.

ABRAMS, M. H., *Natural Supernaturalism: Tradition and Revolution in Romantic Literature*, W.W.Norton & Co.: New York & London 1971.

ACKOFF, Russell, *Redesigning the Future*, New York 1974.

ADLER, Margot, *Drawing down the Moon: Witches, Druids, Goddess-Worshippers, and Other Pagans in America Today*, 2nd ed. Beacon Press: Boston 1986.

———, 'A Response', *Journal of Feminist Studies in Religion* 5:1 (1989), 97-100.

AGRIPPA, Cornelius, *De occulta philosophia: Libri tres* (V. Perrone Compagni, ed.), E.J.Brill: Leiden/New York/Köln 1992.

AHLSTROM, Sydney E., *A Religious History of the American People*, Yale Univ. Press: New Haven & London 1972.

ALBANESE, Catherine L., *Corresponding Motion: Transcendental Religion and the New America*, Temple Univ.Press: Philadelphia 1977.

———, 'Physic and Metaphysic in Nineteenth-Century America: Medical Sectarians and Religious Healing', *Church History* 55 (1986), 489-502.

———, 'Foreword', in: Bednarowski, *New Religions*.

———, *Nature Religion in America: From the Algonkian Indians to the New Age*, Univ. of Chicago Press: Chicago & London 1990.

———, 'The Magical Staff: Quantum Healing in the New Age', in: Lewis & Melton, *Perspectives*, 68-84.

———, 'On the Matter of Spirit: Andrew Jackson Davis and the Marriage of God and Nature', *Journal of the American Academy of Religion* 60:1 (1992), 1-17.

ALEXANDER, Gary T., 'William James, the Sick Soul, and the Negative Dimensions of Consciousness: A Partial Critique of Transpersonal Psychology', *Journal of the American Academy of Religion* 48:2 (1980), 191-205.

ALEXANDER, Kay, 'Roots of the New Age', in: Lewis & Melton, *Perspectives*.

ALEXANDRIAN, *Histoire de la philosophie occulte* (1983), repr. Éditions Payot & Rivages: Paris 1994.

AMADOU, Robert, *L'occultisme: Esquisse d'un monde vivant*, Julliard: Paris 1950.

AMRITO, Swami Deva (Jan Foudraine), *Struikelen over waarheid: over Krishnamurti, Ken Wilber, Da Free John en Gerard Reve*, Ankh-Hermes: Deventer 1982.

ANDERSON, Rodger, 'Channeling', *Parapsychology Review* 19:5 (1988), 6-9.

ANKERSMIT, F. R., *Denken over geschiedenis: Een overzicht van moderne geschiedfilosofische opvattingen*, Wolters-Noordhoff: Groningen 1984.

ANONYMUS, *Index to the Secret Doctrine by H.P.Blavatsky*, The Theosophy Company: Los Angeles & Bombay 1939.

———, 'Witchcraft (Wicca), Neopaganism and Magick', in: Melton, *Encyclopedic Handbook* (ed. 1986).

———, 'Capra und Gorbatschow', *Materialdienst der EZW* 54:5 (1991), 152-154.

ANONYMUS (ED.), *The Spiritual in Art: Abstract Painting 1890-1985*, Abbeville: New York 1986.

———, *Présence d'Hermes Trismégiste* (Cahiers de l'Hermétisme), Albin Michel: Paris 1988.

——, *Hermes Trismegistus: Pater Philosophorum. Tekstgeschiedenis van het Corpus Hermeticum* (Exhibition Catalogue of the Bibliotheca Philosophica Hermetica, Amsterdam), Amsterdam 1990.

ANTHONY, Dick & Bruce ECKER, 'The Anthony Typology: A Framework for assessing Spiritual and Consciousness Groups', in: Dick Anthony, Bruce Ecker & Ken Wilber, *Spiritual Choices: The Problems of Recognizing Authentic Paths to Inner Transformation*, Paragon: New York 1987.

ANTONIO, Michael D', *Heaven on Earth: Dispatches from America's Spiritual Frontier*, Crown publ.: New York 1992.

AYRAULT, Roger, *La genèse du romantisme allemand* vol. II, Paris 1961.

BAAL, J. van, 'Magic as a Religious Phenomenon', *Higher Education and Research in the Netherlands* 7:3/4 (1963), 10-21.

——, *Boodschap uit de stilte/Mysterie als openbaring*, Ten Have: Baarn 1991.

BAAL, J. van & W.E.A.van BEEK, *Symbols for Communication: An Introduction to the Anthropological Study of Religion*. 2nd ed. Van Gorcum: Assen 1985.

BAAREN, Th. P. van, *Voorstellingen van openbaring phaenomenologisch beschouwd: Proeve van inleidend onderzoek, voornamelijk aan de hand der primitieve en oude godsdiensten*, Schotanus & Jens: Utrecht 1951.

——, *Uit de Wereld der Religie*, Van Loghum Slaterus: Arnhem 1956.

BABBIE, Earl, 'Channels to Elsewhere', in: Robbins & Anthony, *In Gods we trust*.

BARKER, Eileen, (ed.), *New Religious Movements: A Perspective for Understanding Society*, Edwin Mellen Press: New York/Toronto 1982.

——, *New Religious Movements: A Practical Introduction*, HMSO: London 1992.

——, 'The New Age in Britain', in: Martin & Laplantine, *Le défi magique* 1, 327-337.

——, 'The Scientific Study of Religion? You Must Be Joking!', *Journal for the Scientific Study of Religion* 34:3 (1995), 287-310.

BARROW, John D. & Frank J.TIPLER, *The Anthropic Cosmological Principle*, Oxford Univ.Press: New York 1986.

BASIL, Robert, *Not Necessarily the New Age: Critical Essays*, Prometheus: Buffalo/New York 1988.

BATESON, Gregory, *Steps to an Ecology of Mind*, Ballantine Books: New York 1972.

——, 'Form, Substance, and Difference', in: *Steps*, 448-465.

——, 'Comment on part V', in: *Steps*, 465-466.

——, *Mind and Nature: A Necessary Unity*, Bantam Books: Toronto etc. 1979/1988.

BATESON, Gregory & Mary Catherine BATESON, *Angels Fear: Towards an Epistemology of the Sacred*, Bantam Books: Toronto etc. 1987.

BECKER, Carl L., *The Heavenly City of the Eighteenth-Century Philosophers*, Yale Univ.Press: New Haven & London 1932.

BECKFORD, James A., 'Holistic Imagery and Ethics in New Religious and Healing Movements', *Social Compass* 31:2/3 (1984), 259-272.

——, 'The World Images of New Religious and Healing Movements', in: Jones, *Sickness and Sectarianism*, 72-90.

BEDNAROWSKI, Mary Farrell, *New Religions and the Theological Imagination in America*, Indiana University Press: Bloomington & Indianapolis 1989.

——, 'The New Age Movement and Feminist Spirituality: Overlapping Conversations at the End of the Century', in: Lewis & Melton, *Perspectives*, 167-178.

BEEK, W. E. A. van, 'Dogon Restudied: A Field Evaluation of the Work of Marcel Griaule', *Current Anthropology* 32:2 (1991), 139-167.

——, 'Dogon religie: Afrika of Sirius?', *Religieuze Bewegingen in Nederland* 28 (1994), 99-113.

BEIT-HALLAHMINI, Benjamin, 'Psychology of Religion, 1880-1930: The Rise and Fall of a Psychological Movement', *Journal of the History of the Behavioral Sciences* 10 (1974).

BELLAH, Robert N., 'New Religious Consciousness and the Crisis in Modernity', in: Charles Y. Glock & Robert N. Bellah (eds.), *The New Religious Consciousness*, Univ. of California Press: Berkeley/Los Angeles/London 1976, 333-352.

BENZ, Ernst, 'Immanuel Swedenborg als geistiger Wegbahner des deutschen Idealismus und der deutschen Romantik', *Deutsche Vierteljahrschrift für Literaturwissenschaft und Geistesgeschichte* 19:1 (1941), 1-32.

——, *Swedenborg in Deutschland: F.C. Oetingers und Immanuel Kants Auseinandersetzung mit der Person und Lehre Emanuel Swedenborgs*, Vittorio Klostermann: Frankfurt a.M. 1947.

——, 'Die Mystik in der Philosophie des Deutschen Idealismus', in: *Schelling: Werden und Werken seines Denkens*, Rhein-Verlag: Zürich 1955, 7-27.

——, 'Die Reinkarnationslehre in Dichtung und Philosophie der Deutschen Klassik und Romantik' (orig. *Zeitschrift für Religions- und Geistesgeschichte* 9:1 (1957), repr. in: A. Resch (ed.), *Fortleben nach dem Tode* (Imago Mundi VII), Innsbruck 1980, 317-356.

——, *Theologie der Elektrizität: Zur Begegnung und Auseinandersetzung von Theologie und Naturwissenschaft im 17. und 18. Jahrhundert* (Akademie der Wissenschaften und der Literatur: Abhandlungen der Geistes- und Sozialwissenschaftlichen Klasse 12), F.Steiner: Wiesbaden 1970.

——, *Franz Anton Mesmer und die philosophischen Grundlagen des "animalischen Magnetismus"*, Akademie der Wissenschaften und der Literatur/Franz Steiner Verlag: Mainz/Wiesbaden 1977.

——, *Kosmische Bruderschaft: Die Pluralität der Welten. Zur Ideengeschichte des Ufo-Glaubens*, Aurum: Freiburg i.Br. 1978.

——, *Les sources mystiques de la philosophie romantique allemande*, Vrin: Paris 1987.

BERLIN, Isaiah, 'The Counter-Enlightenment', in: *Against the Current: Essays in the History of Ideas* (1979), repr. Penguin 1982, 1-24.

BERMAN, Morris, *The Reenchantment of the World*, Cornell University Press 1981.

BERTALANFFY, Ludwig von, *General Systems Theory*, Braziller: New York 1968.

BEVIR, Mark, 'The West turns Eastward: Madame Blavatsky and the Transformation of the Occult Tradition', *Journal of the American Academy of Religion* LXII:3 (1994), 747-767.

BIALE, David, *Gershom Scholem: Kabbalah and Counter-History*, Harvard Univ.Press: Cambridge/Massachusetts/London 1979.

BLAU, Joseph Leon, *The Christian Interpretation of the Cabala in the Renaissance*, New York 1944.

BLAVATSKY, H. P., *Isis Unveiled: A Master-Key to the Mysteries of Ancient and Modern Science and Theology* (1877), repr. Theosophical University Press: Pasadena 1972.

——, *The Secret Doctrine: The Synthesis of Science, Religion, and Philosophy* (1888), repr. The Theosophical Company: Los Angeles 1982.

——, *Collected Writings*, The Theosophical Publishing House: Wheaton n.d.

BLEEKER, C. J., *Godsdienst voorheen en thans: Beschouwingen over de structuur van het geloof*, Servire: Den Haag 1958.

BOCHINGER, Christoph, *"New Age" und moderne Religion: Religionswissenschaftliche Untersuchungen*, Chr. Kaiser: Gütersloh 1994.

BOER, Charles, 'Translator's Introduction', in: *Marsilio Ficino: The Book of Life*, Spring Publ.: Woodstock 2nd ed. 1994.

BOHM, David, 'Hidden Variables and the Implicate Order', *Zygon* 20:2 (1985), 111-124.

——, 'Response to Conference Papers on "David Bohm's Implicate Order: Physics, Philosophy, and Theology"', *Zygon* 20:2 (1985), 219-220.

BOHM, David & Mark EDWARDS, *Changing Consciousness: Exploring the Hidden Sources of the Social, Political and Environmental Crises Facing our World. A Dialogue of Words and Images*, San Francisco 1992.

BÖHME, Gernot, 'Einleitung: Einer Neuen Naturphilosophie den Boden bereiten', in: Gernot Böhme (ed.), *Klassiker der Naturphilosophie: Von den Vorsokratikern bis zur Kopenhagener Schule*, C.H.Beck: München 1989.

BONARDEL, Francoise, *L'hermétisme* (Que sais-je? 2247), Presses Universitaires de France: Paris 1985.

——, 'Alchemical Esotericism and the Hermeneutics of Culture', in: Faivre & Needleman, *Modern Esoteric Spirituality*, 71-100.

——, *Philosophie de l'alchimie: Grand oeuvre et modernité*, Presses Universitaires de France: Paris 1993.

BONIN, Werner F., 'Reinkarnationserfahrung in der transpersonalen Psychologie und unter Einfluss von Drogen', in: Andres Resch (ed.), *Fortleben nach dem Tode* (Imago Mundi Bd. VII), Innsbruck 1980, 293-315.

BONNET, Charles, *Oeuvres d'histoire naturelle et de philosophie*, Neuchâtel 1770-1783.

BORG, Meerten ter, *Een uitgewaaierde eeuwigheid: Het menselijk tekort in de moderne cultuur*, Ten Have: Baarn 1991.

BORSJE, Jacqueline, 'Vrouwenspiritualiteit: Op zoek naar binnen voor kracht naar buiten', *Religieuze Bewegingen in Nederland* 14 (1987), 7-52.

BOURGUIGNON, E., (ed.), *Religion, Altered States of Consciousness and Social Change*, Ohio Univ.Press: Columbus 1973.

——, *Possession*, Chandler & Sharp: San Francisco 1976.

BOWMAN, Marion, 'Drawn to Glastonbury', in: Ian Reader & Tony Walter (eds.), *Pilgrimages in Popular Culture,* MacMillan: London 1993, 29-62.

——, 'Reinventing the Celts', *Religion* 23 (1993), 147-156.

BRADEN, Charles S., *Spirits in Rebellion: The Rise and Development of New Thought* (1963), repr. Southern Methodist Univ. Press: Dallas 1987.

BRANDON, Ruth, *The Spiritualists: The Passion for the Occult in the Nineteenth and Twentieth Centuries*, Prometheus: Buffalo 1983.

BRAUDE, Ann, *Radical Spirits: Spiritualism and Women's Rights in Nineteenth-Century America*, Beacon Press: Boston 1989.

BREARLEY, Margaret, 'Matthew Fox: Creation Spirituality for the Aquarian Age', *Christian Jewish Relations* 22:2 (1989), 37-49.

BRIGGS, John P. & F.David PEAT, *Looking Glass Universe: The Emerging Science of Wholeness*, Simon & Schuster: New York 1984.

BROCK, Erland J. e.o. (eds.), *Swedenborg and his Influence*, Academy of the New Church: Bryn Athyn 1988.

BROEK, R. van den, 'The Present State of Gnostic Studies', *Vigiliae Christianae* 37 (1983), 41-71.

——, 'Gnosticism and Hermetism in Antiquity: Two Roads to Salvation', in: Van den Broek & Hanegraaff, *Gnosis & Hermeticism*.

BROEK, R. van den & G.QUISPEL (ed. & transl.), *Corpus Hermeticum*, In de Pelikaan: Amsterdam 1991.

BROEK, Roelof van den & Wouter J. HANEGRAAFF (eds.), *Gnosis & Hermeticism from Antiquity to Modern Times*, SUNY Press: Albany 1997.

BURNETT, David, *Dawning of the Pagan Moon*, Marc: Eastbourne 1991.

CAMPBELL, Bruce F., *Ancient Wisdom Revived: A History of the Theosophical Movement*, University of California Press: Berkeley/Los Angeles/London 1980.

CAMPBELL, Colin, 'The Cult, the Cultic Milieu and Secularization', *A Sociological Yearbook of Religion in Britain* 5 (1972), 119-136.

CAMUS, Albert, *The Myth of Sisyphus*, London 1955.

CANCIK, Hubert, 'Neuheiden und totaler Staat: Völkische Religion am Ende der Weimarer Republik', in: H.Cancik (ed.), *Religions- und Geistesgeschichte der Weimarer Republik*, Düsseldorf 1982, 176-212.

CANCIK, Hubert, Burkhard GLADIGOW & Matthias LAUBSCHER (eds.), *Handbuch religionswissenschaftlicher Grundbegriffe*, vol. I & II, W.Kohlhammer: Stuttgart etc., 1988

CARPENTER, David, 'Inspiration', in: Eliade, *Encyclopedia of Religion*.

CARPENTER, Frederick I., *Emerson and Asia*, Harvard Univ.Press: Cambridge 1930.

CASAUBON, Isaac, *De rebus sacris et ecclesiasticis exercitationes XVI. Ad Cardinalis Baronii Prolegomena in Annales*, London 1614.

CASSIRER, Ernst, *Die Philosophie der Aufklärung* (1932), Mohr: Tübingen 1973.

CELLIER, Leon, *L'épopée humanitaire et les grandes mythes romantiques*, SEDES: Paris 1971.

CHADWICK, Owen, *The Secularization of the European Mind in the Nineteenth Century*, Cambridge Univ.Press: Cambridge etc. 1975.

CHILD, A. B., *Whatever Is, Is Right*, Berry, Colby & Co: Boston 1861.

CHOWDHURY, Tineke, 'Holisme en parallellisme', in: Chowdhury e.a., *Holisme en New Age-bewustzijn*, 67-102.

CHOWDHURY, Tineke, Niek WISKERKE, Peter van ZOEST & Rob van der ZWAN, *Holisme en New Age-bewustzijn: Fenomenologische, theologische en ecologische aspecten van een nieuwe wereldbeeld*, Elka: Tilburg 1986.

CHRISTY, Arthur, *The Orient in American Transcendentalism* (1932), repr. Octagon Books: New York 1978.

CLARK, Jerome, 'Hundredth Monkey', in: Melton, Clark & Kelly, *New Age Encyclopedia*, 225-227.

——, 'Skeptics and the New Age', in: Melton, Clark & Kelly, *New Age Encyclopedia*, 417-427.

CLARK, Stephen M., 'Myth, Metaphor, and Manifestation: The Negotiation of Belief in a New Age Community', in: Lewis & Melton, *Perspectives*, 97-104.

CLEBSCH, William A., *American Religious Thought: A History*, Univ. of Chicago Press: Chicago & London 1973.

CLIFTON, Robert K. & Marilyn G. REGEHR, 'Toward a Sound Perspective on Modern Physics: Capra's Popularization of Mysticism and Theological Approaches reexamined', *Zygon* 25:1 (1990), 73-104.

COHN, Norman, *The Pursuit of the Millennium*, Secker & Warburg: London 1957.

COLEMAN, Emmette, 'The Sources of Madame Blavatsky's Writings', appendix in: Vsevolod Sergyeevich Solovyoff, *A Modern Priestes of Isis*, Longmans, Green & Co.: London & New York 1895, 353-366.

CONNER, Frederick William, *Cosmic Optimism: A Study of the Interpretation of Evo-*

lution by American Poets from Emerson to Robinson, Univ. of Florida Press: Gainesville 1949.

COPENHAVER, Brian, *Symphorien Champier and the Reception of the Occultist Tradition in Renaissance France*, Mouton: Paris/The Hague/New York 1978.

—— (ed. & transl.), *Hermetica*, Cambridge University Press: Cambridge 1992.

CORBIN, Henry, *Creative Imagination in the Sufism of Ibn 'Arabi*, Princeton University Press: Princeton 1969.

——, '*Mundus Imaginalis* or the Imaginary and the Imaginal', *Spring* (1972), 1-19.

CORSETTI, Jean-Paul, *Histoire de l'ésotérisme et des sciences occultes*, Larousse: Paris 1992.

COUDERT, Allison, *Alchemy: The Philosopher's Stone*, Boulder 1980.

——, 'Renaissance Alchemy', in: Sullivan, *Hidden Truths*, 276-281.

CRAPANZANO, Vincent & Vivian GARRISON (eds.), *Case Studies in Spirit Possession*, John Wiley & Sons: New York etc. 1977.

——, 'Spirit Possession', in: Eliade, *Encyclopedia of Religion*.

CROCE, Paul Jerome, 'A Scientific Spiritualism: The Elder Henry James's Adaptation of Emanuel Swedenborg', in: Brock e.o., *Swedenborg and his Influence*, 251-262.

CROSS, Whitney R., *The Burned-over District: The Social and Intellectual History of Enthusiastic Religion in Western New York, 1800-1850* (1950), Harper & Row: New York 1965.

CROWNFIELD, David R., 'Religion in the Cartography of the Unconscious: A Discussion of Stanislav Grof's Realms of the Human Unconscious', *Journal of the American Academy of Religion* 44:2 (1976), 309-315.

——, 'Toward a Science of Religion', in: Carl A.Raschke (ed.), *New Dimensions in Philosophical Theology* (Journal of the American Academy of Religion Studies 49:1) 1982, 3-16.

CULIANU, Ioan Petru, 'Magic in Medieval and Renaissance Europe', in: Eliade, *Encyclopedia of Religion*.

——, *Eros and Magic in the Renaissance*, Univ. of Chicago Press: Chicago & London 1987.

CULVER, Roger B. & Philip A. IANNA, *Astrology: True or False. A Scientific Evaluation*, Prometheus: Buffalo 1988.

DAN, Joseph, 'In Quest of a Historical Definition of Mysticism: The Contingental Approach', *Studies in Spirituality* 3 (1993), 58-90.

DARNTON, Robert, *Mesmerism and the End of the Enlightenment in France*, Harvard Univ.Press: Cambridge Mass. 1968.

DAVIES, Paul, *God and the New Physics*, J. M. Dent & Sons: London 1983.

——, *The Mind of God: Science and the Search for Ultimate Meaning*, Simon & Schuster: London etc. 1992.

DEGHAYE, Pierre, *La doctrine ésoterique de Zinzendorf (1700-1760)*, Klincksieck: Paris 1969.

——, *La naissance de Dieu: ou la doctrine de Jacob Boehme*, Albin Michel: Paris 1985.

——, 'Jacob Boehme and his followers', in: Faivre & Needleman, *Modern Esoteric Spirituality*, 210-247.

DESROCHE, Henri, *The Sociology of Hope* (1973), repr. Routledge & Kegan Paul: London etc. 1979.

DEUGD, C. de, *Het metafysisch grondpatroon van het romantische literaire denken:*

De fenomenologie van een geestesgesteldheid (with English summary), Wolters-Noordhoff: Groningen 1971.

DIEM, Andrea Grace & James R. LEWIS, 'Imagining India: The Influence of Hinduism on the New Age Movement', in: Lewis & Melton, *Perspectives*, 48-58.

DIJK, Denise, 'The Goddess Movement in the U.S.A.: A Religion for Women only', *Archiv für Religionspsychologie* 18 (1988), 258-266.

DINNAGE, Rosemary, *Annie Besant*, Penguin 1986.

DOBBS, Betty J. T., *The Foundations of Newton's Alchemy or, the Hunting of the Greene Lyon*, Cambridge University Press: Cambridge 1975.

DOBSON, C. C., *Did our Lord visit Britain as they say in Cornwall and Somerset?*, (orig. 1936), repr. Covenant Books: London 1989.

DODDS, E. R., 'The Astral Body in Neoplatonism', in: Dodds (ed. & transl.), *Proclus: The Elements of Theology*, Clarendon: Oxford 1963, 313-321.

DOI, Torakazu, *Das Kegon Sutra: Im Auftrag des Tempels Todaiji aus dem chinesischen Text übersetzt* (4 vols.), Tokyo 1978/1981/1982/1983.

DONGEN, Hein van & Hans GERDING, *Het voertuig van de ziel: Het fijnstoffelijk lichaam; beleving, geschiedenis, onderzoek*, Ankh-Hermes: Deventer 1993.

DRUMMOND, Richard H., *Unto the Churches: Jesus Christ, Christianity and the Edgar Cayce Readings*, A.R.E. Press: Virginia Beach 1978.

DRURY, Nevill, *The Occult Experience*, Robert Hale: London 1985.

——, *The Elements of Human Potential*, Element Books: Shaftesbury 1989.

——, *The Elements of Shamanism*, Element Books: Shaftesbury/Rockport 1989.

DUBOS, Rene, *Man, Medicine, and Environment*, Pall Mall Press: London 1968.

DÜRR, Hans-Peter & Walther Ch. ZIMMERLI (eds.), *Geist und Natur: Über den Widerspruch zwischen naturwissenschaftlicher Erkenntnis und philosophischer Welterfahrung*, Scherz: Bern/München/Wien 1989.

EDMONDS, John W. & George T. DEXTER, *Spiritualism*, Patridge & Brittan: New York 1853.

EIBACH, Ulrich, *Heilung für den ganzen Menschen? Ganzheitliches Denken als Herausforderung von Theologie und Kirche*, Neukirchener Verlag: Neukirchen-Vluyn 1991.

EILBERG-SCHWARTZ, Howard, 'Witches of the West: Neopaganism and Goddess Worship as Enlightenment Religions', *Journal of Feminist Studies in Religion* 5:1 (1989), 77-95.

ELIADE, Mircea, 'The Quest for the "Origins" of Religion', in: *The Quest: History and Meaning in Religion*, Univ. of Chicago Press: Chicago & London 1969.

——, *Occultism, Witchcraft, and Cultural Fashions: Essays in Comparative Religions*, Univ. of Chicago Press: Chicago & London 1976.

——, 'Cultural Fashions and the History of Religions', in: *Occultism, Witchcraft, and Cultural Fashions*, 1-17.

——, 'The Occult and the Modern World', in: *Occultism, Witchcraft & Cultural Fashions*, 47-68.

—— (ed.), *Encyclopedia of Religion*, New York/London 1987.

——, *Shamanism: Archaic Techniques of Ecstasy* (1964), repr. Arkana: London etc. 1989.

ELIOT, C., *Japanese Buddhism*, Routledge & Kegan Paul: London 1959.

ELLENBERGER, Henry F., *The Discovery of the Unconscious: The History and Evolution of Dynamic Psychiatry*, Harper Collins 1970.

ELLWOOD, Robert S., 'The American Theosophical Synthesis', in: Kerr & Crow, *Occult in America*, 111-134.

——, *Theosophy: A Modern Expression of the Wisdom of the Ages*, Theosophical Publishing House: Wheaton/Madras/London 1986.

——, 'How New is the New Age?', in: Lewis & Melton, *Perspectives*, 59-67.

ELLWOOD, Robert S. & Harry B. PARTIN, *Religious and Spiritual Groups in Modern America*, Prentice-Hall: Englewood Cliffs NJ 1988.

EMERSON, Ralph Waldo, *Representative Men: Seven Lectures* (The Complete Works of Ralph Waldo Emerson IV), AMS Press: New York 1979.

EMERSON, Ralph Waldo & Waldo E. FORBES (eds.), *Journals of Ralph Waldo Emerson*, Houghton Mifflin: Boston 1909-1914, vol. 9.

ERNST, Alexander, 'New Age: Ein neuer Weg zu körperlicher und seelischer Gesundheit?', *Materialdienst der EZW* 54:1 (1991), 15-24.

ERTEL, Suitbert, 'Sheldrake's morfogenetische velden getest', in: D.J.Bierman, H.van Dongen & J.L.F.Gerding (eds.), *Fysica en Parapsychologie. Tijdschrift voor Parapsychologie* 59:2/4 (1991), 26-45.

EVANS, Warren Felt, *Mental Medicine: A Treatise in Medical Psychology*, H.H.Carter: Boston 1873.

——, *Esoteric Christianity and Mental Therapeutics*. H.H.Carter: Boston 1886.

FABEL, Arthur, 'The Dynamic of the Self-organizing Universe', *Cross Currents* 37 (1987), 168-177.

FABER, Richard, 'Einleitung: "Pagan" und Neo-Paganismus. Versuch einer Begriffsklärung', in: Richard Faber & Renate Schlesier (eds.), *Die Restauration der Götter: Antike Religion und Neo-Paganismus*, Königshausen + Neumann: Würzburg 1986, 10-25.

FAIVRE, Antoine, *Kirchberger et l'Illuminisme du dix-huitième siècle*, Martinus Nijhoff: The Hague 1966.

——, *Eckartshausen et la théosophie Chrétienne*, Klincksieck: Paris 1969.

——, *L'ésoterisme au XVIIIe siècle en France et en Allemagne*, Seghers: Paris 1973.

——, 'J.C.Lavater, Charles de Hesse, et l'école du nord', *Werkgroep 18e eeuw: Documentatieblad* 23-24, mai 1974, 37-52.

——, *Mystiques, théosophes et illuminés au siècle des lumières*, Georg Olms: Hildesheim/New York 1976.

——, 'Nature: Religious and Philosophical Speculations', in: Eliade, *Encyclopedia of Religion*.

——, 'Magia Naturalis (1765): Théologie de la lumière et de l'électricité dans la "Naturphilosophie" romantique', in: *Lumière et Cosmos* (Cahiers de l'Hermétisme), Albin Michel: Paris 1981, 193-216.

——, *Accès de l'ésotérisme occidental*, Gallimard: Paris 1986.

——, 'Esotericism', in: Sullivan, *Hidden Truths*, 38-48.

——, 'Speculations about Nature', in: Sullivan, *Hidden Truths*, 24-37.

——, 'What is Occultism?', in: Sullivan, *Hidden Truths*, 3-9.

——, 'Théosophie', *Dictionnaire de Spiritualité ascétique et mystique*, Beauchesne: Paris 1990, 548-562.

——, *L'ésotérisme* (Que sais-je? 1031), Presses Universitaires de France: Paris 1992.

——, 'Genèse d'un genre narratif, le fantastique (essai de périodisation)', *La littérature fantastique* (Cahiers de l'Hermétisme), Albin Michel: Paris 1991, 15-43.

——, 'Introduction I', in: Faivre & Needleman, *Modern Esoteric Spirituality*, xi-xxii.

——, 'Ancient and Medieval Sources of Modern Esoteric Movements', in: Faivre & Needleman, *Modern Esoteric Spirituality*, 1-70.

——, 'Le courant théosophique (fin XVIe-XXe siècles): Essai de périodisation', *Politica Hermetica* 7 (1993), 6-41.

——, 'Le courant théosophique (fin XVIe-XXe siècles): Essai de périodisation' (enlarged version), *Travaux de la Loge Nationale de Recherches Villard d'Honnecourt* 29 (Grand Loge National Francaise: Neuilly-sur-Seine 1994.

——, *Access to Western Esotericism*, SUNY Press: Albany 1994.

——, *The Eternal Hermes: From Greek God to Alchemical Magus*, Phanes Press: Grand Rapids 1995.

——, 'Avant-Propos: L'ésoterisme et la recherche universitaire', in: *Accès de l'ésotérisme occidental* vol. II, Gallimard: Paris (forthcoming)

FAIVRE, Antoine & Karen-Claire VOSS, 'Western Esotericism and the Science of Religions', *Numen* 42 (1995), 48-77.

FAIVRE, Antoine & Rolf Christian ZIMMERMANN (eds.), *Epochen der Naturmystik: Hermetische Tradition im wissenschaftlichen Fortschritt*, Erich Schmidt Verlag: Berlin 1979.

FAIVRE, Antoine & Jacob NEEDLEMAN (eds.), *Modern Esoteric Spirituality*, Crossroad: New York 1992.

FAIVRE, Antoine & Wouter J. HANEGRAAFF (eds.), *Western Esotericism and the Study of Religions* (forthcoming)

FESTINGER, Leon, Henry W. RIECKEN & Stanley SCHACHTER, *When Prophecy Fails*, Univ. of Minnesota Press: Minneapolis 1956.

FESTUGIÈRE, A. J., *La révélation d'Hermès Trismégiste* (4 vols.), J.Gabalda & Cie: Paris 1942-1953 (repr. 1983).

——, *Hermétisme et mystique païenne*, Aubier-Montaigne: Paris 1967.

FEYERABEND, Paul K., 'Professor Bohm's Philosophy of Nature', in: *Realism, Rationalism and Scientific Method: Philosophical Papers* 1, Cambridge Univ.Press: Cambridge etc. 1981, 219-235.

FINGER, Joachim, *Gurus, Ashrams und der Westen: Eine religionswissenschaftliche Untersuchung zu den Hintergründen der Internationalisierung des Hinduismus*, Peter Lang: Frankfurt a.M. etc. 1987.

FLORSCHÜTZ, Gottlieb, *Swedenborgs verborgene Wirkung auf Kant: Swedenborg und die okkulten Phänomene aus der Sicht von Kant und Schopenhauer*, Königshausen & Neumann: Würzburg 1992.

FOSTER, George M. & Barbara Gallatin ANDERSON, *Medical Anthropology*, John Wiley & Sons: New York etc. 1978.

FOWDEN, Garth, *The Egyptian Hermes: A Historical Approach to the Late Pagan Mind*, Princeton Univ.Press: Princeton 1986.

FRICK, Karl R. H., *Die Erleuchteten*, Akademische Druck- und Verlagsanstalt: Graz 1973.

——, *Licht und Finsternis* (2 vols), Akademische Druck- und Verlagsanstalt: Graz 1975 & 1978.

FULLER, Jean Overton, *Blavatsky and her Teachers: An Investigative Biography*, East-West Publications: London/The Hague 1988.

FULLER, Robert C., *Mesmerism and the American Cure of Souls*, Univ. of Pennsylvania Press: Philadelphia 1982.

——, *Americans and the Unconscious*, Oxford Univ. Press: New York & Oxford 1986.

——, *Alternative Medicine and American Religious Life*, Oxford Univ. Press: New York & Oxford 1989.

GALBREATH, Robert, 'Explaining Modern Occultism', in: Kerr & Crow, *The Occult in America*, 11-37.

GALE, George, 'Chew's Monadology', *Journal of the History of Ideas* 35:1 (1974), 339-348.

GARDNER, Martin, 'Issness is her Business: Shirley MacLaine', in: Basil, *Not Necessarily the New Age*, 185-201.

GARRETT, Clarke, 'Swedenborg and the Mystical Enlightenment in Late Eighteenth Century England', *Journal of the History of Ideas* 45 (1984), 67-81.

GAULD, Alan, *A History of Hypnotism*, Cambridge Univ.Press: Cambridge 1992.

GAY, Peter, *The Enlightenment: An Interpretation I: The Rise of Modern Paganism* (1966), repr. W.W.Norton & Co.: New York/London 1977.

——, *The Enlightenment: An Interpretation II: The Science of Freedom* (1969), repr. W.W.Norton & Co.: New York/London 1977.

GEBSER, Jean, *Ursprung und Gegenwart* (3 vols.; orig. 1966), München 1986.

GEORGES, A. des, *La réincarnation des âmes: Selon les traditions orientales et occidentales*, Albin Michel: Paris 1966.

GÉRARD, René, *L'Orient et la pensée romantique allemande*, George Thomas: Nancy 1963.

GERDING, J. L. F., *Kant en het paranormale* (dissertation), Parapsychologisch Instituut: Utrecht 1993.

GLADIGOW, Burkhard, 'Pantheismus als "Religion" von Naturwissenschaftlern', in: Peter Antes & Donate Pahnke (eds.), *Die Religion von Oberschichten: Religion—Profession—Intellektualismus*, Diagonal Verlag: Marburg 1989, 219-239.

GLASENAPP, Helmuth von, *Das Indienbild deutscher Denker*, K.F.Koehler: Stuttgart 1960.

GODE-VON AESCH, A. G. F., *Natural Science in German Romanticism*, Columbia Univ. Press: New York 1941.

GODET, Alain, *"Nun was ist die Imagination anderst als ein Sonn im Menschen": Studien zu einem Zentralbegriff des magischen Denkens*, ADAG Administration & Druck AG: Zürich 1982.

GODWIN, Joscelyn, 'A New Series from Britain: "Arkana"', *ARIES: Association pour la Recherche et l'Information sur l'Esoterisme* 5 (1986), 74-80.

——, *The Theosophical Enlightenment*, SUNY Press: Albany 1994.

——, 'Hargrave Jennings and the Philosophy of Fire', in: Martin & Laplantine, *Le défi magique I*, 163-169.

GOETERS, J. F. G., 'Spiritualisten, religiöse', in: *Die Religion in Geschichte und Gegenwart*, J.C.B.Mohr: Tübingen, vol. 6, 255-257.

GOODMAN, F. D., *Ecstasy, Ritual, and Alternate Reality: Religion in a Pluralistic World*, Indiana Univ.Press: Bloomington 1989.

GOODMAN, Russell B., 'East-West Philosophy in Nineteenth-Century America: Emerson and Hinduism', *Journal of the History of Ideas* 51 (1990), 625-645.

GOODRICK-CLARKE, Nicholas, *The Occult Roots of Nazism: Secret Aryan Cults and their Influence on Nazi Ideology* (1985), repr. I.B.Tauris: London & New York 1992.

GOODSPEED, Edgar J., *Modern Apocrypha*, The Beacon Press: Boston 1956.

GOODWIN, B. C., 'A Science of Qualities', in: Hiley & Peat, *Quantum Implications*, 328-337.

GORCEIX, Bernard, *La mystique de Valentin Weigel (1533-1588) et les origines de la théosophie allemande* (thesis), Univ. of Lille 1970.

GORDON, Henry, *Channeling into the New Age: The "Teachings" of Shirley MacLaine and other such Gurus*, Prometheus: Buffalo/New York 1988.

GOUDGE, Thomas A., 'Evolutionism', in: Philip P. Wiener (ed.), *Dictionary of the History of Ideas*, vol. II, New York 1973, vol. II, 174-189.

GRANT, Joan, *Winged Pharaoh* (1937), repr. Berkley Publ.Co.: New York 1969.

GRAßL, Hans, *Aufbruch zur Romantik: Bayerns Beitrag zur deutschen Geistesge-schichte 1765-1785*, München 1968.

GRIFFIN, David Ray, 'Bohm and Whitehead on Wholeness, Freedom, Causality, and Time', *Zygon* 20:2 (1985), 165-191.

—— (ed.), *The Reenchantment of Science: Postmodern Proposals*, SUNY Press: Albany 1988.

GRIM, Patrick, *Philosophy of Science and the Occult*, SUNY Press: Albany 1990.

GROF, Stanislav, *Realms of the Human Unconscious: Observations from LSD Research*, Viking Press: New York 1975.

GROOTHUIS, Douglas, *Revealing the New Age Jesus: Challenges to Orthodox Views of Christ*, Inter-Varsity Press: Leicester 1990.

GUÉNON, René, *L'erreur spirite*, Éditions Traditionelles: Paris n.d.

——, *Le théosophisme: Histoire d'une pseudo-religion* (1922), Éditions Traditionelles: Paris 1986.

GUINET, Louis, *Zacharias Werner et l'ésotérisme maconnique*, Mouton & Co: Paris/The Hague 1962.

HAAR, G. ter, 'Gemeenschapsgodsdiensten', in: Jan Weerdenburg (ed.), *De gods-diensten van de wereld* (Utrecht University: Studium Generale Series), Utrecht 1993.

HACKETT, Rosalind I. J., 'New Age Trends in Nigeria', in: Lewis & Melton, *Per-spectives*, 215-231.

HAICH, Elisabeth, *Initiation*, repr. Seed Centre: Redway 1974.

HALLBERG, Fred W., 'Barrow and Tipler's Anthropic Cosmological Principle', *Zygon* 23:2 (1988), 139-157.

HALLENGREN, Anders, 'The Importance of Swedenborg to Emerson's Ethics', in: Brock e.o., *Swedenborg and his Influence*, 229-249.

HANEGRAAFF, Wouter J., 'Channeling-literatuur: Een vergelijking tussen de bood-schappen van Seth, Armerus, Ramala, en "A Course in Miracles"', *Religieuze Bewegingen in Nederland* 22 (1991), 9-44.

——, 'A Dynamic Typological Approach to the Problem of Post-gnostic Gnosticism', *ARIES* (Association pour la Recherche et l'Information sur l'Ésoterisme) 16 (1992), 5-43.

——, 'Esoterie, occultisme en (neo)gnostiek: Historische en inhoudelijke verbanden', *Religieuze Bewegingen in Nederland* 25 (1992), 1-28.

——, 'New Age en cultuurkritiek', in: J.W.Nienhuys (ed.), *Skepsis in de New Age* (Skeptische Notities 9), Utrecht 1993, 1-29.

——, 'In den beginne was de toorn: Het demonische bij Jacob Böhme', in: Ab de Jong & Aleid de Jong (eds.), *Kleine encyclopedie van de Toorn* (Utrechtse Theologi-sche Reeks 21), Utrecht 1993, 43-56.

——, 'The Problem of "Post-Gnostic" Gnosticism', in: Ugo Bianchi (ed.), *The Notion of "Religion" in Comparative Research: Selected Proceedings of the XVI IAHR Congress*, "L'Erma" di Bretschneider: Rome 1994, 625-632.

——, 'Het verschijnsel New Age: Hoofdlijnen en een dwaalspoor', in: Chris Doude van Troostwijk, Jurjen Beumer & Derk Stegeman (eds.), *'Wij willen het heiden-dom eeren': Miskotte in de 'nieuwe tijd'*, Ten Have: Baarn 1994), 62-104.

——, 'Nieuwe Religieuze Bewegingen', *Religieuze Bewegingen in Nederland* 29 (1994), 1-49.

——, 'Empirical Method in the Study of Esotericism', *Method & Theory in the Study of Religion* 7:2 (1995), 99-129.

——, 'From the Devil's Gateway to the Goddess Within: The Image of the Witch in

Neopaganism', in: Kloppenborg & Hanegraaff, *Female Stereotypes*, 213-242.

——, 'Krishnamurti en "het einde van de tijd": De gesprekken met David Bohm', in: Hans van der Kroft (ed.), *Waarheid zonder weg: 100 jaar Krishnamurti*, Mirananda: The Hague 1995, 170-178.

——, 'On the Construction of "Esoteric Traditions"', in: Faivre & Hanegraaff, *Western Esotericism.*

——, 'Romanticism and the Esoteric Connection', in: Van den Broek & Hanegraaff, *Gnosis and Hermeticism.*

——, 'The New Age Movement and the Esoteric Tradition', in: Van den Broek & Hanegraaff, *Gnosis & Hermeticism.*

HANKINS, James, *Plato in the Italian Renaissance*, Brill: Leiden etc. 1991.

HANSEN, George P., 'CSICOP and the Skeptics: An Overview', *The Journal of the American Society for Psychical Research* 86 (1992), 19-59.

HARRIS, Marvin, *Cultural Materialism: The Struggle for a Science of Culture*, Random House: New York 1979.

HARRISON, John S., *The Teachers of Emerson*, Haskell House: New York 1966.

HARVEY, Graham, 'Avalon from the Mists: The Contemporary Teaching of Goddess Spirituality', *Religion Today* 8:2 (1993), 10-13.

HASTINGS, Arthur, *With the Tongues of Men and Angels: A Study of Channeling*, Holt, Rinehart & Winston Inc.: Fort Worth etc. 1991.

HAWKEN, Paul, *The Magic of Findhorn*, Fontana/Collins: Glasgow 1975.

HEAD, Joseph & S. L. CRANSTON (eds.), *Reincarnation: The Phoenix Fire Mystery*, Julian Press/Crown Publ.: New York 1977.

HEELAS, Paul, *The New Age Movement: Celebrating the Self and the Sacralization of Modernity*, Blackwell: Oxford & Cambridge Mass. 1996.

HEGLER, Alfred, *Geist und Schrift bei Sebastian Franck: Eine Studie zur Geschichte des Spiritualismus in der Reformationszeit*, Freibrug i.Br 1892.

HEMMERING, Hansjörg, 'Über Glaube und Zweifel: Das New Age in der Naturwissenschaft', in: Hansjörg Hemmering (ed.), *Die Rückkehr der Zauberer: New Age. Eine Kritik*, Rowohlt: Reinbek bei Hamburg 1987, 115-185.

HEXHAM, Irving, 'The "Freaks" of Glastonbury: Conversion and Consolidation in an English Country Town', *Update* 7:1 (1983), 3-12.

——, 'The Evangelical Response to the New Age', in: Lewis & Melton, *Perspectives*, 152-163.

HICK, John, *Death & Eternal Life*, Collins & Sons: London 1976.

HILEY, B. J. & F. David PEAT, *Quantum Implications: Essays in Honour of David Bohm*, Routledge & Kegan Paul: London/New York 1987.

—— & ——, 'General Introduction: The Development of David Bohm's Ideas from the Plasma to the Implicate Order', in: Hiley & Peat, *Quantum Implications*, 1-32.

HITCHCOCK, Ethan Allen, *Remarks upon Alchemy and the Alchemists*, Boston 1857.

HOBSBAWM, Eric & Terence RANGER (eds.), *The Invention of Tradition*, Cambridge University Press: Cambridge 1984.

HOELLER, Stephen A., *The Gnostic Jung and the Seven Sermons to the Dead*, Theosophical Publ.House: Madras/London 1982.

HOLMES, Oliver Wendell, 'Agassiz's Natural History', *Atlantic Monthly* I, January 1858.

HOLMYARD, E. J., *Alchemy* (1957), Penguin 1968.

HOLT, Niles R., 'Ernst Haeckel's Monistic Religion', *Journal of the History of Ideas* 32 (1971), 265-280.

HOLZ, Hans Heinz, 'ERANOS—eine moderne Pseudo-Gnosis', in: Jacob Taubes (ed.), *Religionstheorie und politische Theologie. Bd. 2: Gnosis und Politik*, Wilhelm Fink/Ferdinand Schöningh 1984, 249-263.

HOMANS, Peter, 'Psychology and Religion Movement', in: Eliade, *Encyclopedia of Religion*.

HOOVER, Dwight, 'The Influence of Swedenborg on the Religious Ideas of Henry James, Senior', in: Brock e.o., *Swedenborg and his Influence*, 263-276.

HORN, Friedemann, 'Reinkarnation und christlicher Glaube', in: Alfons Rosenberg (ed.), *Leben nach dem Sterben*, Kösel: München 1974.

HOUGH, Peter, *Witchcraft: A Strange Conflict*, Lutterworth Press: Cambridge 1991.

HOWE, Ellic, *The Magicians of the Golden Dawn: A Documentary History of a Magical Order 1887-1923*, Samuel Weiser Inc.: York Beach, Maine 1972.

HOYNACKI, George John, 'Messianic Expectations in Non-Christian Religious Traditions', *Asian Journal of Theology* 5:2 (1991).

HUGHES, Dureen J., 'Blending with an Other: An Analysis of Trance Channeling in the U.S.' (Manuscript 1990).

HUMMEL, Reinhart, *Indische Mission und neue Frömmigkeit im Westen*, Kohlhammer: Stuttgart etc. 1980.

HUNTER, William B., 'The Seventeenth Century Doctrine of Plastic Nature', *Harvard Theological Review* XLIII (1950), 197-213.

HUTIN, Serge, *L'alchimie* (Que sais-je? 506), Presses Universitaires de France: Paris 1951.

——, *Histoire de l'alchimie: De la Science archaïque à la philosophie occulte*, Gérard & Co: Verviers 1971.

ILLICH, Ivan, *Medical Nemesis: The Expropriation of Health*, Pantheon Books: New York 1976.

INGE, W. R., 'The Idea of Progress', in: *Outspoken Essays*, 2nd. series, Longman, Green & Co: New York 1922.

ISAACS, Ernst, 'The Fox Sisters and American Spiritualism', in: Kerr & Crow, *Occult in America*, 79-110.

JACKSON, Carl T., 'Oriental Ideas in American Thought', in: Philip P. Wiener (ed.), *Dictionary of the History of Ideas* vol. 3, New York 1973, 427-439.

——, 'The New Thought Movement and the Nineteenth Century Discovery of Oriental Philosophy', *Journal of Popular Culture* 9 (1975), 523-548.

——, *The Oriental Religions and American Thought: Nineteenth-Century Explorations*, Greenwood Press: Westport & London 1981.

JACOBS, David M., 'UFOs and the Search for Scientific Legitimacy', in: Kerr & Crow, *The Occult in America*, 218-231.

JAFFé, Aniela, *Erinnerungen, Träume, Gedanken von C.G. Jung*, Rascher Verlag: Zürich & Stuttgart 1963.

JAMES, William, *The Varieties of Religious Experience: A Study in Human Nature*, ed. Collins/Fount Paperbacks 1960.

JAMMER, Max, *The Philosophy of Quantum Mechanics: The Interpretations of Quantum Mechanics in Historical Perspective*, Wiley 1975.

JANSEN, Derk, *Op zoek naar nieuwe zekerheid: Negentiende-eeuwse protestanten en het spiritisme*, Thesis Publishers: Amsterdam 1994.

JANSMA, L. G. & P. G. G. M. SCHULTEN, *Religieuze bewegingen*, Martinus Nijhoff: The Hague 1981.

—— & ——, 'Inleiding', in: Jansma & Schulten, *Religieuze bewegingen*, Martinus Nijhoff: The Hague 1981, 3-11.

JANTSCH, Erich (ed.), *The Evolutionary Vision: Toward a Unifying Paradigm of Physical, Biological, and Sociocultural Evolution* (AAAS symposium 61), Westview Press: Boulder 1981.

JANTSCH, Erich & Conrad H. WADDINGTON (eds.), *Evolution and Consciousness: Human Systems in Transition*, Addison-Wesley: Reading 1976.

JEDIN, Hubert (ed.), *Handbuch der Kirchengeschichte* vol. II/1 (1973), repr. Herder: Freiburg/Basel/Wien 1985.

JENCSON, Linda, 'Neopaganism and the Great Mother Goddess: Anthropology as Midwife to a New Religion', *Anthropology Today* 5:2 (1989), 2-4.

JENNINGS, Hargrave, *The Indian Religions or Results of the Mysterious Buddhism. Concerning that also which is to be understood in the Divinity of Fire* (1858), enlarged repr. Redway: London 1890.

JOËL, Karl, *Der Ursprung der Naturphilosophie aus dem Geiste der Mystik*, Friedrich Reinhardt: Basel 1903.

JONES, R. Kenneth, *Sickness and Sectarianism: Exploratory Studies in Medical and Religious Sectarianism*, Gower: Aldershot & Brookfield 1985.

JONSSON, Inge, *Emanuel Swedenborg*, Twayne Publ.: New York 1971.

——, 'Emanuel Swedenborgs Naturphilosophie und ihr Fortwirken in seiner Theosophie', in: Faivre & Zimmermann, *Epochen der Naturmystik*.

——, 'Swedenborg and his Influence', in: Brock e.o., *Swedenborg and his Influence*, 29-43.

JUDAH, J. Stillson, *The History and Philosophy of the Metaphysical Movements in America*, Westminster Press: Philadelphia 1967.

JUNG, Carl Gustav, 'Über das Unbewußte', *Schweitzerland: Monatshefte für Schweitzer Art und Arbeit* 4 (1918).

——, *The Practice of Psychotherapy: Essays on the Psychology of the Transference and Other Subjects* (Coll. Works 16), Princeton Univ. Press: Princeton 1966.

——, *Aion: Researches into the Phenomenology of the Self* (1959), 2nd ed. Routledge & Kegan Paul: London 1968.

——, *Mysterium Coniunctionis*, repr. Princeton Univ. Press: Princeton 1970.

——, *Memories, Dreams, Reflections*, ed. Collins/Fontana 1971.

——, 'Synchronicity: An Acausal Connecting Principle', in: *The Structure and Dynamics of the Psyche* (Collected Works 8), 2nd ed. Routledge & Kegan Paul: London 1969, 417-531.

KAMPEN, N. G. van, 'Determinism and Predictability', *Synthese* 89 (1991), 273-281.

KAMPSCHUUR, Peter, '"Ik vertrouw op het zelfhelende proces": Stanislav Grof en de nieuwe visie op psychosen', *De Ronde Tafel* 14, 1986, 14-18.

KANT, Immanuel, *Träume eines Geistersehers und andere vorkritische Schriften* (Werke in sechs Bände 1), repr. Köln 1995.

KAPLAN, Fred, '"The Mesmeric Mania": The Early Victorians and Animal Magnetism', *Journal of the History of Ideas* 35 (1974), 691-702.

KASKE, Carol V. & John R. CLARK (ed. & transl.), *Marsilio Ficino: Three Books on Life*, Medieval and Renaissance Texts and Studies: Binghamton 1989.

KAUTZ, William H. & Melanie BRANON, *Channeling: The Intuitive Connection*, Harper & Row: San Francisco 1987.

KELLEY, Donald R. (ed.), *The History of Ideas: Canon and Variations*, University of Rochester Press: Rochester 1990.

KELLY, Aidan A., 'Holistic Health', in: Melton, Clark & Kelly, *New Age Encyclopedia*, 214-219.

——, 'Neo-pagans and the New Age', in: Melton, Clark & Kelly, *New Age Encyclo-*

pedia, 311-315.

——, 'Twelve-step Programs and the New Age', in: Melton, Clark & Kelly, *New Age encyclopedia*, 463-470.

——, *Crafting the Art of Magic. Book I: A History of Modern Witchcraft 1939-1964*, Llewellyn Publ.: St. Paul, Minnesota 1991.

——, 'An Update on Neopagan Witchcraft in America', in: Lewis & Melton, *Perspectives*, 136-151.

KENT, John, 'Religion and Science', in: Ninian Smart, John Clayton, Steven Katz & Patrick Sherry (eds.), *Nineteenth Century Religious Thought in the West*, vol. III, Cambridge Univ. Press: Cambridge etc. 1985, 1-36.

KERR, Howard & Charles L. CROW (eds.), *The Occult in America: New Historical Perspectives*, Univ. of Illinois Press: Urbana & Chicago 1983.

KEYES, Ken, *The Hundredth Monkey*, Vision Books: Coos Bay 1982.

KIEFER, Klaus H., 'Goethe und der Magnetismus: Grenzphänomene des naturwissenschaftlichen Verständnisses', *Philosophia Naturalis* 20 (1983), 264-311.

KING, Francis, *Ritual Magic in England: 1887 to the Present Day*, Neville Spearman: London 1970.

KING, Ursula, *Women and Spirituality: Voices of Protest and Promise*, MacMillan: Houndmills 1989.

KIPPENBERG, Hans, 'Apokalyptik/Messianismus/Chiliasmus', in: Cancik, Gladigow & Laubscher, *Handbuch Religionswissenschaftlicher Grundbegriffe* II, 9-26.

——, *Die vorderasiatischen Erlösungsreligionen in ihrem Zusammenhang mit der antiken Stadtherrschaft*, Suhrkamp: Frankfurt a.M. 1991.

KIRVEN, Robert H., 'Swedenborg and Kant Revisited: The Long Shadow of Kant's Attack and a New Response', in: Brock e.o., *Swedenborg and his Influence*, 103-120.

KLIMO, Jon, *Channeling: Investigations on Receiving Information from Paranormal Sources*, Aquarian Press: Wellingborough 1987.

——, 'Channeling Research: A Progress Report with Recommendations', in: *Proceedings of the First International Conference in Paranormal Research*, Colorado State Univ.: Colorado 1988.

KLOPPENBORG, Ria & Wouter J. HANEGRAAFF (eds.), *Female Stereotypes in Religious Traditions*, Brill: Leiden etc. 1995.

KLUCKHOHN, Cl., 'Universal Categories of Culture', in: A.L.Kroeber e.o. (eds.), *Anthropology Today*, Chicago 1953.

KOFFEND, John, 'The Gospel according to Helen', *Psychology Today*, sept. 1980, 75-90.

KOHL, Karl-Heinz, 'Geschichte der Religionswissenschaft', in: Cancik, Gladigow & Laubscher, *Handbuch religionswissenschaftlicher Grundbegriffe* I, 217-262.

KOYRÉ, Alexandre, *Mystiques, spirituels, alchimistes du XVIe siècle allemand*, Gallimard: Paris 1971.

——, *From the Closed World to the Infinite Universe*, John Hopkins Univ.Press: Baltimore 1974.

KRANENBORG, Reender, *De andere weg van Jezus*, Ten Have: Baarn 1994.

KRISHNAMURTI, J. & David BOHM, *The Ending of Time*, Krishnamurti Foundation Trust: London 1984.

—— & ——, *The Future of Humanity*, Mirananda: The Hague 1986.

KRISTELLER, Paul O., *The Philosophy of Marsilio Ficino*, New York 1943.

——, *Eight Philosophers of the Italian Renaissance*, Stanford Univ.Press: Stanford 1964.

KÜENZLEN, Gottfried, 'Psychoboom und Weltanschaaung: Der Glaube der Humanistischen Psychologie', *Materialdienst der EZW* 48:3 (1985), 60-69.

——, 'New Age—ein neues Paradigma? Anmerkungen zur Grundlagenkrise der Moderne', *Materialdienst EZW* 49:2 (1986).

KUHN, Thomas S., *The Structure of Scientific Revolutions*, (1962), 2nd ed. Univ. of Chicago Press: Chicago 1970.

KUNZ, Dora (ed.), *Spiritual Aspects of the Healing Arts*, Theosophical Publ.House: Madras/London 1985.

KURTZ, Ernest, 'Alcoholics Anonymous: A Phenomenon in American Religious History', in: Peter Freese (ed.), *Religion and Philosophy in the United States of America* I, Verlag die Blaue Eule: Essen 1987, 447-462.

LANCZKOWSKI, G., 'Inspiration: Religionsgeschichtlich', in: *Die Religion in Geschichte und Gegenwart*, J.C.B.Mohr (Paul Siebeck): Tübingen, repr. 1986, vol. 3, 773-775.

LANKESTER, Ko, Review of Murry Hope, "The Psychology of Ritual", *Blad O* 6 (1990), 18-19.

LANTERNARI, Vittorio, *The Religions of the Oppressed: A Study of Modern Messianic Cults*, MacGibbon & Kee: London 1963.

LANWERD, Susanne, 'Zur Bedeutung von "Feministischer Spiritualität" in der Literatur des New Age', in: Peter Antes & Donate Pahnke, *Die Religion von Oberschichten: Religion—Profession—Intellektualismus*, Diagonal Verlag: Marburg 1989, 269-277.

LARSEN, Robin e.o. (eds.), *Emanuel Swedenborg: A Continuing Vision. A Pictorial Biography & Anthology of Essays & Poetry*, Swedenborg Foundation: New York 1988.

LASCH, Christopher, *The Culture of Narcissism: American Life in an Age of Diminishing Expectations*, Warner Books: New York 1979.

LASZLO, Ervin, *Introduction to Systems Philosophy*, Harper: New York 1972.

——, *The Systems View of the World*, Braziller: New York 1972.

LATTIN, Don, '"New Age" Mysticism strong in Bay Area', *San Francisco Chronicle*, april 24, 1990.

LAURANT, Jean-Pierre, *L'ésotérisme*, Les Éditions du Cerf: Paris 1993.

LEERTOUWER, L., 'Syncretisme: Over de dynamiek van religieuze verschijnselen', in: Tineke Chowdhury, Wiel Claessens & Wiel Logister (eds.), *Het kosmisch patroon: Het vele en het ene in de godsdiensten*, Tilburg University Press: Tilburg 1989, 5-20.

LEMESURIER, Peter, *This New Age Business: The Story of the Ancient and Continuing Quest to bring down Heaven on Earth*, Findhorn Press 1990.

LESHAN, Lawrence, *The Medium, the Mystic, and the Physicist*, New York 1966.

LESSING, Gotthold Ephraim, *De opvoeding van de mensheid* (J. Sperna Weiland, ed.), Het Wereldvenster: Baarn 1979.

LÉVI, Eliphas, *Dogme et rituel de la haute magie*, Germer Baillière: Paris 1856.

LEWIS, I. M., *Ecstatic Religion* (1971), 2nd ed. Routledge: London & New York 1989.

LEWIS, James R. & J.Gordon MELTON (eds.), *Perspectives on the New Age*, SUNY Press: Albany 1992.

—— & ——, 'The New Age', *SYZYGY* 1:2-3 (1992), 247-258.

LEWIS, James R., 'Approaches to the Study of the New Age movement', in: Lewis & Melton, *Perspectives*, 1-12.

—— (ed.), *The Gods have Landed: New Religions from Other Worlds*, SUNY Press:

Albany 1995.

LINDEBOOM, J., *Stiefkinderen van het christendom*, Gijsbers & van Loon: Arnhem 1973.

LOFLAND, J. & R. STARK, 'Becoming a World-saver: A Theory of Conversion to a Deviant Perspective', *American Sociological Review* 30:6 (1965).

LOVEJOY, Arthur O., 'Bergson and Romantic Evolutionism', *University of California Chronicle* 15:4 (1913), 429-487.

——, 'The Meaning of 'Romantic' in Early German Romanticism' (1916), repr. in: *Essays*, 183-206.

——, 'Schiller and the Genesis of German Romanticism' (1920), repr. in: *Essays*, 207-227.

——, 'On the Discrimination of Romanticisms' (1924), repr. in *Essays in the History of Ideas*, The John Hopkins Press: Baltimore 1948, 228-253.

——, 'Optimism and Romanticism', *PMLA* 42 (1927), 921-945.

——, 'The Meaning of Romanticism for the Historian of Ideas', *Journal of the History of Ideas* 2 (1941), 257-278.

——, *The Great Chain of Being: A Study of the History of an Idea*, Harvard Univ.Press: Cambridge etc. 1964.

LOVELOCK, James, *Gaia: A New Look at Life on Earth* (1979), repr. Oxford Univ.Press: Oxford/New York 1987.

LOVELOCK, James & Sidney EPTON, 'The Quest for Gaia', *New Scientist*, 6 februari 1975.

LUKACS, John, *Historical Consciousness: Or the Remembered Past*, (1968), repr. Schocken: New York 1985.

LUHRMANN, T. M., 'Persuasive Ritual: The Role of the Imagination in Occult Witchcraft', *Archives des Sciences Sociales des Religions* 60:1 (1985), 151-170.

——, 'Witchcraft, Morality and Magic in Contemporary London', *International Journal of Moral and Social Studies* 1:1 (1986), 77-94.

——, *Persuasions of the Witch's Craft: Ritual Magic in Contemporary England*, Harvard Univ.Press: Cambridge Massachusetts 1989.

LÜTGERT, Wilhelm, *Die Religion des deutschen Idealismus und ihr Ende* (4 vols.), C. Bertelsmann: Gütersloh 1923, 1925, 1930.

MANNING, Christel, 'Restoring the Goddess: Z Budapest and Religious Primitivism in America', in: Martin & Introvigne, *Le défi magique* 2, 183-200.

MARIN, Peter, 'The New Narcissism', *Harper's* 251 (1975), 45-56.

MARRS, Texe, *Dark Secrets of the New Age*, Westchester 1987.

——, *Mystery Mark of the New Age: Satan's Design for World Domination*, 3rd ed. Westchester 1988.

MARTIN, Jean-Baptiste & Francois LAPLANTINE (eds.), *Le défi magique. Vol. 1: Esotérisme, occultisme, spiritisme*, Presses Universitaires de Lyon, 1994.

MARTIN, Jean-Baptiste & Massimo INTROVIGNE (eds.), *Le défi magique. Vol. 2: Satanisme, Sorcellerie*, Presses Universitaires de Lyon 1994.

MARTIN, Luther H., 'A History of the Psychological Interpretation of Alchemy', *Ambix* 22:1 (1975), 10-20.

MARTIN, Rachel, 'Swedenborg, Transpersonal Psychology, and Wholeness', in: Larsen e. o., *Emanuel Swedenborg*, 207-213.

MASTERS, G. Mallary, 'Renaissance Kabbalah', in: Faivre & Needleman, *Modern Esoteric Spirituality*, 132-153.

MAYR, Ernst, 'The Idea of Teleology', *Journal of the History of Ideas* 53 (1992), 117-135.

MCCALLA, Arthur, *Expiation, Progress, and Revolution: The Philosophy of History of Pierre-Simon Ballanche* (Ph.D. diss.), University of Toronto 1992.

——, '*Palingénésie philosophique* to *Palingénésie sociale*: From a Scientific Ideology to a Historical Ideology', *Journal of the History of Ideas* 55 (1994), 421-439.

——, 'Illuminism and French Romantic Philosophies of History', in: Faivre & Hanegraaff, *Western Esotericism*.

MCDANNELL, Colleen & Bernhard LANG, *Heaven: A History*, Yale Univ.Press: New Haven & London 1988.

MCGREGOR, Geddes, *Reincarnation in Christianity: A New Vision of the Role of Rebirth in Christian Thought*, Quest Books: Wheaton, Madras & London 1978.

MCGUIRE, Meredith B., 'Religion and Healing', in: Phillip E.Hammond, *The Sacred in a Secular Age: Toward Revision in the Scientific Study of Religion*, University of California Press: Berkeley/Los Angeles/London 1985, 268-284.

MCINTOSH, Christopher, *Eliphas Lévi and the French Occult Revival*, Rider & Co.: London 1972.

——, *The Rose Cross and the Age of Reason: Eighteenth-Century rosicrucianism in Central Europe and its Relationship to the Enlightenment*, Brill: Leiden/New York/Köln 1992.

MCIVER, Shirley, *Ufology in Britain: A Sociological Study of Unidentified Flying Object Groups* (Unpubl. Ph.D. dissertation), University of York 1983.

MELTON, J. Gordon, Jerome CLARK & Aidan A. KELLY (eds.), *New Age Encyclopedia*, Gale Research Inc.: Detroit/London 1990.

——, —— & —— (eds.), *New Age Almanac*, Visible Ink Press: New York etc. 1991.

MELTON, J. Gordon (ed.), *Encyclopedic Handbook of Cults in America*, New York & London 1986.

——, 'The New Age Movement', in: Melton, *Encyclopedic Handbook*, 163-180.

——, 'A History of the New Age Movement', in: Basil, *Not Necessarily the New Age*, 35-53.

——, 'Introductory Essay: An Overview of the New Age Movement', in: Melton, Clark & Kelly, *New Age Encyclopedia*, xiii-xxxiii.

——, 'New Thought and the New Age', in: Lewis & Melton, *Perspectives*, 15-29.

——, 'Paschal Beverly Randolph: America's Pioneer Occultist', in: Martin & Laplantine, *Le Défi magique* 1, 115-129.

MERCIER, Alain, *Les sources ésotériques et occultes de la poésie Symboliste (1870-1914)*, 2 vols., A.-G.Nizet: Paris 1969 & 1974.

MERKEL, Ingrid & Allen G. DEBUS (eds.), *Hermeticism and the Renaissance: Intellectual History and the Occult in Early Modern Europe*, Washington etc., 1988.

MERKUR, Dan, *Gnosis: An Esoteric Tradition of Mystical Visions and Unions*, SUNY Press: Albany 1993.

MEYER, Donald, *The Positive Thinkers: Popular Religious Psychology from Mary Baker Eddy to Norman Vincent Peale and Ronald Reagan* (1965), rev.ed. Wesleyan Univ. Press: Middletown 1988.

MIDDLETON, John, 'Theories of Magic', in: Eliade, *Encyclopedia of Religion*.

MIDGLEY, Mary, *Evolution as Religion: Strange Hopes and Stranger Fears*, Methuen: London & New York 1985.

MIERS, Horst E., *Lexikon des Geheimwissens*, Goldman: Augsburg 1980.

MOLLENKOTT, Virginia Ramey, 'An Evangelical Feminist confronts the Goddess', *The Christian Century* october 20 (1982), 1043-1046.

MOORE, R. Laurence, 'Spiritualism', in: Edwin S.Gaustad (ed.), *The Rise of Adventism: Religion and Society in Mid-Nineteenth-Century America*, New York etc.

1974, 79-103.

——, *In Search of White Crows: Spiritualism, Parapsychology, and American Culture*, Oxford Univ.Press: New York 1977.

——, 'The Occult Connection? Mormonism, Christian Science, and Spiritualism', in: Kerr & Crow, *The Occult in America*, 135-161.

——, *Religious Outsiders and the Making of Americans*, New York & Oxford 1986.

MORRIS, Brian, *Anthropological Studies of Religion: An Introductory Text*, Cambridge Univ. Press: Cambridge etc. 1987.

MOSSE, George, *The Crisis of German Ideology: Intellectual Origins of the Third Reich*, London 1966.

MÜHLMANN, Wilhelm E., *Chiliasmus und Nativismus: Studien zur Psychologie, Soziologie und historischen Kasuistik der Umsturzbewegungen*, Dietrich Reimer: Berlin 1961.

MULLINS, Mark R., 'Japan's New Age and Neo-New Religions', in: Lewis & Melton, *Perspectives*, 232-246.

MURPHY, George L., 'Time, Thermodynamics, and Theology', *Zygon* 26:3 (1991), 359-372.

MURRAY, Margaret, *The Witch-cult in Western Europe*, (1921), repr. At the Clarendon Press: Oxford 1967.

MUTSCHLER, Hans-Dieter, *Physik—Religion—New Age*, Echter Verlag: Würzburg 1990.

NASR, Seyyed Hossein, 'Introduction', in: Seyyed Hossein Nasr (ed.), *The Essential Writings of Frithjof Schuon*, Amity House: Shaftesbury & Rockport 1986.

NEHER, A., 'Vision du temps et de l'histoire dans la culture juive', in: *Les cultures et le temps*, Paris 1975.

NELSON, Geoffrey K., *Spiritualism and Society*, Routledge & Kegan Paul: London 1969.

NETHERCOT, Arthur H., *The First Five Lives of Annie Besant*, Rupert Hart-Davis: London 1961.

——, *The Last Four Lives of Annie Besant*, Rupert Hart-Davis: London 1963.

NEUFELDT, Ronald, 'In Search of Utopia: Karma and Rebirth in the Theosophical Movement', Robert W. Neufeldt (ed.), *Karma and Rebirth: Post Classical Developments*, New York 1986, 233-255.

NEVE, Monika, *"New Age" als Ablenkung? Eine Analyse der New-Age-Bewegung aus anthroposophischer Sicht*, Lazarus Verlag: Raisdorf bei Kiel 1989.

NOLL, Richard, *The Jung Cult: Origins of a Charismatic Movement*, Princeton Univ. Press: Princeton 1994.

NOTOVICH, Nicolas, *La vie inconnue de Jésus Christ*, Ollendorf: Paris 1894.

NÜCHTERN, Michael, *Die Sehnsucht nach Heilung: Über Medizin, Therapie und Weltanschauung* (EZW-Texte: Information nr. 116), Stuttgart 1991.

O'HARA, Maureen, 'Reflections on Sheldrake, Wilber, and "New Science"', *Journal of Humanistic Psychology* 24:2 (1984), 116-120.

——, 'Of Myths and Monkeys: A Critical Look at the Theory of Critical Mass', *Journal of Humanistic Psychology* 25:1 (1985), 61-78.

OLSON, Roger E., 'Rudolf Steiner, Esoteric Christianity, and the New Age Movement', *SYZYGY* 1:4 (1992), 341-353.

OOSTHUIZEN, Gerhardus C., 'The 'Newness' of the New Age in South Africa and Reactions to it', in: Lewis & Melton, *Perspectives*, 247-270.

OPPENHEIM, Janet, *The Other World: Spiritualism and Psychical Research in England, 1850-1914*, Cambridge Univ.Press: Cambridge etc. 1985.

ORNSTEIN, Robert, *The Psychology of Consciousness*, Cape 1975.
——, *Multimind*, MacMillan 1986.
OTTO, Rudolf, *Das Heilige*, repr. Beck: München 1979.
OUTRAM, Dorinda, *The Enlightenment*, Cambridge Univ. Press: Cambridge 1995.
OWEN, Alex, *The Darkened Room: Women, Power, and Spiritualism in Late Nineteenth Century England*, Virago Press: London 1989.
PAGELS, Elaine, *The Gnostic Gospels*, London/New York 1979.
PARKER, Gail Thain, *Mind Cure in New England: From the Civil War to World War I*, Univ. Press of New England: Hanover, New Hampshire 1973.
PECKHAM, Morse, 'Toward a Theory of Romanticism', in: Robert F. Gleckner & Gerald E. Enscoe, *Romanticism: Points of View* (1962), 2nd ed. Wayne State University press: Detroit 1975, 231-257.
PETERS, Ted, 'David Bohm, Postmodernism, and the Divine', *Zygon* 20:2 (1985), 193-217.
——, 'Matthew Fox and the Vatican Wolves', *Dialog* 28 (1989), 137-142.
——, *The Cosmic Self: A Penetrating Look at Today's New Age Movements*, Harper: San Francisco 1991.
PICO DELLA MIRANDOLA, Giovanni, 'Oration on the Dignity of Man', repr. in: Ernst Cassirer, Paul Oskar Kristeller & John Herman Randall (eds.), *The Renaissance Philosophy of Man*, Univ. of Chicago Press: Chicago & London 1948, 223-254.
PIKE, Kenneth L., *Language in Relation to a Unified Theory of the Structure of Human Behavior*, 2nd ed. Mouton & Co.: The Hague/Paris 1967.
PLATVOET, J. G., *Comparing Religions: a Limitative Approach. An Analysis of Akan, Para-Creole, and IFO-Sananda Rites and Prayers*, Mouton: The Hague/Paris/ New York 1983.
——, 'The Definers Defined: Traditions in the Definition of Religion', *Method & Theory in the Study of Religion* 2:2 (1990), 180-212.
PODMORE, Frank, *Mesmerism and Christian Science: A Short History of Mental Healing*, Methuen & Co: London 1909.
POORTMAN, J. J., *Vehicles of Consciousness: The Concept of Hylic Pluralism* (4 vols.), Theosofische Uitgeverij: Utrecht 1978.
PORTER, Roy, *The Enlightenment*, MacMillan: Basingstoke 1990.
PORTERFIELD, Amanda, 'Native American Shamanism and the American Mind-Cure Movement: A Comparative Study of Religious Healing', *Horizons* 11:1 (1984), 276-289.
POYEN, Charles, *Progress of Animal Magnetism in New England*, Weeks, Jordan & Co: Boston 1837.
PRIGOGINE, Ilya, *From Being to Becoming: Time and Complexity in the Physical Sciences*, W.H.Freeman & Co: San Francisco 1980.
PYE, Michael, 'Syncretism versus Synthesis', *Method & Theory in the Study of Religion* 6:3 (1994), 217-229.
PYLKKÄNEN, Paavo (ed.), *The Search for Meaning: The New Spirit in Science and Philosophy*, Crucible: Wellingborough 1989.
QUIMBY, P. P., *The Quimby Manuscripts* (H. W. Dresser, ed.), Thomas Crowell: New York 1921.
QUISPEL, G., *Gnosis als Weltreligion: Die Bedeutung der Gnosis in der Antike*, 2nd. ed. Origo Verlag: Zürich 1972.
——, 'Hesse, Jung und die Gnosis: Die "Septem Sermones ad Mortuos" und Basilides', in: *Gnostic Studies* II, Nederlands Historisch-Archaeologisch Instituut in het

Nabije Oosten: Istanbul 1975, 241-258.

——, 'Gnosis and Psychology', in: Bentley Layton (ed.), *The Rediscovery of Gnosticism, vol. I: The School of Valentinus*, E.J.Brill: Leiden 1980, 17-31.

—— (ed.), *Gnosis: De derde component van de Europese cultuurtraditie*, Hes: Utrecht 1988.

——, 'How Jung Became a Gnostic' (review of Robert A. Segal, *The Gnostic Jung*), *The San Francisco Jung Institute Library Journal* 13:2 (1994), 47-50.

RAND, G., 'Two Meanings of Historicism in the Writings of Dilthey, Troeltsch, and Meinecke', in: Kelley, *The History of Ideas*, 227-242.

RANDALL, J. H., *The Making of the Modern Mind*, Houghton Mifflin Co.: Boston & New York 1940.

RANSOM, Josephine, *A Short History of the Theosophical Society, 1875-1937*, Theosophical Publishing House: Madras 1938.

RASCHKE, Carl A., 'The Human Potential Movement', *Theology Today* 33, 1976, 253-262.

——, *The Interruption of Eternity: Modern Gnosticism and the Origins of the New Religious Consciousness*, Nelson Hall: Chicago 1980.

REISSER, Paul C., Teri K. REISSER & John WELDON, *New Age Medicine: A Christian Perspective on Holistic Health*, InterVarsity Press: Illinois 1987.

RESTIVO, Sal, *The Social Relations of Physics, Mysticism, and Mathematics: Studies in Social Structures, Interests, and Ideas*, D.Reidel: Dordrecht/Boston/Lancaster 1985.

RHODES, Ronald C., 'The New Age Christology of David Spangler', *Bibliotheca Sacra* 144 (1987), 402-418.

RICHTERS, Johanna Maria, *De medisch antropoloog als verteller en vertaler: Met Hermes op reis in het land van de afgoden*, Smart: Heemstede 1991.

RIDALL, Kathryn, *Channeling: How to reach out to your Spirit Guides*, Bantam Books: New York etc. 1988.

RIDDELL, Carol, *The Findhorn Community*, Findhorn Press: Forres 1991.

RIFFARD, Pierre A., *L'ésotérisme*, Robert Laffont: Paris 1990.

RIGBY, Andrew & Bryan S. TURNER, 'Findhorn Community, Centre of Light: A Sociological Study of New Forms of Religion', in: Michael Hill (ed.), *A Sociological Yearbook of Religion in Britain* 5, SCM press: London 1972, 72-86.

RIGHINI BONELLI, M. L. & William R. SHEA (eds.), *Reason, Experiment, and Mysticism in the Scientific Revolution*, London/Basingstoke, 1975.

RIORDAN, Suzanne, 'Channeling', in: Melton, Clark & Kelly, *New Age Encyclopedia*, 97-104.

——, 'Channeling: A New Revelation?', in: Lewis & Melton, *Perspectives*, 105-126.

ROBBINS, Thomas, *Cults, Converts & Charisma: The Sociology of New Religious Movements*, Sage Publ.: London etc. 1988.

ROBBINS, Thomas & Dick ANTHONY (eds.), *In Gods we trust: New Patterns of Religious Pluralism in America*, 2nd ed. Transaction Publ.: New Brunswick & London 1990.

ROBERTS, Jane, *The God of Jane: A Psychic Manifesto*, Prentice Hall Press: New York etc. 1981.

ROBERTS, Peter, 'Is there a Future for the Goddess? Obstacles to the Evolution of Goddess-spirituality in the New Age', *Religion Today* 6:3 (1991), 8-13.

ROBINSON, James M. (ed.), *The Nag Hammadi Library in English*, 3rd ed. Brill: Leiden etc. 1988.

ROBINSON, Richard H. & Willard L. JOHNSON, *The Buddhist Religion*, Wadsworth:

Belmont 1982.

ROSEN, R. D., *Psychobabble: Fast Talk and Quick Cure in the Era of Feeling*, Wildwood House: London 1975.

ROSS, Andrew, 'New Age Technoculture', in: Lawrence Grossberg, Cary Nelson & Paula A.Treichler (eds.), *Cultural Studies*, Routledge: New York & London 1992, 531-555.

ROSSMAN, Michael, *New Age Blues: On the Politics of Consciousness*, E.P.Dutton: New York 1979.

ROSZAK, Theodore, *The Making of a Counter Culture*, Doubleday & Co: New York 1968.

——, *Unfinished Animal: The Aquarian Frontier and the Evolution of Consciousness*, Faber & Faber: London 1975.

——, 'Evolution', in: Eliade, *Encyclopedia of Religion*.

RUDOLPH, Kurt, *Gnosis: The Nature and History of Gnosticism* (orig. 1977), Harper & Row: San Francisco 1983.

RUITENBEEK, Hendrik M., *The New Group Therapies*, Avon books: New York 1970.

RUPPERT, Hans-Jürgen, *Die Hexen kommen: Magie und Hexenglaube heute*, Coprint: Wiesbaden 1987.

——, 'Magie und Hexenglaube heute', *Materialdienst der EZW* 50:3 & 4 (1987), 57-75; 89-104.

——, 'Swedenborg und New Age: Zu einem Ur-Modell alternativer Religiosität neben den Kirchen', *Materialdienst EZW* 57:12 (1994), 353-363.

RUSSELL, Jeffrey B., *A History of Witchcraft: Sorcerers, Heretics, and Pagans*, Thames & Hudson 1980.

RUSSELL, Robert John, 'The Physics of David Bohm and its Relevance to Philosophy and Theology', *Zygon* 20:2 (1985), 135-158.

SANDERS, Annette, '"Morphische Felder" und das "Gedächtnis der Natur"', *Zeitschrift für Parapsychologie und Grenzgebiete der Psychologie* 33:1/2 (1991), 118-123.

SARGENT, J. T., *Sketches and Reminiscenses of the Radical Club*, Osgood: Boston 1880.

SCHLICHTING, Th. H., 'De leer der spiritus of levensgeesten', *Bijdragen tot de geschiedenis der geneeskunde* 19 (1939), 41-55.

SCHLOSSER, J. G., 'Über die Seelenwanderung', in: *Kleine Schriften*, vol. 3, Bey Carl August Serini: Basel 1783.

SCHMIDT, Jochen, (ed.), *Aufklärung und Gegenaufklärung in der europäischen Literatur, Philosophi Politik von der Antike bis zur Gegenwart*, Wissenschaftliche Buchgesellschaft: Darmstadt 1989.

——, 'Einleitung: Aufklärung, Gegenaufklärung, Dialektik der Aufklärung', in: Schmidt, *Aufklärung und Gegenaufklärung*, 1-31.

SCHMIDT, Walter, 'Rebirthing: Rückführung als Rückfall', *Materialdienst der EZW* 54:1 (1991), 25-27.

SCHMIDT, William S., 'An Ontological Model of Development', *Journal of Pastoral Care* 40:1 (1986), 56-67.

SCHMITT, Charles B., 'Perennial Philosophy: From Agostino Steuco to Leibniz', *Journal of the History of Ideas* 27 (1966), 505-532.

SCHNEIDER, Kirk J., 'The Deified Self: A "Centaur" Response to Wilber and the Transpersonal Movement', *Journal of Humanistic Psychology* 27:2 (1987), 196-216.

SCHNURBEIN, S.von, *Religion als Kulturkritik: Neugermanisches Heidentum im 20.*

Jahrhundert, Carl Winter Universitätsverlag: Heidelberg 1992.

SCHOLEM, Gershom, *Major Trends in Jewish Mysticism* (1941), repr. Schocken: New York 1961.

——, 'Zur Geschichte der Anfänge der christlichen Kabbala', in: *Essays presented to Leo Baeck*, London 1954, 158-193.

——, 'With Gershom Scholem: An Interview', in: Gershom Scholem, *On Jews and Judaism in Crisis: Selected Essays* (Werner J. Dannhauser, ed.), Schocken: New York 1976, 1-48.

——, 'Considérations sur l'histoire des débuts de la cabale chrétienne', in: *Kabbalistes chrétiens* (Cahiers de l'Hermétisme), Albin Michel: Paris 1979).

SCHORSCH, Christof, *Die große Vernetzung: Wege zu einer ökologische Philosophie*, Freiburg i.Br. 1987.

——, *Die New Age Bewegung: Utopie und Mythos der Neuen Zeit. Eine kritische Auseinandersetzung*, Gerd Mohn Verlagshaus: Gütersloh 1988.

——, 'Versöhnung von Geist und Natur? Eine Kritik', in: Dürr & Zimmerli, *Geist und Natur*, 342-358.

——, 'Utopie und Mythos der Neuen Zeit: Zur Problematik des "New Age"', *Theologische Rundschau* 54 (1989).

SCHUCHARD, Marsha Keith, *Freemasonry, Secret Societies, and the Continuity of the Occult Tradition in English Literature* (Ph.D.diss.), University of Texas: Austin 1975.

——, 'Swedenborg, Jacobitism, and Freemasonry', in: Brock, *Swedenborg and his Influence*, 359-379.

SCHUMAKER, Wayne, *The Occult Sciences in the Renaissance: A Study in Intellectual Patterns*, Cornell Univ.Press: Ithaca 1972.

SCHURÉ, Edouard, *The Great Initiates: A Study of the Secret History of Religions* (French orig. 1889), Steinerbooks/Multimedia Publ.Corp: Blauvelt, 1961.

SCHUURMAN, R. E., *Tussen technische overmacht en menselijke onmacht: verantwoordelijkheid in een technische maatschappij*, Kok: Kampen 1985.

SCHWAB, Raymond, *The Oriental Renaissance: Europe's Rediscovery of India and the East 1680-1880* (French orig. 1950), Columbia Univ. Press: New York 1984.

SCHWARTZ, Hillel, 'Millenarianism', in: Eliade, *Encyclopedia of Religion*.

SEBALD, Hans, 'New Age Romanticism: The Quest for an Alternative Lifestyle as a Force of Social Change', *Humboldt Journal of Social Relations* 11:2 (1984), 106-127.

——, 'Die Romantik des "New Age": Der studentische Angriff auf Wissenschaft, Objektivität und Realismus', in: Hans-Peter Duerr (ed.), *Der Wissenschaftler und das Irrationale Bd. 3: Beiträge aus der Philosophie*, Frankfurt a.M. 1985, 215-237.

——, 'New-Age-Spiritualität: Religiöse Synthese in der westlichen Welt von heute', in: Dürr & Zimmerli, *Geist und Natur*, 313-341.

SECRET, Francois, *Les Kabbalistes Chrétiens de la Renaissance* (orig. 1964), new ed. Archè/Arma Artis: Milano/Neuilly sur Seine 1985.

——, *Hermétisme et Kabbale*, Bibliopolis: Napoli 1992.

SEGAL, Robert A., 'In Defense of Reductionism' (1983), revised version in: *Religion and the Social Sciences: Essays on the Confrontation*, Scholars Press: Atlanta 1989, 5-36.

—— (ed.), *The Gnostic Jung*, Princeton University Press: Princeton 1992.

SEIFFERT, Helmut, *Einführung in die Wissenschaftstheorie* vol. II, C.H.Beck:

München 1972.

SENIOR, John, *The Way down and Out: The Occult in Symbolist Literature*, Cornell Univ. Press: New York 1959.

SHARMA, Arvind, 'Ecstasy', in: Eliade, *Encyclopedia of Religion*.

SHARPE, Eric, *Comparative Religion: A History*. 2nd ed. Open court: La Salle 1986.

SHARPE, Kevin J., 'Relating the Physics and Religion of David Bohm', *Zygon* 25:1 (1990), 105-122.

SHELDRAKE, Rupert, *Seven Experiments That Could Change the World*, Fourth Estate: London 1994.

SHEPARD, Odell (ed.), *The Journals of Bronson Alcott*, Little, Brown: Boston 1938.

SHEPPERSON, George, 'The Comparative Study of Millenarian Movements', in: Thrupp, *Millennial Dreams*.

SIERKSMA, F., *Een nieuwe hemel en een nieuwe aarde: Messianistische en eschatologische bewegingen en voorstellingen bij primitieve volken*, Mouton & Co: The Hague 1961.

SIGSTEDT, Cyriel Odhner, *The Swedenborg Epic: The Life and Works of Emanuel Swedenborg*, The Swedenborg Society: London 1981.

SILBERER, Herbert, *Hidden Symbolism of Alchemy and the Occult Arts*, repr. Dover Publ.: New York 1971.

SKUTCH, Robert, *Journey without Distance: The Story behind A Course in Miracles*, Celestial Arts: Berkeley 1984.

SLADEK, Mirko, *Fragmente der hermetischen Philosophie in der Naturphilosophie der Neuzeit: Historisch-kritische Beiträge zur hermetisch-alchemistischen Raum- und Naturphilosophie bei Giordano Bruno, Henry More und Goethe*, Peter Lang: Frankfurt a.M. etc. 1984.

SMART, Ninian, *The Phenomenon of Christianity*, Collins: London 1979.

———, 'Asian Cultures and the Impact of the West: India and China', in: Barker, *New Religious Movements*, 140-154.

SMITH, Huston, 'Introduction to the Revised Edition', in: Frithjof Schuon, *The Transcendent Unity of Religions*, Quest Books: Wheaton/Madras/London 1984, ix-xxvii.

SMUTS, J. C., *Holism and Evolution*, MacMillan Company: New York 1926.

SNOEK, J. A. M., *Initiations: A Methodological Approach to the Application of Classification and Definition Theory in the Study of Rituals* , Dutch Efficiency Bureau: Pijnacker 1987.

SPAINK, Karin, *Het strafbare lichaam: De orenmaffia, kwakdenken en het placebo-effect*, De Balie: Amsterdam 1992.

SPERRY, R. W., 'Search for Beliefs to live by Consistent with Science', *Zygon* 26:2 (1991), 237-258.

SPINDLER, Marc R., 'Europe's Neo-paganism: A Perverse Inculturation', *International Bulletin of Missionary Research* 11:1 (1987), 8-11.

SPIRO, M. E., 'Religion: Problems of Definition and Explanation', in: Michael Banton (ed.), *Anthropological Approaches to the Study of Religion*, repr. London 1978, 85-126.

SPRAGUE DE CAMP, L. *Lost Continents: The Atlantis Theme in History, Science, and Literature*, (1954), repr. Dover: New York 1970.

SPRETNAK, Charlene (ed.), *The Politics of Women's Spirituality: Essays on the Rise of Spiritual Power within the Feminist Movement*, Doubleday: New York etc. 1982.

STANLEY, Michael W., 'The Relevance of Emanuel Swedenborg's Theological Concepts for the New Age as It is Envisioned Today', in: Larsen e. o., *Emanuel Swedenborg*, 354-360.

STENGER, Horst, 'Der "okkulte" Alltag: Beschreibungen und wissenssoziologische Deutungen des "New Age"', *Zeitschrift für Soziologie* 18:2 (1989), 119-135.

STEVENSON, I., *Twenty Cases Suggestive of Reincarnation*, University Press of Virginia: Charlottesville 1974.

STEVENSON, I. S.Pasricha & G. SAMARATNE, 'Deception and Self-Deception in Cases of the Reincarnation Type: Seven Illustrative Cases in Asia', *Journal of the American Society of Psychical Research* 82 (1988).

STEYN, Chrissie, *Worldviews in Transition: An Investigation into the New Age Movement in South Africa*, Unisa Press: Pretoria 1994.

STONE, Donald, 'The Human Potential Movement', in: Charles Y.Glock & Robert N.Bellah, *The New Religious Consciousness*, Univ. of California Press: Berkeley/Los Angeles/London 1976, 93-115.

STRIJARDS, C. & O. SCHREUDER, 'Nieuwe Spiritualiteit', in: O.Schreuder & L.van Snippenburg (eds.), *Religie in de Nederlandse Samenleving: De vergeten factor*, Ambo: Baarn 1990.

SUDBRACK, Josef, *Neue Religiosität: Herausforderung für die Christen*, 4th ed. Topos Taschenbücher: Mainz 1990.

——, *Die vergessene Mystik und die Herausforderung des Christentums durch New Age*, Echter Verlag: Würzburg 1988.

SULLIVAN, Lawrence E., 'Healing', in: Eliade, *Encyclopedia of Religion*.

—— (ed.), *Hidden Truths: Magic, Alchemy and the Occult*, MacMillan & Collier: New York & London 1987.

SWATOS, William H., 'Spiritualism as a Religion of Science', *Social Compass* 37:4 (1990), 471-482.

TAFEL, R. L., *Documents Concerning the Life and Character of Emanuel Swedenborg*, vol. I, Swedenborg Society: London 1875.

TALBOT, Michael, 'Swedenborg and the Holographic Paradigm', in: Larsen e. o., *Emanuel Swedenborg*, 443-448.

TALMON, Y., 'Pursuit of the Millennium: The Relation between Religious and Social Change', in: Jansma & Schulten, *Religieuze bewegingen*, 35-61.

TAMBIAH, Stanley Jayaraja, *Magic, Science, Religion, and the Scope of Rationality*, Cambridge Univ.Press: Cambridge etc. 1990.

TART, C. T., (ed.) *Altered States of Consciousness*, Double Day: Garden City N.Y. 1972.

TAYLOR, Eugene, 'Emerson: The Swedenborgian and Transcendentalist Connection', in: Larsen e.o., *Emanuel Swedenborg*, 127-136.

——, 'The Appearance of Swedenborg in the History of American Psychology', in: Brock e.o., *Swedenborg and his Influence*, 155-176.

TEMPLE, Robert, 'David Bohm', *New Scientist* 11, november 1982, 361-365.

TEMPLETON, John M. & Robert L. HERRMANN, *The God Who would be known: Revelations of the Divine in Contemporary Science*, Harper & Row: San Francisco 1989.

THOMAS, Keith, *Religion and the Decline of Magic*, Penguin: London etc. 1971.

THRUPP, Sylvia L. (ed.), *Millennial Dreams in Action: Essays in Comparative Study*, Mouton & Co: The Hague 1962.

——, 'Millennial Dreams in Action: A Report on the Conference Discussion', in: Thrupp, *Millennial Dreams*.

TILLETT, Gregory, *The Elder Brother: A Biography of Charles Webster Leadbeater*, Routlege & Kegan Paul: London etc. 1982.

TIRYAKIAN, E. A. (ed.), *On the Margin of the Visible: Sociology, the Esoteric, and the Occult*, New York etc., 1974.

——, 'Toward the Sociology of Esoteric Culture', in: Tiryakian, *On the Margin of the Visible*, 257-280.

TRINE, Ralph Waldo, *In Tune with the Infinite, or Fullness of Peace, Power and Plenty* (1899), repr. Mandala: London 1989.

TROELTSCH, Ernst, *Die Soziallehren der christlichen Kirchen und Gruppen* (Gesammelte Schriften vol. I), J.C.B.Mohr: Tübingen 1912.

——, *The Social Teaching of the Christian Churches*, vol. II, George Allen & Unwin/ MacMillan: London/New York 1931.

TROMPF, Garry W., 'The Future of Macro-Historical Ideas', *Soundings* 62:1 (1979), 70-89.

——, 'Macrohistory and Acculturation: Between Myth and History in Modern Melanesian Adjustments and Ancient Gnosticism', *Comparative Studies in Society and History* 31:4 (1989), 621-648.

—— (ed.), *Cargo Cults and Millenarian Movements: Transoceanic Comparisons of New Religious Movements* (Religion and Society 29), Mouton de Gruyter: Berlin/New York 1990.

——, 'Introduction', in: Trompf, *Cargo Cults*, 1-32.

——, 'The Cargo and the Millennium on both Sides of the Pacific', in: Trompf, *Cargo Cults*, 35-94.

——, *In Search of Origins*, Oriental Univ. Press: London 1990.

TRUZZI, Marcello, 'Definition and Dimensions of the Occult: Towards a Sociological Perspective', in: Tiryakian, *On the Margin of the Visible*, 243-255.

TURNER, Frank Miller, *Between Science and Religion: The Reaction to Scientific Naturalism in Late Victorian England*, Yale Univ.Press: New Haven & London 1974.

TUVESON, Ernest Lee, *The Avatars of Thrice Great Hermes: An Approach to Romanticism*, Bucknell Univ.Press/Associated University Presses: Lewisburg & London/Toronto 1982.

UNDERHILL, Evelyn, *Mysticism: A Study in the Nature and Development of Man's Spiritual Consciousness* (1955), Repr. New American Library: New York/Scarborough, 1974.

VALLE, Ronald S., 'The Emergence of Transpersonal Psychology', in: Ronald S.Valle & Steen Halling (eds.), *Existential-phenomenological Perspectives in Psychology: Exploring the Breadth of Human Experience. With a Special Section on Transpersonal Psychology*, Plenum Press: New York/London 1989, 257-267.

VANHESTE, Tomas, 'Berichten van een nieuwe tijd: Of hoe de New Age-beweging de natuurwetenschap claimde', *De Gids*, january 1994, 24-36.

VERSLUIS, Arthur, *American Transcendentalism and Asian Religions*, Oxford Univ.Press: New York & Oxford 1993.

——, *The Hermetic Book of Nature* (forthcoming).

VERSNEL, H. S., 'Introduction', in: , *Ter Unus. Isis, Dionysos, Hermes: Three Studies in Henotheism*, Brill: Leiden etc. 1990, 1-38.

——, 'Some Reflections on the Relationship Magic—Religion', *Numen* 38:2 (1991), 177-197.

VIATTE, Auguste, *Les sources occultes du romantisme: Illuminisme, Théosophie 1770-1820. Vol. I: Le préromantisme* (1927), repr. Honoré Champion: Paris 1979.

——, *Les sources occultes du romantisme: Illuminisme, Théosophie 1770-1820. Vol.*

II: La génération de l'empire (1927), repr. Honoré Champion: Paris 1979.

——, *Victor Hugo et les illuminés de son temps*, repr. Slatkine: Genève 1973.

VIVEKANANDA (Swami), *The Complete Works of Swami Vivekananda*, Advaita Ashram: Calcutta 1972.

VOGEL, Stanley M., *German Literary Influences on the American Transcendentalists*, Yale Univ.Press: New Haven 1955.

WAGNER, Melinda Bollar, *Metaphysics in Midwestern America*, Ohio State Univ.Press: Columbus 1983.

WALKER, D. P., *Spiritual and Demonic Magic from Ficino to Campanella*, Warburg Institute: London 1958.

——, 'The Astral Body in Renaissance Medicine', *Journal of the Warburg and Courtauld Institutes* 21 (1958), 119-133.

——, *The Ancient Theology*, London 1972.

WALLER, James & Mary EDWARDSEN, 'Evolutionism', in: Eliade, *Encyclopedia of Religion*.

WALLIS, Roy, 'Betwixt Therapy and Salvation: The Changing Form of the Human Potential Movement', in: Jones, *Sickness and Sectarianism*, 23-51.

WALSH, Roger N. & Frances VAUGHAN, *Beyond Ego: Transpersonal Dimensions in Psychology*, J.P.Tarcher: Los Angeles 1980.

WAPNICK, Kenneth, *The Meaning of Forgiveness: The Meeting Place of 'A Course in Miracles' and Christianity*, Arkana: London 1983.

WARD, William, *A View of the History, Literature and Religion of the Hindoos*, London 1817.

WATSON, Lyall, *Lifetide: A Biology of the Unconscious*, Simon & Schuster: New York 1979.

WAX, Murray & WAX, Rosalie, 'The Magical World View', *Journal for the Scientific Study of Religion* 1 (1962).

—— & ——, 'The Notion of Magic', *Current Anthropology* 4:5 (1963), 495-518.

WEAVER, Mary Jo, 'Who is the Goddess and where does She get us?', *Journal of Feminist Studies in Religion* 5:1 (1989), 49-64.

WEBB, James, *The Occult Underground*, Open Court: La Salle, Illinois 1974.

——, *The Occult Establishment*, Open Court: LaSalle, Illinois 1976.

WEBER, Renée, 'Philosophical Foundations and Frameworks for Healing', in: Kunz, *Spiritual Aspects*, 21-43.

WEEKS, Andrew, *German Mysticism from Hildegard of Bingen to Ludwig Wittgenstein*, SUNY: Albany 1993.

WEHR, Gerhard, *Esoterisches Christentum: Aspekte—Impulse—Konsequenzen*, Ernst Klett: Stuttgart 1975.

——, *Carl Gustav Jung: Leben, Werk, Wirkung*, Diogenes: Zürich 1985.

——, 'C.G.Jung in the Context of Christian Esotericism and Cultural History', in: Faivre & Needleman, *Modern Esoteric Spirituality*, 381-399.

WEISSMANN, Karlheinz, 'Erwachen im Untergrund: Neuheiden unter uns', *Materialdienst EZW* 54:4 (1991), 99-112.

WELLEK, René, 'The Concept of "Romanticism" in Literary History', *Comparative Literature* 1:1 (1949), 1-23; 147-172.

WETERING, Willem Jan van de & Jacques ONDERWATER, *Jomanda: Genezend Medium*, Strengholt: Naarden 1994.

WICHMANN, Jörg, 'Das theosophische Menschenbild und seine indischen Wurzeln', *Zeitschrift für Religions- und Geistesgeschichte* 35:1 (1983), 12-33.

WIEBE, Donald, *The Irony of Theology and the Nature of Religious Thought*, McGill-Queen's Univ.Press: Montreal & Kingston etc. 1991.

WILBER, Ken, 'Sheldrake's Theory of Morphogenesis', *Journal of Humanistic Psychology* 24:2 (1984), 107-115.

——, *A Sociable God: Toward a New Understanding of Religion*, Shambhala: Boulder & London 1984

——, *Grace and Grit: Spirituality and Healing in the Life and Death of Treya Killam Wilber*, Shambala: Boston & London 1991.

WILLIAMS-HOGAN, Jane, 'The Place of Emanuel Swedenborg in Modern Western Esotericism', in: Faivre & Hanegraaff, *Western Esotericism*.

WILSON, Brian R., 'The New Religions: Preliminary Considerations', in: Barker, *New Religious Movements*, 16-31.

WILSON, Daniel J., 'Lovejoy's *The Great Chain of Being* after Fifty Years', in: Kelley, *History of Ideas*, 158-177.

WIRSZUBSKI, Chaim, *Pico della Mirandola's Encounter with Jewish Mysticism*, Harvard Univ.Press: Cambridge/London 1989.

WISKERKE, Niek, 'New Age-holisme en scheppingstheologie: visies op mens en natuur', in: Chowdhury e.a., *Holisme en New Age-bewustzijn*, 139-203.

WOLFAHRT, S., *Erläuterungen zum Mesmerismus*, Berlin 1815.

YATES, Frances A., *Giordano Bruno and the Hermetic Tradition*, Routlege and Kegan Paul/University of Chicago Press: London/Chicago 1964.

——, *The Art of Memory*, Routledge and Kegan Paul: London 1966.

——, 'The Hermetic Tradition in Renaissance Science', in: Ch.Singleton (ed.), *Art, Science and History in the Renaissance*, Baltimore 1967, 255-274.

——, *The Rosicrucian Enlightenment*, Ark: London & New York 1972.

——, *The Occult Philosophy in the Elizabethan Age*, Ark: London etc. 1979.

YORK, Michael, *The Emerging Network: A Sociology of the New Age and Neo-Pagan Movements*, Rowman & Littlefield: London 1995.

——, 'The New Age Movement in Great Britain', *SYZYGY* 1:2-3 (1992), 147-157.

YOUNG, Allan, 'The Anthropologies of Illness and Sickness', *Annual Review of Anthropology* 11 (1982) 257-285.

YOUNG, Arthur M., *The Bell Notes: A Journey from Physics to Metaphysics*, Robert Briggs Ass.: Mill Valley 1979.

ZIMMERMANN, Rolf Christian, *Das Weltbild des jungen Goethe: Studien zur hermetischen Tradition des deutschen 18. Jahrhunderts* (2 vols.), Wilhelm Fink: München 1969 & 1979.

ZINSER, Hartmut, 'Zur Faszination des Schamanismus', *Journal für Geschichte* 1 (1985), 46-51.

——, 'Schamanismus im "New Age": Zur Wiederkehr schamanistischer Praktiken und Seancen in Europa', *Zeitschrift für Religions- und Geistesgeschichte* 39 (1987), 319-327.

——, 'Moderner Okkultismus zwischen Glauben und Wissen', *Zeitschrift für Missionswissenschaft und Religionswissenschaft* 78:4 (1994), 290-301.

ZOEST, Peter van, 'New Age-beweging en holistische wetenschap: terreinverkennende notities', in: Chowdhury e.a., *Holisme en New Age-bewustzijn*, 15-66.

ZUKAV, Gary, *The Dancing Wu-Li Masters: An Overview of the New Physics*, William Morrow & Co: New York 1979.

ZWAN, Rob van der, 'New Age, holisme en theologie', in: Chowdhury e.a., *Holisme en New Age-bewustzijn*, 103-137.

ZWI WERBLOWSKI, R. J., 'Religions New and not so New: Fragments of an Agenda', in: Barker, *New Religious Movements*, 32-46.

INDEX OF SUBJECTS

INDEX OF NAMES